g is hard

* STEVE JOBS IN APRIL 2001.

** By 2008, the company posted revenue of $7.9 billion and net quarterly profit of $1.14 billion. "Apple just reported one of the best quarters in its history, with a spectacular performance by the iPhone—we sold more phones than RIM," said Steve Jobs. "We don't yet know how this economic downturn will affect Apple. But we're armed with the strongest product line in our history, the most talented employees and the best customers in our industry, and $25 billion of cash safely in the bank with zero debt."

Retailing in the Twenty-First Century

Retailing
in the Twenty-First Century

second edition

Jay Diamond
Professor Emeritus, Nassau Community College

Sheri Litt
Associate Dean, Workforce Development
Florida Community College at Jacksonville

Fairchild Books
New York

Executive Editor: Olga T. Kontzias
Assistant Acquisitions Editor: Amanda Breccia
Senior Development Editor: Jennifer Crane
Development Editor: Severine Champeny, Newgen-Austin/G & S
Associate Art Director: Erin Fitzsimmons
Production Director: Ginger Hillman
Associate Production Editor: Andrew Fargnoli
Project Manager: Christine D'Antonio
Copyeditor: Nancy Reinhardt
Photo Researchers: Matthew and Ellen Dudley, Candlepants, Inc.
Cover Design: Erin Fitzsimmons
Cover Art: Photo by Justin Sullivan/Getty Images
Inside Cover Art: © Reuters

Copyright © 2009 Fairchild Books, A Division of Condé Nast Publications, Inc.

First edition published as *Retailing in the New Millennium*. Copyright © 2003 Fairchild Publications, Inc.

All rights reserved. No part of this book covered by the copyright hereon may be reproduced or used in any form or by any means—graphic, electronic, or mechanical, including photocopying, recording, taping, or information storage and retrieval systems—without written permission of the publisher.

Library of Congress Catalog Card Number: 2008924429

ISBN: 978-1-56367-705-2

GST R 133004424

Printed in China

TP15

CONTENTS IN BRIEF

Focus Features Summary   xix

In the News Articles   xxi

Preface   xxv

PART ONE | Introduction to Retailing   1

CHAPTER 1 | Retailing from Its Early Days to the Present   3
CHAPTER 2 | Brick-and-Mortar Retailing   35
CHAPTER 3 | Off-Site Retailing: E-tailing, Catalogues, and Home-Shopping Networks   55
CHAPTER 4 | The Globalization of Retailing   79
CHAPTER 5 | Identification, Analysis, and Research of Consumer Groups   107
CHAPTER 6 | Multiculturalism in Retailing   131
CHAPTER 7 | The Role of Ethics in the Retail Environment   155
CHAPTER 8 | Going Green   173

PART TWO | Management and Operational Controls   191

CHAPTER 9 | Human Resources Management   193
CHAPTER 10 | Loss Prevention   221
CHAPTER 11 | Logistical Merchandise Distribution   239

PART THREE | Retail Environments   257

CHAPTER 12 | Location Analysis and Selection   259
CHAPTER 13 | Designing the Facility   287

PART FOUR | Buying and Merchandising   307

CHAPTER 14 | Buying Domestically and Abroad   309
CHAPTER 15 | Private Labeling and Product Development   341
CHAPTER 16 | The Concepts and Mathematics of Merchandise Pricing   361

PART FIVE | Promotion and Customer Service   385

CHAPTER 17 | Advertising and Promotion   387
CHAPTER 18 | Visual Merchandising   413
CHAPTER 19 | Customer Service   435

APPENDIX | Careers in Retailing and Related Fields   461

FIGURE CREDITS   469

INDEX   471

EXTENDED CONTENTS

Focus Features Summary   xix
In the News Articles   xxi
Preface   xxv

PART ONE | Introduction to Retailing   1

CHAPTER 1 | Retailing from Its Early Days to the Present   3

RETAILING IN AMERICA: A HISTORICAL OVERVIEW OF THE INDUSTRY   4
    Trading Posts   4
    Peddlers   4
    General Stores   4
    Limited-Line Stores   5
    Chain Organizations   5
Focus on . . . Jos. A. Bank   6
    Department Stores   6
Focus on . . . Belk Inc.   7
    Mail-Order Retailers   7
    Supermarkets   8
    Discount Operations   9
    Off-Price Stores   9
    Franchises   10
    Warehouse Clubs   10
    Manufacturer-Owned Retail Outlets   11
    Flea Markets   11
    Boutiques   12
    Kiosks   12
    Category Killers   13
    Hypermarkets   13
    Designer Flagships   13
MAJOR AMERICAN RETAILERS   13
ORGANIZATIONAL STRUCTURES   14
    Traditional Organizational Formats   14
STRATEGIC PLANNING   15
USE OF TECHNOLOGY   16
RETAIL TRENDS   17
    Off-Site Selling   17
    Offshore Expansion   17
    Private Labeling and Branding   17
    Contracting with Upscale Designers for Retail Exclusivity   18
Focus on . . . Joseph Abboud   19
    Contracting with Celebrities to Design Exclusive Retail Collections   19
    Targeting Multicultural Market Segments   20
    Manufacturers Entering the Retail Arena   20
Focus on . . . Liz Claiborne, Inc.   20
    Expansion through Acquisition   21
    New Concepts for Established Retailers   21
    Partnering   22
    Online Apparel Selling Escalation   23
    Global Sourcing   23
    Value Shopping Broadening   23
    Multichannel Retail Expansion   23
    Going Green   23
    Outsourcing Private-Label Production, Design, and Management   23

Refocusing Organizational Structures 24
Broadening the Merchandise Mix 24
Repositioning 24
Site-to-Store Marketing 25

FUTURE RETAILING DIRECTIONS 25
Establishing Town Centers 25
Decreasing Newspaper Advertising Commitments 25
Text Messaging 25
Revitalizing Shopping Streets 26
Utilizing New Technology 26
Mobile Fashion Sales 26
Consumer Shopping Tours 26
3D Online Presentation 26

CAREER OPPORTUNITIES IN TODAY'S RETAIL MARKETPLACE 27

Chapter Highlights 27
Important Retailing Terms 28
For Review 28
An Internet Activity 28
Exercises and Projects 28
The Case of Restructuring the Merchandising Division of a Multichannel Retailer 29
In the News—Panel: Tech-Savvy Retailers Will Thrive 29
In the News—Wholesale Giants Morphing into Retailers 31

CHAPTER 2 | Brick-and-Mortar Retailing 35

TRADITIONAL RETAILERS 36
Department Stores 36

Focus on . . . Macy's, Inc. 38

Focus on . . . Nordstrom 39

Chain Organizations 40

Focus on . . . Gap, Inc. 44

Smaller Stores 46

VALUE-ORIENTED RETAILERS 47
Discounters 48
Off-Price Retailers 48
Manufacturer Closeout Stores 49
Retail Clearance Centers 50

Chapter Highlights 51
Important Retailing Terms 51
For Review 51
An Internet Activity 51
Exercises and Projects 52
The Case of the Off-Price Competitor 52
In the News—The Ins and Outs of Outlets 52

CHAPTER 3 | Off-Site Retailing: E-tailing, Catalogues, and Home-Shopping Networks 55

E-TAILING 56
E-tailing Popularity 57
Online Retailing Today 57
Web Winners 60
Types of E-tailers 60

Focus on . . . Zappos.com 62

Focus on . . . Sephora 64

Multichannel Retailing 65
Virtual Catalogues 66
Interactive E-tailing 66
Internet Fraud 67

CATALOGUES 68
Catalogue-Only Retailers 70
Cataloguers with Brick-and-Mortar Outlets 70

FOCUS ON . . . THE AMERICAN GIRL   70
      Brick-and-Mortar Catalogue Divisions   71
HOME-SHOPPING CHANNELS   71
FOCUS ON . . . HSN, THE TELEVISION SHOPPING NETWORK   72

Chapter Highlights   73
Important Retailing Terms   73
For Review   73
An Internet Activity   74
Exercises and Projects   74
The Case of a Cataloguer's Potential for Expansion   74
In the News—Pick It and Click It   74
In the News—Apparel Now No. 1 Online   75

CHAPTER 4 | The Globalization of Retailing   79

MAJOR GLOBAL RETAILING CENTERS   79
      The United States   80
      The United Kingdom   81
FOCUS ON . . . ABERCROMBIE & FITCH   82
      France   83
      Japan   83
      Italy   84
      Other Major Global Retailing Centers   85
EMERGING COUNTRIES FOR RETAIL EXPANSION   85
      India   85
      Russia   86
FOCUS ON . . . RALPH LAUREN, RUSSIA   86
      China   87
      Vietnam   87
      Ukraine   87
      Chile   87
      Latvia   87
      Malaysia   87
      Mexico   87
      Saudi Arabia   87
      Tunisia   88
      Bulgaria   88
ANALYSIS OF OFFSHORE RETAIL OPERATIONS   88
REASONS BEHIND THE GLOBAL EXPANSION OF RETAILERS   88
      Competition   89
      International Travel   89
      Unique Products   90
      Profitability   90
PITFALLS OF GLOBALIZATION   90
      Economic Downturns   91
      Consumer Differences   91
      Local Competition   91
      Political Risk   91
FOREIGN EXPANSION ARRANGEMENTS   92
      Joint Ventures   92
      Wholly Owned Subsidiaries   93
      Franchising   93
      Licensing   93
LEADING GLOBAL RETAILERS   94

Chapter Highlights   100
Important Retailing Terms   100
For Review   100
An Internet Activity   100
Exercises and Projects   100
The Case of the International Expansion Dilemma   100
In the News—Global Markets Key to Retailing Future   101
In the News—Finding a Home Abroad   103

CHAPTER 5 | Identification, Analysis, and Research of Consumer Groups   107

ASSESSMENT OF CONSUMER GROUPS   108
Demographics   108

Focus on . . . Pottery Barn   111

Social Class   115
Family Life Cycle   117

CONSUMER BEHAVIOR   120
Buying Motives   120
Maslow's Hierarchy of Needs   122

CONSUMER RESEARCH   123
Trade Associations and Organizations   123
Governmental Resources   123
Market Research Groups   124

Focus on . . . ACNielsen   124

In-House Research   124

Chapter Highlights   125
Important Retailing Terms   126
For Review   126
An Internet Activity   126
Exercises and Projects   126
The Case of Price Positioning   127
In the News—Teen Panel Reflects Shifting Spending Habits   127
In the News—In-Store Advertising: Should Psychographic Studies Play a Role?   128

CHAPTER 6 | Multiculturalism in Retailing   131

DEMOGRAPHIC ANALYSIS   132

Focus on . . . Allied Media Corp.   132

STRATEGIES FOR CAPTURING THE MULTICULTURAL MARKETS   134
Merchandising   134

Focus on . . . Zalia   138

Advertising   140

Focus on . . . Arbitron, Inc.   142

Visual Presentation   142
Staffing   143

Focus on . . . Wal-Mart   143

MAXIMIZING THE MULTICULTURAL EFFORT   144

Chapter Highlights   144
Important Retailing Terms   144
For Review   145
An Internet Activity   145
Exercises and Projects   145
The Case of Refocusing the Merchandise Mix   145
In the News—Retail Has Room to Grow in Ethnic Markets   146
In the News—How Do You Say "Got Milk" en Español?   149

CHAPTER 7 | The Role of Ethics in the Retail Environment   155

DEVELOPERS OF ETHICAL STANDARDS   156
Retailer Codes   156

Focus on . . . Stein Mart   156

Focus on . . . Macy's, Inc., Vendor/Supplier Code of Conduct   157

Trade Association Codes   158
Independent Watchdog Agencies   158

Focus on . . . Better Business Bureau   159

AREAS OF ETHICAL CONCERN   159
Advertising   160
Credit   161
Low-Cost Sourcing   161
Conflicts of Interest   161
Counterfeit Merchandise   162

Hiring and Promotion Practices 162
Internal Theft 162
Price Gouging 163
Price Fixing 163
Questionable Products 163
Receiving Room Procedures 163
"Negotiation" Pricing 164
Working-Class Discrimination 164

Chapter Highlights 165
Important Retailing Terms 165
For Review 165
An Internet Activity 166
Exercises and Projects 166
The Case of Taking Substantial Gifts 166
In the News—Is PETA Defanged? Fur Looks Are Back on and off Runways 167
In the News—China Pressure Cooker: Ethical Questions Grow over Low-Cost Sourcing 169

CHAPTER 8 | Going Green 173

THE LANGUAGE OF GREEN 174

AREAS OF GREENING RETAIL 175
Cutting Down on Plastic Bag Usage 175
Energy Efficiency 176

Focus on . . . Giant Eagle 177
Adding Eco-Friendly Products to the Merchandise Mix 177

Focus on . . . Patagonia 179
"Eco-Only" Merchandising 179
Recycling 180
Advertising, Visual Merchandising, and Promotion 180
Purchasing from Eco-Friendly Suppliers 181

Focus on . . . Wal-Mart 182

TRADE ASSOCIATION ACTIVISM 182

THE PROS AND CONS OF GOING GREEN 183

GREEN RESOURCES 183
Chapter Highlights 184
Important Retailing Terms 184
For Review 185
An Internet Activity 185
Exercises and Projects 185
The Case of the Independent Merchant Going Green 185
In the News—Earthly Delights 186
In the News—Leading the Way 188

PART TWO | Management and Operational Controls 191

CHAPTER 9 | Human Resources Management 193

EQUAL OPPORTUNITY EMPLOYMENT 194

THE HUMAN RESOURCES DEPARTMENT 195

RECRUITING AND HIRING EMPLOYEES 195
Recruitment 195

Focus on . . . Target Corporation 198
The Selection Process 201

IN-HOUSE EMPLOYEE TRAINING 203

Focus on . . . Saks Fifth Avenue 203

OFF-SITE EMPLOYEE TRAINING 204
New Sales Associates 204
Executive Trainees 205

Focus on... Von Maur   205
    Support Personnel   206
    Retrainees   206
Focus on... McDonald's   207

EMPLOYEE EVALUATION PROGRAMS   207

COMPENSATION   208
    Straight Salary   209
    Straight Commission   209
    Wage Plus Commission   209
    Salary Plus Bonus   210
    Other Monetary Rewards   210

EMPLOYEE BENEFITS   211

LABOR RELATIONS   211

SUPERVISION TRAINING   212

TECHNOLOGICAL APPLICATIONS   212

Chapter Highlights   213
Important Retailing Terms   213
For Review   213
An Internet Activity   214
Exercises and Projects   214
The Case of Refocusing Training Procedures   214
In the News—H.R. Summit Reveals Employee Woes   215
In the News—Holt Renfrew Turns around H.R. with Tech   218
In the News—The Training Advantage   219

CHAPTER 10 | Loss Prevention   221

SHOPLIFTING   222
    Major Shoplifting Deterrents   222
Focus on... Sensormatic Electronics Corp.   224
    Other Shoplifting Deterrents   225

INTERNAL THEFT   227
    Applicant Screening   228
    Reference Checking   228
    Closed-Circuit TV   228
    Mystery Shopping Services   228
    Drug Testing   229
    Honesty and Psychological Testing   229
    Smuggling Controls   229
    Control of Employee Purchases   230
    Rewards Programs   230
    Prosecution of Dishonest Employees   230

CHECK FRAUD   230

INTERNET THEFT   231
    Fraud Prevention   231

VENDOR THEFT   232

Chapter Highlights   234
Important Retailing Terms   234
For Review   234
An Internet Activity   235
Exercises and Projects   235
The Case of the Missing Merchandise   235
In the News—Retail's Latest Plague: Fighting Back against Shoplifting Gangs   236

CHAPTER 11 | Logistical Merchandise Distribution   239

INTERENTERPRISE COLLABORATION   240
    High-Tech Innovation   240
Focus on... Macy's, Inc., Logistics and Operations   241
    Nonprofit Industry Groups   241
    Outside Marking   242

Focus on... Gymboree 243

VENDOR–RETAILER PHYSICAL DISTRIBUTION 243
    Technological Application for Supply-Chain Performance 245

IN-HOUSE DISTRIBUTION 245
    Centralized Receiving Departments 245
    Regional Receiving Departments 246
    Single-Store Receiving 246

RECEIVING AND MARKING OPERATIONS 246
    Receiving Records 247
    Receiving Equipment 247
    Quantity Checking 248
    Quality Checking 248
    Marking Merchandise 249

Focus on... Monarch Marking Systems 249
    Re-Marking Merchandise 250

Chapter Highlights 250
Important Retailing Terms 251
For Review 251
An Internet Activity 251
Exercises and Projects 252
The Case of the Merchandise Distribution Dilemma 252
In the News—Saks Masters DC Flow-Through 253

PART THREE | Retail Environments 257

CHAPTER 12 | Location Analysis and Selection 259

TRADING AREA ANALYSIS AND SELECTION 260
    Demographic Analysis 260
    Area Characteristic Assessment 262

SHOPPING DISTRICT CHOICES 263
    Central Shopping Districts 264
    Shopping Malls 264

Focus on... Simon Property Group 265
    Festival Marketplaces 269

Focus on... International Council of Shopping Centers 270
    Power Centers 270
    Fashion Avenues 270
    Flea Markets 271
    Airport Terminals 271
    Neighborhood Clusters 275
    Strip Centers 275
    Freestanding Stores 276

SITE SELECTION 276
    Pedestrian Traffic 276
    Neighboring Stores 276
    Competition 277
    Public Transportation 277
    Vehicular Transportation 277
    Parking Facilities 277

OCCUPANCY CONSIDERATIONS 278
    Leasing 278
    Ownership 279

Chapter Highlights 279
Important Retailing Terms 280
For Review 280
An Internet Activity 280
Exercises and Projects 280
The Case of Expansion into a Different Shopping Arena 281
In the News—Mixing It Up 281
In the News—Luxe Goods on the Fly: Accessories Brands Tap Travel Retail for Growth 283

CHAPTER 13 | Designing the Facility 287

EXTERIOR DESIGN CONCEPTS 288

STORE ENTRANCES 289
  Window Structures 290

INTERIOR DESIGN AND LAYOUT 291

Focus on . . . Institute of Store Planners 291
  Interior Design Concepts 292
  Locating the Selling Departments 293

Focus on . . . Bergdorf Goodman 295

Focus on . . . American Girl Place 296
  Departmentalization 297
  Fixturing 297
  Surfacing 299
  Lighting 301
  Locating the Nonselling Areas 301

Chapter Highlights 302
Important Retailing Terms 302
For Review 302
An Internet Activity 303
Exercises and Projects 303
The Case of Redesigning a Store's Interior 303
In the News—Aéropostale Updates Its Box 304
In the News—Maximizing the Assets: Saks Flagship Charts Latest Set of Upgrades 305

PART FOUR | Buying and Merchandising 307

CHAPTER 14 | Buying Domestically and Abroad 309

BUYERS' DUTIES AND RESPONSIBILITIES 310
  Assortment Planning 311
  Purchasing 311
  Merchandise Pricing 311
  Product Promotion 311
  In-House Department Management 311
  Product Development 312

PLANNING THE PURCHASE 312
  Internal Planning Resources 312
  External Planning Assistance 313

Focus on . . . Barnard's Retail Consulting Group 315
  Development of Assortments 316

VISITING THE MARKET TO MAKE THE PURCHASE 323
  Market Week Visits 323

Focus on . . . The Doneger Group 324
  Buying Venues 325

ALTERNATE METHODS OF MERCHANDISE PROCUREMENT 327
  In-House Buying 327
  Catalogues 328
  Business-to-Business Web Sites 328

NEGOTIATING THE PURCHASE 329
  Price Negotiation 329
  Shipping Terms 331
  Delivery Dates 331
  Chargebacks 331

EVALUATING THE BUYER'S PERFORMANCE 332

A DAY IN THE LIFE OF A BUYER 333

Chapter Highlights 334
Important Retailing Terms 335
For Review 335
An Internet Activity 335

Exercises and Projects 336
The Case of the Search for Unique Merchandise 336
In the News—Tackling the Sourcing Conundrum 337
In the News—A Prominent Presence: Walking the Show Floor with Abbey Doneger 338

CHAPTER 15 | Private Labeling and Product Development 341

MANUFACTURER'S BRANDS AND LABELS 342

PRIVATE BRANDS AND LABELS 344
The Proportional Concept 345
The Store-Is-the-Brand Concept 345

Focus on . . . Gap, Inc. 346

The Private Label and Brand Advantage 348

LICENSED PRIVATE BRANDS 348

PRODUCT DEVELOPMENT 350
Company-Owned Production 350

Focus on . . . Mast Industries, Inc. 350

Purchasing from Private-Label Developers 351
Purchasing from National Manufacturers 351
Alternative Private-Label and Brand Acquisition 351

PROMOTION OF PRIVATE BRANDS AND LABELS 353

Chapter Highlights 354
Important Retailing Terms 355
For Review 355
An Internet Activity 355
Exercises and Projects 355
The Case of Determining the Appropriateness of Private Labels 356
In the News—Markets Say Proudly: It's Our Brand 356
In the News—The Power of the Private Label 358

CHAPTER 16 | The Concepts and Mathematics of Merchandise Pricing 361

MARKUP 362
Markup Percent on Retail 362
Markup Percent on Cost 364

FACTORS THAT AFFECT PRICING 364
Supreme Court Pricing Decision 365
The Buyer's Judgment of the Merchandise's Appeal 365
Competition 365
Exclusivity 366
Membership Clubs 367

Focus on . . . Costco 367

The Nature of the Goods 367
Stock Turnover 369
Retailer Promotional Endeavors 369
Company Image 370
Services 370
Pilferage 371

PRICING STRATEGIES 371
Keystone Pricing 371
Keystone Plus Pricing 371
Overall Uniform Pricing 371
Department Pricing 372
Individual Merchandise Pricing 372
Negotiable Pricing 372
Average Pricing 373

PRICE POINTS 373

MARKDOWNS 374
Markdown Causes 374
Timing Markdowns 376
Automatic Markdowns 377

Focus on... Filene's Basement 377
    Determining the Markdown 377
    Markdown Percent Calculations 378

Chapter Highlights 379
Important Retailing Terms 379
For Review 380
An Internet Activity 380
Exercises and Projects 380
The Case of the Markdown Dilemma 380
In the News—Retail Pricing Strategies 381
In the News—The Markdown Blues, Revisited 382

PART FIVE | Promotion and Customer Service 385

CHAPTER 17 | Advertising and Promotion 387

THE SALES PROMOTION DIVISION 388

ADVERTISING 389
    In-House Advertising Departments 389
    External Sources of Advertising Assistance 390
    Advertising Classifications 392
    Advertising Campaigns 393
    Cooperative Advertising 394
    Crossover Advertising 394
    Advertising Media 395
    Advertising Cost Analysis 400

Focus on... SRDS 400
    Evaluation of Advertising 401

PROMOTION 401
    Special Events 401
    "Promoting" the Promotion 405

PUBLICITY 406

MULTIMEDIA CAMPAIGNS 406

Chapter Highlights 407
Important Retailing Terms 407
For Review 407
An Internet Activity 407
Exercises and Projects 408
The Case of the Fashion Entrepreneur with Limited Promotional Funds 408
In the News—The Newspaper Cemetery 408
In the News—Gale Group: Blurring the Lines 410

CHAPTER 18 | Visual Merchandising 413

DEVELOPMENT OF THE VISUAL CONCEPT 414
    The Department Store Approach 415
    Centralized Visual Merchandising 415
    Small Store Visual Arrangements 416
    Freelancers 416

COMPONENTS OF VISUAL PRESENTATIONS 416
    Props 417

Focus on... NADI 418

Focus on... Spaeth Design 418
    Mannequins 419
    Signage and Graphics 419

Focus on ... Clearr Corporation   420
    Lighting   421
    Color   423

DESIGN PRINCIPLES   424
    Balance   424
    Emphasis   425
    Proportion   425
    Rhythm   425
    Harmony   426

THEMES   426

STEPS TO ASSURE VISUAL MERCHANDISING SUCCESS   427
    Component Refurbishment   427
    Timeliness of the Display   427
    Cleanliness of the Environment   428
    Refreshing the In-Store Displays   428
    Continuous Maintenance of Self-Service Fixtures   428
    Merchandise Rearrangement   429

VISUAL MERCHANDISING: THE LINK TO ADVERTISING   429

Chapter Highlights   430
Important Retailing Terms   430
For Review   430
An Internet Activity   431
Exercises and Projects   431
The Case of Creating a Visual Environment to Reflect a New Company Direction   431
In the News—Integrating Art into the Storefront   432
In the News—Redesigning Mannequins for an Upscale Image   433

CHAPTER 19 | Customer Service   435

PERSONAL SELLING   436

Focus on ... Nordstrom   437
    The Rules of the Game   438
    Perfecting the Persona   440
    The Selling Experience   442

OFF-SITE SELLING   445
    Catalogue Selling   445
    Internet Selling   445
    Home-Shopping Selling   446

CUSTOMER SERVICES   446
    Maximizing Shopper Satisfaction   447
    Traditional Customer Services   447
    Customized Services   450
    Call Centers   452
    Guidelines for Better Service   453

Chapter Highlights   453
Important Retailing Terms   453
For Review   454
An Internet Activity   454
Exercises and Projects   454
The Case of Developing a Customer Service Program That Best Serves
    Consumers   454
In the News—Dynamic Web Content: Giving Customers What
    They Want   455
In the News—Merchants Struggle to Define Customer Satisfaction   457

APPENDIX | Careers in Retailing and Related Fields   461

JOB CLASSIFICATIONS   461
    Brick-and-Mortar and Off-Site Job Opportunities   462
    Careers That Parallel Retailing   464

PLANNING FOR THE CAREER 465
  Educational Background 465
  Introduction to the Company 465
  Gaining an Interview 466
  The Interview Follow-Up 467

FIGURE CREDITS 469
INDEX 471

FOCUS FEATURES SUMMARY

The following retail and retail-associated organizations' *Focus* features and segments are interspersed throughout the book, appearing in the chapters most appropriate to emphasize their uniqueness in the industry. Some organizations appear in more than one place in the text.

COMPANY — PAGE

Company	Page
Jos. A. Bank	6
Belk, Inc.	7
Joseph Abboud	19
Liz Claiborne, Inc.	20
Macy's, Inc.	38
Nordstrom	39
Gap, Inc.	44
Zappos.com	62
Sephora	64
The American Girl	70
HSN, the Television Shopping Network	72
Abercrombie & Fitch	82
Ralph Lauren, Russia	86
Pottery Barn	111
ACNielsen	124
Allied Media Corp.	132
Zalia	138
Arbitron, Inc.	142
Wal-Mart	143
Stein Mart	156
Macy's, Inc., Vendor/Supplier Code of Conduct	157
Better Business Bureau	159
Giant Eagle	177
Patagonia	179
Wal-Mart	182
Target Corporation	198
Saks Fifth Avenue	203
Von Maur	206
McDonald's	207

Sensormatic Electronics Corp.	224
Macy's, Inc., Logistics and Operations	241
Gymboree	243
Monarch Marking Systems	249
Simon Property Group	265
International Council of Shopping Centers	270
Institute of Store Planners	291
Bergdorf Goodman	295
American Girl Place	296
Barnard's Retail Consulting Group	315
The Doneger Group	324
Gap, Inc.	346
Mast Industries, Inc.	350
Costco	367
Filene's Basement	377
SRDS	400
NADI	418
Spaeth Design	418
Clearr Corporation	420
Nordstrom	437

IN THE NEWS ARTICLES

PAGE

Chapter 1
PANEL: TECH-SAVVY RETAILERS WILL THRIVE   29
JEANINE POGGI
Women's Wear Daily, APRIL 16, 2007

WHOLESALE GIANTS MORPHING INTO RETAILERS   31
WHITNEY BECKETT
Women's Wear Daily, APRIL 12, 2007

Chapter 2
THE INS AND OUTS OF OUTLETS   52
AMY S. CHOI
DNR, MARCH 26, 2007

Chapter 3
PICK IT AND CLICK IT   74
CATE T. CORCORAN
Women's Wear Daily, JUNE 28, 2007

APPAREL NOW NO. 1 ONLINE   75
CATE T. CORCORAN
Women's Wear Daily, MAY 14, 2007

Chapter 4
GLOBAL MARKETS KEY TO RETAILING FUTURE   101
ROBERT MURPHY
Women's Wear Daily, APRIL 3, 2007

FINDING A HOME ABROAD   103
DAVID MOIN
Women's Wear Daily, APRIL 16, 2007

Chapter 5
TEEN PANEL REFLECTS SHIFTING SPENDING HABITS   127
JEANINE POGGI
Women's Wear Daily, JUNE 11, 2007

IN-STORE ADVERTISING: SHOULD PSYCHOGRAPHIC STUDIES PLAY A ROLE? 128
BILL GERBA
www.wirespring.com, SEPTEMBER 20, 2006

Chapter 6

RETAIL HAS ROOM TO GROW IN ETHNIC MARKETS 146
JEANINE POGGI
Women's Wear Daily, JUNE 11, 2007

HOW DO YOU SAY "GOT MILK" EN ESPAÑOL? 147
CYNTHIA GORNEY
New York Times Magazine, SEPTEMBER 23, 2007

Chapter 7

IS PETA DEFANGED? FUR LOOKS ARE BACK ON AND OFF RUNWAYS 167
ROSEMARY FEITELBERG
Women's Wear Daily, FEBRUARY 14, 2007

CHINA PRESSURE COOKER: ETHICAL QUESTIONS GROW OVER LOW-COST SOURCING 169
EVAN CLARK
Women's Wear Daily, OCTOBER 2, 2007

Chapter 8

EARTHLY DELIGHTS 186
SHARON EDELSON WITH CONTRIBUTIONS BY ROSEMARY FEITELBERG
Women's Wear Daily, APRIL 10, 2007

LEADING THE WAY 188
ELLEN GROVES
Women's Wear Daily, OCTOBER 30, 2007

Chapter 9

H.R. SUMMIT REVEALS EMPLOYEE WOES 215
RACHEL STRUGATZ
Women's Wear Daily, OCTOBER 11, 2007

HOLT RENFREW TURNS AROUND H.R. WITH TECH 218
DENISE POWER
Women's Wear Daily, APRIL 4, 2007

THE TRAINING ADVANTAGE 219
SHARON EDELSON
Women's Wear Daily, APRIL 2, 2007

Chapter 10

RETAIL'S LATEST PLAGUE: FIGHTING BACK AGAINST SHOPLIFTING GANGS 236
EVAN CLARK
Women's Wear Daily, AUGUST 3, 2007

Chapter 11
SAKS MASTERS DC FLOW-THROUGH — 253
www.packagingdigest.com, MAY 1, 2006

Chapter 12
MIXING IT UP — 281
SHARON EDELSON
Women's Wear Daily, JUNE 28, 2007

LUXE GOODS ON THE FLY: ACCESSORIES BRANDS TAP TRAVEL RETAIL FOR GROWTH — 283
KATYA FOREMAN
Women's Wear Daily, JULY 9, 2007

Chapter 13
AÉROPOSTALE UPDATES ITS BOX — 304
JESSICA PALLAY
DNR, APRIL 9, 2007

MAXIMIZING THE ASSETS: SAKS FLAGSHIP CHARTS LATEST SET OF UPGRADES — 305
DAVID MOIN
Women's Wear Daily, MARCH 28, 2007

Chapter 14
TACKLING THE SOURCING CONUNDRUM — 337
EVAN CLARK
Women's Wear Daily, APRIL 9, 2007

A PROMINENT PRESENCE: WALKING THE SHOW FLOOR WITH ABBEY DONEGER — 338
LIZA CASABONA
DNR, APRIL 16, 2007

Chapter 15
MARKETS SAY PROUDLY: IT'S OUR BRAND — 356
JON ORTIZ
www.sabee.com, NOVEMBER 11, 2007

THE POWER OF THE PRIVATE LABEL — 358
WILLIAM GEORGE SHUSTER
www.jckonline.com, MARCH 1, 2007

Chapter 16
RETAIL PRICING STRATEGIES — 381
SHARI WATERS
http://retail.about.com, NOVEMBER 9, 2007

THE MARKDOWN BLUES, REVISITED — 382
TED HURLBUT
www.hurlbutassociates.com

Chapter 17

THE NEWSPAPER CEMETRY — 408
NASEEM JAVED
www.ecommercetimes.com, MAY 23, 2007

GALE GROUP: BLURRING THE LINES — 410
RACHEL STRUGATZ
Women's Wear Daily, JULY 2, 2007

Chapter 18

INTEGRATING ART INTO THE STOREFRONT — 432
DAVID MOIN
Women's Wear Daily, JUNE 26, 2007

REDESIGNING MANNEQUINS FOR AN UPSCALE IMAGE — 433
DAVID MOIN
Women's Wear Daily, MARCH 7, 2007

Chapter 19

DYNAMIC WEB CONTENT: GIVING CUSTOMERS WHAT THEY WANT — 447
JOHN LOVETT
www.crmbuyer.com, JULY 2, 2007

MERCHANTS STRUGGLE TO DEFINE CUSTOMER SATISFACTION — 457
MARIA HALKIAS, AMY CONN-GUTIERREZ
www.dallasnews.com (THE DALLAS MORNING NEWS)

PREFACE

Now that the retail industry is well into the twenty-first century, those involved in its successful management are constantly making adjustments to their business models, strategies, and methods of operation. It seems that almost every day brings new challenges to large and small retailers alike. Whether it is new approaches to maintaining their customer base and attracting new shoppers, keeping abreast of the latest in technology, adjusting their merchandising approaches, or expanding their operations through additional units or off-site involvement, the tasks are formidable and require regular evaluation of business methodologies.

Retailing is now a field where the status quo will generally *not* result in merchants' realizing their fair share of sales or significant profits. While brick-and-mortar outlets still account for most of the industry's sales volume, e-tailing and catalogues are steadily gaining the attention of many consumers. With this in mind, the future seems to be headed in the multichannel direction. There are some exceptions, of course, but most major retailers are following this approach.

In addition to focusing on such areas as buying and merchandising, store location and design, promotional methods and innovations, human resources management, and so forth, this text also covers major retail concerns that few others examine. It includes separate chapters on *The Globalization of Retailing*, which describes how merchants from all over the world are practicing to make their operations available to markets never before served; *Multiculturalism in Retailing*, which addresses the significant growth of the major ethnicities in the United States and their importance to merchants; *The Role of Ethics in the Retail Environment*, focusing on the codes of ethics employed by merchants and how their attention to this timely topic benefits consumers; and *Going Green*, a fast-growing concept that benefits the environment.

The importance of specific retailers and retail-related businesses—and how they have risen above the crowd—are featured within numerous *Focus* features and segments. Merchants like Macy's, Saks Fifth Avenue, Gap, Nordstrom, Spaeth Design, Gymboree, McDonald's, Simon Property Group, ACNielsen, Sephora, Zappos.com, Target Corporation, and many others are featured in the chapters most related to their initiatives.

Also included are "In the News" items at the end of each chapter: articles that have appeared in leading trade and consumer publications or on the Internet. These reprints are timely pieces that cover virtually every aspect of the industry that is important to the retail scene.

To make this book more exciting and give the student a clearer picture of the industry, approximately 250 full-color photographs, tables, and charts are included.

In addition to the complete coverage of the current topics faced by today's retailers, a number of pedagogical devices are used to ensure that readers will benefit from their study of the text. These include:

- *Learning Objectives*, which alert the student to what he or she will be able to master.
- *Chapter Highlights* that give an overview of the important points in the chapter.
- *Important Retailing Terms* that, when mastered, will prepare the student with a vocabulary that is used in day-to-day retailing.
- *Review Questions* that require the reader to recall the materials that have been presented in the chapter.
- *An Internet Activity*, which requires the use of the Internet for its solution.
- *Exercises and Projects* that necessitate some form of industry contact such as company visits, interviews, or observations.
- *Case Problems* that focus on individual businesses facing the challenge of solving problems that are related to the chapter material.

An instructor's guide is also provided, as is a PowerPoint presentation to highlight specific visual items.

Whether the reader is one who merely wants to learn about the field or has already made retailing a career choice, this text provides a wealth of information pertinent to achieving these goals.

ACKNOWLEDGMENTS

We wish to thank the following people and organizations for their invaluable help in the writing of this textbook:

Allan Ellinger, Marketing Management Group; Steve Goodman, Graj + Gustavsen; Marcy Goldstein, JGA Inc.; Donna Lombardo and Steve Kelly, Belk's Department Store; The Doneger Group; Michael Stewart, Rootstein; Ellen Diamond, photographer; Gigi Farrow, fashion consultant; Amy Meadows, Macy's; Tim Wisgerhoff, Saks Fifth Avenue; Manoel Renha, Lord & Taylor; FRCH; Sensormatic Electronics Corp.; International Council of Shopping Centers; The Mills Corporation; Claritas, Inc.; Beth Terrell, Lizden Industries; Billie Scott, Simon Property Group; David Spaeth, Spaeth Design; Brett Wright, NuAmerica Agency; Burnt Ullman, Phat Fashions; Todd Kahn, Sean John Clothing; Chiqui Cartagena, Meredith Integrated Marketing.

Jay Diamond
Sheri Litt

Retailing in the Twenty-First Century

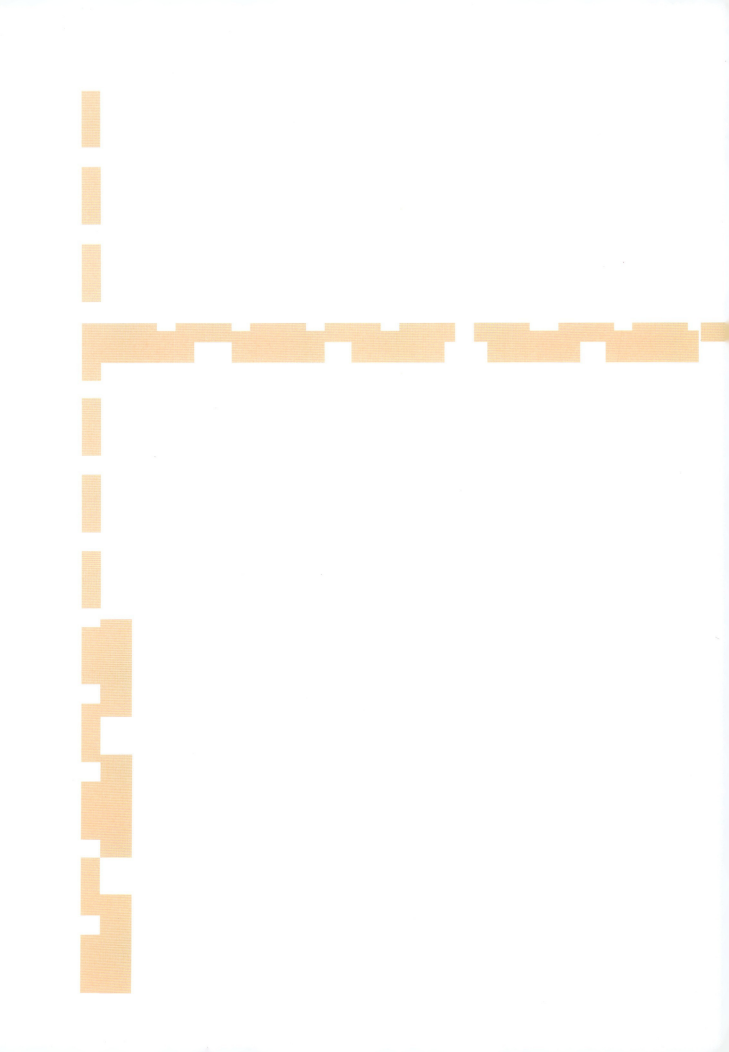

PART ONE

Introduction to Retailing

Retailing today is dramatically different from what it was in the past. Consumers, more than ever before, have avenues for purchasing that are not restricted to the traditional stores and handful of catalogues that not too long ago were the only games in town. Consumers can now satisfy their needs with a wealth of merchandise in creative brick-and-mortar environments that run the gamut from department stores to unique specialty stores, a never-ending number of catalogues that feature every conceivable type of product, Web sites that offer the shopper just about any consumer good that has ever been made in just about any part of the world, and home-shopping networks that feature a wealth of products around the clock. No, retailing is no longer what it once was—a somewhat limited industry with somewhat limited shopping choices—but an exciting, multifaceted arena that affords shoppers unlimited merchandise choices from around the world.

No one can properly explore the present landscape of retailing or its future without a look at the past. In Chapter 1, a historical look at the industry begins with the peddlers who were once the only way that consumers could get their merchandise and traces the evolution that has taken place since then.

Chapter 2 features the various types of brick-and-mortar environments, including traditional department stores, specialty organizations, hypermarkets (a major retail classification in many European countries) as well as "store is the brand" merchants, subspecialty retailers, and franchisers.

Off-site retailing has gained such incredible momentum that it is thought by industry professionals to pose a threat to traditional means of purchasing. Along with an unparalleled number of catalogues to fit every lifestyle, an expansion of home-shopping outlets on cable television, and e-tailing that seems to be taking the world by storm, the shopper has countless ways in which to spend his or her money. These retail entries are extensively examined in Chapter 3.

Chapter 4 provides an overview of the globalization of retailing. Specifically, it examines the phenomenon of merchants from a vast number of countries expanding their operations on foreign shores.

Chapter 5 offers a close inspection of modern consumers and of how they are motivated to make their purchases. Chapter 6 expands upon traditional consumer research, presented in the preceding chapter, with significant attention paid to the various multicultural segments of the marketplace and how their motivations often differ from those of the overall consumer market.

The role of ethics and its importance to today's retailers is featured in Chapter 7, which addresses the many strides merchants are making in these practices. Rounding out this first section is the topic of Chapter 8—"going green"—which underscores the importance of eco-friendly practices by the retailer and the many ways in which he or she can participate in protecting the environment.

CHAPTER 1
Retailing from Its Early Days to the Present

After you have completed this chapter, you should be able to discuss:

- The early days of retailing in the United States and how early retailers differ from today's businesses
- The similarities and differences between department stores and chain organizations
- How two value retail operations—discount operations and off-price stores—differ
- The importance of organizational structure to retailers
- Which retail trends are becoming important in the retail industry
- The major retailers with an overseas presence
- The future retailing directions that are most likely to become trends
- Career opportunities in today's retail marketplace

Retailers today face challenges that never confronted them before. Internet Web sites, vast numbers of global merchandise resource centers, and rapid changes in technology are just some of the issues that merchants must assess in order to make certain that their companies will maintain their competitive edge.

To better understand the new retail environment, which is the second largest industry in the United States and generates sales of $3.8 trillion, it is beneficial to understand how retailing in America has evolved since its infancy and has made necessary transitions to meet the needs of the consuming public.

A look at the history of American retailing, beginning in the sixteenth century, will provide the framework for the principles and practices of modern-day retail businesses.

RETAILING IN AMERICA: A HISTORICAL OVERVIEW OF THE INDUSTRY

In the early years of colonial America, retailers had few avenues through which to reach the market. Practices were primitive, available merchandise was severely limited, and the needs of the customers were extremely basic.

Trading Posts

In the early days of retailing in America, stores as we know them today were not part of the landscape. The American colonies were dealing with the many struggles that developing communities must face. While the needs of the early settlers were minimal in comparison to those of today's consumers, some products were essential to their everyday lives. The first American retail institution, the **trading post**, was established in the early sixteenth century to satisfy these needs. Products manufactured in Europe were available at these outposts along with agricultural products supplied by farmers and pelts supplied by trappers. Currency was not used in the negotiation; instead, goods were traded for other goods in a bartering system. Although this primitive form of retailing is virtually nonexistent today, it is considered to be the forerunner of flea markets. Of course, flea markets in the twenty-first century are not places where bartering is the means of selling, but a place where cash and credit cards are used for purchasing. While many of today's flea markets are actually big business arenas and show no resemblance to the trading posts of the past, there are still some remnants of the old trading posts or swap shops in rural areas where the locals come to buy and sell used items, homemade goods, and farm products.

Peddlers

In extremely remote rural areas, where there were no trading posts, the settlers resorted to buying goods from **peddlers** who went from place to place hawking their wares. They sold such necessities as pots and pans, tools, knives, and foodstuffs, including coffee and tea, that weren't grown by the farmers. As at the trading posts, most of the goods were bartered because people didn't have the currency for outright purchases. The peddlers took a variety of produce and crudely made furniture in exchange for their goods.

In addition to bringing various much-needed items to the farmers, the peddlers also carried eagerly awaited news from the settlements and from Europe. In fact, the peddlers were one of the few ways by which these new Americans could learn about their homelands.

While the merchandise and information peddlers brought to the farmers were essential to their happiness and meager existence, they often came at a dear price. Without competition to serve as a check on prices, many peddlers took advantage of their customers and charged them unfair prices. With the profits they realized from these ventures, some peddlers went on to open stores, and some became major retailing entrepreneurs.

The trading posts flourished for many years, as did the businesses of the peddlers.

General Stores

It wasn't until the early eighteenth century that the first real, permanent retailing establishments came into existence. They were known as **general stores** because their inventory was extremely varied and included goods ranging from food to fabrics. Unlike their predecessors, general stores were operated primarily on a cash basis, although those with good credit were allowed to run up bills that they would pay periodically. Farmers, for example, would get some of their supplies from the general stores and be allowed to pay for them when the crops were harvested and sold. This practice was actually the forerunner to the formal charge accounts that came later.

The physical arrangement of inventory was something of a hodgepodge. Nothing had a set place in the store; as the goods came in, they were put wherever room could be found. The stores also housed the post office and places where people would congregate to exchange news and gossip or just pass the time.

Much like the peddlers who came before them, the general store merchants charged prices that were higher than might be considered fair. With the lack of competition and the population dependent on the general store, these merchants could set their own prices and some became the wealthiest people in town. As goods from overseas became more plentiful and American-made goods became more available, the stores were able to carry a wider assortment of merchandise. The general store didn't face any competition until early in the nineteenth century when a variety of merchandise became even more plentiful. It was this abundance of merchandise that led to the beginning of specialization in retailing. Although the limited-line or specialty store became popular at this time, the general store remained a business venture, especially in the far-flung areas where other retail businesses didn't open more modern facilities. Even today, in the most rural parts of the South, some general stores are still in operation.

Abercrombie & Fitch is an example of a limited-line store.

Limited-Line Stores

By the mid 1850s, merchants started to open **limited-line stores** or **specialty stores** that restricted their offerings to one classification or line. The industrial revolution was now in full steam, and a wealth of goods never seen before was available. Reacting to this abundance of products and the consumers' need to have them, retailers opened limited-line stores in record numbers. Unlike the general store, this new type of store featured a wide variety of goods in one product line, such as shoes, food, hardware, clothing, or millinery, so that customers had an assortment with both breadth and depth to choose from.

The success of the limited-line store has carried over until today. In fact, it is fast becoming the most important segment of the retail industry.

Chain Organizations

Chain store organizations developed shortly after limited-line stores, with the first chain—the Great Atlantic & Pacific Tea Co.—beginning operations in 1859. When the specialty store merchants found success in one geographical area, some expanded their operations to other locations. When these new outlets succeeded, retailers opened still more units. These retailers were "inventing" the **chain store organization.** Simply defined, a chain store organization is a retail business with four or more units, similar in nature,

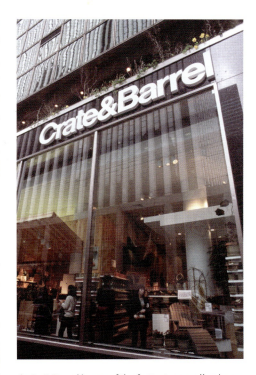

Crate & Barrel is one of the fastest expanding home product chain organizations.

and having common ownership. Chains may specialize in any merchandise category, such as soft goods, home, food, pharmaceuticals, video rentals, music, and so forth. They continue to spread quickly throughout the United States and abroad. Chains like The Limited, Gap, Toys "R" Us, Crate & Barrel, CVS, Pottery Barn, and Abercrombie & Fitch are expanding in record numbers. Not only do they continue to open stores under their company's original name, but many have also established new entities under different names, featuring other merchandise mixes targeted to new market segments.

A case in point is Limited Brands with several thousand stores. Under the Limited umbrella, chain stores like Victoria's Secret and Bath & Body Works are achieving significant success.

> **Focus on . . .**
> **Jos. A. Bank**

ALTHOUGH JOS. A. BANK HAS BEEN IN OPERATION SINCE 1905, its prominence has significantly increased in the last few years. With the goal of bringing quality clothing to the consumer at prices that are 20–30 percent less than the competition, it has always prided itself on customer satisfaction.

Initially a small regional chain, the company has aggressively expanded to become a major force in menswear retailing, with 400 stores throughout the United States. Revenues for 2007 were approximately $600 million, and the goal is $1 billion by 2012.

Significant growth has been realized because of a number of different sound business decisions. One of these was aggressive television advertising. Rarely does a week go by that a major campaign is not seen on the major networks. Commercials announcing special sales, purchasing incentives, and markdowns are the key ingredients of these ads. Given the continued increase in sales volume, their advertising commitment is working.

Unlike other chains, which usually select major malls for their outlets, Jos. A. Bank prefers the small open-air lifestyle centers and boutique malls that are often found in affluent suburbs. Since these locales do not feature department stores, units like theirs are the only games in town that feature menswear.

Merchandise cost is also a factor in the success of the company. Instead of stocking its inventories with nationally branded labels, Jos. A. Bank designs its own products and has them made by outside contractors. The savings realized by eliminating the middlemen are passed along to the consumer, which makes the company extremely competitive. By using the best possible fabrics that their buyers can locate and paying strict attention to construction and fit, it has captured a significant percentage of the retail menswear market.

In addition to the company's store locations, it delivers four seasonal catalogues to domestic and international markets and also has a Web site that offers the latest products as well as closeouts.

The company's goal is to have 600 stores by 2012, which would be more than such marquee chain names as J.Crew, Talbots, Ann Taylor, and Abercrombie & Fitch. After that expansion, it expects to enter the global market.

Department Stores

In the mid-nineteenth century the concept of selling a wide assortment of merchandise under one roof was revived in a new form, the **department store**. Unlike general stores, with their haphazard arrangement of goods, department stores had carefully structured layouts that stocked each merchandise classification in a specific area. Shoppers looking for shoes, for example, could find an assortment of them in an area that had only shoes. Unlike their competition—specialty stores—department stores offered a wide variety of both hard goods and soft goods. A customer could buy a dress, a handbag, bedding, and table linens without having to leave the store. It was **one-stop shopping** at its best. Essentially, the department store is the bringing together of many different specialty stores in a single environment.

The department store format was an immediate success. Companies like Macy's soon began to expand their operations much as their specialty store counterparts had. The additional units opened were smaller versions of the original main stores, or **flagship stores**, and were called **branch stores**. Department store companies developed an organizational structure with central control of management and merchandising philosophies. Thus, the branches were merely selling outlets. All decisions were made at the flagship, which established the rules and regulations to be followed by the branches.

Focus on . . .
Belk Inc.

UNLIKE MOST DEPARTMENT STORES IN THE UNITED STATES, which are public companies and usually part of some major retailing empire such as Macy's, Inc., Belk is the largest privately held department store retailer in the United States. Its stores are located in the southern and southwestern regions of the country.

Founded in 1888 in Monroe, North Carolina, by William Henry Belk, the company is now managed by a third generation: Thomas Belk Jr., who is co-president and chief merchandising officer, and H. W. McKay Belk, co-president and chief operating officer. Under their direction, the company has risen to number 23 in the *Stores Magazine* list of the top hottest U.S. retailers of 2006.

Its rise to retail prominence was due not only to the opening of many new Belk units but also to the acquisition of such companies as Parisian (a Birmingham, Alabama, organization) and Proffitt's/McCrae's (also a southern entity). By renaming these units with the Belk signature, the company entered into many upscale markets such as Atlanta, Georgia, and Charlotte, North Carolina. In these new environments, the company's image is more like that of Neiman Marcus and Nordstrom than of the moderate Belk units that serve smaller markets.

Belk's merchandising approach is now different from what it once was. Today, it includes such brands as Betsey Johnson, Lilly Pulitzer, Juicy Couture, Tahari, Cynthia Steffe, BCBG, and Seven For All Mankind in its merchandise assortments. The company's goal is to upgrade many of its existing units to "premium" or better stores. Augmenting its product mixes are many private labels, which gives the company a degree of exclusivity.

Belk now operates 300 units with estimated annual sales of more than $3 billion. With its increased efforts toward customized service, it expects to generate more customer loyalty and to build a lasting positive image.

Mail-Order Retailers

At about the same time that the department store was achieving success, yet another retailing venture was under way: **mail-order selling**, through which retailers brought merchandise directly to the consumer. Great numbers of Americans lived too far away from stores to patronize them, yet they needed a variety of products. Direct-mail retailers served those needs. Montgomery Ward & Co. published the first mail-order catalogue in 1872; Sears Roebuck & Co. followed suit in 1896. These catalogues featured numerous products in a variety of classifications that rural families could choose from for delivery via U.S. mail. Year after year, with the success of mail-order retailing, these two companies expanded their catalogues until they became **big books** of several hundred pages and contained every conceivable type of merchandise. Although their successes continued well into the twentieth century, both companies eventually disbanded these operations. While sales volume remained stable, the cost of doing business with these enormous books was too high and thus became unprofitable.

Although the huge Spiegel catalogue is still a mainstay in American retailing, the trend in catalogue selling has been toward issuing smaller catalogues numerous times throughout the year. Every department store, most specialty chains, and numerous companies that use only direct selling methods are crowding mail boxes with scores of catalogues that offer a wealth of products. Another change in recent years involves how customers place their orders.

While the term mail order is still used informally for this type of merchandising, the vast majority of purchases are made over the telephone. *Catalogue selling* is therefore a more appropriate term for this type of retailing.

Giant retailer Sears Roebuck & Co. began with a single small location in 1887 and published its first catalogue, limited to watches and jewelry, in 1888.

Supermarkets

Large departmentalized food stores, or **supermarkets**, came on the scene in the early 1930s. Until that time, people shopped for food at grocers, butchers, and bakers. The Great Atlantic & Pacific Tea Co. is credited with developing the supermarket concept with its A & P stores. Other early supermarket chains were Grand Union and Kroger. The notion of one-stop food shopping quickly caught fire, and the race was on for other foods merchants to enter this form of retailing. By the 1950s the supermarket became the dominant force in food sales, forcing many small grocers, butchers, and bakeries to go out of business. So successful were these ventures that more and more units were opened in neighborhoods all across the United States. With their low prices, self-service format, and wide selection of products, supermarkets became the way Americans shopped for food.

The Whole Foods supermarket chain features a wide variety of fine food products.

It wasn't long before supermarkets expanded their inventory into nonfood items, enabling shoppers to purchase many products that once required separate stops at specialty stores such as pharmacies, bookstores, hardware stores, and the like. The availability of nonfood items not only satisfied the needs of the store's customers but also gave the companies a profit advantage. Traditionally, food carries a comparatively low markup and thus a small profit margin. On the other hand, nonfood items enjoy higher markups, thus returning more profit per item to the store.

More and more nonfood items continue to be added to supermarket inventories every day. Greeting cards, paperback books, stationery products, a host of health-care items, plants, hosiery, cosmetics, and tools are commonplace in these stores. Sales for these products continue to increase and help make supermarket retailing a profitable venture.

Discount Operations

In the years immediately following World War II, a new type of retail store was born: the **discount store**, where shoppers could find appliances, cameras, and many other hard goods at prices substantially lower than those charged in the traditional department and specialty stores. The first major discounter, E.J. Korvettes, thrived for many years but has now gone out of business. The discount stores people shop at today are its direct descendants.

Best Buy is a discount operation specializing in electronics.

The discount concept is simple. Stores would lack the usual amenities, featuring instead plain pipe racks and basic counters, and they would provide very few services. In exchange for putting up with the stripped-down environment and lack of services they had been accustomed to elsewhere, customers were offered lower prices. Plainly marked tags with the regular price and the discounted price made it clear to customers that they were getting a bargain.

Today, discount retailing is big business. Companies like Wal-Mart and Target generate an enormous volume of business. These modern discount stores are selling not only hard goods as their predecessors did but also a large variety of clothing, accessories, shoes, food, stationery, records, and garden products—all at discounted prices.

One significant change from their early counterparts is that contemporary discounters offer pleasant shopping surroundings and a host of customer conveniences. The significant volume they achieve enables them to operate in this manner and still turn a profit.

Off-Price Stores

A new type of retail store, the **off-price store**, made its debut on a grand scale in the early 1980s. Frieda Loehmann, founder of the now popular Loehmann's stores, is credited with introducing off-price selling. She began her business on a very limited scale in the 1920s in her home in the Bronx, New York. Each day, Loehmann would go to the Garment Center in Manhattan, where she would buy a few items at greatly reduced prices. She paid cash for the merchandise and was therefore readily welcomed by fashion's top manufacturers. Because she paid low prices and because she had such low overhead, she was able to sell the goods at less than the usual retail price.

Marshalls is one of the leading off-price merchants in the United States.

Day in and day out she followed the same routine. It wasn't long before she opened a store near her home that became a magnet for budget-concious and fashion-concious women throughout the metropolitan area. Like the discount stores, Loehmann's and later off-price stores lacked the amenities of full-price retail outlets.

Today, off-price retailing is a major force in the industry. Along with the Loehmann's chain, companies like Syms, Burlington Coat Factory, Marshalls, T.J. Maxx, and the Men's Wearhouse have outlets all across the country. They are major purchasers in wholesale markets throughout the world, always ready to buy "opportunistically" so that they can satisfy the needs of those seeking bargains. Designer labels and manufacturer brands such as DKNY, Ralph Lauren, Calvin Klein, Liz Claiborne, Guess, and others are mainstays in the off-price merchant's premises.

Manufacturers sell to the off-price retailers as a way to dispose of merchandise that has been left after the traditional store buyers have finished purchasing for the season.

Franchises

In the 1950s, **franchising** began to flourish in the United States—particularly in the fast-food industry with such companies as McDonald's. It was a way for a company to expand with less involvement than required by a chain organization. Under franchising arrangements, the franchiser gives the franchisee the right to open a store that bears the franchiser's name. The franchiser provides the merchandise to the franchisee, trains the new business "partner," and provides the other components necessary for making the franchise a success. In exchange, the franchiser receives a fee, a percentage of sales, and/or a commission on the merchandise sold. The arrangement enables a company to gain a national and international presence while maintaining control over its image without actually opening and operating new units.

Benetton was one of the first clothing manufacturers to expand through franchising.

The concept soon spread to other product classifications such as apparel and accessories. Benetton, the Italian manufacturer and retailer, has expanded into many parts of the world through franchising. Other retailers who use this concept are Athlete's Foot and Mango.

Warehouse Clubs

In the 1980s, the **warehouse clubs** concept was born and began operating in huge industrial-type spaces. Such clubs, where goods are sold at large discounts, were originally established for union members and other large organizations. Today, anyone who pays an annual fee of about $40 can shop at these stores.

Companies like Sam's Club, Costco, Pace, and BJ's are among the largest warehouse clubs, with stores located throughout the country. They offer a vast and ever-changing merchandise assortment. Although the food inventory, which constitutes the largest part of the warehouse club business, is made up of the same product categories throughout the year, buyers can never count on finding the specific brands and products they want. The availability of goods is based upon the buyers' ability to buy at favorable prices. That is, they buy opportunistically.

In addition to foods, warehouse stores carry automotive goods, electronics, outdoor furniture, books, apparel, stationery supplies, cameras, jewelry, and a host of other products. The availability of each merchandise classification at a given time depends on whether the stores' buyers can make deals that will allow them to sell at bargain prices. Another way warehouse clubs keep costs down is by accepting only cash payments; however, some stores (including Sam's Club) do take Discover Card, which has a very low fee.

Unlike other retailing ventures, warehouse clubs sell products only in bulk. Soft drinks, for example, are usually packaged in 24-unit cases; film in 6-packs; and cereals in double packages. To promote food items, as many as a dozen demonstrators prepare samples of hot and cold food at cooking stations on the sales floor.

Warehouse clubs can be extremely profitable despite their low prices because of the money brought in by membership fees. If one considers the huge number of consumers who join these clubs—and pay their dues annually—it is simple to understand their profitability. Thus, unlike other retail ventures where markups need to be high enough to cover overhead expenses and bring in a profit, these retailers need not have high price margins to succeed.

The warehouse clubs continues to thrive and grow, opening new outlets across the United States and in many foreign countries.

Manufacturer-Owned Retail Outlets

At about the same time as off-price retailing and warehouse clubs were in their infancy, consumers were introduced to another new retail operation, the **manufacturer-owned outlet**. With bargain merchandise as the primary draw, shoppers quickly took to these shopping environments.

Manufacturers began to open their own outlets as a way to dispose of unwanted merchandise. Even after selling their leftover inventories to the off-pricers, many still had large quantities of goods in their warehouses. By opening their own stores, designers and manufacturers could "clean out" their inventories to make room for the next season's offerings. Since it is fashion items that quickly change from season to season, it is wearing apparel that led the way in this area of retailing.

Maine Gate Outlet Center is typical of outdoor malls that feature many manufacturers' outlets.

Today, all across the country, numerous outlet centers—usually either outdoor or indoor malls—house the outlets of numerous major designers and manufacturers in a single location. These outlet centers have become favorite destinations for price-conscious consumers. Retail companies that produce their own goods, such as Gap and Banana Republic, are found alongside manufacturers such as Jones New York, Coach, Dooney & Burke, Mikasa, Nine West, Gucci, Perry Ellis, and Liz Claiborne.

Visitors to these outlets find bargain merchandise, often priced as much as 50 percent lower than the traditional retailers, in vast assortments; however the items they find are primarily last season's goods.

So successful are these ventures that many manufacturers are using their leftover fabrics and other materials to produce products especially for these stores.

Flea Markets

Flea markets have their roots in gatherings called swap shops or *swapmeets*, where people bartered their unwanted household items. Swap shops generally took place in rural areas for one day over the weekend. They had no formal structures or continuity. In fact, once someone's goods were sold out, that "retailer" went out of business.

In the early 1980s, the **flea market** took on a new meaning. In parking lots of racetracks, drive-in movies, and other locations that were easily accessible to consumers, vendors began to set up shop with a host of goods that they purchased from manufacturers and sold at very low markups. They were able to market their goods at these attractive prices because their overheads were minimal. Individual spaces cost as little as $40 for the day, with none of the usual expenses for electricity, telephone, insurance, and so forth. The flea market environment is festive and fun, making it a place to bring the whole family. Merchandise offerings included a wealth of items from clothing and foods to household goods and electronics. Many of the markets featured entertainment, fun food, and other enticements.

The flea market concept quickly caught on and flea markets eventually became a regular part of people's shopping routines, not only because of the bargain prices but also for the interesting merchandise assortment. Some flea market vendors carried designer jeans, nationally advertised brands, and other products that could be found—at higher prices—in traditional retail operations. Many flea markets operated in conjunction with farmers' markets that attracted food shoppers with the freshness of their produce.

So successful were these ventures that many of the stall operators opened units at different flea markets, actually becoming chain operations. At many flea markets, the temporary quarters available in the early years have been replaced by permanent structures. For example, in Sunrise, Florida (a suburb of Ft. Lauderdale), more than a thousand vendors hawk their merchandise in permanent buildings as well as outdoor stalls. A wealth of fashion merchandise, expensive jewelry and watches, electronics, and other items fill the shelves and racks. Open every day of the week, the market draws large crowds of shoppers. Another location, operating under the same owners in San Jose, California, is even larger. In each of these environments, entertainment helps to attract the crowds. In the Sunrise Swap Shop, whose name is taken from the early flea market days, a circus performs several times a day and such big-name acts as Willie Nelson and the Gatlin Brothers have appeared. No doubt, when the family has had its fill of entertainment, they head to the vendors to shop.

Boutiques

Catering to affluent men and women, **boutiques** have become favorite shopping places for those seeking high fashion and individuality. Also in the 1980s, just as others were seeking bargains in flea markets and off-price stores, a very small portion of the population headed to these very specialized stores to buy their fashion merchandise. Exclusive apparel and accessories and excellent personal service were the key to the boutiques' success. They can now be found in affluent areas all over the country.

Kiosks

Originating in festival marketplaces like Quincy Market in Boston and South Street Seaport in New York City, the **kiosk** immediately gained favor with the consuming public. Kiosks were like mini stores placed in the aisles and open areas of these marketplaces, where vendors would sell such wares as sunglasses, tee shirts, and other small items from attractive displays.

Today, kiosks are found in the large indoor malls as well as at festival marketplaces. Many do such a thriving business that they have moved into regular retail stores. Lids, a company that sells sports caps with the logos of just about every team in every popular sport, is one company that made the move from kiosk to store.

Kiosks have spread rapidly and are found today in malls, airports, and festival marketplaces.

Category Killers

Another phenomenon that appeared on the scene in the 1980s is the **category killer**. Category killers are extremely large operations that offer enormous selections of merchandise in one classification at discounted prices. Their assortments are so huge that shoppers are almost certain to find the products that meet their particular needs. Examples of such companies are Toys "R" Us, Kids "R" Us, and Best Buy.

Hypermarkets

Fifth Avenue is home to many designers' flagships.

Throughout many European countries, notably France, the **hypermarket** is a major retail classification. Generally it is a very large store with products that range from clothing for the family, toys, and household articles to in-depth offerings of food and food-related items. The leader in hypermarket retailing is France's Carrfour, which has opened units in Spain and South America.

Designer Flagships

Although designer brick-and-mortar ventures are not new to retailing, their presence has become significantly more important since the beginning of the twenty-first century. Haute couture designers, in particular, have opened **designer flagships** on the world's most prominent fashion streets such as New York's Fifth and Madison Avenues, Los Angeles' Rodeo Drive, and Palm Beaches' Worth Avenue. Giorgio Armani, Louis Vuitton, Calvin Klein, and others operate such retail emporiums.

MAJOR AMERICAN RETAILERS

Although retailing is a worldwide business, American companies dominate the landscape. Consisting of such on-site operations as department stores and chain organizations as well as off-site ventures that include catalogues and e-tailing, the U.S. retail industry boasts a wealth of operations that merchandise many product categories in formats ranging from the traditional to the value-oriented. Table 1.1 lists the largest of the retailing giants.

TABLE 1.1
TOP 10 U.S. RETAILERS BY VOLUME, 2006

Company	Headquarters	Number of Units
Wal-Mart	Bentonville, AR	6,779
Home Depot	Atlanta, GA	2,147
Kroger	Cincinnati, OH	3,659
Costco	Issaquah, WA	488
Target	Minneapolis, MN	1,487
Sears Holding*	Hoffman Estates, IL	3,835
Walgreens	Deerfield, IL	5,461
Lowe's	Mooresville, NC	1,375
CVS	Woonsocket, RI	6,202
Safeway	Pleasanton, CA	1,761

Source: *Stores Magazine*, July 2007.
*Includes Sears and Kmart stores.

ORGANIZATIONAL STRUCTURES

The complexity of the retail organization continues to escalate. What was once a rather simple means of organizing a company according to its size, operations, and functions is now significantly more difficult. Retailers of just about every size, except perhaps for the small independents, have adopted new means of reaching their clienteles. Off-site involvement in catalogues and Web sites has compacted their **organizational structures**. The task of making the various retail channels accessible to the consuming public is a formidable one.

Behind the scenes of every retail operation is a management team that structures the organization so that it will be a viable shopping experience for its customers and still maximize the company's profits. Even in the smallest ventures, sole proprietors must carefully establish appropriate procedures.

The approach to organizational structure may differ according to the needs of the company. Whatever the situation, the company must be organized in a manner that addresses all of its functions. In all but the very smallest retail outlets, there are **tables of organization** or **organization charts** that focus on these functions and the divisions that direct each of the company's operations.

Before establishing these functions and divisions and how they should be separated, each must be carefully examined. Only with sufficient coverage of all of the bases will the company run smoothly and efficiently.

The advantages of such charts are numerous. They immediately enable viewers to see the relationships of one division to another as well as the lines of authority, reporting relationships, the various participants in each of the divisions, and so forth.

Traditional Organizational Formats

As previously stated, the size of the operation and its functions play a vital role in its organizational structure. Small stores in no way require the depth and breadth of those formats utilized by the larger organizations. However, no matter how small the company, the careful spelling out of functions is imperative to its success.

Small store organizations most often use single division formats for their operations. That is, the proprietor is the top figure, followed by a manager, with sales associates below them to perform the selling function.

Mid-sized organizations, by necessity, usually have a chief executive officer as head with executives who report to the head and manage such specialized divisions as merchandising and promotion, management, and operations. In fashion operations, there may be a specialist who advises the merchandisers about the status of the fashion market. The roles in these organizations are referred to as **line and staff positions**, with the former the decision makers and producers for the company and the latter, if employed, the advisors. Line and staff operations are typical of mid-sized and large retail operations.

Large-sized organizations, which include department stores and chain organizations, feature the most comprehensive charts and are generally **centralized operations**. That is, decision making occurs at one or more central facilities. These groups include the major department stores that operate flagships, branches, catalogues, and Web sites as well as the chains that operate a thousand or more units and off-site ventures.

The basis of department store tables of organization is the line and staff format, with the line employees being advised by many different staff individuals. Different companies utilize different formats, but all generally have merchandising, publicity, store management, and control divisions. Some have different divisions for their store operations and off-site ventures, whereas others combine them into one general classification. Central headquarters for many department stores is in the flagship, where buyers, merchandisers, advertising personnel, management teams, and other executives make the decisions for the on-site and off-site operations.

The large chains generally have more complicated tables of organization. In addition to the merchandising and sales divisions—which include advertising, buying, and sales—they often also have such divisions as real estate and construction, accounting, transportation, warehousing, human resources, supplies and equipment procurement, and public relations. They also operate on the centralized concept, except that headquarters are not in any store but at a separate central location.

After the table of organization has been developed, it is necessary to spell out the different duties and responsibilities of each title in the structure. In this way, everyone knows his or her role and how it should be carried out.

As a final note, it is important to understand that the best tables of organization are not written in stone. They are reviewed periodically and altered, when necessary, to meet the objectives of the company. In times when retailing practices and procedures are constantly changing and retailers are taking on new challenges, change is often necessary. Overseas expansion, new merchandising formats, and private branding are just some of the trends that might require a new table of organization.

STRATEGIC PLANNING

In an ever-changing retail playing field, it is not appropriate for merchants to continue conducting their businesses in the same old manner. Competition, new retail formats, off-site expansion, and other factors necessitate that those in retailing carefully plan their merchandise sourcing, commitments to advertising, company expansion, potential for globalization, and so forth. To achieve company goals over the long haul and to maximize profits, **strategic planning** is required. It serves as a blueprint for achieving future success.

The plans that retail organizations make focus on their overall picture and include all the activities in which they are involved. Whether the operation is a small independent entrepreneur or a giant in the industry, strategic planning is a must.

Before commencing with an effective plan, the retailer must have an up-to-the-minute understanding of the industry as a whole. A good starting point is information regarding one's competitive environment, what other organizations are doing, the customer base, and the changes currently being made by the industry as a whole. Such information can be culled from in-house management teams, careful examination of trade papers, and contacts with trade associations and marketing consultants. Once the present scene is studied, a strategic initiative is the next stage. It might be a 5-year plan, a 10-year approach, or some period that is suited to the individual company.

Although there are many different approaches to the implementation of a strategic plan, the following steps should be taken by most retailers:

- *Visioning workshops.* These should be held for a few days and should include all of the key players from every part of the organization's present structure. The result should be a host of different ideas that warrant further investigation and whose eventual use may have a positive effect on the company's future.
- *Merchandise diversification or specialization.* Since the backbone of retailing is its merchandise offerings, the plan should focus on the current status of the merchandise mix and how

it could be amended to bring greater attention from customers. It might require "trading up," "trading down," "editing," and so forth.

- *Expansion of existing sales channel.* With so much attention given to the multichannel concept, on-site and off-site outlets should be examined to determine where the most growth can be expected and how the company can alter these **sales channels** to bring greater profitability to the company.
- *Outsourcing considerations.* In a time when in-house activities are sometimes too costly, the use of outside operations to perform certain functions is becoming commonplace. Examples include customer service, call centers, accounting and credit operations, and so forth. Each must be examined to determine if the **outsourcing** route would be more cost-efficient.
- *Merger and acquisition potential.* Instead of opening new stores, the possibility of merging with another retail organization or acquiring an existing retail operation might be considered. Macy's, for example, took the acquisition route in achieving its status as the world's leading department store operation—no doubt a result of careful strategic planning.
- *Creating spin-offs.* Even if expanding an entire operation with new units, exactly as the original, is not warranted, plans for **spin-offs** of particular merchandise categories could be strategically sound. Bloomingdale's has done so with its home furnishing units.

After all of the possibilities have been considered and painstakingly evaluated by the management team, perhaps in conjunction with a specialist in strategic planning such as MMC. A.D. Systems, the plan should be implemented in a timely manner. This should make the company a more competitive one and bring it a fair share of the marketplace.

USE OF TECHNOLOGY

In this time of growth and change and of the ever-growing multichannel playing field, retailers of all sizes and merchandise classifications must stay ahead of the game and continuously "research" their activities to make them competitive. The almost daily introduction of new technological tools makes the smooth running of operations possible. In just about every area—including merchandising, operations, human resources management, finance, and control—retailers are constantly updating their systems and installing new software to refine their tasks and improve their performance.

One of the ways that many of the major retail operations strategically tailor their technology uses is through affiliation with an outside technology group. Even those with significant in-house technical staffing find that interfacing with an outside agency is the best way to proceed. One of the better-known companies to offer such services is Retail Technology Group, a joint venture of leading information systems consultants that entered the marketplace in 1991. Utilizing everything from existing packages to special projects, the company offers diversified, specialized skills in distribution, logistics, merchandise planning, training programs, and catalogue and e-commerce fulfillment. Their client list includes some of retailing's major players such as Bergdorf Goodman, Circuit City, Fortunoff, Loehmann's, Lord & Taylor, Macy's, Saks Fifth Avenue, Bed Bath & Beyond, and The Disney Store.

Moreover, direct involvement with companies like Microsoft, the JDA Software Group, iQmetrix, HR Technology Partners (which markets the Abra Suite programs), Halogen eAppraisal, and the Asymetrix ToolBook program can easily be found online via any search engine such as www.Google.com. Specific technologies will be discussed throughout the text when particular applications (e.g., human resources) are addressed.

In the News . . .

Read the excellent article "Panel: Tech-Savvy Retailers Will Thrive" at the end of this chapter (page 29), which gives up-to-the-minute arguments for improved retail technology.

RETAIL TRENDS

The changes and directions in retailing will more than likely continue in the future. Companies are generally ready to embrace new concepts, expand their offerings, emphasize different motivational techniques to capture the shopper's attention, expand their organizations to new locations at home and abroad, and do anything else that will make their operations more profitable.

Many of these undertakings are based upon industrywide trends. No time in the past has ever been witness to the wealth of innovations and directions that retailing is now experiencing. In this section, we address just some of the trends. Those making a significant impact on the retail scene are discussed briefly, with greater attention given to them in later chapters.

Off-Site Selling

Although brick-and-mortar outlets still account for the vast majority of sales in retailing, the growth of catalogues and Web sites is significant. Except for perhaps very small merchants, retailers are putting major emphasis on **off-site selling**. With the sales generated by these off-site retail divisions growing every year, the trend to continue with their expansion is certain to be a significant part of the retail playing field.

Offshore Expansion

Retailers once stayed in their own "backyards" and opened only domestic stores, but the trend to expand overseas is rapidly growing. Merchants of most every size and product classification are investing in distant places in the hope that they will attract new consumer markets for their merchandise. Every day, trade papers feature news items regarding retailers making the overseas move. It should be noted that such **offshore expansion** is not only by American retailers but also by those based in other parts of the world.

Some of those involved in this trend are Calvin Klein, Zegna, Dolce & Gabbana, Urban Outfitters, Banana Republic, Gucci, Bulgari, H&M, Brooks Brothers, Wal-Mart, Gaultier, Theory, Ralph Lauren, Armani, Tiffany & Co., Cynthia Rowley, Aéropostale, and Gap. See Table 1.2.

It should be noted that some major retailers that have not yet entered the global markets are planning to do so. Target, for example, is eyeing overseas expansion beginning anywhere from 2012 to 2017.

Brooks Brothers is an American company that is expanding overseas.

Private Labeling and Branding

More and more retailers are expanding their private label and private brand collections. They are doing so for several reasons, which include the need to distinguish themselves from competitors who often merchandise the same national brands, to level the playing field with

TABLE 1.2
RETAILERS WITH OVERSEAS PRESENCE

Retailer	Country of Origin	Selected Overseas Expansion
Calvin Klein	United States	Beijing, Shanghai, Tokyo
Ermenegildo Zegna	Italy	Mumbai, New Delhi, U.S.
Dolce & Gabbana	Italy	New Delhi, Beijing, Shanghai, Hong Kong, U.S.
Tiffany & Company	United States	Tokyo, Hiroshima, Beijing, Hong Kong, London
Giorgio Armani	Italy	Tokyo, U.S., London, Munich, Hong Kong
Brooks Brothers	United States	Milan, Paris, London
Bulgari	Italy	Tokyo, U.S.
Wal-Mart	United States	Montreal, Vancouver, Toronto
Gucci	Italy	Mexico City, U.S., Paris, London
H&M	Sweden	Shanghai, U.S., Nice, Hong Kong
Gaultier	France	Hong Kong, Taipei, Dubai, Kuala Lumpur, London
Gap	United States	Japan, London
Ralph Lauren	United States	Moscow, Paris
Banana Republic	United States	London, South Korea
Theory	United States	Paris, Athens
Cynthia Rowley	United States	Tokyo
Urban Outfitters	United States	London, Dublin, Manchester, Stockholm

Vera Wang has signed with Kohl's to produce an exclusive popular-priced collection.

merchants who sell marquee labels at reduced prices, and to provide customers with products that are better tailored to their needs. Examples include Macy's, Bloomingdale's, Dillard's, Saks Fifth Avenue, and other department and specialty chains.

Contracting with Upscale Designers for Retail Exclusivity

The fashion industry is replete with many designers who have achieved success catering to upscale clienteles. In addition to creating these collections, an increasing number of them have signed exclusive agreements with retailers to develop lower-priced lines for their companies. Vera Wang, best known for her bridal collections, has signed on with Kohl's to create a line called Simply Vera at prices that have mass market appeal. Also, H&M continues to go this route with couturiers such as Karl Lagerfeld, Stella McCartney, Roberto Cavalli, and Viktor & Rolf designing exclusive collections for them.

In a complete designer–retailer relationship, Gap, Inc., has hired Todd Oldham, a marquee designer, as their creative director for its Old Navy chain. In addition to overseeing a new direction for its brand, Oldham will also develop a line of merchandise bearing his name.

Brooks Brothers, the perennial choice of discriminating men and women for business attire, has taken a new direction with the addition of a line created by Thom Brown, winner of the 2006 Designer of the Year award by CFDA (Council of Fashion Designers). It is the first time the company has employed the services of a "guest designer" to create a collection. Using the name Black Fleece, it will market sweaters staring at $800, suits from $3,000 to $4,000 and evening wear retailing at more than $5,000. By repositioning its brand with this new couture offering, the company has reacted to the growing trend of using designers with recognized names in order to augment its regular business.

One of the major accomplishments in the exclusivity arena is the deal between Tommy Hilfiger and Macy's. In an unusual move, Hilfiger has agreed to eliminate all of its other accounts (e.g., Dillard's and Bon-Ton) and limit its offerings to Macy's only. The deal is considered to be a coup for Macy's because this is one of the most coveted "names" in fashion.

Joining the fray as both creative director and collection designer is Joseph Abboud, the subject of our next *Focus* segment.

Focus on . . . Joseph Abboud

FOR MANY YEARS, Joseph Abboud has been a marquee-level designer creating menswear collections that have captured many industry awards, including Designer of the Year for two years in a row (1989 and 1990) from the Council of Fashion Designers of America. Embroiled in a lawsuit since 2005 with the JA Apparel Company, which owned the Abboud label, Joseph eventually removed himself as its designer and refrained from creating any new collections.

Lord & Taylor, which has been refocusing its merchandising efforts, has named Mr. Abboud creative director and designer of a proprietary line of tailored clothing, sportswear, and accessories. The hiring of Mr. Abboud is expected to help Lord & Taylor improve its image, which has become somewhat tarnished. His efforts will be directed toward raising the profile of menswear in America.

This private label direction will be the first for Abboud, as previously his collections were sold to the more exclusive stores in the United States and abroad. Abboud's earlier lines were developed by himself with some help from assistants, but the new venture will team him with the menswear merchants at Lord & Taylor. In addition to the creative challenge of designing fashion products, Abboud will also have responsibilities that include presentation on the selling floor as well as marketing and packaging.

Contracting with Celebrities to Design Exclusive Retail Collections

With so many consumers often influenced to purchase products that bear their favorite celebrity signatures, many retailers are entering into arrangements to develop exclusive collections for their operations. Models, athletes, performers, and other notables' collections are becoming more visible on store shelves and racks and on retail Web sites.

With Kohl's success at this game with Daisy Fuentes, other retailers have launched themselves into celebrity fashion, as with the Mervyns line by actress Constance Marie aimed at the Latina market. Other examples include Wal-Mart exclusively marketing the Mary-Kate and Ashley collection, designed by the Olsen twins; Topshop, the British retailer, with its exclusive Kate Moss collection; and M by Madonna for H&M.

Madonna has joined the celebrity crowd that has contracted with retail operations for exclusive distribution.

Targeting Multicultural Market Segments

Liz Claiborne, parent of Juicy Couture, has entered the retail arena with free-standing stores.

Indicators such as the national census and private research disclosures have confirmed the growth of the major ethnicities, and this has motivated many merchants to pay special attention to those market segments. In particular, African Americans, Latinos, and Asian Americans continue to affect overall consumer spending on household products, apparel, accessories, foods, and many other items.

This phenomenon is causing many retailers—such as Sears, Target, Wal-Mart, and Kohl's—to continue investing heavily in advertisements, special products, ethnic designer collections, and promotional endeavors to reach out to these ethnic groups. Every indication is that the trend toward paying special attention to **multicultural market segments** will continue to grow.

Manufacturers Entering the Retail Arena

With so much private labeling on the retail scene, many manufacturers are feeling the pinch with lower wholesale commitments for their brands. In an effort of affected suppliers to offset their reduced sales to retailers, many are opening stores of their own that exclusively feature their lines. Liz Claiborne, Inc., the subject of the following *Focus*, has joined the bandwagon with stores for their Juicy Couture, Lucky Brand, Mexx, and Kate Spade labels; Vanity Fair continues to open North Face units; and Kellwood Co. is opening Phat Farm and Baby Phat in many international locations.

Focus on . . . Liz Claiborne, Inc.

A RELATIVE UNKNOWN IN 1976, the late Liz Claiborne took the industry by storm with her concept of dressing women for work. Together with her husband, a textile professional, and two other partners, she began what was to become a $5 billion public company.

Almost from the start the company had enormous success and had the enviable task of filling and shipping 50,000 units a week! At first it used primarily domestic contractors to produce its merchandise; in the early 1980s, the company expanded overseas in such arenas as Taiwan. It would not be long before the original Liz Claiborne label would be joined by others that included sportswear, accessories, and other fashion classifications.

Recognizing the importance of direct branding, the organization headed in the new direction of opening retail operations. In a just a short time, it established many stores that quickly became household names and attracted a multitude of consumers. Among them are Juicy Couture, Lucky Brand Jeans, and Kate Spade. With stores all over the globe, Claiborne has shown that manufacturers successfully retail their own products.

In addition to these specialty operations, the company also operates closeout stores in which it disposes of its leftovers and slower-selling items. Outlet centers all across America feature these **value shopping** operations.

• •

There is a blurring of the lines between retail and wholesale that is certain to continue. According to industry consultant Robin Lewis, "Direct to the consumer is the future."

Retailing from Its Early Days to the Present | CHAPTER 1

In the News . . .

For the latest in manufacturers and wholesalers entering the retail arena, reading "Wholesale Giants Morphing into Retailers" (on page 31 at the end of this chapter) is a must.

Expansion through Acquisition

There is movement that suggests the better way to expand is by acquisition of existing companies rather than opening new branches from the ground up. Macy's made a success of the concept with its purchase of Marshall Field and the May Company, and other retailers are following its lead. Belk, for example, has gone this route with its purchase of Proffit's/McRae's stores and the Parisian chain. Whole Foods is doing the same in the grocery field via its merger with Wild Oats.

New Concepts for Established Retailers

Instead of opening clones of their regular retail outlets, some merchants are investing in units that feature only one or a few of the merchandise classifications that are found in their traditional stores. In France, for example, Galeries Lafayette has opened units that feature only menswear. In the United States, Bloomingdale's is expanding through specialty units; with the success of its home furnishings store in Chicago, it is opening "home format" stores in many parts of the country. Instead of compartmentalizing the merchandise into such traditional classifications as bedding, the new stores will be organized according to lifestyle. Neiman Marcus has also joined the spin-off craze with a new entry called Cusp. Looking to attract a younger and more fashion-oriented clientele, boutiques that range in size from 7,000 to 11,000 square feet have opened in McLean, Virginia, Los Angeles, California, and Northbrook, Illinois. The merchandise is a subset of what is available at regular Neiman Marcus units. The idea is to attract those women who prefer specialty store shopping to the larger retail formats. Though still in the development stage to discover what's working and what's not, the company's experimental ventures are meeting expectations.

Although Calvin Klein might be better-known for his designs, his company (owned by Phillips-Van Heusen) operates many free-standing regular stores and factory outlets. In a move to highlight its better merchandise components, the organization is opening numerous "white label" stores in which the cream-of-the-crop items will be sold at regular prices. The spin-offs are expected to number 11 by 2012.

Joining the bandwagon for workout clothes and "intimates" is American Eagle with the opening of many Aerie stores. The concept has been so successful that the company expects to roll out 100 units by the end of 2008 and eventually 500 additional stores. Given the success of

Aerie stores is a new concept for American Eagle.

JCPenney and Kohl's in this merchandise classification, American Eagle is betting that a chain devoted to such merchandising is sure to be a winner. And with Victoria's Secret so successful in that arena, other merchants are taking this route.

Still another marquee retail has taken a new route to securing a segment of its existing market and attracting new shoppers to its premises. Tiffany & Co., a household name in luxury jewelry, has decided to enter the retail arena with smaller units whose offerings would be restricted to jewelry ranging from slightly less than $100 to $15,000. This is a departure from its regular store merchandise mixes that market more expensive items. The new stores, Tiffany & Co. Collections, will average about 5,000 square feet in size and will be part of a 70-unit chain by 2009.

Also new is Home Depot's concept of stores that have more appeal to women. Two new test stores, called Home Depot Design Centers, were opened at the end of 2007 in Charlotte, North Carolina, and Concord, California, to "romance and wow the customer." The female customer is targeted with the new concept, which features bath and kitchen showrooms in place of the traditional heavy lumber and building materials. Also, the installations are more extravagant than those seen in traditional Home Depot stores. Color is emphasized, as are products for doors and windows. Also, the Charlotte store features an 11,000-square-foot furniture showroom, the result of a successful test in a Chicago unit.

Some retailers are expanding their operations with spin-off stores that either concentrate on new merchandise categories or appeal to different market segments. Several of these spin-offs are listed in Table 1.3

Partnering

Some major retailers such as department stores are entering into partnership arrangements with manufacturers and other retailers. One of the leading merchants to enter into these contractual **partnering** agreements is Macy's. At the Chicago flagship in the "loop," the practice was initiated by Marshall Field's, which ultimately became a Macy's store. Brands like Thomas Pink opened their own units inside the store to take advantage of spreading their name without opening their own unit. Most recently, Macy's partnered with FAO Schwarz to open a 5,200-square-foot shop in the company's children's department. If the experiment works, it will be followed by more "pop-up" stores in other Macy's flagships.

TABLE 1.3
NEW CONCEPTS FOR ESTABLISHED RETAILERS

Established Merchant	Spin-off	Spin-off Concept
Abercrombie & Fitch	Ruehl	Targeting customers 22–35 years old
American Eagle	Aerie	Concentration on innerwear, dormwear, and fitness clothing
Gap	GapMaternity	Pregnant women
	GapBody	Fitness clothing
Publix	Apron's	Make-ahead meals cooked in "lab" store with famous chefs
	Sabors	Hispanic-themed stores
	Greenwise Markets	Natural and organic foods
J.Crew	J.Crew "at-the-beach"	Smaller shop
	J.Crew "by-the-sea"	Smaller shop
Talbots	Talbot Men's	Menswear
	Talbot Kids	Children's wear
	Talbot Petites	Petite clothing
Bloomingdale's	Bloomingdale's Home + Furniture Store	Home furnishings
Ralph Lauren	Rugby Stores	Shirts, sweaters, chinos, etc.
Barney's	Barney's Co-op	Youth-oriented fashions
Crate & Barrel	CB2	Lower-priced merchandise

Online Apparel Selling Escalation

Although online sales figures pale in comparison with brick-and-mortar sales, many retailers are putting extra efforts into online marketing of apparel and other wearable merchandise. For the first time, Web sales of apparel and accessories have moved into the top spot (excluding travel) and outdistanced computer sales, the perennial leader. In 2006, sales of apparel and accessories reached $18.3 billion and were expected to reach $22.1 billion in 2007.

Retailers such as Neiman Marcus, Macy's, Saks Fifth Avenue, and JCPenney all expect the trend to continue and are revamping their Web sites to capture more of this market.

Global Sourcing

The trend to fill inventories with products from around the world will more than likely continue. In addition to the merchandise that is bought from American resources (most of which is produced abroad), retailers are sure to be sending their product developers and merchandise scouts around the world to search for a wealth of products including apparel, accessories, foods, and so forth. With lower wholesale prices often the draw, this **global sourcing** trend is expected to go forward.

Value Shopping Broadening

Discounters like Wal-Mart, warehouse outlets such as Costco, do-it-yourself centers like Home Depot, manufacturers' closeout stores, off-price outlets, and retailer clearance centers are all expanding and increasing their sales volumes. From every indication, this value shopping trend will continue for bargain-priced goods.

Multichannel Retail Expansion

Except for the very small entrepreneurs who generally restrict their business to brick-and-mortar environments, the name of the game is multichannel retailing. Expanding store operations, producing more and more catalogues, and upgrading Web sites will be commonplace. At every price point, retailers are expanding their multichannel efforts and will continue to do so.

Going Green

Another trend making industrywide gains is addressing the ways in which the environment can be positively affected. Many retailers, both large and small and in all classifications, are making considerable efforts to change their methods of operation and physical needs to protect the environment from hazards. Examples include altering their physical premises by such actions as installing lighter color roofs in place of the black ones that absorb heat, changing to energy-efficient lighting, and redirecting merchandising efforts to include better-performing materials such as organic cotton. The **going green** concept is catching fire, and continued growth is expected.

Outsourcing Private-Label Production, Design, and Management

With costs continuing to spiral upward, especially in the United States, many major retailers have entered the outsourcing market. In the production and design of their private labels and brands, the route taken is generally to contract with an offshore producer who can turn the goods out in a more cost-friendly manner. Some management tasks, such as customer service and accounting, are also being transferred out of the country so that the expenses attributed to these duties can be lowered. It is no longer unusual for a shopper seeking a customer service representative to end up speaking to someone in India, for example, to resolve a dispute.

Refocusing Organizational Structures

Although the trend has been for merchants to expand their empires by adding new concepts, as we have just discussed, some merchants are refocusing their efforts by shedding some of their retail divisions in favor of entering new arenas. A prominent case is that of Leslie H. Wexner and Limited Brands, Inc. By selling The Limited and Express divisions of the company, its future is directed toward the expansion of Victoria's Secret and Bath & Body Works. Not only will the company open more units of these divisions, but the move will enable it to focus on expanding its Internet business and selling products on QVC.

Other notable refocusing efforts have been made by Gap and Liz Claiborne. The former closed its fledgling Forth & Towne, which debuted in 2005. The closure cost the company approximately $40 million but is expected to improve its bottom line. The division, which catered to women 35 and older, never delivered on its potential for profitability. Claiborne Inc. also determined that its U.S. Mexx stores did not have sufficient growth potential. Although Mexx stores worldwide enjoyed annual sales of more than €1 billion, they never achieved real success in the United States.

Broadening the Merchandise Mix

Many retailers are adding new merchandise categories to their assortments. With their customer bases already established, the belief is that overall volume can be increased without opening new units. One of the major product additions to fashion retailer offerings is beauty products. Since cosmetics, fragrances, and skin improvement items are so popular, it is natural to choose these products for inclusion in the merchandise mix.

Gap and Banana Republic have made the jump into these product classifications. GapBody stores are now selling the Bath and Body Collection and GapBody brands; Banana Republic is expanding its fragrance presence with Malachite, a new women's fragrance, and Cordovan, a new men's scent.

Repositioning

The notion of remaining with the "same old, same old" merchandising philosophies is typical of retailing, where the rule is often "if it ain't broke, don't fix it!" Some merchants, however, reposition themselves to improve their bottom lines. Some "trade up" and others "trade down."

JCPenney has taken the repositioning route by adding "power brand" private labels.

Just a few years ago, JCPenney was one of many nondescript department stores that catered to middle America. Although sales were solid for the most part, management decided to take a new route to improving sales. Instead of relying on the somewhat lackluster brands that it had marketed for years, the company took aggressive steps to make it a winner. It plans to add 250 new stores by 2011 and so spread its offerings to more markets. This is not only an expansion but also a new **repositioning**, which includes enhancement of its of its eight "power brand" private labels (e.g., Ambrielle, St. John's Bay, and Stafford), a newly formed Golden Brands concept called American Living (a division of Ralph Lauren), a new addition of Concepts by Claiborne, and further development of jcp.com, its Internet division. Thus far, sales have been better than expected with the repositioning efforts.

Site-to-Store Marketing

By bringing together the concepts of in-store and online selling, the retailer is able to take advantage of both consumer groups. **Site-to-store marketing,** by offering the customer the choice of picking up the merchandise ordered online at the store, increases the potential for more purchases by those opting for the in-person pickup. In a 2-year pilot program, Wal-Mart discovered that the majority of its customers wanted the option. The company then sent an e-mail to its entire network announcing the new concept. Circuit City also uses the program.

FUTURE RETAILING DIRECTIONS

Still in their infancy are the following developments on the retail scene that could conceivably become industry trends.

Establishing Town Centers

In a few places in the United States, outdoor centers have been introduced as major shopping arenas. Filled with a wealth of stores and restaurants, they resemble downtown centers. Simon Property Group, the largest developer of shopping centers in the United States, recently opened a town center in Jacksonville, Florida. Its enormous success has prompted the company to build a second phase with approximately 50 additional retailers and units of established restaurant chains.

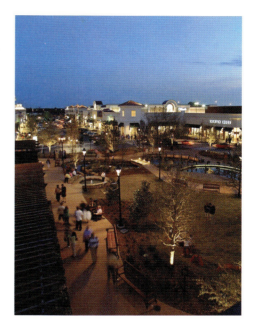

The Simon Property Group has expanded through outdoor "town centers," such as this one in Jacksonville, Florida.

Decreasing Newspaper Advertising Commitments

Retailers across the country are beginning to abandon their commitments to retail advertising. According to an *E-Commerce Times* article entitled "The Newspaper Cemetery," the preference for "moving pictures in the palms of people's hands" has been the cause of this decline. Some industry experts believe that newspaper advertising will become a thing of the past within 10 years.

Text Messaging

As a means of directing shoppers to their Web sites and stores, **text messaging** is starting to attract some merchants. Although little is expected in the way of actual sales from the text message, the conveying of special discount information, rewards programs, and so forth is now being used, although sparingly, by retailers. A pioneer in the field is Moosejaw Mountaineering, a Michigan-based retailer that specializes in outdoor goods. With roughly 230 million Americans using cell phones and about half using them to send or receive text messages, it seems a natural technique for contacting customers. The company reports that the concept is starting to boost sales.

Revitalizing Shopping Streets

In many cities where retailing once reigned on important shopping streets, the environment has become one of abandoned stores. But there are efforts in some of these areas to revitalize them. State Street in Chicago, for example, is getting a facelift in an attempt to restore its former glory. On New York City's lower east side, once a mecca for bargain hunters, big change is on the horizon. With the competition from off-pricers and other value merchants in nearby venues, the area became a ghost town. Today it is being reestablished as an upscale environment with menswear as its centerpiece. Made-to-measure suits retailing for $2,000, $180 shirts, and felt fedora hats for $295 are now offered. BBlessing caters to the media and creative set; Freemans Sporting Goods features made-to-measure suits, pigskin boots, and other upscale items; and First Among Equals specializes in the styles of up-and-coming designers from Japan, Paris, Scandinavia, New York, and California.

Utilizing New Technology

Even though it is one of the most important U.S. industries, retailing has generally been slow to make changes, particularly those that involve new technology. A.G. Edwards consultant Bob Buchanan summed it up best: "I think the problem is we still have a number of retailers out there, including some department stores, that are wedded to legacy systems, much of which is still homegrown." Although it is slow going, retailers are beginning to see the value of new technology for merchandise turnover systems, product management, inventory management, and the like.

Mobile Fashion Sales

The idea of selling directly to the consumer is not new. It has been a staple in the vending of ice cream and other food products for many years. Joining this concept are some vendors of fashion merchandise. In areas such as New York City's meatpacking district, a hot spot for tourists to visit trendy restaurants and clubs, a regular stream of people selling their own designs—from trucks complete with try-on rooms—has become commonplace. In Milan, designer Valeria Ferlini has set up shop in a mobile fashion boutique called the "Ape" (bee in Italian). From her humble beginnings with one Ape, she now operates 30! Her eye is now on Miami and New York.

Consumer Shopping Tours

An innovative way of catering to fashion enthusiasts who do not have the necessary expertise to scout fashion markets for purchases involves taking the clients to various venues and teaching them how to get the biggest bang for their buck. Although the shopping tour concept is not new, it is growing. One company that provides these experiences is Shop Gotham. With most of its clients being tourists from other cities and even other countries, the company takes them on shopping tours to the hottest retail venues and to vendors in New York City's garment center. They even report that Fortune 500 companies are having them make arrangements for the spouses of top executives. Other companies are now beginning to research this mode of shopping.

3D Online Presentation

Although the 3D format is still in the early stages of use, some retailers are using or planning to use this format on their Web sites. At this time, Brookstone is using the technology developed by Boston-based Kinset, Inc., for its online division. It provides shoppers an experience that mimics visiting its physical premises along with interactive options. Kinset is currently negotiating with other merchants to implement the 3D format.

CAREER OPPORTUNITIES IN TODAY'S RETAIL MARKETPLACE

The nature of retailing today is unlike anything in the past. With the coupling of brick-and-mortar operations with off-site ventures such as catalogue sales and e-tailing, the opportunities for a successful career have never been better. Not only are opportunities for lifelong careers in retailing to be found in just about any city and town, but with the expansion taking place across the United States and in major retail centers throughout the world, the choices available in retailing are unrivaled in most other industries.

It is a growth industry with positions at all levels available to both men and women. There are no glass ceilings to hold women back from moving into upper management as there are in many other industries. A close inspection of the retailing industry verifies that if the ability is there, anyone can reach the top.

In the retailing industry, women have every opportunity for advancement.

It should also be noted that what was once a comparatively low-paying field now offers competitive salaries. Unlike other industries, retailing is an arena that allows for quick advancement for those who show promise. Most retail organizations do not require that employees be in a given position for a given length of time before being promoted.

The career opportunities are vast and varied and are waiting to be filled by those who show a willingness to work hard and have the drive necessary for success. A complete overview of the opportunities that await candidates for retailing positions and how to go about securing them is found in the Appendix, Careers in Retailing and Related Fields, where topics such as interviewing, writing résumés and cover letters, and postinterview practices are covered.

CHAPTER HIGHLIGHTS

- During the colonial period and the early years of the United States, retailing was primitive and trading posts, peddlers, and general stores were the only methods of purchasing available to consumers.
- The limited-line or specialty store is the only form of early retailing that remains important in today's marketplace.
- Department stores were the first retail organizations to feature a wide assortment of both hard and soft goods in an orderly fashion.
- The mail-order businesses, initiated by companies like Sears and Montgomery Ward, were the forerunners of today's catalogue operations.
- Off-price operations, discounters, and warehouse clubs are organizations that provide value shopping for the public.
- Designer flagships are becoming more important than ever for those who want to expand their images and show their complete collections.
- Appropriate organizational structures are vital to the smooth and efficient functioning of retail companies.
- Merchants should regularly examine their tables of organization and alter them, when necessary, to meet ever-changing objectives.
- Offshore expansion has become an important tool for all retailers that wish to extend their products to other consumer markets.
- More and more designers are entering into exclusive agreements with retailers and are creating less expensive lines than they typically offer.

- Going green as a retail concept has joined cultural trends toward saving the environment.
- Newspaper advertising commitments by retailers seem to be heading for a significant decrease.
- Retailing is a field that offers seemingly unlimited opportunity for both men and women.

IMPORTANT RETAILING TERMS

big book (8)
boutique (12)
branch store (7)
category killer (13)
centralized operation (14)
chain store organization (5)
department store (6)
designer flagship (13)
discount store (9)
flagship store (7)
flea market (11)
franchising (10)
general store (4)
global sourcing (23)
going green (23)
hypermarket (13)
kiosk (12)
limited-line store (5)
line and staff positions (14)
mail-order selling (7)
manufacturer-owned outlet (11)
multicultural market segment (20)
off-price store (9)
offshore expansion (17)
off-site selling (17)
one-stop shopping (7)
organization chart (14)
organizational structure (14)
outsourcing (16)
partnering (22)
peddler (4)
repositioning (25)
sales channel (16)
site-to-store marketing (25)
specialty store (5)
spin-offs (16)
strategic planning (15)
supermarket (8)
table of organization (14)
text messaging (25)
trading post (4)
value shopping (20)
warehouse club (10)

FOR REVIEW

1. What was the earliest form of retailing in America? How is it different from today's retail operations?
2. In what ways are department stores like trading posts? In what ways are they different?
3. What are some characteristics of a chain store organization?
4. In what ways has catalogue selling changed since it was first introduced in the late nineteenth century?
5. What is the difference between an off-price merchant and a discounter?
6. What is a warehouse club? How does it achieve a high level of profits?
7. How did manufacturers open their own stores?
8. Why are kiosks a method of operation favored by many new companies that want to enter retailing?
9. Why do retailers use organizational charts?
10. How does the small store's organizational structure differ from its large-sized counterpart?
11. What purpose does offshore expansion serve for the retailer?
12. Why are many retailers going the private-label route instead of relying exclusively on products that bear manufacturer's and designer's labels?
13. How important are the multicultural market segments to retailers?
14. What are some of the major classifications of the group of retailers that engage in value shopping?
15. Why are many retailers joining the going green bandwagon?

AN INTERNET ACTIVITY

Use an Internet search engine such as Google to find out about one of America's major retailers (a U.S. chain operation or department store, for example, or any other retail entry). Use what you learn to write a research paper no longer than three pages. The report should include the following:

- History of the company
- Size of the operation in terms of units
- Domestic and overseas presence
- Merchandise assortment
- Methods of doing business with its clientele

The paper should be typed, double-spaced.

EXERCISES AND PROJECTS

1. Write to a warehouse club to obtain information about its operation. Prepare a brief, double-spaced report of no more than two pages. Include the following information:
    - The size of the company in terms of dollar volume

- The scope of its product line
- The membership fee
- The locations served by the company
- Its plans for overseas expansion

2. Prepare a report on retail franchising in the United States. The library houses such periodicals as *The Franchise Annual* that offers a wealth of information on the subject. Include in the report the following:
   - The size of franchising in the United States
   - The most typical types of retail operations that are franchised
   - Franchiser restrictions on franchisees
   - Advantages and disadvantages of franchising
   - The outlook for franchising

The paper should be no more than three typed pages (double-spaced).

THE CASE OF RESTRUCTURING THE MERCHANDISING DIVISION OF A MULTICHANNEL RETAILER

In the early 1900s, Hirsch & Company opened its doors in the northeastern part of the United States. It was, at first, a relatively small specialty store selling women's clothing and accessories. Its market was the upper middle-class female whose tastes were simple yet elegant. Because of the many social engagements frequented by its customers, the store stocked a large assortment of formal apparel. Daytime wear also had a presence in the store.

Not long after the opening, the company began to realize sales far beyond its expectations. Soon the store needed to expand into an adjacent building. As the store continued to succeed, Hirsch & Company investigated the possibility of opening another store 30 miles away. The new unit was opened and offered merchandise in the same manner as the original. It, too, was an immediate success.

Today, the company has become one of the major specialized department stores in the East, with 25 stores carrying high-fashion merchandise ranging from bridge and designer lines to couture collections. The stores also feature numerous private designs.

Wanting to stay current in today's retail scene, the company's management team plans to expand its catalogue operation and to develop a Web site that will make it a multichannel retailer. While everyone in the company is excited about its new direction, many are not sure how the merchandising division should operate. Some believe that the division should be responsible for all of the merchandise purchases, while others believe that separate buyers should be hired for the catalogue and Web site departments. (Currently the buyers purchase new merchandise for the stores as well as the catalogue; because the Web site is new, it's not known whether the same should be done for the new off-site venture.)

Questions

1. What reasons might you offer for keeping the same merchandising format?
2. Would separate buyers better serve the needs of the company? Defend your answer with sound reasoning.
3. Could a variation of these two plans be utilized? What format would it take?

 Panel: Tech-Savvy Retailers Will Thrive
Jeanine Poggi

APRIL 16, 2007

Technology is at the forefront of retail development, but companies must be willing to embrace change to benefit from these advancements, said a panel of industry experts during a roundtable discussion at WWD.

The panel was moderated by Emanuel Weintraub, of the firm that bears his name, and the panelists included: Bob Buchanan, analyst at A.G. Edwards; Vincent Quan, assistant professor at the Fashion Institute of Technology; and Joel Kaplan, president of Cuddle Time, a vendor. The experts weighed in on where technology is leading the fashion industry, how smaller players can get involved and who will come out on top.

It is retailers that are least resistant to change, like American Eagle Outfitters and Nordstrom, that do the best with new technology, Buchanan said.

After Nordstrom set up a new merchandising system about five or six years ago, the company gained a handle on the ownership of goods by door, color, size and style. In the process, Nordstrom's gross margins soared and the retailer drove its merchandise turn from 3.7 times to 4.7 times.

Buchanan said that while American Eagle's high-quality software is valuable, it is more important that the retailer has technicians who know how to use it.

Most companies stumble with technology by not investing enough in proper training, Weintraub added.

American Eagle turns merchandise at a rate of 5.4 times, twice the level of competitor Abercrombie & Fitch. Abercrombie & Fitch is turning goods 2.7 times, down from 6.1 times five years ago. Buchanan attributes this deterioration to management's lack of focus on the business process.

"[Management at Abercrombie & Fitch] has been more focused on the product and building the brand, and I think they are brilliant in that regard. But I think at some point they need to find the right person to evaluate the best software out there and make some decisions, and then also get the process aligned with whatever software they chose," he said.

By using technology to rapidly turn merchandise, retailers see improvements in sales, gross margins and expense ratios.

Retailers who are resistant to technology are only turning goods at a rate of three times or less, Buchanan said.

"I think the problem is we still have a number of retailers out there, including some of the department stores, that are wedded to the old way of doing things. They are wedded to legacy systems, much of which is still homegrown," Buchanan said. "It's OK to fire an old dog who can't learn new tricks when it comes to technology."

Most apparel retailers are still only investing about 1 to 2 percent of their budget in technology, compared with about 5 percent for the rest of corporate America, Buchanan said.

Technology is like the circulatory system of a retailer, feeding the brain, heart, legs and arms and propelling them to operate, Kaplan added.

"With the consolidation of many fashion companies, doing more with less has become a mantra. The streamlining of personnel has created a greater need for systems to ease the crunch. Thus, systems have become the enabler for retailers and vendors to manage their products more efficiently; from allocation to markdown optimization to inventory management. But while these systems help, they do not replace the fashion element," Quan said.

With the industry's emphasis on numbers, buyers and planners must have strong analytical ability.

To educate these future buyers, the Fashion Institute of Technology has added more advance tools to the classroom curriculum.

Recently, FIT partnered with software firm JDA Arthur, and uses Arthur Allocation software, RAPID Planning and E3 Inventory Management applications to prepare students for the high-tech market.

It is not only large-scale retailers that can benefit from and afford the newest technology. Smaller retailers need to invest in software applications, too.

"There is a lot of cool, off-the-shelf software available from third parties and there is absolutely no reason why a small retailer, or up-and-coming retailer, such as Zumiez, can't get the best technology and put it in place," Buchanan said.

For the most part, the fashion industry, which for 20 or 30 years was underinvesting in technology, is finally catching up, the panelists said.

"Eight years ago, very few questions were being asked about technology," Buchanan said. "But now, if you read the current transcripts from Federated or Wal-Mart calls, almost half of the questions being asked are about technology and process."

"My hope is there are other retailers out there that are starting to get into the technology. Kohl's may be one," he added. "We think J.C. Penney may be another."

Wholesale Giants Morphing into Retailers
Whitney Beckett

APRIL 12, 2007

Forget the distinction between wholesaler and retailer. Today's breed are brand managers.

Once simply manufacturing giants, VF Corp., Liz Claiborne Inc., Jones Apparel Group, and Kellwood Co. are mutating into multiheaded beasts, with their direct-to-consumer sides becoming an increasingly large part of their identities.

As traditional retailers consolidated and upped their own production of private label, retailers' reliance on wholesalers has declined.

"Obviously when you look at how much power department stores carry over them, vendors need to do something to get power back in their own hands, but how they do that is up for debate," said Brad Stephens, an analyst for Morgan Keegan & Co. Inc. "Specialty retail is one of the hardest businesses out there, and you can open yourself up for more—not less—risk."

Jones Apparel Group's 1,000-plus retail stores made up about 31 percent of the $4.74 billion firm's sales last year, up from 21 percent in 2005 and 17 percent in 2004, the year Jones acquired Barneys New York. In five years, Jones president and chief executive officer Peter Boneparth would like to see retail contributing between 35 and 40 percent of group revenues—but that doesn't mean the company is walking away from wholesale.

"Everything we do is about balance," Boneparth said. "Our roots are in wholesale. We're a wholesale business, and we aren't abandoning that."

Most of Jones' stores are outlets, but the company is expanding its full-priced segments. Boneparth thinks Bandolino can grow from the 30 stores it has today to 100 within a few years. Still in the beginning retail stages, Anne Klein will get half a dozen new specialty stores this year.

"Our focus is going to be maximizing our productivity in the things we've got," Boneparth said. "The new concept is Anne Klein, but the existing concepts are where we are going to spend a lot of time and energy. The idea is not to open a bunch of doors, but rather to do them profitably. While store numbers are increasing, our goal is to make sure the retail represents the brand properly, because it's the face of the brand on a day-to-day basis."

For Nine West, Boneparth wants to return the retail stores to a double-digit operating margins business—which it has not had of late due to rent increases and "under-investing in the store experience," according to Boneparth. He points to the Nine West store on Madison Avenue in New York that opened in February as the new "cleaner, less cluttered and consumer-centric" model.

The feather in Jones' cap has been Barneys New York, which the firm acquired at the end of 2004 to mixed reviews, but which now seems to have paid off. Opening two flagship stores last year, plus Co-op off-shoots, Boneparth projects Barneys will be a "billion dollar business" in the next three years.

Jones has Barneys, and Claiborne has Mexx, a less-pricey retailer with roots abroad. While about 27 percent of Claiborne's current $4.99 billion business is direct-to-consumer, up from 25 percent in 2005 and 18 percent in 2001, the company projects retail will climb to upwards of 40 percent in the next few years. Claiborne's store numbers today are almost evenly distributed between outlet and specialty stores with about 250 full price and about 200 outlet stores. Going forward, the company speculates growth in the specialty retail sector will outpace outlet growth, so the ratio will be more like 70-30.

Most of that will come from Claiborne "power brands." In the next few years, the group plans to roll out about 100 stores each for Juicy Couture, Lucky Brand and Kate Spade. Under new ceo William L. McComb, Claiborne is closing retail divisions for brands that won't reach that level. Earlier this year, Claiborne said it would shutter the four Mexx stores in the U.S. and the three Laundry stores. The plan is to focus marketing and capital resources—plus attention and man hours—to the brands that have the greatest growth potential.

"It's important to reach 100 stores to have scale and critical mass," said Jill Granoff, group president for direct-to-consumer at Claiborne. "We certainly view retail as a key growth engine."

Granoff, former president and chief operating officer of Victoria's Secret Beauty, joined Claiborne in September in the newly created post, which made her responsible for the company's specialty retail and outlet stores, plus e-commerce Web sites, in the U.S. In McComb's recent shakeup of group presidents' responsibilities, Granoff gained oversight of Lucky Brand and Sigrid Olsen, two of Claiborne's retail power brands. "One of the reasons we brought Jill in was to ensure we aren't wholesalers doing retail," said a spokeswoman for the company.

Granoff is also focusing on how to increase comparable store growth. "The best retailers are the ones with a really compelling shopping experience," she said. "You really have to focus on the retail experience, which is a combination of the product and the shopping environment. You need to scintillate all of the senses – not only what you are seeing, but also what you are hearing, smelling and even tasting. When you are a wholesaler, you focus on the product and not as much on the selling environment."

Analysts agree that other wholesalers could take a page from VF's retail business, with its largely successful North Face and Vans lifestyle stores. VF added company-owned retail operations as a new plank in its growth strategy at the end of 2005, announcing it would grow its stores from about 500 back then, or 12 percent of its business, to about 800 stores, or 18 percent, over about four years. Retail contributed about 14 percent of revenues in 2006. After opening 62 stores last year, the company plans to invest about $45 million in its retail locations this year and open 75 to 100 stores.

A lot changed leading up to 2005 to prompt the manufacturing giant to change its retail strategy. Since 2000, VF has acquired lifestyle brands including North Face, Nautica and Vans—"a lot of brands that have owned monobrand retail potential," noted Eric Wiseman, VF's president and chief operating officer. Its experience with North Face, whose stores have consistently delivered double-digit comparable-store sales growth over the last few years, taught VF the benefits of controlling its distribution channel.

"The brands that we want to acquire should be strong global lifestyle brands," Wiseman said. "Those brands have an owned retail component or at least an opportunity."

Although VF may be "late to the game," as one analyst put it, and garnering a smaller percentage of sales from retail than Claiborne and Jones, which have Mexx and Barneys, the $6.14 billion VF is still doing almost $1 billion a year in direct-to-consumer sales. Wiseman said VF opens stores for three reasons, which the other companies echo:

First, to strengthen brands. "If you look at how any one of our brands is presented by our retail customers, they tend to not bring the whole brand to life in one place," Wiseman said. "We think we can help bring brand strength by putting it all together in an environment like we would like it to be. Because our brands are lifestyle brands, you get to see the lifestyle in our own stores, and consumers respond in those environments."

Second, to improve wholesale business in a geographic market. "Opening the North Face store in New York made our business in New York stronger, so much so we opened a second in New York in the fall," Wiseman said. "When we invest in our retail in the right way, our wholesale business gets better."

Third, to open a brand to new consumers. For VF, retail strategy plays into global strategy. Five years ago, global sales made up about 19 percent of business, compared with about 27 percent this year, and the new target is 30 percent. A lot of VF's store openings are outside the U.S., including India, where Nautica, Lee and Wrangler stores are popping up. "Our own retail stores allow us to introduce the brand to a geographically new market in exactly the way we want to present it," Wiseman said.

For Kellwood, its 2004 Phat Fashions acquisition is helping the group travel globally. Only one of the 10 Phat Fashion doors today is in the U.S., and in the next three years, there may be as many as 50 Phat Fashions stores, which house Phat Farm and Baby Phat, most of which will be international.

Kellwood is actively acquiring more brands that could have retail legs. Both fall 2006 acquisitions, Hollywould will get about 10 new stores in the next few years, and Vince, which currently does not have its own doors, will open a few test stores—though those stores will be domestic.

"Our strategy is to be a brand-focused marketing enterprise," said Robert C. Skinner Jr., Kellwood president, chairman and ceo. "The distinction between wholesalers and retailers is blurring or even disappearing as we all find the best ways to connect with our consumers as we integrate our brands. The Internet, retail consolidation and private label all have changed the landscape to make it advantageous to be a retailer too."

With about 100 stores, Kellwood has been "experimenting" with retail for about two years and will still be in that "embryonic stage of retail" for another year, according to Skinner. Currently Kellwood has outlet and full-price stores for both its Sag Harbor and Koret brands, plus 10 specialty Phat Fashions and two Hollywould stores. Although the majority of Kellwood's stores today are outlet, future openings of specialty stores will outnumber outlet openings. Kellwood does not break out the percentage of its business that comes from direct-to-consumer sales, because "it's not significant," Skinner said. "When it is significant, we'll break it out. I can see it becoming significant." But he added, "We don't consider it to be a race with other wholesalers."

"Wholesalers becoming retailers is just going to accelerate," said consultant Robin Lewis. "The supply chain is going to be absolutely flat. Direct to consumer is the future. There will be no wholesalers or retailers. They will all be brand managers. The words retail and wholesale will be thrown out of the dictionary at least within 10 years, maybe sooner."

John Henderson, a director at Net Worth Solutions Inc. and a former president of Kellwood's Sag Harbor division, cautioned that retail is a competitive, high-risk, capital-intensive business, which requires companies to own the inventory and make long-term commitments on space.

"There's a trend for wholesalers to think retail is more exciting than what they are doing," Henderson said. "Instead of being an opportunity, it can be a distraction. If your business isn't good at wholesale, it most likely won't be good at retail."

Injecting retail into a wholesale business model skews earnings and sales.

"They are in two different worlds in two different cycles but with one reporting period," said consultant Emanuel Weintraub. "The vendor is preceding the retailer by a certain number of months, when you put those together you will have two different sets of numbers, and as vendors' retail businesses grow, the retail numbers are going to be increasingly important. Now the analysts are going to have to dig into those two different sets of numbers and make sense of it. You need a crisp breakout of retail and a crisp breakout of wholesale from firms that have both."

While retailers typically end their fiscal years in January to smooth seasonal disparities, adding January's clearance sales to the robust holiday sales instead of to sleepy February, most traditional wholesalers follow a traditional calendar year, pointed out Margaret Mager, retail analyst and managing director for Goldman Sachs & Co. "Wholesalers need to become even better retailers if they continue to pursue that strategy as specialty retail as a key strategy for growth," Mager said.

VF, which analysts applaud for its appropriately-paced retail growth, was the only company of the four not to take a hit in the first quarter of 2006, while each company grew its retail sector. VF reported a 24.6 percent rise in earnings, while sales rose 5.3 percent in that quarter.

At Jones, first quarter earnings last year dropped 7.8 percent on a 10.8 percent sales gain. Part of the hit came from a 3.7 percent same-store sales drop in its footwear and ready-to-wear stores, excluding Barneys New York.

Claiborne's first quarter of 2006 saw profits fall 34.3 percent on a 3.4 percent drop in sales. The company attributed much of the decline to retail consolidation, but also to its own retail changes.

McComb labeled this not as a problem but rather a reality to be accepted. But planning, particularly when Claiborne returns to giving guidance, is a mutable factor, said Granoff.

"There certainly is a shift in financial planning," she said. "In a wholesaler model, the Christmas revenues are recognized in Q3. There is a shift in timing of when we recognize revenue."

As Claiborne continues to expand its retail segment to its projected 40 percent, this will only become a larger issue, according to analysts.

"The retail business is a black box for Liz," said Elizabeth Montgomery, analyst for Cowen & Co. "This year, they need to anticipate the change in seasonality for the first quarter, especially because they have been adding a lot of stores in the back half of 2006."

As Kellwood inches into the retail game, it too will need to anticipate potential hits in its first quarter, analysts caution. It took a 22 percent hit in its first quarter last year, largely due to restructuring costs.

"Now Kellwood has been testing these retail stores, what is going to happen for Q1?" asked Montgomery. "Q1 is a tough quarter for the retail business, and that's what these companies are finding as they go into retail."

Skinner dismissed the concern. "It's just a reality in retail," he said. "Until we can find a way to make Valentine's Day as big as Christmas, that is."

CHAPTER 2
Brick-and-Mortar Retailing

After you have completed this chapter, you should be able to discuss:

- The present status of brick-and-mortar retailing
- The different types of retailers that fall within the traditional classifications
- The reasons for the success of branch stores in the United States
- Why retail chain organizations are considered to be the most important retail category in the United States
- The different classifications that constitute value-oriented retailing
- The differences between discount operations and off-price retailers
- Why many manufacturers have opened their own outlet centers
- Reasons for the success of retail clearance centers across the United States

Day after day, consumers encounter what seems to be an endless barrage of news reports and advertising that extol the benefits of buying on the Internet. With editorials in newspapers and magazines about the growth and importance of e-tailing and ads for Web sites in print media and television or radio underscoring the ease and satisfaction of making this type of purchase, we are often led to believe that traditional retail stores, and the brick-and-mortar operations by which they are known, have outlived the time when they thrived as the major retail outlets.

However, when we look at the actual amount of money spent making purchases on the Internet it pales in comparison to what is spent in stores. Even though nontravel online retailing reached $200 billion in 2007, it is only a "speck" on the radar screen.

Catalogue shopping, another form of **direct selling**, is also growing in importance. Many brick-and-mortar operations use catalogues to augment their in-store sales, and other companies are exclusively catalogue merchants; but the percentage of retail sales they represent is minimal when compared to buying in stores.

Even with new sources of competition, brick-and-mortar retailers are experiencing enormous growth. Department stores are expanding with the opening of numerous branches, chain stores are extending their reach domestically and overseas, and value-oriented stores such as discounters and off-pricers are finding their way into every region of the United States.

Thus, although the picture presented by some gives the impression that brick-and-mortar retailers should no longer expect significant growth, the sales volumes belie that impression. Sales have never been greater!

Included in the overall brick-and-mortar classification is a wealth of different types of operations. They include traditional retail operations such as department and chain stores and the more recent value-oriented outlets.

TRADITIONAL RETAILERS

Best known among the **traditional retailers** are department stores and specialty chain organizations. These are among the largest retail classifications both here and abroad. Each type serves a specific merchandising need, with the former offering a wide array of products and the latter a more narrow range of merchandise. Every classification of consumer products, ranging from apparel to foods, is available through one of these two types of retailers.

Department Stores

As you learned in Chapter 1, the department store dates back to the end of the eighteenth century. It is still a viable form of retailing, with major companies based in the United States and numerous foreign countries. Many department stores enjoy marquee recognition not only close to home but also at great distances from their headquarters. In America, Macy's and Bloomingdale's enjoy instant recognition all over the country as well as on foreign shores. Similarly, Harrods, in London, is world-renowned and is visited by tourists from every part of the globe. These and other department stores have become "institutions" in their immediate marketplaces and to the tourists who visit the cities they are in.

There are two types of department stores: the full-line department stores and the specialized department stores.

Both types of department stores remain viable forces in retailing, but they now face a great deal of competition from the chain organizations (described later in this chapter). With so many women in the workforce and the ever-growing demands of careers, people have less time to spend searching through huge department stores to find the items they need. The smaller chain units enable customers to move through the store quickly and make the necessary purchases in a short time.

For the same reasons, catalogues and e-tail Web sites have taken some business away from department stores. To meet this competition, many brick-and-mortar stores have created their own mail-order divisions and Web sites to make sure that overall company sales volume continues to climb.

Many of today's department stores, be they full-line or specialized, have embraced the concept of the **store within a store**. That is, they build small shops that feature just one type of merchandise. For example, a designer shop might feature only Ralph Lauren or Chanel or a boutique might sell only upscale intimate apparel. The store-within-a-store concept is that it "feels like" a specialty store: a place where shoppers can go knowing that it stocks the type of goods they want and does not require looking through endless store aisles to find it. This allows customers to complete their shopping more quickly. As a walk through any major department store demonstrates, more and more of these shops are popping up to replace the traditional store layout of one oversized department after another, many of which might need to be scoured before shoppers find what they want.

TABLE 2.1
TOP 10 U.S. DEPARTMENT STORE CORPORATIONS BY SALES

Company	Classification	Headquarters
Sears*	Full-line, specialized	Hoffman Estates, IL
Macy's, Inc.**	Full-line	Cincinnati, OH
JCPenney	Full-line	Plano, TX
Kohl's	Specialized	Menomonee Falls, WI
Nordstrom	Specialized	Seattle, WA
Dillard's	Full-line	Little Rock, AR
Neiman Marcus	Specialized	Dallas, TX
Bon-Ton	Full-line	York, PA
Belk	Full-line, specialized	Charlotte, NC
Saks	Specialized	New York, NY

* Part of Sears Holding, which includes Kmart and is sometimes cross-classified as a chain.
** Originally Federated Department Stores.
Source: *Stores Magazine*, July 2007.

The majority of today's department stores are parts of groups, such as Macy's Inc., which operates Macy's and Bloomingdale's. Other retail operations have only one name for all their department stores; these include JC Penney and Belk.

The ten largest department store organizations in the United States are listed in Table 2.1.

Full-Line Department Stores

Originally, the department store was meant to provide one-stop shopping for consumers. The merchandise assortments featured on the selling floors included a wide variety of both hard goods and soft goods. Patrons could shop for apparel and wearable accessories, move on to sections where furniture was sold, make selections of tableware, and shop for both large and small appliances they might need. Companies like Macy's, Dillard's, Bloomingdale's, and Belk made their reputations as hard and soft goods merchants. To this day, they stock inventories with a variety of products, much as they did in their early days of retailing.

Bloomingdale's is a member of Macy's, Inc., the major department store organization in the United States.

While product diversity is still the forte of the **full-line department store**, many have taken new paths in terms of the product mixes or merchandise assortments. The vast majority of today's department store merchants are concentrating on soft goods and accessories, with less emphasis on hard goods. In department after department, shelves and racks are filled with apparel for the family and a wealth of wearable accessories such as shoes, jewelry, handbags, and the like. Next in importance for most of these retailers are products for the home such as dinnerware, glassware, flatware, bedding, and other items. With the designers who have made their reputations in the apparel field feverishly entering the home furnishings market, these products are gaining a larger share of department store sales. Furniture has remained an important part of the department store's overall inventory for some companies. Bloomingdale's and Macy's, for example, still rely upon their furniture sales to bring in profits to their companies.

Missing from most department store inventories are major appliances. Except at Sears, refrigerators, washers, dryers, and ranges are no longer to be found in major full-line department stores. Now that these products are marketed more successfully at discount chains throughout the country, their profitability for department stores has decreased. Small appliances (such as microwave ovens and food processors) and housewares have taken their place. Many department stores also stock their inventories with a variety of electronics.

> ### Focus on...
> ### Macy's, Inc.
>
> ON SEPT. 1, 2007, one of the major changes in retailing history took place. The name Federated Stores, once the leading department store organization, was changed to Macy's, Inc. Not only was the corporate name changed, but so were the names of the individual groups that were famous in the industry. Retail empires that included Rich's, Marshall Field, and others became Macy's units. The only exception was Bloomingdale's, which retained its name. With the acquisition of the May Company and its more than 400 units, Macy's is now 864 strong. The decision to retain Bloomingdale's was made to maintain it as the only major, upscale, full-line department store in the country.
>
> Key to the success of the company is its commitment to listen and learn from its customer base. They carefully analyze data from all stores in terms of what's selling and what's not. Because customers are not the same in every part of the country, the company feels the study of individual units is essential to its merchandise acquisitions. It conducts online research as well as independent focus groups, where customers and noncustomers are questioned about the Macy's and Bloomingdale's offerings, how they shop, and why they shop. By undertaking these surveys, the company can make any adjustments necessary to improve its bottom line.
>
> One of the fortes of the Macy's and Bloomingdale's operations is their attention to private-label merchandise. In addition to carrying such national brands as Ralph Lauren, Liz Claiborne, DKNY, Calvin Klein, and others, they have created a degree of exclusivity with the development of their own brands. Many of these (e.g., INC, Alfani, Tasso, Elba, American Rag, Karen Scott, John Ashford) have become significant moneymakers for the company. Macy's has also entered into exclusive contractual agreements with such designers as Elie Tahari and Oscar de la Renta, who produce the T Tahari collection and the O Oscar collection (respectively). By adding more and more private labels and designer exclusives, Macy's has been able to significantly distinguish itself from the competition.
>
> Today it is continuing to open more units under the two company names. Together with greater attention to its off-site divisions, Macy's is expected to hold its position as the country's largest full-line department store organization.

Specialized Department Stores

Today, many merchants engaged in department store retailing restrict their inventories rather than carry full lines. Some sell mostly apparel and wearable accessories, while others focus on home furnishings. Saks Fifth Avenue, Neiman Marcus, and Nordstrom specialize in apparel and accessories, while Fortunoff is primarily a home furnishings store.

Although specialized department stores and specialty chains both sell narrow assortments of merchandise, the two types of stores are quite different. A specialty chain might have as many as a thousand units or even more. Each unit is generally a one-story facility with limited floor space. A **specialized department store** usually occupies a multilevel facility with floor space that rivals many full-line operations, and it stocks a vast assortment of goods.

Focus on... Nordstrom

WHEN A POOR BOY FROM SWEDEN ARRIVED IN THE UNITED STATES with only $5 to his name, one would never have guessed that he would eventually become a retail icon. His name was John W. Nordstrom. From difficult beginnings that included a trip to California to labor in mines and logging camps as well as a stay in Alaska to find gold that eventually netted him $13,000, he made his way to Seattle and began his retailing career.

Together with partner Carl Wallin, Nordstrom opened his first retail venture: a shoe store in downtown Seattle called Wallin & Nordstrom that would eventually become the legendary Nordstrom, Inc. With service, selection, quality, and value their goal, the company built a loyal customer base. In 1928, after opening another unit, John Nordstrom retired and sold his share of the company to his sons. Wallin retired a year later and also sold his share to the Nordstrom sons. In 1933, a third son joined the company, which was to become the largest independent shoe chain in the United States.

In the early 1960s, the brothers decided it was time to spread their wings and ventured into the clothing market with the purchase of Best Apparel, a Seattle-based clothing store. Three years later they purchased another apparel operation, eventually renaming the company Nordstrom Best. They soon added men's clothing and children's wear to be able to dress the entire family. In 1968, with the brothers' retirements and the handing off of reins to their children, the company was on its way to becoming a major player in upscale fashion apparel and accessories. In 1971, the company went public and, two years later, formally changed its name to Nordstrom.

Today, Nordstrom enjoys a reputation as the nation's leading service-oriented retail establishment. Its service is renowned and is one of the major reasons behind continued success. With stores throughout many cities in the United States, Nordstrom continues to base its operations on its founders' principles: service, selection, quality, and value.

Branch Stores

When vast numbers of Americans started to leave major cities across the country for the suburbs, many department stores took it as an opportunity for expansion. Stores like Macy's, Bloomingdale's, Dillard's, and Belk seized the moment and opened replicas of their flagship stores. The branches became the salvation of these companies, many of which were seeing business fall off sharply at the main stores.

Today, every mall in the country is home to such branch stores. They are the **anchor stores** in these vast shopping arenas and serve as the attractions that bring in shoppers. Smaller malls have two or more anchor branches, while the majors have as many as six. Old Orchard in suburban Chicago, for example, boasts branches of such stores as Nordstrom, Lord & Taylor, Saks Fifth Avenue, and Bloomingdale's.

Old Orchard, a shopping center located in a Chicago suburb, is home to many of America's branch stores.

The sizes of the branches vary depending on the trading areas they serve and the anticipated needs of the people in that area. Some are small operations while others are nearly as large as the flagships they represent. In general, merchandise offerings fall into the same categories as at the main stores, but the selections are pared down based on the size of the branch and expected sales volume. However, each department store group must decide the proper road to take for branch expansion and must alter its merchandising philosophy to customer demand. Some companies might even eliminate certain departments completely if research shows that they will not fare successfully in the branches. In some cases, different merchandising approaches are used in different branches within the same company. For example, the Bloomingdale's New York City flagship gives a great deal of floor space to its furniture department because the store's success derives in part from this merchandise classification. Many branches, however, lack sufficient space to stock such inventory and customers' need for it is not as great, so the feature inventories are fashion and wearable accessories instead.

The organizational structures of branch stores are worth noting. Unlike the flagship stores where all of the major decision making takes place, the branch is primarily a selling arena. Executives based at the flagship stores oversee merchandising, advertising, special events, and store operations, and they also determine the policies that govern the entire organization. Branch store managers and their subordinates follow these edicts, so very little decision making takes place at the branches. The decisions made there usually involve hiring people in lower-level positions, such as sales associates, determining employee schedules, and so forth. The branch's goal is to turn a profit for the company and leave the steering of the organization to the management team at the flagship.

The health of branch stores, in general, is excellent; more and more of these units are being opened in malls and downtown areas wherever the need arises.

Chain Organizations

In spite of the fact that e-tailing is capturing retail headlines, it is the chain organizations that are fulfilling the needs of the consumer, as shown by their record sales. The chains' concentration on specialized merchandise inventories in small spaces seems to fit the needs of today's shopper. With the vast majority of women working outside the home, the once favorite pastime of many has been abandoned. Instead, people buy only when the need arises and at places where it is quick and efficient to do so. With the continued expansion of such companies and the significant growth in sales attributed to them, it is obvious that the chain organization is the place for retail action and profitability.

By definition, a chain is an organization that has two or more units and is centrally operated and managed. Of course, the chains that most consumers are familiar with are those that have significantly greater numbers of units, with some comprising several thousand stores. Their greatest presence is in women's apparel; menswear; children's clothing; wearable accessories such as jewelry, handbags, and shoes; home furnishings; toys; electronics; food; drugstores; books; pet products; office supplies; computer products; and sporting goods.

Walgreens is an industry leader in drugstore chains.

Chain organizations are big business. Many companies are opening several new units every month, and others are expanding their operations through acquisition. In the drugstore arena, for example, both approaches have been popular. Walgreens, an industry leader, has followed the expansion route in a grand manner. The company now has over 5,000 units, with plans to open a new store every day. In the next decade it expects to have 7,000 stores. On the other hand, CVS and Rite Aid have grown through acquisition. CVS, the largest pharmacy chain, increased the number of outlets by acquiring Eckerd, Revco, and Arbor Drug; and Rite Aid has grown with the acquisition of

TABLE 2.2
TOP U.S. CHAINS,* 2006

COMPANY	SPECIALTY	HEADQUARTERS
Wal-Mart	Clothing, household items	Bentonville, AR
Home Depot	Household products, tools	Atlanta, GA
Kroger	Food	Cincinnati, OH
Costco	Food, household items	Issaquah, WA
Target	Clothing, household	Minneapolis, MN
Sears Holding**	Clothing, appliances	Hoffman Estates, IL
Walgreens	Pharmaceuticals	Deerfield, IL
Lowe's	Household, tools	Mooresville, NC
CVS	Pharmaceutical	Woonsocket, RI
Safeway	Food	Pleasanton, CA
Best Buy	Electronics	Minneapolis, MN
SuperValu	Food	Eden Prairie, MN
Macy's, Inc.***	Clothing, accessories	Cincinnati, OH
Ahold USA	Food, variety	Chantilly, VA
Publix	Food	Lakeland, FL
JCPenney	Apparel, home furnishings	Plano, TX
Staples	Office supplies	Framingham, MA
Rite Aid	Pharmaceuticals	Camp Hill, PA
TJX	Off-price apparel	Framingham, MA
Delhaize America	Variety	Salisbury, NC

* Excluding restaurant chains.
** Includes Kmart and is cross-listed under department stores.
*** Formerly Federated Department Stores.
Source: Adapted from *Stores Magazine*, July 2007.

Thrifty/Payless, Marco, and K&B stores. These two patterns of growth are evident in just about every type of chain operation.

It should be noted that the expansion of chains is not restricted to the domestic market. Many American and foreign companies are vigorously entering overseas venues. At the head of the American list is Wal-Mart, with major growth initiatives in Asia, especially China and South Korea. Wal-Mart is also eyeing Europe. In Germany it purchased the hypermarket Wertkauf, and it is planning for future expansions in that and other European countries.

Although chains, by definition, have specific merchandising and management similarities, they are classified in different ways. They may be categorized by their merchandise assortment or by their pricing policy, as traditional chains or value-oriented chains (off-price stores and discounters). Traditional chains and their product assortments are discussed first.

Traditional Chains

Retailers that buy first-quality goods to sell at standard industry markups are classified here as **traditional chains**. In order of volume, supermarket chains are at the top, followed by drugstores, with home centers and apparel merchants following. Not too far behind are booksellers, computer stores, and toy merchants. Each category is continuously growing in terms of overall units and is showing consumer confidence by virtue of sales increases.

SUPERMARKETS

Three of the top ten retailers in the United States are **supermarket** chains, so it is quite evident that Americans prefer to do their food shopping in these venues. Although competition

Harris Teeter is a supermarket chain noted for its prepared foods.

from warehouse clubs like Sam's Club and Costco is heating up and the entry of online grocers like Peapod and Webvan is drawing away some business, supermarkets are far and away the largest group in the country's top 100 retailers. For all of the hoopla attributed to the Internet, it is certainly not having an impact on brick-and-mortar grocers.

The consolidation of supermarket chains is also a major trend in the industry. Delhaize America, for example, has acquired Hannaford Bros., the largest supermarket chain in New England. Ahold USA, the nation's fourteenth largest retailer, bought U.S. Foodservice, a company that sells prepared foods to supermarkets. Not every attempted acquisition is successful. Royal Ahold's offer to purchase the Pathmark chain, for example, was stopped by the **Federal Trade Commission**. Nonetheless, most industry analysts predict that many more industry takeovers will occur.

The **product mix** at supermarkets continues to change. While packaged food still accounts for the majority of the inventory, other food and nonfood items play a significant role in overall sales. Publix, for example, offers freshly prepared sushi in its stores, and Harris Teeter features a full selection of freshly prepared foods. At many markets, more and more space is being used for in-store baked goods as well as specialty counters that offer a variety of gourmet food items. The inclusion of these foods provides the shopper with more variety to choose from. In addition, the merchant can add a greater markup to these items than to the packaged items traditionally found in supermarkets. Markups on packaged foods are limited because the majority of them are available in any food store. The baked goods and gourmet items, however, are exclusive to the particular stores and can be priced accordingly.

The nonfood and food-related categories include a host of items that help increase overall store sales and result in better profits. Products such as greeting cards, paperback books, stationery, tools, fresh flowers, and other **impulse items** that customers buy without advance planning are usually marked up more than the foods are. More and more supermarket chains are increasing the space allotted for such goods in order to bolster their bottom lines. Specialty grocers such as Whole Foods and Fresh Market also continue to expand.

DRUGSTORES

The retail drugstore industry is lead by CVS, Walgreens, Rite Aid, and Longs. The field, which once was dominated by small independent druggists, has grown into a $20 billion industry, and the local druggist has almost become a distant memory.

The merchandise mix at retail drugstores features a wealth of products that complement the packaged drug and drug-related items and the pharmacy stations that dispense prescription drugs. A visit to any of these emporiums immediately reveals a wealth of food products, stationery, books, greeting cards, cosmetics, photographic equipment, in-house photography developing services, and seasonal merchandise. The expansion into these lines not only helped to increase overall sales but also made the operations more profitable, because markups on many of these items can be greater than on over-the-counter and prescription drugs. Thus they have a positive effect on the bottom line.

CVS is the largest pharmacy chain in the United States.

One current trend in the drugstore industry is the opening of freestanding stores located at corners where

TABLE 2.3
TOP FIVE SUPERMARKET CHAINS IN THE UNITED STATES, 2006

Company	Headquarters	2006 Revenues ($)
Kroger	Cincinnati, OH	66,111,200
Safeway	Pleasanton, CA	40,185,000
SuperValu	Eden Prairie, MN	28,016,000
Ahold USA	Chantilly, VA	24,000,000
Publix	Lakeland, FL	21,700,000

Source: Adapted from *Stores Magazine*, July 2007.

converging roads bring heavy traffic and thus potential customers. Walgreens has led the way in this movement, and CVS, a competitor to Walgreens in many areas, has followed suit. Thus, the corner drugstore is returning in a new form.

HOME CENTERS

When Home Depot came onto the scene in 1978, it revolutionized the retail segment that caters to do-it-your-selfers. With its prime competitor, Lowe's, right behind, it dominates an industry once made up of independent hardware stores. Of course, there are smaller entries in this field such as Menard and 84 Lumber.

Consumers are attracted to **home centers** by the wealth of merchandise found under one cavernous roof and by the low prices that defy competition. A shopper looking for lighting fixtures, tools, machinery, flooring, paint, bathroom accessories, doors, or lumber will find wide assortments to fit their needs. And these operations have now added garden centers to further satisfy the needs of home owners and increase the stores' profits.

Home Depot is the United States' leading home center.

Not only do home centers serve the needs of the individual home owners, they also supply wares to commercial contractors. With separate service areas catering to contractors and vast on-hand inventories, home centers have become the contractors' primary source for building supplies.

The vast majority of the home centers' product mix is made up of practical merchandise. To meet the needs of do-it-yourselfers more concerned with home decorating than home improvement, Home Depot has opened Expo Design Centers. These stores feature up-scale assortments of home decor items that appeal to more affluent consumers. Interior designers and individual consumers alike have made these stores regular stops.

The small neighborhood hardware store has virtually disappeared from this retailing sector. The warehouselike home centers have taken their places and have run with the ball.

APPAREL SHOPS

Who hasn't heard of or visited Gap, Old Navy, Banana Republic, American Eagle Outfitters, Abercrombie & Fitch, or one of the other apparel chains? Each merchant in this classification tries to distinguish itself by product differentiation. While many still rely upon purchasing their goods from a variety of vendors in the hope that they will carry these goods exclusively within their trading areas, many of the larger chains carry only private-label products. This approach

Old Navy, a division of the Gap organization, continues to expand its apparel offerings.

is often referred to as **the store-is-the-brand retailing**. By using this approach and developing their own products, the chains are certain that they will have a unique identity.

Expansion by apparel chains is occurring at a very rapid pace. Whenever a new mall opens, it is certain to house a variety of stores under the Gap, Inc., umbrella, with spin-offs such as GapKids and BabyGap as well as other Gap divisions such as Banana Republic. When malls expand or are restructured, it is certain that these companies will occupy more space than they did originally.

Companies such as Ann Taylor and Talbots are also making major inroads in this fiercely competitive field, though on a smaller scale than Gap. They are opening spin-offs in order to capture new segments of the market. Ann Taylor, for example, has pursued the value market with its Ann Taylor Loft stores, and Talbots has started to cater to apparel **subclassification** with the introduction of Talbot Petites.

An indication of the enormous success of the apparel specialty chains is their 26 percent share of the marketplace, making them the biggest channel of distribution for such merchandise. This success has led manufacturers and designers to enter this arena directly. Recognizing that many of them have loyal consumer followers, they have established retail divisions alongside their wholesale operations. By having their own retail spaces, they can showcase their entire collections and not be restricted by the purchasing budgets of their traditional retail accounts. When a shopper visits a department store, for example, only a fraction of the designer or manufacturer's offerings are featured.

Many **marquee labels**, such as Ralph Lauren, Levi Strauss, Calvin Klein, and others have had considerable success with retail outlets. They continue to open a large number of stores, so it is certain that many consumers are buying directly from them.

Focus on . . . Gap, Inc.

ONE OF THE MOST VISIBLE AND HIGHLY SUCCESSFUL CHAIN OPERATIONS is Gap, Inc., which sells through a number of different stores that feature the corporate name as well as others such as Banana Republic and Old Navy. The organization has grown from a company that was composed of only Gap stores into the giant that it is today. It is one of the largest of the specialty store organizations headquartered in the United States, with more than 3,100 stores and with sales greater than any other chain employing traditional prices.

First, the company expanded its operation by opening divisions that used the Gap name (GapKids and BabyGap, for example), which were designed to satisfy the needs of the shoppers who bought Gap merchandise for themselves. These newer entries immediately found success by using the same merchandising philosophy that brought such acclaim to the original Gap stores where parents bought their own clothes. A walk through most malls in the United States finds outlets from these three units in close proximity to each other, an approach that has enabled Gap to become one of the few retailers to be successful in outfitting the entire family.

Gap stores are thriving not only in the United States but also in many overseas markets, where it has a significant presence. Countries such as Canada, the United Kingdom, France, Ireland, and Japan have Gap stores.

Two of the newer entries in the Gap organization are Banana Republic and Old Navy. Gap acquired Banana Republic more than a decade ago, and it launched Old Navy in 1994. Each unit has won significant acceptance throughout the country.

Banana Republic originally marketed itself with a "safari and khaki" image. The stores were like stage sets of the outback, with bamboo, netting, pith helmets, and rustic jeeps used to foster its environments. Not a trace of that concept is visible any longer. Instead, the company repositioned itself as a marketer of casual, professional, and elegant apparel. As is the case with the Gap stores, Banana Republic carries only products that are created especially for it. No designer labels here, only Banana Republic labels; it is the epitome of the store-is-the-brand retailing. The prices are moderate when compared to those of designer labels but more expensive than the Gap stores. Although some items do resemble the styles of such high-profile designers as Prada, the similarity is said to be only a coincidence. The product developers at the company have a complete understanding of the market it serves and create items that will best serve its customers' needs.

Its customer base is the successful young male and female business executive who wants to purchase sophisticated clothing suitable for casual, daytime, and evening dress. With more than 300 units, many of which are two- and three-story facilities, the company's expansion plans are making it one of the more visible apparel chains in the country.

At the other end of the Gap spectrum is Old Navy. The newest of the company's divisions, it is making one of the loudest splashes in apparel chain history. Since its inception, it has regularly pumped up profits for the corporation. The merchandise, which is intended to appeal to families, bears the lowest prices in the organization. The product mix includes apparel for men, women, and children. The unit has extremely broad appeal and counts as its customers everyone from inner-city teens to baby boomers. Its image is a mix of fun and nostalgia.

After starting in San Francisco with a single unit near Gap headquarters, Old Navy has grown into a major retailer. Each is a cavernous space with huge assortments of private-label merchandise in a wide array of colors piled up on tables or hung on plain racks. The stores' decor features retro graphics and antique trucks.

Gap continues to open Old Navy units that are huge for apparel chain stores. The Old Navy store on 34th Street in New York City, for example, has 150,000 square feet of floor space. The size is not unique to New York City; San Francisco's flagship store occupies 100,000 square feet. Old Navy targets sites of out-of-business retailers in prime locations in an effort to increase its visibility to shoppers.

With these successes in its group, Gap, Inc., continues to be the nation's premier retail apparel chain.

BOOKSTORES

Once a very small part of the retail market, booksellers have reinvented themselves and have become a major force in retailing. Companies like Borders and Barnes & Noble continue to expand with stores that resemble anything but the prototypes of the past.

These stores feature not only a wealth of books in every conceivable category but also lounge areas with comfortable chairs where shoppers can examine their selections before purchasing them, coffee bars where customers can sample a cappuccino and a pastry, and open spaces where entertainers such as storytellers, guitarists, and singers perform. These bookstores have become recreational destinations for families.

Bookstores have become gathering places to examine books while sipping a cappuccino.

Unlike most retail operations that close no later than 9:30 p.m., these stores keep their doors open until 11:00 p.m. It is not unusual to see a great number of people sipping their favorite beverages in the coffee bar and then standing in line to make their purchases at this late hour.

It should be noted that, even though a good deal of book purchasing is accomplished through the Internet, the social nature of the newly created atmosphere in this new type of retail space has made the brick-and-mortar bookstores a profitable venture.

MISCELLANEOUS CHAINS

Many traditional chain store companies specialize in other merchandise classifications such as shoes, eyeglasses, home accessories, jewelry, handbags, toys, museum reproductions, pet supplies, records, and tapes. Some are large chains with many units, while others are smaller chains with only a few units.

As is true with the chain retailers mentioned previously, these retailers are also experiencing considerable growth. Most of them are enjoying success in malls throughout the country and in freestanding units as well.

Smaller Stores

Ever since retailing began, entrepreneurs were in business to cater to the needs of their communities. Many were successful merchants offering a variety of items in relatively small outlets in the main streets of towns and villages. They featured anything from general merchandise to more restricted product lines. As retailing grew and the advent of large-scale retailing took over, many of these merchants grew into larger businesses. But some shuttered their doors, unable to meet the competition from the major players.

Today, smaller retailers still play an important role in the business of selling to the consumer. In every part of the United States and even more so in offshore venues, smaller operations are catering to the needs of their inhabitants. Unlike their large-retail counterparts, who most often have become multichannel merchants, these practitioners primarily operate from single stores.

Although their businesses are relatively small and are run by just a few employees, they are nonetheless performing the same tasks as large retailers. That is, they buy, sell, advertise, promote, merchandise, manage their employees, and so forth.

The vast majority of today's smaller retail operations specialize in one merchandise classification, which might be apparel, accessories, shoes, home furnishings, or specialty foods such as organics and health products. They are usually located on main streets, small neighborhood clusters, strip centers, and places where the giants of the industry do not locate their units. Generally, they are not invited to open in major malls because companies that own and operate giant shopping centers prefer that major merchants inhabit their premises. Also, the cost of doing business in these main shopping arenas is generally prohibitive.

The keys to success of the vast majority of the smaller stores include service, product uniqueness, competitive pricing, personalized attention, and so forth. For those wanting to experience the American dream of self-employment, small store retailing is still a viable choice.

Unlike their large-store counterparts who have access to the latest technological advances, the smaller retailer is often less savvy in these areas. Microsoft Dynamics offers a revolutionary single-store software package that helps bring these entrepreneurs into the twenty-first century's way of efficiently doing business. With the Point of Sale package, these merchants can connect retail and accounting processes, manage and track inventory, automate transactions, deliver personalized service, improve purchasing, better manage employees, and gain control over cash management. Log on to www.microsoft.com/smallbusiness/products/retail-software/point-of-sale for more information.

VALUE-ORIENTED RETAILERS

A steady area of growth in American retailing has been within the segment that provides value to shoppers. Although **value retailing** is not a recent phenomenon, the downturn in the economy of the 1980s provided extra incentive for value retailers to expand and for other merchants to enter the field. After several years of free spending, the recession of the 1980s caused many consumers to rethink their buying habits. In particular, the *yuppies* (young urban professionals) who had come of age in a time of plenty awakened to learn that easy wealth was not the norm.

Capitalizing on the economic downturn, merchants that already catered to the value shopper quickly began to expand their operations with hundreds of new outlets. Joining them were new retailers that wanted to ride this new wave of value merchandising. At the outset of the new millennium, thousands of brick-and-mortar stores of every type were opening everywhere, with value retailers at the head of the pack. Out front were discounters such as Wal-Mart, the nations largest retailer, and Target; off-price merchants such as TJX, with their T.J. Maxx and Marshalls divisions, and category killers such as Toys "R" Us, Best Buy, and Circuit City; manufacturer closeout stores; and retail clearance centers.

TABLE 2.4
TOP 20 U.S. VALUE RETAILERS BY SALES VOLUME, 2006

COMPANY	MAIN PRODUCT LINES	CLASSIFICATION	HEADQUARTERS
Wal-Mart	Household, clothing	Discounter	Bentonville, AR
Home Depot	Home improvement	Discounter	Atlanta, GA
Costco	Food, misc.	Discounter	Issaquah, WA
Target	Clothing, home	Discounter	Minneapolis, MN
Lowe's	Home improvement	Discounter	Mooresville, NC
Best Buy	Electronics	Discounter	Minneapolis, MN
Staples	Office supplies	Discounter	Framingham, MA
TJX	Clothing	Off-price	Framingham, MA
Office Depot	Office supplies	Discounter	Delray Beach, FL
Toys "R" Us	Toys	Discounter	Wayne, NJ
Circuit City	Electronics	Discounter	Richmond, VA
Dollar General	Variety	Closeout store	Goodlettsville, TN
Office Max	Office supplies	Discounter	Itasca, IL
BJ's	Food, misc.	Discounter	Natick, MA
Bed Bath & Beyond	Home products	Discounter	Union, NJ
Family Dollar	Variety	Closeout store	Matthews, NC
Ross Stores	Clothing	Off-price	Pleasanton, CA
Barnes & Noble	Books	Discount	New York, NY
Big Lots	Variety	Closeout store	Columbus, OH
CompUSA	Computers	Discount	Dallas, TX

Source: Adapted from *Stores Magazine*, July 2007.

Unlike the traditional retailers, which are primarily located in major shopping malls and downtown central districts, value-oriented retailers are more likely to be found in **power centers** or **outlet malls**.

> **In the News . . .**
>
> Read the article "The Ins and Outs of Outlets" (on page 52 at the end of this chapter) for a survey of the playing field of value retailing.

A close inspection of the top retailers in the United States shows that many of them are value-oriented. Wal-Mart, Home Depot, and Costco, all three discounters, are near or at the top of the list of specialty retailers. In fact, most of the top retailers of all types are value-oriented companies.

U.S. value-oriented retailers have also been successful abroad. TJX operates Winners outlets in Canada, Sam's Club units are found in Mexico, and Toys "R" Us has a presence in the United Kingdom. Although value retailing has not been an important trend in other countries, the successful entry of these and other companies into foreign markets indicates that this type of merchandising can be profitable worldwide.

Discounters

As explained in Chapter 1, a discount operation purchases merchandise at full price from vendors but sells it at a price lower than that charged by the traditional retailers. They buy early in the season as do traditional retailers, but they discount goods in the hope that greater volume will make up for lower per-unit profit. With discounters like Wal-Mart and Target continuing to increase their market shares, it is obvious that discounting is a major form of retailing in the United States.

Discounting is not limited to one merchandise classification. The giants just mentioned stock a wealth of different items including apparel, small appliances, household products, electronics, and so forth. Others, such as Best Buy, restrict their offerings to electronics, appliances, and other related items. Still others specialize in soft goods.

Stein Mart is a fast growing U.S. off-price retailer.

Off-Price Retailers

Often confused with discounters, off-price retailers are also value-oriented organizations but have a different approach to merchandising. Instead of buying at full prices, these merchants practice **opportunistic buying**. That is, whenever wholesale prices fall, they are there to scoop up the bargains. For example, the fashion industry is a seasonal business, and manufacturers must make room for their new collections to satisfy the needs of their retailers, which must constantly revise their inventories. Even in the most successful companies like Liz Claiborne, Calvin Klein, DKNY, Ralph Lauren, and Tommy Hilfiger, merchandise is always left over at season's end. The only way for these companies to quickly dispose of such items is by offering them at reduced prices. This creates the opportunity for the off-price merchants to buy quality goods at lower prices.

By making only low-cost purchases, off-price retailers are able to offer their customers well-known labels at reduced prices. They buy for less and thus sell for less. Unlike the discounters, which take lower markups, the off-price retailers take markups that are comparable to the traditionalists. It's their ability to "buy right" that allows them to use this pricing structure.

Off-price retailers must operate in a number of ways that are different from other retailers' practices. For example:

- They cannot get merchandise as early as traditional merchants. Since price is their main consideration, they must wait until the manufacturer deems it necessary to rid itself of the goods. Early purchasing at full price enables traditional stores to be the first to receive the goods. The off-price retailers' customers are willing to get the merchandise later in the season in exchange for the lower prices they pay.
- They cannot locate stores alongside those of traditional retailers in major malls and downtown shopping districts. These prime locations purposely exclude off-price retailers, whose price structure would result in unfair competition with the traditional department stores and chain organizations that buy at full price and charge their customers full price.
- Off-price retailers are generally forbidden to mention the names of their vendors in their advertising programs. Instead, they use headlines such as "Closeout of Famous Designer" or "Designer Swimsuits at 40% Less Than Regular Prices" in their ads. Thus, traditional department stores and specialty chains will not be hurt directly if they feature the same items at higher prices.

The major merchandise category of off-price retailers is apparel, followed by wearable accessories. The constant changes of style direction and the seasonal nature of apparel retailing mean that these products must be disposed of quickly by vendors. The out-of-season lines are generally sold as **closeouts**. The merchandise offered as closeouts usually consists of incomplete assortments of colors and sizes, which buyers who represent the off-price retailers must settle for. But there is a trade-off: the prices they pay are well below the original wholesale prices.

Heading the list of off-price retailers is TJX, whose divisions include Marshalls, T.J. Maxx, A.J. Wright, HomeGoods, Winners (Canada), T.K. Maxx (Europe), and Bob's Stores. Collectively, these stores account for approximately half of the off-price retailing business. Others in this category include Stein Mart, Loehmann's, Burlington Coat Factory, Ross Stores, and Syms.

With value shopping on the rise, the outlook for off-price retailing is extremely favorable.

Manufacturer Closeout Stores

Although many manufacturers dispose of their leftover items to off-price retailers, the number of such remaining items may be so great that complete disposal through only these outlets is not practical. Manufacturers' selling of these goods directly began modestly in the late 1970s at locations like North Conway, New Hampshire, and Secaucus, New Jersey. The practice has now grown into a rapidly expanding industry, **manufacturer closeout stores**. All over the United States, nationally recognized manufacturers and designers have opened their own outlets to dispose of slow-selling merchandise. Many of these stores are clustered in such centers as outlet malls. DKNY, Ralph Lauren, Calvin Klein, Liz Claiborne, Nine West, Dooney & Bourke, Mikasa, Gucci, and Geoffrey Beene are among those manufacturers with outlets in such centers. The advantage to manufacturers and designers of owning their own closeout stores is that they can increase their profit by selling directly to the consumer instead of through an off-price retailer.

Rehoboth Outlets on the Delaware shore features manufacturer closeout stores. Its three separate but neighboring malls are managed by Charter Oak Partners, the largest privately owned outlet developer in the United States.

The importance of this form of retailing can be best understood by examining some of the different centers that house these stores and clearance centers. Heading the list of outlet mall managers is the organization that owns a group of malls known as the Mills. Sawgrass Mills, the largest of the group, is located in a suburb of Fort Lauderdale, Florida. It boasts more than two miles of selling space, all under one roof. Featured are closeout stores for Ralph Lauren, DKNY, Nine West, Tahari, Wedgwood, Mikasa, and other brand names. So successful has this venture been that entertainment areas and major restaurants such as the Cheesecake Factory, Rain Forest Café, and Wolfgang Puck have opened branches. Other successful outlet malls are Woodbury Commons in upstate New York, a center for upscale fashion designers; Belz Outlet Centers in St. Augustine and Orlando, Florida; and Freeport, Maine, an outdoor center that boasts many streets lined with designer outlets.

Because of the price structuring of outlet malls, they cannot be located within close proximity to traditional malls or downtown central districts. They are purposely built sufficiently far from traditional shopping locations that they will not compete with them. If the manufacturers opened outlets too close to traditional retailers, this would jeopardize the wholesale operations they depend on, which in turn depend on business from department stores and full-price specialty chain organizations.

Retail Clearance Centers

As discussed earlier, department stores and specialty chains sell merchandise to consumers at regular prices, offering them a wealth of services that justify such prices. Even with the best possible planning, these merchants are likely to be left with unsold merchandise at the end of the season, even after initial markdowns have been taken. With shelf space often limited, retailers must move merchandise as quickly as possible to make space on the selling floor for new items. One salvation for retailers left with slow-selling items is the **retail clearance center**.

Major department stores such as Saks Fifth Avenue, Neiman Marcus, Nordstrom, and Lord & Taylor; specialty stores like the Gap, Banana Republic, and Ann Taylor; and catalogue companies like Spiegel have all entered this arena. Outlets such as Saks' Off-Fifth and Last Call by Neiman Marcus are ringing up record sales. They are not only disposing of the slow sellers from their regular stores at the clearance centers but also—in spite of the lower prices being charged—are making a profit because of the high turnover.

In spite of all of the hoopla regarding off-site selling, brick-and-mortar retailing is alive and well and making progress on both the traditional and value-oriented fronts.

Specialty stores like Gap have entered the retail clearance arena.

CHAPTER HIGHLIGHTS

- Brick-and-mortar retailers are the most important segment of the retailing industry in terms of overall sales.
- The best known of the traditional retailers are department stores and specialty chains.
- Department stores are classified as either full-line operations or specialized companies.
- Many traditional department store companies have expanded their organizations through acquisitions.
- Department stores started operating branches because of population shifts to the suburbs across the nation.
- The drugstore retail segment is now dominated by a few giants such as CVS and Walgreens, and the vast majority of small druggists have closed their doors.
- Bookstores have become entertainment centers where live performances and cafes share space with the book inventory.
- The greatest movement in retail sales has been away from traditional retailers to value-oriented retailers.
- Off-price merchants, discounters, manufacturer closeout stores, and retail clearance centers are the components of value retailing.
- Because of their price structure, off-price retailers must locate their stores away from traditional shopping malls.
- Major companies like Saks Fifth Avenue, Neiman Marcus, and Nordstrom have had enormous success in selling excess inventory at their own clearance centers.

IMPORTANT RETAILING TERMS

anchor store (39)
closeout (49)
direct selling (35)
Federal Trade Commission (42)
full-line department store (37)
home center (43)
impulse item (42)
manufacturer closeout store (49)
marquee label (44)
opportunistic buying (48)
outlet mall (48)
power center (48)
product mix (42)
retail clearance center (50)
specialized department store (38)
store within a store (36)
subclassification (44)
supermarket (41)
the-store-is-the-brand retailing (44)
traditional chain (41)
traditional retailer (36)
value retailing (47)

FOR REVIEW

1. What does the term *brick-and-mortar retailing* mean?
2. In what way do the two department store types differ?
3. Why was the department store concept so successful when it was introduced to American consumers?
4. Why have most department stores discontinued their appliance departments?
5. Define the *store-within-a-store* concept used by department stores. Why has it achieved such success?
6. Identify the department store company discussed in this chapter that started as a small operation and has grown to be a major player.
7. What trend led department stores to expand by opening branch stores?
8. Why have the specialty chains become the most successful of today's brick-and-mortar operations?
9. Describe one method supermarkets have used to increase their overall profits.
10. What does the term *the-store-is-the-brand* mean?
11. Name one method that stores like the Gap and Banana Republic have used to differentiate their merchandise from that of other retailers.
12. Discuss some features that bookstores have added to make the stores more exciting for their clienteles.
13. What are the major differences between discount operations and off-price retail outlets?
14. Why don't discounters and off-pricers locate their stores in traditional shopping malls?
15. What does the term *manufacturer closeout store* mean?

AN INTERNET ACTIVITY

Select five of your favorite brick-and-mortar retailers, making certain that you are familiar with the merchandise in the stores you choose. See if these retailers have Web sites. Go to the Web sites to find out what merchandise is available.

Develop a table with the following column headings:

- Name of the store
- Major merchandise categories in stores
- Merchandise available on Web site

Compare the merchandise available at the brick-and-mortar stores with the merchandise available through the Web site. Prepare a double-spaced report.

EXERCISES AND PROJECTS

1. Write to or visit the public relations department in a full-line or specialized department store organization to learn about the topics listed below. Use this information to write a two-page, double-spaced report:
   - The company's history
   - The merchandise mix it offers its clientele
   - The store's target market
   - Other means of transacting business, such as catalogues and a Web site
   - Potential for overseas expansion

2. Visit an off-price outlet store to find out what nationally advertised manufacturer and designer brands it stocks. Prepare a chart with headings as shown below to record the information. List at least ten brands. Price tags usually show the regular price along with the price at the off-price store.

   Store _____
   Location _____

Brand	Regular Price	Outlet Price

THE CASE OF THE OFF-PRICE COMPETITOR

Clements Department Store has been successfully operating five traditional stores in the South for many years. It opened its first unit in 1945 and subsequently expanded to four other locations, each within a radius of 200 miles of the flagship store. The company is a family business with four generations involved at present. Until recently it did not have any direct competition, an unusual position for a department store to be in. Of course, there were specialty stores in the area, and households could make purchases from the many catalogues they received regularly. Many families have also begun to make purchases over the Internet. When all is said and done, however, most customers were faithful to the company and called upon it for most of their buying needs. The merchandise assortment was substantial for the trading area, and the clientele was sufficiently satisfied to pay the prices asked.

Last year, the situation at Clements changed. What was once the perfect retailing situation was altered by the opening of a highly visible new operation, The Smart Shopper, an off-price venture that sold merchandise bearing many of the same labels carried by Clements but at lower prices. Although the merchandise offered at the new company wasn't generally available at the same time as at Clements and the size and color assortments were not complete, the brand-name merchandise was still there for the taking.

The new venture was located in the same area as the five Clements stores and adjacent to a major highway, making it within easy reach of the customers who frequented any of the Clements stores. The Smart Shopper immediately became a destination for curious shoppers who wanted to learn what bargains might be found. Sales began to fall at each of the Clements stores.

Each member of the Clements family in the management team reacted differently. Steve Clements, its founder, felt that loyal customers would return once their curiosities were satisfied and that no changes should be made. His daughter Julia, senior vice president, felt that playing the waiting game was dangerous and that the results would be harmful to the company. She believed an aggressive advertising campaign was necessary to bring the shoppers back to the stores. Bill Reilly, Julia's husband and general merchandise manager, felt an aggressive approach would be necessary to meet the new competition. His plan was to play The Smart Shopper's game and introduce off-price merchandise.

As sales begin to slip even more, the three are still trying to come up with a solution to the problem.

Questions

1. With whom do you agree?
2. What other approaches should the company take to bring the customers back to them?

The Ins and Outs of Outlets
Amy S. Choi

MARCH 26, 2007

NEW YORK—There's big and there's small, but is there any room left in the middle?

Of the dozens of midsize outlet developers that used to build centers in the U.S., only two major players, Tanger Factory Outlet Centers and Prime Retail, remain today as their own independent entities. Tanger is the only real estate investment trust in the segment. Other companies either devoured each other, collapsed under poor management, or both.

Chelsea Property Group, for example, acquired Konover Property Trust for $180 million in 2001, only to then be acquired by Simon Property Group in 2004 in a blockbuster $3.5 billion deal. It is currently the largest operator of outlet malls, with 14 million square feet domestically and an additional three million square feet internationally. In the past few months, Simon, which is the country's largest mall REIT, has also snatched up The Mills Corp. for some $7.9 billion, taking control of the ailing company and its portfolio of mixed entertainment-retail and outlet centers.

"I wouldn't eliminate the acquisition of Tanger as a possibility," said Craig Schmidt, vice-president of Merrill Lynch. "There's a real possibility that General Growth or Macerich could do the same thing that Simon's done."

Tanger, which did not return calls for comment, was also a contender for the Mills portfolio. Though the company kept mum due to confidentiality issues, it completed due diligence "and submitted our proposal to acquire a significant portfolio from a public REIT that was exploring its strategic alternatives," said Frank Marchisello, CFO, on a recent conference call with Wall Street.

"We always look at every portfolio that comes available, particularly in an area that might be closely aligned with ours where we feel we can add value," said Stanley Tanger on the call. "We feel that's our responsibility to our shareholders and also to ourselves."

But even as Tanger seeks out new acquisition opportunities, it and Prime are likely targets for shopping center and mall REITs hungry for growth.

"Consolidation is a trend that's going to continue," said Josh Podell, vice-president of real estate for Jones Apparel. "I wouldn't be surprised at all if the traditional developers expressed interest in the Primes and the Tangers of the world. It creates a sense of being vertical."

That verticality can of course help an owner grow in a number of ways, not the least of which is capturing tenants for one format while leasing them for another. According to Philip Ende, vice-president of leasing at Chelsea, the company is often introduced to brands from Simon. Tourneau, for example, is opening its first outlet in Chelsea's Desert Hills Premium Outlets in Cabazon, Calif.

It may also encourage retailers who don't have an outlet store to open one.

"Simon has some of the best malls. Chelsea has some of the best outlets," said Podell. "If you can get into the top tier of both the full price and outlet centers, why wouldn't you? If you can go into the Forum Shops and Woodbury Common, it's the best of both worlds."

Other observers don't believe that the verticality in ownership could lead to more stores for retailers.

"The outlet industry is extremely retailer-driven," said Linda Humphers, editor-in-chief of *Value Retail News*, an International Council of Shopping Centers publication. "If they don't want to open a store, they won't open a store."

Consolidation has other ripple effects, one being the proliferation of individual landlords that own just one or two outlets.

"As Chelsea and Prime and Tanger beef up their tenancy they spin off centers that don't fit their high profile," she said. "Those centers are bought by the little guys—because of consolidation we're seeing more owners, not fewer owners."

The numbers show how disparate outlet ownership is despite the consolidation of the past decade. Chelsea, the largest operator of outlet space, controls only about 25 percent of the 55 million-square-foot outlet market, and Tanger has only about half that. In the mall industry, by contrast, some 80 percent of the malls are owned by just a handful of the major REITs.

As they spin off their properties, major developers are focused on growing their core asset base[s], which are often focused on luxury vendors and target aspirational shoppers. Chelsea, for example, recently broke ground on its Houston Premium Outlets, which will open in 2008, and expects to open centers in Rio Grande, Philadelphia, Seoul, and Osaka this year. It is also expanding its Orlando, Las Vegas, and Gotemba, Japan, projects. Tanger plans to break ground soon on a project in Long Island, N.Y., and has plans to invest up to $36 million to expand four of its existing centers in Barstow, Calif., Branson, Mo., Gonzalez, La., and Tilton, N.H. Prime Retail completed a 200,000-square-foot expansion of its marquee property in San Marcos, Texas, and is currently revamping an older outlet center in

Orlando. The first, 500,000-square-foot phase of Prime Outlets Orlando is expected to open in August.

"Shoppers don't want to shop a number of outlet centers," said Schmidt. They want to go to one that offers as much as possible. Smaller outlet centers are disadvantaged just because they can't offer a broad enough variety of retailers."

Owners are also beginning to incorporate lifestyle elements into their centers. At Prime Outlets Gaffney, in South Carolina, for example, Prime Retail added a family entertainment center that includes a movie theater and bowling lanes. Chelsea has vastly increased the number of specialty tenants and kiosks on its properties, and is considering how to best improve the food mix.

"It just depends on where the outlet is, and how much local traffic there is," said Bob Brvenik, president of Prime Retail. "But some outlets operate more like a local mall, and in those situations you clearly want to add more amenities."

Still, all of this activity may not be enough for some vendors.

"Because there are so few outlet centers being developed, a lot of traditional outlet retailers are going to nontraditional outlet venues to open up stores," said Podell. "Some alternatives are power centers, downtowns, even some lifestyle centers.

"I think it's an incredibly important part of any real estate strategy," he continued. "You can reach new customers, shed merchandise and grow your bottom line. From a growth standpoint, there are only so many malls you can go to, so you need to look to different avenues. Outlet centers are that avenue."

CHAPTER 3
Off-Site Retailing: E-tailing, Catalogues, and Home-Shopping Networks

After you have completed this chapter, you should be able to discuss:

- The effects of the three major off-site retailing classifications on brick-and-mortar retailing
- The fundamental components that must be addressed when starting a Web site
- The multimedia approach to retailing
- The ways in which interactive e-tailing better serves the needs of the customers
- Why catalogue shopping continues to appeal to consumers
- Ways in which businesses that were formerly catalogue companies are expanding their businesses
- Why home-shopping channels continue to experience record sales

Among modern retail professionals all across the United States, a topic of interest is the recent increase in customer spending in venues other than the brick-and-mortar stores. More and more shoppers are choosing to make purchases electronically, through catalogues, and via the numerous home-shopping networks on television. These retail outlets are making significant gains in their share of the consumer dollar, but it is too early to tell if their presence will result in the demise of brick-and-mortar stores. At this time, the percentage of off-site consumer spending pales in comparison with in-store shopping. However, with the considerable efforts of countless businesses now embracing **off-site purchasing** as a means to satisfy consumer needs and bring a profit to their companies, it is obvious that this trend will not only continue but also gain momentum.

During the past few years, with the advent of **electronic retailing**, a new language has been created. Consumers have come to hear and use new words, words that hadn't existed in the recent past. The new terminology includes such terms as *dot-com*, *search engine*, *Web site*, and *e-tailing*, and its use has become commonplace on the lips of industry professionals and consumers alike. Whenever discussions about retailing in the new millennium take place, these terms are involved. Although e-tailing has generated a great deal of excitement and enthusiasm in the industry, the verdict is still out on its actual long-term success and on where it will lead future generations of retailing.

Long before anyone dreamed of electronically filled orders for consumer goods, those unable or unwilling to go to stores took care of their buying needs through catalogues. Although the granddaddy of them all, the Sears catalogue, has ceased publication, catalogues are alive and well in the United States and are bringing in record sales. In fact, even Sears published a Christmas catalogue in 2007. Major department stores are constantly expanding their direct marketing efforts, and catalogue-only companies are featuring merchandise heretofore rarely found in catalogues. Whether it is the traditional merchandise offerings such as apparel and housewares or unusual items such as original artwork and rare plants, an abundance of goods can be found in catalogues. American households today are regularly bombarded with unsolicited catalogues; and the catalogue business is certain to gain even greater momentum than it has already realized.

Rounding out off-site retailing are the television "programs" that sell a variety of products to consumers. Cable channels devoted to shopping programs include QVC (quality, value, convenience), HSN (home shopping network), and Shop at Home. The variety is not as great as at other off-site ventures, with jewelry being the most common offering, followed by women's apparel. Day by day and hour by hour, customers are placing orders in record numbers, making these programs a viable outlet for some vendors. Akin to the shopping programs is the **infomercial**, a form of advertising that reports the virtues of a particular product such as a cooking device or workout equipment in a time block—such as a half hour—more usually associated with entertainment programs. Although limited somewhat to specific types of merchandise, it too has had considerable success in selling its wares via television.

Through these off-site selling shopping venues, retailers are able to offer consumers many alternative methods of making purchases.

E-TAILING

With the vast majority of American households owning computers and most having access to the Internet, electronic retailing or "e-tailing," as it is generally called—is a natural medium for selling merchandise to consumers. Retailers run multimillion dollar advertising campaigns to bring shoppers to particular Web sites to look for the products they need. Retailers hope customers will find what they want, buy it, and return again and again for additional purchases. As in any fledgling industry, the proliferation of e-tailers has been enormous. The number of entries in this retailing format is without rival among retailing venues. Not a day goes by without another Web site being launched. As in the case of brick-and-mortar organizations, the fittest survive and the others fail.

The growth in online retailing is significant. In 2007, according to Shop.org, Internet sales exceeded $200 billion. Also, according to a Harris poll, nearly 80 percent of U.S. adults go online, spending an average of 11 hours a week on the Internet.

The e-tailing industry is divided into two parts: those that do business on-line exclusively, **Web site–only retailers**, and those that are divisions of either brick-and-mortar retailer or catalogue operations. Each type of operation will be discussed more fully later in the chapter in terms of the benefits of its approach to e-tailing and likely future directions of the concept.

E-tailing Popularity

Although shopping in stores is generally the preference of consumers, a number of factors have made shopping online extremely popular. Among them are the following:

- *Saving time.* With the ever-increasing number of women in the workforce and with many consumers working more than one job, time for traditional shopping is more limited. Where store visits were often looked upon as social outings, the practice has steadily declined.
- *24/7 availability.* Unlike most retail operations (except for the 24-hour supermarket), shopping in stores is restricted to certain hours. Although evening hours and Sunday openings have expanded the shopping times, there's no comparison to e-tailing. Consumers can access their favorite Web sites, or search the Web for products, at any time.
- *Large selections.* Companies that are Web site–only merchants often have significantly broader merchandise offerings that do their store counterparts. At www.Zappos.com, for example, the shoe selection is greater than in any onsite retail operation.
- *Global reach.* Not only can customers access domestic Web sites, they can also shop virtually anywhere in the world on the Internet.
- *Comparison shopping.* With price often a purchasing consideration, many consumers like to know if they are paying the lowest price for a product. With only a few "clicks" they can quickly research identical products or those that are similar in nature.
- *Bargain prices.* E-tailers often focus on low prices to attract the shopper's attention. Such outlets as designeroutlet.com and bluefly.com offer bargains as their means to generating business.

Zappos.com is the largest "Web site–only" shoe merchant.

In the News . . .

"Pick It and Click It," an article that appears on page 74 at the end of this chapter, should be read now to gain a more complete understanding of the rationale behind Internet shopping.

Online Retailing Today

Continuing on its path to becoming a very important part of the retailing industry, the growth of online retailing is being realized by those companies that exclusively use the Internet to sell as well as by those that are multichannel merchants selling in stores and catalogues. Table 3.1 shows that the eight major Internet outlets include merchants from each of these classifications.

Consumer Planning for Online Purchasing

According to an October 2007 survey in *Stores Magazine*, consumers plan their purchases before actually making them. Such planning is perhaps to ascertain the benefits of the products or to make comparisons with retailers' offerings. In fact, according to research undertaken by PowerReviews, there is a trend toward individuals becoming "social researchers." In their "Social Shopping Study 2007," 65 percent of the respondents were identified as social researchers

TABLE 3.1
THE BIG EIGHT INTERNET OUTLETS

Company	Classification	Primary Products
Amazon.com	Web site–only	Books, media
eBay.com	Web site–only	Miscellaneous goods
Wal-Mart	Multichannel	Apparel, household
JCPenney	Multichannel	Apparel, home products
Target	Multichannel	Apparel, home products
Kohl's	Multichannel	Apparel, accessories
Sears	Multichannel	Household, apparel
Overstock.com	Web site–only	Variety

Source: *Stores Magazine*, October 2007.

because they collect, analyze, and manage information about shopping choices. The facts uncovered during this study included the following statistics:

- 78 percent of respondents indicated they spent more than 10 minutes reading product reviews.
- 86 percent of the respondents found customer reviews extremely or very important.
- 76 percent found that "top-rated product" lists were extremely or very important.
- 64 percent researched products online more than half of the time, no matter where they bought the product.
- 93 percent reported that they are more likely to start their shopping on a Web site that offers "social navigation"—cues to help find and understand information in real and virtual environments.

Given such important consumer information, online retailers must take the findings seriously enough to make certain that their Web sites feature consumer reviews.

A number of different online resources may be used to undertake product research, as shown in Table 3.2.

TABLE 3.2
TOP 10 WEB SITES USED BY CONSUMERS TO RESEARCH PRODUCTS

Web Site	Consumer Popularity*
Google.com	26.0
Amazon.com	6.8
Yahoo.com	5.8
eBay.com	3.0
ConsumerReports.org	2.2
WalMart.com	1.8
MSN.com	1.6
Manufacturer's Web site	1.3
Ask.com	1.1
AOL.com	1.0

* Percentage of respondents reporting use.
Source: *Stores Magazine*, October 2007.

Product Classification Popularity

Right from the very beginning, the purchase of computers, travel, books, and CDs accounted for the majority of online shopping. Today, this has changed. According to a study conducted by Forrester Research, Inc., the top spot (excepting travel purchases) now belongs to apparel and such fashion items as shoes, jewelry, and other wearable accessories. In fact, apparel and fashion online sales reached $18.3 billion in 2006 and were expected to reach $22.1 billion in 2007.

> **In the News . . .**
>
> Reading "Apparel Now No. 1 Online" (on page 75 at the end of this chapter) will give you a complete overview of the importance of apparel to online merchants.

Innovative Directions for Web Sites

Retailers are just beginning to understand the importance of transforming their Web sites into exciting and informative venues, just as merchants do in their brick-and-mortar outlets. Eye-catching window displays, signage that motivates purchasing, "personal shoppers" who make the customer's in-store experience a meaningful one, and special events that arouse motivation to buy are just some of the tools that distinguish one merchant from the other. In order to become more effective, online shopping also requires the company's special attention. Some of the more recent innovative tools that are starting to surface include the following.

LIVE CHATS

The use of instant messaging is one way for the prospective purchaser to have his or her questions answered. It has become a powerful tool for transforming doubts and objections into sales. The shopper, when needing a little more information, can use this direct communication tool to contact a company employee.

PERSONALIZING THE PRODUCT

Some merchants are finding a market for customized products that can be purchased online. SteveMadden.com can assist the customer in designing her own high-heel shoes; FreddyandMa.com will likewise accommodate handbag needs by helping design the perfect one; and Zafu.com, using a different personalized approach, takes customer's measurements and steers them to jeans retailers who have the products that guarantee a sure fit. According to Marshall Cohen, retail analyst for the NPD Group marketing research firm, a consumer who is involved in the design and/or fit of a product will buy it 72 percent of the time as compared with 23 percent for fashion purchases in general.

SteveMadden.com helps customers design their own high-heel shoes.

CUSTOMIZING THE FIT

Trying on many different pairs of jeans or any other wearing apparel is standard for most shoppers. It is, however, an experience that often takes considerable time. With time so precious these days, many have resorted to online purchasing only to be frustrated when the garment arrives but doesn't fit properly. In an effort to reduce merchandise returns and better satisfy shopper's needs, myShape.com offers a variety of designer ready-to-wear items to fit the customer's body shape. After a customer completes the shape analysis questions, appropriate styles are shown that will accommodate different body shapes. The system is not foolproof, but it does cut down on returns.

Eddie Bauer offers customers its version of customized fit.

Companies like Eddie Bauer, L.L.Bean, and Lands' End are all offering their versions of customized fit. Also making an important inroad into customized fit is Intellifit. Customers who use this service are required to go to any one of a number of specific shops (e.g., Levi stores) to be measured. From this measurement a "print" is created, and brand-name clothes can be identified that match this print. The process guarantees a perfect fit.

GRAPHICAL MERCHANDISING

Simply showing products to the consumer online doesn't always work. Different people have different needs for the same product. In the home furnishings arena, for example, the same couch may serve different purposes. One shopper might need it in a particular setting or in a specific color while another might have entirely different requirements for the same product. The furniture giant Thomasville uses Scene 7's system, which allows the shopper to see the couch in different settings. Draping applications is another area where specific use can be seen. After implementing this application, Thomasville reported a 1,100 percent increase in its online traffic.

RESEARCHING "CART ABANDONMENT"

In stores, the sight of abandoned shopping carts is unusual. Shoppers most often select their products, fill their carts, and take them to the checkout counter. In online shopping, however, abandoned carts are far more numerous. The shopper merely exits the Web site without completing the purchase. In an attempt to discover why this phenomenon is so prevalent, many online merchants are using research to determine the causes. Doubts about shipping charges, price, security, and so forth can be uncovered via online surveys. By understanding consumer concerns, the retailer can address this issue.

NAVIGATIONAL CHANGES

Logging on to a Web site doesn't always guarantee consumer comprehension in terms of how to navigate it. Without simple navigational solutions, empty shopping carts are often the result. At Bath & Body Works, research into its Web site indicated a need for change. The number of categories was reduced, old terminology was replaced to coincide with shifts in the marketplace, and some features were moved to more visible places on the page. These changes yielded significant results.

TARGETING THE HISPANIC MARKET

A news report shows that Hispanic consumers account for 11 percent of all e-shopping in the United States. Given that this is a growing segment for online buying, more and more retailers are designing their Web sites to motivate these consumers to purchase. Most still use only English on their Web sites but feature products that will have greater appeal to Latinos. However, retail giants such as Wal-Mart and JCPenney use some Spanish on their Web sites.

Web Winners

Consumer satisfaction is the driving force behind Web site popularity. Table 3.3 shows satisfaction scores for the highest-rated merchants as reported by the research firm ForeSee Results.

Types of E-tailers

Exploring the many retailer sites on the Web reveals three basic types of companies: organizations that use the Internet exclusively to conduct all of their business, catalogue companies that use the Internet to bring additional sales, and brick-and-mortar operations using a multimedia approach that includes a Web site to augment sales.

TABLE 3.3
WEB WINNERS

Rank	Web Site	Score	Remarks
1	LLBean.com	79	Founded in 1912 by Leon Leonwood Bean, this family-owned company based in Freeport, Maine, now generates sales of $1.5 billion, with an increasing percentage from the Web site. In addition to ordering turtlenecks and tote bags on the site, online customers can find information on state, national and international parks.
2	Zappos.com	79	Online shoe retailer Zappos expects to post sales of $800 million this year, up from just $1.6 million in 2000. The site carries 500 brands and stocks two million pairs of shoes, and the company has become known for fast delivery, free returns and superior customer service.
3	Cabelas.com	78	Cabela's calls itself the "World's Foremost Outfitter" of hunting, fishing and outdoor gear and apparel. Founded in 1961, the publicly traded company posted sales of $2.06 billion in 2006.
4	jcp.com	76	JC Penney is the country's largest online apparel and home retailer, with sales from JCP.com up 24 percent in 2006 to $1.29 billion. The site gets about 520,000 visitors each day, a number that jumps to 920,000 during the holiday shopping period.
5	Target.com	76	Known for its stylish advertising campaign and emphasis on cheap-chic design initiatives, including its ClearRx pharmacy packaging, Michael Graves housewares and Go International partnerships with designers, Target last year posted revenue of $59.49 billion. The company operates 1,500 stores and Target.com.
6	eBags.com	75	Online retailer eBags sells a wide range of backpacks, handbags, luggage, wallets, messenger and duffel bags from more than 200 brands like Samsonite, JanSport, The North Face, Eagle Creek, Victorinox, and Nike.
7	EddieBauer.com	73	Outdoor lifestyle brand Eddie Bauer sells apparel and accessories in approximately 390 stores, as well as online and through catalogues. In February, shareholders nixed a deal to sell the publicly traded company to affiliates of Sun Capital Partners Inc. and Golden Gate Capital.
8	Nike.com	73	Shoppers can custom design their own sneakers and athletic apparel with the NikeiD feature on this elegantly designed Web site. On the new NikePlus.com site, runners can sync their iPod to the site and track the histories of their workouts, including distance run and calories burned.
9	Nordstrom.com	73	Founded in 1901 as a small shoe store in Seattle, there are now 98 full-line Nordstrom stores and 50 Nordstrom Rack off-price outlets, in addition to the company's online and catalogue business. The company is known for its stellar customer service.
10	REI.com	73	REI was founded as consumer cooperative in 1938 by a group of 23 mountaineers, and it now rings up more than $1 billion in sales. Anyone can make purchases on its Web site or in its 80-plus stores, but cooperative members receive a portion of the company's profits based on a percentage of their annual purchases.
11	Talbots.com	73	At the end of fiscal 2006, specialty chain Talbots operated 1,125 retail stores, in addition to its Web site and distributing 48 million catalogues during the year. The company offers updated classics for men, including sportswear, golfwear and suit separates.

Note: Top online retailers of apparel and accessories ranked by satisfaction score (ranging from 0 to 100) as assessed by the research firm ForeSee Results. Sites with identical scores are listed alphabetically.

eBay.com is a global Web site operation where products are bought and sold exclusively through the Internet.

Spiegel offers one of the better-known direct marketing catalogues to consumers.

Web Site–Only Retailers

Many companies began their operations as exclusively e-tailing businesses. These Web site–only retailers, or **e-commerce businesses**, use neither stores nor catalogues for the sale of their merchandise. Some of these businesses feature a wealth of products that surpass those available at the largest department stores, while others restrict their offerings to one or two merchandise classifications.

One of the better known global Web site–only operations is eBay.com. The concept behind eBay is to host electronic auctions in which registered members bid for a vast number of products that are put up for sale by other members. The Web site boasts more than 4 million different items up for sale at any given time. Not only has it become an American institution, it is also achieving international marketing recognition through eBay Australia, eBay Japan, and other divisions. Potential purchasers scan the various offerings within a chosen category, make a bid, and learn whether or not that bid is the winning one. Its attractive format has led to worldwide acceptance by consumers.

Designeroutlet.com was one of the first companies to sell fashion merchandise at deeply discounted prices on the Internet. The site was started by a few fashion executives with more than 50 years of combined experience in the fashion industry. It offers overstocked merchandise from most major designers, including such internationally recognized labels as Ralph Lauren, Prada, Dolce & Gabbana, Fendi, Adolfo, and Nicole Miller at prices far below the original retail prices.

The offerings are updated every two weeks, making it worthwhile for fashion-conscious shoppers to make frequent, repeat visits. Each item is shown in full color so customers feel they know what they're getting. Once customers select an item, it goes into a shopping basket, where it remains until the purchaser is ready to check out. A final look at the selections allows customers to change their orders up to the last minute. The company accepts returned merchandise, making it a safe place to shop.

With fashion enthusiasts often too busy to visit the many off-price fashion retailers in person, the designeroutlet.com Web site fills an important need. It allows the targeted shoppers to buy fashion goods in their limited spare time and in the comfort of their homes.

One of the fastest-growing Web site–only retailers is zappos.com, the subject of our next *Focus*.

Focus on . . . Zappos.com

WHEN COMPANY FOUNDER NICK SWINMURN walked through a San Francisco mall in 1999 looking for a pair of shoes, the concept of Zappos.com was born. Unable to satisfy his needs after visiting many stores, he returned home without a pair of shoes. At home, he looked on the

Internet only to find more disappointment. While there were many "mom and pop" stores selling shoes online, there was no major specialist in this merchandise classification.

With little more than a desire to fulfill an unmet need, Nick quit his job and began what has become an industry leader. Initially offering only shoes, Zappos.com has since spread to offer other fashion merchandise for men, women, and children.

The growth of the company has been phenomenal. In 7 years it went from realizing $1.6 million in sales to about $800 million. The company's enormous success, according to its CEO and founder, was due in part to:

- Concentrating on customer retention with the use of no-cost return shipping
- Keeping accurate inventory records
- Providing service and selection over price
- Maintaining centrally located warehouses to guarantee prompt delivery
- Using in-house staff instead of outside consultants to improve customer service, operations, and advertising
- Relying on word-of-mouth endorsements

By offering a wealth of merchandise that includes more than three million pairs of shoes in addition to handbags, clothing items, and accessories, Zappos.com has been able to satisfy the needs of a growing number of return customers and is attracting new ones every day. Moreover, they are responsive to shoppers, maintaining a call center that carefully handles problems and makes certain that all questions are properly answered.

The company's goal is to one day be the most important online merchant for fashion merchandise.

Cataloguers with E-tailing Operations

As most consumers know, numerous retail operations specialize in direct marketing via catalogues, including such major companies as Spiegel, Fingerhut, and Lands' End. They market to consumers who have limited time for shopping, do not live within easy reach of the major shopping centers, or prefer the convenience of shopping from home. By providing quality merchandise and excellent customer service, many catalogue companies have developed large numbers of loyal clients. Though some of these companies also operate closeout centers, the basis of their business is serving their customers through catalogues, which are updated periodically.

L.L. Bean is a high-profile catalogue company with e-tailing exposure.

In the new era of electronic retailing, the vast majority of these companies have augmented their catalogue sales with Web sites. The online product selection pales in comparison to that of some Web site–only retailers, but the sales results have been promising enough to merit further on-line expansion. Spiegel.com offers items ranging from wearing apparel for the family to electronics, whereas Lands' End has limited its range of offerings to casual clothing. Sears acquired Lands' End in order to expand its own presence in this segment of the apparel market.

Today most retailing professionals agree that having a Web site is necessary to remain competitive. With buying more and more in the hands of young consumers who are comfortable with the Internet, it is essential for cataloguers to embrace this selling venue. Not only that, but other market segments are beginning to feel at home surfing the net. Senior citizens who were not at first receptive to the computer are now beginning to understand its benefits and are turning to the Internet as a means of keeping up with the world. Many of these seniors first went online for the latest news and financial information but are now using the Internet to buy goods. Although many continue to use catalogues for shopping, they are finding that the Web can more quickly satisfy their needs.

Segments of the population other than those mentioned here comprise catalogue shoppers who have now turned to the Internet for many of their purchases.

Bricks and Clicks

A fairly new entry in the changing jargon of the new millennium is **bricks and clicks**. The term is used for brick-and-mortar stores that have developed Web sites as an added means of reaching consumers. *Bricks*, of course, refers to the physical store and *clicks* to the simple task of clicking a mouse to order the desired goods.

In a variation on e-tailing, shoppers at a self-checkout kiosk in a Giant Eagle supermarket buy their purchases online within the brick-and-mortar store.

The roster of retailers that have developed Web sites is staggering. Full-line department stores like Macy's, more specialized department stores like Saks Fifth Avenue, and apparel chains like Gap are just a few of the many that have recognized the need to become e-tailers.

The breadth and depth of the merchandise mix is minuscule in comparison to what is available in the stores. However, the actual sales that result from the Web site are not its only purpose. Most merchants believe that electronic exposure will motivate satisfied shoppers to visit the store to make future purchases. So, in a sense, one of the drawbacks to shopping at brick-and-mortar retailers' Web sites—that they offer only a limited number of products—is a strength for the company. Customers will come to the store to select from the wider assortment of goods.

Another purpose is to extend the company's reach beyond its geographical area. The Internet reaches consumers in areas without physical access to stores. Many retailers are using their Web sites to build a market in areas where they might open brick-and-mortar units in the future—if data from the Web site indicate enough consumer interest. The level of interest is easy to measure by analyzing Internet sales in terms of online purchasers' zip codes.

Focus on...
Sephora

Sephora is a rising star in the bricks-and-clicks arena; customers can shop for its products on the computer or in a store.

IN JUST A FEW SHORT YEARS, Sephora has become a major player in the highly profitable cosmetics industry. Industry professionals and consumers alike are heralding its presence. Rarely has a company made such an immediate impact all over the globe.

Formed in 1993, Sephora was acquired as a division of Moët Hennessey Louis Vuitton (LVMH), the world's leading luxury products group in 1997. With the LVMH empire including such internationally recognized names as Christian Lacroix, Givenchy, Kenzo, Louis Vuitton, and Guerlain, Sephora is a good fit. Sephora benefits not only from its association with such a stellar roster but also from the fact that the parent company is extraordinarily well funded and is ready to make significant investments to assure the division's future success. Sephora is currently the leading chain of perfume and cosmetics stores in France and the second largest in Europe with stores in Luxembourg, Spain, Italy, Poland, Germany, and the United Kingdom. In Asia it is represented with outlets in Japan and is now opening new stores across the Asia–Pacific region. The Sephora retail concept arrived in the United States in 1998 with the opening of its 21,000-square-foot flagship store in New York City and a second store in Miami. The flagship store has caused great concern to its neighbor, Saks Fifth Avenue, which has long been the premiere purveyor of luxury cosmetics in New York.

The Sephora stores are distinctively different from their competitors. They offer a complete line of international fragrances, cosmetics, and "well-being" products, arranged alphabetically to provide the browser with an easy way to discover what is available without having to undertake a time-consuming search for a given brand. Sephora—with such innovations as the Top Ten Fragrance Wall; a Fragrance Organ, where shoppers can test and compare fragrances; the Cultural Gallery, a section that features exhibits related to beauty; a Treatment Library, which showcases a variety of products to meet any special care needs; the Lipstick Rainbow, a display of 365 shades; the Nail & Polish Spectrum, an array of 150 shades packaged in practical miniature bottles—is truly the "temple of beauty."

Launched in October 1999, Sephora.com extends the Sephora retail beauty concept to a wider audience. Through this e-tail venture, the company hopes to create a haven of unique beauty and knowledge for the whole world to share. The company spends many millions in advertising campaigns to ensure that its presence on the Web will gain immediate attention. By using two of fashion's superstars, Kate Moss and Carmen Kass, in its print media campaigns, the company associates recognizable faces with its image.

Since the Web site's launch, it has met with overwhelming success, averaging more than a million "hits" a day. Often the site is so busy that would-be customers find it difficult to access. To make Sephora.com an even bigger player in the crowded Internet beauty arena, the upscale e-tailer has entered into a broad-based alliance with Yahoo!, the medium's most heavily trafficked Web site. With Yahoo! reporting more than 50 million site visits each month, it is a place where Sephora will be able to maximize its exposure.

Multichannel Retailing

In this day of highly competitive retailing, it is essential that merchants expand their operations and take advantage of the different consumer channels available to them. Each channel offers a different opportunity for shopping. Store visits are time consuming, but for most types of merchandise large segments of the population still favor this way of making their purchases. Catalogues provide a leisurely means of shopping without having to travel to stores or be limited by store hours. The Internet can be accessed from the workplace as well as from the home, providing even more convenience to shoppers.

American Girl has made great sales gains as a multichannel retailer, first selling products through a catalogue and later expanding to a flagship store and online shopping.

Thus, the way a company can achieve the greatest retailing exposure is by becoming a **multichannel retailer**. To do so, it must have brick-and-mortar outlets, a catalogue division, and an Internet Web site. Most typically, a brick-and-mortar retailer embraces first catalogue selling and then e-tailing. This is not always the case, however. American Girl, one of America's most visible retailers of specialized dolls and accessories, was first and foremost a catalogue operation. It then spread its wings with a flagship store in Chicago and a Web site.

An analysis of July 2000 data in the *Wall Street Journal* shows that while online sales have escalated in all categories, it is the multichannel retailers that are getting most of these dollars. In fact, the difference in online sales by multichannel retailers and online sales by Internet-only retailers is staggering. In all but three classifications, the multichannel retailers have far outperformed the Web site–only companies. In the product classifications of event tickets, computer hardware/software, apparel/sporting, and flowers/cards/gifts, the multichannel merchants had an edge of at least 80 percent.

Although the Internet will most certainly remain an active channel for selling directly to consumers, by itself it does not yet have enough power to compete with multichannel retailers.

Multichannel Integration Technology

The integration of stores and other sales channels such as Web sites and catalogues is very important in today's retail arena. Multichannel retailing support that fully integrates these outlets is available in RetailStore 3.0 software. The program runs on a variety of point-of-sale hardware platforms and, in addition to other capabilities, helps sales associates locate merchandise, fulfill the customer's order, and make the sale. Often, when products are not available in one store, the system quickly locates them in other units of the company so that the sale will not be lost.

Virtual Catalogues

The next section is about real catalogs that you can hold in your hand. Not surprisingly e-tailers have borrowed the concept to introduce the **virtual catalogue**, which simulates a printed catalogue to show products on the Internet.

America Online is a major player in the virtual catalogue business. Its Shop@AOL Web site is filled with selected items from AOL's merchant partners, including Macy's.com, Gap.com, Bluefly.com, eBags.com, jcp.com, and other high-profile retailers. Shop@AOL brings together a wealth of products and makes purchasing easier for the shopper than if he or she had to examine each and every catalogue or Web site of the individual merchants. An AOL Web site/virtual catalogue simply called *The Basics* offers women guidance in building a wardrobe and features the merchandise needed to carry out this task, including apparel and accessories that can be coordinated to create a complete wardrobe. If shoppers need additional information about the goods shown, they can access the Web sites of the particular stores through a link at the AOL site.

Interactive E-tailing

Although Internet sales continue to spiral upwardly in many classifications, some e-tailers in the fashion arena are experiencing growing pains. Unlike product information available online for books, CDs, and computer software, information for apparel is not sufficient to motivate shoppers to buy; they want to feel the texture of the fabric, try on the item, examine how it is made, and perhaps even consult an expert. Of course, for jeans and other basic apparel products, little selling effort is needed to make the sale. For fashion-forward apparel such as designer clothes, customers seem to feel the lack of real-time communication with a "live" fashion consultant.

Shopping Consultants

Many e-tailers are finding solutions to this problem that involve making their Web sites more interactive. LandsEnd.com, for example, offers two interactive services. One makes it possible to interact online with a company representative. The other allows the customer to speak to a customer service representative through a voice telephone connection. Since the offerings at Lands' End are rather basic, the communication needed to make purchasing decisions is rather straightforward, and both modes of communication appear to address customers' concerns.

More and more dot-coms are adding interactive sections to their Web sites so that shoppers in every merchandise classification will be able to buy with greater ease and have less reason to return the products that they have chosen.

Virtual Try-Ons

When shoppers buy apparel in a store, they have the opportunity to try it on before making a final decision. When they shop for apparel online they do not have that opportunity and must make a buying decision based on an imagined "picture" of how the outfit will fit and how it will flatter the figure.

Or at least that used to be the situation. Now, many e-tailers have solved the problem by adding virtual mannequins that correspond to the shopper's actual figure. The shopper creates his or her likeness by entering the appropriate measurements. The personalized mannequin so created permits the shopper a **virtual try-on** of any item the e-tailer sells.

At Lands' End, "my virtual model" is offered as a 3D rendering of a human figure based on the individual's entered body measurements. The technology is provided by a Montreal-based company, My Virtual Model Inc. In addition to the body measurements, there are options for face shape and complexion.

Productive Web Site Navigation

All too often, potential purchasing on the Internet is frustrated by poor design of the Web site and the difficulty of navigating it. Few shoppers have time to spend figuring out how to make a purchase. If the buying procedure is too difficult or there are too many pages to view, the results are often negative. That is, the shopping spree is abandoned in the middle of an attempted purchase.

It is important to build the Web site so that it is easily navigated. In the *E-Commerce Times* of July 3, 2007, Darrell Long gave the following advice on how to avoid losing the shopper:

- Java script–based navigation should be avoided, since many users have Java script disabled within their Web browsers.
- The desired page should be no more than two clicks away from the home page.
- Using a site map will act as a directory and allow search engines to access any other page.

Internet Fraud

One reason many potential purchasers do not buy online is that they are not certain that the transaction will be secure; that is, they fear that computer hackers will break in, learn credit cards numbers and other personal information required for e-tail transactions, and then use this information to make purchases—or even "steal" their identities. While some say security is not a major problem, estimates indicate that nearly 10 percent of online sales involve the fraudulent use of credit cards or debit cards. At Beyond.com, one of the earliest online sellers of computer software, the matter was significantly worse. Nearly half the retailer's sales were made to people using fake or stolen credit card numbers!

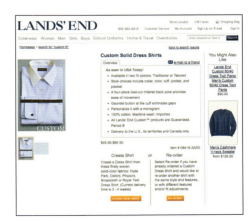

Lands' End was one of the first retailers to offer a virtual try-on service.

Today, new technologies are being introduced to fight fraud and make consumers more comfortable about making Internet purchases. This development is absolutely essential for an industry that is expected to reach more than 40 million households in the United States, to produce $108 billion in revenue, and to account for 6 percent of all consumer spending—according to a study in 2000 by Forrester Research of Cambridge, Massachusetts.

One of the leaders in developing this new technology is CyberSource in San Jose, California. CyberSource systems assist merchants in screening out fraudulent transactions by calculating risk factors. They examine 150 features of a potential sale to determine the relative risk involved. The process takes less than 10 seconds and cuts the losses from fraud to less than 1 percent.

It is virtually impossible to eliminate all online purchasing fraud, just as it is impossible to do so at brick-and-mortar retailers. Yet experts agree that some simple steps can reduce the risk even further. NEWrageous, a marketing service company in Olney, Maryland, has developed a list of tips for e-tailers on how to prevent fraud. These tips include:

- Be wary of orders with different bill-to and ship-to addresses.
- Be cautious about orders that are larger than the typical purchase.
- Be cautious about orders that indicate next-day delivery.
- Be careful about international orders.
- Whenever there is a doubt, telephone the customer for additional information.

One way by which the industry is hoping to reduce credit card fraud is by accepting checks, just as is done at brick-and-mortar stores. By using one of the many check-guarantee companies that are in the business of taking the risk out of accepting checks, retail Web sites can allow customers to pay by check instead of charging their purchases.

Red Envelope is a unique catalogue featuring accessories for the home.

CATALOGUES

When the early catalogue pioneers such as Sears and Montgomery Ward first introduced their big books, it was for the purpose of reaching people who were not in close proximity to stores. Today, Sears is no longer in the direct-mail business and Montgomery Ward is no longer in business at all. This abandonment on the part of the industry's founders has not led other companies to close their direct marketing divisions. The likes of Spiegel and Fingerhut are reaching households in record numbers with big books and a wealth of smaller and more specialized catalogues, proving that catalogue retailing is alive and well and here to stay.

In terms of specialization, more and more catalogues are joining the fray with a host of unique offerings. Although some of these merchants have other outlets, by and large it is their catalogue operations that bring the most sales to their companies. See Table 3.4 for a listing of some of these catalogues.

There are many reasons for the popularity of catalogue buying:

- First and foremost, catalogue shopping is easy, while in-store shopping has become more time consuming than ever before. Department stores, for example, continue to increase their merchandise inventories even as they reduce the number of sales associates. With so

TABLE 3.4 CATALOGUES WITH UNIQUE OFFERINGS	
Company	**Selected Product Offerings**
Sundance	"Outdoorsy" apparel, home furnishings
Journey's	"Folksy" apparel and shoes
Harry & David	Food gift baskets
Company Kids	Apparel and home furnishings for children
Frontgate	Unique home products
Pendleton	Quality classic apparel
Wine Country Gift Baskets	Food and wine baskets
Discovery Channel	Unique creative gifts
PBteen	Home products for teenagers
Red Envelope	Accessories for the home

much to see and so little personal attention available, the once pleasurable event of a shopping expedition has become a time-consuming chore.

- The difficulty of shopping at brick-and-mortar retailers is more of a problem because women are working outside the home. In record numbers they are actually performing two jobs, one in their place of business and the other at home tending to their family's needs. This situation gives them less time to visit the stores, requiring that they find alternative ways to make purchases.
- Catalogues' visual presentations have become increasingly sophisticated, and the quality of the merchandise offered is getting better and better. Shoppers are now able to evaluate each offering easily and to shop with confidence.
- Catalogue shopping is not limited by store hours. It may be done at any time—at home at the end of the day, for example, or during the lunch break at work.
- Ordering is simple. With most ordering possible 24 hours a day and given the availability of knowledgeable company representatives ready to answer questions, purchases are easily made.
- Specialized catalogues are available to meet individual shoppers' particular needs. Literally hundreds of catalogues routinely bring consumers offerings that are difficult to find at the brick-and-mortar stores. One catalogue might feature only natural fibers, another may offer a vast assortment of writing implements, and so on for virtually any product classification.
- Catalogue sellers have generous return policies, so buyers can feel safe that they will not be "stuck" with merchandise that does not live up to their expectations.

Lillian Vernon is still considered by many to be a catalogue-only retailer despite having launched a Web site.

The catalogue industry is divided into three categories: catalogue operations with little or no other outlets, catalogue companies that also sell through brick-and-mortar stores and/or online, and brick-and-mortar organizations with catalogue divisions.

As discussed earlier in the chapter, most retailers today use a multichannel approach that combines brick-and-mortar outlets, Web sites, and catalogue selling. The following discussion divides catalogue companies according to their primary means of doing business.

Catalogue-Only Retailers

With the Internet such an integral part of retailing, it is unlikely that any business that relies exclusively on direct marketing will be able to compete. Spiegel, Lillian Vernon, and Fingerhut—all of which used to be strictly catalogue companies—are operating Web sites. While their Web sites do bring sales, the companies are still classified as catalogue companies.

Nonprofessionals have come to believe that, with online purchasing becoming more and more popular, the catalogue company is heading for extinction. However, Internet sales currently account for less than 1 percent of all retail sales, and those businesses that are exclusively online operations are less likely to compete in today's retailing arena than those that have other outlets as well.

Cataloguers with Brick-and-Mortar Outlets

Many companies began as catalogue operations, fully intending to remain exclusively in that retailing segment. They believed they could achieve their goal of reaching a certain segment of the population in just about any trading area without opening stores.

Now, however, several of these catalogue companies are also increasingly opening up stores to sell their goods. One such venture is The American Girl, a division of Pleasant Company.

Focus on . . .
The American Girl

IN 1986, PLEASANT COMPANY INTRODUCED THE WORLD TO ITS EXCITING new concept of dolls by mailing its first consumer catalogue to a selected market. Joining the dolls in the catalogue a year later were historical fashions for the dolls to wear. With the wide acceptance of the catalogue, the company introduced a magazine that was filled with stories about their collections. Year after year, new additions were made to the line, and business continued to boom. The catalogue was its only means of transacting business until 1998, when American Girl Place, a store that featured the entire collection of dolls and accessories, opened in Chicago and later in New York City.

This new brick-and-mortar retail division was an immediate success. The multistory brick-and-mortar outlets are actually a combination sales arena and entertainment center. They are places where little girls could come not only to make purchases but also to spend a few hours being entertained. The stores have tearooms with "high chairs" for the dolls, so they can share the refreshments with the girls, as well as theaters with live productions.

Crowds are so large that customers must wait in lines that snake around the buildings to gain entrance to the store. Little girls, with their dolls and parents in tow, wait patiently for a chance to visit the store. At peak periods, such as Saturdays and holidays, the sight of several hundred people in line is commonplace.

In addition to the catalogue, magazine, and American Girl Place stores, the company also publishes and markets American Girl books, promotes special charity events, and features a Web site for access by those wanting to purchase online.

It is the stores, however, that have become the centerpiece of this retailing empire. They enable new customers to learn the American Girl concept firsthand and old customers to play out their fantasies through their on-site adventures with their dolls.

Recognizing that their loyal clientele is constantly aging, with many early devotees now in their adolescent years, a "Daughters" newsletter was introduced in 1999 for parents of this age group. It aims to help parents understand the growing pains of their adolescent children and make meaningful decisions concerning their upbringing.

Now a subsidiary of Mattel, Inc., Pleasant Company continues to operate all its divisions, including the American Girl, independently.

Other companies that started as catalogue operations are also expanding their operations with brick-and-mortar stores. Patagonia, a company that specializes in ski apparel and accessories, has opened full-price and outlet stores in many parts of the country; J. Jill, a women's apparel specialty catalogue, has a growing number of mall stores; and J.Crew now has a wealth of stores across the United States in addition to its catalogues.

One reason these direct-mail companies are opening stores is that retail stores can show an even greater selection of the goods than catalogues can. By exposing shoppers to a wider selection, they hope to increase the average number of sales per customer.

Brick-and-Mortar Catalogue Divisions

Victoria's Secret Holiday catalogue.

It is hard to find a store anywhere in the United States that doesn't send out a catalogue. Perhaps the only remaining members of the store-only category are small, independent merchants that feature limited assortments and appeal to small market segments in limited trading areas. Most other retail institutions have embraced catalogue merchandising, with department stores and specialty chains leading the way. Early on, the direct-mail retailers sent out catalogues only during a few peak selling periods such as Christmas, Easter, late summer (back-to-school), and so forth. Today, department stores such as Macy's, Lord & Taylor, Belk, and Dillard's each send more than 30 catalogues through the year. Chain stores also use direct mail extensively, and their numerous catalogues reach consumer households in record numbers. Some even issue catalogues that offer totally different merchandise from the store. Victoria's Secret stores, for example, specialize in *innerwear*. In contrast, its catalogues feature a more diverse product line.

Although most brick-and-mortar operations would prefer in-store visits, they have come to recognize that catalogue selling not only brings sales to the company but can also motivate off-site shoppers to make a trip to the store where more merchandise is available. The larger selection can in turn lead to larger purchases.

Retailers often find that a catalogue that replicates the merchandising concept of the store may not be on target for the direct-mail customer. As a result, more and more of them are creating independent divisions to address the special needs of their direct-mail clientele.

HOME-SHOPPING CHANNELS

At any hour of the day or night, shoppers can tune into a variety of television "programs" through which they can buy merchandise comfortably and conveniently. **Home-shopping channels**—such as HSN, the television shopping network; QVC; and Shop at Home—fill TV screens with a wealth of merchandise ranging from jewelry and apparel to sporting goods and products for the home. It is an industry that continues to achieve record sales by catering to a segment of the population that responds quickly to "bargain" prices.

HSN, the television shopping network, allows people to shop without leaving their homes for products they see on television.

Today, home-shopping channels are more sophisticated than they once were. By and large, the items are developed primarily for the programs. They are produced with the audience in mind and marketed in a way that motivates quick purchases. One of the on-screen devices shopping channels use is an inset that changes rapidly to show the available quantity of an item, how many remain unsold, and how quickly they are selling. Shoppers wishing to avoid being closed out respond to this "selling" message.

Of significant importance to these shopping arenas are the celebrities who appear to sell their own products or those of other producers. With our society smitten by celebrities and "sold" by their endorsements, this marketing approach works. Whenever a well-known individual makes an appearance, sales grow.

Another reason for this medium's success is its interactive format. Callers may speak directly to anyone making the sales pitch—including a celebrity. Other shoppers listen in on the conversations and are often motivated to buy the items being discussed.

The home-shopping-channel format had already reached unprecedented heights when these organizations began their own Web sites featuring the same products. With this innovation, the medium has become even more important. Many shoppers feel more comfortable making Internet purchases, and regular viewers can avail themselves of the merchandise when they are away from the home because a TV is not necessary. Users may quickly log on to their favorite home-shopping Web site from work during lunch break, for example.

Focus on . . .
HSN, the Television Shopping Network

SINCE ITS INCEPTION AS THE PIONEER OF HOME-SHOPPING PROGRAMMING IN 1977, HSN has maintained a leadership position in the industry. First introduced to a small audience in 1977, the company's programming has achieved enormous success in the market it serves. Today, HSN is on 24 hours a day. It reaches 90 million households in the United States, accounting for $3.29 billion in sales, and countless others through affiliation with countries across the globe such as SHOP Channel Japan and TVSN Ltd. China.

Headquartered in St. Petersburg, Florida, in a 500,000-square-foot facility and with fulfillment centers strategically located throughout the world to ensure accurate, on-time delivery, the company continues to realize significant success. It employs more than 2,000 customer care experts and more than 1,700 fulfillment personnel.

In an effort to direct its viewers to specific merchandise, the cable channel features a schedule of times when each product classification will appear. In this way, potential customers may plan to watch during the period when the described products are sold. With the signing of major personalities from different areas such as cooking, performing, modeling, designing, and hair styling to market their products, HSN has broadened its audience.

Once known for its attention to "cubic zirconium," a somewhat demeaning term used to describe low-end, "chintzy" merchandise, the company has started to reposition itself by adding more marquee name designers and cooking notables to its roster. Celebrity chefs such as Todd English, Emeril Lagasse, and Wolfgang Puck, hair stylist Ken Paves, actors Suzanne Somers and Susan Lucci, fashion designers Randolph Duke, Wayne Scott Lucas, and Carlos Falchi, and supermodel Lauren Hutton each appear selling their own products. Because so many Americans are influenced by personality endorsements, such appearances often motivate them to buy.

Exclusive branding is also key to the company's success. Products available only to HSN watchers come from Sephora, Scoop, Kodak, Samsung, JVC, Epson, Fugi, Cuisinart, Reebok, Samsonite, and Perlier. Partnering with fashion leaders such as Michael Kors, Seven for All Mankind, Tina Knowles, and David Rodriguez have also increased the popularity of HSN. Their next targets are the likes of Donna Karan, Calvin Klein, and Ralph Lauren, which have stayed away from the shopping networks so far.

The company's present strategy is to become even more fashion savvy. In addition to runway presentations, all fashions are now photographed on models. Since these new shows began airing, the number of new customers has increased significantly. In fact, after the Scoop Style show there was a 25 percent increase in new purchasers, with sales amounting to an increase of 12 percent.

Recognizing the value of the Internet, the company also markets its offerings via hsn.com. This is an interactive site that provides shoppers with the same 25,000 products featured on the cable program.

CHAPTER HIGHLIGHTS

- Before launching a new e-tail business, the e-tailer must determine the merchandise assortment to be offered for sale and design a Web site of the size and scope to fit its needs.
- The three categories of e-tailing ventures are Web site–only e-tailers, brick-and-click companies that have both stores and Web sites, and catalogue companies that augment their sales with Web sites.
- In order to remain competitive, more and more retailers are using a multichannel approach.
- Many brick-and-mortar merchants expect their off-site operations to result in more customers' shopping at their stores.
- The present overabundance of retailers on the Internet will probably be reversed as many Web site operators are forced to abandon their businesses.
- Interactive e-tailing, which enables the customer to have questions directly answered, is becoming more and more popular.
- Internet fraud remains a problem in the industry and accounts for significant losses.
- Some early cataloguers such as Sears have ceased to publish their big books.
- Home-shopping channels, many of which have added Web sites, continue to increase their sales volumes.

IMPORTANT RETAILING TERMS

bricks and clicks (64)
e-commerce business (62)
electronic retailing (55)
home-shopping channel (71)
infomercial (56)
multichannel retailer (65)
off-site purchasing (55)
virtual catalogue (66)
virtual try-on (67)
Web site–only retailer (56)

FOR REVIEW

1. Why have many e-tailers added interactive features to their Web sites?
2. With their catalogue operations so successful, why have retail giants added Web sites to their businesses?
3. Define the term *brick-and-click*.
4. Explain how multichannel retailing has helped merchants expand their sales volumes.
5. What is a virtual catalogue?
6. What are virtual try-ons? How do they benefit consumers?
7. What can e-tailers do to reduce fraud on their Web sites?
8. Describe the difference between big books and the catalogues most retailers now use to reach their clienteles.
9. How extensive are the catalogue divisions of most major department store organizations?
10. Describe how the Home Shopping Network has expanded its Internet operation.

AN INTERNET ACTIVITY

Explore three Web sites that are divisions of major retailers such as department store chains or organizations. Determine the following for each site:

- The depth and breadth of its offerings
- The types of visuals used
- What, if any, interactive devices are used
- Whether it is possible to create a virtual mannequin
- If the Web site is affiliated with any other Web site

Arrange the information in a three-column table as follows.

	Store A[1]	Store B[1]	Store C[1]
Merchandise			
Visuals			
Interaction			
Virtual Mannequins			
Web site Affiliation			

[1]Insert name of store.

EXERCISES AND PROJECTS

1. Compare the merchandise assortments and formats of five catalogues mailed to your home. Focus on the following:
   - The breadth and depth of the offerings
   - The quality of the illustrations
   - The clarity of the order form
   - Any tie-ins with other retailing channels such as Web sites
   - Any warranties

   Write summaries of your findings. Each summary should be typed, double-spaced, on a separate sheet of paper.

2. Compare the operations of two home-shopping channels. Show your findings on a table as follows:

	Channel A[1]	Channel B[1]
Product Mix		
Shopper Interaction		
Celebrity Presence		

[1]Insert name of home-shopping channel.

THE CASE OF A CATALOGUER'S POTENTIAL FOR EXPANSION

The last 50 years have seen significant growth in the catalogue operation of Dreams for the Home, Inc. When it first began operation, the merchandise mix was a simple assortment of such home accessories as lamps, mirrors, framed prints, and throw pillows. As its years in business brought a continuous increase in business and customer requests for new items, the company's product assortment increased. New merchandise classifications, such as table linens and bedding, were added, bringing even greater sales to Dreams for the Home. Today, some decorator furnishings—such as wine racks, accent tables, ready-made draperies, statuary, and other items—have been added to the collection.

Last year the company was less successful than in the past. For the first time, sales leveled off. While this might be a fluke, management believes it might be time to consider multichannel retailing. Thoughts have centered on entering the Internet with a Web site devoted to all of the company's catalogue offerings, starting a brick-and-mortar operation, or using a combination of all three channels to reach its market. Session after session has been concluded without any definitive decision about the future direction for Dreams for the Home.

Questions

1. Should the company rest on its laurels and continue to sell exclusively by catalogue?
2. What are pros and cons of opening brick-and-mortar stores?
3. Is the Internet a viable option for this company?

Pick It and Click It
Cate T. Corcoran

JUNE 28, 2007

Shopping online saves time and, although many women like to try on clothes in stores before they buy, they are increasingly flocking to the Internet to purchase apparel, shoes and accessories.

"The Internet is the megadepartment store, super-Wal-Mart open 24/7," said Marilyn Machlowitz, a New York-based executive search consultant who dreamed of living near Manhattan stores as a child but now buys 75 percent of her wardrobe online. "If you're a working parent, there just aren't enough hours" to shop in stores, she said.

Faster connections, better imaging and a wider variety of merchandise available online helped push apparel into the number-one spot online last year, edging out computers, books and music (but excluding travel) for the first time, according to a report last month from retail analyst Sucharita Mulpuru of Forrester Research Inc.

Last year, 8 percent of all apparel was sold online, up from 5 percent the year before. This year, 10 percent of apparel sales will take place online, Forrester predicts.

Ruth Sinanian, an assistant at NBC, works long hours and concurs she doesn't have time to shop in stores. In the last year, the lure of free shipping and no tax, plus unique, smaller labels, prompted her to do most of her shopping online at such sites as Shopbop, Zappos and beauty retailer Skinstore.

"I'm busy at work, and on the weekends there's so much stuff to do," she said. "There are a lot of interesting smaller labels I don't see everywhere else. I like getting something nobody else is going to have, even Barneys," she said, referring to Shopbop exclusives like the Dahl line by Alison Kelly of "Project Runway."

In this year's WWD survey, 38 percent of women said their chief reason for shopping online is that it saves time. At the same time, 67 percent of women said that when they don't shop online, it's because they prefer to try things on and feel the fabric and see the workmanship up close. But 62 percent of women said they do buy clothes and accessories for themselves online.

Satisfaction with 'Net shopping is increasing, which could reflect the recent improvement in imaging—a key to selling visual products such as fashion.

Over the past year, many major retailers have added zoom, multiple views and detailed product descriptions. They are able to support better imaging because high-speed Internet connections are becoming common at home. In this year's survey, 25 percent of women said they rate their Internet shopping experience as excellent, up from 22 percent the year before.

If she can find it online, Machlowitz buys multiples of a product she likes or replenishes items that have worn out, such as shoes, lipsticks and pants. Her personal shopper, Kathryn Finney of "The Budget Fashionista" blog and book, found her the perfect pair of black wool Jones New York pants on sale at Bloomingdale's for $99, and she then bought eight pairs at Overstock for $44 each.

If more merchandise were available online, such as the Bitten by Sarah Jessica Parker line or a certain exercise top she found at Wal-Mart, Machlowitz would buy more after trying it at home, she said. "I do think there is an interplay between online and offline. Once you have seen the stuff [in person], you feel braver about it."

In the last year, Machlowitz has bought more online because she has been busier and her trust of online shopping has increased, she said.

Blue Nile, Overstock and Piperlime are among her favorite Web stores. "They send it so quickly and they wrap it so exquisitely. It's an extremely pleasant experience to open the container. It feels like a present," she said. "That's part of the secret of online."

• •

Apparel Now No. 1 Online
Cate T. Corcoran

MAY 14, 2007

Last year was a watershed moment for apparel online.

Apparel sales moved into the top spot online for the first time in 2006, overtaking computers but excluding travel, according to a report due to be released today from the National Retail Federation.

Last year, online sales of apparel, accessories and footwear grew 61 percent compared with the year before, according to the report. Forrester Research Inc., which conducted the study, projects growth will slow down this year to 21 percent. In 2006, Web sales of apparel, accessories and footwear reached $18.3 billion, and are expected to grow to $22.1 billion this year.

Retailers and analysts predict massive growth in online revenues in the category in the next five years. At the same time, competition is increasing and requirements to succeed are changing rapidly.

If the first decade of e-commerce belonged to the pure plays and the innovators, the second decade may well turn out to be the era of the established brands — particularly those with brick-and-mortar stores and deep pockets to keep up with the latest technologies to enhance the customer experience.

It's not enough to throw up a pretty Web site anymore, said Brendan Hoffman, president and chief executive officer of Neiman Marcus Direct. "You need proper customer care 24/7, phone calls, live chat."

Even though the pie is getting bigger, "there could be a shakeout for other reasons," said Rich Last, director of new business development for jcp.com at J.C. Penney and a member of the NRF's Shop.org board, which commissioned the study from Forrester. "This is such a quickly evolving business, you really have to stay ahead of it and on top of it — not just putting up a Web site, but continually improving and investing in it. Some will be better than others at it."

Established online players — including specialty sites such as Neiman Marcus and Net-a-porter, and department stores such as J.C. Penney and Macy's — report robust profits and growth rates of 20 to 70 percent in their online businesses.

Key reasons for the growth of apparel, accessories and footwear online are new sites, liberal shipping policies and rich imaging, according to Forrester.

High-speed broadband access at home is now common. At the same time, the ability to offer zoom and multiple views became de rigueur last year, with many luxury and department store retailers adding them to their sites for the first time.

"Customers have better monitors and views of the product," said Last. "That may not make a big difference in the selling of books, computers and travel reservations online, but for selling apparel and home products, they are significant factors, so I think we're about to see a whole other wave occur."

The overtaking of computers and software represents a significant shift.

"If you were looking for a sign [shopping for apparel online] has become mainstream, this is the sign," said Scott Silverman, executive director of Shop.org. "It's not a technology thing anymore. It's really something the general population is taking part in."

"It's a huge market," said Shopbop CEO Bob Lamey, whose online-only contemporary shop flew under the radar until its sale last year to Amazon.com. "I think for all online retailers, there is still a tremendous amount of tailwind behind the business."

Although Madison, Wis.-based Shopbop does not break out financials, Lamey said the business is "very profitable" and its growth rate is in the high double digits. A former options trader who briefly owned an outdoor store, Lamey opened Shopbop in 1999 and the business became profitable in 2002.

Another established online pure play that's doing well is Net-a-porter. The company has not released earnings for 2006, but founder Natalie Massenet said sales were up more than 70 percent last year. Profits before taxes also grew, despite the cost of expanding its U.S. operations with a distribution center here, she added. In 2005, the company's revenues reached 21.3 million pounds, or $40.5 million.

Federated Department Stores also experienced impressive growth in its online business, which was up 38 percent to $620 million in 2006 from $450 million the year before. A major factor in its growth was the acquisition of May Department Stores, which took Federated and its Macy's nameplate into new geographical markets and propelled new customers to the Web site, said a Federated spokesman.

Saks Fifth Avenue also did well, with a growth rate of about 35 percent, said Denise Incandela, senior vice president of Saks Direct. Last year, the company changed its online assortment and bought broad and deep in designer ready-to-wear, handbags, shoes and contemporary. The last three are "our biggest groups and the drivers of the business," said Incandela. The company also added product detail pages with richer imaging and keeps working to improve customer service and editorial.

"The pie is continuing to grow," said Incandela. "Retailers are investing in the business in a big way because the opportunity is significant. That's good for all of us, because as more customers are shopping online, the pie is getting bigger. We are attracting new customers, and repeat customers are spending more."

The strong numbers turned in by these retailers are not surprising, given the overall growth rate for apparel online. Nonetheless, there remains plenty of room for more apparel sales to shift online. For instance, 41 percent of all computers and software sales take place online, whereas only 8 percent of apparel, accessories and footwear do, said Forrester. Online sales of apparel are projected to reach 10 percent of all apparel sales this year, according to the firm.

Footwear and contemporary are two key categories that have experienced major growth and increased competition last year. Industry pioneer Girlshop closed its doors, while dozens of small brick-and-mortar boutiques offering little-known designers went online and Shopbop offered everyday free shipping after Amazon acquired it. Free shipping is now standard in footwear, noted the NRF report, and shoe stores that opened online in 2006 include Amazon's Endless, Gap's PiperLime and eBags' 6pm.com.

Retailers are always looking for ways to make the shopping experience more interactive. A surprising number of them are already adding next-generation technologies (loosely known as Web 2.0), which include video and user-generated content such as customer-written product reviews, blogs and profiles and social networking. Amazon has been the undisputed leader in this area in its book business, but apparel retailers are not far behind. For instance, Macys.com added user reviews in September, and since then more than 50,000 reviews have been posted, with an average of 225 going up a day. They add a lot of value and credibility to the site, and let customers know if something runs big or small and inform merchants if there is a problem, said the Federated spokesman.

J.C. Penney has been online since 1990, and is moving forward with new technologies to enhance the customer experience at its $1.3 billion site. The retailer plans to add social networking, user reviews, and video this year, said Last. The department store last year added the ability to look up merchandise at local stores online, an achievement for a department store, whose many legacy systems and departments are usually too sprawling to integrate. The company also completed its rollout of Internet-enabled point-of-sale systems last year, to assist sales of bras and locate products.

Neiman Marcus has also been considering how to add interactivity to its site, and plans to add video to its virtual trunk shows this season and is mulling live chat with designers and store executives.

"Potentially, there's a lot of value with that," said Hoffman. "It just has to be done within the Neiman Marcus experience."

The retailer rang up online sales of $400 million in fiscal 2006, ended in July. A big reason for its booming business is being able to extend its brand to customers who live outside its store areas, said Hoffman.

Online stores are driving a huge amount of business to brick-and-mortar stores, said Patti Freeman Evans, retail analyst with Jupiter Research. "The retailers who can capture that customer have an opportunity to grow their business."

Having brick-and-mortar stores gives customers the ability to return items that don't fit, and reduces marketing costs.

Web purveyor Bluefly cited marketing costs as a factor in its continued losses, reported this week. Its revenues grew 31 percent to $77.1 million in 2006, but the cost of marketing and executive bonuses resulted in a loss of $12.1 million for the year.

"If we were a store, we could count on people walking by, but it's a pull site, so you have to continue to invest in a marketing campaign to let [people] know you're there," said Melissa Payner, president and CEO of Bluefly.

Nonetheless, having brick-and-mortar stores is no guarantee of success, said Lauren Freedman, president of consulting company the e-tailing group. "In a year's time, the merchandising requirements for any one category can change. Also, there's a cost associated with that." The bar moves very quickly, she said, adding, "But at the end of the day, fashion is a large category and the only way is up."

CHAPTER 4
The Globalization of Retailing

After you have completed this chapter, you should be able to discuss:
- The major global retail centers
- Emerging countries for international retail expansion
- The difference between Russia today as a retail destination and what the country once was in terms of retailing
- Factors such as the percentage of sales by retailers in foreign operations
- Reasons for global expansion by retail operations
- Conditions that affect the profitability of globalization
- Foreign expansion arrangements that retailers use to enter overseas venues
- The leading global retailers and the countries they have entered

The retail playing field is broader than ever before in most parts of the world. Globally, it reaches nearly every part of the population through brick-and-mortar operations, catalogues, cable television, and the Internet. Companies expand not only within their countries of origin but also (and increasingly) to foreign shores. Rarely does a day go by without the announcement of a retail operation expanding outside its domestic trading area. Except for smaller businesses, the trend is for globalization. Merchants in just about every product classification are either jumping on the overseas expansion bandwagon or planning to do so within the next few years.

Department store branches, specialty clothing chains, couture emporiums, boutiques, discount operations, off-price outlets, supermarkets, specialized food stores, catalogue companies, and warehouse clubs are spreading their wings with more and more **retailing "doors."** Just about every form of retailing has undergone significant expansion at home and abroad and so, indeed, the global retailing landscape is without boundary.

MAJOR GLOBAL RETAILING CENTERS

Marquee retail names dot the globe in many parts of the world and are frequented by residents as well as visitors. Harrods in London, Macy's in New York, and Galeries Lafayette in Paris are just a few that enjoy international reputations. They and scores of others populate the retail landscapes of their countries. The major players maintain a dominant presence on their domestic shores, but they are not the only **global retailers** who are enjoying success. The following sections provide an overview of the countries that are prominent in today's global retail environment.

> **In the News . . .**
>
> Read the article, "Global Markets Key to Retailing Future" (on page 101 at the end of this chapter) to learn about the strategies of the retail industry's principal firms.

Harrods, in London, is a world-renowned retailer.

The United States

In terms of major retail operations, the United States is unparalleled. Throughout the country, just about every large city either is home to a retail giant or is represented by branches of renowned retailers. Most important in terms of dollars earned and populations served are New York City, Chicago, San Francisco, Atlanta, Los Angeles, Miami, Dallas, Houston, and Boston. These cities encompass a vast number of department stores, specialty organizations, big box merchants, and supermarkets as well as a host of independent boutiques. They run the gamut from the industrial giants such as Wal-Mart (the world's largest retailer) and marquee department stores such as Macy's and Bloomingdale's to companies that serve smaller, specialized clienteles.

The shops are located in a multitude of environments and locations ranging from downtown central shopping districts to regional malls. They cater not only to the region's permanent residents but also to the multitude of visitors who flock there for business purposes or merely to experience its wealth of museums, theaters, and points of interest.

H&M, a European retailer, has opened many stores in the United States.

In addition to its home-grown retail companies, the United States is also host to merchants from all over the world. Companies like H&M, a European retailer of modestly priced clothing, have opened units throughout the United States and have attracted huge audiences for their products. At the other end of the spectrum are such couture ventures as Chanel, Fendi, Hermès, Gucci, and Burberry, whose presence on America's major fashion streets—New York City's Fifth and Madison Avenues, Palm Beach's Worth Avenue, Chicago's North Michigan Avenue and Oak Street, and Beverly Hills' Rodeo Drive—are generating record sales.

Of course, retailing in the United States is not exclusively in brick-and-mortar stores but also in catalogue operations and e-tailing ventures. The former is either a division of a major department store or chain organization or a "catalogue only" venture. The merchandise assortments offered by these two retailing formats include the same product classifications as stores at every conceivable price point (recall the discussion in Chapters 2 and 3).

The United Kingdom

The United Kingdom includes England, Scotland, Wales, and Northern Ireland. Although England is the dominant retailing location with London its major venue, the other U.K. countries are also home to many retail operations. Unlike the United States, where value shopping is plentiful via off-price and discounting formats, shopping fare in the United Kingdom is primarily traditional in nature. That is, prices reflect the standard markups that retailers need to turn a profit. In addition to department stores, chain operations, and sole proprietorships, the United Kingdom is home to many mixed-merchandise stores that sell a combination of products such as foods, soft goods, and books.

Department stores range from Harrods, perhaps the best-known store in the world with its wide assortment of upscale, unusual offerings that include antiquities and gourmet foods, to the House of Frasier, a company that operates stores selling mainstream goods under several different names in the same way that Target does. Many of the country's department stores contain leased departments, which are spaces rented out to merchants who determine their own merchandise mixes.

Also at the upscale level is Selfridges, a London landmark. In order to recapture some of the clout it enjoyed in the past, the company has recently re-invented itself. After a $20 million investment, it has once again become a fashion favorite for men and women. At the center of its new format is the Wonder Room, a 20,000-square-foot showcase with everything from diamond necklaces and wines to artifacts and art. For the upscale shopper there is a wealth of shops-within-a-shop that house such couture collections as Vuitton, Gucci, Prada, and Dior. In-store themed events give it a unique ambience. Rounding out the new format is the men's shop, which Selfridges touts as the biggest men's store in the world.

Specialty chains flourish in the United Kingdom. For example, Body Shop, an important retailer in the United States, is actually a British company and is one of the nation's most successful nonfood chains. Fortnum and Mason is another favorite. Its products include apparel and fashion accessories, but it is perhaps best known for its food delicacies. High tea at Fortnum and Mason is a highlight, with residents and tourists from all over the world stopping their routines to partake of the company's elegant tea service.

A $20 million investment returned Selfridges to its days of glory.

In addition to the brick-and-mortar operations that abound in the United Kingdom, the mail-order business continues to flourish. The emphasis is on *big books*, much like those popularized in the early twentieth century by Sears and Montgomery Ward in the United States. However, the method of purchase from these catalogues differs from how it is practiced in the United States. The vast majority of the merchandise is not sold directly to the consumer but through **agent order takers**. These agents show the catalogues to prospective customers, many of whom are members of their own families, and place orders for them. In return for the services they provide, the agents are paid a small commission. The largest of these companies is Great University Stores, which sells mostly apparel.

Smaller catalogues are now becoming more common in the United Kingdom. They are similar to the catalogues that are popular in the United States and generally number less than 100 pages. They feature specialized, branded merchandise assortments. Unlike the big books, these catalogues employ the direct channel of distribution in which potential customers receive them directly and order without the aid of a middleman.

Marks & Spencer is a famous U.K. mixed-merchandise store.

In addition to the independent mail-order catalogues, traditional brick-and-mortar merchants are also entering the fray. Marks & Spencer, a household name in the United Kingdom, entered this market in 1996 with a large variety of housewares and clothing and continues to benefit from this expansion.

Food retailing is big business in the United Kingdom. Led by Tesco and J. Sainsbury, the focus is on service and innovation rather than price competition as in the United States. These two giants, as well as other companies, offer their customers "loyalty cards" that give them small discounts for their patronage. Other typical programs include community outreach in the form of donating computers to schools. Not only have Tesco and Sainsbury remained giants in their native country, but they have also expanded to other countries. The former has entered many European countries while the latter has entered the United States with its acquisition of Shaw's, a supermarket chain.

The aforementioned mixed-merchandise stores round out the major retail classifications. The most famous is Marks & Spencer, whose large inventory includes food, soft goods, housewares, and cosmetics.

The United Kingdom's powerful retailing presence has attracted many branches from around the world. In addition to IKEA from Sweden and Benetton from Italy, scores of others are heading to U.K. shores. The U.S. presence in the United Kingdom has been evident with the success of Sears, Blockbuster, and Toys "R" Us, and the invasion of American retail operations continues apace. The first-ever Banana Republic in Europe is set to open in London on fashionable Regent Street, and there are plans to open many more units in the European market. Wrangler recently opened a flagship on Carnaby Street, a template of its planned stores for many parts of Europe. Also making a splash in the United Kingdom is Abercrombie & Fitch, the subject of the next *Focus* feature.

Focus on . . .
Abercrombie & Fitch

WHEN IT FIRST OPENED ITS DOORS IN NEW YORK at the turn of the twentieth century, this company's merchandise mix was targeted toward those involved in elite sporting expeditions. Celebrities such as Clark Gable, Charles Lindbergh, Greta Garbo, John Steinbeck, and Katharine Hepburn were known to be patrons of the store. With an outdoor feeling of nature in the store and similar environments featured in its catalogue, the company sought to appeal to outdoorsmen. Equipment for skiing, archery, scuba diving, badminton, camping, and boating filled its floors and direct-mail pieces. With its success, the retailer opened stores in Chicago, San Francisco, Short Hills, Bal Harbour, Oak Brook, and other venues throughout the United States. Although it achieved early success, the company eventually went bankrupt in 1977 and was purchased by Oshman's, a sporting goods merchant. When Abercrombie & Fitch was still unable to turn a profit, it was acquired by The Limited, which had a successful track record for turning out new companies such as Express and Victoria's Secret.

In the 10 years that followed this 1988 acquisition, The Limited organization refocused the retailer's concept and transformed it into a store that catered to teenagers and college students. In 1999, The Limited took it public and divested itself of the company.

Today, Abercrombie & Fitch enjoys success all across the United States. Not only its stores but also its Web site have captured the hearts and minds of the 18–22 age segment. Given the high sales volume from British shoppers on the Internet and their familiarity with the stores when visiting the United States, the company decided to enter the European market with a store in London.

The shop opened on fashionable Savile Row, the home to traditional tailors of fine clothing. Crowds waited for hours for the store to open, with lines snaking around the corner. It is a 13,000-square-foot selling arena steeped with the merchandise for which the company is famous and manned by shirtless males wearing flip-flops, T-shirts, and jeans. Their female counterparts were dressed in hot pants and tube tops. With blasting music, it was reported that the opening had a fraternity atmosphere. The prices were about twice those in the United States, but the armfuls of clothing carried by many patrons suggested that prices didn't matter.

France

A fashion mecca with Paris at its focal point, France is a haven for native shoppers as well as tourists. One of the major retail classifications is the department store, headed by Galeries Lafayette, Printemps, and Bon Marché. Each is headquartered in Paris and has branches throughout the country. Although they carry a variety of different products, fashion is the leader.

Of course, when fashion enthusiasts think of France, they immediately focus on couture merchandise. Couturier shops line its most fashionable streets, such as Avenue Montaigne, and include Christian Lacroix, Missoni, Claude Montana, Valentino, Yves St. Laurent, and Jean Paul Gaultier. In Paris and in Cannes, St. Tropez, and other French cities, boutiques offering couture collections or **prêt-à-porter** (ready-to-wear) merchandise are alive and well and satisfying the fantasies of natives and visitors from all over the globe.

The **hypermarket** is another type of retailing venture that is popular in France. Selling product lines in addition to food, these giant markets turn a better profit than food stores because nonfood items have higher markups. Carrefour is the leading hypermarket in terms of sales, and it has earned global acclaim by opening units in other parts of Europe and South America.

Printemps is a major French department store.

Japan

Retailers in Japan have a different kind of relationship with their suppliers than do U.S. retailers: it is more of a partnership in which suppliers take responsibility for inventory replenishment. Sales associates, who are employees of the vendors and are paid by them, provide their managers with information about product requests at the retail level and other information that would affect decisions about what inventory the retailer should carry. Often the vendors actually refurbish the stock and share in visual merchandising and other store promotions. In many cases, unsold merchandise can be returned to the supplier.

Takashimaya is one of Japan's oldest department stores.

Japanese department stores are the outgrowth of the **kimono stores**, which sold fabrics to be tailored into garments, and the **terminal stores**, which were located in railroad terminals and sold convenience goods. Little by little, many of these merchants expanded their operations into department stores. One of the oldest, Takashimaya, has expanded into international markets and now has outlets in New York City and elsewhere.

Other major department store retailers are Mitsukoshi and Seibu, based in Tokyo, and Hankyu, based in Osaka. They sell general merchandise to customers from every age group. Unlike in U.S. department stores, here food occupies a large area in every store. The stores are extremely service oriented, providing everything from information about the products they sell to assistance with party planning.

More important than department stores in terms of size are supermarkets and superstores. Although both types carry a wide assortment of products, the former leans more toward food and the latter carries more generalized merchandise. The largest stores in these categories are Daiei, which is the largest retailer in Japan, and Ito-Yokado.

Convenience stores are comparatively new to this country. Their inventories range from prepared foods to books and magazines. The are considerably smaller than the department stores and superstores, operate many hours of the day, and are welcomed by the vast majority of Japanese as places where they can satisfy most of their basic needs. The largest store in this group is the Seven-Eleven Japan Co.

In addition to its home-grown retail operations, Japan features more and more companies from around the world. America's Tiffany & Co. has a significant presence in Japan, with still more units planned over the next few years. Fashion designer Cynthia Rowley, who has a presence in 28 shops-in-shops in Japan, is opening a flagship in Tokyo. The most formidable entry into Japan is a major undertaking by Giorgio Armani. Joining the likes of Gucci, Bulgari, and Dior, Armani has opened a 12-story, 65,000-square-foot tower in the Ginza section of Tokyo. Featured are the Giorgio Armani collection, Emporio Armani, and the Casa line. Surrounded by the Armani/Ristorante and Armani/Prive and the Armani/Spa, it is expected to reach unprecedented levels of sales.

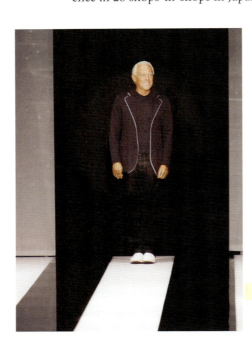

Italian designer Armani is one of the better-known retailers of fashion.

The numbers that attest to Japan's significance in retailing are staggering. According to the Japan Council of Shopping Centers, in 2006 there were 2,759 shopping centers in operation with total sales of $223.58 billion.

Italy

With fashion such an important part of the Italian landscape, a large number of boutiques may be found in most parts of the country. Jewelry and leather shops are among the most popular, especially for tourist consumption. In Florence, for example, the famous Ponte Vecchio—which spans the Arno River and is frequented by visitors from around the world—shop after shop features an enormous variety of 18-carat gold jewelry. Also in that area are leather boutiques and couturier shops that feature the creations of such famous Italian designers as Armani as well as branches of upscale fashion emporiums from France and other countries. Rome is also home to couture emporiums. Clustered in the streets that extend from the famous Spanish steps are shops that offer designer labels from both Italy and Paris. Rounding out the couturier offerings are the boutiques found on Milan's Via Montenapolene.

Other Major Global Retailing Centers

Holt Renfrew is a leading Canadian department store.

Although the countries just discussed are the major entities in the global market, other countries continue as forces in retailing. In a variety of classifications such as department stores, specialty operations, food markets, and so forth, their presence is important in the overall retail environment.

In Canada, the dominance of companies based in other parts of the world is extremely evident. Although Canada is home to such upscale department stores as Holt Renfrew and La Maison Ogily as well as a wealth of specialty stores, more and more of the Canadian market is filled with stores from the United States. Wal-Mart's share of nonfood items is more than 50 percent, and its presence in food retailing is on the rise. Other American companies with a Canadian presence include Sam's Club, Home Depot, Lowe's, Sears, Costco, and Best Buy. The one area in which Canada is weak is Internet sales.

Germany is increasing its retail presence with an emphasis on high-fashion boutiques. The German economy has soared ever since the Berlin Wall fell, helping retailers achieve record sales.

Greece has its share of large and small stores. In Athens and on the numerous Greek islands, shops that deal in precious jewelry, leather goods, and rugs dominate the retail scene. Sales continue to climb for Greek retailers that cater to tourists, many of whom come to shop while on cruises.

EMERGING COUNTRIES FOR RETAIL EXPANSION

Ready to compete against countries with proven retail track records are others that have shown significant growth in retail sales. According to A.T. Kerney's Global Retail Development Index Report, countries that were once not considered viable by foreign retailers are attracting many types of retail operations. The 12 leading countries and the stores that have taken the plunge to open there are discussed next.

India

In the news because of its popularity as an outsourcing capital for American business, India's newfound wealth has given rise to an influx of offshore retailers. And because retailers from other countries are now able to own a 51 percent majority stake in joint ventures with local partners, India has become a place where retail expansion is at an all-time high. Luxury products and fashion goods are dominant in the merchandise assortments of the foreign investors. Hermès, Lacoste, and Tommy Hilfiger from the United States as well as Marks & Spencer from the United Kingdom are examples of retailers that have staked claims in India.

Russia is one of the more recent openings for Ralph Lauren stores.

Russia

A growth in wealth has prompted many upscale retailers from other countries to enter the Russian market. The British department store Debenhams is there along with the fashionable jeweler Kieselstein-Cord, Alberta Ferretti (with two Russian flagship stores), Prada, Armani, and Brioni. The big news is Ralph Lauren's investment in Russia, which is the subject of the next *Focus* segment.

Focus on . . .
Ralph Lauren, Russia

TO FASHION ENTHUSIASTS AROUND THE WORLD, the name Ralph Lauren immediately brings to mind the epitome of style, elegance, and grace. Few designers have gained the reputation that Ralph Lauren has as the master of low-key yet elegant dress. Devotees all over the globe collect his designs as one would collect treasures. With timelessness one of the keys to his creations, Ralph Lauren's popularity continues to soar. Consumers are known to wear his designs for many years as if they were newly purchased. With boutiques in most major fashion capitals and selections in department stores and fashionable specialty chains, the time seemed right for expansion into uncharted waters.

Russia is a location once considered inappropriate for the Ralph Lauren experience. Yet with segments of the Russian population now wealthier than ever and ready to satisfy their fashion appetites, it was a country ready for this American icon. To make an initial impact, Lauren decided to simultaneously open two locations: one in downtown Moscow and the other just outside the city. The flagship at Tretyakovsky Passage, a luxury shopping destination, is housed in a stately building complete with a white façade and blue awnings. Reminiscent of the Madison Avenue flagship in New York City, it features old-world interiors. A grand staircase, vintage oil paintings, wood paneling, and other antique-like features surround the merchandise offerings.

The assortment features all of the Lauren collections with special emphasis given to the Purple and Black labels, the epitome of upscale clothing. Given the wealth of some of today's Russian families, these two collections are expected to entice consumers to the store and help achieve sales goals.

Although the success of this undertaking is still in question, the Lauren touch seems to be just what the Russian elite have been waiting for.

China

With its middle class expected to grow significantly over the next 10 years and given their penchant for fashion, China is ripe for more overseas retailers to set up shop. In addition to the government-owned establishments called **friendship stores**, many new retailers are entering China. American brand names that are famous in other parts of the world—such as Calvin Klein, Stuart Weitzman, and Coach—can now be found in China.

Vietnam

An increase in per capita income has made this country an attractive place for offshore retailers to expand. The emphasis has been on upscale marquee retailers such as Gucci, Louis Vuitton, Burberry, Ermenegildo Zegna, and Lacoste.

Ukraine

Although a majority of the retail operations in the Ukraine consist of family-owned stores in undistinguished shopping venues, this country's residents are now embracing malls as their favored places to shop. Most of the foreign companies that have entered this market are in the midprice range. Such retailers include Swatch, Timberland, Adidas, Esprit, Metro, and Rewe.

Chile

Although the Chilean-based supermarkets and hypermarkets are still the most successful shopping destinations, many international retailers are making their way there. In Santiago, for instance, shops include such couture-level names as Ferragamo, Versace, Polo, and Valentino as well as the world-famous, popular-priced fashion emporium, Zara.

Latvia

With a significant GDP growth of 12 percent in 2006, this country is attracting the attention of many global retailers. Particularly in Riga, cafes, designer hotels, and boutiques are making certain that there are places to open businesses. The uniqueness of the city—with its cobblestoned streets, medieval architecture, and Art Nouveau interiors—makes it a perfect setting to attract tourists. Designer shops include Armani, Gianfranco Ferre, and MaxMara; midlevel fashion retailers include Benetton, Zara, and Mango.

Malaysia

In many of this country's shopping arenas, including one of the world's largest (the Kuala Lumpur City Centre), shoppers are patronizing some of the world's leading fashion retail operations. Already there are branches of Chanel, Gucci, Hermès, and Prada.

Mexico

In addition to Mexican chains such as Sanborns—which features a variety of products along with eateries in each of its units—and American giants like Sears and French companies like Carrefour, a great number of upscale retailers have joined the fray. Luxury foreign shops such as Louis Vuitton, Christian Dior, Chanel, Tiffany & Co., and Cartier are opening in record numbers The shopping malls that house these new entries are extremely successful.

Saudi Arabia

High oil prices have contributed to this country's significant growth. Together with its tax-free status and enormous tourist trade, Saudi Arabia's economy in general has grown a great deal. Leading the way with offshore retail companies is Carrefour, which plans to open more than 20 hypermarkets in the next 10 years. Apparel merchants such as Harvey Nichols, Nike, Zara, Mango, and DKNY are frequented by the Saudi Arabian population.

Tunisia

Although the **souks** (colorful open markets that deal in everything from spices to jewelry) lead the way, the French Carrefour hypermarkets have made an impact on the retail scene. Along with Gap, they are the major foreign retailers.

Bulgaria

As a new member of the European Union, this country has seen vast economic growth. Nike, Puma, Geox, Sephora, and Marks & Spencer all have stores in the bustling capitol of Sofia. Ready to join this market is France's Carrefour.

ANALYSIS OF OFFSHORE RETAIL OPERATIONS

Tables 4.1 and 4.2 make it evident that many countries are expanding past their original borders of operation. In terms of percentage of sales from foreign operations, the current leaders are Germany and France. These two countries also lead all others in terms of the number of different countries harboring overseas operations. Of course, future growth may show different trends.

REASONS BEHIND THE GLOBAL EXPANSION OF RETAILERS

Having made their initial successes in their native countries, many retailers are finding profitable situations offshore and thus are readying themselves for even greater expansion of their empires. The reasons for this global expansion are numerous and include: a significant amount of competition at home; the existence of markets where international travelers are becoming repeat visitors; unique product offerings not found elsewhere; and (of course) the potential for increased profits.

TABLE 4.1
PERCENTAGE OF SALES FROM FOREIGN OPERATIONS

REGION EXTRACTED FROM	PERCENTAGE 2000	PERCENTAGE 2005
Top 250	12.6	14.4
Africa/Middle East	20.2	13.0
Asia/Pacific	4.2	6.0
Japan	0.8	1.2
Europe	26.9	28.1
France	36.8	34.8
Germany	32.4	36.0
United Kingdom	17.1	14.6
Latin America	12.2	7.6
North America	4.2	7.1
United States	3.6	6.2

Data based only on those companies for which data existed for both years.
Sources: published company data and Planet Retail.

TABLE 4.2
AVERAGE NUMBER OF COUNTRIES OF OPERATION

Region Extracted From	2000	2005
Top 250	5.0	5.9
Africa/Middle East	8.0	8.8
Asia/Pacific	2.7	3.4
Japan	2.4	2.6
Europe	8.6	9.9
France	11.8	15.7
Germany	10.3	12.7
United Kingdom	9.0	7.6
Latin America	1.4	1.9
North America	2.9	3.5
United States	3.0	3.7

Figures exclude Dell, Avon, Alticor (Amway) and AAFES, whose global or near-global coverage would skew the averages.
Sources: published company data and Planet Retail.

Competition

When competition in a specific country is particularly stiff, it may inhibit retailers from expanding operations. In the United States, for example, competition is keen in almost every part of the country. While many American companies succeed despite the competition, their profits are lower because of it. By entering less saturated retail venues where competition is minimal, the chances for acceptance and eventual profitability are greater.

Canada is one of many countries that foreign retailers are entering aggressively. According to Richard Talbot of Talbot Thomas Consultants International, Canada is "under retailed compared to the U.S." In light of this analysis and those of other consulting organizations, American retailers including Gap, Banana Republic, Wal-Mart, and many others have opened Canadian branches. These companies are betting that their operations will be profitable because of lower retail saturation in Canada than in the United States.

International Travel

People from virtually every part of the world regularly leave their countries and travel to other regions. Many are business executives whose work takes them to foreign countries; others are tourists who are seeking to experience the excitement afforded by overseas travel.

Some cities such as New York, Paris, Rome, Hong Kong, and London are international destinations for world travelers. Now, many newer venues such as Dubai and Russia have joined them as places for tourists to visit. During these trips, the vast majority of visitors head for the stores to bring back remembrances of their adventures. Each city has its own high-profile retailers—as well as others representing overseas merchants—that travelers seek out during their visits. Bloomingdale's in the United States, Au Printemp in Paris, and Harrods in London are just a few of the retailers that have reputations outside of their countries. Chain stores like Gap, Victoria's Secret, and Banana Republic in the United States, French Connection and Nicole Farhi in France, and Benetton in Italy also attract a great deal of attention from tourists. Knowing that they already have name recognition and a strong image abroad has motivated many companies to open stores around the world. With business travel and tourism at an all-time high, it is a safe bet that such global expansion will continue to escalate.

Unique Products

The fashion industry is one segment of retailing in which products are unique. Designers the world over have captivated international audiences with their imaginative and unique styles. The collections they offer to their clientele are singular combinations of silhouettes, color harmonies, textures, and construction details. Individuality is the key to the success of these designers, leading fashion devotees around the globe to seek out their creations.

Uniqueness of design is a Dolce & Gabbana forte.

In order to capture a share of the international fashion market, designers such as Dolce & Gabbana, Giorgio Armani, Calvin Klein, Ralph Lauren, and Fendi have established networks of boutiques outside their native countries. The trend for this type of retailing venture is definitely upward, as designers open shops in record numbers at fashionable addresses worldwide.

Profitability

The key to success in business is profitability. When domestic markets are significantly saturated, companies in that market segment are less able to increase profits unless they seek out new markets. It is then time to consider overseas expansion. In order to expand their horizons, many businesses, including retailers, look elsewhere to establish new units. Those countries (reviewed previously in this chapter) emerging as major retailing venues are examples of this expansion.

The potential for profit in some regions is greater than in the country of a company's origin. In Germany, for example, the average net profit margin is only 2 percent, which makes offshore expansion all the more inviting. Table 4.3 shows the average net profit margin by region or country.

PITFALLS OF GLOBALIZATION

Even the most carefully conceived plans for growth do not always bear fruit. Many merchants have learned that international expansion does not always result in success. The renowned French fashion emporium Galeries Lafayette, for example, met with heavy losses after opening a branch in New York City.

TABLE 4.3
AVERAGE NET PROFIT MARGIN BY REGION OR COUNTRY, 2005

Region Extracted From	Average Profit Margin
Top 250	3.5
Africa/Middle East	4.0
Asia/Pacific	2.9
Japan	2.6
Europe	4.0
France	3.7
Germany	2.0
United Kingdom	5.5
Latin America	4.4
North America	3.4
United States	3.5

Sources: published company data and Planet Retail.

Some of the pitfalls of globalization are as follows.

Economic Downturns

It is difficult to foresee the future direction of the economy. Recessions are always a possibility anywhere in the world, and expansion during these times plays havoc with the best-laid plans. The following are just two examples of what can occur. Analysts were taken by surprise in 1998 when Asian capitals had serious business declines that significantly affected American retail interests. When Mexico devalued the peso in 1994, it was a nightmare for companies (such as Wal-Mart) that had high hopes for retailing units. Because currency devaluation happens only rarely, businesses were not prepared to handle the ensuing crises.

Of course, most often these economic problems are short-lived. As we see today, both the Asian and Mexican markets are considered sound investments for offshore retailers. India, China, Vietnam, and Mexico are all considered good bets for retail expansion.

Consumer Differences

People's needs, tastes, and habits often differ from country to country. What might have satisfied the retailer's consumer clientele at home might not satisfy potential customers abroad. Food preferences, for example, are not uniform throughout the world. If close attention isn't paid to these details, domestic success might translate into offshore failure.

Local Competition

Sometimes retailers try to expand their operations into other countries without carefully assessing domestic operations that could seriously hurt their plans. When Galeries Lafayette opened in New York City, it found itself in a saturated retail environment with no room for another competitor. Knowing that the new store would be surrounded by such stellar performers as Macy's, Bloomingdale's, Lord & Taylor, and Saks Fifth Avenue, the company should have realized that failure was likely. Its shortsightedness and inability to recognize the competitive forces it faced led to disaster. Even with the prestige it enjoyed in France, the American competition was too much for Galeries Lafayette to succeed.

Galeries Lafayette in New York was a failure because of the competition it faced from American retailers.

Similarly, Benetton, which made an early splash into American retailing but had short-lived success, did not have the staying power to compete with such companies as Gap and Limited. These domestic merchants had a better understanding of U.S. consumer needs and were able to address them quickly. Unable to withstand the competition from the locals, Benetton's numbers soon diminished. Today, although it still has a presence in the United States, it is by no means at the level Benetton first enjoyed.

Political Risk

Throughout the world, history has regularly shown some degree of political unrest. At this time, for example, the Middle East is a hotbed of uncertainty. Many parts of that area are considered ripe for retail expansion, but merchants must carefully assess the possible effects of the wars being waged and only then decide whether the time is appropriate for their companies to expand there. Foresight is critical even when unrest is the dominant motif. Few knew that countries like Vietnam would emerge as arenas for global retail expansion. Risk is a factor that must be considered when political uncertainty is the order of the day.

> **In the News . . .**
>
> A complete analysis of the hurdles faced by U.S. retailers moving into global arenas is discussed in "Finding a Home Abroad," an article reprinted on page 103 at the end of this chapter.

FOREIGN EXPANSION ARRANGEMENTS

There are many ways for retailers to approach entry into foreign markets. These include joint ventures, wholly owned subsidiaries, franchising, and licensing. A company must weigh and measure the benefits of each plan and select the one that is best suited for its specific goals. Of course, legislation in the target country often dictates the manner in which expansion can take place. Before any programs earmarked for offshore consideration can come to fruition, it is essential for the foreign retailer to study carefully the requirements of the country it is considering and so determine whether its expansion plans are feasible on those shores. The principal routes to be considered are discussed in the following sections.

Joint Ventures

In a **joint venture**, two or more businesses act as partners for the purpose of starting a new business. The partners may be retailers who operate their own stores or a retailer and an investment company. By entering into a joint venture with a native business, a company from another country can avoid some of the risks of international expansion. For example, a retailer that is successful in one country might not have the necessary knowledge of consumer preferences and governmental requirements in the other country to succeed there. For instance, Liz Claiborne, Inc., which opened Mexx stores (a highly successful chain in Europe) in the United States, failed to replicate its success overseas. Never able to capture the attention of the American market, the company decided to close its outlets in the United States. In the joint venture approach, a combination of the foreign retailer's capital and technical know-how and the local business's understanding of what is needed for success in its country would give the foreign operation a better chance to succeed.

Galeries Lafayette, the French department store stronghold, is once again expanding outside of its domestic borders. After failing in the United States, where it attempted to "go it alone" instead of joining with an American company, it is now taking the joint venture approach by partnering with Lebanon's Gard Investments and Emaar Properties to open a store in Dubai. Because the latter two companies are experts in the Middle East, the new venture is likely to succeed.

The AX Armani Exchange is expanding into many global venues.

AX Armani Exchange is also expanding into numerous global arenas. The company formed a joint venture for the purpose of managing its expansion outside the United States. Together with billionaires Christina Ong and her husband Ong Beng Seng, Armani formed a joint venture company called Presidio Holdings Ltd. to target such new markets as Japan, China, South America, and the United Kingdom. The company has already opened stores in Abu Dhabi, United Arab Emirates, São Paulo, and Rio de Janeiro.

Other global joint ventures include France's Printemp department stores in Taiwan, America's Wal-Mart in Mexico, Japan's Sogo in Taiwan, the Netherland's Makro in Beijing, and America's McDonald's all over the world.

Wholly Owned Subsidiaries

Many retailers create a **wholly owned subsidiary** in order to open a store in a foreign country. With this approach, companies avoid establishing any formal affiliations with other businesses. In this way they assume complete control and all risks associated with the venture and are able to maximize profits. Some retailers take this approach so that they needn't divulge their business practices to partners. Of course, some nations forbid foreign businesses from being sole owners within their borders. In such circumstances, joint ventures are the only way to develop a presence in that country.

The Gap Stores, Inc., is one company that expands overseas via wholly owned subsidiaries and franchising (discussed in the next section). In Japan, Gap owns its own stores whereas the units are franchised in the Middle East.

Franchising

Under a **franchising** agreement, the franchiser gives the franchisee the right to open a store that bears the franchiser's name. The franchiser usually provides the merchandise to the franchisee, trains the new business "partner," and provides other components necessary for making the franchisee a success. In exchange, the franchiser receives a fee, a percentage of the sales, and/or a commission on the merchandise sold. This arrangement enables a company to gain an international presence and to maintain control over its image without actually owning the new units.

McDonald's is the epitome of franchising.

Franchising is commonplace in the fast-food industry, with McDonald's reigning as king of these operations. In the soft goods arena, the Italian manufacturer and retailer Benetton has expanded into many parts of the world through franchising. With more than 2,000 units in its own country, Benetton has franchised more than 3,000 additional units in the United Sates, France, and Asian countries. Others that have used this approach in clothing and accessories are America's Athlete's Foot with units in Canada and Australia; Spain's Mango with stores in Greece, Portugal, and France; Canada's Mad Science Group with units in the United States; and the aforementioned Gap, which is slated to open franchises under the Gap and Banana Republic marquees in South Korea under an agreement with Shinsegae International.

Although franchising has been a major approach for retailers, few designer boutiques have taken the plunge. An exception is Tom Ford, which (in addition to creating collections) has opened a flagship on New York City's Madison Avenue. While expanding into other locales with fully owned units, this company is using the franchise approach to reach many global markets. Moscow, Zurich, St. Moritz, Hong Kong, Beijing, Kuwait, Dubai, and Qatar will have these franchised units.

Licensing

Similar to franchising, in **licensing** a retailer offers its company's name and expertise for a fee or royalty. Typically, the licensee purchases merchandise from the licensor, but this is not always the case. The arrangement does give the licensor overseas exposure, but it may be risky because the licensee might not properly operate the business and thus cause image problems for the licensor.

Saks Fifth Avenue has two overseas licensed stores and is presently looking for more locations. The licensed operations are now in Riyadh (Saudi Arabia) and Dubai. High on the list for further licensed expansion are Beijing and Macao in China as well as Mexico.

LEADING GLOBAL RETAILERS

After considering all the positives and negatives regarding globalization, many established retailers have entered offshore markets. While some of these major entities have pursued varying degrees of overseas expansion, others have remained within their countries of origin. Even with their decision to forgo such expansion, companies such as Kroger, Target, Lowe's, Albertson's, and CVS have remained at the uppermost levels of gross sales. Some, however, have not closed the door on overseas expansion; for instance, Target is considering such a move in the near future. It should be noted that global expansion runs the gamut from just two countries—as with Safeway, Inc., which has stores in the United States and Canada; and Walgreens, with units in the United States and Puerto Rico—to companies that have entered many foreign markets—such as the French chain Carrefour and Metro AG from Germany.

It should also be noted that the range of retail formats run from single-classification operations such as Home Depot and Lowe's, which specialize in home improvement, to multiclassification organizations that feature a substantial number of formats, such as Sears Holding and Rewe-Zentral AG.

Table 4.4 lists the top 20 global retailers. They are listed according to rank (based on sales), and the table shows their countries of origin, formats, countries of operation, and 5-year sales increase.

Carrefour, the French chain, is a major global retailer.

TABLE 4.4
TOP 20 GLOBAL RETAILERS

DT RANK (FY 05)	NAME OF COMPANY	COUNTRY OF ORIGIN	2005 GROUP SALES* (US$MIL)	2005 RETAIL SALES (US$MIL)	2005 GROUP INCOME/ (LOSS)* (US$MIL)	FORMATS	COUNTRIES OF OPERATION	5 YR RETAIL SALES CAGR % (LOCAL CURRENCY)
1	Wal-Mart Stores, Inc.	US	315,654	312,427	11,231	Cash & Carry/Warehouse Club, Discount Department Store, Hypermarket/Supercenter/Superstore, Supermarket	Argentina, Brazil, Canada, China, Germany, Japan, Mexico, Puerto Rico, S. Korea, UK, US	11.6%
2	Carrefour S.A.	France	92,778	92,778	1,788	Cash & Carry/Warehouse Club, Convenience/Forecourt Store, Discount Store, Hypermarket/Supercenter/Superstore, Supermarket	Argentina, Belgium, Brazil, China, Columbia, Dominican Republic, Egypt, France, French Polynesia, Greece, Guadeloupe, Indonesia, Italy, Malaysia, Martinique, Oman, Poland, Portugal, Qatar, Reunion, Romania, Saudi Arabia, Singapore, S. Korea, Spain, Switzerland, Taiwan, Thailand, Turkey, Tunisia, UAE	2.8%
3	The Home Depot, Inc.	US	81,511	81,511	5,838	Home Improvement	Canada, Mexico, Puerto Rico, US, Virgin Islands	12.3%
4	Metro AG	Germany	69,396	69,134	808	Apparel/Footwear Specialty, Cash & Carry/Warehouse Club, Department Store, Electronics Specialty, Hypermarket/Supercenter/Superstore, Other Specialty, Supermarket	Austria, Belgium, Bulgaria, China, Croatia, Czech Rep., Denmark, France, Germany, Greece, Hungary, India, Italy, Japan, Luxembourg, Moldova, Morocco, Netherlands, Poland, Portugal, Romania, Russia, Serbia and Montenegro, Slovakia, Spain, Switzerland, Turkey, Ukraine, UK, Vietnam	5.0%

(Continued)

TABLE 4.4
TOP 20 GLOBAL RETAILERS—continued

DT RANK (FY 05)	NAME OF COMPANY	COUNTRY OF ORIGIN	2005 GROUP SALES* (US$MIL)	2005 RETAIL SALES (US$MIL)	2005 GROUP INCOME/ (LOSS)* (US$MIL)	FORMATS	COUNTRIES OF OPERATION	5 YR RETAIL SALES CAGR % (LOCAL CURRENCY)
5	Tesco plc	UK	68,866	68,866	2,837	Convenience/Forecourt Store, Department Store, Hypermarket/Supercenter/ Superstore, Supermarket	China, Czech Rep., Hungary, Japan, Rep. of Ireland, Malaysia, Poland, Slovakia, S. Korea, Taiwan, Thailand, Turkey, UK	12.8%
6	Kroger	US	60,553	60,553	958	Convenience/Forecourt Store, Hypermarket/Supercenter/Superstore, Other Specialty, Supermarket	US	4.3%
7	Target Corp.	US	52,620	52,620	2,408	Discount Department Store, Hypermarket/Supercenter/ Superstore	US	7.4%
8	Costco Wholesale Corporation	US	52,935	51,862	1,063	Cash & Carry/Warehouse Club	Canada, Japan, Mexico, Puerto Rico, S. Korea, Taiwan, UK, US	10.4%
9	Sears Holdings Corp (formerly Kmart Corp)	US	49,124	49,124	858	Department Store, Discount Department Store, Home Improvement, Hypermarket/Supercenter/Superstore, Other Specialty	Canada, Guam, Puerto Rico, US, Virgin Islands	5.8%

The Globalization of Retailing | CHAPTER 4

DT RANK (FY 05)	NAME OF COMPANY	COUNTRY OF ORIGIN	2005 GROUP SALES* (US$MIL)	2005 RETAIL SALES (US$MIL)	2005 GROUP INCOME/ (LOSS)* (US$MIL)	FORMATS	COUNTRIES OF OPERATION	5 YR RETAIL SALES CAGR % (LOCAL CURRENCY)
10	Schwarz Unternehmens Treuhand KG	Germany	45,891[e]	45,891[e]	n/a	Discount Store, Hypermarket/ Supercenter/Superstore	Austria, Belgium, Croatia, Czech Rep., Denmark, Finland, France, Germany, Greece, Hungary, Rep. of Ireland, Italy, Luxembourg, Netherlands, Norway, Poland, Portugal, Romania, Slovakia, Spain, Sweden, UK	13.0%
11	Aldi GmbH & Co. oHG	Germany	45,096[e]	45,096[e]	n/a	Discount Store, Supermarket	Australia, Austria, Belgium, Denmark, France, Germany, Rep. of Ireland, Luxembourg, Netherlands, Slovenia, Spain, Switzerland, UK, US	4.5%
12	Rewe-Zentral AG	Germany	51,933	44,039[e]	n/a	Apparel/Footwear Specialty, Cash & Carry/Warehouse Club, Discount Store, Drug Store/Pharmacy, Electronics Specialty, Home Improvement, Hypermarket/Supercenter/Superstore, Other Specialty, Supermarket	Austria, Bulgaria, Croatia, Czech Rep., France, Germany, Hungary, Italy, Poland, Romania, Russia, Slovakia, Switzerland, Ukraine	3.0%

(Continued)

TABLE 4.4
TOP 20 GLOBAL RETAILERS—continued

DT Rank (FY 05)	Name of Company	Country of Origin	2005 Group Sales* (US$Mil)	2005 Retail Sales (US$Mil)	2005 Group Income/(Loss)* (US$Mil)	Formats	Countries of Operation	5 Yr Retail Sales CAGR % (Local Currency)
13	Lowe's Companies Inc.	US	43,243	43,243	2,771	Home Improvement	US	18.2%
14	Walgreen Co.	US	42,202	42,202	1,560	Drug Store/Pharmacy	Puerto Rico, US	11.4%
15	Groupe Auchan SA	France	41,855	41,180	1,216	Discount Store, Electronics Specialty, Hypermarket/Supercenter/Superstore, Supermarket	China, France, Hungary, Italy, Luxembourg, Morocco, Poland, Portugal, Russia, Spain, Taiwan	7.1%
16	Albertsons Inc.	US	40,358	40,358	446	Convenience/Forecourt Store, Discount Store, Drug Store/Pharmacy, Supermarket	US	1.9%
17	Edeka Zentrale AG & Co. KG	Germany	41,347e	39,445e	n/a	Cash & Carry/Warehouse Club, Convenience/Forecourt Store, Discount Store, Home Improvement, Hypermarket/Supercenter/Superstore, Other Specialty, Supermarket	Austria, Czech Rep., Denmark, Germany, Russia	4.9%

DT RANK (FY 05)	NAME OF COMPANY	COUNTRY OF ORIGIN	2005 GROUP SALES* (US$MIL)	2005 RETAIL SALES (US$MIL)	2005 GROUP INCOME/ (LOSS)* (US$MIL)	FORMATS	COUNTRIES OF OPERATION	5 YR RETAIL SALES CAGR % (LOCAL CURRENCY)
18	Safeway, Inc.	US	38,416	38,416	561	Supermarket	Canada, US	3.7%
19	CVS Corporation	US	37,006	37,006	1,225	Drug Store/Pharmacy	US	13.0%
20	AEON Co., Ltd	Japan	39,562	36,978	258	Apparel/Footwear Specialty, Convenience/Forecourt Store, Department Store, Drug Store/Pharmacy, Home Improvement, Hypermarket/Supercenter/Superstore, Other Specialty, Supermarket	Canada, China, Hong Kong SAR, Japan, Malaysia, S. Korea, Taiwan, Thailand, UK, US	10.6%

Rank determined by Fiscal 2005 Retail Sales.
*Group Sales and Income/Loss may include results from non-retail operations.
CAGR = Compound Annual Growth Rate
Name after forward slash is retail segment of parent company.
Name in parentheses is former name of company.
n/a = not available
ne = not in existence (created by merger or divestiture since 1999)
e = estimate

CHAPTER HIGHLIGHTS

- The United States is the major retailing country in the world with the United Kingdom, France, Japan, and Italy closely following in importance.
- In addition to the global leaders, emerging nations such as India, Russia, China, and others are making their marks with offshore expansion.
- In terms of percentage of sales from foreign operations, leading the pack are Germany and France.
- Retailers choose to expand overseas because of domestic competition, the familiarity of their companies due to significant international travel, the uniqueness of their products, and the potential for profitability.
- Even with the continued overall success of global expansion, retailers must consider the potential pitfalls before making such a commitment.
- There are several foreign expansion arrangements for retailers, including joint ventures, wholly owned subsidiaries, franchising, and licensing.
- Some of the leading U.S. retailers such as Target and Kroger have not yet entered overseas markets.

IMPORTANT RETAILING TERMS

agent order taker (81)
franchising (93)
friendship store (87)
global retailer (80)
hypermarket (83)
joint venture (92)
kimono store (84)
licensing (93)
prêt-à-porter (83)
retailing "doors" (79)
souk (88)
terminal store (84)
wholly owned subsidiary (93)

FOR REVIEW

1. Which are today's major global retailing countries?
2. Describe the term *big books* as it is known in the United Kingdom. Which American stores once used big books?
3. What is an agent order taker?
4. How are loyalty cards used in the United Kingdom to motivate shoppers?
5. From which form of Japanese retail operations have department stores evolved?
6. Name, in order of importance, the three leading "emerging" countries for retail expansion.
7. What are so-called friendship stores?
8. In addition to domestic competition, international travel, and profitability, what has prompted many retailers to expand into foreign countries?
9. What are the political risks for retailers seeking to open branches offshore?
10. How does a joint venture differ from a wholly owned subsidiary?

AN INTERNET ACTIVITY

Use a search engine such as Google to explore the activities of a major retailer who has entered an offshore venue. Write a research paper that includes the following:

- Company history
- Presence in overseas venues
- Operational formats
- Number of domestic and overseas units

The paper should be typed and double-spaced.

EXERCISE AND PROJECTS

1. Select a country that American retailers have entered with branches of their operations. In a three-page typewritten paper, indicate the stores that have made the plunge, their merchandise mixes, and whether these new offshore branches required refinement of and/or adjustment to their American operations. Trade periodicals, the Internet, and contacting the public relations departments of stores could provide the necessary information.
2. Prepare a research paper on any one of the three major methods used by retailers to expand their operations oversees. Make certain that all of the pros and cons of the chosen expansion plan have been presented.

THE CASE OF THE INTERNATIONAL EXPANSION DILEMMA

One of the established junior sportswear chains in the United States, Gallop & Company, has been in business since 1950. Beginning as a modest single-unit organization, its success has resulted in a retail company of 950 units. It first opened in Roanoke, Virginia, and has since become a coast-to-coast operation. Now that this type of company is facing stiff competition in the United States, its plans for further domestic expansion have just about come to an end. More specifically, giants like The Limited and Gap have claimed most of the prime real estate, leaving little room for Gallop & Company to open more domestic units.

Gallop's aggressive management team wants the company to grow and has decided to look offshore for new locations. Those responsible for the expansion program are in agreement that Canada would be a good place to begin. However, there is some disagreement as to which expansion arrangement would be most beneficial for the company to pursue. John Gallop, the president and CEO of the organization and a third-generation chief executive, believes the best road to take would be a joint venture with a high-profile Canadian business. The second in command, Helen Avidon, disagrees. She firmly believes that, given the company's expertise, a wholly owned subsidiary would be ideal. Yet another opinion comes from the COO, Marc Litt, who thinks the company should expand through some form of licensing.

All economic indicators suggest that the time is ripe to begin global expansion, but the management team has not yet reached a decision concerning the best method to employ. Each member of the executive team has given several plausible reasons for his or her recommendation.

With time of the essence for preempting any other competitor from staking a similar claim in Canada, it is imperative that a final decision be made soon.

Questions

1. List the pros and cons of each form of expansion: joint venture, wholly owned subsidiary, and franchising.
2. Which approach do you believe would best serve the interests of the company? Defend your answer with facts and analysis.

Global Markets Key to Retailing Future
Robert Murphy

APRIL 3, 2007

BARCELONA—Emerging markets are transforming the landscape of the retail industry, as more players eye expansion in the fast-growing economies of China, India and Russia, said executives at the World Retail Congress here last week.

"This is the best time ever to be in the retail industry," said Sir Terry Leahy, chief executive officer of Britain's Tesco. "There are more opportunities than ever."

Several retailers said they wanted to bridge into rising markets, including Carrefour ceo Jose Luis Duran, who repeated that the French hypermarket operator was in talks with potential partners to open in India and it was going to enter Russia, too.

Duran said those markets would hold great potential. "We see a huge opportunity to grow internationally, whether in Poland, Brazil or China," he said.

Terry Lundgren, chairman, president and ceo of Federated Department Stores, also said he was in the early stages of investigating the "global expansion" of the Macy's and Bloomingdale's banners.

"It would have to be a meaningful opportunity," stressed Lundgren, who added it was only a matter of time before a major U.S. retailer became bullish about overseas expansion.

Saks Fifth Avenue and Harvey Nichols already have opened stores in the Middle East, and this month France's Galeries Lafayette said it would kick-start its own international expansion strategy with a store to open in Dubai. Saks, which operates its overseas stores with a franchise partner, also is planning to launch a store in Shanghai, and Harvey Nichols has one in Hong Kong.

Delegates at the conference prominently mentioned the importance of finding the right formula to crack into markets in Asia, and they bemoaned regulations that created red tape barriers to business.

Pascal Lamy, director of the World Trade Organization, spoke via video link to warn of the ramifications of a failure in the current Doha round of global free trade talks, which are struggling with agricultural subsidies and tariffs.

"Globalization has formidable advantages," said Lamy, as he outlined the political dangers of disagreement on the round, which, he said, would require great political will from the United States and the European Union if an agreement was to come by yearend.

"[An agreement] is doable, it's not yet done and we need political traction for a final breakthrough," said Lamy. He added: "Failure of the round is a scenario which we all need to have in mind. If we are really responsible, given the state of negotiations, we need to consider this scenario."

For retailers, Lamy said the consequences of a failed round would undermine the WTO system and its series of safeguards against protectionism, while a successful conclusion would, besides doing away with tariffs, begin a cycle to diminish regulatory restrictions in real estate ownership or in the types of products foreign retailers can carry.

Adapting to emerging markets marked a significant subject of debate among speakers, with many outlining the importance of tailoring an offer to local demand and finding the right partner with whom to do business.

Carrefour's Duran, for instance, told how the retailer had staved off a downturn in its business in Argentina a few years ago by abandoning a centralized pricing system and creating a flexible store-by-store alternative, while also catering product assortments especially for each store. Carrefour, as a result, has logged three years of double-digit growth in Argentina, Duran said.

Considering many retailers, from Carrefour to Tesco, already have entered China aggressively, delegates emphasized the attraction of India as Asia's next great frontier—though China remains largely untapped and a great source of potential growth.

"Asia is going through profound change," said Ravi Thakran, group director of Southeast Asia for LVMH Moët Hennessy Louis Vuitton. "No market gives brands the opportunity of Asia today."

"But there isn't one Asia," he said. "The challenge is to get deeper understanding [of the consumer landscape]."

For instance, Thakran said while one part of India gravitates by heritage to pomp and show, another is prone to understatement. Another obstacle for retailers is to challenge the intricate web of mom-and-pop shops in India that have cultivated direct relationships with their clientele for years.

But the potential rewards largely outweigh drawbacks. After all, the population boom alone in Asia is enough to tempt retailers to aggressively grow in the region.

Jim O'Neill, global head of economic research at Goldman Sachs International, gave a detailed presentation on the shape of the world's population in 2025 and what it would mean for the global economy.

"Population changes have become the key to the future of world growth," he said.

Although O'Neill said although the world's current wealthiest consumers would remain the wealthiest in the near future, some countries are growing at such a rate that they will join the elite club soon.

Russia, for instance, could become as rich as the world's wealthiest nations in per capita household income by 2025, O'Neill said. Korea also is on track to become as wealthy in per capita income as the U.S. or Japan.

Although the opportunities of emerging markets dominated a large chunk of the conference, it was hardly the only focus. Green consumption and the information revolution also got attention.

Tesco's Leahy, for instance, said the way in which retailers deal with environmental concerns might become the biggest single issue in the future.

"Customers are more and more aware of climate change," he said. "I think we need to give customers the tools to do something, too."

How exactly more acute consumer concerns about the environment will be played out commercially is anyone's guess. But already a green consumer agenda has had an impact at retail with huge growth of organic foods and green clothing, executives said.

"We need a huge change," said Leahy, adding that Tesco was taking steps to open green stores. "We are a high carbon industry."

Another British retailer moving to improve its environmental commitment is Marks & Spencer, which has pledged to be carbon neutral in five years and to eliminate its waste to landfill in that same period.

Strangely enough, the Internet is playing a significant role in rising green concerns. That's because more consumers use the Web to connect to retailers and inform themselves about retailers' practices and products, making for a highly sophisticated consumer.

"Sophisticated people expect us to understand their needs," said Concetta Lanciaux, the former head of human resources at LVMH and an adviser to the luxury group's chairman, Bernard Arnault.

"Consumers are becoming more demanding in quality and fashion," said Pablo Isla, Inditex's ceo.

Wrapping up the event, the congress honored international retailers with prizes during a black-tie gala dinner. Kate Moss, who did not attend, was named the consumer icon of the year.

Meanwhile, other honorees included the most innovative store format (American Girl Place), best retail destination (Dubai's Mall of the Emirates) and the retailer of the year (Inditex).

Finding a Home Abroad
David Moin

APRIL 16, 2007

U.S. retailers entering overseas markets often overestimate or underestimate demand.

The misfires stem from a lack of knowledge about some of the business and political complexities and nuances of mostly uncharted territory. But that hasn't chilled the desire of most companies to tap into growing economies across the globe.

Take Brooks Bros.' opening day in Santiago, Chile, last April. "We were surprised by the depth of what was shopped," said Claudio Del Vecchio, president and chief executive officer. "Shoppers bought everything—shirts, suits, shoes."

Typically, a Brooks Bros. opening overseas is marked by far less exuberant spending across categories; shirt sales can comprise as much as 70 percent of the total. Shirts are less expensive than most Brooks Bros. products and readily identified as embodying the spirit of the brand, so they're an easy impulse buy, Del Vecchio explained. As customers become more familiar with the assortment, the selling evens out across categories, and shirts average out to some 30 percent of sales.

In Germany, Wal-Mart was far too optimistic. The retail giant was up against restrictive building codes, scarcity of land for new stores and a lack of a critical mass to leverage costs, a sluggish economy and, most important, tough competition from local chains Aldi, Tengelmann and Metro. Last July, Wal-Mart announced the sale of its ailing German retail business to Metro AG and took a $1 billion charge in the second quarter to cover the exit. Wal-Mart last year also left South Korea, where it was losing money.

But the world's largest retailer has fared better in Brazil, Canada and Mexico. And despite some setbacks on the world stage, Wal-Mart recently bought a 35 percent stake in Taiwanese retailer Trust-Mart, which will more than double Wal-Mart's retail footprint in China, and entered India with a retail joint venture with Bharti Enterprises Ltd., a New Delhi conglomerate. Under the deal, structured to capitalize on loopholes in India's restrictions on foreign direct investment, it is said Wal-Mart will provide logistics and sourcing expertise and Bharti will franchise retail units.

Gap Inc.'s international sales have been generating negative comps. To minimize risk, last year Gap shifted from a strategy of strict ownership of the stores to signing with franchise partners better acquainted with the markets. Deals have been struck in the Middle East and Asia. Gap still owns its stores in Japan.

Saks Fifth Avenue had a different strategy. The company secured a prime piece of real estate in China for a 300,000-square-foot store, which will be the chain's largest location except for the Manhattan flagship. It's an historic building in the Bund district of downtown Shanghai. Initially, the plan was to open before the 2008 Summer Olympics in Beijing. But Saks hit a snag last month. Roosevelt China Investments Corp., which will own the store, said it terminated its sublicense agreement with I.T. Ltd., the company designated to operate the Saks unit. Now Roosevelt must find another operator, delaying the opening until 2009.

Undeterred, Roosevelt said it was considering additional licensed Saks stores in Beijing, Macao and other cities in China. Saks has two overseas stores, both licensed units, in Riyadh, Saudi Arabia, and in Dubai in the United Arab Emirates. Saks also plans to open stores in Mexico.

Other mass and high-end specialty retailers are pushing ahead with overseas expansion, following the lead of luxury brands such as Ralph Lauren and Brooks Bros., which have been targeting real estate in such high-end locations as New Bond and Sloan Streets in London, Rue du Faubourg Saint-Honoré in Paris and the Ginza in Japan.

"There's definitely a lot of interest from American retailers looking to go abroad," said Robert Cohen, a retail broker at Robert K. Futterman Associates, who helped CP Shades enter the London market seven years ago, and recently landed Chrome Hearts a location on the Avenue Montaigne in Paris. "Chrome Hearts is considering other luxury streets in different European cities. They definitely have an appetite for more deals."

Last fall, Brooks Bros. opened a flagship on Regent Street in London, where it also has a smaller store. Flagships also opened in Paris and Seoul last fall, and two weeks ago, another flagship opened in Milan.

Abercrombie & Fitch opened a London flagship last month on the corner of Burlington Gardens and Savile Row.

"Our long-term goal is to roll out stores, and we are working on it," Michael Jeffries, chairman and ceo, said at the launch. "But we're not looking for world domination. We want the business to grow naturally, and we're humble—and cautious—in whatever we do."

The youth specialty retailer is searching for a flagship site in the Ginza or Omotesando sections of Tokyo, and will have a local manager to supervise future A&F stores in Japan. Abercrombie envisions a multi-level Tokyo unit of more than 20,000 square feet opening in fall 2008.

Last year, three Abercrombie & Fitch stores and three Hollister units were launched in Canada. "These stores really surprised us," Michael Kramer, A&F's executive vice president and chief financial officer, said at a recent Bear Stearns' Retail, Restaurant and Consumer conference. "We anticipated them opening to great volume, but not anywhere near what they did. These stores have not slowed down to any lower than three times our average store here domestically and they continue to perform."

As a result, Hollister is accelerating its international rollout. Hollister is targeting malls, while the Abercrombie & Fitch brand is focused on measured development of big flagships on prime real estate in major cities.

"You have seen a lot of retailers laying on the side of the road in terms of their international development," Kramer said. "Why? Because they went in there and one day they woke up and said, 'I want to be international,' and it was really more of a marketing ploy than a profit ploy. You can ask them whether their hurdle rates were the same or how much more diluted were they, or did they really bank on the future. We are not going to do it that way. We are going to be slow and measured and try to develop relationships with not only brokers but these owners and developers, to be able to get in on the ground with regards to Tokyo, Milan, Madrid, the U.K."

He added that the merchandise was not going to be at all different from what's in U.S. stores. "What has made us successful is that we are a Western brand."

Distribution is one of the challenges of Abercrombie's overseas strategy.

"Until we really get a full understanding of what our business is and in terms of the quantity, we are outsourcing our distribution center to a third party," Kramer said. "Most of the product that is going to be in the London stores is going to be shipped to the U.S. and then shipped back over. China, because of customs, we are not able to."

Another U.S. giant, Target, had resisted publicly talking about international growth—but no longer.

"It makes sense five to 10 years down the road," Robert Ulrich, Target's chairman and ceo, told analysts last week. Target would consider India and China when the populations are more affluent and educated. And Canada has been on the radar for a decade. To enter that market, Target would need to take over a large cluster of stores from another retailer, in one block, he noted.

Urban Outfitters is making inroads in Europe. The retailer has three stores in London, and one unit each in Dublin, and in Glasgow, Manchester and Birmingham in the U.K. The company opened a store in Stockholm and another in Copenhagen last year. In the fall, Urban launched a European market Web site. The five-year objective is 30 to 40 stores across the Continent. The company, which has favored high street locations, will begin situating stores in malls in the fall, at Bluewater in Greenhithe, a London suburb, and at the Dundrum Shopping Centre outside Dublin. The company is also firming up plans to enter Germany and Belgium.

The key to success abroad, said Ted Marlow, Urban Outfitter's president, is "understanding the market from a local perspective." A buying staff, based in London, complements Urban's assortments with local products. "In Denmark and Sweden, we've tried to have a lot of sensitivity to different cultures. We look for individual lines or designers that are popular in the market."

Christine Chen, vice president of equity research at Needham & Co., cited three top retailers for their aggressive international expansion: Guess, Abercrombie & Fitch and Polo Ralph Lauren. "These retailers are going international because they are looking for growth and realize that brands are global, thanks to the Internet and technology.

"Another retailer who you wouldn't really expect as an international figure, but is really pushing overseas expansion, is Urban Outfitters," Chen said. "They already have stores in Europe and Canada and have seen tremendous success in these locations. I expect they will also eventually move to Asia, as well.

"None of these retailers I mentioned are anywhere near saturation in the U.S., but they don't want to fall into the trouble Gap is seeing—getting too big and then struggling, looking for areas of growth. Retailers want the best locations overseas, but space is limited and they need to get in early or other retailers will snatch up the real estate. Guess and Ralph Lauren are partnering with licensees to help negotiate the real estate transactions, since locals are able to get better deals and know the area."

As for Brooks Bros., door to door overseas, the styles don't change and the woodsy, polished look of the store stays uniform, though the product mix may be different. However, the operating strategy is tailored to the market. It's a combination of company-owned, joint ventures, wholesaling and shops-in-shops. "When you decide to open more stores, you have to trust some local expert. That's why we don't mind partnering with a local partner," Del Vecchio said. "In London, we have partnered with a strong local developer and operator of other stores.

"We are not tapped out in the U.S.," Del Vecchio continued, "but certainly the long-term potential is less here than internationally." Brooks Bros. operates 105 full-price stores in the U.S., and has room for another 30 to 40. Overseas, Brooks Bros. operates 121 stores. Key markets are Japan, where there are 70 full-price stores; China, with 14; Taiwan with five, and Italy and London with two each.

"We expect the U.K. to become a very important market, shorter term," Del Vecchio said. "Longer term, Hong Kong and China is the biggest opportunity. Five years from now, it will be a very different world market. The priority now is Europe, which is ripe and ready to embrace the Brooks Bros. brand."

—With contributions from Sharon Edelson and Jeanine Poggi

CHAPTER 5
Identification, Analysis, and Research of Consumer Groups

After you have completed this chapter, you should be able to discuss:

- The importance of consumer research and analysis for today's retail organizations
- How the study of demographics helps retailers better understand the needs of the consumer
- How the characteristics of geographic region affect inventory decisions
- Why it is necessary for retailers to study various age classifications and how these groups make purchases
- How lifestyles affect the shopping requirements of consumers
- How different social classes approach their purchases
- The importance of understanding the family life cycle to preparing merchandise assortments
- The difference between rational and emotional buying motives
- The importance of the patronage motive to retailers
- The manner in which Maslow's Hierarchy of Needs affects consumer spending
- The different approaches retailers take to consumer research

Whenever a shopper walks into a store, logs on to a Web site, or peruses the pages of a catalogue in search of something he or she needs, a sale seems to be within easy reach. If, however, the individual can't find what he or she is looking for, then it is likely that the merchant didn't work hard enough when planning the available assortment. How many times have consumers who were eager to buy come away from in-store or off-site venues disappointed? Is it merely the mood of the shopper that prevents purchasing, or is it the retailer's poor planning that results in a lost sale? Or, is it the fault of the manufacturers that developed products without regard to consumer preferences that led the retailer to stock merchandise that never really had a chance to sell?

The educated merchant who toils in today's highly competitive retail arena must carefully investigate the forces that motivate consumers' buying behavior. Taking chances without understanding the real needs of potential customers often leads to losses rather than profits. A walk through any store filled with markdown racks immediately signals that the merchant failed to identify the likes and dislikes of the clientele. Of course, there is no such thing as perfect planning. Retailers, no matter how carefully they have planned, will always be left with broken sizes, colors that didn't catch the shopper's fancy, or a few items that simply didn't catch on. Some of this is to be expected, but it should not be a dominant part of the retailer's selling experience. In order to maximize profits, every merchant, no matter what product classification is being offered, must pay strict attention to his or her consumer market. Guesswork must be eliminated and replaced with educated decision making. The age-old axiom that the customer is king (or queen, for that matter) still applies today. By understanding the concepts of consumer behavior and, more specifically, the patterns of motivation and habits, a retailer is likely to address customer needs and thereby maximize profits.

The merchant has at hand a variety of different tools to safeguard against unfortunate merchandising errors. These tools include a host of traditional, fundamental concepts concerning consumer motivation and behavior, such as demographic analysis, Maslow's Hierarchy of Needs, motive assessments—which are both rational and emotional—class structures, and lifestyle categories. Knowing the details of each, and properly applying them to the company's specific situation, will more than likely prove to be a fruitful experience.

ASSESSMENT OF CONSUMER GROUPS

Every educated retailer understands that it is virtually impossible to satisfy the needs of everyone in his or her trading area. No matter how attractive the merchandise, how value-oriented the product mix, or how complete the assortment might be, it is simply a matter of fact that not everyone will be motivated to buy in one store, through one catalogue, or on one Web site. Different age groups, for example, will respond differently to a company's product mix, as will people with different lifestyles. Reality teaches us that retailers must appeal to specific segments or groups in order to achieve success.

Demographics

Briefly defined, **demographics** is the study of various characteristics of the population such as size, geographic concentration, age, occupation, education, lifestyle categories, and income. Retailers can learn about their consumer market by carefully studying these demographic factors. Although generalizations about the typical customer in the trading area cannot be assumed to apply to each individual shopper, demographic information helps retailers predict the kinds of merchandise that will sell well within their market. By and large, most brick-and-mortar organizations need not explore the population in its entirety—unless they are giants in the industry, like Wal-Mart and Sears, which seem to have boundless trading areas. Cataloguers and e-tailers also have the potential to sell just about anywhere. With the world potentially their trading area, they should know the specifics of the makeup of the entire population. Most stores, however, need to concentrate only on the trading areas they serve.

Sales potential is based upon the size of the population served by the business. In addition to studying current population figures, it is imperative to determine population trends, that is, whether the numbers are growing or declining. In this way, merchandise plans for the future will more accurately address the needs of the retailer's changing consumer base.

Retailers can obtain a wealth of figures from the federal government, trade associations, such as the **National Retail Federation**, or, if funds are available, from any one of the many marketing research firms in the United States.

Geographic Location and Climate

Where people live is also an important factor in determining what they will buy. This is particularly essential in assessing the specific apparel needs for the family. In the southern tier of the United States, consumers have greater year-round needs for swimwear and other warm-weather clothing based on that part of the country's climate. If the company has the majority of its units in such a region, these purchasing needs are easy to assess. If, however, the retailer is a brick-and-mortar one whose outlets stretch into numerous geographic regions, more of an in-depth study must be done. Gap, for example, with stores located from coast to coast and abroad, must tailor its merchandise mix according to the regions in which the stores are located. Whereas jeans are a principal product for every unit in the chain at all times, winter-weight outerwear would be required inventory for the northern-based stores while lighter outerwear would be more suitable for stores in warmer climates.

Population Concentration

Consumers who live in densely populated cities have different needs from those in suburban areas, who, in turn, seek different merchandise from rural populations. Even supermarket retailers must carefully address consumer needs based upon population density. Stores in major metropolitan areas, for example, tend to have a greater affinity for gourmet foods, while stores in outlying regions require greater emphasis on staples. City dwellers, who typically live closer to their favorite supermarket than do suburbanites or rural populations, often make smaller, more frequent purchases rather than stock up on a weekly grocery shopping trip.

For off-site ventures, geographic concentration is generally widespread. Of course, in cases where the products are oriented to more selective areas such as lawn and garden products, the efforts generally focus on suburban regions. If direct-mail pieces, for example, were targeted to just about any region, those reaching inner-city dwellers would bring virtually no sales.

Each merchant must study different regions and determine which ones have the greatest sales potential. By using only today's figures on geographic concentrations, the retailer will not have sufficient information for future merchandise planning. It is imperative that projection analysis be utilized for future years to see if the current geographical findings are heading for change.

Age Classifications

The merchandise needs of one age group are by no means identical to those of the others. Food is a constant in every household, but it is obvious that there are numerous differences in the requirements of each group. Cereal, for example, is generally a staple in all age categories, but the type preferred by each age varies considerably. The sugar varieties are naturally targeted to children, while the more health-oriented are directed to more mature audiences.

Apparel is another merchandise classification that requires analysis by age group. Although both teenage girls and their mothers wear skirts, the styles and hemlines worn by each group differ. The younger set is usually more taken with the trendy silhouettes. If the fashions of the time indicate one trend, this group is ready to buy. On the other hand, the moms generally take a more middle-of-the-road approach.

In these and most other product groupings, age plays a major role in consumer acceptance. It is therefore necessary to study these age classifications in order to make the proper merchandise decisions.

Age groups are segmented in a variety of ways. Some classify the groups with the use of such designations as **baby boomers** (born between 1945 and 1959), **generation X** and **generation Y** (ages 18–34 at the turn of the century) to study their differences. The United States Department of Commerce uses a more traditional breakdown that segments the groups into children, teenagers, young adults, young middle-aged, older middle-aged, and elderly. It should be noted that each methodology offers a good deal of information for the retailer. The study of each one will provide research that is sometimes overlapping but still benefits decision making.

Information on these classifications is regularly updated by the Department of Commerce and is easy to obtain from the federal government.

CHILDREN

This category comprises those from birth to age 13. Knowing whether the trading area contains large numbers of families with children is important to retailers in establishing their overall merchandising policy. Although the needs are different for infants and preteens, there is a great deal of similarity in the general needs of each group. If more detailed data is needed to make better merchandise judgments, it might be appropriate to confer with trade organizations, such as the National Retail Federation, or to employ the services of a market research firm.

Toys "R" Us is an example of a store focused on the children age group.

In general, the younger members of this group have neither buying nor decision-making power when it comes to purchasing. However, there is a tendency for children to influence the purchases that are being made for them.

Specific foods such as the aforementioned sweetened cereals, frozen pizza, and a host of soft drinks are part of the likes of the young. Because television targets the young with a wealth of advertising, it is imperative that the food retailer stock these products in great breadth and depth.

Clothing is no longer relegated to the basics. Children are influenced by what they see on television and in the preteen magazines. The styles are more fashion-oriented and the colors no longer remain within the staple range.

Stores like Kids "R" Us, GapKids, and Limited Too have focused on this age group. From the expansion of these companies, it is evident that the children's market is constantly growing.

TEENAGERS

Retailers who specialize in trendy clothing regularly target their wares to the teenage market, the 13- to 19-year-olds. No other age classification presents quite the same interest in this merchandise. Avid followers of the trends depicted in publications such as *Seventeen* magazine, teenagers purchase just about anything that is new. The price points they are attracted to are at the lower end of the scale, enabling them to buy more items, and they prefer to buy at specialty stores such as Wet Seal.

A large portion of this age group also makes shopping treks to stores like Gap, American Eagle, and Old Navy for clothing. Unlike the trendy merchants, these retailers provide the teenager with a wealth of jeans, T-shirts, sweats, khakis, and other items that are central to their wardrobes.

In addition to being great consumers of apparel, teenagers are the largest purchasers of compact discs. As loyal fans of the ever-growing number of rock groups around the world, they buy just about any recordings that these musicians offer. A visit to stores like Tower Records, Best Buy, and Borders immediately reveals that the vast majority of the CD inventory is aimed at the teenage market.

With more and more teenagers working after school, their purchasing power continues to increase.

In the News . . .

"Teen Panel Reflects Shifting Spending Habits," an article written on the findings uncovered by studying a large group of teenagers, is featured on page 127 at the chapter's end and should be read at this time.

YOUNG ADULTS

The vast majority of those in the 20–34-year-old age group are interested in fashion merchandise. They are either finishing college and heading for the work world or are already employed in a full-time career. Their apparel needs are divided into three categories: career clothing, special occasion apparel, and leisure attire. With incomes relatively high, this group is able to afford more expensive merchandise than those in the same age group years ago.

The favorite places to shop for apparel and accessories are Banana Republic, Gap, Ann Taylor, J.Crew, and The Limited.

Home furnishings have also become extremely important to this age group. Whether they are unmarried and live alone, share with other singles, or are married, they have significant home furnishing needs. The places where they shop are unlike the places where people in past generations shopped for these needs. Instead of the traditional stores that their parents frequented, this group heads for more contemporary merchants, such as Crate & Barrel, IKEA, Pottery Barn, Pier 1 Imports, and Restoration Hardware. In addition to the enormous selections available at these stores, delivery is generally immediate. People in this age group often want their purchasers right away and don't want to wait months for delivery. By responding to these needs, the present-day home furnishings retailers have replaced many of the old-timers like W.J. Sloane.

Young adults are the primary market for stores such as J.Crew because of their normally high incomes and need for a variety of clothing types.

Focus on . . .
Pottery Barn

ONE OF THE MAJOR SUCCESSES IN THE HOME FURNISHINGS' ARENA is Pottery Barn. It was established as a single-unit store in lower Manhattan in 1949. Its goal was to offer home furnishings that were exceptional in comfort, style, and quality at affordable prices. Unlike other home furnishing retailers, who bought their inventories from numerous vendors, Pottery Barn's approach was to sell merchandise that was designed exclusively for its needs by an in-house creative team. Its formula for success was immediately embraced by a large number of New Yorkers seeking to find more exciting products for their homes that were generally unavailable at traditional retailers.

After success with its first unit, the company continued to expand. Not only did the expansion focus on adding stores from coast to coast, it also focused on expanding the product offerings. Originally concentrating on small items such as picture frames, glassware, dinnerware, decorative accessories, and gift items, the merchandise mix now incorporates all items necessary to furnish a home.

On the selling floor, through catalogues, and on its Web site, Pottery Barn features a host of furniture for every room in the house. These items are accessorized with lamps, rugs, wall hangings, artwork, candles, paper flowers, and all of the products that were introduced in the store's original concept.

For those with limited time to shop, the company's Web site exquisitely presents decorated rooms that are replete with everything needed to make them a comfortable setting. The room designs change with each season. Not only is an overview of a room featured, but the shopper can also zero in on an item for closer inspection with a mere click of the mouse. The Web site is also arranged in a manner that allows the Pottery Barn catalogue shopper to get a closer look at the items featured in the book.

Pottery Barn is a company that has achieved success by tailoring its products to the needs of an ever growing segment of the home furnishings market.

Young adults are also very important to physical fitness apparel and outdoor retailers. Workout clothing and running shoes, for example, rank among this group's top purchasing needs. Stores like Sports Authority and catalogues like L.L.Bean cater to this group.

Finally, members of this group are also major purchasers of computer products, frequenting such stores as Office Depot, CompUSA, Best Buy, and Staples.

YOUNG MIDDLE-AGED

The Polo Ralph Lauren stores are frequented by young middle-aged shoppers.

The 35–49 age group represents a great deal of spending power in America. Those with careers in such areas as investment banking, computer engineering, e-commerce, law, and medicine have paid off their college loans and are ready to enjoy the rewards of their labors. They are now able to purchase a host of expensive products. Luxury automobiles, high-fashion apparel, precious jewelry, original art, and exotic travel are just a few of the areas this group indulges in.

Stores like Saks Fifth Avenue, Neiman Marcus, Bloomingdale's, and a host of others are regular haunts for this group. With many of them having limited time to shop, they have become one of the major segments of the e-tail community. Shopping on line is second nature to many in this age classification.

This group is also likely to dine in the most fashionable restaurants. The result is an enormous increase in upscale dining establishments.

OLDER MIDDLE-AGED

World-famous boutiques like Hermès have opened units in fashionable shopping areas to cater to affluent older middle-aged clientele.

Like their counterparts in the previous age segment, these individuals are also able to afford the luxuries of life. Many have reached the pinnacle of success and continue to enjoy their accomplishments by making extravagant purchases. Of course, a large number in this group are retired and armed with significant sums of money.

Those who are affluent patronize the luxury emporiums of the world. Not only are American merchants beneficiaries of their wealth, but so also are many global merchants. Extensive travel to foreign shores brings them within reach of the British, French, and Italian designers. This group also frequents posh dining establishments, treating themselves to everything and anything they want. The explosion of upscale retailing is evident in many of America's fashionable shopping areas. New York City, for example, has witnessed the opening of numerous world-famous designer boutiques to cater to the city's affluent residents as well as to tourists.

Of course, not everyone in this age classification is privileged. Many are middle-income wage earners and retirees who spend more cautiously. Value shopping is clearly what motivates many in this group. The off-price retailers such as Marshalls, T.J. Maxx, Syms, and Stein Mart all cater to this class. Especially for those on restricted budgets, these stores offer great values on high profile manufacturer goods and marquee labels. Discounters such as Target, Wal-Mart, and Kmart are regular stops on their buying jaunts. This is also the age classification that regularly visits clearance centers across the country to make purchases.

ELDERLY

Most in this age group are retirees. The "gray heads," as they are known, spend rather cautiously. Many relocate into retirement communities. Fashion is not generally a must for them. They seek more functional purchases. They spend a great deal on health products, making them the major markets for companies like Walgreens and CVS. Typically, the elderly are cautious shoppers, buying only what they deem to be the necessities of life. Even those with more wealth than they ever imagined tend to become careful spenders. As a group, the elderly are considered to be difficult shoppers.

This group dines out a lot, but value restaurants are their usual destinations. Travel is prevalent in this age group, but again, value is important.

Occupations

A very important part of today's purchasing decisions involves the consumers' occupations and where they spend their time carrying them out. It is obvious that the investment banking community and those that make up the various trades have different needs, especially when clothing needs are considered. Those retailers who target the former group must concentrate on suits and accessories such as business shirts, ties, and dress shoes.

In today's work environment, changes in appropriate dress have caused many retailers to refocus their inventories. **Casual Friday**, when the business suit is left home, has in many firms spilled over into other days of the week. The emphasis on proper dress, even in the legal profession, has given way to more relaxed business casual clothing all week. Merchants who cater to this group must adjust the inventory levels of more formal attire and begin to stock sports coats, contrasting trousers, open-collared shirts, and slip-ons to serve the needs of male clientele—as well as pant-suits and casual dresses for working women—in order to maximize sales.

Many companies permit employees to "dress down" at least once a week. As this employee goes about her normal job, she is also functioning as a model for the casual apparel that her employer sells.

Another phenomenon that has affected retailers in terms of career clothing needs has been the continuous increase of those working at home. Many consumers spend their days at computers in home offices rather than in traditional workplaces. Jeans and T-shirts and even sleepwear have become standard dress for these people, since they need not interface with others. Because of this ever growing trend of at-home employment, many restaurants must re-address their markets. Office furniture suppliers are finding a greater need for scaled-down desks and chairs to fit home offices, and many have increased their sales because of this new business environment. An examination of retailers such as Staples and Office Depot reveals a significant expansion of the home office departments.

Even in major department stores, the last bastions of proper dress in retailing, the dress code has changed. Selling-floor personnel were once relegated to wearing basic colors and traditional apparel. Now, just about anything goes as long as it reflects good taste.

Merchants must continually reevaluate their consumer markets based on the changing needs of their occupations. Inventories must then be adjusted to satisfy those needs.

Lifestyle Profiles

A great deal of research has been undertaken to examine people's attitudes and lifestyles and how these affect their purchases. Although studies that categorize attitudes and lifestyles surface regularly, none have had as great an impact on retailing as the VALS™ study.

VALS, SRI Consulting Business Intelligence's psychographic segmentation system, is widely used throughout the marketing community. It is regularly updated via surveys that investigate consumer attitudes and motivations. Specifically, the use of VALS assists retailers in:

- Identifying their target markets
- Uncovering what the target group buys and does in their lives
- Locating the areas in which the largest segments of the target market live
- Identifying the best ways in which to communicate with the target groups
- Gaining insight into why the target group acts the way it does

The system categorizes consumers into eight specific profiles. They are *Actualizers, Fulfilleds, Achievers, Experiencers, Believers, Strivers, Makers,* and *Strugglers*. Each classification represents a different set of interests, motivations, and habits for those in the group. For example, the Achievers collectively are attracted to such premium products as innovative electronics, purchase a variety of self-help publications, and are avid readers of business periodicals. Strivers are image focused, spend a great deal on clothing and personal care products, carry a large credit card balance and are avid television watchers. Strugglers, or those with the least amount of financial resources, are loyal brand shoppers, read the scandal tabloids, and clip coupons for purchases.

By understanding these psychographic categories and singling out those that relate to their client base and potential markets, the retailer is better able to determine such factors as location expansion, merchandise assortments, price points, advertising formats, and media consideration.

A greater detailing the VALS concept is available on the Web at www.sric-bi.com/VALS, and in the following diagram.

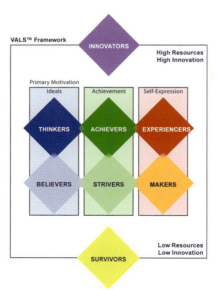

American consumers generally fall into one of these eight profiles.

> **In the News . . .**
>
> The article "In-Store Advertising: Should Psychographic Studies Play a Role?" (on page 128 at the end of this chapter) should be read now to gain a perspective on psychographics.

Income

Although many of the preceding classifications indicate personal consumer preferences based upon such characteristics as lifestyle, age, and occupation, it is an individual's income that ultimately plays the most significant part in whether or not a purchase can be made.

While one might like to purchase a Mercedes Benz, wealth plays an important role regarding the purchase. Similarly, individuals often are motivated by the fashion advertisements in *Elle* magazine. But though the styles are exciting, many must opt for less expensive apparel that will fit their budgets. Even when food is the product in question, income may play an important role. For example, with so much of the population in the workforce there is less time for food preparation. A good alternative would be to buy freshly prepared dinners. Of course, many of these items are pricey and thus limited to those with greater resources; the frozen dinner alternative might be the answer for those with smaller disposable incomes. Brochures that stimulate thinking of vacationing in exotic, far-away shores make many consumers consider taking the plunge. Of course, once costs are examined, it is the affluent who actually take the trip.

Education

Whatever a person's income, his or her level of education may also make a difference in purchasing decisions. The more formally educated are more likely to recognize the need for specific products. For example, advanced degrees provide entry into such fields as law and investment banking. This individual is required to dress a certain way. Politicians and advertising executives, for example, often patronize stores like Brooks Brothers for their clothing.

Additionally, the well educated are more likely to purchase a variety of books. With so many in this class at the upper levels of employment, they find their time too limited to visit bookstores. Instead, the online approach is utilized. Such Web sites as Amazon.com and BarnesandNoble.com are the beneficiaries of the educated market.

With more and more students graduating from college and with increasing numbers going on to graduate and professional schools, the need for retailers to appeal to these groups continues to increase.

Social Class

All over the world, the various nations' populations are divided into separate **social classes**. The distinctions, as we know them in the United States, are based upon such factors as income, goals, education, attitudes, and sometimes birthright. Being born into significant wealth and ongoing social standing that has passed from generation to generation, for example, immediately places offspring in the upper-upper class.

By studying each of the traditional groups that make up class structure, the retailer is able to get a better look at the specific goods and services generally required by them. The retailer can then set up a merchandising and management plan that will have the potential for success.

The American class structure is made up of the upper, middle, and lower classes. Each of these three classifications can be further divided into two subcategories.

Upper Class

This group represents the wealthiest in America. It accounts for approximately 3 percent of the population and is wealthier today than at any other time in history. With the evolution of new technology toward the end of the twentieth century, more citizens have reached billionaire status. Microsoft's Bill Gates, for example, with an estimated wealth of $60 billion, rose from the lower-upper class to achieve this status.

UPPER-UPPER CLASS

This segment of the upper class accounts for about 1 percent of the population. In order to be counted as a member of this group, one's wealth must be inherited. They are the socially elite families in American society. Purchasing is often understated. There is an emphasis on quality, and cost is never a factor. They live in the most affluent enclaves, such as Park Avenue in New York City; South Hampton, New York; and Palm Beach, Florida. Travel is to exotic global destinations, where they often have their own vacation homes. Education is taken at the elite schools at home and abroad. Couture labels, fabulous jewelry, and anything they desire is there for the taking. They are members of country clubs that are restricted to families with considerable prestigious backgrounds.

LOWER-UPPER CLASS

Although members of this group do not have the credentials of the upper-upper class, such as family history, they are often wealthier. They are the **nouveau riche** of our society, having come upon their fortunes through hard work. Rock stars, investment bankers, and business tycoons are part of this group. Their purchases are often extravagant and rarely understated. They are the buyers of couture clothing, luxury automobiles, and lavish travel. Many in this class reveal their successes by indulging themselves in purchases that are obvious to the world. They belong to the wealthiest country clubs—but not those reserved for the upper-upper class families. They have homes in many prestigious locales such as East Hampton, New York, and Beverly Hills, California. They frequent retailers like Bergdorf Goodman and Saks Fifth Avenue, the couture houses abroad, and Harry Winston for their jewels. Travel is taken in places not frequented by the masses, where they often own their own vacation villas. They are considered to be **conspicuous spenders**.

One retailer favored by the upper-upper class is Tiffany & Co.

The lower-middle class frequents value merchants such as Wal-Mart and Sam's.

Middle Class

The middle class accounts for approximately 42 percent of the U.S. population. However, its two segments are distinctively different in terms of their shopping needs.

UPPER-MIDDLE CLASS

This group is considered by many retailers to be the best consumer market in the country. They are concerned with education and often send their children to private schools. They are always trying to gain upward mobility to the lower-upper class. Their financial resources are not unlimited, but they do tend to spend a great deal on expensive, tasteful merchandise. They are the purchasers of luxury cars, designer clothing—albeit not the couture variety—and a host of services. Designer labels such as DKNY, Ralph Lauren, and Calvin Klein are among their favorites, with shopping undertaken at major department stores like Bloomingdale's. They are considered to be intelligent shoppers and often turn to the closeout centers of Neiman Marcus and Saks Fifth Avenue to buy the headline labels at a fraction of the original costs. They are members of country clubs, travel extensively, and spend considerable leisure time on the golf course.

LOWER-MIDDLE CLASS

Distinctly different from those at the upper spectrum of this group, the lower-middle-class has a more modest income and is more cautious about spending. They purchase automobiles that provide them with economy and durability, have a strong sense of value, and are frequent purchasers at stores like Target, Wal-Mart, and Kmart. Off-price centers are also their favorite destinations because they can get more for their dollar. They are the do-it-yourself crowd and flock regularly to stores like Home Depot for their household needs. Although they do travel somewhat, the mode is usually by car to more localized areas. They are loyal sports enthusiasts and attend the games of their favorite teams.

Lower Class

In terms of real income, most Americans continue to occupy the lower class category. With approximately 55 percent of the population, they account for more than half of the consumers in the United States.

UPPER-LOWER CLASS

Without question, price is the most important consideration for this group. Whether it is apparel, home furnishings, food, or anything else, price is first and foremost. They regularly scout the discount outlets and off-price centers for bargains, most often choosing the major chains such as Wal-Mart, Target, and Kmart in which to shop. Wholesale clubs such as Sam's, Costco, and BJ's are other destinations they are likely to patronize for a major portion of their everyday needs. Instead of utilizing the Internet and catalogues as alternatives to brick-and-mortar retailers, many turn to cable television. They are, in fact, the targeted market for home-shopping channels.

LOWER-LOWER CLASS

Shopping needs other than those necessary for survival are unimportant to this group. They will buy clothing only as needed, and then it must be serviceable items. Secondhand and thrift shops are the arenas for many of their purchases.

Family Life Cycle

Another type of methodology that retailers use to assess their markets is the **family life cycle**. This concept is based upon the premise that families can be grouped according to the age and family status of the heads of households. Specifically, it addresses the composition of families and how the specific family units affect such purchases as clothing, accessories, home furnishings, food, automobiles, pharmaceuticals, housing, physical fitness equipment, travel, and recreation.

The classifications within the family life cycle have changed throughout the years. In the early 20th century, most households fell into traditional categories; today, however, household categories include more unconventional segments.

Childless Singles under Age 45

This group represents an excellent market for many retailers. Collectively, they are a group that has a great deal of discretionary income because they support only themselves. After the rent and utilities have been paid for, the remainder of purchasing generally concentrates on clothing, cosmetics, physical fitness products and memberships, recreation, entertainment, dining in restaurants, automobiles, and travel. Those at the upper end of the income scale are generally fashion conscious and often choose marquee designers such as Ralph Lauren, Joseph Abboud, Calvin Klein, Donna Karan, and the wealth of new fashion creators that grace the pages of *Women's Wear Daily*. They generally take their meals in better restaurants, join upscale fitness centers, purchase the latest cosmetics by cosmetologists such as Bobbi Brown, and travel to famous clubs around the world that cater to singles. Value and bargain shopping is not their preoccupation; instead they choose brick-and-mortar merchants or convenient off-site retailers. In terms of automobiles, many fancy BMWs, other foreign cars, and a host of SUVs.

Of course, not everyone in this group is enjoying the financial resources that enable "frivolous" spending. Even though they need only concern themselves with their own needs, the approach to shopping is more cautious for the less affluent. They head for Banana Republic and Gap as well as stores like Ann Taylor. They patronize department stores as well as specialty stores, and they frequent less expensive restaurants. Their automobiles might more likely be American-made sports cars.

Childless Singles 45 and Over

This has become a large segment of the population with more and more individuals opting to remain single. Many maintain their own premises while others participate in shared households, a classification known as **multiple-member/shared households**.

Much like their counterparts who are under age 45, they too live exciting lifestyles without the responsibility of dependents. Many in this group are employed in the new technology fields, are self-employed, or work in the legal, investment banking, and medical professions. They spend in a manner that is similar to those in the preceding group and frequent many of the same retail institutions. Of course, as they age, their purchases tend to become more conservative. They drive Mercedes Benz automobiles, take numerous vacations, and generally spend money on whatever pleases them. Those with less prosperity are still the targets of many merchants because their purchases are only for themselves.

Single Parents

The significant increase in the U.S. divorce rate and the number of unmarried mothers have made this group one that is constantly growing. Members of this group have the task of supporting themselves and children who may or may not live with them. They often have considerable stress in making their incomes last until the next paycheck. Women, in particular, find their discretionary purchasing power eroding. Typically earning less than their male counterparts and burdened with the rearing of children without the benefit of a mate, they find it difficult to make ends meet. Thus, they are the value shoppers who frequent such discounters as Wal-Mart and Target as well as off-price merchants like T.J. Maxx, Burlington Coat Factory, and Marshalls. They generally eat at home and only dine out for special occasions. They purchase modestly priced cars and take limited, less costly vacations. A small segment of the single mother group has better incomes and can therefore spend without as much caution.

Single fathers have similar problems. Unless they are in the high-income group, they are saddled with child support payments and sometimes spousal support, both of which render them unlikely to spend on anything but essentials.

Multiple-Member/Shared Households

This is a fast-growing stage in the family life cycle. With the cost of living spiraling upward, more and more people are choosing to live with others to whom they are not connected by marriage or family. In big cities like New York, Chicago, and San Francisco, where apartment rentals are soaring, several people sharing a single residence has become commonplace.

This is a diverse group that includes singles who live together, eventually planning marriage; members of same-sex relationships; members of the opposite sex without any amorous connections; and two or more sets of single parents whose children reside with them. They are of no particular age group.

Given the diversity of those in this classification, their purchasing characteristics vary considerably. For example, singles who live together with the intention of marrying often have considerable disposable income because of their shared expenses for housing. The arrangement leaves plenty of cash for necessities as well as luxury items. Even more buying potential is in the hands of members of long-term same-sex relationships. They have dual incomes and typically have no plans for child rearing, which could cost a great deal. Those in this arrangement often buy cars like the BMW Z3, wear the best clothing from stores like Barneys, take lavish vacations, and in general are the dream customers for upscale merchants. Of course, spending by the two single-parent families that share common living facilities is usually restricted, making them less attractive to merchants.

Single-Earner Couples with Children

This classification has shown the most radical drop in recent years. Except for those with young children of preschool age, most couples have dual incomes. Even those with young children are opting for day care so that the family income can be maximized. Unless the single earner has a professional career or is in some high-paying arena such as investment banking or new technologies, the income generated doesn't allow for many luxuries. Not only must they provide for themselves, they must address the needs of their offspring.

Those with limited budgets choose their purchases carefully and patronize the retailers that offer value. Discount outlets, off-price stores, and warehouse clubs are the main venues for many of their needs. Once the children are of school age, the situation tends to change with the marital partner returning to work.

For the smaller number of affluent single-earner families, their disposable incomes enable them to buy from traditional retailers where price doesn't play a major role.

Dual-Earner Married Couples with Children

Depending on the ages of the children, these couples have different buying needs and spend their dollars in many different ways. Those with children at home have significant expenses. Some choose preschool programs for their children while others elect for private schooling once their offspring reaches the kindergarten age. The vast majority, of course, utilizes public education.

By comparison with the preceding classification, this group is better off financially and is far more appealing to retailers. With a dual income and one household they are generally able to satisfy their needs. The more affluent may shop at Banana Republic and Gap, while their lower-income counterparts may have to settle for Old Navy.

Two cars are typical for many of these families. They eat out more than families in earlier generations, spend money on family vacations, and often buy on the Internet and from catalogues because their days are filled.

Many in this group are funding their children's college education or are looking to do so in the future. In either case, with the escalating costs of higher education, these families are often termed *cash poor*. College tuition takes a big bite out of their incomes, leaving them less to spend on items other than the basics.

Childless Married Couples

The age groupings in this category range from the young to the elderly. Typically, these couples are better off than those with children since they generally have two incomes and have little responsibility other than themselves. In every age grouping, clothing expenditures, food requirements, automobile choices, entertainment preferences, travel, and home furnishings are easily affordable—although tastes undoubtedly differ. They are usually the purchasers of luxury products and shop at traditional retailers.

Travel is particularly extensive for the older members of this group. A look at the numerous extended cruise itineraries, for example, indicates that there is a need for this type of venture. These couples have the financial capacity and, since they are often retired, the time to enjoy themselves.

Automobiles for most in this group are in the luxury class, with the younger consumers generally choosing European imports such as Audi or BMW. Their older counterparts elect full-sized American cars such as Cadillac or Lincoln.

Empty Nesters

As couples age and their children grow up and move out, many couples enjoy the **empty nester** status. Expenses for this group are minimized and purchasing needs maximized. They often choose to purchase products and services that they couldn't afford in years past. Some families continue to earn dual incomes, making them even more likely to be free spenders. Others become single-income families when one spouse retires.

As the group ages its needs begin to change. Often smaller residences are chosen, country clubs are joined, and travel becomes more extensive. They are still in need of clothing, but their choices might be of a more conservative nature.

With the size of this market constantly growing, more and more vendors are coming to recognize them as a viable segment and are producing goods specifically to meet their desires. Prescription medication is not their only need. There is also a host of goods and services that are still relevant to their lives. Many, for example, are still willing and able to buy fashionable merchandise, although their size requirements may have changed. Liz Claiborne, a collection that features a wealth of different styles aimed at middle-aged women, also produces a larger-sized line for the more mature female. By concentrating on this market, retailers are able to satisfy their loyal customers who have moved into a new grouping.

It should be noted that people move in and out of these lifestyle classifications many times during their lives. As incomes change, so do the needs of their families. No group has members with exactly the same characteristics, as we have discussed. It is therefore imperative for retailers to carefully examine each group in terms of their differences and to utilize other market assessment tools when determining appropriate product mixes.

CONSUMER BEHAVIOR

In addition to examining the demographics of their markets, retailers must consider consumer buying motives and behavior. By undertaking this investigation, they will be better able to appeal to their customer base and prospective clienteles.

Buying Motives

What motivates consumers to purchase? Is it price? Is it to gain a social advantage? Is it quality? Is it for safety reasons? The answer to all of these questions is yes! Is each purchase product based upon a single buying motive? This answer is no! In the case of the purchase of a Jeep

Grand Cherokee, for example, some might consider purchasing it because it is practical. Others might be motivated to buy because of the "coolness" it provides. These are both viable motives for buying. But different people purchase the same product for different reasons. Buying the jeep for practical reasons is known as a **rational motive**. Purchasing the jeep for the purpose of status is known as an **emotional motive**.

Rational Motives

Such factors as practicality, quality, price, durability, serviceability, care, adaptability, and warranties constitute rational buying motives. The very essence of value shopping is based upon the idea that consumers are looking for merchandise that offers many of these qualities. Discounters like Wal-Mart and Target have built enormous retail empires by providing their customers with items that are competitively priced, provide serviceability, and feature quality. Similarly, the off-pricers such as Marshalls and T.J. Maxx offer their customers prices that cannot be duplicated elsewhere. By utilizing the rational approach, these merchants are finding that their sales volume is soaring.

Although rational purchasing has been a constant in many consumer product groups, it hasn't always played as important a role in apparel as it does today. In the 1980s, the **yuppies** (a word used to describe young urban professionals with large incomes) were often called conspicuous spenders. Price was rarely a consideration in their purchasing habits. They bought anything that satisfied their egos and brought status to them. The economic recession at the close of the 1980s dealt a blow to this group, and some believe it responsible for inducing a more rational approach to shopping. Today's young executives, having faced a similar boom-and-bust economy, typically spend more wisely. Although able to afford higher-priced merchandise, a large number may be seen shopping in stores like Old Navy, where fashion and value are featured.

Other goods that are purchased based on rational motives include computers, electronics, packaged food, and home office equipment and supplies. Stores like Office Depot, OfficeMax, Staples, Circuit City, and Best Buy have built mega-retail operations based on rational purchasing principles.

Emotional Motives

Many retailers use emotional motives to target their customers. Merchants realize that by appealing to their customers' desire for prestige and status, they can gain significant profits.

In the case of automobiles, there is a segment of the population that is motivated by status to purchase certain models. A Lexus, Mercedes, or BMW may receive a high performance rating, but it is often the name on the car that drives such a purchase.

Apparel and wearable accessories are other merchandise classifications where prestige often takes the forefront. Would the sales for Ralph Lauren's Polo products be as high if the insignia were removed from the outside of the garments? How successful would the signature bags of Louis Vuitton be if the ever-present logos were taken off the bags? These are vinyl handbags that bring large profits to the company. Similarly, the fabrics, embellishments, handwork, and limited production that make up famous couture creations don't really account for the costs of the garments or their popularity with consumers. It is often the prestige of attending the couture collection openings in Paris, Milan, and London and the chance to be seen by the press that motivates purchases.

Dining in certain restaurants is also a prestigious event. It is often difficult to obtain a reservation at a globally famous restaurant even though the cost of a meal is outrageous. Being seen in such a venue brings enough prestige to the patrons to make the eating expense worthwhile.

Today, retailers all over the world are creating excitement in their stores by adding home furnishing lines that bear the signatures of famous worldwide apparel designers. Names like Ralph Lauren, Versace, Calvin Klein, and Bill Blass are helping these retailers generate sales in departments like bedding and housewares. It should be mentioned that many industry professionals attribute the birth of the prestige label to Pierre Cardin. By capturing the public's attention with his revolutionary bubble dress in the 1950s, he was quickly catapulted into fame. Through his ingenuity, he transformed his business into a fashion empire via the licensing route. It wasn't long before everything from watches and sunglasses to household furnishings bore his signature. Status was now available in more modestly priced merchandise that the masses could afford. By combining rational and emotional purchasing motives, some retailers have been able to appeal to a segment of the population that insists on value but is also motivated to buy merchandise that offers them prestige and status.

Patronage Motives

Patronage motives address where consumers shop. There are numerous factors that make up this motive classification. They include convenience, service, price, salesperson availability, liberal exchange policies, and merchandise assortment. A merchant that offers any or all of these is appealing to the clientele and has established a level of comfort for them. When this comfort level becomes expected by shoppers and the company provides it, the end result is customer loyalty. Knowing exactly what to expect each time they shop, customers return again and again. This is the dream for every merchant.

Not only are brick-and-mortar retailers satisfying their customers with positive shopping experiences, but so are many off-site merchants. With the latter group trying to capture a share of the consumer market that doesn't have time to visit the stores, service has become an important part of the purchasing decision. Shoppers want the convenience of shopping on-line or in catalogues and they also expect speedy delivery. Slow delivery, especially at peak selling periods like the Christmas season, has made many consumers anything but satisfied shoppers.

It is the task of each merchant, whether it is a brick-and-mortar operation or an off-site company, to determine the consumer's needs and to provide them with a level of service that makes them a loyal customer.

Maslow's Hierarchy of Needs

The American psychologist Abraham Maslow conceived a major theory on motivation. His concept, known as **Maslow's Hierarchy of Needs**, has been widely accepted by retailers and other marketers. Maslow theorizes that people attempt to satisfy five levels of needs beginning with the most important (physiological needs) and ending with the least important (self-actualization needs). As individuals reach each level, the next level in the hierarchy is likely to be pursued.

Viewed as a pyramid, the most basic of the levels—at the bottom of the pyramid—are the **physiological needs**, which include such requirements as food, water, shelter, clothing, and sexual satisfaction. Retailers attempt to cash in on these requirements by stocking a host of products to satisfy them.

The next level incorporates the **safety needs**. Automobile salesmen point out the value of air bags to a potential customer. Similarly, life insurance agents underscore the importance of policies that provide for loved ones.

Continuing upward are **social needs**, which merchants address through advertising. Ads that show the benefits of cosmetics, jewelry that makes the wearer more socially appealing, and cars that will affect the social status of the driver all fall into this classification.

At the next level are the **esteem needs**. It is this segment that sells the consumer on such purchases as first-class travel, belonging to upscale health clubs, and cars that will make one the envy of others.

The pinnacle of the scale concerns **self-actualization needs**. The retailer concentrates on products and services that show how individuals may maximize their potential. Education, symphony subscriptions, and self-employment workshops are part of this level.

It should be noted that the bottom level of Maslow's Hierarchy of Needs is the broadest and most attainable. Each subsequent stage becomes narrower, indicating that the higher needs are more difficult to attain.

CONSUMER RESEARCH

The world's largest retail trade association, the National Retail Federation, provides research studies for members.

With all the theories available for retailers to study their target markets, there is often a need to examine research studies that address the potential customers. Major trade associations, such as the National Retail Federation, often undertake these studies. When a major retailer wants to find specific information regarding their own potential customers, the services of an outside agency are often employed or the research may be conducted in-house.

Trade Associations and Organizations

There are numerous trade groups serving the needs of retailers with research studies. These organizations address a host of subjects, the scope of which is dependent on their missions. The National Retail Federation (NRF) is the largest retail organization in the world. Its goal is to serve its membership in every aspect of retailing. Among its many endeavors is research. Studies are regularly conducted and made available to its members, which include some of the largest merchants in the world. By subscribing to the organization, merchants are able to obtain any studies NRF has conducted. By logging on to NRF's Web site, www.nrf.com, would-be members can assess the group's offerings.

Other more specifically oriented trade groups include the Institute of Store Planners (www.ispo.org), the National Association of Sales Professionals (www.nasp.com), the International Mass Retail Association (www.imra.org), and the Fashion Group International (www.fgi.org).

Governmental Resources

Each level of the United States government conducts research involving endless subjects. Included are studies that deliver factual information on consumers. The federal government, through the Census Bureau, provides a wealth of information on population, an area that retailers need to examine with regard to their consumer bases. A great number of important charts, tables, and graphs that concern the population are easily available at the Census Bureau Web site (www.census.gov). An excellent hard-copy source is the Statistical Abstract of the United States, which features the same information and is available at most public libraries.

Market Research Groups

There are numerous research organizations dedicated to conducting studies that provide information on consumer motivation and behavior. Among the better known are SRI International, a consulting firm that specializes in market segmentation systems (www.sri.com), the Gallup organization, which (among other things) offers consumer measurement studies (www.gallup.com), and ACNielsen, the world's largest provider of market research (www.acnielsen.com).

> **Focus on . . .**
> **ACNielsen**

THE ACNIELSEN CORPORATION is a globally structured organization that represents more than 9,000 clients in more than 100 countries. Their expertise lies in the measurement of competitive marketplace dynamics, understanding consumer attitudes and behavior, and developing advanced analytical insights that generate increased sales and profits.

Retail measurement by the organization provides continuous tracking of consumer purchases at the point of sale through scanning technology and in-store audits. Clients that subscribe to its services receive detailed information on actual purchases, market shares, distribution, pricing, merchandising, and promotional activities—all of which are vital to the success of any retail organization. The company also offers consumer panel services that provide detailed information on actual purchases made by household members as well as their retail shopping patterns and demographic profiles. This data is culled from 126,000 households in 18 countries.

In addition to these general studies, the company also engages in customized research. This service includes quantitative and qualitative studies that deliver vital information and insights into consumer attitudes and purchasing behavior. The company believes that taking what consumers say at face value is insufficient. By reading between the lines and grasping the subtle nuances of what is said—or often left unsaid—the analysis is more meaningful for problem solving. Additionally, the company conducts studies that measure customer satisfaction and brand awareness, which is important to the success of the private labels featured by most major retailers. In the case of private-label merchandise, ACNielsen provides test marketing services that launch new products or reposition existing brands. Its overall service helps retail managers to gauge product penetration, evaluate overall product performance, and analyze the effectiveness of promotional endeavors. The company also engages in research that measures a retailer's own brand versus competitive brands.

In-House Research

Many of the retail giants have their own **in-house research** departments. These departments investigate a wide range of areas for the company including consumer research. Identifying potential customers and addressing the problems involved in appealing to them is of paramount importance to any in-house team. Once the problem has been defined and identified, the team is ready to begin the gathering of data. Like their outside counterparts, in-house teams utilize many different tools in finding solutions to the problems they are charged to investigate. These tools are described next.

Questionnaires

The researchers carefully develop a list of questions. The formats used in questionnaires include personal interviews, telephone, mail, and the Internet. The intended audience dictates what format is used. For example, although the Internet is gaining in popularity for consumer research, it is not used when the target market is an older generation. Many senior citizens are either computer illiterate or not interested in the technology. Therefore, this tool probably wouldn't elicit enough responses to make the survey reliable.

Observations

This technique involves watching people and recording their actions. A retailer trying to determine the effectiveness of a new type of visual presentation in the store would use **observation research**. Someone would record the number of individuals who have shown interest in the presentation.

Personal interviews are an important way of gathering consumer information in-house.

Focus Groups

The **focus group**, or consumer panel as it is sometimes called, is a technique in which a retailer invites a small representative group of customers to assemble and answer questions about such areas of concern as merchandise assortments, price points, service, visual presentations, and advertising. These panels are formed either sporadically or on a regular basis. More and more merchants are using the latter approach because it gives them regular feedback on the store.

Research Samples

In order to make any study a meaningful one, it is imperative to select a **research sample** or representative group of the body of people being investigated. Then there is no need to elicit information from each and every customer but only from the fraction of those in the sample. It is very much like the polls used to predict political elections. In a presidential election for instance, the sample used might consist of only 1,000 individuals. If the sample is carefully chosen then the predicted results will likely prove to be right.

Once the sample has been selected and the data has been collected by the chosen methodology, it is time for processing and analysis. It is the analysis that is extremely important. If the data is properly used, then the retailer can make the necessary adjustments that will better serve the needs of the consumer and make the business more profitable.

The power of consumers is such that they will either make or break a retailer's opportunity for success. The extent of competition in retailing gives the shopper what seems like unlimited venues for their selections. If not satisfied by one company, there are many others to choose from until a level of satisfaction is achieved.

CHAPTER HIGHLIGHTS

- The study of demographics provides retailers will a wealth of information that helps them address their customers' needs.
- Since different geographic locations dictate different shopper needs, it is important to understand the specifics of the communities a retailer serves. For example, colder climates will certainly have different merchandise requirements than warmer climates.
- The study of age groups is imperative to determine what the specific needs of each group are. Except for a limited number of products, different ages have different needs.
- Lifestyles generally play an important role in assessing consumer needs. An investment banker and a farmer might have the same annual income of $100,000, but each will spend this money differently.

- The multiple-member/shared household category is one of the fastest growing segments of the family life cycle.
- Consumers make their buying decisions based on rational or emotional motives. The retailer must determine which plays the more important part in purchases of the goods offered.
- The retailer must study Maslow's Hierarchy of Needs in order to better serve the needs of potential customers.
- Consumer research is accomplished in many different ways, which include in-house research, outside marketing research firms, and trade associations.
- The vast majority of consumer research is accomplished through the use of questionnaires, observations, and focus groups.

IMPORTANT RETAILING TERMS

baby boomer (109)
casual Friday (113)
conspicuous spender (116)
demographics (108)
emotional motive (121)
empty nester (120)
esteem needs (123)
family life cycle (117)
focus group (125)
generation X (109)
generation Y (109)
in-house research (124)
Maslow's Hierarchy of Needs (122)
multiple-member/shared household (118)
National Retail Federation (108)
nouveau riche (116)
observation research (125)
patronage motive (122)
physiological needs (122)
rational motive (121)
research sample (125)
safety needs (122)
self-actualization needs (123)
social class (115)
social needs (122)
yuppie (121)

FOR REVIEW

1. Is it possible for a retailer to plan so perfectly that there will not be any merchandise left for markdowns? If so, how can this be accomplished?
2. What is meant by the term *demographics*?
3. What source might a retailer use first to find out general information about the portion of the U.S. population that might affect its business?
4. Why is it important for Web site retailers to learn about the different geographic concentrations in the United States?
5. How important is it for merchants to study the needs of different age classifications in his or her trading area?
6. In what ways did companies like Pottery Barn change the nature of home furnishing retailing?
7. How has casual Friday changed the merchandising philosophies at some major retailers?
8. Why is the study of lifestyles so important for the retailer to understand?
9. Explain the VALS concept and how it helps retailers with their merchandise planning.
10. Are there any other factors besides income that are needed to determine the type of products that a consumer will be likely to purchase?
11. How does the lower-upper class differ from the upper-upper class in their purchasing habits?
12. Which social class is considered to be the conspicuous spenders in our society?
13. Which social class makes up the majority of the population in the United States?
14. What is meant by the classification "multiple-member/shared households"?
15. Differentiate between rational and emotional motives.
16. Can the same product choice be influenced by both an emotional and a rational motivation?
17. What does the term *patronage motive* mean?
18. According to Maslow, which needs must be first satisfied before one can move on to the next stage?

AN INTERNET ACTIVITY

Select one of the Web sites listed in the Consumer Research section of this chapter and determine what type of service is provided to the retailer. After you have logged onto the Web site of your choice, prepare a paper that addresses the following:

- The overall mission of the Web site
- The cost, if any, to gather information from the site
- The different types of information provided
- The depth of the information available
- Your impression of the Web site's assistance in providing research information

Your response should be not more than three double-spaced typed pages.

EXERCISES AND PROJECTS

1. Prepare a list of questions that could be used in a survey to determine whether a ladies' clothing retailer in your community should expand into menswear. An actual questionnaire takes a great deal of refining and input from more than one

individual, but your assignment is only to write the questions that might be used. Include ten questions that you consider important to the survey. Each should be multiple choice, giving the respondent three or four options to choose from.

2. Select a retailer in your community and determine to which social class or classes it is appealing. Construct a chart and record the following information: name of store, location, type of store, merchandise assortment, and price lines. In a summary statement, include which social class or classes are being targeted and discuss your reasons for this conclusion.

THE CASE OF PRICE REPOSITIONING

Sibena is a 15-unit ladies' specialty chain located in Nebraska. Headquartered in Omaha and with stores within a 200-mile radius, it opened its doors 25 years ago and has been a successful venture. Throughout the years, the customer base has been extremely loyal. Sibena provides excellent customer service and merchandise assortments that have always satisfied the needs of its clientele, resulting in excellent profits for the owners. The price points for the company are generally moderate, with a smattering of higher-priced merchandise in each of its classifications. For example, the bulk of the sweater inventory features items priced from $30 to $50, with just a few items marked as high as $75.

This region of the country has begun to realize greater prosperity. Sales have never been stronger. During their semiannual analysis of the sales figures, buyers recognized a fast turnover of the higher-priced items. Merchandise at the upper price points had begun to check out even faster than the bulk of the inventory.

At the semiannual meeting of the management team, a new merchandising approach was introduced. Beverly Nadler, the general merchandising manager, offered a plan that would change the price structure at Sibena. The new concept eliminated the lower price points and featured a much more expensive line of merchandise. Some agreed to the repositioning of price points; however, the general consensus was to proceed slowly. After considerable discussion, the idea was tabled until the new concept could be further studied.

Questions

1. Should the company desert its present pricing structure in favor of the new idea? Why or why not?
2. How should the management team go about determining if the plan would be successful?

Teen Panel Reflects Shifting Spending Habits
Jeanine Poggi

JUNE 11, 2007

Teens are spending less of their part-time paychecks and allowance on clothes and accessories and more on filling up their tanks and eating out.

This was the consensus of a group of 17- and 18-year-olds from Ramapo High School in Franklin Lakes, N.J., during a teen panel at Piper Jaffray's Annual Consumer Conference in New York last week.

With a majority of high school students juggling school, extracurricular activities and organized sports, the mall is no longer the number-one after-school or weekend destination. Instead, teens are opting to spend their free time at restaurants, working at a part-time job or at friends' houses.

The 17 students on the panel said that when they eat out, they choose restaurant chains such as Chili's, California Pizza Kitchen, Houlihan's and TGI Friday's. But the most popular food craze among the panelists is sushi, and they cannot make it through the day without a trip to Starbucks.

These teens haven't given up apparel shopping altogether, however. Most said they spent the same amount on clothes this year as they did last year, and would stock up for the back-to-school season.

When they do hit the mall, they prefer to shop at specialty stores over department stores, citing specialty stores' inviting environment and cooler image, as well as cheaper prices.

Urban Outfitters, Free People, Pacific Sunwear, Hollister, Ruehl, American Eagle Outfitters and Quicksilver are among their favorite stores.

The young men said that "every guy at school has a pair of Birkenstocks," while the young women said they wore surf-inspired Reefs. But none of them seemed to get the Crocs craze, saying they would "never wear plastic shoes with holes to school."

Most of the panelists are heading to college in the fall, and they are looking for zip-up hoodies, jeans and layering items. Denim was still a staple, since it is easy to wear, comfortable and can be dressed up or down, the panelists said. But these teens were looking for quality, not quantity, in denim purchases, and chose True Religion and Seven Jeans.

MAC is the most sought-after cosmetics brand in the "higher-quality" beauty products for its bright colors and cheap prices. But the young women also liked the good-for-your-skin qualities of Bare Escentuals and Nars and Clinique.

When asked what brands or trends filled their closets five years ago, that they would no longer wear, the female panelists all said Juicy Couture T-shirts and Coach.

One panelist said she had a collection of small handbags when she was younger, but now had "better things" to spend her money on. The young women said Coach had become too preppy and was better suited for an older customer. While rising prices at the pump may affect how their parents allocate funds, teens say that while they may be spending more on gas, they are not curbing their spending to fill up their tanks.

"When I get a paycheck, I will still spend the money, regardless if I have gas to get home," one 18-year-old Best Buy employee said.

Most of the teens said they did not even know what the prices were until they finished filling up their tanks and saw the hole in their wallet.

Having their own cars gives them the freedom to do more things, leaving less time for television or surfing the Internet. All the panelists said they watched less television this year than they did last year, and rarely listened to the radio since they had iPods.

And while the newspaper industry has feared the death of print, more than half the teens claimed they read newspapers frequently.

But what teens are really searching for is a place to "hang out" with their friends; a place that is like their living room, but without the parents.

"There are no places that really cater to us. All you investors get us a place we can go to just lay back," one male panelist said.

In-Store Advertising: Should Psychographic Studies Play a Role?
Bill Gerba

SEPTEMBER 20, 2006

Whether you're working with digital signs or static POP displays, creating in-store advertising content is hard work. Aside from making sure that the appropriate information about product quality, price, and availability is properly conveyed, marketers need to consider the design and readability of the message, target specificity, and how the content contributes to the retail experience. Plus, you have to ensure that the in-store ad is effective during the 3-7 second "first moment of truth," when a shopper begins to make her purchase decision. In the course of discussing these challenges with some of our customers, we happened upon a subject that periodically makes the rounds in the advertising world: psychographic segmentation.

The basics of psychographic segmentation are pretty straightforward, and I particularly like how NetMBA defines the term:

Psychographic segmentation groups customers according to their lifestyle. Activities, interests, and opinions (AIO) surveys are one tool for measuring lifestyle. Some psychographic variables include:

- Activities
- Interests
- Opinions
- Attitudes
- Values

In the broader realm of marketing and advertising, psychographic segmentation focuses on identifying the likes, opinions and attitudes of a particular group of people and creating messages that cause people to identify with those ideas. This is distinct from *demographic* segmentation strategies like sociocultural and socioeconomic targeting, which look at customers based on age, gender, etc. (for example, Wal-Mart's recent announcement that they would design the store experience around certain key demographics). If we were in academia, I might mention how the concept of "archetypes," or prototypical ways of representing larger (and less homogeneous) groups, has a long and storied tradition in the field of human cognitive psychology, starting with the work of Carl Jung in the early 20th century, and leading up to many of the most prevalent models for learning and memory in use today. Unfortunately, one of the main academic arguments against archetypes, namely that you need large numbers of them and a deep level of detail for each one, can also limit their practicality in the advertising world.

Despite these challenges, properly applied psychographics can play a powerful part in developing effective digital signage content and other in-store advertising techniques. At-retail media is dynamic and visually-oriented, and digital signs in a high-traffic location may be viewed by hundreds or even thousands of individuals from any number of different demographics. Individual target specificity in this scenario is impossible, and demographic targeting could be very difficult as well. However, what if the content were able to address multiple demographic constituencies by addressing their *psychographic* commonalities? Sound like a bunch of psycho-babble? Here's an example of how it might work in the store:

Imagine that you want to advertise a packaged rice side dish on digital signs in a national supermarket chain, where the customers span multiple disparate demographic groups. Instead of creating separate versions of a commercial spot focusing on demographic differences (e.g. showing different races, different ethnic foods on the table, different social classes, etc.), you might instead create a single version of the ad using images catering to a particular psychographic profile. For example, across multiple demographic groups there is a feeling that homemade meals are more valuable or somehow better than a pre-packaged or take-out meal. Home-cooked meals require effort on the part of the cook, and therefore represent not only sustenance, but also the value of the cook's time and their care for the meal being delivered.

In this example, our target customer is someone trying to recreate these positive feelings in their home, regardless of that shopper's age, gender, family size, or how much time they have to prepare dinner. To reach them, we might utilize a group of images (featuring different demographic groups) showing the product being cooked, featured as part of a larger home-made meal, and bringing a family, a group of friends, or a couple on a dine-in date closer together. By associating the product with concepts, attitudes and opinions that are popular across many demographic groups, a single spot can do the work of many. This technique also reduces the amount of content that needs to be developed and managed, which in turn helps to rein in costs and reduce complexity (an important but often overlooked detail of large retail networks).

There are some who put psychographic segmentation in the same category as phrenology or psychoanalysis—popular theories that seemed to be confirmed at one time, but haven't held up over subsequent decades of more careful study. I think that most of the dissent comes up when trying to use psychographic segmentation to create artificial archetypes of the "average" consumer, family, etc. The thought here is that if you fill your product packages with images of totally unremarkable, average people engaged in the desired activities (and hence sharing the same interests, etc.), the product will be able to resonate with the widest possible buying audience. You won't necessarily be compelling the strongest identification with your product, but instead you'll cast a very wide, shallow net. That's the theory, anyway.

In practice, and as illustrated by this great entry at Design Observer, this method doesn't really work very well, especially not in such an ethnically and racially diverse country as the US. Instead of images of "average" people, we instead get creepy images of bland, blank-staring, and wholly unremarkable people that seem "permanently arrested in an incessant state of euphoria," as Design

Observer so accurately notes. Some of these images are even computer-generated, using an algorithm designed to blend the traits of various ethnic groups into a single portrait. That creepy kid on the front of a box of Life cereal? Yeah, I'm willing to bet that's supposed to be a psychographic archetype.

Fortunately, the tendency to use psychographics as a generic, thoughtless substitute for demographic segmentation seems to be going away, and more savvy marketers are successfully employing psychographic techniques to communicate values, ideals and opinions to the right group of shoppers. And while demographic segmentation will likely continue to be the primary means for creating targeted messages on large digital signage networks, the proper use of psychographics offers the opportunity to do more with less. By building the imagery of different ideals and opinions into content that can appeal to multiple demographic groups, an in-store advertising campaign can be expected to deliver greater relevance to consumers, lower production cost, and higher incremental sales lift for marketers.

CHAPTER 6
Multiculturalism in Retailing

After you have completed this chapter, you should be able to discuss:

- Why the "one size fits all" philosophy in retailing is no longer appropriate for today's operations
- The demographics of the multicultural consumer markets
- The anticipated growth of different ethnicities in the near and distant future
- Which exclusive arrangements some retailers have made in terms of merchandise offerings
- The two major ethnicities that are primary markets for specific food products
- The different advertising media used to attract the multicultural markets to the retailer's stores
- Which factors must be considered by retail advertisers when creating ad campaigns
- Why it is better to use specialized agencies rather than the mainstreamers when planning advertising
- The importance of minority staffing in retail operations

As we just learned in the preceding chapter, retailers of every size and classification must continuously assess their clienteles and potential consumers to make certain they are completely aware of their demographics and behavioral motivations. By doing so, retailers are able to make adjustments to their merchandise mixes, promotional endeavors, shopping services, and any other practices that will best motivate the consuming public to patronize them. This is where the concept of **multiculturalism** comes into play.

Whereas the past principles and practice of most retailers were once designed with a **"one size fits all" philosophy**, today's diverse customer base requires a much different approach to determine consumer needs. In this era of **ethnic diversity**, it is essential that the different ethnicities be carefully evaluated to determine if their wants and needs are being met. By engaging in multicultural research, retailers will learn how to best appeal to the segments of the population they serve.

Today, retailers in many parts of the United States have large minority populations in their trading areas. There are many different **ethnic minorities** that make up the population, but

Minority shoppers make up a large part of the consumer population.

three top the list in terms of numbers and buying power: African Americans, Latinos, and Asian Americans. Each group has shown significant growth in recent years and often requires products that differ from those required by the mainstream consumer. Thus, careful analysis of these groups has been undertaken by most of the major department stores, chain organizations, supermarkets, direct marketing merchants, and others in order to ensure that they are aware of how best to serve these groups.

Every part of a retailer's operations—including merchandise offerings, advertising and promotional endeavors, visual merchandising, staffing, and so forth—must be examined in terms of multicultural appeal to determine if it is on the right track to maximize profits in today's **diverse marketplace**.

In the News . . .

An excellent article entitled "Retail Has Room to Grow in Ethnic Markets" (found at the end of this chapter on page 146) should be read at this time.

DEMOGRAPHIC ANALYSIS

A likely starting point in the retailers' quest to understand the size and scope of minority segments of the population is the study of demographics. By learning about population characteristics and traits, appropriate planning can take place.

Major retailers often use outside marketing research firms to assess population trends and make recommendations regarding the best ways to attract the principal **ethnicities** to patronize their operations. Once such research group is Allied Media Corp., the subject of the next *Focus* feature.

Focus on . . .
Allied Media Corp.

IN AN INDUSTRY REPLETE WITH AGENCIES that primarily service mainstream companies, Allied Media Corp. (AMC) is one devoted exclusively to multicultural communication. Today it is extremely important for companies, especially retailers, to reach the expanding marketplace for ethnic populations, and AMC has been at the forefront of such endeavors. Specifically, they supply advertisers wishing to reach the various ethnic markets with a variety of programs. Whether it is the African-American, Hispanic, Asian-American, or any other important ethnic consumer group, AMC is capable of assessing media outlets that best serve them and of developing plans that range from market research to creative production to single ads and campaigns.

The company's methodologies include the following:

- Developing market research plans for ethnic markets that help clients achieve their goals
- Offering media consulting that takes the clients' campaigns from initial concept through actual execution

- Placing media orders, collecting tear sheets, and monitoring the media outlets to make certain that advertising commitments are implemented in a timely manner
- Managing a company's communications issues to make certain that good press relations are maximized
- Providing professional production for both print and broadcast advertising
- Making available direct marketing consumer lists that zero in on the ethnic consumers who meet the client's requirements

Its expertise has made AMC one of the leading companies that can deliver a client's message and bring about positive results.

• •

The giants in the industry may also maintain **in-house research** divisions that conduct their own investigations, or they may work in conjunction with independent research groups to make the studies. Whatever approach is followed, it is likely to begin by studying the number, potential **buying power**, and **household mean income** of different ethnic populations.

A likely starting place for demographic analysis is the Census Bureau, which conducts surveys of the general population every 10 years. Even if the figures are not current, researchers can scientifically estimate the approximate numbers for a particular time. With the most recent survey numbers dating back to the 2000 census, adjustments must be made to bring the figures up to date.

Using the 2000 figures as an example, we can assess the importance of the three largest minority groups in contrast with the Caucasian population and study these groups for their relevance to the present time. The findings, based upon a general population of 293 million, are as follows.

Population (millions)

Caucasians	216.9
African Americans	36.4
Latinos	35.3
Asian Americans	11.9

Buying Power (billions of dollars)

Caucasians	6,219.8
African Americans	572.1
Latinos	452.4
Asian Americans	296.4

Household Mean Annual Income (dollars)

Caucasians	61,237
African Americans	40,068
Latinos	42,410
Asian Americans	70,221

Other research is used to augment the figures derived from the Census Bureau's findings. This is often in the form of original research involving such approaches as questionnaires, focus groups, and/or observation instruments.

Such research has been conducted by ACNielsen, with its SCANTRACK ethnic service that evaluates the effectiveness of micro-marketing efforts targeted to population segments with specific ethnic characteristics; Unilever; Meredith Integrated Marketing, a communications marketing organization; and NuAmerica, an agency that specializes in minority promotion. The following observations have been made.

Los Angeles is home to the American Apparel headquarters.

- The vast majority of the ethnic population resides in five states.
- The six major Hispanic markets are Los Angeles, Miami, San Antonio, Chicago, New York City, and Houston; and the four largest African American markets are Atlanta, Baltimore/Washington, Chicago, and Memphis.
- By 2010, minorities are expected to constitute a full third of the American population.
- Hispanic buying power is expected to reach $1 trillion by the end of this decade.
- By 2020, the three major ethnicities are expected to have grown at six times the rate of the nonethnic population.
- By 2050, one in four workers will be Hispanic.

Given these figures and the previous observations, it is evident that retailers serving areas of substantial minority population must develop a marketing strategy to attract these groups to their operations.

STRATEGIES FOR CAPTURING THE MULTICULTURAL MARKETS

If retailers cling to their "one size fits all" marketing strategies for attracting new consumers to their stores, catalogues, and Web sites, then they will most likely fall short in their efforts to capture ethnically diverse **market segments**. In advertising, visual presentation, staffing, merchandise assortments, and all other practices, plans must be altered to make certain that multicultural communities are properly taken into account.

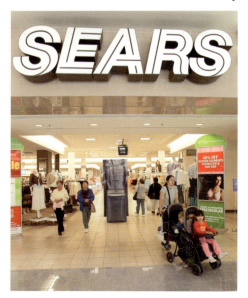

Sears is making major efforts to appeal to minority shoppers.

In the News...

"How Do You Say 'Got Milk' en Español?" (on page 147 at the end of this chapter) is an article that explores how to market American brands to a diverse Hispanic immigrant population. It should be read now to gain a better appreciation of the problems associated with multicultural marketing.

Merchandising

No matter what the product classification might be, African Americans, Latinos, Asian Americans, and other minorities often require different products to fill their needs than does the general Caucasian population. To motivate these ethnic groups to buy, retailers must develop specific merchandise assortments for apparel and accessories, cosmetics and fragrances, and foods. The approach should involve either **merchandise exclusivity** or the promotion of well-known brands.

In the fashion arena, which accounts for significant sales from ethnic minorities, companies such as Sears, JCPenney, Target, and Wal-Mart are making significant adjustments to their operations to make certain that they are motivating the diverse populations who might purchase from them. Table 6.1 addresses the ways in which many retailers are actively pursuing the Hispanic population in the United States.

Apparel and Accessories

In the fashion industry, more and more retailers are entering into contractual agreements with celebrities of different ethnicities. Kohl's, a Wisconsin-based merchant, seems to have hit the jackpot with collections designed by Cuban native Daisy Fuentes. With a significant following of Latinos who became familiar with her first as news anchor at Telemundo and then as host of *MTV Latino*, her name became one with whom this ethnicity could relate. Together with Kohl's, she introduced collections of apparel, jewelry, handbags, swimwear, and other fashion products. These offerings helped to increase the Hispanic customer base for the store.

Although exclusive arrangements such as the Daisy Fuentes–Kohl's partnership are becoming more and more popular in the retail arena, this is not the only route by which apparel and accessories can be designed and targeted to reach multicultural audiences. Many other ethnic personalities from the entertainment world have entered the fashion market with collections of their own.

Daisy Fuentes restricts her collection exclusively to Kohl's.

The Hispanic market has been enriched with the designs of guitarist and singer Carlos Santana as well as one of the hottest Latina actresses, Jennifer Lopez. Their collections are being featured in numerous stores across the country, not in just one retail organization as in the case of Daisy Fuentes. Their brands, and others, have caught fire with the Hispanic community and sometimes "cross over" to other market segments who admire their talents.

There are two marquee names notable in the African-American fashion design arena: Sean "Diddy" Combs and Russell Simmons have taken the fashion world by storm. The former's apparel line, Sean John, is an enormous success with both African Americans and other consumer segments. The latter's efforts, under the Phat Fashions labels Phat Farm and Baby Phat, are being successfully sold all over the country. Each has more than reached its anticipated sales goals.

Asian Americans have long established themselves as design forces in apparel and accessories. Award-winning designers such as Anna Sui and Vera Wang, in particular,

Sean "Diddy" Combs has taken the fashion arena by storm.

TABLE 6.1
COURTING THE HISPANIC CONSUMER

RANK	STORE	PERCENTAGE	REMARKS
1	Wal-Mart	56	"Hispanics have a greater affinity for Wal-Mart than any identifiable segment of the U.S. population," H. Lee Scott, chief executive officer, said at a conference. He pointed out that over 1,000 Wal-Mart stores have predominantly Hispanic shoppers, and that his organization is working to continue to reach out to Hispanic consumers.
2	Target	34	Earlier this year, ImpreMedia, the number-one Spanish-language newspaper and online publisher, said its flagship publication, *La Opinión*, had entered a multiyear partnership with Target that calls for the retailer's ad inserts to be placed in *La Opinión* and *La Opinión Contigo*, two of its Los Angeles-based newspapers. Target operates nearly 100 stores in the L.A. area, the largest Hispanic market in the country.
3	JCPenney	20	In July, JC Penney presented three Hispanic students with college scholarships—each worth $15,000 at Univision's annual Premios Juventud awards show for exceptional youth. Penney's is the official retail sponsor for Premios Juventud. The company is also taking other strides to reach its Hispanic consumers: Last year, six of its associates were featured in "Samos J.C. Penney," a special advertising section in *People en Español*.
4	Kmart	20	In August of 2003, the Troy, Mich.-based retailer, owned by Eddie Lampert's Sears Holdings Corp., unveiled its exclusive Thalia brand at select stores nationwide. The collection, created by Mexican pop star Thalía Sodi, is aimed at a young, female ethnic audience. *Hispanic Market Weekly* said in June that, in an effort to connect with Hispanic consumers, Kmart has returned to a staple: The Blue Light Special is back.
5	Dollar General	19	With nearly 1,400 of its 8,000-plus stores located in Texas and Florida alone, Dollar General is getting the word out to southern Hispanic communities in the U.S. The company prides itself on a diverse employee workforce. "We recognize that diversity is a business imperative" reads the firm's mission statement. The retailer's stores average roughly 6,900 square feet, and 30 percent of merchandise is priced at $1 or less.
6	Dollar Tree	18	At Dollar Tree, specific items may change weekly, but one thing's for sure: "Every item you find in our stores is priced at $1.00 (or less), every day," according to the company. Dollar Tree currently has more than 3,200 locations across the U.S. The *Arizona Republic* reported earlier this year that the Phoenix metro area has witnessed a number of dollar-store chains popping up in order to cater to the Valley's growing Hispanic population.

RANK	STORE	PERCENTAGE	REMARKS
7	Sears	17	Though Sears Holdings Corp.'s Hispanic magazine, called *Nuestra Gente* (*Our People*), shut down in 2005, the company hasn't slowed in its outreach to Hispanic shoppers. Sears was one of the first retailers to market credit cards to Latinos: The store card's section of the Web site provides the option of reading details entirely in Spanish.
8	Kohl's	16	Kohl's Corp. has taken on well-known Hispanic entertainers to help lift its awareness within Hispanic communities. Actress Daisy Fuentes has an exclusive collection with Kohl's, including sleepwear, shoes and clothing. And 30-year veteran journalist Cristina Saralegui, who is recognized as one of the most influential role models for Hispanic women, signed on in January to feature a line of home furnishings called Casa Cristina.
9	Best Buy	15	According to Forrester Research's Hispanic Consumer Technographics report, Minneapolis-based Best Buy has almost 2.8 million Spanish language-preferring Hispanic customers. And in August, Best Buy's executive vice-president of emerging business and strategy, Kal Patel, was the opening keynote speaker for the Hispanic Retail 360 Summit. "The fabric of America is changing. And that means the fabric of our company must change," Patel said.
10	Macy's	15	Macy's recently embarked on a promotional campaign that included spots targeting Hispanic consumers. According to its most recent Diversity Report: "It's critical to our business success to grow our relationships with our multicultural core customers. To solidify those relationships, we strive to integrate diversity into five critical business areas: work force, marketing, communications, supply chain and strategic community partnerships."
11	Sam's Club	15	Wal-Mart's version of the warehouse-retail-chain format also ranked highly with Hispanic consumers. Last year, select Sam's stores in Florida, Illinois, New Jersey, Nevada, and Texas began carrying TúYo Mobile phones. The provider is IDT Telecom's prepaid wireless service specifically designed for the mobile communication needs of Hispanic consumers. Advertisements in local Spanish-language newspapers were placed to promote the service.
12	Family Dollar	14	Matthews, N.C.–based Family Dollar has worked hard to place its locations in areas that cater to Hispanic consumers. For example, the company, which opened a location in Pecos, N.M., in June, said it chose Pecos for a new store based on demographics, proximity to competition, and ethnicity. The company operates more than 6,400 stores in the U.S.—a typical store format ranges from 7,500 to 9,500 square feet.

Note: Top retail destinations of Hispanic consumers as assessed by Scarborough Research. Stores with identical percentages are listed alphabetically.

Flori Roberts cosmetics is in the business of catering to African-American women.

have regularly captured the attention of their consumer counterparts as well as other market segments.

Cosmetics and Fragrances

With a wealth of different products ranging from the popular-priced varieties found in pharmacies to the more costly varieties marketed in department stores, sales have soared for cosmetics and fragrances produced with specific ethnicities in mind. Cosmetics in particular have become important products because people of color require specific formulas and colorations to enhance their complexions.

Leading the way are those products targeted toward the African-American market. The offerings come from two different manufacturing groups. One group is companies that are strictly in the business of creating products for ethnic minorities, and the other consists of well-known manufacturers who produce cosmetic collections for both the mainstream market and for the ethnic market. Flori Roberts and Patti LaBelle are examples of companies that produce products exclusively for minorities. Bobbi Brown is just one of many cosmetic companies that create product lines for mainstream America and the multicultural markets.

The Hispanic community, with complexions similar to those of Caucasians, often purchase mainstream brands. However, brands such as Zalia—featured in the next *Focus* segment and created by Monica Ramirez, who is of Peruvian descent—are capturing a large percentage of the Hispanic market.

Focus on . . .
Zalia

A FIRST-GENERATION AMERICAN OF PERUVIAN DESCENT who achieved fame as a beauty pageant winner and a professional makeup artist, Monica Ramirez realized her vision and dream with the creation of a cosmetics line called Zalia. Her frustration with the limited products that were available for Latinas motivated her to correct the situation. After extensive research, Monica founded the company that today is one of the leading firms dedicated to providing Hispanic women with products best suited for their skin tones.

By dedicating her time to product refinement and promoting the line through personal attendance at charitable functions, Monica has advanced her philosophy of self-esteem, self-growth, and success for her Latina sisters. In addition to reaping the benefits of the company's profitability, she also re-invests 3 percent of its profits to charities that help Latinas and entrepreneurs.

Unlike other companies that have entered into exclusive relationships with major retailers, Zalia sells its products to department and specialty stores as well as through its own Web site, www.zalia.com.

• •

Although sales of specific cosmetics for the Asian-American consumer are insignificant in comparison to those of African-American and Hispanic products, they are starting to gain some momentum. Zhen Cosmetics and Skinlight Cosmetics Ltd. have joined the fray and have achieved moderate success.

Food Products

With specific tastes and appetites for foods that are not typically found in food markets, ethnic foods have become an extremely important category to a growing list of supermarkets and specialty food merchants.

Whereas apparel and cosmetics are major specialty items for the African-American population, their desire for certain ethnic foods is not generally a must. For canned goods and other packaged products, where packaging plays an important role in attracting attention, the fact that African Americans speak English makes the use of other languages on the packages unnecessary.

In contrast, the Hispanic and Asian-American populations are major purchasers of food products. Not only are their food requirements specific to their ethnic eating habits, the need to label the foods in different languages makes marketing them more involved for the manufacturers and merchandising them more difficult for food retailers.

The *bodega* is a small independent grocery store that caters to the Hispanic population.

The Hispanic community spends more on food purchases than the non-Hispanic communities. With their households generally larger, they reportedly spend about 17.5 percent of their disposable incomes on flour, rice, sugar, fats, and oils. Although they most often patronize the major supermarkets in their areas, they also buy their foods at local **bodegas** (small independent stores that are owned by and cater to Latinos). In both of these retail classifications, the goods sold generally include Spanish versions of the package's messages. With the size of this market so large, food producers are willing to provide such special labeling.

It is the Asian-American communities that have the best assortment of specialty foods available to them. In both supermarkets and specialty food stores, Chinese, Korean, Vietnamese, and other minorities are able to get all of the foods they require for their diets. As the size of these populations increases, the necessity for their traditional foods also continues to increase.

Retailers in African-American, Hispanic, and Asian-American trading areas must regularly evaluate the sizes of their customer bases and stock sufficient assortments to satisfy their needs.

Advertising

In trading areas that have large percentages of minority consumers, generic advertising is no longer considered appropriate. In fact, ethnic radio, television, and newspapers today reach more than 64 million people, about half of whom prefer them to the mainstream press. Whether the advertising is in print or broadcast format, its production must carefully consider the use of minority images, written messages that utilize language that will capture the attention of the **multicultural markets**, and spoken words in the native tongue of these consumers. Cultural sensitivity is extremely important in developing such ads.

A mix of newspapers, magazines, radio, television, and direct marketing pieces should be used to make certain that all constituencies are addressed. African Americans, Latinos, and Asian Americans each have their own newspapers and magazines as well as broadcast outlets that specifically appeal to their needs. The following are some of the considerations necessary to maximize the effectiveness of an advertising campaign.

Newspapers

First and foremost is the selection of the right newspapers to reach the retailer's targeted audiences. Each of the three major ethnicities has a significant number of newspapers that are directed toward it. In New York City, where there are a significant number of African Americans, the *Amsterdam News* leads the way; in Philadelphia it is the *Philadelphia New Observer*, and in Michigan it is the *Michigan Citizen*. Of course, in most other parts of the country with large minority populations, there are usually ethnically oriented newspapers in which retailers can place their advertising campaigns.

The *Amsterdam News* leads the way in advertising to African Americans.

Similarly, Latinos and Asian Americans each have their own consumer newspapers. In the Asian communities, where so many different languages are spoken, there are Chinese, Korean, and other newspapers.

In addition to choosing the appropriate newspapers, care must be exercised to create ads that speak directly to these consumers. Models in ads, for example, should be African American, Hispanic, or Asian American as appropriate. The advertising copy must use the language with which these consumers are familiar. Using a layout that was initially intended for the general population and merely inserting minority images in place of Caucasian figures is not sufficient. By contracting with agencies—such as NUAMERICA in New York City—that specialize in ethnic advertising and marketing, advertising is more likely to bring results.

Magazines

JET magazine is a leader in the African-American community.

The number of ethnic minority magazines continues to grow in the United States.

Two of the major ones are *JET* and *Ebony*, both produced by Johnson Publishing Company. They reach African-

TABLE 6.2
TOP 10 HISPANIC MAGAZINES

Rank	Title	Publisher	Total Dollars	% Share of Dollars
1	People en Español	Time, Inc.	$38,651,534	28.5%
2	Latina	Latina Media Ventures, LLC	$27,088,261	20.0%
3	Selecciones	Reader's Digest	$14,811,300	10.9%
4	TV y Novelas	Editorial Televisa	$10,852,270	8.0%
5	Vanidades	Editorial Televisa	$10,126,050	7.5%
6	Hispanic Business	Hispanic Business, Inc.	$8,312,894	6.1%
7	Healthy Kids en Español	Meredith Corporation	$6,932,493	5.1%
8	Ser Padres	Meredith Corporation	$6,787,300	5.0%
9	Hispanic Magazine	Hispanic Publishing Associates	$6,507,525	4.8%
10	Vista	Vista Publishing Corp.	$5,625,080	4.1%

American audiences all over the United States and are excellent places to advertise products targeted to this audience. Other high-profile publications directed African-American audiences include *Essence*, *Black Men*, and *Black Enterprise*.

Equally important are the Hispanic magazines, which include *Latina*, *People en Español*, *Selecciones*, and *Vanidades*. Like their African-American counterparts, these publications feature a wealth of product advertisements. Table 6.2 lists the top-ranked Hispanic magazines.

Rounding out the ethnic minority magazine offerings are the Asian-American publications such as *Jade*, *Hyohen*, *Audrey*, *Asiance*, and *aMagazine*. Because there are many different languages spoken by the Asian community, there is a wealth of different magazines in each of the major languages.

As in the case of newspaper advertising, attention must be paid to properly creating the layouts that will achieve the best sales results.

Television

When television advertising is used to reach non-Hispanic minority communities, there are not any specific stations that directly focus on them. As a rule, the audiences are general in nature. If the commercials are to attract minority shoppers, then they must have some elements that "speak to" those markets. For example, the models in the commercials should show a mix of ethnicities. If African Americans, Latinos, and Asian Americans are being targeted, then the ads should employ actors from these minority groups. If just one group is being courted, then just the appropriate models should be used.

In the case of the Hispanic audience, there are two Spanish-speaking networks in the United States that speak exclusively to it: Telemundo, with 15 stations and 35 affiliates; and Univision, with 50 stations and 43 affiliates. As the size of the Hispanic population continues to grow, so does the importance of these networks in reaching this ethnic audience.

Radio

The use of radio advertising continues to increase, especially with the ethnic minority consumer. It is especially important as an outlet for the Hispanic audience. In a recent study undertaken by Edison Media Research and Arbitron, findings showed that radio is "most essential" for 24 percent of Latinos as compared with 17 percent for the overall U.S. market.

Given the large number of stations directed specifically to Hispanic, African-American, and Asian-American listeners, radio is a sure winner if used properly. This means selecting the right stations at the right time of day. Arbitron, Inc., the subject of our next *Focus* feature, is a company that helps with those decisions.

Focus on . . .
Arbitron, Inc.

ONE OF THE LARGEST COMPANIES SERVING AS AN INTERNATIONAL MEDIA and marketing research firm for the radio industry is Arbitron, Inc. Its focus is on radio broadcasters, networks, advertisers, advertising agencies, and the online radio industry in the United States and Europe. Through their Scarborough Research joint venture with ACNielsen, Arbitron also provides media research services to the broadcast television, cable, newspaper, and online industries. The company's objective is to help media companies, advertisers, and marketers understand media audiences and reach consumers more effectively.

One of its goals is to help retailers target their multicultural efforts more precisely. One way is by helping them select, from all of the available media outlets, which is best suited to their needs and, within these outlets, which programs will help them best target their prospective customers. Arbitron accomplishes this by:

- Identifying the events and sponsorship opportunities that best match the retailer's customers' best interests
- Finding out who's buying the competitor's products so that their client could compete more effectively
- Making better-informed channel decisions with information on retail and product consumption
- Improving media strategy by identifying what media the retailer's consumers use

According to Arbitron CEO Steve Morris, the company's overall aim is "completely customer-focused. Everything is built around helping clients achieve their goals, grow their businesses, and maximize return on investment."

Direct Marketing

The use of direct marketing pieces is especially important to the multicultural consumer. It is especially useful if they are developed with African-American, Hispanic, and Asian American shoppers in mind. As with other media, the layouts should have relevance to these markets by using models, graphics, and copy that will motivate them to buy. Agencies that specialize in ethnic advertising are best suited to create the appropriate direct marketing pieces.

Visual Presentation

Visual merchandising is an important tool used by retailers at points of purchase. It involves the proper use of window displays to motivate the shopper to enter the retail premises as well as interior displays, graphics, and signage to further stimulate their interest in the merchandise.

One of the key elements in visual presentation is the use of mannequins. In recent years, more and more retailers have incorporated ethnic mannequins into their window and interior presentations. This is especially important if a significant portion of the clientele served consists of ethnic shoppers. By using African-American, Hispanic, and Asian mannequins, the shopper is made to feel that the displayed merchandise is being addressed to him and her. Many mannequin manufacturers—including Goldsmith, Inc., and Rootstein—now produce a variety of men's, women's, and children's ethnic mannequins.

Graphics and signage of a multicultural nature are also key to making the shopping environment ethnic-friendly. Stores like Kohl's feature large graphics of Daisy Fuentes, the Hispanic celebrity, whose collections are featured in the store. This is just one more way to make the ethnic shopper feel at home.

 Staffing

In stores across the country, merchants are making certain that their selling floors are filled with sales associates of different ethnic backgrounds. A mix of these minority employees is necessary to properly service the multicultural clienteles that continue to grow in numbers. It is especially important in those areas that are patronized by a large number of African Americans, Latinos, and Asian Americans. Wal-Mart is a leader in bringing Spanish-speaking associates to the selling floor: 54 percent of its employees speak Spanish.

Minority representation is imperative not only for those who interact with shoppers but also for those in management positions. In this way, buyers, merchandisers, managers, and other key personnel can be involved in the decision making that affects their shopping counterparts.

Wal-Mart, the subject of our next *Focus*, has been singled out because of its commitment to multicultural staffing.

Focus on . . .
Wal-Mart

AS THE WORLD'S LARGEST RETAILER, Wal-Mart has made so many retail initiatives that the company is regularly in the headlines of numerous trade and consumer periodicals. Its selection by *Working Mother* magazine as the "2007 Best Company for Multicultural Women" is an industry accolade that underscores their commitment to ethnic minorities. The award celebrates companies that establish groundbreaking diversity policies and programs to encourage the hiring and advancement of African-American, Hispanic, Asian-American, and Native American women.

In an industry that is finally recognizing the need for ethnic minority individuals on the selling floor to properly interact with shoppers who have special needs, such as conversing in Spanish, Wal-Mart has taken ethnic placements to the next level. Its overall employee roster of more than 826,000 females is extremely diverse, with more than 237,000 African Americans, 154,000 Latinas, 41,000 Asian Americans, and 15,000 Native Americans.

In the June edition of *Working Mother*, the magazine that profiled the company's ethnic diversity numbers, Wal-Mart was honored as a result of its unique programs for multicultural women. The initiatives were established to advance the growth and development of women and minorities within the company, with one consequence being an astounding 40 percent of female managers.

The company also has a Diversity and Inclusion Training program that teaches associates how to work with and value all cultures and backgrounds.

MAXIMIZING THE MULTICULTURAL EFFORT

In addition to demographic analysis for developing strategies that best capture the multicultural consumer markets, there is much daily informal research in which members at all levels of a retail organization should engage in order to keep abreast with developments. To be most effective, it is necessary for merchandisers, buyers, store and department managers, and sales associates to regularly participate in appropriate "investigations." These may include the following:

- Perusing multicultural publications to read editorial columns, examine product newspaper and magazine advertisements of competing companies, and scan competitor direct marketing pieces toward the end of gaining a firsthand perspective of what is being marketed to their readers.
- Viewing the Spanish-speaking television networks Telemundo and Univision to determine what products are being advertised to this ethnic market.
- Information exchange between sales associates and ethnic consumers so that their wants and needs are met. Oftentimes shoppers come to buy but are dissatisfied with the company's offerings. In their discussions with the store's visitors, sales associates could learn about what shoppers are seeking. The information could then be passed on to department managers and then to the buyers and merchandisers. In this way, if a sufficient number of similar requests are made, the buying team could adjust its inventories to meet these requirements.
- Setting up regular meetings between those on the selling floor and their supervisors to discuss the potential for adding products that are sought by multicultural consumers.
- Establishing focus groups comprising the different ethnicities to determine if their needs are being met.

It is only through such efforts that the retailer's merchandise offerings and methods of operation that affect these consumer groups can be met. This is another way of helping to maximize profits.

CHAPTER HIGHLIGHTS

- With the continued growth of multicultural market segments, demographic studies are necessary to make certain their shopping needs are met.
- There are six major Hispanic markets in the United States.
- The three major ethnicities are expected to grow at six times the rate of the nonethnic population through 2020.
- By 2050, one in four workers will be Hispanic, which means that retailers must learn how best to appeal to them.
- More and more retailers are entering into exclusive arrangements with minority celebrities to design collections for them.
- The African-American female consumer is the most important ethnicity for cosmetics and fragrances.
- Latinos and Asian Americans are the major purchasers of special food products.
- Selecting the right newspapers and magazines is important for capturing the attention of ethnic minorities.
- Ad agencies that specialize in multicultural advertising are a better choice than the mainstream agencies for reaching ethnic markets.
- Radio is more important in reaching the Hispanic audience than any other ethnicity.
- In visual presentations, the use of ethnic mannequins is essential.
- The establishment of multicultural focus groups is one way to learn about minority wants and needs.

IMPORTANT RETAILING TERMS

bodega (139)

buying power (133)

diverse marketplace (132)

ethnic diversity (131)

ethnic minority (131)

ethnicity (132)

household mean income (133)

in-house research (133)

market segment (134)

merchandise exclusivity (135)

multicultural market (140)

multiculturalism (131)

"one size fits all" philosophy (131)

FOR REVIEW

1. What is meant by the "one size fits all" merchandising philosophy?
2. Which are the three major ethnic minorities in the United States in terms of population numbers and buying power?
3. With what information does the retailer generally begin study of ethnic minorities when determining their importance to the company?
4. Do any retailers maintain in-house research staffs? Which types?
5. From which resource can a retailer determine the sizes of the ethnic minority populations?
6. Which instruments are used to conduct original research?
7. How large is the Hispanic population expected to be in comparison with overall workers?
8. Which Hispanic celebrity creates exclusive collections for Kohl's?
9. What is meant by the term *crossover acceptance*?
10. Why have special cosmetics lines achieved so much success within the African-American community?
11. In addition to special foods being marketed to Asian Americans, what other feature in food marketing is used to increase sales?
12. How do Asian-American newspapers differ from those targeted to African Americans?
13. What care must be exercised in multicultural advertising to make certain that is appreciated by the groups being targeted?
14. Name the two major Hispanic television stations.
15. In what way are fashion merchandise visual displays being made most effective?
16. How can proper retail staffing increase sales to ethnic minorities?
17. Is the establishment of focus groups important to the proper satisfaction of minority shopping needs?
18. How can sales associates help their retail organizations make certain that their shoppers' needs are met?

AN INTERNET ACTIVITY

Use an Internet search engine to find a particular retail operation, or a specific retailer's Web site with which you are familiar, and assess the company in terms of its attention to the multicultural consumer. Using the information gathered, write a paper that touches upon the following:

- Special merchandise collections that have been created by ethnic designers
- Web site features that are designed to attract multicultural consumers
- Departments that have multicultural "sounds"

The paper should be no more than three double-spaced typed pages.

EXERCISES AND PROJECTS

1. Visit a store in your immediate trading area to observe the different tools that are being used to attract minority shopper attention. These could include signage, graphics, ethnic sales associates, and so forth. In addition to writing a three-page summary paper on your observations, you should take photographs of these indicators to include in your report.
2. Using resources such as the Census Bureau or studies that you might find on the Internet, research a particular city in the United States to determine the depth and breadth of its minority population. Include the following in a written report:
   - Population figures
   - Ethnicity breakdowns
   - Multicultural buying power

THE CASE OF REFOCUSING THE MERCHANDISE MIX

Thirty years ago, The Pampered Woman opened what was to become an extremely profitable retail venture. It chose a downtown central district for the store and built a retail facility that would become one of the primary destinations for upscale fashion enthusiasts. Initially the merchandise assortment was filled with marquee labels such as Calvin Klein, Donna Karan, Ralph Lauren, and Anne Klein.

With its continued success, the company expanded its premises by taking over adjacent properties and eventually covered an entire city block. Its multilevel operation was a venue for fashion shows, charity events, celebrity promotions such as in-store designer appearances, and so forth. It was one of the more profitable retailing ventures in the city.

Ten years ago, The Pampered Woman's consumer base started to change. The customer mix was no longer strictly Caucasian but also included African-American customers. Profitability remained solid, but management observed that the mix was starting to become more African American–oriented and that the price points being requested were a little below what was typically merchandised.

Always ready to make any changes to operations that would maintain the company's profitability, management decided to study the changing population and decide whether to alter its merchandising philosophy. The in-house research team decided to study matters to determine how The Pampered Woman could retain its loyal followers and also appeal to the growing African-American clientele.

Suggestions at the research department's meetings with merchandising managers, buyers, and the fashion director included carrying high-profile ethnic designer labels such as Phat Fashions, developing private labels that featured African-American celebrity signatures, and hiring an African-American personal shopper.

After many such meetings, some of the management team's members suggested that the impending decision to change the company's strategies was too important to leave to the in-house research staff. They thought an outside agency would better serve their needs. Others wanted to keep the research in-house.

At this point they all knew that change was necessary but still had not decided which approach to take.

Question

Should the company seek outside help to study the situation or should it keep the research efforts in-house? Defend your position with sound reasoning.

Retail Has Room to Grow in Ethnic Markets
Jeanine Poggi

JUNE 11, 2007

NEW YORK—Retailers must find new ways to target ignored minority groups if they want to keep up with the purchasing power of that rapidly expanding population.

Ethnic markets can be one of the most profitable ventures for retailers and developers, but currently remain largely untapped, said Anthony Buono, executive managing director of retail services at CB Richard Ellis, at the International Council of Shopping Centers annual conference in Las Vegas in May.

"In the United States, ethnic markets remain the biggest opportunity, but the least understood," he said. "There is a lot of money to be made by developers and retailers."

With different cultural beliefs and traditions, however, each demographic requires unique services and merchandise.

"Everyone just bulks each ethnic group into one single category," said Monique Tapie, communications director at Global Advertising Strategies, a marketing consulting firm. "They will target Hispanic, but not people from Mexican or Puerto Rican descent."

By ignoring major demographics, such as Asian-Americans, Hispanics and Eastern Europeans, retailers run the risk of losing new and future customers who have tremendous buying power and who frequently purchase designer, brand-name merchandise.

According to a survey conducted by Global Advertising Strategies, the household incomes of South Asian Americans average $90,000 annually, making them the most lucrative ethnic group in the U.S. In addition, the buying power of this group is slated to reach $77 million in 2008 in the Tristate area alone.

"Strong in cultural beliefs, but flexible in mainstream lifestyle, the South Asian community occupies a niche that is challenging to reach, yet promises to deliver loyal customers in a community that continues to grow rapidly," said Global Advertising Strategies, a marketing consulting firm.

South Asian Americans travel and eat out frequently, are big purchasers of big-ticket electronics and are willing to pay for a high quality of life, Global Advertising said.

But the retail dynamic in the Asian market is vastly different from that of typical American retail centers, making it hard to cater to this population.

"Asians are used to shopping in [stores that are] three stories or more, while in America, most shopping malls and stores are only one or two stories," said Scott Kaplan, senior managing director of the western region for retail at CB Richard Ellis.

One of the largest ethnic demographics, the Hispanic market stretches across California, Arizona, New Mexico and Texas, and into Chicago and New York.

But since most Hispanic youths want to be a part of American culture, especially those who come from Mexico and South America, retailers must find ways to subtly connect with these customers, said Derick TeeKing of Fleming + TeeKing Strategic Advisors LLC.

"Maybe they will make a shoe that is white with green and red embellishment or have products that are more colorful," TeeKing said.

In this sector, it is not only the Hispanic retail tenants that are succeeding, but stores like Starbucks, Panda, T.J. Maxx and Applebee's, which have a large Hispanic following.

"There tends to be the stereotype that Latinos are cheap. But that is not true. They are actually spending more or just about as much as suburban whites," TeeKing said.

"Wall Street is chasing Hispanic developers," Kaplan said. "Originally, they did not want to bank on these developers because they believed the Hispanic market had a lower income. But this is not the case. Retailers are doing well and the tenants' credit are strong."

Retailers and developers are beginning to recognize the importance of downtown locales, and that they can do well in these markets once they find solutions to city issues such as small spaces, security and parking.

According to the Brookings Institution, a Washington nonprofit research group, $3 trillion in public and private funds over the next decade will be invested in U.S. urban communities.

"Traditional retailers would never go into urban markets, but if you do it right, the volumes kick [those] of the suburbs," Kaplan said.

"People are starting to realize that the population is shifting in the U.S. Whether it's the illegal or legal population, it is growing," said Christine Chen, specialty retail analyst at Needham & Co.

While money is being invested across the U.S. to redevelop urban areas, not enough is done by retailers to market products to ethnic markets.

Companies are not using their marketing budgets to do direct marketing to ethnic groups, according to Global Advertising's Tapie. She added, "It costs seven times less to market to ethnic communities then it does in mainstream media. There are over 20 Russian cable television channels that are not being used to sell and market products."

And while the moderate players like department stores and mass merchants are starting to see the potential for these markets, luxury retailers have not jumped on board.

"What will be interesting is to see if the higher-end retailers start catering to these demographics and move into urban centers," Chen said.

How Do You Say "Got Milk" en Español?
Cynthia Gorney

SEPTEMBER 23, 2007

"That boy over there?" John Gallegos said. "Straddler. His mother is a Learner. She's going to be talking to him in Spanish. Watch."

Gallegos stood quietly, in the wide central part of a mall, pretending to look at nothing. The mother and son passed close by. She had dark red hair and was leaning on the boy's arm; he was 14 or so, and in blue jeans. Gallegos was right. The mother was chatting amiably in Spanish. Gallegos tilted his head toward four teenagers shambling along. "Those kids? All Straddlers," he said. "Well, the guy with his cap backwards—he might be a Navigator. He's probably more English-media-consuming."

The mall was in the city of Downey, which is part of Los Angeles. It was an ordinary California midrange shopping center: clean floors, Starbucks, hip apparel chains. Gallegos had come in to examine a clothing store he thought might become a new client. He's a *publicista* an adman. He runs a 60-person agency called Grupo Gallegos in Long Beach. His agency wins awards for its commercials, which are funny, edgy and require translating into English when international judging committees study them. This particular week, in the middle of summer, Grupo Gallegos work was advertising *leche, transporte de autobuses, pollo, ropa interior, servicio de Internet de alta velocidad, consultorios médicos, gimnasios* and *pilas* that would be California Milk Processor Board milk, Crucero bus lines, Foster Farms chicken, Fruit of the Loom underwear, Comcast high-speed Internet service, Quick Health medical clinics, Bally fitness clubs and Energizer batteries, which the Gallegos people had decided to promote via a long-faced Mexican man who walks down the street explaining that as he has figured out that he's immortal (scenes of him being mashed by a plummeting second-story sign, impaled on a spear in a museum, etc.), he requires an especially durable battery for his camera.

Grupo Gallegos advertising runs on Spanish-language television, Spanish radio, in Spanish magazine pages and on Spanish or bilingual Web sites. Some of these enterprises are housed in places you might expect them to be: New York, Miami, Los Angeles, Houston. Many are not. There's full-time Spanish television broadcasting now in Anchorage; Salt Lake City; Little Rock, Ark.; Wichita Falls, Tex.; Indianapolis; Savannah, Ga.; Boston; Oklahoma City; Syracuse, N.Y.; and Minneapolis. The area encompassing Portland, Ore., now has 10 Spanish radio stations, while four years ago it had only 3. The July issue of *ESPN Deportes*, with Hugo Sánchez on the cover, had a Gallegos underwear ad inside; so did the gossip magazine ¡*Mira!*, with Angélica Rivera on the cover; and a *People en Español* with RBD on the cover; and a *Men's Health en Español*, whose cover article promised that James Bond would show readers how to be an *hombre de acción*.

If the only name on that list that sounds familiar is Bond's the others are, respectively, the Mexican national soccer team coach, a *telenovela* star and a wildly popular pop-music group then Gallegos is interested less in selling you products, since you are likely not Hispanic, than in pointing out the exploding spending power of the demographic that is. The estimate worked up by the Association of Hispanic Advertising Agencies for 2007 is $928 billion. Those are dollars spent inside this country by Hispanic consumers, American-born citizens as well as green-card residents and the undocumented, on things they want or need: batteries, iPods, laundry soap, lawn chairs, motor oil, Bulova watches, new-home loans, Volvos, takeout pizza, cellphones, power saws, swimming pools, deodorant, airline tickets and plasma TV's. It's $200 billion more than was spent two years ago. Propelled by continuous immigration and larger family size, the dual factors that are making the Hispanic population multiply faster than any other in the United States, the spending figure is expected to top a trillion dollars within the next three years.

In comparison with some of his colleagues in Hispanic advertising, in fact, John Gallegos runs a moderate-size shop. There are more than a hundred United States ad agencies, not including the *publicistas* in Puerto Rico, that now work almost exclusively in Spanish. The bigger Hispanic agencies have accounts like McDonald's (*Me encanta*, which roughly translates to "I'm lovin' it"), and Chevrolet (*Súbete*, "Get in"). Bounty's slogan in English, "The quicker picker-upper," appears in Spanish as *Con Bounty sí puedes*—"With Bounty, yes you can." T-Mobile does *Estamos juntos*, "We're all together." Toyota does *Avanza confiado*, "Advance confidently." Wal-Mart reportedly spends more than $60 million a year on reaching Hispanics, and for some years the Wal-Mart Spanish tag line, composed by a Houston agency called Lopez Negrete Communications, was *Para su familia, de todo corazón. Siempre.* Which lofted the blunt English "Low prices, always," into a line enduring enough for a tombstone: "For your family, from the heart. Always."

From this vantage, the grim admonitions of anti-immigration groups are hard to hear distinctly; they're drowned out by the sound of cash registers. At the Grupo Gallegos office there's a closet full of display cards on which fragments of information have been written out in black ink. The cards are frequently rifled through and arranged onto giant poster boards, and the first time I visited the Gallegos offices this summer, the boards from the most recent presentation were still leaning against a wall; the prospective client was a food company. The boards said things like:

LEARNERS: foreign born, Spanish dominant, 3 av kids, 65% rent

STRADDLERS: immigrated young, 4 av HH size, blue collar/semi prof, bilingual/mostly Spanish

NAVIGATORS: English dominant, some Spanish, 78% at least some college, semi prof/prof, 60% own home, HH inc $76K

The towers of information, with arrows here and there for emphasis, were taller than I am. They included Learner/Straddler/Navigator particulars on sour-cream usage (Navigators buy the most). The Senate immigration bill was collapsing during the weeks I spent watching Grupo Gallegos at work, and the Gallegos office sometimes felt like a prism in which the information generating so much political argument was continuously being refracted and reassembled into something vigorous and celebratory. "You ask: the guy who just came across the border with a coyote, do I want to go after him, too?" Gallegos once said to me. "Well, he's going to get a job. He's going to work. He's going to start buying products and contributing to the economy. So while he might not be viable for a Mercedes today, I can introduce you to people who came here illegally or legally, with nothing, and are now driving a Mercedes. Advertising is aspirational. I want to aim ahead of where my audience is. Unless it's the equivalent of beef to Hindus, I always say, any product and any service should be sold to Latinos in this country."

Gallegos happened to be sitting in an office conference room at that moment with two account executives, an immigrant from Argentina named María Maldini and an immigrant from Mexico named Ken Muench, and they both considered this.

"Is there a beef-to-Hindus equivalent?" Maldini asked.

"Not that I've been able to find," Gallegos said.

"Sleepovers," Muench said, and smiled.

"True," Gallegos said. "My parents wouldn't let me sleep over at friends' houses. I still won't let my 8-year-old. You have to be *very* high on the acculturation curve to do sleepovers."

The Grupo Gallegos office stretches across the sixth floor of a building one block off the beach. It has conference rooms and odd corner spaces that are enclosed by red curtains, like indoor Bedouin tents, so the creative guys on deadline can go slouch inside on stuffed chairs and pull the curtains around them and stare at their open laptops, looking desperate. The preferred Gallegos term for this state is *en el fondo del mar*, at the deepest depths of the sea. The creative guys wear blue jeans and T-shirts and tend to be unshaven. The office chatter eddies around the Gallegos workspace in Mexican Spanish, Argentine Spanish, Colombian Spanish, Puerto Rican Spanish, Cuban Spanish and the lispy Castillian Spanish of Spain, which is spoken fluently by, among others, a woman of Korean ancestry who grew up near Barcelona. It's all extremely modern and confusing. John Gallegos, who is 40, was born in Los Angeles to a family from the Mexican state of Zacatecas; he and the other United States-born Hispanics at the agency slide back and forth between languages, frequently midsentence. "O.K., *aquí está el problema que tenemos* when we really start looking at the brand."

One morning I walked into a red-curtained corner as Curro Chozas, one of the art directors, was saying in Spanish: "Tutankhamen, Charlie Chaplin, Mozart, George Washington—whatever. Anyway, whoever he is, he rips open his shirt. VRROOOM! It's a bird! It's a plane! No! It's George Washington!"

Chozas is from Madrid. He talks very fast and is good at sound effects, so the *vrrooom* made everybody jump. On the stuffed chairs were a copywriter named Saúl Escobar, who's from Mexico, and one of the creative directors, Juan Pablo Oubiña, who's from Buenos Aires and was listening to Chozas while staring at his own feet. Oubiña has a shaggy dark hair and a melancholy countenance, even when he's greatly amused. Escobar and Chozas spent the previous days imagining a set of Dadaist spots placing famous characters from history in interesting situations with speedy things, strapped-on rockets and race cars and so on; this was promoting high-speed Internet service from Comcast, for which a previous campaign had featured wallets so grateful for Comcast's low prices that they leapt from their owners' possession and flew through the air in order to protect them from mishaps like spilled ketchup or reaching pickpockets.

Escobar and Chozas were tag-teaming now, waiting for a reaction.

"Napoleon Bonaparte, for example," Chozas said. "Lassie. Mahatma Gandhi."

"That would get my attention, Gandhi with the race car," Escobar said.

"Napoleon's too hard," Oubiña said.

"You think more people will recognize Gandhi than Napoleon?" Chozas said.

"Pancho Villa," Escobar said.

"There must be 200 ads with George Washington in them," Oubiña said. He stretched and scrunched his hair. "Cleopatra would be better known than Napoleon."

"Let's go ask somebody," Chozas said.

They trooped out. Oubiña has a college degree, owns his home, has a wife-one-child HH size, is more comfortable speaking Spanish than English, would be white-collar if he actually wore collars and at 38 has lived in this country for less than a third of his life; for these and other reasons, he is a Straddler, he told me, with certain Learner/Navigator undercurrents. At Grupo Gallegos, they all think this way. ("Navigator, with Learner mother and Straddler father," one account director said crisply, when I asked her to label herself: she's a 34-year-old professional; they came from Mexico when she was 6; her father manages well now in English; her mother doesn't.) It was Oubiña who led the preparation for the first Grupo Gallegos ad I ever saw, last spring, during one of my periodic *telenovela* binges. The tagline was *Toma leche*, "Have some milk." The ad was vastly more entertaining than my *novela*, and I thought I appreciated what the challenge had been; the counterpart English campaign was "Got Milk?" and I was pretty sure that asking people in Spanish whether they have milk is a bad idea, since I had once learned the regrettable way that if you use Spanish to ask a male Mexican grocer, "Do you have eggs?" you are inquiring as to his testicles.

In this instance, as it turns out, *Tiene leche*? may or may not be a vulgarity about breast milk, depending on situational context, but that wasn't the real challenge at all. Translation alone rarely is. (The famous Chevy Nova story, about how General Motors bungled its 1960s Latin American car marketing because nobody figured out in time that *no va* means "doesn't go," has been reclassified as urban legend; there was a Mexican gasoline called Nova, debunkers point out, and besides, *no va* is not the way a Spanish speaker would typically say a car doesn't work.) The real challenge, for Grupo Gallegos, was how to sell more milk to as many kinds of Hispanics as possible without alienating any of them or boring all of them. Also, as a point of creative honor, the Gallegos people didn't want to look lame alongside the English "Got Milk?" campaign, which is internationally regarded as one of the brilliant ad runs of the last 20 years. That campaign's big idea, to use adspeak, was deprivation; the San Francisco agency Goodby, Silverstein, stumped about how to draw attention to a product as familiar and soporific as milk, had decided to play with the comic horrors inherent in discovering the milk carton was empty. In one of the most celebrated of the "Got Milk?" ads, a history buff who knows the name of Alexander Hamilton's killer grabs the phone to answer a radio quiz question and win a load of money, but he can't make himself understood because his mouth is jammed up with peanut-butter sandwich and he's completely out of milk.

But this would have been a gross misfire in Spanish—and not simply because an El Salvadorean immigrant, for example, is probably unfamiliar with both Aaron Burr and peanut-butter sandwiches. The whole theme was wrong, especially for people who have abandoned their home countries to migrate hundreds of miles north for work. "There's already enough deprivation," Oubiña told me. "It wasn't funny."

Everybody at the agency wanted to be memorable and sharp, though; they were not going to stick Mamá in her kitchen lovingly pouring milk for the children while exchanging smiles with *Abuelita*, as grandmas are called in Spanish. For some years now, that has been the standard these-are-Latinos cue when Hispanic agencies are doing the work. You don't see dumb Anglo-generated clichés in these ads, like strategically placed tortillas or businessmen wearing sombreros. In Hispanic-made commercials the clichés are homegrown; the United States in general appears as a splendidly cheerful, up-by-the-bootstraps sort of place, full of suburban homeowners and hardworking men with pickup trucks, and an impressive amount of the time somebody has also figured out how to stage all this amid a warm multigenerational family, with *Abuelita* helping demonstrate the merits of the product. It's referred to in some agencies as "Abuelita advertising." It makes Oubiña a little crazy. "Look how she's dressed," he said in exasperation, replaying on his computer an *Abuelita* ad for cooking oil. Technically there was no *abuelita* in this one, just a beautifully-outfitted mamá in a spotless kitchen, experiencing overwhelming joy because of the health benefits the oil was bringing her family. "I would never make this ad," Oubiña said. "It looks like 750,000 other brands. On any team I lead, there is never going to be a kitchen with somebody exclaiming, 'Mmmm, how delicious!'"

The milk problem sent Oubiña and Escobar and Chozas into the deepest depths of the sea for a while, until it occurred to them to improvise with the opposite of deprivation: maniacal consumption, with the ensuing calcium-and-vitamins overload. They thought up a town where gravity is unreliable, causing the locals to float matter-of-factly along 30 feet in the air until they suddenly crash to the ground; their bones are exceptionally strong, though, because they drink so much milk, so they get right up and stroll away. Same thing with powerful teeth (a town where bus riders bite the straps hanging overhead) and hair with the strength of steel. Big success: satisfied client, international award for the gravity spot. "I just don't want to do old-school Hispanic advertising," Oubiña said. "I'm not trying to sound like an artist here. If I thought that, I'd be out of work by the end of the year. I'm just talking from a strategic point of view. You have to put something out there that hasn't been seen before."

On his desk Oubiña had a plastic Energizer bunny, which fell over after he wound it up and was now on its back, drumming and flailing. The agency had won awards for its Energizer ads too, but now they had a new campaign to develop, and Oubiña was grappling; he had to write a 15-second television spot that was eye-catching, praised the battery, contained a comic punch line that would make perfect sense to Hispanics and allowed *el conejito*—the little rabbit—to do its marching act across the screen. He was also supposed to try to help make the brand iconic for Spanish speakers. That was the word they were using at the agency;

they had discerned that in English, people will use "going and going, like the Energizer bunny," but that nobody makes *como el conejo Energizer* references of a similar nature, which means that in Spanish the battery is still a battery, not an icon or a simile or a feeling about life. This was perhaps a situation they could rectify. "In advertising it's not easy to be different," Oubiña said, and sighed. "It takes 10 times as much work."

You can track part of the modern history of United States Hispanics, in a way, through the proliferation and escalating ambition of this country's *publicistas*. Forty years ago, they were mostly a small group of Cuban-exile ad executives in New York and Miami, talking American agencies into letting them translate ad copy into Spanish. Then all-Hispanic agencies started opening up here, trying—often to no avail—to persuade clients that there were enough Spanish speakers in this country, with enough disposable income, to merit whole campaigns aimed directly at them. "I used to have clients who said, 'I don't want those people in my store,'" the Gallegos media director, Ken Deutsch, who is one of the agency's only non-Hispanics, told me. "It was all: 'Gardener.' 'Criminal.' Or just: 'They don't have money.'"

Then the 2000 United States Census data began going public, and in its wake came the rattling headlines: at 15 percent of the present United States population, or 44 million people (factor in an estimated 9 million Latin American illegal immigrants), Hispanics now outnumber African-Americans. Their populations are multiplying so fast in certain parts of the country—nearly a 1,000 percent increase in Atlanta, for example, between 1980 and 2000—that one recent report used the term "hypergrowth." More than half come from or have origins in Mexico, but the array of homelands is extensive; when Grupo Gallegos got the Fruit of the Loom account a few years ago, Favio Ucedo, the Argentine chief creative director, decided to Hispanicize the four fruit guys, all of whom hover around in the ads offering underwear advice, via some mother-country humor that in Spanish constituted a collective private joke. He made Apple Guy and Leaf Guy Mexicans, hiring Mexican actors and giving them script lines that indicated they were the group leaders. Red Grape Guy became a Caribbean, dark-skinned and the best dancer, with the lilting half-swallowed Spanish of Puerto Rico or the Dominican Republic. There had to be a South American, Ucedo decided, so he tipped his hat to his countrymen's unfortunate reputation elsewhere in Latin America and made Green Grape Guy an ego-inflated, overbearing Argentine, a caricature Ucedo knew Mexicans especially would relish.

Gallegos brought Ucedo with him seven years ago when he left the Hispanic agency where he worked before deciding to start his own shop; and one day when we went driving around Los Angeles Gallegos talked with some agitation about *Abuelita* advertising—not that he's unilaterally opposed to it, he said, or feels anything but the greatest affection for his own *abuelita*, who as it happens now lives with his parents. "Latinos *are* more family-centered than the population in general," he said. "But is that the beginning and end of us? No. And if that's the only thing you put into a commercial to make it Latino, the commercial is boring."

We were crossing the flat southeastern swath of the city where Gallegos lived as a child until his parents moved the family to a more middle-class and also less Hispanic area in neighboring Orange County. Gallegos narrated as he drove. "Here's the church where my mom and dad got married. . . . Here's Nix Check Cashing, where I used to bring my grandfather. . . . Look at that store with the wheel rims. That's a big thing with Latinos. The cars have *rims*." He chuckled. He was in his own car, a silver Lexus with entirely ordinary rims. He was wearing khaki pants, brown leather shoes, and a blue button-down shirt hanging loose. He's a registered Republican, though he says he now leans Independent. He majored in business at the University of Southern California, where he was a catcher on the baseball team. His wife, Palma, is half second-generation Italian, half came-over-on-the-Mayflower descendant; Gallegos is still such a devoted U.S.C. football fan that when they were engaged, he advised her to time their wedding date outside the football season or he would never be able to go away with her for their anniversary.

"Here's the grammar school where my aunt went," Gallegos said. He uses English automatically, unless he's around people who prefer Spanish, and as I looked at him in profile I contemplated the crash course in advertising that I was receiving at his agency. One of the first tasks the Gallegos researchers undertake when the agency begins a campaign is clarifying who the "bull's-eye target" is—whether the ads should be aimed most directly at Learners, say, for whom some clever reference to their newness in the United States might help. (They did a Tecate beer ad recently in which a young working man named Basilio puts up politely all day with mangled English versions of his name—"Hey, Basedo!" "Hi, Basyloh!"—and finally walks into a bar full of Latinos, where everybody, hoisting Tecates, gets it right.) Bull's-eyeing a Straddler in Spanish made intuitive sense, too: you're here, you're acquiring and *nos entendemos*, we understand each other.

But Spanish advertising aimed at a person like Gallegos, who lives fully and prosperously in the English-speaking United States—why make the effort? Why wouldn't a company regard him as a frequent-flying, golf-playing, John Grisham–reading Lexus driver and assume they've got his attention every time he picks up an airline magazine or watches college football on English-language TV? Whenever Gallegos and I talked about this, he'd ask why anybody should bother targeting ad campaigns specifically at women. "You can see the same ads the men see," he would say.

During his "Galaygos" period, the years in elementary and middle school when teachers regularly mispronounced his surname and he gave up trying to correct them, Gallegos—it's supposed to sound like *gah-YEH-gos*—stopped speaking Spanish to anyone outside his family, desperate to blend in. It was in his parochial high school that he began to "reacculturate," as the marketing terminology puts it; there, in the early 1980s, ethnic-identity badges had become chic, and the Anglo kids got his name right. "Then I became John Gallegos again," he said. There are certainly Hispanics in this country who know no Spanish—born-heres who were never chewed out by their elders in Spanish; never curled up on a couch with a favorite aunt to make fun of the scheming women on the *telenovelas*; have zero consciousness of *Sábado Gigante*, the beloved cornball variety show, which broadcasts live from Miami and is the longest-running weekly entertainment program on TV, in English or Spanish. But the percentage who have had the language assimilated out of them completely is strikingly small—a national survey last year found that fewer than 5 percent of United States Latinos say they can neither read nor converse even a little in Spanish. Gallegos regards this degree of monolingualism, to be blunt about it, as their loss.

"Here's my neighborhood," he said suddenly. The streets were curving now, with broad-leafed trees and wide, well-tended lawns—$850,000 around here for a teardown, Gallegos observed. He was quiet for a minute. His agency has done advertising aimed at Hispanics who live in communities like his own; on occasion, when they think it's appropriate, they'll do the work in English as well as Spanish. But if there's any single net that can be draped across the length and breadth of American Hispanics, it's the Spanish language itself, and like his *publicista* colleagues, Gallegos is perplexed at American truculence about assuming that full integration into this country requires leaving the native language behind—that bilingualism in the United States is something to be overcome on the path to success, rather than cultivated and celebrated as a success unto itself. The most famous immigrant in California, Gov. Arnold Schwarzenegger, had just a few weeks earlier set off a small uproar at a National Association of Hispanic Journalists convention by declaring that he knew the best way for Hispanic immigrants to learn English well enough for life in the United States: "Turn off the Spanish television," the governor said.

We sat in front of Gallegos's house, which is white, spacious, Cape Codish. There's a swimming pool in the back. The children were away taking martial-arts classes or learning classical piano. The whole tableau looked like a public service announcement for American upward mobility, and Gallegos knew it. "I'm the poster boy for what they think it should be like, right?" he said. "I guarantee you Arnold wouldn't have a problem with me. Registered Republican. Thriving young businessperson. Big donor to my university. But they don't know that I grew up in the environment they don't want to have—watching Spanish television. We speak Spanish to this day. We speak Spanish in the house."

He started the car. "If you really like me, what you're going to get is me promoting what I grew up with, which is more diversity," he said. "Careful what you wish for."

Gallegos invited me to a family dinner at his parents' house the night before I left Long Beach. His mother, María Elena, had made *coctel de camarones*, shrimp cocktail flavored up with chopped avocados and tomatoes; and *carnitas*, shreds of fragrant pork spooned with fresh salsa into tortillas. She swore this was nothing special. Gallegos's father, who is also named John and worked his way up through various businesses while Gallegos and his sister were children, owns a company that makes light fixtures. His mother works at a public elementary school, as a bilingual liaison for parents who aren't comfortable in English. "She's a great bridge," Gallegos said, as his mother handed him a plate of food in the kitchen. "That's all I do, too. We're a bridge for the consumer."

When Gallegos's grandmother came in he kissed her on the cheek, addressing her with the respectful *usted* instead of *tu*, and everybody sat. The conversation ricocheted between Palma, who doesn't really speak Spanish; Gallegos's grandmother, who doesn't really speak English; his children, who understand Spanish but respond in English; his mother, who speaks both languages but prefers Spanish; and his father, who speaks both languages but prefers English. Nobody found this disorienting, including me; my father is from Mexico, the son of Warsaw Jews who fled in the 1920s to Mexico City, and our extended family gatherings used to sound like the Gallegoses', except with Polish thrown in when my grandparents wanted to mutter to each other in private. Like many immigrants' children, I tend toward complicated feelings about language, heritage and the wages of fitting in, and I had come across something I was interested in showing Gallegos: copies of two United States newspaper advertisements, circa 1910—one for Woodbury's Hair Tonic and the other for the Equitable Phonograph Company. Both, except for a few truncated phrases ("Greasy dandruff? Hair coming out?"), were entirely in Yiddish.

Gallegos's parents studied the ads, examining the lettering closely—Yiddish is written in Hebrew characters—and Gallegos looked over their shoulders. A century ago, like Italian and German and Chinese, Yiddish was a vibrant language of daily life and commerce in the United States, read all over the Eastern states in the pages of the Jewish Daily Forward. When Gallegos's grandchildren replay his agency's gravity ad, I wondered, will it look to them like these? Will Spanish in the United States have been recast by then as the language of the aged *abuelitos*, saluted in selective identity-establishing vocabulary words and the names of foods and holidays? What will his sons and daughter be speaking at their own family dinner tables?

"Anything's possible," Gallegos said. He traced one finger down the outline of the Woodbury's bottle. "But I think there's a difference. There was a massive ocean between those people and their home countries. And technology prevented people from staying in touch." No immigrant group in United States history has ever had what this era's Spanish speakers have, in fact: an international border that can be crossed on foot; constant back-and-forth traffic and inexpensive phone communication to the countries of origin; the Internet, on which the Mexican daily Excelsior can materialize onscreen every morning and two clicks turns the entire Google landscape to Spanish; multiple networks of non-English broadcast programming with enormous audiences; and a long lineup of corporations eager to court these people's spending money in any manner that works.

It was dark by now, and María Elena Gallegos rose to bring dessert: a plate of sweet rolls, *pan dulce*, made by a Mexican bakery nearby. "Both," Gallegos finally said. The languages his children will speak, he meant—what they'll work in, what they'll dream in at night, how they'll live. "Everybody will speak English," he said."I think it's not going to be either-or. I think we might become a bilingual nation. And I don't think that's a bad thing."

CHAPTER 7
The Role of Ethics in the Retail Environment

After you have completed this chapter, you should be able to discuss:
- Retailer-based codes of ethics
- The different situations that involve conflicts of interest
- What is generally considered appropriate as a gift from vendors
- Why it is important for companies to establish codes of conduct for their employees' interactions with vendors
- How the Better Business Bureau helps merchants with codes of ethics
- Some of the major areas of concern regarding misleading advertisements
- What is meant by *bait and switch*
- How internal theft can be curtailed
- How the receiving room might be a location where unethical practices occur

Many of the headlines in the media today, and in the past few years, speak of the unethical practices that have pervaded our society. The culprits have been in the business arena, politics, advertising, medicine, and other areas. Not only are some of these practices illegal as well as unethical, but they often do irreparable damage to individual careers and to the organizations they represent. Staying on the right track is a moral given, leading the way to more successful outcomes.

Retailers, in particular, have a responsibility to "do the right thing" for their investors, employees, and customers. To remain a viable and profitable company, ethical business practices are a must. Sometimes, the areas of concern are subject to governmental regulation and include advertising, conflicts of interest, price gouging, price fixing, counterfeit merchandise, and hiring practices.

More and more retailers are instituting ethical standards in their operations. Some are merely informal practices that develop as needed, while others are carefully written documents created by in-house management teams or, in some cases, outside organizations. Other standards are written by trade associations and independent watchdog agencies and are often adopted by retailers. Whichever route is taken in the development of these **codes of ethics**, it is most important that everyone in a company's employment—from the CEO down to sales associates on the selling floor—be aware of the standards that have been established in these documents.

DEVELOPERS OF ETHICAL STANDARDS

Codes of ethics are developed by a number of different groups, as described in the preceding paragraph. The documents produced range from those of a general nature, which merely suggest that employees should act in an honorable manner when carrying out their duties and responsibilities, to more detailed formats that specify expected behavior in every possible business situation.

Retailer Codes

In the major organizations, carefully spelled-out codes of ethics are the general rule. Larger operations usually promulgate documents that cover policy makers as well as lower-level employees who perform duties such as selling, stock keeping, and so forth. Senior executives such as financial officers who make monetary decisions and merchandise managers, store managers, and others who regularly interact with outside vendors are the primary subjects of most company codes of ethics. Belk, Inc., one of the larger department store organizations in the country, subscribes to a code that emphasizes honest and ethical conduct, accurate periodic reporting to the SEC and other appropriate governmental agencies, and compliance with applicable laws, rules, and regulations.

Chain organizations are no exception when it comes to developing codes of ethics. A medium-sized chain that has an unusually detailed code is Stein Mart, which operates 263 stores in 30 states and the District of Columbia. The *Focus* segment that follows underscores the importance of complying with the basic tenets of honesty and integrity.

Focus on . . . Stein Mart

THE CORNERSTONE OF THIS CHAIN'S ETHICAL CODE is voluntary compliance in every aspect of the operation, including conflicts of interest, relationships with vendors and suppliers, relationships with governmental officials, insider trading, and discrimination.

In a 14-page document, the company's CEO specifies the store's commitment to appropriate ethical practices, the route it takes to weed out offenders, and its pursuit of legal sanctions against offenders.

The essence of the Stein Mart code of ethics may be summarized as follows:

- *Compliance with laws*. The company is in compliance with all statutes, regulations and other applicable laws wherever its business is conducted.
- *Conflicts of interest*. The company mandates avoidance of any activity that interferes with its best interests. Even the appearance of any impropriety will not be tolerated. **Conflicts of interest** concern relationships with any supplier (or any firm doing business with the company) and any decisions by employees to secure a personal financial interest in any transaction between them and relatives who are principals, directors, officers, or associates of other companies.
- *Gift taking*. No monies, excessive hospitality, free or discounted services, use of facilities, loans, or gifts that exceed $50 in value may be accepted by any employee. The exception is gifts worth less than $50 that may be offered as promotional rewards by suppliers.

- *Maintenance of accounting records and controls.* Individuals at all levels of the company who are involved in record keeping and control must make certain that all accounts information, records, and books are supported by appropriate documents in auditable form.
- *Reporting violations.* Concerns about possible unethical or illegal activity must be reported to the employee's immediate supervisor. If anonymity is desired, the company's law firm may be contacted with the understanding that no retaliation will take place.
- *Confidentiality of information.* Unauthorized use of any company information is prohibited. This includes accounting reports, supplier identities, business methodology, personnel records, and stockholder lists.
- *Intellectual property.* Assets such as trade secrets, trademarks, logos, copyrights, and so forth are considered to be the company's **intellectual property** and shall be protected. These assets cannot be shared with any individuals or other companies unless authorization has been received.
- *Discrimination and harassment.* Equal opportunity is a commitment from the company for all levels of employment. Derogatory comments based upon racial or ethnic characteristics will not be tolerated.
- *Political contributions.* No expenditures or contributions of any value may be made to political candidates in the Stein Mart name.
- *Relationship with vendors.* No employee may give any money, gifts, excessive hospitality, or so forth to any associate or agent of any vendor. However, gifts of a reasonable amount (under $50) may be appropriate if it is a promotional item or memento.
- *Vendor samples.* These items are not to be considered as gifts, and their personal use is not permitted.
- *Relationship with government officials.* Any offers or authorization of payments of anything of value to political parties or officials is not allowed. All relations with governmental officials shall be conducted in an ethical manner.

Belk offers one of the most comprehensive codes of ethics.

Compliance with these standards is the duty and responsibility of all employees at Stein Mart. Any person who violates these conditions is subject to severe disciplinary action, which may include termination of employment.

Codes of this nature should be published and made available to all employees. Those who are aware of ethical violations are encouraged to bring their observations to the responsible supervisors and/or appropriate committees who have the responsibility of imposing penalties such as reprimands, demotions, or dismissal.

Some companies have established rules and regulations regarding codes of conduct that apply primarily to doing business with their merchandise suppliers. Typical of these codes is that of Macy's, Inc., the subject of our next *Focus*.

Focus on . . .
Macy's, Inc., Vendor/Supplier Code of Conduct

AS THE WORLD'S LARGEST DEPARTMENT STORE ORGANIZATION, Macy's employs thousands of merchandisers and buyers who deal directly with vendors around the globe. These are the people who work for the store divisions of Macy's and Bloomingdale's, the direct-mail catalogue operations, and the company's Web sites.

The goal of Macy's is to "do business only with those manufacturers and suppliers that share the company's commitment to fair labor practices, including adherence to laws that protect workers and their salaries, both in the United States and abroad."

Manufacturers who supply Macy's must comply with all laws of the country in which the merchandise is produced. This includes laws against child or forced labor and against unsafe working conditions. In order to make certain these conditions are understood, the company lists them as a condition of sale on every purchase order. By signing these purchase orders, the vendors are made to understand that these are contractual agreements and that any violation is subject to legal action.

To further ensure that these conditions of sale are adhered to, each supplier must annually sign an agreement to this effect. Any vendor who does not comply is automatically eliminated as a supplier.

Macy's is an enormous user of private-label merchandise for which it has manufacturing agreements with outside contractors at home and abroad. These manufacturers' factories are regularly inspected to make certain that working conditions are up to established standards and that laws prohibiting child and forced labor are not being violated.

If any violations of the law are recognized, the company notifies the U.S. Department of Labor (for domestically produced products) or the appropriate foreign government. Merchandise in question is immediately returned to noncomplying vendors, and future shipments are either cancelled or delayed pending resolution.

Trade Association Codes

Various retail trade associations promulgate codes of ethics for members that have not established their own documents. Such codes generally consist of suggested ethical approaches for the membership to use in their own operations. Some retailers use these **trade association codes** as guidelines; others strictly adhere to them.

The National Association of Ethical and Responsible Independent Retailers (NAERIS) is an organization that aggressively investigates consumer complaints against member retailers and also offers dispute resolution. Association members are required to:

- Promptly honor all guarantees
- Clearly, honestly, and accurately represent all products, services, terms, and conditions
- Deliver products as presented
- Never malign the good name or business reputation of another member
- Fairly represent their products to the public within any advertising
- Communicate in a respectful and courteous manner
- Respond to inquiries and complaints in a timely fashion
- Maintain appropriate security policies and practices to safeguard customer information

Independent Watchdog Agencies

Another group that provides retailers and other businesses with codes of ethics consists of **watchdog agencies**, the most well known of which is the **Better Business Bureau** (BBB). Although it has no *legal* jurisdiction, the BBB is considered to be one of the most powerful groups in solving business disputes. One way in which it helps companies maintain high standards and meet customer expectancies is by interacting with businesses to direct them toward practices that foster ethical principles. The following *Focus* explores how the BBB promotes ethical practices through the services it provides.

> ### Focus on . . .
> ### Better Business Bureau
>
> **THE BBB IS A PRIVATE, NONPROFIT ORGANIZATION** established in 1912 to monitor and report marketplace activities to the public. Each local bureau is licensed by the Council of Better Business Bureaus and is governed by its own local board of directors. Funding for BBB activities is primarily derived from local business support. The 138 bureaus in the United States, Canada, and Puerto Rico have a uniform goal: to help establish an ethical marketplace by monitoring standards for truthful advertising, investigating and exposing fraud against consumers and businesses, and providing information to consumers before they purchase goods and services.
>
> The BBB works toward promoting ethical business practices by:
>
> - Issuing reliability reports on business in response to inquiries. The BBB receives more than 6,500 inquiries each day through a Voice Response System and via the Internet.
> - Investigating advertisements that appear to violate regulations and seeking corrections where appropriate.
> - Mediating and arbitrating disputes between buyer and seller.
> - Reporting on charitable and soliciting organizations.
> - Issuing alerts about schemes and frauds that attempt to victimize consumers and businesses.
> - Cooperating with law enforcement and regulatory agencies to deal with businesses that do not respond to self-regulation.
> - Promoting intelligent buying through consumer and business education.
> - Encouraging the public to "Do business with BBB members" through cooperative advertising campaigns in newspapers and television.
>
>
>
> The Better Business Bureau is an independent watchdog agency concerned with business ethics.
>
> The Better Business Bureau provides dispute resolution services, promotes honest advertising, and offers educational materials to the public; it also promotes honest selling practices and self-regulation within the business community. In addition, the BBB informs the public about consumer scams and fraudulent business behavior.

AREAS OF ETHICAL CONCERN

As previously noted, ethical practices should play a role in every facet of the retail operation. Whether it concerns employees or customers, "walking the straight and narrow" will foster better relationships among employees, provide shoppers with a high comfort level, and ultimately help the company achieve profitable goals. The following sections discuss the major areas of concern regarding unethical practices.

Advertising

The principal way in which retailers alert consumers about product offerings is by advertising. The use of newspapers, magazines, direct marketing catalogues, television, radio, and company Web sites all incorporate information and products that help consumers with shopping decisions. If a merchant uses basic advertising principles in its media offerings, then customers are likely to seek out the merchandise in person or to place orders via telephone or the Internet. If the advertised merchandise is ethically presented in terms of product description, accurate price information, comparison with similar merchandise in the marketplace, and so forth, then those who are attracted to the ads are likely to make purchases and to keep the items they have paid for. If, however, misleading ads were used to attract attention and motivate purchasing, then the result might be returned merchandise, distrust of future advertisements, poor company image, bad-mouthing the retailer, and even reporting the misrepresentation to legal authorities.

Newspaper advertising is often the source of unethical ads.

There are several areas of concern in regard to retail advertising. These include **bait-and-switch** practices, misleading price claims, and **puffery**. Advertising abuses of this nature will more than likely cause consumers to avoid the companies that use such misleading approaches.

Bait and Switch

Sometimes merchants run ads that feature goods at unusually low prices as a means of motivating shoppers to come to the store. When the customer arrives, the featured goods are "sold out" and the retailer pushes some other product that is more profitable. The automobile industry is notorious for using this practice. The ad typically features a very low-priced model, but in reality it is not the car the dealer wants to sell. High-pressure sales tactics take over in an attempt to sell a model that is more profitable. Although unlawful in most states, this practice continues to be employed.

Yet bait and switch is not only illegal, it is unethical as well. Merchants that resort to this tactic run the risk of alienating shoppers. Advertised items should be readily available to those who have been motivated to come to the store, and the seller should make every effort to tell the customer of that product's benefits. If the profit margin for such items is too little, then the company shouldn't feature it in its ads.

Misleading Price Claims

In order to motivate shoppers to look further at their merchandise, some retailers use misleading words to imply that significant savings will be realized if the goods are purchased. These claims include the use of such terms as **list price**, which implies (often wrongly) that this is the normal selling price; "up to," which can actually mean that just one item is selling at a significantly reduced price; "lowest price," which is often not verifiable and may exist only in the mind of the advertiser; and "this week only," which may falsely suggest that a reduction in price is only temporary.

Advertisements that feature sale merchandise frequently use a variety of price declarations such as **comparative price** and "value." These are often pricing gimmicks that have no actual validity. A retailer may believe that its merchandise is comparable to that of another retailer and is selling for less, but rarely can this be verified. If such terminology is used, the merchant should have factual information on hand for customers who question the claim.

False and misleading claims will result in consumer mistrust and may have long-lasting consequences, such as discouraging the shopper from believing or responding to future ads.

Puffery

The use of superlative terms is either objective or subjective. Objective claims are statements of fact that can be measured, as with quality and performance. Subjective claims are merely opinions but are often used to describe quality and/or service in the view of the advertiser. Such puffery should never be used because it is generally misleading.

Credit

One of the areas in which customers are sometimes misled is credit. As a way of life for a significant number of Americans, the use of "plastic" to make purchases is often fraught with misconceptions. Retailers must comply with the **Truth in Lending Act** and **Regulation Z**, which require that all credit terms be clearly and conspicuously disclosed, but some employ unethical practices nonetheless. For example, a merchant may show the terms of the credit in an inconspicuous place, even though this is not lawful.

Although easy credit is a boon for shoppers who are short of cash, it is essential that they receive accurate information regarding payment and other stipulations such as late fees. Failing to act ethically will only bring unhappiness on the part of the customer and possibly legal ramifications for the merchant.

Credit card applications should clearly state a store's credit terms.

Low-Cost Sourcing

Many retail giants have engaged offshore suppliers to produce their goods because of the price advantages they receive. Lower costs are achievable overseas in part because of the lower wages paid to workers there, but the products themselves are coming under question. As foreign-made items ranging from toys to foods increasingly find their way onto store shelves at extremely favorable prices, the quality is becoming more and more suspect. In fact, harm is a potential risk when these items are used.

Many questions have surfaced regarding the ethics of offshore merchandise procurement. Is it only a matter of getting these products at bargain prices, or is it also necessary to make certain that they are not toxic or otherwise harmful?

In the News . . .

"China Pressure Cooker: Ethical Questions Grow over Low-Cost Sourcing," an article found on page 169 at the end of this chapter, should be read carefully now to learn about the ethical dilemmas faced by retailers with regard to overseas sourcing.

Conflicts of Interest

Supplying the retailer with the best available merchandise is a sure way to satisfy the needs of the store's patrons. It is expected that professionalism will prevail when purchases are made by buyers and merchandisers, yet this is not always the case. From time to time, retail employees who are charged with product procurement will stray from objective decision making and fall into the trap of buying goods that yield personal favors. That is, instead of carefully shopping the lines to choose the best products, buyers are sometimes motivated to procure less desirable items because of a personal gain.

This is clearly an unethical practice. It is unfair to honest vendors and, in the long run, to customers because they are then not given the best merchandise assortment to choose from.

Counterfeit Merchandise

Watches, designer handbags, sunglasses, fine art, **logo** apparel, and jeans are just some of the products that have come to market but are not "the real thing." Although there are retailers that knowingly try to pass off such **counterfeit merchandise** as the real thing, even seasoned professionals are sometimes unable to distinguish the real from the fake. Those who willingly purchase counterfeits are not only participating in an unethical scheme but are also subject to legal penalties. A retailer that includes—knowingly or otherwise—counterfeits in its product mix could lose both consumer trust and the potential for future business.

In order to make certain that they are not duped by purveyors of such imported goods, retailers should purchase only from vendors of known integrity. By doing so, there will be little chance that counterfeit goods will find their way to the selling floor.

Many designers such as Louis Vuitton have been plagued with counterfeit merchandise.

Hiring and Promotion Practices

Although discrimination has diminished in many businesses, minority groups still find upward mobility difficult. Companies such as Texaco have made news regarding charges of discrimination against African-American employees. Texaco paid more than $140 million to settle the class action complaint and has made other efforts to correct the injustices, including the creation of an Equality and Tolerance Task Force.

Not only are discriminatory practices illegal, immoral, and unethical, but they attract such bad press that it eventually reduces profits of the businesses in question. Groups like the NAACP have called for people to boycott such companies. This attention is not welcomed by retailers and other business enterprises and can be avoided when genuinely unbiased hiring and promotional practices are carried out.

Texaco has made news regarding charges of discrimination.

Internal Theft

Although shoplifting by people posing as customers is an unethical practice that results in significant losses for the retailer, the notion of in-house or **internal theft**, carried out by employees, is even more troublesome. Such theft (known in the trade as "inventory shrinkage") definitely affects the company's bottom line. Some employees have the audacity to offer low wages or dissatisfaction with supervisors as the reasons for their dishonesty, but nothing justifies these actions.

Internal theft can be reduced by taking any or all of the following measures:

- More thorough applicant screening
- Checking references
- Using closed-circuit TV to monitor employees at work
- Using mystery shopping services
- Employee drug testing
- Controlling employee purchases
- Offering rewards to those who report suspected employees
- Prosecuting dishonest employees as an example to others

Price Gouging

A common unethical practice is to raise the price of goods during emergency situations. For example, when a hurricane is about to strike, merchants of lumber (which is needed to protect windows) may quickly raise their prices. Such **price gouging** is against the law in many states, where retailers that employ this practice may be fined. Even where it is not against the law, price gouging is unfair to consumers, and offending retailers may well lose customers. This is another case where an unethical practice could affect future sales and profitability.

Price Fixing

It is unethical (and illegal, in most states) for two or more retailers in a competitive environment to conspire to charge the same prices. From time to time, competing supermarkets have been found fixing milk prices. Such **price fixing**, when discovered by consumers, generally leads to a boycott of the involved stores.

Questionable Products

Occasionally, products are manufactured and marketed that carry disturbing ethical implications. Of particular concern has been the production of fur garments. Questions involving declining species and the potential for brutality in the capture of some animals have been discussed by consumers and merchants alike for many years. Is the sale and use of these furs ethical? It is an issue that may never be entirely resolved.

In the News . . .

The article "Is PETA Defanged? Fur Looks Are Back on and off Runways" (on page 167 at the end of this chapter) should be read now to see what retailers are doing about selling these items.

Receiving Room Procedures

When buyers place orders with vendors, they expect to receive the merchandise exactly as described on the purchase order. In practice, however, suppliers all too often (either purposely or accidentally) make **short shipments** to the retailer, submitting invoices that charge for more than the retailer receives. Sometimes the vendor's shipping

Receiving rooms are places where improprieties have surfaced.

Price negotiation is a typical practice at automobile dealerships.

clerks engage in unethical practices such as helping themselves to some items. Whatever the case, it is at the retail receiving facility that special care should be taken to verify that the orders have been properly charged to their company.

Most retailers have developed systems to make certain that they have been properly charged. Whether by *direct quantity check*, *blind quantity check*, or *semi-blind check* (as more fully discussed in Chapter 11), it is incumbent upon the checkers to make certain that the actual shipments coincide with the invoice billing. It is at this stage where unethical practices sometimes occur.

Receiving clerks may be remiss in their roles as merchandise "counters." Instead of making an item-by-item count of what was received and comparing it to the vendor's invoice, they might only pretend to make the count. Often this may lead to shortages, and so the retailer, without this knowledge, pays an inappropriate amount. Not only is lax counting an unethical practice, it also affects the company's bottom line.

"Negotiation" Pricing

Although the vast majority of sales strategies are based on a single given price, in some retail industries **negotiation pricing** is the name of the game. In the automobile showroom, a customer entering the premises is often able to negotiate a price that is lower than the asking price. The better the negotiator, the better the price! Although this has become standard practice in the auto industry, the ethics of the technique are questionable. Why should an individual who hasn't mastered the art of negotiation pay more than someone who has? Often, dealers have legitimate reasons for negotiating: a trade-in for a customer's old car, a large down payment, or the purchase of a car at the end of the season. However, retailers who abuse this pricing technique are doing a disservice to their customers. Not only is this practice unethical, it can also cause a lack of public trust. If, after paying a certain price for an automobile, a customer learns that someone else paid less at the same dealership for the same car, then his or her business will probably be lost to the company forever. Negotiating prices is bad business and could hamper future profits. Saturn, on the other hand, doesn't allow price negotiation. The company has captured a significant market with this strategy.

Working-Class Discrimination

Especially in the grocery industry, the same items often cost working-class people more than what is charged in more affluent markets. This practice occurs because many in this lower class do not have cars and cannot take costly public transportation that would take them to and from more competitive shopping arenas where prices are lower.

Merchants who exploit this segment of the population are doing so at the expense of those incapable of finding their goods elsewhere. This unethical practice is used even by well-known supermarkets that employ **zone pricing**.

No matter how many publications or news programs uncover this practice, the problem still exists. Businesses continue to take chances in exploiting their customers and hoping they will not be caught.

CHAPTER HIGHLIGHTS

- Codes of ethics range from documents that merely suggest employees should act in an honorable manner to more detailed formats that prescribe specific behavior.
- Major retail organizations often subscribe to codes that address such topics as compliance with laws, conflicts of interest, gift taking, and so forth.
- Many trade associations promulgate codes of ethics for members that have not created their own documents.
- Some watchdog agencies, such as the Better Business Bureau, provide retailers and other businesses with codes of ethics.
- Advertising is a major area in which unethical or dubious practices are used.
- Bait and switch is a notorious practice whereby an item is advertised to lure the shopper, who is then urged to purchase a more profitable item.
- Merchants may attempt to conceal credit terms by placing them where they are unlikely to be seen.
- Counterfeit merchandise in a retailer's product mix could eventually result in loss of consumer confidence.
- Internal theft is costing merchants billions of dollars.
- The receiving room is where many losses can occur, but these can be reduced by establishing proper "checking" systems.
- Price negotiation is not prevalent but is still practiced by auto dealers, for example; its use can reduce future profits.

IMPORTANT RETAILING TERMS

bait and switch (160)
Better Business Bureau (158)
code of ethics (155)
comparative price (160)
conflict of interest (156)
counterfeit merchandise (162)
intellectual property (157)
internal theft (162)
list price (160)
logo (162)
negotiation pricing (164)
price fixing (163)
price gouging (163)
puffery (160)
Regulation Z (161)
short shipment (163)
trade association codes (158)
Truth in Lending Act (161)
watchdog agency (158)
zone pricing (165)

FOR REVIEW

1. In which areas have unethical practices been discovered in recent years?
2. What is a code of ethics and how does one code differ from another?
3. For major retail organizations, what procedure is usually undertaken to spell out codes of ethics?
4. Describe a typical conflict of interest that is addressed in retailer codes.
5. Why is it generally unethical for retail executives to take gifts of a substantial amount from vendors?
6. What is meant by the term *intellectual property*?
7. What types of retail organizations are likely to adopt codes of ethics that have been written by trade associations?
8. What is a watchdog agency?
9. What is the Better Business Bureau?
10. How is the practice of "bait and switch" used by retailers?
11. Define the term *puffery*.
12. How is the term *list price* often misused by sellers?
13. Does the term *comparative price* have any validity?

14. With what Federal law must retailers comply in regard to consumer credit?
15. In what product classifications is counterfeit merchandise most prevalent?
16. How can internal theft be curtailed?
17. What is meant by the term *price fixing*?
18. How can "direct quantity checking" improve a retailer's bottom line?
19. Why is it dangerous for a merchant to engage in negotiation pricing?
20. What is zone pricing?

AN INTERNET ACTIVITY

Using a search engine such as Google, research some of the major retail organizations in the United States to learn about their codes of ethics. Select one that has not been used in the text and describe the most important elements of the document.

Some of the following areas should be addressed:
- A brief history of the company and its retail classification (e.g., department store, chain organization)
- The essence of the various aspects of the code
- Reporting procedures to alert unethical activities
- Penalties for unethical practices

The paper should be no more than five typewritten, double-spaced pages.

EXERCISES AND PROJECTS

1. Visit a merchant to determine if it has a code of ethics. Select one that does and briefly describe if the code is its own document or the work of another agency. The details of the code of ethics should be summarized and readied for discussion with the class.
2. Write to a watchdog agency *other* than the Better Business Bureau to determine if it provides codes of ethics for retailers and other businesses. If so, outline the details of the code.
3. Select a product (such as a handbag, sunglasses, or wristwatch) in order to make a comparison between the genuine item and a counterfeit. The real ones are available from legitimate retailers, while the fakes are often seen in flea markets or at street vendor stands. Carefully examine two that seem to be the same for the purpose of discovering differences.

THE CASE OF TAKING SUBSTANTIAL GIFTS

Since 1965, when it first opened its doors, John Stewart has enjoyed a reputation as being one of the finer men's clothing stores in the Midwest. Starting with a single store, it has grown into a chain of distinction that now features 28 units, a catalogue operation, and an Internet Web site. Its locations are in Illinois, Missouri, Michigan, and Indiana. With the success of its catalogue and Web site, the company enjoys business from all over the country.

Originally family-managed, today's management team includes people unrelated to the founding family. Although the heirs to company founder John Stewart are still involved in the operation at its highest management levels, the merchandising and buying team consists of "outsiders." Many have been with the company for as long as 20 years, but some arrived as recently as last year. Given its merchandise mix of tailored clothing, coats, suits, sportswear, haberdashery, and shoes, the task of supplying the company with the right merchandise is formidable. There are five merchandise divisions as well as 30 departments each headed by a buyer; there are also assistant buyers for each department.

New lines are always being introduced into the inventory, but the tried-and-true collections have dominated, as has the "personality" of the company's image. Ranging from more traditional styling to some contemporary offerings, the overall mix has remained basically the same since the company began.

Last year, with the hiring of Steve Adams to merchandise "contemporary casual"—a department that caters to a younger shopper—the product offerings took on a new look. Not only were some of the successful lines reduced in size, but untried collections began to come aboard in large numbers. However, sales did not reach anticipated levels. In fact, the results were dismal in comparison to the rest of the store.

Confronted by the divisional merchandise manager, Hank Wilcox, Adams felt it was his right to buy as he thought appropriate and that sales would eventually rebound. This failed to occur. Adding to the confusion was the lateness of merchandise arrivals and some less-than-quality goods.

Upper management has thus become suspicious about Adams's purchasing decisions. Were they simply bad judgment or rather a case of unethical gift taking? Before taking any action, some investigation seemed in order.

Question

How might the company investigate Mr. Adams to make certain that no impropriety was taking place?

Is PETA Defanged? Fur Looks Are Back on and off Runways
Rosemary Feitelberg

FEBRUARY 14, 2007

NEW YORK—Let the fur fly.

That seemed to be the motto of designers showing during New York Fashion Week last week, and the buyers, editors and socialites sitting in the front rows. Whereas in past seasons the luxury material seemed as taboo in certain fashion circles as overweight models, this fashion week, there was more fur on display—in ways both bold and discreet—than there has been in years.

In addition to ubiquity on the runway, there was Christian Louboutin in a fur-lined down vest, Bergdorf Goodman's Roopal Patel in a tie-front fur vest, Joanna Mastroianni snug under a Mongolian lamb hat and Judith Giuliani playing it safe in a full-length fur. Though unintentionally, the female trio that accompanied Burt Tansky to Friday's Carmen Marc Valvo show was a candid snapshot of how fur has caught on with women of all ages. Tansky's wife, Rita, wore a full-length coat, his daughter opted for a shorter version and his granddaughter sported a shearling.

But the Neiman Marcus Group chief executive officer said the interest is driven by shoppers. "I think the customer wants fur—it's a luxury."

Of course, designers want the four-digit and five-digit sales that accompany fur to keep going. Last year, fur items rang up $1.82 billion in retail sales—a slight increase compared with 2005, according to the Fur Information Council of America. But given the unseasonably warm winter many regions of the country had last year, that tally wasn't bad, said executive director Keith Caplan. "The focus was on more fashion-oriented pieces—capelets, shrugs, stoles and accessories. Obviously, those pieces are lower-priced than a fur coat, so you have to sell more of them."

What the masses of fur all over the runways for fall means to People for the Ethical Treatment of Animals remains to be seen. The group has raised plenty of ruckus in past seasons, but this fashion week's demonstration amounted only to fliers being passed out before one show, and the group's sponsorship of Marc Bouwer's fur-free show.

"It's a sad commentary that instead of wowing fashion editors, buyers and consumers with actual design talent, some designers threw fur on anything, from dresses to handbags to hats, to get attention for their runway shows this season," a PETA spokesman said, contending, "even when much of it will be translated to faux fur for retail."

He claimed that Polo Ralph Lauren, Ann Taylor, Jones Apparel Group, Limited Brands and Kenneth Cole were not using fur. In Europe, Stella McCartney, Vivienne Westwood, Comme des Garçons and Katharine Hamnett were just a few of the designer labels with fur-free policies, the PETA spokesman added.

Calvin Klein went fur-free as of this spring, but a company spokeswoman could not say if it stemmed from PETA.

The prevalence of fur on the runways was not missed by animal rights activists. IMG staffers received their share of unsolicited e-mails. One executive showed one that read, "Have you ever looked into the eyes of an animal being skinned alive for the fur industry? If not, I can send you the videos. Or, is it about money . . . only money matters?"

By last weekend, PETA's efforts were focused on Cleveland and Columbus, where a crew of naked activists climbed into a giant bed, holding signs that read, "Fur – Out, Love – In." The pre-Valentine's Day pitch was part of PETA's "I'd Rather Go Naked Than Wear Fur" campaign that was introduced in the Nineties.

Just as designers were unabashed about their fondness for fur, fur-wearing women seem unconcerned about the threat of animal activists.

Celine Dion wasn't making any apologies when she turned up at the J.Mendel fashion show in a fur-trimmed coat. Asked if she had any reservations about attending due to animal rights activists, she said, "No," adding she takes responsibility for "what I say, what I do and what I wear."

"Project Runway" critic Tim Gunn said seeing Vanessa Williams backstage at Dennis Basso's show reminded him of an exchange they had on the red carpet at the Golden Globes, when he was covering it for "The Today Show." Gunn said when he commented on the big fur she was wearing, Williams shot back, 'I didn't kill it.'"

That said, the former chair of the department of fashion design at Parsons The New School for Design noted the school also works with PETA. "I really think it's important for people to have choices, especially when there are so many great synthetic substitutes for fur." (Gunn was just hired as chief creative officer of Liz Claiborne Inc.)

"But now, there are these horror stories that have made me wince about the synthetics that are coming from dog fur in China," Gunn said before Basso's show.

Whether or not that is true, he said the origins of every product should be detailed on its label. "Let the truth be told so consumers can decide. There is an incredible amount of misinformation out there," Gunn said. "I was discussing something about China with my students. I told them, 'If a country doesn't have human rights, why would you expect them to have animal rights?'" Gunn said.

Bouwer was one designer during fashion week who tried to make a statement about not using fur. Bouwer, who once used fur and leather, said he would stop using all animal-based materials, including wool, in his fall collection. That made him the first designer to show completely free of animal fibers.

Bouwer was bucking the tide, though. And all the fur was welcome news to many retailers, including Ginny Hershey, senior vice president and general merchandise manager of Bergdorf Goodman, who noted, "The treatments are much more sophisticated."

Badgley Mischka offered a cream plucked mink and fox coat, J.Mendel created a white silken lamb coat with a white fur raccoon hood and Isaac Mizrahi designed fox clogs.

Of course, what appeared to be a fur free-for-all on the runways was not by chance. Saga Furs has been rounding up young designers to get them better acquainted with the latest techniques, lining up potential manufacturers and making skins available to them. Rodarte, Doo.Ri and Jason Wu are among the newest names on its roster, and Peter Som, Derek Lam and Proenza Schouler have been around for the past few seasons, said Charles Ross, director of international operations for Saga Furs.

In addition, longtime Saga collaborators like Michael Kors, Oscar de la Renta, Carolina Herrera, Carmen Marc Valvo and Badgley Mischka had a wider assortment of fur pieces on their runways, Ross said. Should any of the 15 to 25 designers Saga works with each season have a special request—an unusual color, an uncommon treatment or a limited number of skins—Saga taps its international network to get things done at the quality designer's demand, Ross said. What really appeals to them is the high-ticket sales.

"The category sold very well at the designer level last winter. They shipped early and sold early," Ross said. "Maybe there was global warming in early December, but it's been frigid in February. Plus, a lot of women who buy a designer fur don't just stay in New York. They travel the world."

And fur is one look that disposable fashion retailers can't knock off, said noted fashion consultant Robert Burke. "Fur has been prominent in so many runway shows. Part of the explanation for this is the real emphasis on luxury. Contemporary companies and H&M have been so quick to copy things. But this is something they can't copy with any real authenticity."

As a former retailer, Burke also understands that fur can help boost the bottom line. "Stores are always looking for a way to bring up the average price point."

Marylou Luther, who hit the shows in a fur she bought in the Seventies, said she had never seen designers showing so much fur. That's saying something, considering she has been attending shows since Yves Saint Laurent introduced his first collection for Christian Dior in 1958. "I can't say it's because of our cold weather because these collections were planned months ago."

The threat of PETA is less of a factor, she said. "More and more women aren't worried about PETA—just wearing fur is almost an expression of independence, as if [women are thinking] no one is going to tell me what not to wear."

Nicole Fischelis, vice president and fashion director at Macy's East, said, "I think more is not enough. There was a lot of fur last winter as well. But last year was more about flat fur and this year is more about volume and fur trimming."

Fur-trimmed items in Macy's Birger Christensen-run fur salon are bestsellers year after year, she said. Having grown up around furriers—her father was one and her brother Gerard is one—she thinks fur design to be a craft, not a controversy. "There are other causes in our world that I wish people would demonstrate as violently for."

Bergdorf Goodman's senior vice president and fashion director Linda Fargo said people justify wearing fur. "What about leather? What about plastics?" she asked.

Personal preferences aside, Fargo praised the inventiveness shown in new designs like Proenza Schouler's hats.

Not everyone sees furs as the next big thing. Saks Fifth Avenue vice president and women's fashion director Michael Fink considers the category to be part of the fashion landscape. "In the last few years, people have been wearing fur freely if they want to. But it hasn't stuck out as a major trend this season. I'm just seeing it as another texture in a very monochromatic season," he said.

That all-inclusive mind-set is just what sold longtime fur designer Basso on his Bryant Park debut last week. After 23 years of specializing in fur and throwing lavish fashion shows that often attracted or "finale-d" with a major celebrity, Basso decided it was time to show the versatility of his work and introduce a ready-to-wear collection. "I've always handled fur in a creative manner. Other designers are just beginning to do that now."

IMG doesn't necessarily hire extra security for fur-heavy shows, but is said to have more manpower out front, where ticket holders check in. Many designers take it upon themselves to hire extra security for any number of reasons—to safeguard jewelry, protect the designer, take insurance precautions or deal with celebrities. At Basso, security was beefed up at the entrance and some were asked to show their tickets with seat assignments as many as five times. Once showgoers were inside, security guards were buckled down in each aisle during the presentation. Asked if the extra manpower was there to handle any animal activists, one guard, who asked not to be named, said, "Of course."

China Pressure Cooker: Ethical Questions Grow over Low-Cost Sourcing
Evan Clark

OCTOBER 2, 2007

Low prices are coming at a cost that consumers and fashion companies can no longer ignore.

Globalization and relentless retail competition among the likes of Wal-Mart, Target, H&M, Kohl's, Gap and Macy's might have turned supply chain "efficiency" into a high art, but the pressure on factories has spurred a slew of sweatshops, industrial pollution and consumer safety concerns that many expect ultimately will increase prices.

At the same time, rising wages in China are only increasing pressure on manufacturers there as they strive to maintain the nation's status as the world's low-cost factory across a variety of product categories. This could result in even more shortcuts being taken by suppliers as they subcontract out more of their production.

Recent safety recalls of Chinese-made toys, bibs and toothpaste prompted consumer outcries and governmental reviews in both the U.S. and China that could lead to new regulations in both countries. The misery and human toil of sweatshops never fails to resonate with Western consumers at some level, and the green issue has gained traction in the last year, especially with tales of industrial pollution making front-page news.

What is becoming clear in these scandals is [that] the relentless drive toward lower and lower prices—whether it's a toy or T-shirt—in turn comes at a price, be it greater pollution, displaced populations or possible safety hazards.

"This is potentially hugely important—all these issues do become lumped together," said Charles Kernaghan, director of the National Labor

Committee, a watchdog group that has uncovered worker abuses, such as those discovered in special Jordanian trade zones last year. "If there are a few more recalls [of Chinese products], then I think we're going to see some real change."

While these issues rarely impact the luxury or high-end designer world, they could come to bear more and more on designers and celebrities as they increasingly strive to broaden the bandwidth of their brands, be it Karl Lagerfeld for H&M, Vera Wang for Kohl's or Sarah Jessica Parker for Steve & Barry's. And, while none of these brands have been involved in these issues up to now, consumers are unlikely to give any company a pass on product safety in the long run.

"When it comes to the point where children are sucking on a toy with lead paint on it, that's where they draw the line," said Kernaghan. "What will the Congress, what will the administration do to guarantee the safety of these products? It's something that's so powerful and so frightening to people [that] it does bring it right into their home."

Paul Charron, former chairman and chief executive officer of Liz Claiborne Inc., said China has had such incredible growth, it's "like the Wild, Wild West."

"There's a lot of pollution in the Pearl River Delta," Charron said. "There has been unbridled growth without appropriate checks and balances. I think that period of unbridled, undisciplined growth is about to be over."

It isn't just China. Much of the apparel supply chain relies upon the developing world, where it can be difficult for companies to get a handle on their suppliers. But now consumers want companies to do just that, and they might start expecting even more guarantees that firms aren't polluting or otherwise cutting corners, just as they did with sweatshops in the past.

"The balance is tipping a bit and now we do have product safety and climate change and environmental stuff on the front burner as we didn't before," said Barbara Franklin, commerce secretary under former president George H.W. Bush and a consumer product safety commissioner in the Seventies.

"Right now, there are some different points of view, what we expect and what the developing world's trying to do," said Franklin. "It's just one of the fault lines between developed and developing as we become more and more global."

The cultural differences or levels of development that have contributed to environmental and other problems require more of a multifaceted understanding from companies.

"A lot of the sins of the father are now coming back to haunt the sons and daughters," said Elaine Hughes, president of executive search firm E.A. Hughes & Co. Sourcing executives have had to evolve beyond their traditional role as experts of the technical aspects of making goods overseas, she said.

"They need to be a little more well rounded in understanding the supply chain and logistics pieces to it," said Hughes.

As a result, fashion companies are starting to take a broader look at ethical standards in their sourcing practices.

"What we've been doing has been focused on labor and safety in the factories," said Laura Wittman, vice president of compliance and human rights at Jones Apparel Group. "However, we do anticipate expanding that to consider environmental and other areas."

The intertwining of product safety, environmental and sweatshop concerns marks a significant evolution in the sourcing landscape navigated by fashion brands, retailers and importers in general. The combination of the three issues might be enough to awaken the consumer in ways worker conditions alone rarely have.

So far, apparel hasn't been caught up in the product safety scandal beyond an investigation by the government of New Zealand into unsafe levels of formaldehyde reportedly found in some Chinese-made apparel. Most apparel consumer safety issues are centered on flammability and drawstrings that could choke children.

However, there seems to have been some interest on the part of fashion companies to make sure their goods don't contain harmful substances.

"The last four months have been crazy," said Dina Dunn, marketing agent for the International Oeko-Tex Association, who has been working to establish a U.S. business for the Zurich-based firm that tests textiles for harmful substances. "Now, they're coming to us. There are a lot of people talking about it. Right now it's toys, but it's not going to be long until apparel gets onto that list."

Given the catch-as-catch-can nature of Washington politics and policy making, fashion companies could get caught up in the sweep of changes, even if they avoid a consumer safety scandal.

For instance, Sen. Susan Collins (R., Maine) said the Senate Homeland Security and Governmental Affairs Committee would investigate the safety standards not only for children's toys, but also clothing in the current Senate session.

When it comes to new standards, industry tends to favor voluntary guidelines and a market-based approach in which the ultimate consumer would punish brands whose policies fail to keep their goods and supply chain up to snuff. That might no longer be enough, though.

"We've seen too many instances in which companies can counter any bad publicity with clever P.R.," said Robert Reich, who tackled sweatshop issues as former president Clinton's labor secretary, in response to e-mail questions. "Moreover, it's far from clear that consumers are willing or able to keep the pressure on companies to clean up their acts."

Big changes, though, are going to require some kind of buy-in from the consumer/voter.

"If Congress is going to make any headway, the public has to be willing to pay more—in the form of a carbon tax if we want to avoid global warming, for example, or higher prices if we want higher wages and better working conditions," said Reich, now a professor of public policy at the University of California at Berkeley. "There's the rub. And I'm not sure the public is willing to bite these bullets quite yet."

Consumers have indicated that they are willing to pony up more money for goods produced ethically, or for products labeled organic. Anecdotally, this can be seen by a proliferation of fashion lines at least claiming to be "green," though that means different things in different instances, and charging a premium. The same applies to the beauty industry.

More scientifically, a 1999 survey by Marymount University showed that 86 percent of the people polled would pay an extra dollar on a $20 apparel purchase if it were guaranteed to not come from a sweatshop. Similarly, three-quarters of consumers would avoid shopping at a store they knew to sell goods produced under sweatshop conditions.

That attitude, if extended to environmental and safety issues and brought fully to bear, could increase pressure on brands.

Harmful chemicals that might work their way into fashions on store shelves and into waterways outside of factories are also a worker safety issue. Such a connection helps give industrial pollution a human face, which makes combating it an easier sell to the consumer.

"The antisweatshop movement probably hasn't paid enough attention to this," said Bob Jeffcott, policy analyst at the Maquila Solidarity Network, which agitates for worker rights. "We have to make sure the consumers are also equally aware of the impact of these dangerous chemicals used in the production of these products."

Unions also are taking note and planning to mobilize.

Bruce Raynor, general president of apparel union UNITE HERE, said the spate of tainted products from China is a serious blow to the sourcing status quo.

"This is not going to go away," said Raynor. "This is the biggest major development since the sweatshop issue."

Raynor pointed to Wal-Mart and said the company was being impacted by campaigns highlighting its business practices to consumers. Wal-Mart, the world's largest retailer, has come under fire for its antiunion efforts, its health care benefits and conditions at overseas factories.

"The consumer is the boss and the consumer is now making judgments about sourcing," said Raynor, who described the legacy of tainted consumer goods as the "third leg" that will force the debate to a new level.

"We need to see campaigns led by unions and student organizations," he said. "You're going to see consumers react with their buying power."

If interest groups are going to use ethical sourcing habits to nudge consumer behavior or attitudes on trade issues, they are going to have to make the issue "real" to shoppers.

"Until they can take it and turn it into something people can see, touch and feel—if they can take that message and make it concrete, then it's more likely to effect the way people think, but otherwise it's abstract," said Laura Peracchio, professor of marketing at the University of Wisconsin in Milwaukee.

They also are going to have to appeal to the early adopters—not just celebrities, but fashion-minded people who set trends. Consumers generally don't move quickly, though.

"Behavior is slow and hard to change," stressed Peracchio.

It also might be hard to change the dynamics between manufacturers, vendors and retailers. As John Eapen, chairman of the American Apparel & Footwear Association's environmental task force, told WWD in August: "You have to honor and reward suppliers that have the know-how, that have the knowledge level and have the resources to do the right thing. [If] you go for the cheap stuff, this is what you get. When you don't have the relationship and you don't pay them properly, they're trying to cut corners and you can get into trouble. When you have 2,000 suppliers, somebody's going to cheat you."

In the end, though, the bottom line might be that ethical sourcing, no matter how engaged the consumer is, is just good business. The implementation of such practices across the industry could result in what Wal-Mart has found with its push for more environmentally friendly practices and products: The push has resulted in cost savings across the board.

"I'm seeing a rapid trend toward long-term sustainable enterprise that may increase costs somewhat," said Steven Jesseph, ceo of Worldwide Responsible Apparel Production, a nonprofit organization specializing in certification of ethically sourced goods.

"When you start imposing systems at a factory, is there a cost involved? Yes, but there are also efficiencies that are gained," said Jesseph, who retired from Sara Lee Branded Apparel in 2005 as vice president of compliance and risk management. "It therefore becomes an investment and there is a return on investment."

As with everything else in business, companies simply can't afford to take their guards down.

Kevin Burke, ceo of the American Apparel & Footwear Association, however, said the increase in freer trade after the elimination of a global system of quotas in 2005 has streamlined the supply chain and made it easier to source goods responsibly.

"There are not as many factories making products as there were," said Burke. "Now they can have long, steady relationships with factories. There are fewer and fewer bad players. They can't afford to be in business anymore."

CHAPTER 8
Going Green

After you have completed this chapter, you should be able to discuss:

- The overall concept of "going green"
- Terminology used by industry professionals and the media to describe the "green" movement
- The implications of such concepts as carbon footprint, sustainability, eco-conscious production, and others
- Why the use of plastic bag has become such an important issue for supermarkets
- How retailers can become more energy-efficient
- The advantages of including eco-friendly products in a retailer's merchandise mix
- How merchants are using advertising, visual merchandising, and promotion to become more eco-friendly
- How suppliers are becoming more eco-friendly
- The pros and cons of going green
- Several resources that can guide retailers in their quest to become more environmentally sound

As a way to help preserve the environment or as a marketing ploy, merchants of all sizes and classifications are joining the bandwagon and **going green**. From giant retailers such as Wal-Mart and Home Depot to independent entrepreneurships, and from trade shows that supply these retailers to designers and manufacturers that produce the merchandise for retail distribution to the facilities creators that plan physical retail environments, a host of concepts are being used to foster the concept of "green."

Garment hangers made from recycled paper, clothing brands produced using organic materials, wind power in factories, innovative fabrics, reusable shopping bags, the recycling of plastics and paper waste, and energy-efficient compact fluorescent light bulbs are some of the directions that retailers (and the suppliers they buy from) are taking in their everyday operations to join the green bandwagon.

In selling the concept of **environmentally friendly**, each of these business entities uses a number of different means to promote the concept. These include consumer advertising in print and broadcast media, in-store signage, public relations releases to the editorial press,

Home Depot is a leader in "green" retailing practices.

online messages, special employee training, and trade paper ads that are intended to reach their retailer base.

From all indications and for whatever motivations, retailers across America are making every effort to do their share in preserving the environment.

THE LANGUAGE OF GREEN

Discussions of the green movement, advertisements that speak to it, and programs that address the concept all involve the use of terminology that is often not fully understood by consumers and business people. In order to develop a better understanding about what retailers and writers on the topic are speaking of, it is essential to have a working knowledge of the "green" language. The following terms are frequently employed:

Going green is used to describe business entities that have embraced the concept of environmental initiatives such as the use of organic materials in production, energy-saving measures, the replacement of plastic packaging, and so forth.

Organic cotton is a fiber that is cultivated without the use of synthetic fertilizers, chemical herbicides, insecticides, or genetically modified seeds.

Organic labeling involves the use of specific terminology on products such as apparel. The use of the words "100% organic cotton" means that only 100% organically produced cotton was used in the product. Variations on the label include the terms "organic cotton," which means that a minimum of 95% of the fiber was organically produced, and "made with organic cotton," which signifies that at least 70% of the product is organic.

Carbon footprint, according to www.Carbonfootprint.com, is defined as "a measure of the impact human activities have on the environment in terms of the amount of greenhouse gases produced, measured in units of carbon dioxide."

Eco-friendly is used to describe wearable products, physical environments, household products such as light bulbs, and so forth that contribute to protection of the environment.

Sustainability, according to the U.S. Environmental Protection Agency (EPA), is "the ability to achieve continuing economic prosperity while protecting the natural systems of the planet and providing a high quality of life for its people."

Third-party certification refers to independent certifying bodies that oversee claims of an organic nature. These include Leadership in Energy and Environmental Design (LEED), the U.S. Department of Agriculture, and others.

Environmental activism is a term that describes the different programs and approaches that businesses use to protect the environment from harm.

Environmental responsibility implies the obligation that businesses have to make the environment safer.

Carbon neutral, as defined by the *New Oxford Dictionary*, is "a state where a person or institution has reduced its carbon emissions where possible, and then purchased a carbon offset for its remaining emissions, bringing its carbon footprint down to zero."

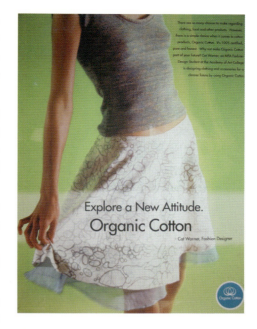

Organic cotton has become an important fiber for green-conscious manufacturers.

Eco-conscious production means that the manufacturing processes used by producers involve the use of energy-saving devices, materials of an organic nature, and so forth.

Reusable supplies are products that can be used again and again, such as the fabric shopping totes offered by some supermarkets.

Understanding these terms will help you make better sense of the environmental-saving issues addressed in the balance of this chapter.

AREAS OF GREENING RETAIL

Although the green concept is relatively new to most retail operations, it is being embraced by more merchants every day. Some have already undertaken full-scale programs to make themselves eco-friendly, while others are just getting into the game by introducing one or two concepts into their daily routines. The following sections describe those green initiatives that are evident in today's retail scene.

Cutting Down on Plastic Bag Usage

A walk through many of the outdoor Provençal markets in France reveals that visitors carrying their own shopping bags is the norm. All sorts of food items are purchased and inserted into fabric bags that are used over and over again. In many traditional European food markets, this is also the means of packing a customer's purchases. This type

Anya Hindmarch designed a canvas bag that is eco-friendly.

of bagging is now carrying over to many of America's supermarkets and other food stores. The ubiquitous use of plastic has become a sore point for environmentalists. Landfills are being inundated with this material, which is known to cause mountains of waste.

All over the country, the use of plastic is being replaced by other materials. The attention that this trend is receiving is evident in many places. Accessories designer Anya Hindmarch designed a white canvas tote that boasts the statement "I'm not a plastic bag." The tote was launched in the Los Angeles namesake boutiques of the designer, where the bag sold for $15, and it later surfaced in New York, New Jersey, and Canada. The next step was to release 20,000 more bags to Whole Foods locations in New York, New Jersey, and Connecticut. Now a fashion symbol that speaks of exclusivity and excitement, the bag is being used and reused in place of the plastic variety by fashion-savvy consumers. Here a simple product has helped people participate in the "green" movement.

In another attempt to curtail the use of plastic bags, IKEA charges $0.05 for a plastic bag and endorses the purchase of its reusable "Big Blue" IKEA bag. The goal is to cut back on use of the plastic variety, which amounts to 380 billion bags each year according to the EPA. The main culprit is the high-density polyethylene varieties, which number about 100 billion a year.

IKEA is a retailer engaged in several "green" practices.

The IKEA campaign promises to donate revenues from bag purchases to American Forests, a conservation organization that plants trees and restores forests. It is expected that its blue bag will be used again and again, reducing the need for the disposable plastic variety to the tune of 50 percent. The project is intended to reduce litter, lessen the need for more landfills, and help declutter the environment.

Tops Markets, a grocery chain, has joined other retailers like Wegmans and Save-A-Lot in the quest to reduce the number of plastic bags used in their stores and to encourage their customers to switch to environmentally friendly reusable totes. Although Tops was keen on making this transition from traditional bagging, its customer base also encouraged this move in the new direction. With a significant number of requests from its customers who increasingly embraced environmentally friendly products, Tops decided to make the move. The initial order of 25,000 reusable bags promptly sold out at 99 cents each.

The switch to reusable bags is by and large a shopper's choice. Although many have been encouraged to go this route, it is still up to the discretion of the consumer to heed the warnings caused by the mounting problems associated with plastic. In some locales, however, bans on plastic have been initiated by local legislatures, with many more now following suit. San Francisco enacted a ban that forbids plastic bag usage in large grocery stores and drugstores. As of this writing, similar measures are being considered in Boston, Baltimore, Oakland, Santa Monica, and Steamboat Springs.

Energy Efficiency

Inefficient lighting is one of the major areas of environmental abuse. Conventional incandescent bulbs, a mainstay in homes and businesses alike, are draining our energy supply. In their place, consumers and business users are turning to compact fluorescent light bulbs, which can last up to ten times longer than the incandescent variety. IKEA has been selling these **energy-efficient** bulbs for more than 10 years. They use 80 percent less energy than traditional bulbs while providing the same amount of light and a reduction in electric bill expenses.

Giant Eagle, a supermarket chain, utilizes environmentally friendly premises.

In retailing, the use of white and colored light is essential in display windows to enhance the featured products. Although this is important to the success of a display, conventional lighting is costly and energy-abusive. A study undertaken by the Lighting Research Center resulted in a major way in which light energy can be reduced. Light emitting diodes (LEDs) have been found to cut energy use as much as 50 percent while attracting more shopper attention. In its detailed study, the Lighting Research Center (in conjunction with the Los Angeles Department of Water and Power) surveyed 700 individuals over a period of eight weeks to evaluate the effectiveness of the LED systems. In a major Los Angeles store that used the new lighting, there was a 30 percent reduction in power usage. Moreover, 74 percent of the shoppers found the new lighting eye-catching, 84 percent agreed that the display windows were visually appealing, and 91 percent confirmed that the visibility of the displays was not diminished.

Reaching new heights in eco-friendly facilities is Giant Eagle, the subject of the following *Focus*.

Focus on . . .
Giant Eagle

THE SUPERMARKET INDUSTRY WITNESSED SOMETHING NEW in ways to become more energy-efficient when Giant Eagle opened its unit in Brunswick, Ohio. No only was energy on the minds of the company and the design team that created the store, but so were many other "green" conditions. It was the first supermarket to achieve the LEED designation—Leadership in Energy and Environmental Design—a certification awarded by the United States Green Building Council.

In addition to the use of energy-saving fluorescents, the company went several steps further to reduce energy costs and usage. More than half of the store's electrical energy is supplied by wind-generated power. Fifty large skylights allow for an efficient balance between fluorescent lights and day lighting. Sensors installed within each skylight measure the daylight throughout the day and adjust the fluorescent lighting accordingly.

In addition to these energy-saving concepts is the use of a reflective white roof that reduces heat. In traditionally built roofs, which are usually black, the heat is absorbed and brought into the store. This necessitates more air conditioning, which is costly and wastes energy. Giant Eagle also used cabinetry and paneling made of renewable wheat in place of wood. And with carpet that contains no volatile organic compounds, the store is a model for the green retail phenomena.

• •

Also innovative in its energy-efficient store design is the British retailer Tesco, which has opened convenience stores on the West Coast. The company has installed what amounts to a power plant in its distribution center that employs photovoltaic solar panels generating 2 megawatts of electricity and capable of serving nearly a fifth of the building's power needs.

Adding Eco-Friendly Products to the Merchandise Mix

From grocers like Whole Foods to luxury merchants like Barneys, the move to bring eco-friendly products to the merchandise assortments is in high gear. All across the board, retailers of every classification are stocking their shelves with eco-conscious lines. The demand for such items increases daily, and retailers have responded by devoting more space to these items.

Barneys's goal is to offer its customers the opportunity to make eco-conscious decisions when shopping for luxury items. Much of the merchandise in the company's 17 stores incorporates organic fabrics and or sustainable and environmentally friendly processes. Julie Gilhart,

Whole Foods was an early proponent of eco-friendly products.

Barney's sells a "green" collection called *Loomstate*.

Patagonia is one of the leading producers of eco-friendly merchandise.

Senior VP and fashion director, reports that some of the biggest designers in the industry are "going green." At the moment, Barneys sells organic collections from 3.1 Phillip Lim and Stella McCartney. Of significant importance to the company is a collection called *Loomstate for Barneys Green*. It is a collection of dresses, knits and T-shirts all made from environmentally restorative materials and fabrics such as certified organic cotton and wool. The collection is identified with a special hangtag indicating that both Barneys and Loomstate will donate a percentage of their sales to the 1% For The Planet. There are also several skincare and cosmetics lines that are offering green products, beginning with the composition and extending to the packaging.

The Swedish-based retail operation H&M is making important strides to add large numbers of environmentally-appropriate lines to its merchandise assortment. The goal is to use 600 tons of organic cotton annually, which is 30 times more than its current use of the fiber. Together with the World Wildlife Fund and Organic Exchange, H&M is fully engaged in promoting the use of organic cotton.

In the News...

"Leading the Way," an article that appears on page 188 at the end of this chapter, should be read now to learn how many European retailers are taking a leadership role in the green movement.

• • • • • • • • • • • • • • • • • • •

In the grocery arena, Whole Foods is a major player in the sale of eco-conscious products. In addition to food offerings that feature organic products, the company is expanding its "Under the Canopy" collection of clothing and bathrobes. Organic cotton, soy, bamboo, silk, and wool are used in the items.

In the News...

The article "Earthly Delights" (on page 186 at the end of this chapter) focuses on the increased demand for eco-conscious merchandise and should be read at this time.

• • • • • • • • • • • • • • • • • • •

Patagonia, the subject of our next *Focus*, is a company that manufactures many of its own goods and sells them primarily in its own stores. It is considered one of the nation's leading outlets for eco-friendly products.

Focus on . . .
Patagonia

ONE OF THE MORE ECO-SAVVY COMPANIES IS PATAGONIA. With stores all across North America, a Web site, and a catalogue that not only markets environmentally appropriate clothing and gear but also features articles on saving the environment, it is one of the earliest entries into retailing to participate in environmental activism.

Patagonia's mission statement best summarizes the goals of the company: To "build the best product, do no unnecessary harm, use business to inspire and implement solutions to the environmental crises."

Patagonia began as a small company that made tools for mountain climbers. It still makes clothing for climbers but now also dresses skiers, snowboarders, surfers, fly fishermen, and trail runners. Its designs stress simplicity, utility, and—wherever possible—materials that are eco-friendly. The company donates its time, services, and at least 1 percent of sales to hundreds of grassroots environmental groups all over the world who work to reverse the tide. It uses recycled polyester and organic cotton instead of the pesticide-intensive variety.

Dedicated to building products and working with processes that cause the least harm to the environment, Patagonia evaluates raw materials, invests in innovative technologies, and polices its waste. In addition to the aforementioned 1 percent of sales donations, it engages in "Common Threads Garment Recycling." In this program, customers return their worn out garments for recycling.

Other areas of environmental-related participation include the following:

- Membership in the Conservation Alliance, a group of 70 companies that each contribute annual dues to a central fund that distributes the monies to environmental groups
- Maintenance of grants programs to fund innovative groups that have been overlooked by other corporate donors—groups that advocate radical and strategic steps to protect habitat, wilderness, and biodiversity
- Membership in Organic Exchange, a nonprofit organization committed to expanding organic agriculture with a specific focus on increasing the production and use of organically grown fibers such as cotton
- Participation in environmental activism, including the selection of an environmental crisis every one or two years for study

Patagonia is LEED certified. The designation is awarded to companies that have erected green buildings that balance environmental responsibility and resources efficiency and that address the comfort and well-being of their staffs.

"Eco-Only" Merchandising

Retailers have received a lot of favorable press coverage about including eco-friendly products in their merchandise assortments. Some have taken the concept a step further, going green by offering **eco-only merchandise** exclusively. The list of retailers subscribing to this approach is short but continues to grow.

Greenloop is a retailer that exclusively features products manufactured by companies committed to social responsibility. The vast list of apparel and accessories employ sustainable textiles, many of which are recycled. Their production employs renewable energy gases, or-

Greenloop is an eco-only merchant.

ganic farming, and sweatshop-free manufacturing. Although the end products offered by Greenloop are eco-friendly, their design does not sacrifice style and fashion. The company's on-site store is in Portland, Oregon, but the bulk of its business is transacted via its Web site, www.thegreenloop.com.

Pangaya describes itself as an online eco-chic retailer that cares about sustainability and fashion. Its merchandise selection includes women's and children's clothing, accessories, home furnishings, skin care products, and gift items. The company features organic and natural products that are made in sweatshop-free environments and donates 1 percent of its annual sales to environmental causes.

Recycling

Landfill eyesores are becoming all too common in the United States. Filled with a number of different products that don't break down, these mountains of trash are causing significant environmental concern. Imbedded in these ever-growing landfills is potentially toxic refuse such as inkjet and toner cartridges, cell phones, digital cameras, and dead batteries.

More and more environmentally friendly retailers are joining the recycling bandwagon to eliminate these mounds of waste that can cause ecological damage. Staples' green initiative includes a program that makes it easy for customers to recycle the aforementioned products. IKEA is also involved in recycling with its "Free Take Back" program. Shoppers are encouraged to bring their used fluorescent lights (which contain mercury) for free disposal. Each store offers recycle bins in which the burned-out tubes and bulbs are stored before being recycled into new products.

Gant, in its Fifth Avenue flagship, is launching a *Patterns of Green* lecture series.

Advertising, Visual Merchandising, and Promotion

One of the surest ways of bringing the "green" message to the consumer is through advertising, visual merchandising, and promotion. The mere inclusion of eco-friendly products, and initiatives that are environmentally sound, may go unnoticed unless attention is drawn to them.

In an effort to spread the news about their green involvement, retailers are using the media, store windows, promotional endeavors, online messages, and so forth to an increasing degree. Barneys New York, for example, has used its display windows to extol the virtues of being environmentally friendly. Its 2007 display windows presented a green theme featuring a tribute to the heroes and champions of the green movement. The display mascots included Rudolph the Recycled Reindeer and Frosty the Fair Trade Snowman. Supplemental to the visual merchandising are packaging and gift cards made of recycled materials as well as shopping bags with a green message.

On the promotion front, Gant—in its redesigned flagship store on New York's Fifth Avenue—is launching a *Patterns of Green* lecture series. Many of today's most influential green pioneers will be engaged to inform the community on environmental responsibility. Kicking off the series was Robert F. Kennedy Jr. with a talk aimed at benefitting the Waterkeeper Alliance.

A unique way of promoting environmentally sound products has been employed by Home Depot in all of its stores. In April 2007 the company introduced a new labeling program for about 3,000 products, such as light bulbs and natural insect killers, that promote energy conservation, sustainable forestry, and clean water. By 2009, the initiative is expected to include 6,000 products, representing 12 percent of the chain's sales, and become the largest green labeling program in the United States. The items will be identified with the "Eco Options" brand tag. In order to motivate suppliers to get on the ecology bandwagon, Home Depot has promised to give them prominent shelf space and aggressive marketing in weekly newspaper inserts.

Every indication is that more and more retailers who understand the benefits of green merchandising, store design, and eco-friendly concepts are using the aforementioned promotional activities to foster the movement.

Purchasing from Eco-Friendly Suppliers

Every day the roster of those manufacturers who take steps in the direction of eco-friendliness is growing. Marquee brands such as Nike, Perry Ellis, and Levi's are adding products to their lines that are eco-friendly and are also implementing business practices that lessen harmful effects on the environment. Materials such as organic cotton, bamboo, soy, and coconut are being used to produce shirts, underwear, sports apparel, and accessories.

Nike sells a variety of eco-friendly products.

The reasons for this activism are twofold. One is the desire to do something that will help save the environment; the other is a response to consumer awareness. In 2001, an NPD Group research project found that 6 percent of respondents were interested in purchasing eco-friendly products; in 2006, this number rose to 18 percent.

One problem with using organic fibers, for example, is that the garments made with these materials are more costly. Although sticker shock is a reality, it is expected that—given increased public awareness regarding environmental issues—the eventual results will be positive.

The implementation of environmental safeguards is also being addressed by some vendors. For example, Liz Claiborne, Inc., uses some wind power for its New Jersey warehouse and distribution center. The North Face is another manufacturer committed to The Conservation Fund's *Go Zero* program to neutralize its carbon footprint. By paying for the planting of enough trees to offset its hazardous emissions, the company hopes to address the problem of global warming. Timberland expects to become carbon neutral by 2010 after introducing its *Green Index*. This program measures greenhouse gas emissions that result from production, the presence of hazardous substances, and the reduction of resource consumption from using recycled, organic, and renewable materials.

Prana, an outdoors brand owned by Liz Claiborne; Quiksilver; Volcom; Sole Technology, Inc., owners of action brands Entries and ThirtyTwo; B.U.M Equipment; Atman, a Russell Simmons line; Gant; Louis Vuitton; and Bamford & Sons are just a few of the other companies that have started to make changes that will help preserve the environment. With many retailers now addressing eco-friendliness in their merchandise assortments and advertising campaigns, their commitment to buying from suppliers who support these concepts is increasing.

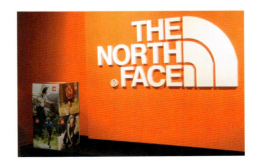

North Face is committed to The Conservation Fund's *Go Zero* program.

The world's largest retailer, Wal-Mart, is a leader in the green initiative. Dozens of changes by the company are making them environmentally friendly, as discussed in the next *Focus* segment.

> ### Focus on . . .
> ### Wal-Mart
>
> **ALTHOUGH MANY ARE CRITICAL OF SOME OF WAL-MART'S PRACTICES,** there is a general consensus that the company is on the right path to becoming an industry leader in helping to improve the environment.
>
> Wal-Mart's initiatives run the gamut from simple, commonsense solutions to more involved approaches. Simply by dimming its lights between midnight and 6 A.M., the company realizes significant energy savings. Other changes and directions are more profound. These include:
>
> - Requiring that some of its suppliers change product designs to comply with new environmental standards
> - Reducing the packaging for its Kids Connection toy line, which will result in the use of 720 fewer freight containers
> - Changing the light bulbs in its display of ceiling fans to energy-efficient compact fluorescent lights
> - Investing $500 million annually in sustainable technology
> - Retrofitting older stores with more efficient lighting and ballasts that reduce the use of energy 15 percent
> - Opening an environmentally friendly store in McKinney, Texas, that incorporates cutting-edge green technologies, including alternative energy sources
> - Requiring that suppliers change their distribution routes to help save gas
>
> The company is presently considering the elimination of those suppliers who do not comply with its eco-friendly demands. It is a safe bet that, given Wal-Mart's clout, these demands will be met.

TRADE ASSOCIATION ACTIVISM

The Collective is a premier menswear trade store.

We have discussed how many manufacturers have embraced green principles in their production, how retailers have included more and more eco-friendly items in their merchandise assortments and factored environmental considerations into the running of their operations, and how certifying agencies (such as LEED) have helped oversee business claims regarding environment protection. Now trade associations are beginning to help spread the message.

At the 2007 trade exposition of The Collective—a premier men's trade show—a panel with four well-versed participants addressed the audience of retailers about how they could provide eco-friendly products to their customers and why going organic may prove to be a worthwhile effort. Topics included how the eco-friendly trend will trickle down to the consumer as well as the obligation of merchants to educate their customers about green concerns.

THE PROS AND CONS OF GOING GREEN

Although the advantages of environmental awareness are regularly extolled in the media, some retailers remain skeptical. Before listing the negatives, we summarize the positives as follows:

Advantages
- A positive image is established by those embracing the various manifestations of "green." Consumers in ever-growing numbers are reacting positively to environmentally committed merchants through loyalty and regular patronization.
- The sense of acting ethically is a benefit of going green. In a time when ethics are in question in many aspects of business and other arenas, those who follow eco-friendly principles are likely to be considered ethical business people.
- Operating costs are reduced when, for example, a company employs energy-efficient lighting or charges for disposable plastic shopping bags.
- The quality of life is enhanced by participation in green programs. The ecosystem is protected and enhanced.

Disadvantages
- Some of the kinks, as in new eco-sound environment design, have not yet been worked out.
- Manufacturers that subscribe to the use of green materials are limited in number and don't always offer the essential products of a retailer's merchandise mix.
- Products that are manufactured in eco-friendly environments are often costlier than those that are traditionally produced, making them too expensive for some customers.

Although from every indication the green concept is on an upturn, it is still too early to proclaim its success for retailers.

GREEN RESOURCES

We have seen that the green movement is gaining momentum with retailers and the industries that service them. Although many of the larger merchants have departments that study environmental advancements, others do not. Smaller retailers can still obtain valuable information on the topic by logging on to Web sites that offer advice on everything from energy efficiency to eco-friendly products. Some of these are governmental or nonprofit sites, while others are for-profit resources.

Governmental and Nonprofit Web Sites
- The U.S. Department of Energy Green Power Network (www.eere.energy.gov/greenpower) offers information about green power providers, products of a green nature, issues that provide protection to the consumer, and the policies that affect green power markets. It is operated by the National Renewable Energy Laboratory of the U.S. Department of Energy.
- The National Renewable Energy Laboratory (www.nrel.gov) offers information regarding renewable energy and energy efficiency.

- The World Resources Institute (www.wri.org) is a nonprofit think tank that helps society conduct itself in a manner that protects the environment. Of paramount importance to their goals are reversing the degradation of ecosystems, providing information about natural resources and the environment, and protecting the environment from greenhouse gases.
- The U.S. Green Building Council (www.usgbc.org) helps interested parties with the tools they need to leverage green building. It oversees LEED, the accepted benchmark for green building performance.
- The Sustainable Style Foundation (www.sustainablestyle.org) offers a daily showcase for green products and covers sustainable style information and resources.

For-Profit Resources
- Fabulously Green (http://fabgreen.com) tracks the latest trends, styles, and products in eco-friendly fashion and accessories.
- StyleWillSaveUs (www.stylewillsaveus.com) is an independent digital magazine concerned with stylish, organic, eco-friendly, and sustainable products.
- TreeHugger (www.treehugger.com) is a blog that addresses everything green; it provides the latest updates on green trends.

The resources listed here constitute only a fraction of what is available on eco-friendly matters. Using an Internet search engine and entering such key words as "eco-friendly," "environmentalism," or "saving the environment" will yield a wealth of other Web sites for further exploration.

CHAPTER HIGHLIGHTS

- The "language of green" offers many new terms that are becoming commonplace in discussions about the environment and are now regularly used by retailing professionals and the media.
- Plastic bag usage has become a major concern for eco-friendly supermarkets, many of which have chosen alternate means of packing.
- Energy efficiency is a challenge that has been taken on by concerned retailers in their own premises and through their product offerings.
- More and more retailers are adding eco-friendly products to their merchandise mixes to protect the environment and attract green-aware customers.
- Recycling is the order of the day for retailers, such as IKEA, that are concerned with preserving the environment.
- Through advertising, visual merchandising, and other promotional endeavors, merchants are spreading the word about the importance of environmental concerns.
- Many retail suppliers are using raw materials that are eco-friendly and production methods that are less harmful to the environment.
- Trade associations are beginning to address issues associated with the environment.
- While the advantages of going green are significant, there are also disadvantages for the retailer.

IMPORTANT RETAILING TERMS

carbon footprint (174)
carbon neutral (175)
eco-conscious production (175)
eco-friendly (174)

eco-only merchandising (179)
energy-efficient (176)
environmental activism (175)
environmentally friendly (173)
environmental responsibility (175)
going green (173)
organic cotton (174)
organic labeling (174)
reusable supplies (175)
sustainability (175)
third-party certification (175)

FOR REVIEW

1. What is the motivation for retailers to go green?
2. What is meant by going green?
3. How does organic cotton differ from regular cotton?
4. Explain the term *carbon footprint*.
5. Describe some of the measures taken by retailers to become eco-friendly.
6. How have manufacturers become more eco-conscious in their production?
7. Explain how many retailers have cut down on the use of disposable plastic bags in their operations.
8. How have retailers employed energy-efficient lighting for their premises?
9. What are some of the ways in which facilities have become more energy-efficient?
10. What is meant by the term *eco-friendly product*?
11. What are some of the initiatives undertaken by Patagonia to assist environmental causes?
12. What is the "eco-only" merchandising concept?
13. Describe IKEA's light-bulb recycling program.
14. Discuss Home Depot's labeling of products that are environmentally sound.
15. In addition to organic cotton, what other materials are being used by fashion manufacturers in their eco-friendly products?
16. What are some of the pros and cons of going green?

AN INTERNET ACTIVITY

From the *Green Resources* section of the chapter, select one of the Web sites that pay special attention to environmental protection. For the chosen site, discuss the following:

- The nature of the Web site (governmental, nonprofit, or for-profit)
- The scope of the organization's activities
- The targeted group
- The products discussed on the Web site
- Its goals and aspirations

The material should be summarized in a typewritten paper no more than three pages long.

EXERCISES AND PROJECTS

1. Visit a local supermarket to determine the depth and breadth of its commitment to protecting the environment. Through observation and pre-arranged interviews with company representatives, address all of the areas in which they are presently involved and the areas that they expect to tackle in the future. Present your findings in a report that will be delivered to the class.
2. Visit an apparel store in your community to see whether any of its garments' tags speak to the topic of eco-friendliness. Using a sample of these tags (obtained with the store's permission), prepare an oral presentation for the class.
3. In a shopping mall, downtown area, or any other shopping venue, examine the window and interior visual presentations to determine which ones are eco-friendly. With the merchant's permission, photograph these presentations for class discussion.

THE CASE OF THE INDEPENDENT MERCHANT GOING GREEN

In spite of competition from major players in the retailing industry with their numerous units, catalogues, and Web sites, Fashion Plus—a single-unit specialty store—continues to meet its challenges. Successful ever since its opening ten years ago, the company has developed a business that remains profitable. Its merchandise assortment is replete with designer and bridge collections, all of which are fashion forward. (Bridge collections are lines that have price points just below those of designer collections.) Fashion Plus also offers a small selection of couture merchandise for affluent clientele seeking more exclusivity. Like most small, independent fashion emporiums, it does not merchandise private-label collections because these offerings require considerable monetary commitments.

The premises of the store occupy approximately 10,000 square feet in a single-level environment. Two major display windows flank either side of their entranceway, with interior showcases and fixtures making up the inside of the store.

With all of the trade papers, such as *Women's Wear Daily*, featuring articles on the importance of retailer participation in helping to save the environment, the store's owner, Kathy Parker, feels obliged to do her part in the war against environmental abuse. She and her manager, Don Phillips, are in the process of trying to figure out how Fashion Plus can become more eco-friendly. Given its limited resources, replacing the roof on the building owned by the company would be too costly; becoming an "eco-only" operation could jeopardize the success of its current merchandise mix.

Although hiring a consultant could be helpful, such expense is considered inappropriate for their business. Kathy and Don are scanning the media and logging on to environmentally oriented Web sites for ideas. For now, they still haven't made any changes in the running of their company.

Questions

1. Is there any reason for such a small company as Fashion Plus to get on the eco-friendly bandwagon?
2. How can the company make changes that would be environmentally sound at a modest cost?

Earthly Delights
Sharon Edelson with contributions by Rosemary Feitelberg

APRIL 10, 2007

As demand increases, retailers are devoting more space to eco-conscious lines.

It's getting easier to be green.

Al Gore and friends have made global warming the cause du jour in certain circles, celebrities are driving Toyota Priuses in Hollywood and organic food products are finding their way to mainstream supermarket shelves and even Wal-Mart. Caring about the environment isn't just for treehuggers anymore. So, with their cups of fair trade coffee and cage-free egg omelettes, consumers are now reaching for clothing made from organic cotton or natural fibers such as hemp. Retailers are happy to oblige.

In March, Barneys New York unveiled Loomstate for Barneys Green, an ambitious green collection designed by Rogan Gregory, who also teamed up with Bono and his wife, Ali Hewson, to create Edun.

"Loomstate for Barneys Green is a sexier version of what we're doing in our main line," said Scott Hahn of Loomstate. "There are more dresses and edgier silhouettes, and tops have asymmetrical shapes and architectural lines."

Hahn added that, for fall, the line also will offer outerwear, organic cotton and free-range alpaca sweaters, as well as an eco jean in unwashed 100 percent vegetable-dyed cotton. "It's an authentic, raw kind of jean that's symbolic of this whole pure movement," he said.

The Loomstate for Barneys Green collection carries a hangtag signifying that both Barneys and Loomstate will donate a percentage of their sales to the 1 Percent for the Planet environmental organization.

Consumer reaction to the line has been strong. "We sold 400 pieces [of Loomstate] last week," Julie Gilhart, senior vice president and fashion director of Barneys, said late last month. "We bought a lot. There's not a style that's not selling."

The store is working hard to promote the brand, and eco-friendly apparel in general. Introducing customers to the idea of green clothing requires "a lot of education and a lot of hard work," Gilhart said. "We're doing seminars in all stores and sending out written information to sales associates." Barneys put a full-page ad for Loomstate in the New York Times and will feature it in the upcoming Co-op catalogue.

In addition to Loomstate for Barneys Green, the specialty chain is launching two new cosmetics brands—one organic and one all natural—developing a line of handbags and featuring shoes from Stella McCartney.

Sweden is one of the more environmentally conscious countries in the world, and Stockholm-based H&M has developed initiatives aimed at conserving the planet's resources. Last month, the retailer launched a stylish organic cotton collection, which retails from $34.90 to $59.90. "Sustainability is on everyone's mind today," said Lisa Sandberg, director of communications in the U.S. "The product is moving well in all our stores."

One of H&M's goals is to use 600 tons of organic cotton this year versus 20 tons last year. For the past five years, H&M has worked with the World Wildlife Fund and Organic Exchange, as well as governmental agencies, to promote the use of organic cotton.

On another front, H&M plans to donate 10 percent of sales of guest designer Kylie Minogue's collection to Water Aid, a nonprofit organization whose mission is to provide safe water and sanitation to indigent people. Minogue's styles will bow on May 10.

Sandberg also noted that clothing that doesn't pass the company's quality-control standards is donated to charity, with "millions" being given away in the U.S. alone.

Already sold at Whole Foods, spas and yoga boutiques, organic clothing line Under the Canopy is looking to expand its reach. In October, Origins will begin carrying select Under the Canopy clothing and bathrobes at all stores and counters. Made from cotton, soy, bamboo, silk and wool, the collection emphasizes style along with natural fabrics. A red camisole with embroidery and a ribbon tie, made of 100 percent soy, is as soft and fluid as any jersey. There's an embroidered banded blouson made of bamboo and an organic cotton gray shirt with a contrasting light gray yoke. Under the Canopy is targeting high-end specialty stores with a new edgier collection called 108, which includes tunic dresses in muted shades made of soft soy and organic cotton voile.

Diesel's ad campaign, "Global Warming Ready," uses images of sexy male and female models cavorting in well-known tourist destinations. But there's something wrong with these pictures. A tropical garden has grown around the Eiffel Tower, New York and Rio de Janeiro are practically submerged under water, Mount Rushmore looks like a Hawaiian beach and the Great Wall of China is surrounded by a giant desert. There's no mention, however, of the fibers used to make Diesel's jeans.

Levi Strauss & Co., on the other hand, has been promoting every natural aspect of its Eco jeans, which feature 100 percent organic cotton, natural dyes and a tag made of recycled paper and printed with environmentally friendly soy ink. The jeans, which are part of the company's Capital E label, have green stitching accents.

American Apparel, which is known for its antisweatshop position, sells Sustainable Edition, a line of organic cotton T-shirts and baby clothes.

At Nordstrom, organic cotton can be found in the store's private label collection. "Nordstrom joined the Organic Cotton Exchange in 2004," said a spokeswoman. "Since that time, our goal has been to use some percentage of organic cotton in at least 5 percent of all Nordstrom private label products. We have achieved that goal and are now setting new goals to increase our use of organic cotton in our products."

Nordstrom features Amber Sun separates made of organic cotton in the Narrative department and Halogen T-shirts with 5 percent organic cotton in its TBD section, along with organic cotton sleepwear and robes. Organic cotton and bamboo items will launch in activewear in the summer, and the store offers 100 percent organic luxury bedding and towels in its housewares department.

Nordstrom is heeding the call to eco-consciousness in other ways, as well. The company in April began printing its catalogues on recycled paper and gift boxes are made of 100 percent paperboard stock with a minimum of 40 percent post-consumer content.

Wal-Mart last year doubled its organic food offerings and launched the George Baby line of 100 percent organic cotton infant clothes. The retailer is offering organic T-shirts in the junior department as well as Hanes sleepwear.

Finally, there's Ekovaruhuset, an organic fair trade boutique on New York's Lower East Side indicative of the grass-roots nature of the green movement. Ekovaruhuset, which opened four months ago and is the younger sibling of a Swedish store by the same name, showcases green designers who screen-print fabric and sew, weave and crochet one-off items for the store. For spring, Ekovaruhuset will feature an organic collection from As Three.

"We're trying to make the whole organic thing very interesting and sexy," said Melissa Kirgan, an Ekovaruhuset designer.

When the store first opened, consumer interest was slow to build. "Now there's all these eco tours with buses coming down here and other eco-friendly stores are opening nearby," Kirgan said.

Leading the Way
Ellen Groves

October 30, 2007

Recognizing the potential for cost savings and new markets, European retailers are taking a leadership role in the green movement.

There are rumblings of a green retail revolution in Europe.

Retailers are going beyond just stocking environmentally friendly and ethically oriented products and are repositioning themselves as completely eco-conscious from the factory floor to the eco-friendly store. From introducing organic private label apparel collections to reducing their factories' carbon footprints, retailers are polishing up their ethical credentials, often on several fronts at once.

PPR, which owns Gucci Group and the La Redoute catalogue, recently introduced a new department grouping environmental, social and diversity initiatives. The department—the first of its kind for a French company listed among the country's 40 biggest publicly traded firms, according to its chief executive officer Laurent Claquin—underscores a general move toward a more holistic view of ethical concerns.

For retailers, that means going beyond just offering the token handful of ethical apparel lines they've made available to their customers up to now. German department store Karstadt, for example, plans to introduce its own sustainable label next year. Also, according to industry sources, Galeries Lafayette will debut an eco-fashion concept, including a private label ethical clothing line, in the spring.

"There's no point offering a pair of organic socks, if 99 percent of the offer isn't [organic]," said Hélène Sarfati-Leduc, head of textile projects for Yamana, a sustainable development consultancy.

Similarly, some stores are delving deeper into environmental issues and ensuring their work practices reflect a renewed commitment to green matters.

In the U.K., this month Marks & Spencer unveiled its first green store, which uses energy-efficient appliances, while Tesco began opening stores with carbon footprints some 60 percent lower than its traditional outlets.

"Retailers can't compete on price alone anymore with Asian imports bringing prices down," Sarfati-Leduc said. "They have had to find another way."

More executives are realizing that communicating a meaningful message to customers can only be achieved by tackling environmental and social issues together.

"It's not one versus the other," said Karstadt's ceo, Peter Wolf.

Marks & Spencer's five-year eco-plan, dubbed "Plan A" and announced in January, was a catalyst for that approach.

"While some organizations were very cautious about making high-profile claims, a ceo like [Marks & Spencer's] Stuart Rose really took a leadership stance and broke ranks," said Rita Clifton, chairwoman of New York-based branding consultancy Interbrand Corp.

Such major players throwing their weight behind ethical and environmental issues is key to the trend becoming mainstream going forward, according to executives.

"The more companies—Carrefour, for example—with huge power that get involved, there's a competition effect, encouraging others to do the same," said Olivier Ven, apparel quality manager for La Redoute. The retailer carries its own fair trade cotton lines and supports ethical designers through its annual prize "Tackling Ethical Fashion with La Redoute." The winner gets to design a collection exclusively for La Redoute.

While big business may make the difference in the future, it's the demands of individual consumers that are bolstering the ethical movement today, according to retailers. A TNS Worldpanel Fashion study this August found about 7.1 million British consumers feel ethical issues are important, but that availability of products is poor.

Executives hope to tap that market.

"We keep our fingers on the pulse of what customers want," said Allan Wragg, category technical manager of Tesco's clothing division, which is expanding its fair trade and organic brands. "If we give [consumers] a T-shirt that looks good and that is also a positive and environmentally sound product, it makes the customer feel that they are doing their bit."

And consumers increasingly want to get involved.

"Twenty or 30 years ago if you were interested in ecology, people looked at you like you were a hippie," said PPR's Claquin. "The phase we are in now is the realization that global warming is something we can't avoid, we can't pretend it does not exist and even on our own scale, on a daily basis we can change what we do."

Unpredictable weather, such as the poor summer in the U.K., has brought the issue of climate change even closer to home, added Jane Shepherdson, who introduced fair trade brand People Tree at Topshop when she was buying director there.

"It's now much more immediate," she said. "People are thinking about their choices a little bit more."

"No retailer can sensibly ignore that sort of market as they did for most of the 1990s," said Richard Perks, senior retail analyst at London-based Mintel.

Although Perks found the core of green consumers has grown only slightly in 20 years, retailers are hedging their bets on its future importance.

"It's like the Internet," said Karstadt's Wolf. "In the beginning, everyone said it wouldn't amount to much. The question is: Do you want to be a late follower or a first mover?"

While green approaches are costly—Marks & Spencer's Plan A weighed in at 200 million pounds, or $410 million at current exchange—executives say such strategies can reduce long-term costs.

"If you do things right, you can actually make cost savings on things like packaging," said Tesco's Wragg.

Some companies are still taking a soft approach when it comes to communicating on green issues, as they're wary of seeming hypocritical if they vaunt their positives, while ignoring areas yet to be improved.

"The reason is that if I speak about some good actions I'm taking, people will try to find what I'm doing that's bad," said Yamana's Sarfati-Leduc.

Tesco was recently lambasted by the media for not fully backing collections by Katharine Hamnett, amid speculation the eco-fashion designer had stopped working with the retailer.

Consumer polls have so far been kinder. Earlier this month, the U.K.'s first Climate Brand Index, which grades consumer perception of brand performance on climate change run by London's The Climate Group, ranked Tesco as number one. Marks & Spencer and Sainsbury's were also in the top five.

Social responsibility claims are met with more skepticism, however. Forty-five percent of Brits don't believe the ethical claims made by high-street fashion stores, according to TNS.

"They need to be able to prove what they say and be more transparent to consumers," said Katharine Hamnett, who declined comment on her Tesco deal.

Companies can boost credibility by taking a long-term approach.

Marks & Spencer is working on a lingerie factory in Sri Lanka that will run on renewable energy, while Tesco is helping build lower-energy factories in East Africa, Sri Lanka and Bangladesh. Retailers are already influencing the supply chain.

"You even see farmers saying, 'We need to get more organic [or fair trade] cotton to fill our Marks & Spencer orders,'" said Shepherdson. Marks & Spencer will introduce 20 million fair trade cotton garments over the next year.

"When companies like Inditex are asking their suppliers to respect environmental and social aspects, it's affecting the whole supply chain," said Gildas Minvielle, head of the Economic Observatory for the Institut Français de la Mode.

And future shoppers seem set to be even more demanding when it comes to ethical and environmental issues.

"In the U.K. there's a lot of pressure in education to make kids more green and ethically aware," said Mintel's Perks. "That should work into attitudes as they get older although how much that sticks, whether they rebel against it, remains to be seen."

Future rebellions aside, businesses are responding to today's already demanding consumer.

"We've got to do this because it's good for the planet, it's what our customers expect of us," said Tesco's Wragg.

—With contributions from Lucie Greene, Tosin Mfon and Melissa Drier

PART TWO

Management and Operational Controls

Before any business can operate successfully and return a profit to its investors, it must establish management and operational controls that will enable it to carry out its goals in the most efficient manner. The most talented individuals must be selected to manage these functions. In particular, the speedy distribution of the merchandise and its safeguarding are imperative to achieving the levels of success envisioned during the formation of the organization.

In Chapter 9, Human Resources Management, the role of human resources managers and their staffs are explored, underscoring their importance to the retail organization. The various roles of these managers are explained in detail.

One of the major obstacles plaguing merchants of every size and classification is shoplifting and internal theft. Chapter 10, Loss Prevention, addresses these problems as well as the ways in which today's merchants are coping with them.

In Chapter 11, Logistical Merchandise Distribution, discussion centers on the all-important matter of how the merchandise ordered by buyers and merchandisers reaches the selling floors.

Once these managerial endeavors and operational controls have been carefully accounted for and are working satisfactorily within the organizational structure, the company is ready to face the challenges of operating a retail business in the new millennium's competitive environment.

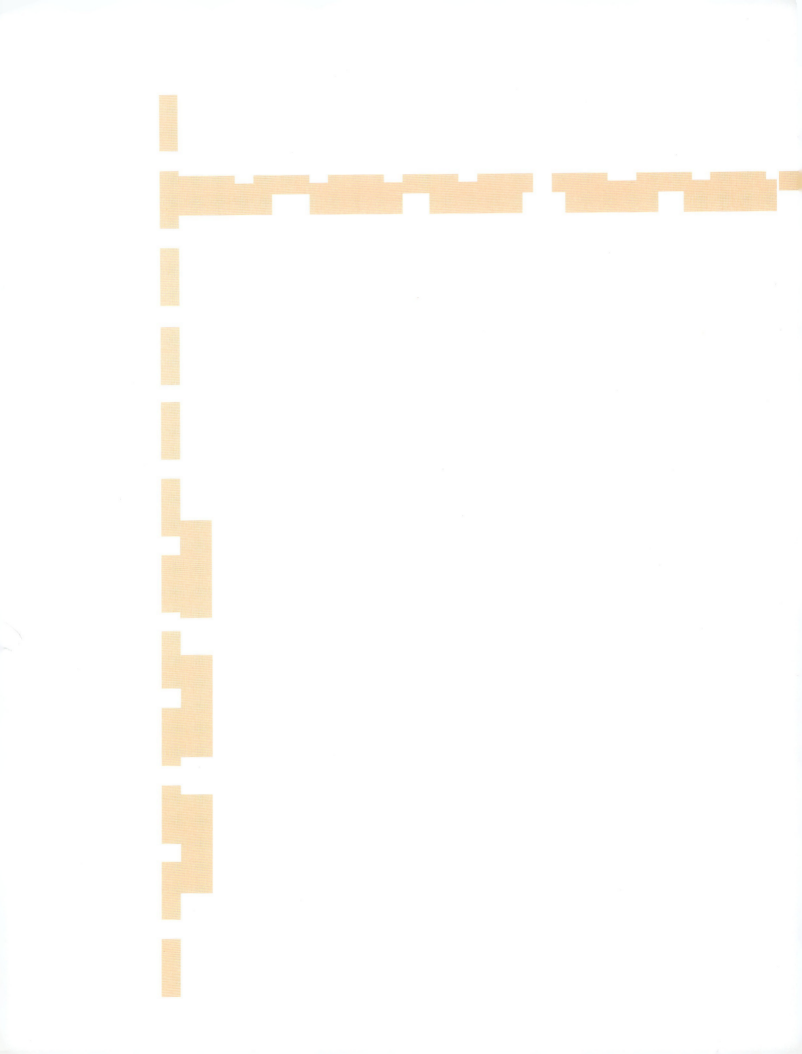

CHAPTER 9
Human Resources Management

After you have completed this chapter, you should be able to discuss:

- The various functions of the human resources department
- The concept of job analysis and how important it is in the recruitment of employees at all levels
- Which specific routes human resources managers take to find the most competent employees for their companies
- How the selection procedure is used to make certain that the most qualified candidate is hired
- Why training of employees is so vital to the success of a company and how that training is carried out
- The manner in which employee evaluations are performed at all levels
- Why different remuneration systems are employed in the industry
- What types of benefits are being offered to today's retail workers

Staffing a retail organization with the most qualified people is the responsibility of the human resources department. Today, this challenge is greater than ever before. Since multichannel retailing is the direction in which most of the larger organizations are headed, proper staffing has become even more critical. Not only must personnel be recruited and trained for every division of the store, but the same must be done for the company's off-site ventures, such as catalogues and Web sites. These relatively new approaches to retailing, coupled with the expansion undertaken by retailers, make the task a difficult one to accomplish.

The level of difficulty of store and off-site staffing varies according to the economy of the time. In the late 1980s, for example, retailers had few problems finding an experienced **employee pool** to draw from because the country was in the midst of an economic recession. With unemployment at significant levels at the time, individuals who would have opted for other careers were willing to consider one in retailing. The number of college graduates was at an all-time high, giving human resources managers a wealth of people from which to choose.

Staffing problems vary from year to year. As retailers entered the new millennium, finding individuals with the most potential to fill positions became more difficult. Because the economy was booming unlike any other time in the past, other industries were offering more financial rewards and incentives. The difficulty in hiring qualified people for retail positions reached critical levels. College graduates were being enticed to enter careers that paid more and often demanded less. It was a buyers' market, and retailers had to use their bag of tricks to convince people to consider retail careers. Whether it was in the recruitment of management level employees or those who might be needed as part-time sales associates, the task of staffing was a formidable one.

Toward the end of 2001, with a recession in place, it became easier to recruit people at all levels. Many employed by the dot-coms were out of work and turned to retailing for employment. Thus, the tasks of hiring are not a constant. In reality the problem is one of supply and demand. If the job applicant pool is large, then the responsibility of finding suitable employees is relatively simple. If, on the other hand, the pool has shrunk to very low numbers, the challenge of staffing is extremely complex. In the early part of the twenty-first century, human resources managers were much less stringent in their evaluation of potential employees than were their counterparts who made these decisions in other times. It wasn't a matter of carefully screening applicants for the positions; it was more a matter of using all of their expertise to find workers and motivate them to come on board. Oftentimes, managers settled for those who were willing to take the job.

Since 2007, recruitment at all levels has been relatively easy. With more and more jobs being lost to outsourcing, the employee base has broadened.

As we will learn in this chapter, retailers—and, more specifically, those entrusted with staffing—follow a set of principles in searching for individuals with the most potential to meet the needs of their companies. These principles inform a road map or plan that addresses all of the aspects of staffing such as recruitment, training, employee evaluation, compensation planning, and benefits and services.

In the News . . .

"H.R. Summit Reveals Employee Woes," an article reprinted on page 215 at the end of this chapter, should be read at this time.

EQUAL OPPORTUNITY EMPLOYMENT

Throughout the years, there has been considerable discussion regarding the rosters that make up the many different industries in the United States. Many believe that unfair advantages have been given to male Caucasians, especially in the upper reaches of management. Minorities and women have often complained that, while the jobs at the bottom of the ladder have been relatively easy to come by, there was little room at the top for them. In most fields, women rarely break through the **glass ceiling**. Even if a woman reaches a mid-management level position, the top of the ladder is often unreachable. Some women who have achieved a level of success in upper management positions find that rewards and compensation are not the same as those of their male counterparts.

The federal government, even with the passage of legislation such as The Equal Pay Act, hasn't been able to guarantee the same monetary rewards for men and women. The Civil Rights

Act protects people from discriminatory practices, but it still hasn't completely removed the biases in some industries.

Although employment opportunities continue to increase for minorities and women in most industries, few surpass retailing in terms of offering unbiased opportunity for advancement. An examination of the retailing arena shows that women and minorities are engaged in every level of employment, including the highest positions in the company. General merchandise managers, buyers, promotion executives, store managers, and fashion directors are just a few of the senior level and mid-management positions that these groups have obtained. Retailing continues to set an example for other fields of employment as the leader for advancement based on ability.

THE HUMAN RESOURCES DEPARTMENT

Except for smaller retailers, the industry utilizes human resources departments to manage all aspects of recruiting and maintaining a staff. The tasks are ones that involve every level of employment. In some instances, human resources focuses on the actual hiring of people for specific positions. In the area of selling, for example, employee selection is usually at the human resources department's discretion. Armed with a **job specifications** profile developed by merchandise department managers, employment managers simply hire those individuals who meet the pre-established criteria.

In positions that are above the selling and stock levels, human resources is often the initiator of the recruitment process but doesn't usually make the hiring decision. Once the department has found the prospects and screened them, the actual hiring decision is left up to the discretion of the supervisor for the vacant position. For example, divisional merchandise managers make the final decision for new buyers, and buyers have the ultimate say as to who their assistants will be.

RECRUITING AND HIRING EMPLOYEES

As mentioned previously, recruitment problems change according to the economics of the time. In any case, it is up to the human resources department's recruitment specialists to set up a plan that provides the best results. By understanding exactly what duties each position requires, they can select the most qualified candidates for company employment.

It all begins with **job analysis**, an investigative research procedure that involves cooperation from the various managers in the stores' numerous divisions. Once the specifications of each position—such as its title, level of technical knowledge, and duties—have been determined, the information is condensed into a format known as a **job description**. This simplifies the first stages of the recruitment process. Instead of having to make personal contact with those supervisors who have a vacancy, the employment manager refers to the specific description of the job that is to be filled. Each job description is kept in a computer file that may be quickly retrieved, making the process one that is fast and accurate.

Recruitment

There are numerous sources from which potential employees may be drawn. It is the professional human resources specialist who, from experience, knows which ones will have the greatest potential for bringing the right prospect to the company. The sources are of two types: internal and external.

Typically, a job description looks like this:

Massey & Lowell, Inc.

Division: Merchandising

Title: Buyer

Department: Men's Active Sportswear

Immediate Supervisor: Menswear Divisional Merchandise Manager

Professional Experience: Five years as an assistant buyer

Duties and Responsibilities:

- Purchase of new merchandise
- Six-month plan development
- Visits to domestic and foreign markets
- Analysis of computerized reports
- Adherence to open-to-buy parameters

A job description, like this one for a buyer, gives specific information and requirements for the position.

Internal Sources

Since the turnover rate is particularly high at the lower levels of retail employment, it is appropriate to elicit leads from current employees—that is, to conduct **internal sourcing**. If someone on the company's staff is a satisfied employee, it is relatively safe to assume that his or her recommendations will result in capable new candidates. Those currently employed by the company understand the plusses of working for the organization and could pass such information on to friends and relatives. Those who are satisfied employees often act as good will ambassadors for the operation. In order to motivate those on the retailer's team to make recommendations, many companies offer bonuses for their cooperation.

Upward mobility is the goal of many who have careers in retailing. Most retailers use the incentive of **promotion from within** to attract better people to fill their positions. With employees already on board who know the workings of the operation, this is a pool that is often tapped to fill positions that are higher on the ladder. An assistant buyer might be promoted to buyer, a department manager to a group manager, or a division merchandise manager to general merchandise manager. While this track might serve the needs of the company, it isn't always used to fill upper-level positions in the company. Relying solely on in-house workers may result in overlooking the potential for people outside of the company to bring in new ideas learned elsewhere. It is therefore essential that a combination of inside and outside sourcing be considered.

External Sources

There are many different external recruitment sources. **Outside sourcing** includes the more traditional formats such as **classified ads** and the relatively newer ones such as the Internet. Each serves the retailer to find appropriate candidates seeking employment.

Classified ads in local newspapers and trade publications are one way employers recruit potential employees.

CLASSIFIED NEWSPAPER ADVERTISEMENTS

Classified advertisements have been regularly used ever since the earliest newspapers were published. It is generally considered the most effective method to fill vacancies. Want ads, as they are often referred to, offer many advantages to the retailer. First, it is a relatively inexpensive tool to use. Second, the ad can be placed about 24 to 48 hours before newspaper publication, making it a fast technique to announce job openings. Third, if the ad is carefully developed, it can help eliminate less desirable candidates. Fourth, there are many newspapers, ranging in size from the local publications to nationally recognized ones. Every city, no matter what its size, publishes a paper that can be used for recruitment. Finally, newspapers such as the *New York Times* are read all around the country, extending the scope of the retailer's employee search. Of course, the disadvantage of using classified advertising is that it doesn't provide for any prescreening apparatus, as employment agencies do.

TRADE PUBLICATION WANT ADS

These ads are often used by retailers when they need to fill a management level position. *Women's Wear Daily* and *VM+SD* are just some of the trade papers that feature these ads. Since they are generally read by retailing professionals, it is the perfect place to seek employees. *VM+SD* is a monthly periodical that specializes in visual merchandising. Individuals in that aspect of the industry regularly read it and are well aware of the career opportunities section.

WEB SITES

The Internet has become important in reaching potential job applicants. With the computer playing a part in the everyday lives of most everyone in the United States, it has become a tool for employers to reach future employees. Recruiting sites such as Monster.com, Careerpath.com, and Gottajob.com are regularly used by such retail giants

Web sites like www.monster.com bring together huge numbers of employers and job candidates.

as Sears, JCPenney, and Best Buy. Other popular career Web sites include Yahoo! Hotjobs, Job-central.com, and CareerBuilder.

More and more retailers are also using their own Web sites to attract the attention of potential employees. Looking at any number of the major retailers in the country, you will find sections of their Web sites that invite users to investigate job opportunities with the company. The Target Corporation offers one of the more detailed of these Web sites.

Focus on . . .
Target Corporation

ONE OF THE FASTEST GROWING RETAIL ORGANIZATIONS in the United States is the Target Corporation. Expansion all across the country and a tremendous sales increase make the challenge of recruitment a formidable one.

In order for all its divisions to continue on a path of success, the company is always in a recruitment mode. Whether it is looking to fill a vacancy at the top of the organizational structure, at the mid-management level, or at a low-level position, the Target Corporation must find ways to attract competent workers to join its team. One of the methods that Target uses is the Internet. While many retailers use Web sites to promote their businesses and sell specific products, few use them to carefully spell out job opportunities for every division of the organization.

The home page of the company's Web site, (www.targetcorp.com) makes a general statement to prospective customers. At the top of the page, a display banner features, among other areas of interest to consumers, a section on careers. Interested parties can then access this section to learn more about opportunities in the company. Within this section, prospective applicants can find out more specifics about the company, including "employer of choice" (which briefly spells out the status of Target in relation to the overall retail industry), "benefits, diversity policy, awards, and technology services," and separate sections for each of its store divisions.

Those who might be interested in the company's benefits package, for example, might select that area before any other. It outlines programs such as 401(k) plans, pharmacy discounts, insurance, alternative work arrangements, and vacations. The next screen lists information on a wealth of careers, including advertising, assets protection, merchandising, finance, and store leadership. If someone is interested in merchandising, for example, a click on that page outlines the company's merchandising career path. If a potential candidate is interested in a career at a particular store, a full description of the company, its locations, and job opportunities can be also accessed with a mere click of the mouse. Additional screens outline how to apply and where résumés may be sent for further consideration.

All of the written information on the site is surrounded by photographs of smiling faces, company logos, charts, and a map featuring the locations of the company's major markets.

By focusing its recruitment efforts on the Internet, the Target Corporation attracts potential employees who might otherwise never have pursued a career with the company.

EMPLOYMENT AGENCIES

An **employment agency** is a company that specializes in matching job candidates to specific positions. There are both private and governmental agencies. In the private sector, some specialize in specific areas of employment such as retailing. Many of these companies focus on the lower to mid-management levels of employment, while others, the **executive search firms** or **headhunters** as they are often called, deal exclusively with the recruitment of upper-level management. Employment agencies advertise in consumer and trade papers and also make significant contacts via the Internet. For entry level and mid-management personnel, the site www.careersinretailing.com serves as host for the biggest merchants such as Best Buy, Toys "R" Us, Dillard's, JCPenney, Bed Bath & Beyond, and Sears. By scrolling through the Web site, viewers can find answers to questions concerning career paths, how to get started in retailing, and the potential for employment in every segment of the industry.

There are also Web sites offering executive search services that alert potential executive candidates to specific recruiters. When individuals log on to these Web sites, they are presented with a number of different executive recruitment organizations. For retailers, the biggest advantage to using employment agencies is that the agencies prescreen applicants for them. Applicant credentials, such as previous employment histories, are carefully scrutinized before a recommendation is made to the retailer. This saves the retailer a great deal of time and effort when seeking qualified candidates, since companies need only interview those who have been recommended by the agencies. In most cases, retailers pay the fees required by the employment agency only if they actually hire the recommended individuals.

EDUCATIONAL INSTITUTIONS

These are excellent resources for employee recruitment. High schools, technical schools, colleges, and universities all play an important role in the placement of their graduates. Retailers use a variety of methods to attract graduating students. One of the most popular ways of attracting future graduates is through **internship** programs that allow for the assessment of individuals who are still in school and will be seeking full-time employment upon graduation. One such company that utilizes the internship route is Kmart. By logging onto www.kmartcorp.com/corp/careers2/general/college.stm, soon-to-be graduates can learn about opportunities that await them at Kmart. By clicking on "Send Us Your Resume," an interested candidate can fill out a form and send their credentials to the company for consideration. By using this standardized form, the human resources department can quickly determine if the applicant has the proper credentials to be considered for the program. Those who meet the company's criteria are invited to interview.

Regular meetings with key faculty who serve as prescreeners for career candidates, participation in career days and job seminars, and the development of posters and brochures that can be delivered to the campus and outline the benefits of joining a specific company are other ways that retailers recruit at educational institutions. Continuous communication with the educational institutions also helps fill part-time positions for key selling periods such as Christmas. Often these temporary employees are later given full-time opportunities with the company.

WALK-INS

Going from store to store seeking employment is known as a **walk-in**. The invitation for such pursuits often comes from a sign in a store window. In times when employment is already at high levels, the signs might indicate **signing bonuses** to motivate potential employees to find out more about available jobs. Many retailers agree that those who are self-motivated enough to seek employment via a walk-in often make very capable employees. On the other hand, many of these prospects do not fit the company's hiring profiles because of a lack of experience and end up wasting the recruiter's valuable time. It is, however, a good method for attracting part-time help and seasonal workers. Some merchants have installed employment kiosks on their selling floors to inform shoppers of available jobs. The kiosks are replete with computer terminals that enable the user to complete an application form. Once the form has been completed, the respondents are directed to the human resources department in the

"Now hiring" signs outside stores attract walk-ins.

In-store employment kiosks are helpful because they promote job openings and allow the manager to screen candidates before meeting with them.

store. These kiosks not only attract attention but also give the employment manager time to quickly assess candidates and make a preliminary determination before he or she arrives at the human resources department. Best Buy, one of the largest electronics retailers in the United States, uses attractive tear-away cards in its stores to motivate people to apply for jobs. The information on these cards instructs candidates on how to apply by phone 24 hours a day and promises that the call will take only 3 to 6 minutes of their time. In order to motivate would-be employees, the card spells out some of the reasons why Best Buy is a wise career choice.

TELEVISION PROGRAMMING

This has become an excellent tool to quickly announce job openings in a variety of industries. Local television stations, such as WTWN in Jacksonville, Florida, dedicate a specified amount of time during their regular schedule to inform viewers about employment opportunities in the general area. Specifics such as the company's pay structure, hours of employment, and job specifications are clearly noted for each available position. Instructions on how to contact the company and apply for the job are provided.

INDUSTRY CONTACTS

This is an excellent, informal approach to use when a specific type of employee is needed to fill a vacancy. When a store buyer is looking for an assistant, one resource might be to contact a resident buying office merchandiser who often interacts with assistant buyers. Similarly, a manufacturer might give this same buyer information about people who might be right for the position. Since both of these industry contacts regularly meet with assistant buyers during their daily routines, they are able to assess their capabilities and make recommendations concerning their potential worth to a company.

While each of these sources merits consideration from the company's employment managers, not every one brings equal results. That is, a particular retailer might find that classified advertising is most suitable for its needs, while another might get better results from an employment agency. The use of all of these resources to fill one position might not be a sound approach to use. The costs are considerable, so attention should focus on just one or two ways to fill the vacancy.

The seasoned human resources director keeps records of the successes and failures of the various sources of recruitment. Then, when a hiring need arises, the route that has brought the most favorable results in the past can again be utilized. Of course, different job titles might require different search techniques. The records might indicate that sales associates have been best secured through classified ads whereas buyers have been more successfully recruited through industry contacts. Good record keeping will save the retailer both time and money in the recruitment process.

In the News . . .

Be sure to read the article "Holt Renfrew Turns around H.R. with Tech" on page 219 at the end of this chapter.

The Selection Process

When the employment sources have produced job applicants, the retailer is ready to begin the **selection process**. This procedure attempts to match a candidate to the requirements of a position. Typically, the route used to ultimately select the individual with the most potential is a six-step screening process. Not every company follows the same plan, and most tailor one to fit their own needs. It should also be noted that the best planning procedure might necessitate curtailment in times of low unemployment. When an employee pool is low, it is often necessary to circumvent some of the steps in the established procedure and make less scrutinized selections.

The following steps are followed by most retailers in their selection process:

1. Reviewing a résumé is generally the first step. Except for bottom-rung jobs such as sales associates and stock personnel, a résumé that includes all of the applicant's educational, professional, and personal information is required. This document enables an employment expert to evaluate the candidate's background and to determine whether there is a potential fit. Those deemed worthy of consideration will be invited to go on to the next step.

A typical retail job application.

2. Application forms are then generally completed by those who have passed the first stage. For lower level positions, this often serves as the first step in the procedure. In any case, the forms address such areas as personal information, educational achievements, professional accomplishments, and so forth. Once completed, the applications are carefully examined to see whether or not further screening is appropriate. It should be noted that today's application forms are quite different from those used in previous years. Questions regarding age and marital status, for example, are forbidden by law. After the applications are reviewed, a decision is made in terms of the applicant's match with the company's requirements.

3. Most companies then schedule **preliminary interviews**. This is actually the first time in which a face-to-face meeting is held between the potential new employee and a representative of the human resources department. It is often a brief meeting that merely serves the purpose of further screening the applicant. For sales associates positions, this is often the first and last interview. Since the job specifications are listed on the job description, it is only necessary to determine whether the candidate possesses such attributes as good communication skills and dresses appropriately to meet company standards. This type of interview is sometimes referred to as a *rail interview*, a reference to the barrier separating the interviewer from the candidate. For more challenging positions, this interview serves only to determine whether a more intensive one is in order. The résumé and job application are both used as a basis for some of the questions that will be asked. By conducting these preliminary discussions, the interviewers will save time for the busy upper level executives who are engaged in a host of other activities. Of course, the preliminary review must be carefully executed to make certain that only those who meet the minimum standards are asked to continue in the selection process.

4. An extremely important part of the procedure is **reference checking**. It is often done at this point so that only those whose backgrounds have been cleared move onto the next stage. The résumé and application are used to conduct the reference search. Educational institutions are contacted to make certain that the prospect attended during the indicated dates and that the level of education declared is accurate. Many secondary and postsecondary schools do not provide such information to third parties, so the candidate must provide official documents that verify his or her educational record. Former supervisors are also contacted to verify the employment information listed on the résumé and application. Technically, the only information that may be obtained is the validity of the candidate's past employment and the dates he or she worked for the company; anything else might be considered an invasion of privacy. One way in which more and more retailers and other businesses are learning about an applicant's past is through the use of public record information. The leader in such investigative research is US Search.com. Employers wishing to check a candidate's past record may do so by logging onto the company's Web site, www.1800ussearch.com. Through customized searches, the user can quickly learn what he or she needs to know before considering a particular individual for employment. If the information checks out, the candidate moves on to the next stage.

5. Some form of testing is used by most retailers. The interview process can give the human resources representative only a feeling about the applicant. It cannot measure such competencies as mathematics skills, logical reasoning, or problem solving. Specific abilities are needed for each job, and these skills can be assessed by testing. The testing may be conducted by the retailer's in-house experts or by outside agencies that

specialize in the field. In addition to testing in areas such as computer literacy, personality, intelligence, and aptitude, testing may also be used to determine an individual's capacity to perform a certain type of job. Today, a great deal of emphasis is also placed on drug testing. Drug problems have become so rampant that most retailers use drug testing as a standard procedure in employee screening. Companies like Home Depot, for example, make applicants aware of their drug testing requirement as a condition of employment by posting large signs throughout the store. Any trace of drug usage immediately rules out the candidate's chance for employment. If drug tests are negative and the other standardized tests are completed satisfactorily, then the candidate is ready for the next stage in the process.

6. Final interviews are conducted for managerial level positions by the supervisor of the specific department. In cases where the position is one of great importance, a group or team interview might be conducted. In some instances, a series of interviews are used to assess the candidate. In either case, the final interview is a lengthy one. If the screening process was carefully structured, there should be just a few candidates who will be considered for the job. The time involved in this process usually ranges from a few hours to a few days. The actual interview sessions generally take place in formal environments such as the supervisor's office or in a conference room if several company executives are involved. Sometimes off-premises locations, such as restaurants, are used to evaluate the candidate's demeanor in social situations.

7. Choosing the successful applicant is the task of the supervisor to whom the new employee will report. The actual decision may be spontaneous but more than likely will take a great deal longer. Test results might need to be re-evaluated, opinions of others might be warranted, or a closer look at references might be in order. Once a candidate is selected, he or she may be required to take a physical examination as a condition of employment. If everything checks out, the prospect is invited to join the retailer's team.

IN-HOUSE EMPLOYEE TRAINING

The purpose of employee training is usually twofold. It is used to introduce new employees to the company and also to retrain those on staff who have been promoted or need to learn new systems or procedures. Those who are already on board may participate in individual instruction or group seminars, depending upon the scope of the new activities. The amount of training necessary before the new employee can assume his or her role in the company varies from job to job and from retailer to retailer. Some merchants use formal **in-house training** sessions to familiarize the worker with his or her expected duties and responsibilities. Others may subscribe to on-the-job training, where those who have just joined the business are immediately put on the firing line. A recent innovation that is gaining in usage is the subject of the following *Focus*.

Focus on . . .
Saks Fifth Avenue

ONE OF THE LEADING U.S. UPSCALE RETAIL FASHION EMPORIUMS IS SAKS. With more than 110 stores in the United States alone, it understands the value of having highly trained people in its employ. Training of a traditional nature had always been the route the company took in training employees at all levels until it introduced E-Learning.

With 16,000 employees, $2.9 billion in annual sales, and 3,000 new hires each year, the task of training was a formidable one. Training the in-store personnel along with those who work in the corporate locations was difficult until the new program was put in place. Not only was it important for those on the selling floor to understand the fashion picture, which changes every few months, it was also imperative for upper level management to stay informed about changing customer preferences so that the merchandise assortment would address the changes. Being able to keep abreast of the big picture by understanding and analyzing trends is paramount in satisfying the needs of its customers.

Sales associates and floor managers participate in the E-Learning program, which teaches them about the product, how to use the point-of-sale system, and how to develop the necessary relationship skills to interact with customers.

Senior merchandising executives participate in an online simulation that tests their knowledge of analyzing profitability of business plans and finances. The E-Learning plan consists of four sections, each representing a different clothing season. In this simulation, participants are given $1 million to spend as a merchant over the course of the four seasons. They are provided with hypothetical information about the seasons and are asked to make decisions on merchandise purchases. At the program's end, they learn about their potential for profit based on their decisions.

In addition to training in-store personnel, Saks prepares those who are involved in multi-channel challenges such as interacting with online shoppers. The goal is to "win the talent war" by finding the proper talent in the first place and then retaining that talent so that long-term relationships can be forged.

OFF-SITE EMPLOYEE TRAINING

Although the bulk of training is still accomplished in-house by a variety of methods and for people at all levels of employment, there is a trend for outside groups to do the training for retailers. Of course, learning of a general nature has always been accomplished by courses given at educational institutions, with some specialization in fields such as product knowledge.

This **off-site training** has become more formalized through the collaboration of colleges, trade organizations, and specific retailers. Atlantic Cape Community College in New Jersey has teamed up with the National Retail Federation (NRF) to offer training to future retail employees. The focus of the program is improving customer service while providing jobs for the unemployed. Operating in the Hamilton Mall in Mays Landing, it is one of 24 training programs sponsored by the NRF. The facility houses two classrooms, a computer lab, a conference room, and offices for the teaching staff.

The cooperation of such merchants as Kmart, Marshalls, Macy's, Lowe's and Home Depot—who have agreed to hire the program's graduates—has been excellent. By hiring these "trained" individuals, a company has some assurance that their better understanding of retailing will translate into becoming better employees.

New Sales Associates

Those on the firing line are the retailer's sales associates. They are primarily found on the selling floors, but many also work in catalogue divisions or on Web sites, where live interaction with a company representative may be necessary. In any case, the better trained the associate is, the more likely it is that a sale will be made. All too often, merchants shortchange sales associates in terms of training. Some use only a 2- or 3-hour session to offer the basic knowledge necessary to sell, while more progressive companies may develop sales training programs that last a full week.

The training at this level of employment may take a number of forms. The program might utilize professional videos that initially introduce the newcomer to the business and then concentrate on selling practices. The value of such visual presentations is that they not only teach selling techniques but also may be used over and over again. Guess, Inc., uses a combination of video and CD-ROM instruction in the training of its sales staff. Impressive sales improvements have been made since the program's inception. Presented in an MTV format because the sales associates generally range in age from 18 to 25, the presentations are slick, fun, and brief.

One of the methods that best simulates an actual selling demonstration is **role-playing**. The concept involves two participants; the sales associate and the shopper. The two engage in a presentation that involves a particular product or service. Trainers evaluate every step of the way, beginning with greeting the customer and ending with a sale. In this way, the evaluator can reinforce the positive aspects of the sale while pointing out and correcting the negatives. The arena for such role-playing is a setting that simulates the actual selling environment. If the new sales associate tried his or her approach in a department with a real shopper, there might be some risk of turning the potential customer into one whose needs were not satisfied. It is important in this type of training to make certain that the consumer role-player acts in a manner that approximates a realistic presentation.

In the News . . .

"The Training Advantage," an article featured on page 219 at this chapter's end, should be read now to better understand the value of training.

Executive Trainees

Most major retailers utilize formal training programs for the people whom they expect to become managers in their companies. From large department store groups to food franchises, such programs are vital to the future success of the companies.

Executive or management training programs use a variety of techniques to train the future leaders of retailing. Typically, the programs offer a combination of formalized classroom work coupled with on-the-job training. Specifically, lectures, videos, case problem solving, programmed instruction, demonstrations, and role-playing make up the training techniques used. Macy's Executive Development program is considered to be one of the better programs in the country. Its on-the-job training involves placement in a sales supervision environment; conferences with key executives that cover every aspect of the company's endeavors, such as merchandising, sales promotion, and store management; counseling to provide answers to questions about the company; performance reviews; and a rotational plan that moves **executive trainees** from area to area.

Sales support personnel are a retailer's representatives to the public. Their training must include human relations skills to ensure customer satisfaction, which is an essential ingredient of profitability.

Some smaller department store organizations offer executive training programs whose scope rivals those of the industry giants. One such program is that of Von Maur, a 22-unit department store that is the subject of our next *Focus*.

Focus on... Von Maur

Von Maur, a small department store chain, offers executive training that rivals programs of the industry giants.

STARTING IN A SMALL 20 × 50–FOOT STORE IN DAVENPORT, IOWA, this company has gone on to become one of the more important upscale department stores to serve the Midwest. The company remains under the leadership of family members and has no plans to pursue the merger-and-acquisition route followed by so many of today's department stores.

In addition to specializing in marquee-label brands and providing the best possible service to its customers, the company prides itself on grooming future executives to carry on the long-established Von Maur traditions. One of the major undertakings used to meet the challenges of today's competitive retailing is the company's renowned executive training program. By incorporating classroom instruction with hands-on training, it regularly turns out productive managerial talent.

Specifically, Van Maur engages its trainees in interactive workbook experiences, designs challenging business analysis projects, holds weekly meetings between trainees and store managers, utilizes scheduled training at their corporate offices, introduces participants into the fundamentals of buying, and uses "job shadowing" as a learning tool.

The track taken at the company for upward mobility involves 3 to 6 months as a sales associate and 3 to 9 months as a department manager. Then, after careful analysis, candidates are moved into management or merchandising positions. Throughout each stage of development, trainees are evaluated and made ready for the next stage until the final assignment is made.

Given the company's promotion-from-within philosophy, successful candidates have the opportunity to achieve such levels as merchandise manager, regional director of stores, and even vice president of the firm.

Support Personnel

Throughout a retail organization are many who operate in support positions such as cashiers, stock people, unit control, and customer service. Their responsibilities, while neither management nor sales, are extremely important to the overall functioning of the company. Cashiers, for example, must be trained to make certain that the right prices are being charged, especially when markdowns have not been noted on price tags.

Many of the support staff are trained using real machinery, equipment, and other tools in simulations. A computer-driven cash register is used to train new users, for example, and a forklift is used to train personnel in placing stock on hard-to-reach warehouse shelves.

Retrainees

It should be understood that the initial training a new employee receives is sometimes not sufficient for his or her tenure at a company. New computer systems might be installed that require retraining of those who will use the system. Transfers and promotions also necessitate retraining. When a sales associate is promoted to a junior merchandising position, there is generally a need for training. Often this is on-the-job training, where all the fundamentals and tasks of the new challenge can be learned firsthand.

No matter which employees are being retrained, there are numerous advantages of such efforts:

- Improving competency levels makes employees more productive in their assigned duties and responsibilities.
- Well-trained employees need less supervision, allowing managers to focus on their own activities.
- Sound training, particularly for those on the selling floor, helps present a better image of the store to the shopper.

Focus On... McDonald's

IT WOULD BE HARD TO FIND ANYONE IN THE UNITED STATES who hasn't eaten at or at least heard of McDonald's. For that matter, with its worldwide expansion to a vast number of cities all over the globe, the recognition has become even greater. Ray Kroc, its founder, mortgaged his home and invested his entire life savings to open the initial restaurant in Des Plaines, Illinois, in 1955. Who would have believed that the company would become one of the most amazing entrepreneurial stories in business history.

McDonald's Hamburger University is a state-of-the-art training facility.

In order to bring the company to this enviable position, emphasis has always been placed on having the best possible management team. To be sure the team was trained properly, McDonald's opened Hamburger University. Located in Oak Brook, Illinois, the university has grown to become a worldwide training center that exclusively instructs personnel employed by McDonald's Corporation or by McDonald's independent franchisees. Founded in 1961, it has come a long way since the company's first training facility, which was located in the basement of a McDonald's restaurant in Elk Grove Village, Illinois. Since then, the university has moved twice, and the average size of a class has grown from 10 to more than 200.

Today, more than 65,000 managers in McDonald's restaurants have graduated from Hamburger University, now located in a 130,000-square-foot, state-of-the-art facility that employs 30 resident professors. Because of the organization's international scope, translators and electronic equipment help the professors to teach and communicate in 22 languages at one time. In addition to its international headquarters, the company manages ten international training centers in England, Japan, Germany, and Australia.

It is such attention to training that has enabled the company to remain a leader in this highly competitive business arena.

EMPLOYEE EVALUATION PROGRAMS

The breadth and depth of evaluation procedures vary from retailer to retailer. Small companies such as boutiques, where the number of employees is low, usually forgo formalized methods of evaluation. Supervisors generally talk to their employees about their positive and negative traits in an informal manner, if they discuss them at all. In larger operations, the procedure is a formal one. Evaluation forms are central to evaluating employee progress. These forms are generally filled out by the individual's supervisor in conjunction with a human resources specialist. The reasons for such programs, whether formal or informal, are numerous. They include:

- Determining whether or not the employee has performed satisfactorily
- Deciding if the present position is appropriate for the worker or if he or she might better serve the company in a different capacity
- Evaluating the employee for a promotion and monetary rewards
- Determining if the individual has mastered the job for which he or she has been hired or if further training is needed
- Terminating the employment of those individuals who have not performed according to specifications outlined in the job description

Sound programs provide for regular and continuous evaluations of employees. These evaluations should be positive experiences, correcting shortcomings while underscoring the challenges that have been effectively met. By implementing a sound system that addresses all of the standard elements of evaluation, a retailer can ensure that its employees are apt to perform at their highest potential.

COMPENSATION

The method of compensation used by retailers should reflect the needs of both the employer and the employee. The employee must be satisfactorily compensated to be properly stimulated to do his or her best for the company. If the remuneration system is carefully determined, it should provide the following benefits to the employer:

- Maximize the output of the individuals on the payroll
- Reduce employee turnover, which can reduce training costs
- Motivate an individual's performance, which can lead to in-house promotions and eliminate the need to look outside of the company for new personnel

For the employee, a sound compensation plan should offer the following:

- An incentive to provide an honest on-the-job performance
- Reduced incentives for internal theft
- An incentive to remain with the company instead of regularly seeking higher salaries elsewhere
- The heightening of morale
- The maintenance of a good standard of living

With these requirements in mind, management must establish a system that best suits the different jobs that are found within the company. Different levels of work necessitate different levels and types of compensation. For example, sales associates, department managers, buyers, merchandise managers, and sales promotion directors are each paid differently. Some are paid according to the number of hours worked in a week, some with salary and commission plans, and others by set salaries and bonus incentives. In each of these methods, it is essential that management assess the standards established by the industry so that they can meet or beat the competition and thus hire and retain the best people.

Of course, employers must obey the laws governing employee compensation. The federal government, as well as many state governments, has established a minimum wage. At the present time, the federal minimum is $6.55 per hour; in July 2009 it will rise to $7.25. In Santa Cruz, California, however, with the cost of living so high and a labor shortage, the minimum is $11.00 per hour. At times of greater prosperity, the minimums never really come into play because starting salaries are generally higher. On the other hand, if unemployment figures escalate, the minimum wage is often paid to new personnel.

Straight Salary

Many merchants use this arrangement to pay their staffs. It is particularly common with sales associates and some levels of management. This system of compensation has advantages for the employer and employee. For the employer, it establishes regular expenses. For the employee, it provides a steady income. On the other hand, it also has disadvantages. It doesn't motivate employees and so may lead to minimal commitment from the staff. And, as a fixed expenditure, it sometimes costs more than the value of the actual job performance. Because the salary is fixed and steady, employees find this arrangement favorable. Since the costs are easy to compute, this type of payroll works best for management.

Straight Commission

Unlike the straight salary plan, which affords safety and security to the employee, straight commission employees must perform in order to earn their salaries. There is no guarantee at the end of the week that the sales associate who sells on commission will receive a paycheck. This does, however, provide the employee with the incentive to perform to his or her highest potential in return for a greater salary than if he or she were being paid a predetermined amount.

Nordstrom was one of the first merchants to use the straight commission system for sales associates.

More and more retailers have introduced straight commission to their sales associates. This is particularly true for the sale of high-ticket items such as designer clothing, major appliances, and computers. Those being paid in this manner must be well trained and ready to spend every available moment trying to make the sale. It provides the experienced, professional seller with the opportunity to earn more than the standard salary common to retailing, bringing the company the potential for more business.

Nordstrom, the leading upscale retailer of fashion merchandise, was one of industry's first to introduce the system. Not only has it resulted in better monetary rewards for its employees, but it has also helped to establish the highest levels of customer service in retailing. Employees quickly learn that when you provide excellent customer service, a customer is likely to buy more. Following Nordstrom's lead, companies like Saks Fifth Avenue and Bergdorf Goodman have opted for the straight commission plan in many of their departments.

Wage Plus Commission

The best of both worlds for many employers and employees is the system that offers a guaranteed wage along with an incentive for better performance. A great number of retailers who have experienced lackluster commitments from their employees have turned to this method.

By paying the minimum wage, and adding the opportunity for more money, merchants find that sales associates are ready to meet and greet more customers.

The commission rate varies from store to store and from department to department. It might be as little as 1 percent or as much as 5 percent, with small-ticket item commissions at the bottom of the scale.

Salary Plus Bonus

Department managers, store managers, buyers, and merchandise managers are sometimes rewarded with bonuses in addition to their established salaries. When their departments, divisions, or individual stores surpass anticipated revenues, they are sometimes awarded extra compensation. This plan motivates managers not only to work harder but also to encourage better performances from their subordinates.

The system usually sets a specific minimum goal for each manager to achieve. Once that amount is met, a bonus based on the excess is given to the supervisor. Often the bonus amount is based upon an escalating scale. For example, if the measured time period is a month and the expected sales are $300,000, then the manager whose department sells $330,000 would be rewarded perhaps an extra 1 percent of the additional $30,000. If sales of an additional $75,000 are realized, then the incentive might result in 2 percent. There is no specific plan used by all retailers; most simply use the one that best addresses its needs.

Table 9.1 summarizes and compares the benefits of the four major compensation plans for both the employer and employee.

Other Monetary Rewards

In an effort to maximize the performance of their staffs, retailers offer some other types of incentives. These include **profit sharing**, which enables employees to share in the success of the company. By providing this type of monetary gain, employees are encouraged to maximize their work effort because they will share the rewards. Another example is the extra money that comes for selling slow-moving merchandise. Small stores often reward **P.M.s**, or prize money, for items that the company is eager to sell. Typically, most sales associates try to sell the hot items first because they are easier to move. When given the extra incentive of prize money, many place their efforts on the less desirable merchandise. Contests and other promotional endeavors also bring extra pay to employees. The person who sells the most swimsuits in a week, for example, might be the recipient of a monetary prize.

TABLE 9.1
BENEFITS OF COMPENSATION PLANS

Plan	Employer Benefit	Employee Benefit
Straight Salary	Easy to formulate, regular costs, simple bookkeeping	Guaranteed income, easy to understand
Straight Commission	Motivates better performance, improved customer service, salaries in line with performance	Easy to understand, better pay for better performance
Wage Plus Commission	Provides some incentive so productivity increases, better customer service	Offers higher income, fairly stable wages
Salary Plus Bonus	Increases productivity	Opportunity for greater monetary rewards

More and more retailers, whether they are small entrepreneurs or the retail giants, have come to recognize that, with the proper incentives, sales will increase and customers will be treated to better service.

EMPLOYEE BENEFITS

While most people are motivated to work for one company rather than another because of the paycheck offered, there is a growing trend to consider benefits as part of the package. The extremely high cost of health insurance, for example, has made it an important requirement for families. Those companies that offer sound medical plans have often been able to use this benefit to attract capable workers even though actual salaries might be lower than elsewhere.

Most retailers also offer pension plans as another incentive. Not only do today's workers want benefits while they are employed, they also want the security of being able to have a quality life upon retirement. In the not-too-distant past, many retailers didn't offer pensions except perhaps to their management teams. Today, most retailers provide some sort of retirement package. People looking at a retailing career generally compare one pension program to another before making a final choice.

One of the most important duties of the human resources benefits manager is to develop programs that help attract qualified candidates. At one time, classified ads merely focused on the wages being offered. Today, there is considerable emphasis on the overall benefits package to entice people to apply for jobs.

At the Target Corporation, human resources has developed a program that is one of the most complete in the industry. The features of this plan are as follows:

- Pretax salary set-asides to help pay for dependent care
- Childcare resource and referral information
- Alternative work arrangements such as telecommuting, **job sharing**, work at home, and flextime
- Time off to care for a sick child or seriously ill family member
- Maternity leaves
- 401(k) plan and employee **stock options**/stock ownership plan that includes a dollar-for-dollar match for the first 5 percent of salary
- A pharmacy discount program including mail-order access for maintenance prescriptions
- Vacation values programs that feature discounts on airfare, car rental, and hotel stays
- Automobile and homeowner's insurance through payroll deduction at group discount rates

Without programs of this nature, it is unlikely that retailers will be able to attract qualified employees to fill their needs and remain competitive in the field.

LABOR RELATIONS

Satisfying employees is key to their performance. Those who are pleased with their working conditions are more likely to perform better on the job; those with issues are more than likely not to. The human resources (HR) department is assigned the responsibility of making certain that there is a comfort level in the business environment that is beneficial to both management and labor, and HR personnel must be sufficiently competent to resolve employee problems and relieve any tensions that might hinder performance.

Problem solving is an ongoing challenge in major companies. It might be a relatively simple task between a manager and a subordinate or one that involves **collective bargaining**. Most major retailers have labor unions concerned with trying to improve working conditions, salaries, and benefit plans. Human resources managers are called upon to participate in the drawing up of employee contracts and to settle disputes when these contracts are violated. The role is a sensitive one requiring sympathetic handling in order to prevent slowdowns or, at the extreme level, employee strikes.

SUPERVISION TRAINING

Human resources leadership is often called upon to establish guidelines in order to foster a better understanding between management and subordinates. All too often, those who are inexperienced in dealing with the people in their charge create problems that imperil satisfactory working conditions. Most confrontations can be easily resolved if there is an understanding of human relations and of the manner in which unpleasantries can be avoided. To achieve an environment that maximizes the highest level of excellent behavior on the part of both supervisors and their subordinates, HR experts, with the benefit of sound psychological and behavioral training, often provide a set of principles and provisions to be addressed. These include:

- Developing an orientation package that outlines, among other things, the importance of each employee to the success of the company
- Setting up an appointment between the new worker and his or her supervisor to make certain that responsibilities are carefully discussed
- Preparing a set of goals expected of each new employee
- Informing employees of the procedure to be followed in case of disputes
- Recognizing the need to be a team player
- Developing a recognition program that singles out employees who have performed above and beyond expectations

TECHNOLOGICAL APPLICATIONS

One of the more important tools used by many retailers in their human resources departments is the *Asymetrix ToolBox* program. It is a hands-on program for point-of-sale (POS) systems and is an excellent computer-based tool for training new employees. It is especially useful at holiday time periods, when retailers often add temporary employees to the selling floor. With little time for traditional training, the program helps give those new to the company a better insight into some of the company's rules and regulations. It features excellent graphic displays regarding proper dress, the details involved in making cash and credit card sales, return and exchange policies, customer service, and so forth. At the conclusion of the program, users are given quizzes for reinforcement purposes.

Halogen Software has produced a program called *Halogen eAppraisal*, which retailers and other businesses are using in their evaluation of employee performance, training and development, and other HR-related areas. With the click of the mouse, employee performance is tracked. A live demonstration of the program can be seen by logging onto www.halogensoftware.com/eappraisal.

Abra HRMS is an industry leader in human resources management. It is an affordable information system that addresses recruiting, training, and other areas of concern for retailers. For more information on these areas of human resources, an overview is offered by www.hrtechpartners.com/abra-software.html.

CHAPTER HIGHLIGHTS

- Even with the passage of key legislation by the federal government, there is still a disparity in pay between men and women who perform the same job.
- The tasks of the human resources department include recruitment, training, evaluation, compensation, benefits, and labor relations.
- The recruitment problem is greatly affected by the economics of the country. In times of low unemployment, many retailers lessen their standards so that they can have enough staff to carry out the company's tasks.
- In order to hire the right person for a job, the human resources specialists undergo investigative research known as job analysis.
- Retailers recruit either by looking internally for people to fill higher positions or by using outside sources to fill vacancies.
- Although classified ads help to alert individuals of a company's available positions, more and more major retailers are turning to the Internet for recruitment purposes.
- Employment agencies aid merchants in recruiting because they carefully screen applicants, saving employment managers a great deal of time and effort.
- The selection process typically involves a series of screening devices that helps lower the number of candidates being considered for the available position.
- Much time is saved by using online companies that check the credibility of job applicants. In this way, those who fail the test can be quickly eliminated from consideration.
- Training at the retail level is a two-part project; it trains new employees and retrains those on the staff when the need arises.
- In addition to the traditional methods of using trainers, many retailers are utilizing CD-ROM and video packages to instruct new employees and current employees who have been promoted to new positions.
- The evaluation of employees should be an ongoing process so that individuals can learn and correct their weaknesses and be rewarded for jobs well done.
- Compensation plans range from straight salaries to those that motivate employees through incentives such as commissions and bonuses.
- Because of the competitive nature of retailing salaries, more and more companies are offering extensive benefits packages to encourage employee longevity.
- The human resources department plays an important role in labor relations by resolving conflicts and sustaining a working environment that encourages better job performance.

IMPORTANT RETAILING TERMS

classified ad (196)
collective bargaining (212)
employee pool (193)
employment agency (198)
executive search firm (198)
executive trainee (205)
glass ceiling (194)
headhunter (198)
in-house training (203)
internal sourcing (196)
internship (199)
job analysis (195)
job description (195)
job sharing (211)
job specifications (195)
off-site training (204)
outside sourcing (196)
P.M.s (210)
preliminary interview (202)
profit sharing (210)
promotion from within (196)
reference checking (202)
role-playing (205)
selection process (201)
signing bonus (199)
stock options (211)
walk-in (199)

FOR REVIEW

1. Why is the problem of staffing greater today than it was in the past?

2. How does the concept of supply and demand affect the human resources department in its hiring practices?
3. What is meant by the term *glass ceiling* as it relates to promotions?
4. Why is it necessary for the human resources department to perform job analyses?
5. What is the difference between the terms *job specification* and *job description*?
6. Describe the concept of promotion from within. Why do most retailers utilize this method?
7. How have Internet Web sites assisted employment managers in their search for new employees?
8. Why are many retail organizations willing to use employment agencies to fill positions even though it is costly?
9. How can educational institutions assist in the recruitment process?
10. List the steps that most of the retailers use in the selection process.
11. How does the preliminary interview differ from the final interview?
12. Why are many retailers using Internet search firms as part of the screening process?
13. In addition to training new employees, why is it necessary to sometimes train employees who are already working for the company?
14. Explain the importance of employee evaluations to the employer as well as the employee.
15. Why are more and more retailers adding commissions to the compensation plans used to pay sales associates?
16. When does it sometimes become necessary for municipalities to establish a minimum wage that exceeds the one set by the federal government?
17. Define the term *P.M.s* and explain why some retailers use this system.
18. What role have benefits packages played in the hiring and retention of employees?
19. Why are human resources managers involved in labor relations?

AN INTERNET ACTIVITY

Pretend that you are ready to graduate and have chosen retailing as your career goal. After some consideration, you have decided to pursue opportunities with two major retailers.

Go to their official Web sites and access the career opportunities area. Carefully scroll down each page in the career sections to compare their recruitment procedures.

Prepare a chart with the following headings, indicating the tools used by each.

Recruitment Procedures	
Name of Retailer	Name of Retailer

When the chart is completed, select the retailer that you think offers the better package for recruitment procedures. Note the reasons why you think it is the better choice.

EXERCISES AND PROJECTS

1. Examine the classified advertisements of the major newspaper in your area. Select three ads for the same type of position and analyze the contents of each. The ads should be attached to an 8-1/2 × 11 sheet of paper with the job title at the top of the page.

   For each ad, note whether the following have been indicated:
   - Salary
   - Benefits
   - Working hours
   - Experience required
   - Academic requirements

   Select the ad that you think best describes the employment opportunity and note the reasons for your choice.

2. Pretend that you are seeking part-time employment in a store while you are still attending school. Using the walk-in approach, choose three stores that you think would suit your preference. Go to the employment office and tell the representative of your desire to work part-time. Using the information gathered at the meeting, evaluate each retailer in terms of its approach to you.

   Each evaluation should address such aspects as courtesy, length of interview (if any), and application availability.

   Once the task has been completed, select the retailer you think was best organized and indicate your reasons for choosing it.

THE CASE OF REFOCUSING TRAINING PROCEDURES

Hewlett's started out as a small chain operation in the West in 1950. It began as a single-unit company that featured a limited number of sporting goods items such as golf equipment and tennis rackets. Year after year, the company grew not only in size but also in terms of its product mix. Three years ago Hewlett's was operating 462 stores from coast to coast, that in addition to golf and tennis equipment, sold a wealth of exercise products, camping equipment, and apparel appropriate for these activities.

Two years ago, the company expanded its operation into a multichannel organization, adding catalogue and Web site divisions. Although these divisions are still in their infancies, the outlook is excellent for their success.

The running of such a huge operation has had its problems, many of which are presently being resolved. The only one that still needs refinement is the training program. Until now, Hewlett's left the training of employees to the human resources management team at the company's headquarters. There the team developed guidelines for store managers to follow when orienting new employees to the company. Although this plan had some degree of success, it took time away from the managers.

Elaine Salter, the human resources director for the company, suggested to Hewlett's CEO that a plan might be considered to change its training program from one that used managers to one that centered exclusively on using CD-ROMs and video presentations. She was asked to study the existing programs, but none were available that specifically fit the company's needs. Further investigation revealed that customized packages would cost approximately $200,000.

Her presentation to the management team received mixed reactions. Jack Slaughter, the CEO, thought the costs were too high and that they should leave well enough alone. Sam Jacobson, the chief trainer, was of the opinion that individual instruction is better but perhaps a general video used by many businesses could also be employed. Ms. Salter, recognizing the need for more training based on the multichannel expansion, believed that the new methodology was a must if the company wanted to remain profitable. The problem has yet to be resolved.

Questions

1. With which executive do you agree? Why?
2. Is there another plan that could be utilized? What would that plan be?

H.R. Summit Reveals Employee Woes
Rachel Strugatz

OCTOBER 11, 2007

NEW YORK—Workers in the apparel and retail industry are not feeling the love from their bosses.

And from the corporate human resources perspective, the difficulties of recruiting and retaining workers—especially younger ones—have never been greater.

According to a job satisfaction survey conducted and sponsored by WWD, 24 Seven Inc. and C-Suite Inc., and presented at the first WWD Human Resources Leadership Forum this month, just 12 percent of the respondents said they felt valued by their employers. Speakers at the conference said the challenge of recruiting and retaining talent was enormous. Dissatisfied employees, high turnover and generational differences in the workplace as well as aging workers are among the issues facing companies.

The unhappiness of many in the workforce, depending on age, appears to stem from the struggle to balance work and lifestyle, a sense that the talents of individuals aren't being properly used and that they are underpaid and a bad match with their firms, Barbara Marchetti, president of C-Suite, said in an interview.

"People don't feel that their full bandwidth of skills and experiences are being utilized ... the number-one reason people are unhappy in organizations is because they feel it's a cultural mismatch," she said. "They just don't fit in ... not being recognized for a job well done can also cause unhappiness."

The survey, which didn't break down the reasons for dissatisfaction, found that technology

On the Move

Percent of respondents searching for jobs monthly or more frequently	
Retail/E-Commerce/Store Level	68
Design and Technical Development	63
Planning and Merchandising	61
Sales and Marketing	58
Production and Product Development	55
Operations and IT	50
Executive Level	42

Job Satisfaction

Percent of respondents satisfied in their current position	
Executive Level	71
Operations and IT	66
Sales and Marketing	60
Planning and Merchandising	58
Design and Technical Development	51
Production and Product Development	50
Retail/E-Commerce/Store Level	42

Change Is in the Air

Percent of what respondents say a company values most today

Sales	66.1
Product Development/Design	48.5
Merchandising	40.7
Marketing	36.5
Management	32.1
Manufacturing	25.6
Distribution	21.2
IT	15
H.R.	12

was having the greatest impact on the careers of respondents.

"We're talking about various components of the job, from concept to store," Marchetti said. "Some facet of a role or department, whether it is production, design, manufacturing or logistics will either be augmented or replaced by technology."

Individuals said top-line growth was the number-one priority of their employers.

"What we gathered from this survey is that change, change, change is clearly the theme of the day, the week, the year, the decade," Marchetti said during the conference, which was attended by human resources professionals from all aspects of the industry, including designers, retailers and suppliers.

"I think it's very telling to see that technology was the number-one factor [impacting careers] and if you look at it, technology actually drives other areas [such as consolidation and operations]," Marchetti said. "Technology clearly affects retail consolidation, outsourcing and manufacturer consolidation. So technology has played into each of these areas."

The survey also showed that 91 percent of employees in a retail/e-commerce/store-level position would consider switching jobs if offered a more competitive salary. Additionally, at the retail level, 61 percent of employees are in pursuit of better quality of life, which explains why there is such a high turnover rate in the retail sector of the industry, Marchetti said.

In vertical/single-label retailers, 63 percent of the respondents were satisfied in their current positions, and 58 percent in multilabel specialty stores were satisfied. As far as years in the industry, those with fewer than five years were only 53 percent satisfied in their current position, and those with 20 years or more of experience were 65 percent satisfied.

In addition to the presentation by Marchetti, the half-day conference, held here, included presentations by Larry McClure, senior vice president of H.R. at Liz Claiborne Inc.; Casey Priest, vice president of marketing at The Container Store, and William Cody, chief talent officer at Urban Outfitters.

The Container Store, the nationwide retailer that boasts holding a spot on Fortune's list of the 100 Best Companies to Work For since 2000 and held the top spot for two of those years, prides itself on not having an H.R. department, according to Priest's presentation. The 40-store chain has a Cherry Hill, N.J., unit opening later this year and plans for six additional store openings in 2008.

Priest said The Container Store's core competency is "astonishing customer service" while abiding by the foundation principle that "one

What Motivates People to Move

Percent of respondents saying they would consider moving for the following reasons (by age):

	Under 25	25-34	35-44	45-59	60+
Better Salary	93	90	84	78	69
Better Job/Position/Company	79	75	60	59	50
Better Growth Potential	78	73	62	57	44
Better Commission/Bonuses	55	48	38	34	25
More Prestigious Brand/Company	56	49	35	27	13
Better Health Benefits	43	32	31	34	31

Source: WWD.com, 24 Seven and C-Suite. There were 1,257 respondents. The survey was conducted between Aug. 23 and Sept. 6.

great person equals three good people." She cites this, as well as selective hiring processes, creative recruiting ideas and 241 hours of formal training as paramount to the retailer's growing success and turnover rate of less than 10 percent a year, which compares with an industry average of over 75 percent.

"We receive about 40,000 applications a year, and we'll only hire about 6 percent of those who apply, so we're highly selective. We have a very intense interview process: You start with a phone interview, then you do a group interview where we see who really speaks up and who has an affinity for selling, and there's a visual merchandise exercise as well. Then you have a one-on-one interview," said Priest, who stressed that the company makes sure to respond whether or not the applicant receives the job.

"So, why don't we have an H.R. department?" Priest asked. "Well, it's because we're all in the business of H.R. and people, and people are the most important thing. That's what drives your business, and we believe that if you take care of your employees, everything else comes. If the employees are taken care of, then the customer is taken care of, then finally the shareholder is taken care of."

Cody, a Wharton School alum who joined the Urban Outfitters team in April 2007, focused on the Generation Y component of the workforce and how to successfully recruit students into the retail sector in his presentation. Cody illustrated a cohort of contradictions he feels are infectious among young adults joining the workforce today, labeling them as a "community of individuals" and "selfish loyalists" as well as "ambition with a safety net," referring to the generation's reliance on their parents.

"Probably the most troubling to anyone who is involved within business or within the talent field is job surfing. When I look at it from the Wharton School's perspective, the graduate who graduated in 2007 will have 2.5 jobs by the time they hit their fifth reunion, so that's on average a change of jobs every 18 to 20 months. So, from a talent perspective, you're dealing with someone who thinks it's perfectly all right to change jobs very frequently after they graduate college and that's a tremendous challenge for any industry," said Cody.

Cody referred to a survey conducted by Michigan State University that found that 50 percent of students would have no problem backing out after accepting a job to take something better. This information supports the results from the job satisfaction survey, which found that 93 percent of the under-25 age bracket would consider moving jobs for a better salary.

In hopes of rendering the term "job surfing" obsolete among the Gen-Y set, Cody proposed "hyper-rotational programs" that are focused on young employees. The idea is to give them little snippets of experience from different aspects within the company from 18 months to two years, depending on the department. "Instead of job surfing, create the wave within your own company," said Cody.

Liz Claiborne's McClure opened his presentation with a short film about Kate Spade, Lucky Brand Jeans, Mexx, Liz Claiborne and Juicy Couture, some of the most lucrative brands within the company that produces nearly 250 million pieces of apparel each year.

McClure explained the importance of recognizing talent, and aligning it with the goals of the company, which is aimed at bringing value to the market.

"We're designed to win," McClure said. "It's all about our product and our talent, it's about how you design everything we do, every process, every product, every function."

McClure offered details of the leadership charter of the brand leviathan, which employs 15,000 associates worldwide. "You start by inspiring a vision and defining a code and talking about values and behaviors," he explained. "It's how you build capacity, build the muscle and tone, and the ability of the organization is to respond to all of the challenges we have in the workforce."

McClure went on to say, "Then it's a matter of directing the resources, such as time, money and people. These are all things you can allocate, which is what you're expected to do as a leader when it comes to managing our business. At the end of the day, it's all about delivering value."

Holt Renfrew Turns around H.R. with Tech
Denise Power

APRIL 4, 2007

Three years into a human resources overhaul, Holt Renfrew reduced turnover by one-third, improved employee satisfaction 14 percent and inspired workers to recommend others for jobs like never before—from four internal referrals in 2004 to 200 per year.

Those successes gave rise to an enviable problem. Prospective job candidates began flocking to the upscale Canadian department store through every portal imaginable: online ad, store, career fair, phone, friends and old-fashioned paper application.

Streamlining the application process became a practical necessity, and Holt turned to a Web-based system that culls job applications from all sources. The software, from San Francisco-based Taleo, interrogates candidates with role-specific questions in order to sort them into three buckets for Holt Renfrew. The buckets range from "what were they thinking" unqualified candidates to "dream employee" to "interesting, but. . ." found somewhere in between.

When Holt opens its next store May 31 in Vancouver, the 160 available job positions will draw 5,000 applications, said Mark Derbyshire, vice president of human resources. The software's ability to incorporate role-specific questions that change dynamically based on an applicant's responses can replace the screening interview that would happen by phone, bringing greater efficiency to the hiring process.

"I don't think [this technology] is a silver bullet," Derbyshire said. "It's not. I think it's a great tool that, if you get everything else right, will work fine. We didn't need Taleo three years ago because no one was standing in line to come work here."

Derbyshire, who joined the company as it was embarking on the human resources overhaul, said "fit" is key to finding the right employees who are happy and make customers happy. A worker who was a superstar in one company's culture may not shine so brightly at another, he said.

"Hiring is 90 percent of H.R.," he said. "You hire the right people and everything is going to work. You can train a turkey to climb a tree but it's easier to hire a squirrel. If we hire the squirrel, he will innately know what to do."

Holt Renfrew has introduced 34 human resources initiatives in three years with the intent to fix what was broken, from communication and incentives to development and e-learning to transparency and commission, Derbyshire said.

In three years, the company has gone from nonexistent e-learning to more than 200 employee tutorials built on the development platform from Telus of Vancouver. Holt also offers employees a Telus-based "360 degree" co-worker evaluation, where employees can solicit input from peers, superiors and subordinates anonymously for their own edification—not to be shared with corporate.

Employee satisfaction has improved dramatically since chief executive officer Caryn Lerner came on board in 2004 and started pushing change.

"At that time we had a significant number of [employees] who were dissatisfied on every level with us as an organization, yet they showed up for work every day. Eight percent of the company couldn't stand us. What do you think that is going to mean to the customer? I mean, 'I don't like anything about Holt Renfrew but here I am to service you and make sure you feel like you have a good experience,'" Derbyshire said.

Three years later, the company has come a long way. Turnover is down, satisfaction is up and employees regularly refer friends for jobs.

The Training Advantage
Sharon Edelson

APRIL 2, 2007

NEW YORK—Consumers gripe about dismal service in stores and retailers pledge to improve the shopping experience, but few actually succeed.

Men's Warehouse, however, has been dedicating time and resources to training, and reaping the rewards. Suits University, a training program for the retailer's salaried sales associates and managers, prepares employees to be "wardrobe consultants" rather than simply salespeople, by teaching corporate values, sales and product information.

About 20 times a year, 30 employees from across the country travel to Men's Warehouse's corporate headquarters in Fremont, Calif.—the company built a separate facility for Suits U in the late nineties.

Sales associates participate in the program any time during the first year of employment. They must have worked for the company for at least 30 days. The sessions, which run from Sunday through Friday, are intense.

"We have 32 hours of classroom training, half of which consists of selling," said founder and chief executive officer George Zimmer. "When I say selling, we call it 'Selling With Soul.' It's part of our culture. We don't sell up or sell an expensive product when a less expensive one would suffice. We represent the customer."

In addition, the sales associates learn about tailoring and how to fit customers for clothes.

"This employee group [sales associates] is thought of as replaceable and turnover is high," Zimmer explained. "They're very appreciative of the training. We give them their average commission and base salary for a 40-hour week while they're at headquarters. A lot of them think of it as a vacation."

Recreational time is well thought out and built into the program. The groups spend a day at Monterey Bay and have dinner in San Francisco. "They bond over the course of the week," Zimmer said. "After the program they remain friends. The biggest benefit is the off-time, meals and evenings, when this group of 30 men and women with a couple of corporate executives just sits around and talks."

Suits U costs Men's Warehouse under $1 million a year to implement, or about $1,500 per person. Zimmer thinks it's money well spent.

"The long-term dividend is high," he said. "There are salespeople in every class who come for training and are really lost. They don't know what they're doing. After the program, a light bulb goes off in their head. They show a 30 percent or 40 percent improvement. A lot of people are very good when they arrive. It's hard to say we make them better. I do believe it's one of the reasons we have one of the lowest shrinkage rates in the retail industry."

The savings on low shrinkage and a smaller security department "is a significant number," Zimmer said. "There are other ways this type of investment pays off. We have lower [staff] turnover. That means many things in terms of continuity with customers and employees. It's hard to achieve."

A testament to the program is the fact that 90 percent of the company's store managers started out as sales associates.

Men's Warehouse was number nine on a list of top rated companies in "New Dynamics That Create and Build Retail Competitive Advantage," a report for the National Retail Federation Foundation by Kanbay Research Institute. KRI took 300 leading companies with annual sales of over $100 million and applied a set of benchmarks, such as stable or increasing market share and high return on investment, for five consecutive years. Only 15 firms made the cut: UPS, Dollar Tree, Dollar General, Walgreens, Kenneth Cole, Petco, Kohl's, Target, Men's Warehouse, PetSmart, Office Depot, eBay, Apple Stores, Macy's and Hasbro.

Gary Williams, president of KRI, said Men's Warehouse is the only apparel retailer he's come across with such a strong commitment to training. "Macy's approach is on a regional basis," he explained. "In terms of customer desire for merchandise, the regional approach could do very well. From a training perspective, the more consistency you have, the better. We've seen that consistent training can be enormously beneficial to driving sales. You just don't see that [training] in the apparel industry. Why? It could be because apparel retailers over-focus on costs."

Zimmer's people-centric approach is evident in other aspects of employee relations. Many companies might terminate an underperforming employee, but Zimmer often tries to find a more creative solution.

"When we have people who are not necessarily succeeding in a position, we see if their skills would work in another capacity before we fire them," he said. "A fellow here used to be in charge of a large group of stores [as a manager] but it wasn't working out. He was such a great guy we brought him into the corporate office and put him in charge of employee complaints. He's done an amazing job. I recognized him at a holiday dinner last year and 800 people stood up and applauded."

Zimmer also believes store managers can use a refresher course. Every year, the firm's 2,000 managers descend on the Fremont headquarters—in eight groups of 250. The groups are taught to solve problems and make good decisions through various exercises. "Our stores are small enough that they're really like neighborhood clothing stores," Zimmer said. "We want the store manager to handle a customer's problem. When you do solve problems you have greater customer loyalty."

CHAPTER 10
Loss Prevention

After you have completed this chapter, you should be able to discuss:

- How inventory shortages have affected the retailer's profitability
- The numerous deterrents to shoplifting that are being used by merchants all over the globe
- Techniques that human resources managers use to reduce internal theft
- How employees are being trained and motivated to cut shoplifting losses
- The different types of electronic surveillance systems that retailers are using in their stores
- The technologies used to cut losses from fraudulent Internet purchasing

Merchants all over the world entered the twenty-first century plagued with enormous losses due to shoplifting and theft by unscrupulous employees. More than $30 billion per year is lost, with the largest portion of that being attributed to internal theft. It is reported that the public is perpetrating 92 percent of the thefts. However, the 7 percent stolen by employees is valued at more than 9 times what is lost through shoplifting. The final 1 percent of losses comes at the hands of vendors who are also involved in cheating their customers through short shipments. These alarming statistics also reveal that losses due to theft range from 1 to 8 percent of sales. Given a company's sales figures, the resulting dollar losses may run into millions for a retailing giant.

Most honest shoppers don't realize that they are actually paying for these crimes. In order for retailers to turn a profit, it is necessary for them to calculate their expenses and use them, along with the cost of the merchandise, as the basis for determining how much they must charge for their goods. One of these expenses is dollar loss due to theft. Thus, if a merchant determines that theft amounts to 5 percent of sales, then he or she must adjust prices to reflect that 5 percent loss.

With the realization that these figures have reached staggering proportions in every retailing classification—department stores, specialty chains, and supermarkets—the industry has started using more deterrents than ever before. A combination of educational approaches to loss prevention and new technology shows promise that the future will be brighter for merchants. Whether the focus is on a retailer's brick-and-mortar operation, Web site, or catalogue division, closer control of such losses is taking center stage.

This chapter will concentrate on the two major groups that cause the losses—company employees and shoplifters. In addition, check fraud (estimated to cost $10 billion), shortages due to dishonest vendors, and Internet fraud will also be addressed.

SHOPLIFTING

Those who enter stores posing as customers but steal rather than pay for merchandise are called **shoplifters**. You might think that such individuals are suspicious, scruffy-looking characters, but this is not the case. There is no stereotypical shoplifter. He or she is often well-dressed and looks exactly like a typical shopper making a legitimate purchase. The shoplifter needs to be able to move through the store without attracting undue attention. Those with less than proper grooming are often suspect and are carefully scrutinized by store employees. Shoplifters come from all walks of life. They include professional business people, members of the clergy, educators, celebrities, students, and a host of others. Some commit the crimes because of drugs and other problems associated with economic pressures, while others perform the act because of **kleptomania**—a psychological problem that causes an irresistible urge to steal. Some act alone in their endeavors, satisfying personal needs without making payments, while others are parts of professional teams that set out to steal just about anything that can bring them a profit when resold. Many professional shoplifting gangs steal to order. Accomplices place their orders and pay these shoplifters for the delivered merchandise.

One cause of the escalating shoplifting problem is that today's retail environments almost encourage theft with their many open counters and airy merchandise displays. Another is the shortage of sales associates found in many stores. With easy access to the merchandise and few eyes in place to deter the thefts, shoplifting is relatively simple.

Recognizing the seriousness of the situation, merchants are arming themselves with many different deterrents to control the problem.

> **In the News . . .**
> "Retail's Latest Plague: Fighting Back against Shoplifting Gangs," an article that appears on page 236 at the end of this chapter, should be read now.

Major Shoplifting Deterrents

Retailers have three major options available to them in the prevention of shoplifting. Security guards and video surveillance systems, anchoring merchandise in place, and tag and alarm systems.

Security Guards and Video Surveillance Systems

The strategic placement of security guards at stores' entrances might deter some people from trying to leave with goods they haven't purchased. The visibility of the guard is somewhat of a deterrent, but it also makes the honest shopper nervous. Because of this, many retailers have steered away from using guards, except for those that deal in high-volume, low-priced merchandise.

Instead, many use some type of **video surveillance system**. Typically, **closed-circuit television (CCTV)** involves the installation of video cameras in prominent places in the store. The system observes shoppers and records their actions. Through observation by security guards, the offenders can be easily identified. This system is especially helpful when suspects are recorded in the act more than once. Repeat offenders are often apprehended in this way. By analyzing the tapes, retailers are able to learn the patterns of shoplifters and come up with solutions to the problem. The more sophisticated, state-of-the-art models in use today are hidden in places such as smoke detectors, sprinkler systems, thermostats, and clocks. From these vantage points a security guard can use a camera that has the capability of panning and zooming to follow the suspect. Stores that do not have sufficient resources for security guards to man the camera may use automatic panning devices to perform the task.

Anchoring Merchandise in Place

If you have ever shopped for an expensive item such as a leather jacket, you may have noticed that the item is locked in place with security cables. Although this technique secures the products, it also makes it difficult for customers to closely examine them and try them on. Accessibility to the merchandise is possible only when the keeper of the keys is available. Oftentimes, finding a sales associate who can assist the customer is impossible. Discouraged shoppers often leave the area frustrated. In this instance, the merchandise has been protected but the sale has been lost.

SpeedDome® ultra is a high-speed programmable dome camera system that clearly focuses on people, even in the dark.

Tag and Alarm Systems

Better known as **electronic article surveillance (EAS)**, this system is considered to be the most effective method for protecting the retailer's inventory. When used in conjunction with closed-circuit television, it is the best protection that the industry has developed to date. The technology identifies articles as they pass through a gated area in the store. If unpurchased merchandise leaves the store, an alarm system is triggered. Today, according to the Association of Automated Identification Manufacturers, there are more than 800,000 EAS systems installed throughout the world.

There are three major types of EAS systems used by retailers. Each involves the use of a label or tag that is attached to an item. Once the customer pays for the item, the tag is either deactivated or removed. A **detacher** is used to remove the **hard tags**, and a scanner is used to deactivate a disposable paper tag by swiping it over a pad or handheld scanner. If the tag is not removed or deactivated, an alarm will sound when the item is removed from the store.

One of the more effective types of tag devices is one that contains **ink reservoirs**. If these tags are not removed by a detacher, ink will spill onto the item and permanently damage it. Recognizing that the article will be destroyed, the perpetrator generally moves on to another area of the store.

Ultra Max® anti-theft system, pictured here, is the world's most innovative electronic article surveillance system.

The most widely used device is known as the **radio frequency (RF) system**. This system involves gates at the store's entrances and exits. When a shopper passes through the gates, an alarm will sound if the sensor tag hasn't been removed. Sometimes an automated message is sounded telling the shopper to return to the department for tag removal. Of course, those who don't intend to pay for the items attempt to quickly exit the premises. Sometimes invisible systems are used instead of entry gates. This technique involves using an antenna loop around the store's door, leaving it virtually undetectable by shoppers. Although this might serve the needs of some upscale retailers who do not want a visible system to clutter their entrances, the system has not proven to be as effective as the visible type. In fact, there is proof that a visible system is more of a deterrent to theft.

Another system that is dominant throughout Europe and widely used in U.S. pharmacies and supermarkets is the **electronic magnetic (EM) system**. In this technology, a magnetic, iron-containing strip with an adhesive layer is attached to the merchandise. The strip is not removed at checkout, but is deactivated by means of a scanner that uses a high magnetic field. Those who try to bypass the gates at the store's entrances without having the strip desensitized will trip an alarm. One feature of the system is that if goods are returned, the procedure can be reversed to restore the strip instead of applying a new one.

The newest system to be used is the **acousto-magnetic (AM) system**, which has the ability to protect very wide store exits and allows for high-speed label application. Stores like Home Depot are using acousto-magnetic tags from Sensormatic Electronics Corp., the largest surveillance system manufacturer in the United States.

Focus on...
Sensormatic Electronics Corp.

ONE OF THE largest companies dedicated to protecting retailers' inventories is Sensormatic Electronics Corporation, a division of Tyco. Founded in 1966, it has grown to employ more than 5,700 people and has an annual revenue of more than $1 billion. The company designs, manufacturers, sells, services, and supports the world's most advanced lines of fully integrated electronic article surveillance (EAS), video surveillance, access control, **electronic asset protection (EAP)**, and security management systems. Sensormatic not only addresses the needs of the retailing industry, it also services consumer goods manufacturers who apply the Sensormatic antitheft tags to their products before they are shipped to their customers' stores. Retailers in more than 113 countries have used Sensormatic products, with 93 of the top 100 retailers around the globe counted as clients.

A shopper who walks through a store is likely to come upon one of the company's more widely used products: hard tags. These tags are affixed to the items and must be removed upon purchase. Some of the tags are equipped with ink reservoirs that, if not properly removed, will spill ink on the garment and permanently damage it. The alarm-equipped gates through which shoppers pass are most often part of a system that has been installed by Sensormatic.

One of the company's innovations is the smartEAS system, which comprises **radio frequency identification device (RFID)** and EAS systems, offering retailers the ability to implement customer self-checkout, enhanced inventory management, and stock cycle counts, as well as new antidiversion, return-fraud, and merchandising programs. This technology has been adopted by many retailers who have implemented (or are actively exploring) customer self-checkout.

Retailers are always able to explore new product offerings of Sensormatic and obtain customer service at its Web site, www.sensormatic.com.

Some of the components of the EAS systems include:

- Disposable paper tags that can be imprinted with a **bar code** containing a host of information, including price
- Reusable, hard plastic tags referred to as **alligators**
- "Benefit denial" tags, which feature ink reservoirs that damage the garment if the tag is improperly removed
- Scanners that deactivate the merchandise tag
- Detachers that easily remove the hard tag from a garment

Other Shoplifting Deterrents

While the aforementioned systems are becoming commonplace in most major retail enterprises, others have also been used by giants in the industry as well as the smaller companies that have neither the need for such elaborate methods nor the capital available to install such systems.

Inktag® releases permanent ink onto the merchandise if customers illegally remove the tags.

Two-Way Mirrors

Although **two-way mirrors** have raised invasion-of-privacy issues in the retailing industry, they are still being used in some stores. In order to prevent any lawsuits, management usually posts signs alerting the shoppers that such mirrors are being used in fitting room areas.

On one side, these mirrors are used by customers in an ordinary manner, while the other side allows employees to watch the customers. When they are used, most retailers report a decrease in shoplifting.

The Radio Frequency Identification (RFID) system is a technology used by many retailers.

Magnifying Mirrors

It is mostly the smaller retailers who use **magnifying mirrors** in their attempt to spot shoplifters. The mirrors are strategically placed in areas that are generally concealed by merchandise racks. Store personnel are able to check these concealed areas for potential shoplifters by watching the mirrors. Even if the perpetrators are hard to spot, the mirrors often act as psychological deterrents. They serve a purpose for the merchant who cannot afford the costs of more sophisticated surveillance systems.

Control Access

One of the ways in which shoplifters remove merchandise from the store involves the fitting room. After they have selected a number of garments to try on, they head for the changing area and begin their scheme to steal merchandise. Some have been known to put several outfits on, one on top of the other, and leave the store without paying for them. Others have left their own clothing and replaced it with the store's merchandise. Still others merely enter these rooms wearing baggy, oversized apparel and stuff the new items into them.

Through **control access** to these areas, retailers have significantly reduced theft. One method is to lock the fitting rooms and to open them only when a sales associate has counted the garments that a shopper will try on. He or she gives the customer a plastic number that is equal to the number of items taken into the room. When the customer leaves the room, the associate must reconcile the number of pieces taken out with the plastic marker. If employees

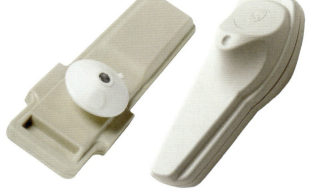

Supertag® is the world's most widely used hard tag.

carefully check the shoppers in and out of the fitting rooms, this system will reduce shoplifting. Gap and Old Navy use this method, as do many department stores.

Special Coded Signals

Some of the major department stores use a **coded signal** that alerts their store detectives to potential thefts. It is a method that involves the use of a signal that is sounded over the store's loudspeaker system. The code is one that is understood only by the employees in the store. A sales associate or manager might initiate the action by dialing a number that is directly linked to the store's security office. Another technique involves the witness of the potential crime using the store's speaker system to alert the in-house security team. In either case, using a code alerts the proper authorities of a problem without causing undue alarm to the customers.

Warning Signs

Warning signs help to deter shoplifters.

Some merchants post **warning signs** that help to deter shoplifting. These retailers usually sell value or discount merchandise and attract large numbers of shoppers to their stores. At the store's entrance or other strategic locations, signs are posted that state, "Free ride to the police station if you take merchandise without paying for it." Another might warn that "Those people committing in-store theft will be fully prosecuted." Such signs are an excellent method for deterring the theft of small items. It is usually the youthful offender who, given such a warning, refrains from committing the crime.

Another type of warning sign is found in the area of the fitting rooms. These signs alert shoppers to the fact that store security officers regularly patrol the area. Hence, some might think twice before stealing.

Price Awareness

A common practice that costs the retailer significant losses is **ticket switching**. Instead of stealing the merchandise outright, some thieves replace one store ticket with a lower-priced one. Professionals often have the same tools that the merchant uses to tag goods and merely remove the original tag and replace it with their own. Sometimes they take tags from other goods on the selling floor and use them on the merchandise they want.

In order to stop such practices, the retailer must make certain that the staff is familiar with merchandise prices. It is sometimes a difficult problem to correct, especially when numerous part-timers are employed. Additionally, with the use of scanners, many cashiers rarely look at the prices and simply charge the amount printed on the receipt.

Only through regular training sessions for cashiers can ticket switching be effectively combatted.

Incentive Award Programs

There is virtually nothing as effective as awarding someone with something meaningful for special performance. An **incentive award program** can be an effective tool to deter theft. When an employee has alerted the security team to a potential crime, recovers merchandise that has been earmarked for theft, provides information about a person suspected of shoplifting, or provides good prevention information, an award system is in order. Some retailers use a method that gives points to employees who have assisted in deterring shoplifting. The points may be used to redeem store merchandise.

Employee Workshops

Many retailers use workshops to educate new employees about shoplifting and how they might assist the company in combatting the problem. Through lectures given by managers and security personnel and through the use of video programs, a greater awareness emerges. Sometimes the sessions are followed up with quizzes to make certain that the staff understands all the issues that were covered. For example, the rights and wrongs of apprehension are generally discussed, such as never falsely accusing the suspicious-looking shopper and leaving the actual detainment of the criminal to the security team. In most states, a shopper who is apprehended wrongfully can bring a lawsuit against the retailer.

Awareness Bulletin Boards

The placement of bulletin boards in areas where employees congregate has helped to control shoplifting. The bulletins on these boards highlight theft prevention techniques and also post congratulatory notes to those employees who have assisted in apprehensions.

Although training sessions are quite helpful, their impact is quite short lived. On the other hand, the bulletin boards are always there to remind employees of how they can help the store. These boards should be updated regularly to feature new methods being instituted to prevent shoplifting. They can also be used as reminders of the incentive award programs offered by the company and how employees might personally benefit from the point system program.

Used either in combination or alone, all these techniques drastically reduce shoplifting and help reduce costs that would otherwise be passed on to the company's honest clientele.

INTERNAL THEFT

As previously emphasized in the chapter, store employees account for significantly greater merchandise shortages than do shoplifters. There are many reasons why the problem of **internal theft** continues to exist.

- An employee feels stealing is justified because his or her wages are lower than expected.
- An employee is dissatisfied with his or her immediate supervisor or the company itself.
- Because an employee knows the company's systems, he or she take advantage of that knowledge for personal gain.
- Security officers are so preoccupied with would-be shoplifters that they spend little time watching employees.
- Unsupervised workers are often the only ones working in the stockrooms.
- Employees may be aware of the company's lax prosecution of offenders.

There are many types of internal theft that continue to plague retailers. It is not only the stealing of merchandise but also ringing up sales for lower amounts, aiding and abetting friends by charging for only some of the items being purchased, applying higher than appropriate discounts to merchandise, and allowing ticket switching to take place.

The total elimination of internal theft is impossible, but there are several approaches that merchants use to significantly reduce the problem. When each of the deterrents and controls becomes part of an overall plan, significant curtailing of internal theft is possible.

Applicant Screening

A sound approach to the reduction of internal theft is to begin by screening those people who are being considered for positions in the company. Whether it is someone who is applying for a part-time sales associate's job or a top-level management role, careful assessment of the candidate's past is essential. When applications for employment are examined, often they are quickly skimmed and not thoroughly studied. It is at this point that management can actually prevent suspicious candidates from joining the staff. For example, if a résumé indicates brief stays of employment with numerous companies, there might be reason for concern.

Since screening is often a time-consuming task, many retailers are making use of outside sources to check the backgrounds of potential employees. In Chapter 9, www.1800ussearch.com was featured as a leader in this type of investigation. For a nominal fee, this company (and others) will provide different levels of research that range from typical formats to more customized approaches.

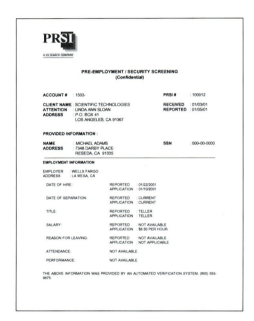

Online searches help retailers with applicant screening, usually a time-consuming process.

By using the employment application to give its investigators basic information such as name and address, the external source can make the necessary background checks. Once these inquiries are completed without incident, it is then appropriate for the human resources staff to move the applicant to the next level in the selection process.

Reference Checking

Merchants generally require that those seeking employment supply references. In most states, inquiries may be used only to verify the dates of employment and nothing more. In others, a more thorough questioning is allowed to determine the reasons a former employee left the company. In the latter situation, the candidate's honesty can be assessed; in the former, this must be done via use of the previously mentioned outside search sources. If any doubt about the individual's trustworthiness is uncovered, it is at this point that consideration of the application should be terminated.

Closed-Circuit TV

As we learned earlier in the chapter, most large retailers use cameras on the selling floor to record potential theft by shoplifters. The use of these cameras doesn't stop there. More and more merchants are investing in such installations to also check the honesty of their employees.

Mystery Shopping Services

Many major retailers use the old-fashioned method of checking on their employees' honesty: **mystery shoppers**. For a fee, a company sends people to the store to pose as customers. This is often the standard procedure when a newly added staff member has been with the company for a few weeks. When the shopper makes a purchase, the individual being evaluated is observed as the sale is taking place. Any irregularity, such as ringing up the wrong amount or failing to put cash in the register, is immediately reported to a manager who is standing by.

Shoppers are also used in cases where suspicion surrounds a particular staff member. Whatever the uncertainties might be about this employee, careful scrutiny is used to determine whether or not an impropriety has occurred.

Drug Testing

As discussed in Chapter 9, more and more companies are resorting to drug testing for new employees as part of the selection procedure as well as random drug tests for those already on the staff. There seems to be a correlation between drug abusers and internal theft. Many users are in need of funds to support their habits and increase their incomes by stealing merchandise and selling it for cash.

In order to ascertain the drug status of a potential employee, retailers often use outside companies to conduct the tests. For those already on staff who are required to undergo unannounced testing, many retailers make use of drug screening kits to conduct tests on their premises. One of the largest suppliers of drug testing materials is Noble Medical. Merchants can log on to its Web site, www.noblemedical.com, to learn about its entire product line.

The sign on the door of this Home Depot store informs potential employees that the retailer tests applicants for drug use.

Honesty and Psychological Testing

Another tool that retailers use to evaluate a candidate's potential for theft is testing. In particular, many rely upon the results of honesty and personality testing to make certain that those being considered for employment meet the ethical and moral requisites of the company. One source that companies such as Tandy Corporation and KFC use is Personnel Profiles, Inc. It administers a variety of tests such as Wonderlic, Thurston, Stanford-Binet, Strong-Campbell, and its own creation, The Achiever. The latter measures six mental aptitudes and ten personality dimensions, each of which is essential in employee screening to assess whether candidates are likely to commit crimes within the company.

Smuggling Controls

One of the ways in which a great deal of merchandise has been stolen by employees is to place it in a refuse container ready for disposal, only to retrieve it once it is outside of the store. Stock personnel have the responsibility for bringing goods to the selling floor and have total control of the items from the time they leave the receiving centers. By reserving an item or two in trash containers, they are able to collect them at the close of the day. Maintenance people, whose responsibility it is to clean the retailer's premises, also have considerable opportunity to participate in internal theft. Many of them perform their duties while the store is closed and are in close proximity to the merchandise that is stocked on racks and shelves. Left alone in an area, they are sometimes tempted to make their own selections without paying for them.

In order to reduce the internal theft attributed to this method of stealing, some merchants have installed systems for locking up the trash receptacles. Other merchants are going a step further by installing **through-the-wall security systems**. Those responsible for trash removal must place the items to be discarded through an opening in the wall that is connected to a compactor. Any attempt to smuggle stolen items from the premises in this manner will be eliminated.

Control of Employee Purchases

Most retailers offer attractive discounts to their employees for purchases made from the company. While this is certainly a benefit that sometimes motivates an individual to take a job with specific retailer, it also has resulted in the loss of merchandise that hasn't been paid for. If the employee transaction takes place on the selling floor and the items are then packed and brought to the individual's locker, along the way some other items may be placed in the package.

To stop this from happening, most retailers require that all employee purchases be retrieved at a behind-the-scenes location that is carefully controlled. Often, a security person who oversees the claiming of such merchandise mans the station. These counters are close to the employee entrances, making them inaccessible to the store's selling areas.

Rewards Programs

One of the most difficult problems that often confronts retailers is how to encourage honest employees to report criminal actions of their associates. While it is less troublesome for many to alert the security staff to potential shoplifters, revealing the names of fellow workers who are engaged in theft is another matter. An employee may be unwilling to report an associate because of friendly relationships that have been established or because he or she is fearful of reprisals from the culprits.

To motivate individuals who have witnessed internal theft, many retailers have established programs that offer them monetary rewards for their assistance. Essential to the success of such methods is the assurance that the person reporting the crime will remain anonymous and not be later called to testify against the perpetrator. This guarantee often convinces the honest staff member to help.

Prosecution of Dishonest Employees

It is essential for any merchant to quickly take action against anyone found guilty of internal theft. The offenders must be swiftly terminated—not only to make them pay for their misdeeds but also to put others on notice that dishonesty will not be tolerated by the organization. Slaps on the wrist or second chances do not work. A reputation for laxity on the part of management sends a poor message to other employees.

A company's position and procedures on internal theft should be spelled out during its orientation program for new employees. In this way the immediate warning will serve to deter possible moral and ethical violations. Of course, the information should be tactfully offered in a manner that doesn't sound threatening. Trained human resources personnel are best suited for such disclosure to make certain that the employer–employee relationship that is about to start will be beneficial to both parties.

According to statistical studies by such companies as Sensormatic Electronics Corporation, addressing internal theft by some or all of these techniques can help lower criminal activity.

CHECK FRAUD

Along with the losses due to shoplifting and internal theft is the problem of **check fraud**. Estimated to cost retailers in the United States more than $6 billion annually, it is yet another "bite" that retailers must make up for by increasing their selling prices to customers. The number of checks that are marked and returned because of such reasons as "account closed" and "counterfeit" is staggering. The phenomenon is considered to be one of the fastest growing problems affecting the U.S. financial system. But with checks estimated to account for approximately a third of retail spending, merchants can't simply refuse to accept them as payment.

TeleCheck, a leading provider of check services, offers several ways in which they believe check fraud can be reduced. Some of these include:

- Establishing a check acceptance policy that details required forms of identification along with dollar limits
- Accepting only checks with printed information such as name, address, and phone number
- Comparing the signatures on the ID and check to make certain they match
- Carefully checking the driver's license to make certain that it has not been altered
- Refusing to accept second-party or third-party checks
- In cases of suspicion, calling the financial institution to verify authenticity and confirmation of available funds
- Using a check verification or guarantee service

One of the better ways of curtailing the acceptance of fraudulent checks is by training employees at the time of their hiring. By using classroom teaching, instructional CDs, role-playing, and E-Learning technology (as outlined in Chapter 9), the problem could be alleviated.

Of course, there is no foolproof way to avoid all bad checks. However, if the "rules" established by a company are carefully followed by employees, the problem will be substantially reduced.

INTERNET THEFT

The phenomenon of the Internet as a viable outlet for consumer goods has not only given merchants a new way to reach targeted markets, it has also created a new arena for fraud. Numerous scams have been utilized to defraud merchants of payment for goods. So significant is **Internet fraud** that its curtailment has become one of the major challenges of retailers who sell on-line. There are no actual figures on the amounts lost due to these practices, but the most recent opinions of experts estimate the losses to be about 10 percent of sales. This figure is greater than for internal theft and shoplifting combined. At the present time, MasterCard is in the process of setting up a procedure that will help combat these crimes.

To make matters even worse for Internet merchants, they are 100 percent responsible for fraudulent Internet credit card transactions, even when the credit card company has authorized the sales. Martaus and Associates, a payments research and consulting firm, predicts that with the problems now spiraling upward, card companies will be forced to rewrite the rules for Internet payments.

The main reason criminals attempt online fraud is the anonymity factor. The Internet makes it easy for them to ply their trade. Tom Arnold, chief technology officer for San Jose, California–based CyberSource observes, "Nobody knows who you are."

To soften the blows of this fraud to retailers, a new Web site and Security Program (WiSP) offers insurance policies for companies selling on-line. It covers many types of losses at costs that range from $4,000 to $50,000 a year.

Fraud Prevention

One of the challenges of Internet businesses is to sharply reduce this problem. At this point in time, new techniques are surfacing to do just that.

Equifax Check Solutions has introduced PayNet Secure, a complete payment processing service for Internet sales. The key to the service is its customer authentication and certification components. The first time a consumer makes an online purchase from a PayNet Source client, he or she is asked a series of routine questions such as name, address, age, and so forth. Using the responses, Equifax checks the customer against the consumer credit base it maintains and also against internal and external databases, such as lists of bad check writers. It then proceeds to ask other questions such as the identity of his or her mortgage lender. Once the company validates a consumer, he or she is given a password that precludes similar security scrutiny in future online transactions involving any PayNet Secure merchants. The system is intended to help "ferret out fraudsters."

Although the overwhelming number of transactions are made with the use of credit cards, some purchasers want the option of paying by check, just as they do at the brick-and-mortar operations. A joint venture between TeleCheck Services and Payment NET offers guarantees to Internet merchants to safeguard against fraud by check.

San Diego–based HNC Software has developed another technique that is being used by the industry. The company, a pioneer in the use of neural network technology to predict consumer credit behavior, introduced eFalcon, a fraud detection system that can be installed by online merchants. Online transactions are run through eFalcon, which provides a statistical score reflecting the possibility that the transaction is fraudulent. The scoring process is based upon detailed transaction information and behavior profiling, and it takes less than a second to complete during the normal card authorization process. If the probability of fraud is high, the system offers further verification suggestions. It asks the consumer to provide the CVV2 number, which is the three digits after the account number on the back of the credit card. Fraudulent users most likely will not have these numbers, indicating that the purchase is being illegally made.

NETrageous, a Maryland-based firm, has developed a list of scam prevention tips for online merchants that is available on a public-service Web site, www.ScamBusters.com. Among some of the tips offered to merchants are the following:

- Be wary of orders with different "bill to" and "ship to" addresses.
- Be especially cautious about orders that are larger than typical order amounts and orders requesting next-day delivery.
- Don't accept orders from customers using e-mail services without first requesting additional information, such as the name of the card-issuing bank, which can provide further assurance that the transaction is legitimate.
- Pay close attention to international orders, and take extra steps to validate orders before shipping products to foreign addresses.
- If in doubt, telephone the customer to confirm the order.

At the time of this writing, more approaches to the prevention of Internet fraud are surfacing. However, just as in-store fraud cannot be totally prevented, it is unlikely that the Internet fraud problem can be 100 percent eliminated.

VENDOR THEFT

A problematic area in which losses may be prevented is one that involves vendor transactions. The troubles attributed to this type of loss are not always due to intentional misdeeds but may come as a result of poor handling by manu-

Sometimes shipping clerks miscount the goods during packing, leading to shortages for the retailer.

facturer and wholesaler personnel. Specifically, the two major areas are improper billing and merchandise shortages in shipments. Of course, vendors—like retailers—have staff members who are dishonest and who sometimes intentionally omit the shipping of a few pieces for which the account has been billed.

The problem will continue at its present annual level of $2 billion if merchants are lax in making corrections. Before the methods that may be used to control the losses are examined, the following specific causes should be addressed:

Theft of merchandise in transit is a cause of shortages.

- *Improper billing.* The vast amount of invoicing that takes place often results in charging the retailer more than the actual shipment requires. It might be keying in the wrong price for the merchandise or billing for more pieces than were actually shipped. The invoice is then in error. This may be an honest mistake or one that was intentional. Whatever the reason, the retailer is charged more than it should be.
- *Merchandise shortages at vendor premises.* When shipping clerks are packing orders it is possible that they will not fill the order exactly as the invoice reads. They might, intentionally or otherwise, pack fewer items into the carton than have actually been ordered. Sometimes quick handling of the orders results in a miscount, with the retailer bearing the burden of being overcharged. Other times the causes are due to the dishonesty of vendor employees. Just as retailers are confronted with unscrupulous employees, so are the vendors.
- *Shipping point theft.* Occasionally packages shipped by vendors are not carefully sealed. When such conditions are evident, the shipping company's handlers may find ways to remove merchandise from the cartons, leaving a shortage. More and more theft is being attributed to the period between goods leaving the vendors and reaching the merchant's premises. Only by careful packing can such theft be reduced.

Retailers may substantially reduce losses that come as a result of vendor improprieties by establishing a careful system that checks every aspect of incoming merchandise and invoices. Such systems should include the following elements:

Invoice checking with the original order is imperative in making certain that a vendor's figures are correct.

- *Careful checking of invoices.* The staff whose responsibility it is to post the amounts due to the vendor must not rely upon the totals that have been determined by the vendor's billing department. Each invoice must first be compared to the original order to make certain that the prices correspond. In some cases, the price charged might differ from what the buyer had previously negotiated. Once this step has been addressed, computations should be made to make certain that there are no errors. If there are any discrepancies, the matter must be resolved with the vendor before the invoice can be made ready for payment.
- *Merchandise counts.* Those in the receiving areas must make certain that the merchandise indicated on the packing slip is exactly what has been shipped. Too often, receiving clerks merely unpack the goods without actually making certain of the contents. Some retailers use a method known as a *blind count*. This system provides the clerk only with the numbers

of the items that have been ordered, not the expected amounts. The clerk is then required to indicate the exact amount of each item that has been received. This amount is then compared to the invoice that has been received by the accounts payable department. At this time, if there are differences, the matter can be resolved by notifying the vendor.

- *Package examination.* When the merchant receives merchandise, it is imperative that each package is carefully scrutinized to make certain that it has not been tampered with. Any package that shows signs of a tear or opening should be called to the attention of the vendor. The receiving clerk should then either note the situation when he or she signs for the shipment or return the questionable package to the vendor.

When retailers carefully address all of the circumstances and conditions that involve losses due to shoplifting, internal theft, check fraud, Internet fraud, and vendor misrepresentation, their losses will likely be reduced. The end result will be better prices for shoppers and more profit for the company.

CHAPTER HIGHLIGHTS

- Internal theft, shoplifting, Internet scams, and vendor misrepresentation in invoicing account for more than $30 billion in losses to retailers each year.
- Video surveillance systems that involve closed-circuit television are being used by most major retailers to watch and record the actions of shoplifters and dishonest employees.
- Most merchants who deal in high-ticket soft goods agree that the best method of curtailing shoplifting is to use electronic article surveillance (EAS) systems.
- Most EAS systems yield excellent results, especially those that use inktags to deter theft.
- Incentive programs are being used by retailers to motivate their employees to report suspected shoplifters.
- Internal theft accounts for greater retailer shortages than shoplifting does.
- One of the ways in which employers are reducing internal theft is by using outside agencies, such as www.1800ussearch.com, to prescreen job applicants.
- Many retail operations use rewards programs to encourage staff members to report suspicious employees to the security division.
- In order to reduce Internet fraud, more and more companies are developing plans to more carefully assess Web site transactions.
- Industrywide, shortages that come at the hands of inappropriate vendor billing and inventory shortages amount to $2 billion each year.

IMPORTANT RETAILING TERMS

acousto-magnetic (AM) system (224)
alligator (225)
bar code (225)
check fraud (230)
closed-circuit television (CCTV) (222)
coded signal (226)
control access (225)
detacher (223)
electronic article surveillance (EAS) (223)
electronic asset protection (EAP) (224)
electronic magnetic (EM) system (224)
hard tag (223)
incentive award program (226)
ink reservoir (223)
internal theft (227)
Internet fraud (231)
kleptomania (222)
magnifying mirror (225)
mystery shopper (228)
radio frequency (RF) system (224)
radio frequency identification device (RFID) (224)
shoplifter (222)
through-the-wall security system (230)
ticket switching (226)
two-way mirror (225)
video surveillance system (222)
warning sign (226)

FOR REVIEW

1. How much has the retail industry lost as a result of shoplifting and internal theft in the past year?
2. Who is typically the cause of more theft, the shoplifter or the company employee?

3. Define the term *kleptomania*.
4. Describe how a video surveillance system works and how it helps to reduce shoplifting and internal theft.
5. Briefly describe electronic surveillance systems and how they help retailers deter shoplifting.
6. In what way has the ink reservoir system made EAS systems even better?
7. What does the term *alligator* mean when referring to antitheft systems?
8. How does a retailer prevent theft of merchandise that is taken into a fitting room?
9. How are specially coded systems used to alert store security of potential shoplifters?
10. In what ways have retailers motivated employees to help control shoplifting?
11. Describe how the latest techniques in applicant screening help to reduce internal theft.
12. Define the term *mystery shopper* and tell how it helps to reduce internal theft.
13. Why has drug testing become such an important part of the recruitment process in the retail industry?
14. Other than drug screening, what kinds of tests help to evaluate the honesty of job candidates?
15. How does the through-the-wall security system reduce internal theft?
16. How large is the check fraud market?
17. What are some ways retailers can reduce check fraud?
18. Why has the advent of Internet shopping resulted in so many losses for the merchant?
19. Name two companies that have developed techniques to reduce Internet fraud. Describe their techniques.
20. How can a vendor contribute to a retailer's losses?

AN INTERNET ACTIVITY

Pretend you are a recently hired human resources specialist whose expertise is in recruitment. Your main role is to develop resources that will carefully screen job applicants before any face-to-face interviews take place.

Using any Internet search engine, find five Web sites that run background checks on people. For each site that you find, note the following: Web site, services offered, and cost.

EXERCISES AND PROJECTS

1. Using either the Internet or Yellow Pages, research three companies that specialize in surveillance systems. Through direct contact with the companies or by examining their Web sites, gather information about particular products they produce that may help retailers. Request brochures or catalogs from these companies to share with other students in the class. Using the information obtained, write a brief report telling about each company's approach to surveillance systems.

THE CASE OF THE MISSING MERCHANDISE

Cannon & Abbott started a small mail-order company in the Southwest in 1972. Initially, Cannon & Abbott specialized in a very small model stock that exclusively sold women's wear through quarterly catalogues. The company operated out of a central warehouse that housed and shipped all of the merchandise.

The product line concentrated on women's apparel for both missy and junior sizes and accessories that included hosiery, handbags, gloves, scarves, and jewelry. In 1990, Cannon & Abbott expanded its offerings to include men's clothing and children's wear. The success of these lines helped make the company one of the more profitable of its kind in the industry. The company's success demanded considerable physical expansion. It moved from a small, three-story warehouse to several buildings. Its growth, while providing considerable profits for the company, also caused a number of problems.

The first problem was finding capable employees who could carefully carry out the responsibilities required of them. The second, and more serious, involved internal theft. Unlike retailers who operate out of brick-and-mortar locations and deal with shoplifters every day, Cannon & Abbott needs to secure their merchandise only to prevent employee theft. When the company was small, the problem was almost nonexistent. Now, however, the problem has become extremely widespread.

The management team has just held a meeting to determine how the problem should be addressed. Some of the suggestions include:

- Calling the entire staff together to see if anyone could give information about the culprits.
- Pretagging the merchandise with alligators and requiring that employees pass through surveillance portals when leaving the premises.
- Conducting a security check on everyone employed by the company.

At the conclusion of the meeting, there wasn't a consensus about how the situation should be remedied.

Questions

1. Do any of the suggestions merit further consideration? Defend your answer.
2. What other approaches could the company take to eliminate internal theft?

Retail's Latest Plague: Fighting Back against Shoplifting Gangs
Evan Clark

AUGUST 3, 2007

Hot goods are becoming a hot issue for retailers.

Every year thieves—many of them employees—walk out of stores with apparel, jewelry and other merchandise estimated to be worth more than $30 billion, taking with them a hefty chunk of the industry's profits.

Often, the money made from reselling the goods online, to fences or returning them for rebates at the store helps fund criminal enterprises that prey on the ultimate of soft targets: retailers that aim to draw as many people as possible through their doors.

"It all comes to be another tax on the consumer," said Dan Doyle, vice president of loss prevention and human resources at department store chain Bealls Inc. "They end up footing the bill on all this. As a consumer who's concerned about higher prices, they should be mad as hell about the fact that they're out there stealing this stuff and selling it."

Far removed from the shoplifting commonly attributed to adolescents who are looking for a thrill or a freebie, the gangs targeting stores are sophisticated enterprises.

"This is their job, they have people who work for them and potentially people who work for them," said Doyle, explaining the multilayered structure of the syndicate. "They either take orders or they go out and steal stuff knowing they have a market to sell it—the Internet sites that allow people to sell merchandise somewhat anonymously. It isn't like you have to walk into a back alley where you're exposed."

Streetwear, denim, swimsuits, junior fashions and jewelry are all hot items to swipe, he said.

The gangs have a new, formidable foe: the Federal Bureau of Investigation, which has focused more attention on organized crime as of late. In conjunction with retail trade groups, the FBI helped establish an online tracking system to help stores protect themselves and aid law enforcement in capturing and prosecuting criminals.

The organized groups come in all shapes and sizes, from gangs such as MS-13, a violent street gang with Latin American roots, to organizations that use everyone from illegal immigrants to all-American types. Bealls was even hit by a group of strippers who were stealing from stores around Florida and selling the goods to a fence.

"Typically, the organizations that we look at or law enforcement looks at are dozens of people working together," said Brian Nadeau, who until last month was a supervisory special agent in the FBI's major theft unit before transferring to the bureau's inspection management unit.

The groups have "boosters" who steal the product, as well as fences who move the goods, people who determine what stores will be hit and scouts who get the lay of the land beforehand. Often there are drivers behind the wheel of a getaway car.

Boosters will go into stores, distract the salespeople, perhaps by setting a small fire in the back of the store or spilling something, grab thousands of dollars worth of merchandise and sneak out, only to go directly to another store, perhaps in another state along a major highway.

To combat the gangs, Nadeau has preached collaboration, even among retail rivals.

Hence the Law Enforcement Retail Partnership Network, or LERPnet, an online database that is just gearing up and connects retailers with each other and law enforcement. Companies from Bealls and Mervyns to Saks Fifth Avenue, J.C. Penney and Wal-Mart are part of the program.

Stores using the network can post descriptions and vital statistics on suspected thieves and get alerts when there has been criminal activity nearby. The authorities will also soon be able to look into the database to hopefully connect the dots to catch bad guys.

"Loss prevention people now have the ability to share this information with each other almost real-time, as it's happening," said Nadeau. "This will give the ability for a retailer in one state to quickly know that the same problem happened 45 minutes or an hour ago in another state and then notify law enforcement."

Being part of the network frees loss prevention executives from having to get approval from their superiors to share notes with their competitors.

"Law enforcement has not, in the past, been focusing heavily on organized retail theft," said Nadeau, noting the concentration was instead on areas such as drugs.

Shoplifting gangs targeting stores are getting more attention now, in part because of the FBI's new program.

The Web-based approach has helped Mervyns capture professional shoplifters.

"You want to be able to heighten your team's awareness of who's out there," said Mike Keenan, director of loss prevention at Mervyns. "The value to the industry is if one loss prevention team takes out a group, that benefits all the other retailers, too. The more retailers that participate, the more valuable the system is."

If LERPnet helps authorities tie one robbery to another, a larger case can be brought against the professional criminal who, with just a slap on the wrist, might go undeterred.

"If they're back out and released, they just start out again," said Keenan. "As long as they're in jail, they're not stealing from us."

Despite growing awareness on the part of retailers, there is much room for improvement industrywide.

"Many retailers don't have vast in-store loss prevention resources," said Read Hayes, director of the Loss Prevention Research Council and co-director of the University of Florida's loss prevention research team. "They're not catching bad guys—taking prisoners, in other words."

While some large chains do have a strong loss-prevention apparatus, Hayes said most retailers are not set up to deal with organized gangs.

"They probably do not have a real handle on the scope or dynamics, and they don't have the infrastructure or resources to attack it," he said, noting a good place to start for stores is to understand how much they are impacted by theft through surveillance and research.

Though often not connected to an organized gang, employee theft is also a big drain on stores. "There's clearly an employee component [of theft] throughout the supply chain, not just in stores," said Hayes, noting retailers estimate that employee theft accounts for 30 to 40 percent of their inventory shrinkage.

The excitement and buzz that brands create around their products attract not only shoppers, but thieves who have a great incentive to steal.

Stolen goods fetch about 30 cents on the dollar on the street, 70 cents on the dollar if they're sold online or, for the more enterprising, 100 percent plus tax if they're returned to the store, said Joseph LaRocca, the National Retail Federation's vice president for loss prevention.

"They're going from store to store in the mall, they're loading up shopping bags, they're going from mall to mall and stealing up to $10,000 a day," said LaRocca. "These groups are very sophisticated and they, for the most part, slide in and out of stores without ever being noticed."

In addition to sophisticated surveillance of stores and malls, boosters come prepared with plans to distract employees, or tools such as jackets or "booster bags" lined with tin foil to confound antitheft sensors.

"There are shopping lists that these groups will create," said LaRocca. "The things that the goods have in common is they're highly desirable, they're easily resold in person or over the Internet."

The ease of selling goods online is a sore spot for stores.

"EBay has done very little to assist retailers' investigations, stating that their platform is merely a way to connect buyers and sellers," claimed LaRocca. "Retailers have repeatedly asked for assistance in the identification of sellers who offload their brand goods or items believed to be stolen or fraudulently obtained, and there has been little to no response."

The online auction site did not return calls for comment.

Security experts said they could virtually stop theft tomorrow, but acknowledge that increasingly draconian protections would make customers feel unwelcome in the stores.

One antidote to being ripped off might lie within stores' grasp, though.

"If we just keep doing what we're already supposed to be doing, it's going to control organized crime—good customer service," said Chris

McGoey, a Los Angeles-based security consultant. "Having people on the floor it has been proven time and time again, increases sales and reduces losses. The store looks much better, it's in stock, everything works, everyone's happy. The only downside is that you're spending some money up front to get the benefits later of increased sales and reduced inventory shrinkage."

CHAPTER 11
Logistical Merchandise Distribution

After you have completed this chapter, you should be able to discuss:

- The concept of interenterprise collaboration
- The manner in which electronic data interchange benefits both the supplier and the retailer
- How information is gathered through the use of a vendor managed inventory system
- The extent to which nonprofit organizations have been involved in improving the efficiency of the entire merchandise supply chain
- Why many major retail organizations use outside marking
- What role a centralized receiving department plays in retailing
- Why some companies use regional receiving facilities to distribute goods to their stores
- How the concept of intermodal transportation facilitates the shipping of merchandise from vendor to retailer
- The concept of barcoding and the role it plays in merchandise distribution

One of the vital components of any retailing venture is merchandise distribution. Before any purchasing is done or any merchandising plans are considered, a company must address the problems of getting merchandise to the selling floors in the brick-and-mortar operations or to the stockrooms of cataloguers and e-tailers in a timely fashion. If merchandise is not available for sale when the consumers' needs arise, it is likely that sales will be lost.

Inventory management decision making has become the focus of the retailing industry, and greater profits can be realized by addressing the problems associated with this part of the business before they occur. Unlike the retailers who preceded them, today's merchants have the benefit of numerous sophisticated technological advances to make the transition from vendors to their own warehouses a smoother and simpler one.

Not only has the physical movement of the goods become easier, but so has the relationship between the supplier and merchant in terms of order processing and fulfillment. By dovetailing the retailer's and manufacturer's efforts in these areas, the former is able to reduce the amount of merchandise on the selling floor, resulting in a more profitable turnover rate, and the latter is able to respond to retailer merchandising needs as they arise. Through such programs as **electronic data interchange (EDI)** and **Quick Response (QR) inventory planning**, retailers and vendors regularly exchange information via their computers. Other routes available to both of these channel partners are accessed via the Internet.

The practice of merchandise planning requires that a retailer interface with its vendors and also address the in-house problems associated with merchandise distribution. These include the physical receipt and handling of incoming goods, the manner in which shipments are scrutinized, and the marking of individual items. For brick-and-mortar operations, there are also problems associated with moving the goods onto the selling floors and transferring them to various units of the company if the receiving facility is a centralized one. For catalogue and Web site retailers, the problem is a little different because the merchandise doesn't move to a selling floor; it remains in the warehouse awaiting a customer order.

Today, retailers are investing millions of dollars to upgrade the systems that concern merchandise distribution. After doing so, they can reap the benefits afforded by these programs in terms of greater profitability for their companies.

INTERENTERPRISE COLLABORATION

By developing and maintaining close business relationships, vendors and retailers are better able to serve each other's needs. This makes their companies more profitable and creates an **interenterprise collaboration**. Whether it is the brick-and-mortar operations that seek better turnaround times in merchandise acquisition or the Internet Web sites that want to reduce the time it takes for goods to be delivered from manufacturer to consumer, a closer relationship is the key.

This clerical worker for a vendor is checking a merchandising request from a retailer.

High-Tech Innovation

Merchants and manufacturers are involved in numerous technical innovations that make merchandise analysis and delivery more beneficial to both parties. Electronic data interchange, as it is commonly known in the industry, is an excellent tool for improving a retailer's purchasing plans. The process provides for the electronic exchange of machine-readable data in standardized formats between one organization's computers and another's. It eliminates the need for a lot of paper pushing by retailers to get their goods shipped from vendors. Whenever ordering, invoicing, and shipping take place, EDI enables the task to be accomplished more quickly, saving time, energy, and ultimately cost. With the use of laser scanners, satellite linkups, and wireless systems, retailers and suppliers can communicate as never before. One e-tailer that uses an EDI system is eBags.com. The company uses a system supplied by RnetEC, of Sacramento, California, that has given it greater control of its integration with suppliers and has significantly reduced the time it takes to fill customers' orders. With customer purchase orders filled directly from suppliers, the delivery time has been reduced from a week or longer to only 1–3 days. The eBags system consists of a virtual area network that features a standard interface through which the e-tailer can communicate with vendors, sending machine orders and shipping information as electronic documents. Every major retailer—whether it is a brick-and-mortar merchant, cataloguer, e-tailer, or participant in multichannel retailing—participates in one of the many available EDI systems.

Another technology that is affecting retailer–vendor relationships is **vendor-managed inventory (VMI)**. By using scanners at the retail level, manufacturers can gather information about the sales of their products through stores, catalogues, and Web sites, replenishing inventories on a continual basis. Thus, the vendor is actively involved in making replenishment decisions for the retailer. Among the major companies who are significant users of VMI are JCPenney, Kmart, and Wal-Mart.

Through the use of Quick Response inventory systems, order processing and delivery can be greatly improved. In these systems, the manufacturer keeps close watch on the retailer's inventory levels and makes production decisions that will result in delivery of goods whenever it anticipates the merchant will need them. By participating in this methodology, the retailer is able to reduce the amount of merchandise it has on hand, knowing that the manufacturer will be able to quickly restock the store's inventory. This enables the retailer to capitalize on a better stock turnover rate, which can translate into higher profits. With the proper use of an EDI system and mutual trust between the retailer and its supply vendors, Quick Response planning is easily achieved and is evident at most every major type of retailing classification in operation today.

Focus on . . .
Macy's, Inc., Logistics and Operations

THE LOGISTICS AND OPERATIONS DIVISION WAS FOUNDED IN 1994, when the company was then Federated Department Stores. Now, as part of the new Macy's, Inc., structure, it serves the needs of all Macy's and Bloomingdale's stores.

The primary responsibility of Logistics and Operations is to ensure the efficient and timely flow of goods to the selling floors of all stores, ensuring that the right merchandise is delivered to the right locations at the right time. The system involves operating distribution centers, coordinating transportation and shuttle deliveries, handling vendor returns and merchandise liquidation, delivering large-ticket items such as furniture to customer's homes, and fulfilling Internet and catalogue orders.

In 2001, Macy's Logistics and Operations was among the first in retailing to adopt "Six Sigma" (6σ) quality improvement techniques to focus on a particular population segment, expand operating capabilities, and improve processes. The division is also heavily involved in EDI with vendors employing state-of-the-art material handling systems in its distribution centers. Macy's is considered the current leader in pursuing the benefits of RFDI (radio frequency identification) technology to help speed the flow of goods through distribution centers and other facilities.

When Macy's, Inc., acquired such other retail giants as the May Company and Marshall Field's, the challenges facing Logistics and Operations were monumental. It was necessary to dismantle the systems used in these acquired retail operations and then to fit them into the logistics and distribution functions used by Macy's.

The division strives for continuous improvement in people, processes, and technology to reduce supply chain and logistics costs while simultaneously working to enhance service, speed, and accuracy.

Nonprofit Industry Groups

Several groups have formed in order to improve the efficiency of the entire merchandise supply chain. Two of the principal groups, both of which are nonprofit organizations, are the **Voluntary Interindustry Commerce Standards Association (VICS)** and the **Collaborative**

Planning, Forecasting, and Replenishment Committee (CPFR). Each has initiated specific guidelines and recommendations that hope to foster closer supplier–retailer relationships.

CPFR is a trade organization with a large number of participating suppliers and retailers on its roster. Some of the merchants represented are Best Buy, Kmart, JCPenney, Safeway, Sam's Club, Staples, Wal-Mart, and Walgreens. The vendors include Gillette, Kraft Foods, Inc., Levi Strauss & Co., Nestlé, Ralston-Purina, and Ocean Spray Cranberries.

The mission of CPFR is to take a global leadership role in the ongoing improvement of products and information within the general merchandise retail industry supply chain. It hopes to provide an environment for dynamic information sharing, integrating both the demand-side and supply-side processes (linking manufacturers, retailers, and carriers) and to effectively plan, forecast, and replenish customer needs through the total supply chain. Early participants such as Wal-Mart and the Sara Lee Corporation have found considerable success through CPFR participation.

VICS, organized in 1986, has also worked continuously to improve the efficiency of the entire supply chain. It has established cross-country standards that simplify the flow of product and information in the general merchandise classification for retailers and suppliers alike.

The organization is made up of senior executives who have proven that a timely and accurate flow of product and information between companies significantly improves their competitive positions. They believe that implementation of VICS technologies and QR partnerships by committed participants will improve their bottom lines.

The goal of VICs is to create solutions, with input from its many member companies (e.g., Best Buy, Kmart, Wal-Mart) that will improve processes throughout the supply chain. Members believe that businesses that fail to adopt the available technology will be moving backward.

Through regularly produced newsletters, participants learn about the current issues that confront supply chain management.

Outside Marking

Although most retailers have their own in-house marking facilities in their receiving areas, more and more of them opt for goods to be ticketed by either the vendors or freight carriers.

Many vendors pre-ticket merchandise for their retail accounts to save time.

This **outside marking** allows merchants to get the goods onto the selling floor more quickly. Either the retailer or the company that is doing the actual ticketing may supply the price tickets.

Those who prepare their own tickets send them on to the manufacturers before the goods come off the production line. In this way, no time is lost and they can be immediately affixed prior to shipment. The manufacturers also save the retailers time by placing the garments on hangers, putting them into individual plastic bags or boxes, or utilizing other merchant-preferred formats. If it is the carrier that pre-tickets the items, the supplier must send the goods to the shipping point for processing. Traditionally, standard goods are ticketed in this manner. Since retailers must often replenish such standard goods as hosiery and basic men's dress shirts, and since price fluctuations for these goods are relatively uncommon, price tickets may be prepared in advance of the goods' production. This, too, is a time saver.

It should be understood that, whenever outside marking is used, the information on price, sizes, colors, and merchandise classification is provided by the retailer. The outside sources merely follow instructions.

Focus on . . .
Gymboree

GYMBOREE, AN APPAREL RETAILER THAT SPECIALIZES in children's clothing, uses an allocation system that tailors merchandise distribution to the 600+ stores in its chain. The objective of the company is to improve margins on inventory by sending the most appropriate goods to the units where they will be best utilized. The premise is based upon the company's belief that, unless a store-by-store allocation is undertaken, much of the merchandise will find itself in places where it won't sell in quantities necessary to produce a profit.

Unlike the practice of most companies, which allocate goods on a "store cluster" basis—where groups of stores receive identical inventories—this system addresses individual needs. Gymboree believes that the typically used cookie-cutter distribution approach is far too imprecise to maximize profits. If its units were clustered, then the company feels that some would perform above average and some below average. The technology employed is from JDA Software Group of Scottsdale, Arizona, and focuses on the exact needs of each individual unit.

Since the implementation of its new system, task time has been reduced by 25 percent. Distribution plans, based upon the reports that are generated by the methodology, are drawn up one week in advance of shipping. Not only has time been saved in the allocation process, but also the needs of each store are being more accurately addressed.

Gymboree management stresses that its intention is not necessarily to reduce inventory levels, as many big box retailers are apt to do, but rather to send the goods where they will be needed most.

VENDOR–RETAILER PHYSICAL DISTRIBUTION

Moving goods from supplier to retailer is a major concern for both parties in the distribution channel. Time is generally of the essence, making it imperative that the products get into the hands of the retailer and onto the selling floor—or in the warehouse for catalogues or Web sites—as soon as possible for consumer ordering.

Merchants and suppliers alike have a number of different transportation modes from which they may choose. Their selection depends upon the origination of shipping point, the amount

TABLE 11.1
COMPARISON OF MODES OF TRANSPORTATION

	Trucks	Railroads	Air	Water Carriers
Transportation costs	High	Average	Very high	Very low
Door-to-door service	High	Average	Average	Low
Speed of delivery	High	Average	Very high	Very low
Schedule maintenance	High	Average	Very high	Average
Location availability	Very high	High	Average	Low
Shipment frequency	Very high	Low	Average	Very low

of merchandise to be delivered, how urgently the goods are needed, and the available shipping facilities where the goods have been purchased.

Overall, the choices are trucks, railroads, air, and water carriers. The retailer must analyze factors such as cost, speed of service, dependability, location, availability, and frequency of shipments before any decisions are made. Within each transportation systems there is generally a choice of shippers with whom transportation arrangements can be made:

- *United Parcel Service.* A company that offers regular or express service in most parts of the globe.
- *Federal Express.* A major transporter of goods that need overnight delivery.
- *United States Postal Service.* The post office has numerous options: parcel post, an inexpensive delivery method; priority mail, a service that promises 2- or 3-day delivery; and express mail, the fastest of the methods.

In many situations there is a need for **intermodal transportation**. This refers to the need for two or more modes of transportation in order to move the goods more efficiently. For example, a trucking company might be needed to bring the order from the vendor to the air carrier and then to another trucker once the merchandise has arrived at its destination. Thus, for example, orders placed in France might take the route of a local trucker picking up the packages and delivering them to Air France, which upon arrival in the United States would have the goods picked up and delivered to the retailer by a company such as American Freightways.

Federal Express is a major carrier that guarantees overnight delivery.

Table 11.1 offers a comparison of the different modes of transportations in terms of the features of their services.

Technological Application for Supply-Chain Performance

Timely delivery of merchandise from vendor to retailer is extremely important. When selling seasons are limited, as with fashion merchandise and other "perishables," it is vital that the goods arrive at the stores for in-house distribution in a timely manner. Anything short of on-time delivery often results in markdowns. IBM has introduced a supply-chain system on its IBM System p5 595 server that promises to revolutionize supply-chain efficiency. This server enables JDA Software to run critical supply-chain and other retail applications in a variety of demanding contexts. JDA Software Group is the global leader in helping retailers and other businesses in their supply-chain endeavors. Both www.ibm.com and www.jda.com offer more information on supply-chain operations.

IN-HOUSE DISTRIBUTION

Although the trend of supplier–retailer supply-chain cooperation is on the upswing, many companies still utilize in-house staffing to handle some of the distribution details. Needless to say, the major retailers interface with their suppliers via EDI, QR, and VMI to help manage order processing and its fulfillment. However, other merchants maintain departments that address some of their needs such as inventory checking and marking. Of course, small retailers generally rely upon less technically oriented systems for the entire process of getting the goods from suppliers to the selling floors.

The major retail organizations that have in-house installations use either a **centralized receiving** department to process the goods before shipping them on to all of the individual units in the company or **regional receiving** departments that receive and mark the goods for stores in their districts.

Centralized Receiving Departments

In many major department stores and chain organizations, receiving and marking the goods from the vendors is accomplished at a centralized location that facilitates the movement of goods to their stores. There are several good reasons for this type of merchandise distribution:

- *Better physical control of merchandise.* Retailers go to great expense establishing facilities that handle all the company's incoming merchandise. With the use of a wide variety of technological tools that interface with such programs as EDI and VMI, merchandise management is more likely to be better controlled. Receiving managers solely concerned with merchandise distribution are making certain that the goods are: properly accounted for, processed for entry into the company's inventory system, and made ready for quick movement onto the selling floors. In contrast, when store or department managers—who have other responsibilities—must handle merchandise that is sent directly to the stores in the chain or department store organization, the system is less efficient and might result in improper handling that could lead to losses.
- *Better financial control of merchandise.* Centralized receiving departments work closely with the company's control division to ensure that goods are accounted for in the various merchandising systems. If there are any discrepancies, the regular interfacing of these two important areas of the business can quickly address them. This reduces the risk of

shortages, damages, and other problems that might be overlooked under less centralized arrangements.

- *Sophisticated equipment and supplies.* When companies subscribe to centralized receiving plans, they invest in machinery and supplies that are generally state-of-the-art and then continuously upgrade them as new systems come on the market. This assures the continued prompt movement of goods from their locations to the selling floors.

Regional Receiving Departments

Some retailers who have enormous numbers of units segment their receiving operations into regions or districts. These facilities are responsible for supplying goods to a number of stores that might cover one section of the country or, perhaps, a few states. In either case, the buyer prepares separate purchase orders for each of the regions. The suppliers then ship the goods to the respective receiving departments.

Retailers who use the regional approach often do so because of the time saved in getting the goods from receiving to the selling floors. If a large company with coast-to-coast stores employs a totally centralized approach, then merchandise movement may take longer than if the receiving warehouses were in closer proximity to stores in a specific region. Because time is of the essence—especially for fashion merchandise, which has a built-in perishable factor—the faster an item gets onto the selling floor, the more time it will have to be sold.

Single-Store Receiving

In some organizations, the receipt of goods is undertaken by the individual stores in the group. Of course, small and independent entrepreneurs have no other choice but to receive the merchandise that has been ordered directly from the suppliers.

Supermarkets are among the retailers that subscribe to direct receiving for many of their items. They might purchase produce from local farmers for each of their units, making centralized receiving impractical. Even if some of the products, such as canned goods, are first sent to centralized warehouses for redistribution to the units in the chain, the actual marking of the items generally takes place in the individual stores. Stock personnel can be regularly seen marking goods in the aisles. Marking at the centralized warehouse would require unpacking and repacking, both costing a great deal of time. The store manager, or an assistant, merely checks the delivery—to make certain that it is exactly what has been ordered—records the delivery, and makes it ready for marking.

OshKosh B'Gosh, a retail apparel chain with 130 units, subscribes to the concept of individual store receiving departments. The company uses a software receiving package from Datavantage that incorporates the receipt of goods from suppliers. Each store is able to determine the contents of the carton by scanning the barcode on the outside. The system links up with the corporate inventory management system, which was developed by STS Systems of Pointe-Claire, Quebec.

RECEIVING AND MARKING OPERATIONS

Once the merchant puts a receiving system in place, it is necessary to install a plan that will physically address the tasks involved in getting the goods properly recorded, marked, and transferred to the selling departments.

The plans involve the actual receiving of the goods, checking the contents to determine if they are exactly as indicated on the purchase orders, making certain that invoices agree with the amounts that have been received, marking the items with the prices that have been established by the buyers, and moving them to where they will be featured in the store.

> **In the News . . .**
> The article entitled "Saks Masters DC Flow-Through," found at the end of this chapter on page 253, is an excellent summary of one retailer's efforts and should be read at this time.

Receiving Records

When the merchandise that has been ordered is ready for shipping to the retailer, the manufacturer or the shipper might tag it, or it may come to the merchant without any ticketing. In any event, the goods are delivered to the company's centralized, regional, or individual receiving facilities.

Receipt of the goods might be informal, as in the case of small stores. Since the merchant is often the buyer or at least has total familiarity with the goods that have been purchased by an associate, a formal **receiving record** is generally not necessary. If the company has many units, a more formal recording device is used.

This record lists all pertinent information regarding the shipment, including the name of the shipping company, date and hour of arrival, number of pieces in the shipment, delivery charges, amount of the invoice, name of the department that ordered the merchandise, and the condition of the packages. Each piece of information is vital: in cases of disagreement between retailer and supplier, there must be sufficient evidence to make a settlement.

Cartons that are damaged, for example, must be noted since there is the potential for losses. A slight opening could be sufficient for an item or two to be stolen. An order might comprise several dozen or more pieces, and only physical counting will reveal if all have been received. Here too any discrepancies must be noted. If delivery charges seem out of line with typical shipping costs then this, too, should be addressed in writing so that adjustments to the invoice can be made. It is at this stage of the process—when the delivery receipt has been signed—that the shipment becomes the property of the retailer and must be paid for according to the terms agreed upon. If suspicious circumstances are not resolved at this time, the merchant is responsible for payment even if shortages are discovered later.

Receiving Equipment

Once handlers at the **receiving dock** have approved receipt of the goods, they are then moved to an area housing a variety of equipment that will be used in the checking process. Moving the goods is accomplished via means of hand trucks, movable racks, or—as in the case of many major companies—on conveyor systems. By using the latest automated technology, efficiency is maximized. In small stores it should be noted that the packages are carried by hand either to multipurpose back rooms or right onto the selling floor, where sales clerks undertake the receiving process.

The destination for goods in larger retail operations is replete with **stationary tables** on which the goods are sorted and processed for delivery to the warehouse or selling floors, **portable tables** that have wheels to expedite the procedure, or **conveyor systems** that quickly and easily handle the movement of the goods.

Saks Fifth Avenue uses a national distribution center that houses state-of-the-art receiving equipment. After goods have been received and the numbers have been entered into the computer, the merchandise is moved as a function of how the goods were packed by the supplier. Those that are **flat packed** in cartons are placed on roller conveyors to a processing center, where paperwork is completed to generate the appropriate tags used to mark the items. In the next area the cartons are opened, tags are affixed, and the cartons are repacked for shipment to the stores. Once the packages have been coded for identification purposes, an automated system moves the goods to chutes that take them to the loading dock and ultimately to the stores. Hanging garments are placed on a **trolley conveyor** that moves the goods through the same stages as the flat-packed merchandise. After processing, the garments are placed in metal cages for shipping to the stores.

Integration with a sophisticated computer system enables the company to know exactly what has been received, where it is in the system, and when each store has received the goods. It is this type of system that enables retailers to achieve a savings in both processing and transportation costs.

Quantity Checking

Once the goods pass the receiving stage, one or more pieces of equipment are used to check the quantities. This stage is of the utmost importance in verifying that the contents of packages are in agreement with the packing slips or invoices. Only a physical inspection of the flat package's contents will reveal if the vendor has faithfully filled the order. When the shipment comes on hangers that have been placed on merchandise racks, the same inspection step is necessary. There are three basic techniques that are used in quantity checking, as follows:

- **Direct quantity check.** In this system, the checker uses the vendor's invoice to make certain that the amounts indicated are actually present and that the colors, sizes, and prices are accurate. Although this is the most widely used checking technique because it is quick, it also has a distinct disadvantage. Careless checking could result because the checker might merely give the contents a quick once-over and not really count everything that has arrived. He or she might then sign off on the delivery, suggesting that everything in the containers is in agreement with the invoice.
- **Blind quantity check.** This method is designed to minimize checking errors. The checker must prepare a list of the items in the package that has been received without the benefit of the invoice. Although it slows down the process somewhat, this method forces checkers to perform their job. Most retailers who use this system prepare forms that have such headings as style number, merchandise description, color, sizes, and total number of items in the package.
- **Semiblind quantity check.** This technique utilizes the best features of the two other plans. The person responsible for checking quantities is given a packing slip that lists the styles that are in the delivery but not the quantities. Thus, the checker is obligated to make a physical count, which will later be compared with the actual invoice, but need not tabulate all the items' characteristics.

Quality Checking

It is relatively easy for trained people in the receiving department to make certain that shipments comply with the purchase orders in terms of quantities and prices, but **quality checking** is another matter. In small stores, verifying that the merchandise received is exactly the same as the samples from which they were ordered is a relatively simple matter. The buyer is often the store's proprietor and is generally on the selling floor, readily available to examine the shipments.

In larger companies, the buyers are generally far from the receiving areas and are unable to examine shipments. In fact, where central receiving is utilized, the buyer might be hundreds of miles from the warehouse. Many retailers now use quality control experts to examine shipments and assess their conformity to the original purchase order requirements. These people are trained to evaluate the merchandise and determine if it meets company standards. Whereas inspection of nationally known brands rarely turns up inferior goods, products from lesser-known vendors are sometimes of poor quality. This problem is especially prevalent in goods that come from overseas sources.

If a system isn't in place to assess quality, then unsuspecting shoppers could make purchases but later return them because of poor wear. This could lead to the loss of customers.

Once the receiving task has been completed, the information—in the form of either an invoice or packing slip—is sent to the control department for processing. The merchandise is then sent on to be ticketed. Of course, if the supplier has made the goods "floor ready," they are moved to the selling floors or to in-house storage areas. Some retailers divide the merchandise into two parts. One portion is sent to the selling department and the other to a behind-the-scenes stockroom, where it is placed in bins or on racks until it is needed on the selling floor. The trend in retailing has been to eliminate backroom stocking wherever possible. Goods that are ordered are generally readied for floor placement. If more merchandise of the same type is needed, then reorders are placed. This generally results in a better stock turnover rate, a concept discussed in Chapter 16.

Marking Merchandise

Assuming that the merchant undertakes the ticketing procedures, an in-house procedure must be developed. In small stores, many proprietors still use the handwritten method. Given their minimum merchandising requirements and their close customer contacts, this method is sufficient.

The other retailers choose from a variety of automated systems that are on the market with the computer as their centerpieces. The tags may be computer generated or printed by handheld equipment. In any case, the computer is essential in that, with the use of scanners, the tag's information is transferred, stored, and eventually used for inventory printouts.

The devices shown here are examples of marking equipment for retailers.

The tickets list not only the prices but also a host of other essential inventory control items that help buyers and merchandisers refine their purchasing decisions. The more complete the information, the more likely the merchant will be able to address the customer's needs.

Typically, the labels or tags include department number, classification of the good, its style or subclassification, vendor name, size, and (of course) the price. Stores that are value oriented, such as the discounters and off-pricers, often list the store's "regular price" on the ticket along with the price at which it sells for elsewhere.

If you examine the merchandise tags at many of the large retailers, it is obvious that much of the information is coded. In this way the merchant doesn't give away any merchandise secrets to the competition, which might be comparison shopping. The only items on the tags that are easily recognized are the price and the size. Many tagging systems also feature the use of barcodes. Recognized as a series of thick and thin black vertical lines, these are printed codes storing merchandise information that is recorded once the sale is made.

 Focus on . . .
Monarch Marking Systems

MONARCH MARKING SYSTEMS, headquartered in Miamisburg, Ohio, is a wholly owned subsidiary of Paxar Corporation, which has been in business since 1890. It has more than 300,000 customers in the retail supply chain in over 100 countries. Manufacturing plants have been established in nine countries, making it the largest international marking brand in the world. They offer an unmatched reservoir of expertise and are always on the cutting edge of producing products that make the retailer's merchandising operation more reliable.

Monarch provides marking systems for leading retailers such as Brooks Brothers, Federated, Kmart, Nordstrom, Office Max, Saks, Sears, Talbots, Wal-Mart, and Gap. They offer barcode products (stationary and portable), printers, markers, tags and labels, software, and support services as well as identification and price-marking products such as handheld marking systems that are ideal for price/date marking and promotional labeling.

Through continuous innovative research, Monarch has been able to solve the problems of individual major retailers. American Eagle, for example, reports how Monarch's DOS-based Pathfinder Ultra handheld marking unit has revolutionized its price changing process. No longer must the company rely on a time-intensive, manual procedure involving a good deal of guesswork on the part of the store's sales associates. Pathfinder Ultra has significantly improved efficiency.

A problem encountered by most major retailers who utilize barcode applications for their products is that vendors apply inaccurate labels and tags on boxes. Through another Monarch innovation, ComplyLine was born. The system allows suppliers to download the requirements of every major retailer, determining exactly what barcode information each requires. With every merchant having its own requirements that are designed to increase its own efficiency and improve customer service, marking is made simple with Monarch ComplyLine service. In this way, vendors can reduce operating costs and improve profits by complying with retailer demands. For the retailer, the system captures more accurate point-of-sale data to track inventory flow, provides inventory counts, and improves the accuracy of automated stock replenishment. These benefits of the ComplyLine service have enabled Monarch to attract such clients as JCPenney and Wal-Mart.

The company has made acquiring their products and services easier than ever. Its Web site, www.monarch.com, features most of their products as well as online assistance for questions.

Re-Marking Merchandise

No matter how carefully buyers plan their purchases and select what they believe will be the most desirable merchandise, mistakes are often made. A walk through any store immediately reveals racks and shelves that feature markdowns.

Retailers must re-mark every single price tag that has been designated for clearance. There are two methods used by merchants. One is simply done by hand by a sales associate. The clerk generally draws a line through the original price and marks the new price with a different color ink. Some stores use a handheld machine that quickly adjusts the prices.

It is only by complete and competent handling of goods that the retailer will avoid the pitfalls of sloppy merchandise distribution and thus be the beneficiary of greater profits.

CHAPTER HIGHLIGHTS

- Interenterprise collaboration has enabled retailers and vendors to work together to better determine merchandise needs.
- High-tech innovations such as EDI make merchandise analysis and delivery more beneficial to both retailers and suppliers.
- Through VMI, vendors are able to gather information about their products once they have been shipped to the retailer and also to process reorders more quickly.
- Quick Response technology allows the manufacturer to monitor the merchant's inventory and anticipate future merchan-

dise needs. This benefits the retailer, who is able to reduce the amount of merchandise on hand knowing that the vendor will react quickly to replenish the store's merchandise.
- Nonprofit industry participation to improve the efficiency of the supply chain continues to broaden, with such groups as VICS and CPFR playing key roles.
- Outside marking is becoming more prevalent in the industry because it enables the retailer to move the merchandise more quickly onto the selling floor.
- Most chains use centralized receiving facilities to check and mark their goods.
- Receiving records are kept to assure that the right merchandise was delivered and that the prices invoiced are the same as on the purchase order.
- The blind method of checking incoming merchandise is designed to minimize errors.
- Quality control personnel are often assigned to receiving areas to make certain that the quality of the goods is identical to the samples from which they were ordered.

IMPORTANT RETAILING TERMS

blind quantity check (248)
centralized receiving (245)
Collaborative Planning, Forecasting, and Replenishment Committee (CPFR) (241)
conveyor system (247)
direct quantity check (248)
electronic data interchange (EDI) (240)
flat packed (247)
interenterprise collaboration (240)
intermodal transportation (244)
outside marking (243)
portable table (247)
quality checking (248)
Quick Response (QR) inventory planning (248)
receiving dock (247)
receiving record (247)
regional receiving (245)
semiblind quality check (248)
stationary table (247)
trolley conveyor (248)
vendor-managed inventory (VMI) (241)
Voluntary Interindustry Commerce Standards Association (VICS) (241)

FOR REVIEW

1. Why do suppliers and retailers participate in interenterprise collaboration for merchandise distribution?
2. What is EDI, and how does it affect the retailer's purchasing plans?
3. In what way can vendors gather information from the retailer using a VMI system?
4. How does a QR system help the vendor in terms of satisfying the merchant's merchandise needs?
5. What role have nonprofit industry groups played in improving efficiency between retailers and vendors?
6. Why have many retailers opted to use outside marking services instead of relying upon their in-house resources?
7. Why do most major chain organizations utilize central receiving departments in their operations?
8. What is the advantage of using regional receiving locations to distribute goods to stores?
9. Why do most supermarket chains rely on direct receiving and marking of products from vendors instead of using a centralized distribution system?
10. Why are receiving records important?
11. Discuss the different types of receiving equipment that retailers use in marking and moving their merchandise.
12. Distinguish between the direct and blind methods of quantity checking.
13. How do retailers make certain that the quality of the merchandise received is the same as what was shown in the sample line?
14. What are the advantages and disadvantages of using air express for merchandise delivery?
15. How do merchants change the tags of items whose prices have been reduced?
16. Why do some merchants utilize intermodal shipping arrangements?

AN INTERNET ACTIVITY

One division of a retail operation that is constantly looking to upgrade its equipment is the department responsible for merchandise handling and distribution. Many manufacturers of products that help make merchandise handling and distribution more efficient are making significant use of the Internet to tell regular and prospective clients about the availability of new products. One such company is Monarch at www.monarch.com.

Using this Web site, or any other that deals specifically with distribution and marking products, research the company's products and complete the table below. Be prepared to deliver an oral report on your findings.

Company name _____
Web site _____

Products	Description	Uses

EXERCISES AND PROJECTS

1. Contact a major retailer that has a unit in your city and ask for permission to observe its merchandise receiving and tagging operations. Be sure to tell the company representative that this is an assignment for a college course.

    Take notes during your visit and ask if you can photograph the operation. When you have gathered all the information, it should be organized into a typewritten paper of approximately three pages in length. Be sure to include the following in your report:
    - The exact names and uses of each piece of equipment
    - The costs of each
    - Training necessary to operate the equipment
    - Output that is tied into the computer for merchandise reports
    - Photographs that you have taken

2. Visit a retailer and observe the various types of price tickets that are used on the company's merchandise. Carefully examine each type and record the exact information that is printed or written on it. If there have been markdowns taken on some goods, record the manner in which they have been changed on the tag.

    After your observations are completed, write a two-page paper about the information you gathered.

    Note: Be sure to bring identification with you and explain that you are participating in a school research project.

THE CASE OF THE MERCHANDISE DISTRIBUTION DILEMMA

When the Archers first opened their retail business in 1973, they never expected it to become one of the fastest growing sporting goods companies in southern California. After initial success with their first Outdoorsman store, they began to open many more units. In addition to expanding into other parts of the state, they crossed into Nevada, New Mexico, Arizona, Oregon, and Washington. At the present time, the Outdoorsman has 150 units.

When the company began operation, merchandise receiving was a simple matter. All packages were delivered to the back room of the store, where cartons were opened and merchandise was counted, checked against purchase orders, tagged, and then put onto the selling floor. The operation consisted primarily of hand recording and was overseen by Tom Archer, the company founder. As the organization began to grow, Mr. Archer found it necessary to embrace a new merchandise distribution concept. It was no longer feasible for each store to receive shipments; a centralized system would better serve the company.

After considerable research, a location in the middle of the company's trading area was chosen for the new distribution center. At the time, the chain was still primarily located in southern California and had 60 stores. An automated system was installed, replete with the latest in receiving and marking equipment. Every item was tagged in a way that allowed the information to be fed into a computer so that merchandising reports could be produced.

Now that the company has 150 stores and its geographic coverage has extended to several states, it seems that there might be yet a better method of merchandise distribution. The management team, still headed by Tom Archer, has undertaken the task of determining whether or not the distribution requirements could be better addressed. Some of the proposals that have been made are:

- Using a regional approach. Stores could be divided into districts or regions, with each location serving a specific number of stores.
- The centralized arrangement, now in use, could be enlarged to handle the merchandise.
- A system where each store would receive goods directly from the vendors could be arranged.

At this point in time discussions continue, but no solution has been found that satisfies all members of the management team. The company has employed the services of a research organization in the hope that it could make a meaningful determination in regard to merchandise distribution.

Questions

1. If you were the lead researcher in the study, how would you begin to evaluate the problem?
2. Which approach would you suggest, and why?

Saks Masters DC Flow-Through
Packaging Digest

May 1, 2006

Manufacturers, distributors and retailers talk a lot about flow-through, but few practice it. Flow-through, also known as cross docking, involves the flowing of goods directly from receiving to shipping without the labor-wasting steps of putting the goods away and later picking them. Saks, Inc., is one company that has aggressively adopted flow-through as the operating system for one of its key distribution centers located in Steele, AL. It has literally built this DC operation around flow-through, with material-handling system integration by Siemens Logistics and Assembly Systems, Inc. (www.usa.siemens.com/logisticsassembly). Since the facility was completed a few years ago, Saks has not only mastered this advanced logistics capability, but the facility has also become a showpiece of flow-through performance and efficiency and a blueprint for how to do DC flow-through properly, with the statistics to back it up.

Saks is one of the country's premier retailers, operating 386 luxury, specialty and traditional department stores, including Saks Fifth Avenue, Bergner's, Boston Store, Parisian, McRae's, Herberger's and several other chains, in 40 states, with annual revenues of more than $6 billion and nearly 55,000 associates. The company's stores offer a wide selection of fashion apparel, accessories, cosmetics and decorative home items and feature assortments of unique designers and brand names.

The company started its journey to flow-through in 1997, when it began creating an idea of where it wanted to go. At that time, Saks had doubled in size through various mergers over a 10-year period, and they were left with different systems at their DCs. They wanted to have common applications across their distribution network, rationalize the network to reduce transportation costs and slowly move to state-of-the-art facilities. Saks hired IBM Global Services (www-ibm.com/services) to help with the selection process. By the end of 1999, they had chosen Siemens L&A as the systems integrator for material handling, as well as the supplier of conveyor systems, high-speed sortation equipment and the material-handling control system.

One of the most interesting decisions Saks made after Siemens L&A was selected was to allow them to design the material-handling system first and then to design the building as a shell that wrapped around the automation. No other company has approached an automation project in quite the same way. On the outbound side, Siemens came up with a unique design, where conveyors heading to dock doors criss-cross back and forth, instead of having a central conveyor line from which packages are diverted to shipping doors. While this design led to longer conveyor systems, it allowed the building to be much narrower and saved a significant amount of money in the construction of the building.

"The logistics solutions Siemens developed for Saks' DC worked well, because we tailored them to Saks' individual needs," says Ken Ruehrdanz with Siemens. "Complex design tasks, like this project, require thorough preparation, so we started the support process right from the earliest stages, helping Saks to define its project objectives. We employed proven procedural models for proposed-system data analysis, and then prepared performance specifications to compare potential solutions, both in terms of investment and operational costs. For Saks, it made more logistics and financial sense to construct the building around the material-handling solutions that we were arriving at through our analysis process.

"Optimum flow-through performance, such as exists with the Steele DC, required significant upfront engineering to arrive at a flawless integration of mechatronics, which is a holistic approach embracing mechanical, electronic and information technology components. Siemens' state-of-the-art control systems, high-speed sortation equipment and conveyor systems all had to integrate perfectly with the postulated and existing warehouse-management system information technology capabilities. Designing the optimum system requires detailed knowledge in all core and peripheral disciplines, including plant engineering, material and information flows, system engineering and control technology. The success of the flow-through system within the Steele DC was positively impacted by Siemens' ability to deliver a turnkey capability throughout these disciplines."

At Saks, merchandise is delivered, not on pallets, but in cases. Ninety-six percent of cases move through the facility to shipping without being put away. This percentage could be even higher, but Saks has learned that it makes sense to retain a small amount of inventory at a central DC in order to replenish stores quickly with hot-selling items, instead of managing cross-store shipments or having to use a reverse-logistics process.

The key to flow-through is that information must flow in advance of merchandise. That information takes the form of Electronic Data Interchange (EDI) and portal-based Advanced Ship Notices (ASNs) from suppliers and 214 electronic manifests from Saks carriers. More than 90 percent of shipments are preceded by ASNs. Saks, like other leading retailers, does levy chargebacks if suppliers do not send UCC 128 ASNs, do not properly label cartons or short Saks, or if trucks do not arrive on time. To practice flow-through, supplier reliability is critical. Saks' success in this area is based on years of working with suppliers to improve their performance. For suppliers that cannot afford EDI, Saks provides an internet-based application that allows even the smallest suppliers to generate ASNs, UCC labels and the necessary packing slips. ASNs offer strong advantages in preplanning DC operations. These advantages are magnified when combined with flow-through processes.

A visitor to Saks' highly-automated, 180,000-sq-ft DC in Steele would see mainly 55-ft trailers being unloaded across 16 receiving docks. Based on the bar-code label and its pre-existing association with an ASN, most cases flow from inside the trailer via conveyors to the appropriate receiving line. A single inbound trailer might contain goods destined for 100 different stores, so the cases are typically routed to about 80 outbound trailers (some trucks deliver to more than one store). While it is critical that inbound trailers be moved as quickly as possible from the dock, trailers on the outbound docks may take as long as a day to be fully loaded as they incrementally receive cases from different inbound trucks.

In some cases, when a trailer is filled, but delivery is not scheduled until later in the week, a trailer will be pulled away from the dock and placed in the yard for a brief period of time. The trailer, in effect, becomes a miniature warehouse. The constraint is the store; if the store lacks the labor to get the merchandise to the floor, there is no sense in delivering the goods. Saks requires vendors to send shipments in a floor-ready format (on hangers and then boxed) to help reduce labor at the store level.

On the shipping dock, workers "tunnel load" the trucks. They group cases for one store on one side of the truck, for example, and goods for another store on the opposite side. Or, if goods were destined for delivery to the same store, products from one selling zone (like men's apparel) would be grouped separately from women's apparel. While building the load, a tunnel down the center of the truck is created by not filling that area with cases.

This base-process flow is automated through the use of a conveyor system integrated with a high-rate sorting system. Telescopic conveyors that extend into the trucks are used at receiving. Different types of receiving equipment are used, because the trucks that are arriving have a variety of factors attached to the shipment that affect how fast they can be unloaded.

Goods move up a conveyor to a mezzanine level, where they are merged onto a sliding-shoe sorter operating at 540 ft/min. The cases then move onto an inbound sorter station that routes packages to value-added processing stations located directly below this station or on to shipping. A vision system captures an image of every bar code, reads the bar code, measures the length of the package and determines how many packages should go on a particular value-added processing divert lane.

Next to this station is a PC loaded with system-monitoring software that shows the conveyor layout. If a particular module is not performing correctly, that module's icon turns red on the computer screen. It is an internet-enabled system, so corporate headquarters in Jackson,

MS, can also view the system status simultaneously.

Cases headed for the shipping docks are printed with the store number and department by ink-jet printers. This information is used by truck loaders to correctly load trailers that will contain goods moving to more than one store. Cases are then sent to the shipping sorter, which diverts them to the appropriate shipping lines. Packages move down from the mezzanine level to the shipping docks on gravity-controlled conveyors designed to extend into trucks to speed truck loading. The conveyor system is engineered to recirculate cases on the shipping side if workers are not able to keep up with the amount of cases flowing to them, and thus prevent the overhead conveyor from becoming blocked. An indicator light adjacent to a particular gravity-fed conveyor comes on if the conveyor is fully loaded with cases. This allows a manager to reposition workers and eliminate the bottleneck.

The speed with which cases move through the facility is impressive. If the cases are not diverted to value-added processing, they move through the facility in seven minutes.

Not all cases flow through the facility in the manner described above. Saks has a sophisticated inbound auditing process. Audited cases are diverted to an audit area. For some suppliers, 40 percent of inbound cases are audited. If there is no ASN associated with a shipment, Saks will scan each piece of merchandise. For suppliers with excellent reliability, few, if any, inbound goods need to be audited. The audit logic is contained in an add-on module to the WMS solution that was built with detailed input from Saks.

Certain products require Value-Added Services (VAS) and they are also diverted to a special area. VAS tasks include price ticketing, putting security devices on expensive goods and shipping some apparel on hangers. At the Steele DC, diverted product is processed and then reintroduced onto the conveyor system.

Flow-through's greatest advantage is labor savings. At the Steele facility, the combination of common systems, material-handling equipment and flow-through processes allows 45,000 cases/shift to be processed. In the past, a facility with the same square footage could process 15,000 cases/shift at best. The labor cost per carton has since dropped dramatically for Saks. The cost of handling a carton is $0.14 when it arrives as part of an ASN shipment, but $1.40 for cases shipped without ASNs. The initial projection was that the payback period would be three years. Subsequent analysis showed that the project actually had a payback of 18 months.

Labor savings are partially the result of better capacity planning and smoother labor utilization. Flow-through, as practiced by Saks, resembles Theory of Constraint (TOC) processes used in manufacturing operations. A human planner can enable a steady flow of work by visually monitoring activity and by scheduling the unloading process to maintain a steady beat of activity. If the VAS area is busy, for example, a trailer that has a high percentage of ASNs can be unloaded, which means less work for the VAS processors.

The planner indicates which trailer moves to which inbound dock by making a selection in the Yard Management System (YMS). The YMS's alerting capabilities aid labor productivity. If an inbound dock is open for more than five minutes, a manager is alerted on a pager. Similarly, if a truck will arrive late to a yard, managers are alerted. Prior to the implementation of the YMS, turn time was 10 to 12 min. The YMS solution reduced it to seven minutes or less.

Flow-through took two days out of the Saks' supply chain, while increasing its ability to flex deliveries to the stores. It can ship as often as warranted, based on volume. For its larger stores, in peak season, this means twice daily. The service standard, even for VAS merchandise, is to receive goods and ship them out within a four-hour window. Saks' flow-through system has also increased store replenishment accuracy. Each time they increase the percentage of goods moving via flow-through, replenishment accuracy is also increased. The value of flow-through is greatly increased by procurement programs that emphasize more frequent, smaller buys that better reflect consumer demand. If retailers do not have "open-to-buy" programs in place, they will not gain the full advantages of flow-through.

Saks' new flow-through DC operation at Steele represents an example of what can be done to solve distribution challenges, when innovative planning and engineering, state-of-the-art material-handling systems, IT interfacing and overall turn-key system integration are brought together and flawlessly orchestrated.

This case study is an adaptation of an ARC Advisory Group brief titled Mastering Flow-Through.

PART THREE

Retail Environments

In addition to establishing an organizational structure determining the depth and breadth of the store's staffing, management must select an appropriate location in which to operate and plan a design for the premises that will best serve the needs of the targeted shoppers. These decisions must be implemented before opening the store. Unlike offsite operations that need only a viable center from which executives and rank-and-file personnel will operate, the brick-and-mortar organizations must make certain that their environments will be perfectly located and designed to attract customers, thereby earning a fair share of the consumers' disposable income.

In Chapter 12, the emphasis is on location analysis (the trading areas that must be assessed before any location decision can be made), the types of retail arenas that are available for merchants to choose from, and the specific sites within these arenas that best serve their needs.

Contemporary retailing demands that an individualistic approach be taken to facilities design so that each merchant will operate from an environment that is different from the others. In Chapter 13, a wealth of design principles are explored. If these principles are carefully followed, the creative team will deliver a facility that significantly enhances the company's merchandise offerings. While some traditionalists rely upon conventional methods of store design, others have embraced newer concepts such as themed environments. Both of these approaches—and others—will be explored to show how retailers are able to distinguish their premises from those of the competition.

CHAPTER 12
Location Analysis and Selection

After you have completed this chapter, you should be able to discuss:

- The importance of demographics in the selection of a trading area
- The concept of geodemographics and how it is used by merchants to assure that they have targeted the best markets for their company
- The role that area characteristics play in determining the potential of a retailer's trading area
- Why downtown or central shopping districts have remained important as retail locations
- How outlet malls have grown to become one of the more important venues for value shopping
- The concept of the festival marketplace and how it differs from standard shopping malls
- Some of the factors that must be addressed before a specific site is chosen to open a brick-and-mortar operation

Whenever retailing experts are asked what the three most important considerations for success in the industry are, many reply, "location, location, location." This response should apply to anyone with the intention of opening a brick-and-mortar operation. Before anything else is considered, the exact location must be determined. Too many inexperienced entrepreneurs have found that, by being in the wrong place, their businesses never got off the ground.

Planners at the major companies fully understand the necessity of being in the right place. The giants in the industry generally maintain their own in-house real estate departments that investigate location opportunities and assess them for new units. Others turn to marketing research experts who, for a fee, conduct studies before they make recommendations to their clients. In either case, the approach must be a scientific one where a host of different criteria are addressed, with the final decisions resting with top management.

The choices today are numerous. Merchants have the option to choose malls of every size and configuration both in cities and suburban areas; downtown shopping districts in the major and smaller cities; mixed-use centers that incorporate stores, entertainment offerings, residences, and commercial offices; festival marketplaces that are composed of shops and eateries in revitalized, unique areas; power centers where high-profile merchants dominate the scene; neighborhood clusters that generally feature small operations; or freestanding stores.

With so much opportunity, the retailer should be able to find the sites that are best suited for its type of organization. Before a specific site can be selected, research initially focuses on selecting the general trading area in which the company chooses to operate, then moves on to the type of shopping district that will best serve the company's needs, and ultimately concludes with selecting the exact site where the organization can open its doors to the consumer.

If the study is carefully conducted, then the location will serve the merchant well when his or her merchandising concepts are applied.

TRADING AREA ANALYSIS AND SELECTION

The United States—and, for that matter, the entire world—comprises general trading areas in which retailers may choose to establish business outlets. A trading area might be an entire country, a region of a country, a city, or a community within a city. Many major retailers such as Wal-Mart are expanding their businesses into overseas arenas and therefore must consider the entire globe as their potential trading area. On the other hand, smaller merchants generally narrow their markets to more restricted locales such as a particular city. Whether it is the establishment of a new retailing venture or the expansion of one that already exists, the task of selecting a trading area is a formidable one for retailers of all sizes.

Demographic Analysis

The actual procedure usually begins with **demographic analysis**, a study of the trading area's demographics (see Chapter 5). Some of the specifics of the population investigation must center on the following elements:

- *The size of the population and its potential for expansion.* Current figures are insufficient by themselves. Statistical models must be used to determine whether the number of people in the area will remain constant or whether it will increase or decrease. The southern tier of the United States, for example, continues to serve as a place to which retirees flock for their later years. Projections indicate that states like Florida will maintain their population growth because of the number of senior citizens who move to warm climates during their retirement years. As a result, this trading area is a must for merchants who count seniors as their customers. Geographic projections are easily obtainable from the Census Bureau, which studies the U.S. population every 10 years. Trade associations also conduct population analysis so that they can provide statistics to their members who are considering expansion programs. Of course, major retailers might address the problem by conducting their own investigations that concentrate more specifically on their own needs.
- *The dominant ages of the population in a specific region.* This is extremely important to the success of most retail businesses. The needs of the young contrast considerably with those of the elderly. While most general trading areas consist of across-the-board age classifications, some have heavier concentrations in one age group than in another. Southern New Jersey and Southern California, for example, are experiencing significant growth as retirement communities. With the number of planned communities for the elderly on the rise in these regions, it is an obvious place for merchants who count on this group as a major part of their customer base to expand. On the other hand, major cities such as New York, Boston, and Chicago are experiencing enormous population growth with younger consumers. This

fact has encouraged companies like Banana Republic, Gap, Abercrombie & Fitch, and Ann Taylor to undergo considerable expansion in these trading areas.

- *The size and makeup of the family.* This is also an important factor to consider. It cannot be assumed that every region of the country is made up of typical households. Whereas the typical family in one city may consist of two parents and two children, other cities might be quite different. In major cities, there are large numbers of families that are by no means traditional. A family might consist of two unrelated people, a married couple without children, or a single-parent home with children. Researchers are finding that "typical" is no longer the standard in American culture. Thus, careful research must be undertaken to discover the different types of families that constitute the trading area being considered and whether or not the retailer who contemplates expanding there will have the appropriate goods to satisfy their needs.

- *The stability of a trading area in terms of seasonality.* The vast majority of general trading areas are traditionally composed of consumers who reside there year-round, but some areas are primarily made up of part-timers who call these places home for only a short part of the year. Palm Springs, California, and Southampton, New York, for example, are areas where the population isn't constant throughout the year. Each caters to a clientele that frequents these resort towns for just a few months of the year. In such cases, only those merchants who can profit in such short seasons should consider expanding into these regions.

- *Income.* This is a vital concern for any retailer to address before a trading area can be considered. Data on per capita and family earnings are available from the Census Bureau. Consumer spending is directly related to their incomes. If a particular trading area is at the upper level of the income ladder, such as is the case in Beverly Hills, California, or Palm Beach, Florida, then high-profile boutiques and designer shops can consider these areas excellent locations. On the other hand, if the median income in a geographic area is at the lower levels of the earnings scale, then value-oriented stores such as Kmart and Wal-Mart will be best suited to these locations.

- *The type of residences in which consumers reside.* If the majority of dwellings are apartment buildings, retailers of outdoor furniture wouldn't find a market for their goods there. In contrast, if the region is dominated by single family homes that are situated on large lots, then outdoor specialists would likely succeed in their ventures.

One concept that retailers often use in their demographic studies is a segmentation system that involves clustering descriptions. One of the major sellers of this information is Claritas, Inc., based in San Diego, California. This company and other researchers of this nature believe that most variations between neighborhood types can be explained by social rank, household composition, mobility, ethnicity, population density, and housing information. The Claritas segmentation system, called PRIZM (Potential Rating Index Zip Code Market), defines neighborhoods in terms of 62 different codes assigned

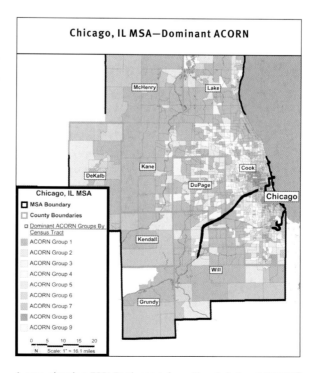

A map showing ESRI Business Information Solutions' ACORN® lifestyle classification segments.

to 15 social groups. These codes are used to describe consumer behavior and categorize individuals with similar characteristics. Five-digit ZIP code descriptions form the basis of the predictions and are available free on the Claritas Web site (www.claritas.com). Another major player in this type of **community segmentation** is ESRI Business Information Solutions, which features the ACORN® (A Classification Of Residential Neighborhoods) product. A view of its offerings is available on the Internet at http://www.infods.com.

From either of these services, a retailer seeking to open a new business, or expand an existing one, may discern where it has the most potential for success based upon the characteristics of the consumers that reside in a particular location.

Population explosion has made Las Vegas a major shopping location for retailers.

Area Characteristic Assessment

Once the demographics have been thoroughly analyzed, it is important for the retail research team to investigate the trading area under consideration in terms of its characteristics. The characteristics that must be assessed include the following:

- *The amount of competition that already exists there.* The lack of any competition might be an indicator that the area doesn't warrant stores of this nature. Of course, if there is a great deal of competition then this might signal that another store, similar to what is already in place, is one too many to achieve success. If there are existing stores, their operations should be evaluated in terms of how the new merchant's operation will be similar or different. **Me-too stores** run the risk of being unable to distinguish themselves from what is already there and thus might not be able to compete successfully.
- *Area accessibility.* This is extremely important. The type of roadways that are in place must provide easy access to the stores so that a sufficient amount of customer traffic will be generated. Major malls are always located in areas that are adjacent to highway networks and convenient for vehicular traffic to reach the stores. Public transportation is also essential if the proposed trading area is in the city. Unlike suburbanites, who generally rely upon their automobiles to bring them to shopping areas, residents of the cities often depend upon buses and trains. The retailer who is considering a particular trading area must assess each of the available modes of transportation and whether they are sufficient to bring in the numbers of people necessary to be successful.
- *Area attractions.* The availability of area attractions should be evaluated in terms of drawing potential shoppers. Other than the residents who call certain cities their home, visitors often provide another segment of the population that accounts for a great deal of purchasing. Tourists generally spend more on their vacations than they would at home. New York City—with its abundance of museums, theaters, and other attractions—provides its retailers with a constant flow of out-of-town consumer traffic; Orlando, Florida, home to Disney World and other theme parks, is a mecca for a host of different types of retailers; and Paris, with it's legendary historical attractions, is a natural environment for the tourist to purchase a wealth of mementos.
- *Area growth.* This is another signal that helps retailers consider expansion. Throughout the United States there are numerous cities that continue to awaken and have population ex-

plosions. Las Vegas, Nevada, for example, once a place frequented exclusively by gambling enthusiasts, has not only expanded its environment to become a place where entire families can be entertained, it has also become a city where permanent residence is significantly increasing. Many southern cities such as Charlotte, North Carolina, and Jacksonville, Florida, are realizing enormous population increases that make them excellent locations for retail expansion. Very often, these areas have been underserved by the retailing community. They make for excellent choices for retailers because of the lack of competition.

New York City, with its abundance of exciting attractions, is home to many world-famous retailers.

- *The availability of educational institutions that offer the business programs essential to training retailing managers.* If a retailer is to succeed, then it must be able to recruit skilled personnel to run the business. If colleges and universities do not offer curricula that could provide the number of trained specialists needed to run a business, then it must look elsewhere to fill its management ranks. This is sometimes problematic, especially when the economy is at full employment levels and relocating isn't a benefit to employees. Colleges and universities are also excellent providers of specialized training courses that fit the specific needs of retailers. If, for example, there is a need for better understanding of computer operations, the educational institution could provide such training. The success of any company depends on its employees' performances.
- *Local laws that could improve or hinder sales.* These should be assessed. Sometimes local legislation limits store hours or imposes certain restrictions that prevent the retailer from maximizing sales. Occasionally, the laws actually benefit merchants. Delaware, for example, has no sales tax. This sales-tax advantage serves as an inducement to consumers from neighboring states in the mid-Atlantic region, giving the retailer an extra customer base from which to draw.

Once the demographics have been evaluated along with the area's characteristics, a decision can be made as to the viability of the region as another company outlet. Of course, some areas do not score perfectly in each of the assessment criteria. In those cases, management must determine whether or not the shortcomings will negatively affect the retailer's potential success.

SHOPPING DISTRICT CHOICES

A close inspection of the places where retailers open their outlets immediately reveals that there is an abundance of shopping district choices available. A century ago, this was not the case. The choices were either the downtown central district, which was the dominant location, or the main street of the town or village where merchants set up shop. This radically changed in the middle of the twentieth century, when families began relocating from the inner cities to the suburbs. As the population began to move from its urban environments to outlying areas, retailers began to follow in record numbers. Recognizing that shopping convenience was the factor that motivated many consumers, it was necessary for retailers to head wherever their customers moved.

Department store branches abounded everywhere, while the downtown flagships continued to serve the needs of those who remained in the cities and also functioned as company headquarters, where buyers, merchandisers, and other key executives continued to make decisions for the main store as well as the newly opened branches. Chain organizations also headed into the new towns that consumers called home. They, too, opened stores in record numbers to serve these newly formed communities.

It would not be long before a host of different shopping districts would emerge as viable places for retailers to open new companies or expand their existing operations. Today, we see a variety of different types of retailing formats that serve every segment of the population.

Central Shopping Districts

Often referred to as downtown, **central shopping districts** are the main places in a city where people shop. They house the flagships of many department stores as well as a large number of other retailers. Macy's, for example, has the centerpiece of its vast empire located in New York City's midtown area. With their stores located within the center of the business community, retailers are able to serve the needs of those who commute to work from outlying areas along with those who call the city their home. In addition to the region's regulars, the tourists and business visitors who frequent these locales add significant numbers of people to the shopping population.

Chicago's "Magnificent Mile" is a renowned central shopping district, housing such retail giants as Neiman Marcus and Saks Fifth Avenue.

There are other reasons why these areas have remained important retailing centers, including:

- A significant amount of public transportation, which provides a steady stream of shoppers.
- A vast number of stores that generally feature a variety of merchandise at all price points.
- A wealth of pedestrians who pass by the stores while going to and coming from work. During lunch breaks, in particular, the streets of these avenues are filled with these potential customers.
- A large number of restaurants and entertainment venues that draw people to the area.

While these are advantageous conditions, the central districts also have disadvantages:

- For those who prefer to come to these locations with their own automobiles, parking facilities are often minimal.
- Those who live far from the downtown areas must often face considerable traffic on the roads, making the trips very time consuming.
- Some inner cities, while still serving as viable business communities, are experiencing high crime rates that make shoppers feel insecure.

Even with these negatives, the United States is experiencing a renaissance in their cities that makes them excellent outlets for retail enterprises. Chicago, for example, has recently witnessed an enormous investment by retailers in their downtown area. Nordstrom has opened a major unit that has attracted significant numbers of customers. In New York City, Saks Fifth Avenue undertook an extensive renovation of its midtown unit, and numerous designer shops have opened flagships in the city. Even in the smaller cities, downtown revitalizations have made these areas places to which shoppers are returning in record numbers.

Shopping Malls

The history of the **shopping mall** is attributed by most industry professionals to the Highland Park Shopping Village in Dallas, Texas, which opened its doors to the public in 1931. It was by no means as extravagant as today's malls, but it had the requisites of the **controlled shopping center**, as do all of the malls now in operation around the country. It had a unified image, was under the management of a single owner, and occupied a site that was not bisected by public streets.

Through the years, as different malls were introduced to the public, innovative concepts were introduced to make these shopping arenas superior to those that preceded them. Some of these included:

- The introduction of nighttime shopping, which took place at the Town & Country Shopping Center in Columbus, Ohio, in the 1940s.
- The first two-level center at Shoppers World in Framingham, Massachusetts, in 1950.
- The first fully enclosed mall, Southdale Center in Edina, Minnesota, in 1956. The advantage of climate control enabled consumers to shop in comfort year-round.
- Regional malls like The Galleria in Houston, which opened in 1972 and was the forerunner of the many large malls that now operate in the United States.
- Faneuil Hall Marketplace, developed by the Rouse Company in Boston in 1976 became the first festival marketplace in the country.
- The country's first urban **vertical mall**, Water Tower Place, which in 1976 debuted on Chicago's Michigan Avenue, the hub of its downtown shopping district.
- Potomac Mills opened in northern Virginia in 1985. It was the first of many enclosed factory and retail **outlet centers** to open in the United States.
- **Power centers**, arenas that house about six category killers, came into prominence in the mid-1980s.
- Following on the success of the West Edmonton Mall in Canada, America witnessed the opening of its own **mega-mall** in Bloomington, Minnesota.
- The opening of major outdoor malls such as Simon's Town Center in Jacksonville, Florida, has been extremely successful.

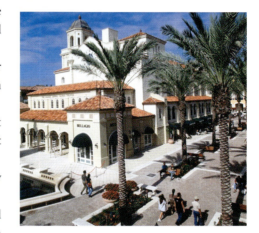

Simon has developed new outdoor "Town Centers" such as this one in Jacksonville, Florida.

The number of shopping malls that continue to open all across the United States is evidence of the strength of this retailing concept. Most every format, as will be discussed, is still in existence, with more and more existing malls undergoing extensive renovations and expansions.

The mall phenomenon that is sweeping the country is due in part to the involvement of the Simon Property Group, the nation's largest developer of shopping centers.

Focus on . . .
Simon Property Group

FOUNDED IN 1960, Simon continues to expand on its history of innovation and creativity in developing the highest quality retail properties in North America. At the present time, the company manages a retail network that generates more than $30 billion in annual sales. The group owns more than 380 properties consisting of regional malls, community/lifestyle shopping centers, premium outlet centers, specialty and mixed-use centers, and international properties. Within these shopping arenas, the group holds more than 20,000 retail leases. Adding to these staggering numbers is the fact that half of all Americans shop in Simon malls, accounting for approximately 2.5 billion mall visits each year. One million employees work for retailers at Simon malls.

The types of retail operations that are either owned or managed reflect the industry's entire spectrum. These include high-fashion boutiques, specialty stores, designer shops, department stores, mass merchants, category killers, discounters, and manufacturer's outlets.

In the Simon portfolio are some of the country's most productive and recognizable properties. Included are The Forum Shops at Caesars Palace in Las Vegas, a high-fashion shopping arena; The Mall of Georgia, a 1.7-million-square-foot super regional mall; Mall of America, America's largest mall, which incorporates shopping with unique entertainment venues; and Town Center in Boca Raton, Florida, an upscale shopping environment.

One of the innovative techniques that Simon Properties uses involves branding. Much like the retailers who have established their own merchandise brands, Simon has adapted the concept to publicize its malls. While each of the shopping arenas maintains its own identity, they are all tied together by specific elements. It all begins with the Simon name, which is emblazoned on mall entry doors, parking lot banners, and signs. Also visible in every one of their properties is a pledge signed by each member of the mall staff to provide superior shopping with special incentives and amenities. One such incentive that rewards shoppers for their patronage is the Mallperks Program. Participants in the plan are awarded points for their purchases that can be redeemed for rewards.

With its unrivaled success as a retail developer, the organization believes that "giving back" is also one of its obligations. Through the Simon Youth Foundation, it fosters economic and career development in youth by implementing focused and appropriate educational initiatives and programs. Specifically, it provides students with the opportunity to learn and receive a high school diploma in a nontraditional setting—the shopping mall—and enables students to participate in internships at mall retail stores. They also award scholarships for continuing education.

The company's expansion continues to soar, with many more mall openings and the acquisition of other properties that are already in existence.

Traditional Shopping Malls

Old Orchard in suburban Chicago is a traditional mall that features many well-known anchors.

Every major region of the United States has at least one traditional shopping center that serves the needs of its residents. A consumer generally needs to travel no more than twenty miles from his or her home to arrive at a shopping arena that is anchored by two or more department stores, has a host of stores that are units of nationally prominent specialty chains, and features single-store operations that are unique to its locale. Included in these arenas are the obligatory food court, restaurants, and some entertainment facilities.

Initially, these retail environments began as outdoor, single-story operations. Although most of today's major malls are housed in enclosed structures, there are many throughout the country that still successfully operate outdoors. Two extremely successful ventures are Old Orchard in suburban Chicago and The Falls in Miami. Some outdoor malls occupy two stories, such as The Esplanade in Palm Beach and the Bal Harbor Shops in Bal Harbor, Florida.

Today, with the benefit of climate control, the vast majority of the traditional malls are enclosed. They provide customers the convenience of being able to comfortably shop no matter what the weather is like outside. Many malls that began as outdoor centers have enclosed their premises. Roosevelt Field in Garden City, New York, was one of the major malls to enclose its premises after it was in business many years.

Many malls are also undergoing significant expansions to their regular configurations so that they may better serve the communities in which they are located. Roosevelt Field, for example, first added a second floor and then further expanded to include new anchors such as Nordstrom. Beginning as a modest shopping center, it now is one of the largest in the United States.

Vertical Malls

Amid the clamor of both vehicular and pedestrian traffic in some downtown areas of major cities, vertical malls are rising because of the lack of traditional street-level space. Chicago led the way with the first high-rise, Water Tower Place. It is anchored by Macy's and features a mix of many specialty stores such as The Limited and Gap. It is also unique in that its eight retail floors are topped by the Ritz Carlton Hotel. Its success spawned other vertical configurations in Chicago, including Chicago Place, anchored by Saks Fifth Avenue and a host of other merchants, as well as 900 Michigan Avenue, which is anchored by Bloomingdale's and is home to a small unit of an upscale supermarket, Bockwinkles.

Except for the anchors that occupy a portion of these malls' main floors, the stores are on upper levels, resulting in lower rents than if they occupied street-level space.

Mixed-Use Centers

Building on the traditional mall concept, developers began to expand their environments with centers that, along with shopping facilities, featured commercial districts and housing. The idea was based on the realization that a captive audience was on the premises and would more than likely patronize the surrounding stores.

Copley Place in Boston was one of the earliest of these **mixed-use centers**. It is anchored not only by large department store branches but also by two hotels and four office buildings in addition to the private residences. By virtue of the two hotels, it has the advantage of reaching visiting tourists, and with the businesses and apartments located in the facility it has a built-in customer base.

Gambling Casino Malls

One of the fastest growing mall locations is within the boundaries of gambling casinos, most notably in Las Vegas and Atlantic City. High-end retailers such as Louis Vuitton, Gucci, and Ferragamo are already realizing record sales, with many others ready to join the fray.

Retailer locations generally require a "10- to 25-mile radius restriction" before opening other units, but this is not the case here. Merchants are opening units in several casino environments that are merely a few hundred feet from each other. With patrons often restricting their visits to one or two casinos, it makes sense for these retailers to

High-end retailers such as Gucci have opened boutiques in Las Vegas, Nevada.

open several units. For example, a visitor who stays at the Wynn will probably not go to Caesar's Palace to shop—hence the need for many units of the same company to locate in several nearby places.

It should be noted that this phenomenon is not restricted to the American casino scene. In the gambling meccas of Macau, the same practice is followed.

> **In the News...**
>
> "Mixing It Up," an article that appears on page 281 at the end of this chapter, should be read at this time.

Potomac Mills was the first of the Mills group's outlet malls.

Opry Mills is a major enclosed outlet mall.

Outlet Malls

Joining the traditional shopping centers, where regular pricing is expected and customer service is the forte, manufacturer's outlets and off-pricers have joined forces to open value-oriented malls. In locations all across the United States, a multitude of indoor and outdoor shopping venues continue to account for enormous success.

The earliest of these entries were in Reading, Pennsylvania, and Secaucus, New Jersey, where many manufacturers opened warehouses to sell off slow-moving inventories. The concept was quickly embraced by consumers, who learned of the stores by word of mouth. There was no formality in these arenas; each vendor acted independently, establishing their own days and hours of operation.

Today, the outlet phenomenon is an ever-expanding concept. Retailers wishing to dispose of items that weren't sold in regular stores, along with manufacturers who must make room for the new season's arrivals, have each opened units in the outlet malls.

The largest of the indoor environments is part of the Mills group, a venture now owned by Simon Property Group. Beginning with its first entry, Potomac Mills in Northern Virginia, the group has expanded into arenas that feature as many as 2 million square feet under one roof. The largest and most successful of these malls is Sawgrass Mills, located in a suburb of Ft. Lauderdale, Florida. Occupying enormous spaces are Off-Fifth, Saks Fifth Avenue's clearance facility, and Last Call, the Neiman Marcus closeout center. Also in residence are manufacturers of marquee labels—such as DKNY, Ralph Lauren, and Calvin Klein—and upscale specialty retailers that include Barneys New York. Also prominent are enormous food courts and well-known eateries such as the Cheesecake Factory, along with entertainment facilities that feature multiplex theaters.

Outdoor value-oriented malls continue to open all over the country. There, too, consumers are treated to the closeout offerings of retailers and manufacturers. Names like Coach, Ann Taylor, Gap, Calvin Klein, Mikasa, Liz Claiborne, Nautica, and Brooks Brothers dominate.

Akin to these planned shopping meccas are locations that evolved because of a **popular area destination**. Initially, these sites served the purposes of unique retail operations that were not value-oriented. One such place that has become a major shopping stop on the East Coast is in Freeport, Maine, where LLBean is headquartered. With this enormous brick-and-mortar operation, open 24 hours a day all year round (except for Christmas Day), the crowds that come to patronize it are tremendous. No matter the time of day or night, the parking lots are filled with campers, mobile homes, and cars. With LLBean as its centerpiece, Freeport soon became a haven where outlets of well-known companies set up shop. Dooney Bourke, Patagonia, Banana Republic, Cole-Haan Shoes, Dansk, Ralph Lauren, and Calvin Klein all operate closeout or factory stores that are in close proximity to the landmark retailer's facility.

Outlet arenas such as these now include more than 14,000 factory stores and 350 shopping centers. The names and locations of each are readily available to shoppers at www.outletbound.com, where store names, locations, brands or product category, phone numbers, hours of operation, and basic directions can be accessed with a click of the mouse.

Mega-Malls

With the opening of the West Edmonton Mall in Canada and Mall of America in Bloomington, Minnesota, North Americans were introduced to the concept of the mega-mall. Occupying about 4 million square feet of space, they offer a wealth of shopping and entertainment to the families that frequent them. Aside from the Nordstrom, Bloomingdale's, and Sears anchors and more than 500 specialty stores, Mall of America features a tremendous mix of restaurants, movie theaters, a water park replete with waves, a miniature golf facility, and many night clubs.

While these two massive retail arenas initiated the mega-mall concept, they are not alone. Others have joined the fray, albeit on a smaller scale. The Mall of Georgia opened to great fanfare in 1999, with a 1.7-million-square-foot site. It is a planned development that occupies 500 acres and includes apartments, a power retail center, a village concept, an open air concert venue, an Imax 3D theater, and a 90-acre nature park. Anchors include Nordstrom, JCPenney, Macy's, and Dillard's. With Georgia-inspired architecture, store facades draw upon the state's small-town retail history. Broken down into five mall zones are Atlanta, the North Georgia mountains, the Piedmont area's manufacturing heritage, the plains made famous by Jimmy Carter, and the coastal areas. Each features its own design; for example, the Atlanta zone is a replica of Union Station, the city's main post–Civil War train terminal. Also unique to the mall concept is the clustering of stores according to price points. This plan enables shoppers with limited time or budgets to quickly head for their area of interest.

Festival Marketplaces

It was the redevelopment of the waterfront area in Boston that gave us the first **festival marketplace**. Specifically, the Rouse Company totally refurbished historic Faneuil Hall to create Quincy Market, the center of this new shopping arena. The term *festival marketplace* was coined to describe centers that offered festive settings along with places to shop and innovative eateries.

With the immediate success of the Faneuil Hall venture, other unique centers began to spring up. In old railroad terminals and downtrodden or underutilized waterfront warehouses, other festival marketplaces were born. South Street Seaport in New York City soon became a destination for tourists to make purchases and enjoy the sights. Once home to the Fulton Fish Market that served the city's seafood restaurants, it now features Pier 17, a shopping facility, cobblestone streets reminiscent of earlier times, and numerous restaurants whose themes replicate the former fish market. St. Louis' Union Station was refurbished into another of these marketplaces. HarborPlace in Baltimore was yet another festival marketplace that replaced an eyesore, the city's seedy waterfront area.

The success of these enterprises has made them popular all over the country. Many cities have erected festive settings that provide a renaissance in otherwise forgotten places.

The entrance to Bayside Marketplace, a Rouse Company festival marketplace in Miami, welcomes shoppers with its attractive local architecture and greenery.

Focus on...
International Council of Shopping Centers

FOUNDED IN 1957, the International Council of Shopping Centers (ICSC) has thousands of members in more than 75 countries. ICSC's members include shopping center owners, developers, managers, marketing specialists, investors, lenders, academics, public officials, and (of course) retailers.

Its principal aim is to assist members in the development of their businesses through professional education, conferences and conventions, publications, research, and legislative action. Specifically, the council:

- Collects and disseminates information pertaining to the techniques of profitable operations, which serves to improve the individual shopping center and the industry
- Studies economic, marketing, and promotional conditions that affect the shopping center industry
- Promotes the prestige and standing of members as reputable specialists in the field of shopping center development and management
- Encourages research on the architecture and design of shopping centers and on the development of improved management and maintenance methods
- Promotes the role of shopping centers in the marketing of consumer goods and services

In carrying out its vital role in the shopping center industry, the ICSC organizes more than 250 conferences a year where as many as 75,000 individuals participate. The council also offers more than 70 books, reports, audio books, and computer disks to its members on a variety of topics ranging from retailing and architectural design to marketing and management issues. On one of its Web sites (www.retailernews.com), ICSC connects subscribers to the latest in industry developments. In order to keep the professionals in the group up to date about industry happenings, ICSC offers an educational component—the University of Shopping Centers. It is specifically designed as a continuing educational forum whose curriculum covers asset management, retailing, finance, lease administration, development, design, architecture, construction, law, technology, and a host of other areas of specialization. Through distance learning, ICSC is able to reach the far corners of the globe.

Among the many high-profile members of this organization are Mall of America, Sawgrass Mills, The Forum Shops, Desert Hills Premium Outlets, and Pier 39.

Power Centers

These are small shopping venues occupied by about six high-profile category killers. Typically they feature retailers such as Borders Books, Bed Bath & Beyond, Best Buy, CompUSA, Office Depot, Sports Authority, Toys "R" Us, and PetsMart. Each of these merchants advertises heavily and draws large crowds of shoppers to the premises. The centers usually occupy from 225,000 to 500,000 square feet. The key to the success of these centers is that they offer a wealth of merchandise at value-oriented pricing structures, guaranteeing that there will be something to satisfy each shopper's needs.

Fashion Avenues

In many of America's most affluent communities there are **fashion avenues** that feature a number of upscale shops. The marquee names on the storefronts include internationally renowned designers such as Hermès, Louis Vuitton, Giorgio Armani, Chanel, Yves St. Laurent, Calvin Klein, and Ralph Lauren.

Rodeo Drive in Beverly Hills, California, is one such fashion avenue. With the film and television industry located close by, it has remained a destination for the rich and famous. Worth Avenue in Palm Beach, Florida, is also a thriving street of fashion. The city's inhabitants include social elites like the Kennedys. Lining the streets and waiting to cater to the whims of the upper-upper class are many of the same stores that are found in Beverly Hills.

Other prime fashion avenues are New York City's Madison and Fifth Avenues. The former is housed primarily by designers who feature the latest in fashion-forward merchandise, upscale boutiques, and art galleries. The latter features the flagships of Saks Fifth Avenue and Lord & Taylor and a host of designer emporiums. Since New York City is home to some of the wealthiest families in America, a place where many international businesses are headquartered, and a spot where tourists visit each day in record numbers, these avenues are a natural place for fashion devotees to satisfy their desires.

An overview of the priciest retail streets in the United States is given in Table 12.1.

Power centers generally house about six high-volume retailers such as Office Max, PetsMart, and Bed Bath & Beyond.

Flea Markets

The antithesis of the fashion avenue is the bargain arena housing flea markets and swap shops. In the vast parking fields of racetracks and drive-in movies, vendors line the aisles with stalls that feature everything from electronics to apparel and accessories. The atmosphere is much like a carnival, making it a fun place for the entire family to shop for value merchandise.

The smaller of these markets tend to operate limited hours such as weekends. The major flea markets, such as the Swap Shop in a suburb of Fort Lauderdale, Florida, operate daily and feature more than 1,000 vendors. The Swap Shop has booths that are surrounded by a circus and a stage that spotlights a variety of entertainers.

Many of the vendors who own these businesses may actually be considered chain operators in that they have branches in several different markets. Most, however, are individual entrepreneurs who use this type of selling as a means to supplement their incomes.

Airport Terminals

Today's travelers are finding that many of the flights they have booked require airport stopovers. Often, these plane changes require stays that last a few hours. Add to this the ever increasing delays due to security checks and inclement weather, and the result is a terminal filled with people with nothing to do but wait for their departures.

Enter the age of airport shopping. Once housing only newsstands, bars, restaurants, and duty-free shops, these locales are now home to retailers like Gap, Victoria's Secret, The Museum Shop, Wilson's Leather, and many others. Although the phenomenon is relatively new in the United States, European airports have long catered to the traveler. In London's

TABLE 12.1
THE MONEY STREETS

Rank	Locale	City	Rent per Square Foot	Remarks
1	Fifth Avenue	New York	$1,350	"By global standards, New York's Fifth Avenue ranks with the most expensive streets in the world," said Moore of Colliers. "London, Paris, Hong Kong, and Tokyo have considerably higher rents than any other street in the U.S., but Fifth Avenue falls right into step with these global cities." Fifth Avenue has long been touted as one of the most popular shopping streets in the country. The corridor boasts specialty stores like Bergdorf Goodman and Saks Fifth Avenue, as well as flagships for major brands such as Prada, Fendi, Cartier, Tiffany & Co., and Louis Vuitton. Mega-flagships from Giorgio Armani and Gucci are in the pipeline. And The Disney Store, FAO Schwarz, The Apple Store, and the NBA Store surely cater to all those tourists.
2	Union Square	San Francisco	$485	This area of San Francisco evolved into the city's premier shopping district following the great earthquake and fire of 1906. Today, five major department stores can be found there, including Macy's, Neiman Marcus, Nordstrom, Saks Fifth Avenue, and Bloomingdale's, which opened last year as an anchor to the newly expanded Westfield San Francisco Centre on Market Street. Along with its second anchor, Nordstrom, other stores in Westfield include Juicy Couture, Coach, Kiehl's, and H&M. Nearby is the Crocker Galleria, which houses Polo Ralph Lauren and Versace. Last month, Barneys New York opened its sixth full-line store of 60,000 square feet in a six-floor building at Stockton and O'Farrell Streets. Surrounding these shopping hot spots is a plethora of upscale hotels, including the Four Seasons-San Francisco, Sir Francis Drake Hotel, and the Westin-St. Francis.
3	Rodeo Drive	Los Angeles	$480	The stretch of shops and boutiques on Rodeo Drive begins at Wilshire Boulevard to the south, and runs north to Santa Monica Boulevard. "The stores here are just getting more and more fabulous," said Moore. "High-end retailers here can afford to pay these rents." Giorgio Armani, Badgley Mischka, Bottega Veneta, Christian Dior, and Dolce & Gabbana are among some of those high-end retailers, while fine jewelry names like Van Cleef & Arpels, Cartier, Harry Winston, and Bulgari lure shoppers with their baubles and gem contributions to the upscale neighborhood.

Location Analysis and Selection | CHAPTER 12   273

RANK	LOCALE	CITY	RENT PER SQUARE FOOT	REMARKS
4	Kalakaua Avenue	Honolulu	$360	Located just off of Waikiki Beach in Honolulu is Kalakaua Avenue, Hawaii's famed shopping corridor. With over 111,000 square feet of selling space, retail complex 2100 Kalakaua Avenue offers some of the best-known luxury brands in the world: Gucci, Yves Saint Laurent, Coach, Tod's, Bottega Veneta, and Hugo Boss can all be found here. Five years ago, Chanel arrived here with a 12,450-square-foot flagship—the three-story space was designed by architect Peter Marino. Prada boasts a total of five stores in Hawaii, which include its newly renovated two-level freestanding flagship on Kalakaua Avenue.
5	Michigan Avenue	Chicago	$250	"The density of the area's first-rate shopping is, quite simply, unmatched anywhere," said Frommers.com. The corridor's nickname, "Magnificent Mile," refers to the mile-long stretch of North Michigan Avenue between Oak Street and the Chicago River. Designer names line this street one after another. Beginning at Michigan Avenue and Oak Street, shoppers will find Chanel and Louis Vuitton, with Giorgio Armani just a few steps away. "The next block of Michigan Avenue has a New York vibe, thanks to the world's largest Polo Ralph Lauren—a four-floor, wood-paneled minimansion," said Frommers.com. Other nearby tenants include Tiffany & Co., Neiman Marcus, Crate & Barrel, and Burberry. Neighborhood tourist draws include Niketown and the Virgin Megastore.
6	Las Vegas Boulevard	Las Vegas	$210	Perhaps shopping isn't the first thing people think of when they travel to Sin City, but maybe it should be. With hotel casinos, such as The Forum Shops at Caesars Palace, Grand Canal Shoppes at The Venetian, Mandalay Place, Via Bellagio, and Wynn Esplanade offering plenty of upscale luxury brands in their spaces, it's hard to avoid the growing retail development here. The latest hotel casino to break ground is The Palazzo, a 643-square-foot, 53-story extension of The Venetian Resort Hotel Casino and the Sands Expo complex on the Las Vegas Strip. It will feature The Shoppes at The Palazzo, where more than 50 international boutiques are housed, from Ferragamo and Christian Louboutin to Coach and Ralph Lauren. Barneys New York will anchor the luxury complex. The Palazzo is scheduled to open on Dec. 20.
7	Lincoln Road	Miami	$120	Only three years ago, annual rents along this retail corridor in Houston were roughly $66 per square foot. Situated just west of Houston proper, Westheimer Road expands the shopping area further with specialty retailers, superstores and galleries. Popular stand-alone shops include Tootsies Highland Village (men's and women's apparel), The Arrangement (home furnishings), and Antique Pavilion, an upscale multidealer shop with a plethora of antiques. The road also includes the Galleria Mall, which features a luxury lineup including Neiman Marcus, Saks Fifth Avenue, Louis Vuitton, Burberry, Chanel, Christian Dior, and Ferragamo.

(Continued)

TABLE 12.1
THE MONEY STREETS—(continued)

RANK	LOCALE	CITY	RENT PER SQUARE FOOT	REMARKS
8	Westheimer Road	Houston	$120	"I think Miami has some of the best retail in the country," said Moore. "We're seeing some great tourism here, there are tons of restaurants and art galleries, and the apparel retail scene is excellent. I can see these rents climbing significantly." Located in Miami's South Beach, Lincoln Road is considered the best people-watching street in the area. Specialty stores include Anthropologie, Miss Sixty, Arden B., Lucky Brand Jeans, and Bebe. And the Lincoln Road Mall is a pedestrian-only street mall in South Beach, which features jewelry, art galleries and restaurants like SushiSamba Dromo and La Lupa di Roma.
9	Prospect/Girard	San Diego	$100	A bevy of specialty shops lines this retail hot spot, located in La Jolla—San Diego's most upscale neighborhood. Warwick's La Jolla is a family-owned shop that features books, artisan jewelry and stationery, while Michele Coulon's Dessertiere, another family-owned shop, offers gourmet French cakes and confections. New and noteworthy boutiques that have recently entered the area include Elizabeth's Closet, which carries women's wear brands like Twelfth Street by Cynthia Vincent, Rock Revival and We the People, and Emilia Castillo, a high-end home decor and jewelry shop. Meanwhile, tired shoppers can stop at one of the neighborhood spas like GAIA Day Spa and C Spa, which are also located here.
10	Walnut Street	Philadelphia	$100	The majority of shops, restaurants and art galleries located on Philadelphia's busy Walnut Street are located between Broad Street and 18th Street. Walnut Street also features Rittenhouse Row, an upscale shopping district that boasts some of the biggest names in the business, including Burberry, Tiffany & Co., Cole Haan, Polo Ralph Lauren, and Diesel. And on nearby Chestnut Street, The Shops at Liberty Place is a retail complex which features J.Crew, Ann Taylor Loft, and Jos. A. Bank, plus Express, Nine West, and Victoria's Secret.

Note: Priciest retail streets in the United States (ranked by rent per square foot) as reported by Colliers International, a Boston-based real estate brokerage company; only one retail corridor is listed for each metro area. Ties are listed alphabetically.

Heathrow Airport, numerous small stores surround an outpost of the world-famous Harrods. At France's Nice Airport, designer boutiques of Hermès and Gianni Versace are bordered with numerous upscale jewelers and perfumeries.

Pittsburgh International Airport was one of the first in America to get in on the airport shopping mall game. Apparel and accessories stores, gift shops, bookstores, golf shops, and restaurants are in abundance, catering to those waiting for their connections. Its more than 10 merchants have access to about 60,000 passengers daily and are averaging per-passenger sales of approximately $10. Jumping on this bandwagon are LaGuardia Airport in New York City and Ronald Reagan National Airport in Washington, D.C., where annual sales average $950 per square foot.

Airports are becoming major shopping venues for travelers, who often have lots of time to spend shopping because of flight delays. Shops at London's Heathrow Airport are shown here.

This is more than three times the business of an average mall store, where the figure is closer to $275 per square foot. Chicago's O'Hare Airport, a hub for United Airlines, is another that is moving forward with significant expansion.

As is the case for conventional merchants, those in airport retailing benefit if they are in key locations. In hubs, where plane changing is a given, passengers are forced to linger longer and have time to peruse the shopping facilities. Heavy international traffic is also a plus. The best locations are in spots beyond the security checkpoints.

In the News . . .

The article entitled "Luxe Goods on the Fly: Accessories Brands Tap Travel Retail for Growth," is featured on page 283 at the end of this chapter and should be read now.

Neighborhood Clusters

Neighborhood clusters are unplanned locations that are either replete with stores that provide services to their clienteles or shops that offer a broad selection of apparel and home furnishings. Unlike the malls that are set up in a controlled fashion, where the developer determines the number of retailers in each merchandise classification that will make the center profitable, these venues are anything but controlled. Generally consisting of buildings that have no central ownership, each landlord has the freedom to rent to anyone he or she desires.

In some small cities and towns, these clusters typically feature a grocer, bake shop, dry cleaner, beauty salon, and pharmacy. They are places that the locals frequent on a daily basis. Other clusters might be more oriented toward apparel or accessories and feature small specialty shops, haberdasheries, boutiques, or jewelry shops. Most of the stores are independently owned and operated, but occasionally there is a chain present.

Strip Centers

In communities all over the country, the main shopping outlets are located in **strip centers**. The types of stores found in these configurations are similar to those situated in neighborhood clusters. There are, however, some differences between them. Unlike the unplanned clusters, strip centers are owned by a single developer who maintains control regarding tenancy. This means that he or she determines the tenant mix that will make the center profitable for those who have leased the premises.

Another feature of this type of location is the availability of parking. Unlike the neighborhood clusters, which rely on street parking for shoppers, this arrangement makes store access simpler.

Freestanding Stores

The concept of a single retail entity situated all by itself is not prevalent in the retail scene. Most merchants want to locate their stores in places where others operate so that each can bring its own customer traffic there. Thus, the consumer is more likely to visit places where there are several shopping options.

The only type of retailer that still subscribes to the **freestanding store** concept is the one that, by virtue of its reputation, can draw vast crowds of shoppers to its location. These stores can be located just about anywhere they choose as long as the public will be able to access the premises. The major warehouse clubs such as Sam's Club, Costco, and BJ's are proponents of such venues. Their merchandising philosophies and reputations, which are based upon value, bring the crowds in masses. They need not rely upon other retailers to attract the crowds.

SITE SELECTION

Within every shopping district there are particular locations that are better than others. The difference between one place and another may contribute to the success or failure of a company. Each merchant's needs are unique and are generally based upon its retailing format. Supermarkets, for example, need convenient parking facilities, whereas boutiques may prefer quiet, secondary streets where there is less hustle and bustle. In order to make certain that the best possible site has been selected, competent research is needed before any final decision is made.

The factors addressed in site selection include pedestrian traffic, neighboring stores, competition, transportation, and parking facilities.

Pedestrian Traffic

Stores that thrive upon passersby for their success must first consider the amount of pedestrian traffic at the site. Not only are the numbers important, but so is the composition of the people in terms of age and income. Tower Records, for example, generates a large portion of its revenue from sales of rock music CDs and thus would benefit from a downtown site that is regularly seen by passing teenagers. Even in the malls, there are some sites that get more pedestrian traffic than others. Each mall has main arteries and secondary spurs. The former are traversed by the vast majority of the shoppers and so, of course, are more productive in terms of providing potential shoppers. The latter are seen by a lesser number but might serve the purposes of a retailer with little competition in the area, making it a destination that people will seek out.

A store that is situated on the corner of a street is assured of greater pedestrian traffic and visibility because of the converging traffic produced by the intersection.

Pedestrian traffic is vital to the success of retailers because of the number of people who see stores as they pass by.

Neighboring Stores

A retailer who is rewarded with a site adjacent to a department store is usually guaranteed a steady stream of potential customers. Since department stores rely heavily on advertising to attract potential customers, surrounding merchants are the beneficiaries of the traffic generated by such promotional endeavors.

Another plus would be a site that is bordered on both sides by stores that sell complementary merchandise. The ladies' accessories boutique that is located between an apparel shop and a shoe store will have a regular flow of customer traffic.

It is also better if the stores that lie next to each other feature merchandise at the same price points. An upscale men's clothing store would not benefit from a next-door neighbor that sells low-priced shoes; nor would a high-end children's boutique gain traffic generated by a nearby value-oriented merchant.

Although these are all sound considerations in site selection, it should be understood that the ideal situation isn't always available. Oftentimes vacancies in existing shopping centers do not provide the optimum neighboring stores. In newly built arenas, such as malls, the chances of leasing optimal space are more likely because developers are aware of the benefits of complementary neighboring stores.

Competition

The number of competitors carrying similar merchandise is an important factor. If there are too many, the competition might be too keen to make the new entry a viable one. Breaking into an area that has established businesses of the same nature requires some amount of uniqueness to lure customers away from the established companies. Unless the new store has something unique to offer, it is unlikely that a success can be made in that locale.

Public Transportation

Stores that are located at bus stops or subway exits are treated to a steady stream of potential shoppers. It is especially favorable if the mass transit system is one that brings shoppers from outlying areas, since this broadens the merchant's trading area.

In downtown areas, where private transportation is limited because of increased driving time due to heavy traffic, public transportation is more likely to bring a more relaxed consumer population to the store. These customers will have time to spare for some shopping either before or after work.

Vehicular Transportation

Many shopping sites are visited by consumers who drive their own automobiles. If the location under consideration is one of these, it is important to count the number of vehicles that visit the area as well as the types of vehicles. In this way, an assessment can be made of the incomes and lifestyles of the automobile owners and, based on that information, of the type of merchandise they would probably want to purchase.

Parking Facilities

One of the keys to the success of the suburban shopping center is the availability of parking. Shoppers are generally guaranteed places to park their cars and so have easy access to the stores of their choice. Similarly, strip centers and power centers provide ample parking for customers.

In major downtown shopping arenas, on the other hand, shoppers who prefer to use their automobiles often find parking problematic. On-street parking is hard to come by and, where available, private parking garages are often expensive. In some major cities like Chicago, the vertical mall developers addressed this problem by building parking facilities adjacent to the malls themselves. On-premises parking is available at 900 Michigan Avenue, where Bloomingdale's is the anchor store; at Water Tower Place, home to Macy's; and at Chicago Place, where

Saks Fifth Avenue is the main store. Not only are the costs of parking relatively modest, but it is also convenient for the shopper.

Convenient and abundant parking is essential where supermarkets are located. Shoppers must be able to move shopping carts to their cars when they have finished making their purchases. Stores such as Home Depot and Lowe's also consider only those locations that provide ample parking to accommodate the often cumbersome purchases made on their premises. Without such facilities it would be impossible for them to sell in large quantities.

Specific sites are evaluated by using a rating system and a checklist that addresses each of the factors to be considered. The form shown on this page is typical of those used in such evaluations.

OCCUPANCY CONSIDERATIONS

There are two choices available to merchants when it comes to making arrangements for the occupancy of a retailing outlet: they may either own their own premises or lease it. While ownership generally provides fewer restrictions, the opportunity is not always available.

SITE SELECTION EVALUATION FORM

Factors	Rating
Pedestrian Traffic	People per hour _____
	Ethnic composition _____
Neighboring Stores	Types _____
Competing Stores	Number _____
Public Transportation	Types _____
Vehicular Transportation	Types of Cars _____
	Number of Vehicles per Hour _____
Parking Facilities	Number of Parking Spots, Total _____
	Covered _____
	Outdoor _____
General Impression of Site	_____

This site selection evaluation form helps retailers make informed decisions concerning the potential benefits of a given site.

Leasing

Retailers whose primary locations are in shopping malls, for example, must lease space from the developer. These are primary locations for large department stores and chain organizations and are generally chosen in lieu of owning their own structures. Although there are numerous restrictions by which tenants must abide, the major department stores that anchor these malls are in a position to dictate their own terms. Since they are the venues that bring shoppers to the malls, these **anchors** are often in the driver's seat. The benefit of having a Macy's, Bloomingdale's, Lord & Taylor, or Nordstrom is so important to the developer that these companies are generally awarded concessions that make occupancy worthwhile. Others who wish to take advantage of the traffic that is generated in these malls are less likely to obtain the same considerations afforded the anchors. They must be willing to adhere to the rules and regulations established by the mall operators in exchange for the advantages that such locations provide.

In the strip and power centers, leasing is also the order of the day. Developers often accommodate merchants by offering them the amount of space they need to properly function before the structures are built. In this way they can have their facility tailored to fit the retailers' specific needs.

Leasing costs vary from one shopping center to another. The rent is usually on a "cost per square foot" basis. The merchant pays the set price each month. Other arrangements might involve a fixed rental rate plus an additional amount based on the retailer's sales; a percentage of profits is one typical method. **Graduated leases**, with escalating rent clauses built into the agreement, are also commonplace in the industry. Maintenance costs that cover expenses of the structure and care for it are sometimes part of these agreements and are over and above the amounts called for in the leases.

Whatever the arrangement is for a property that is leased, the retailer must carefully assess all of the costs to determine if the outlay is worth the investment.

One consideration that must be addressed when leasing retail space is the **rule of occupancy** established by the lessor. Regular hours and days of operation as well as uniformity of exterior signage are just some of the rules that must be followed. Retailers are often forbidden to follow their own instincts in such matters under certain leasing agreements.

If the established conditions are inappropriate for the merchant, then he or she will either have to look at another leasing possibility or consider property ownership.

Ownership

Some retailers opt to own their own premises. This frees them to proceed with the property as they please and not be restricted by real estate developers. The practice includes ownership by small retailers as well as the industry giants.

From the downtown central districts to neighborhood clusters and large tracts of land in suburban areas, individual buildings stand in which retailers operate their businesses. On fashionable streets such as New York City's Madison Avenue and on main and secondary streets that are found in cities and towns all across America, merchants open their doors for business.

Occupants range from small independent entrepreneurships to giants in the industry and include every size business in between. It might be a boutique, a supermarket, a specialty store, department store, or a big box retailer. Major retailers such as Home Depot, Lowe's, and Best Buy often purchase tracts of lands on which they set up shop. Downtown flagships, such as Macy's Herald Square in New York City, own the buildings in which they are housed. Sam's Club and Costco purchase acreage to open their value-oriented retail warehouses.

Each of these companies finds this form of occupancy more favorable to its bottom line. These retailers also benefit by being able to establish their own hours of operation and any other guidelines deemed imperative to the success of their business.

CHAPTER HIGHLIGHTS

- Most industry professionals agree that location is the single most important factor in a brick-and-mortar operation's success.
- In assessing the viability of a location, a retailer must start by conducting demographic research.
- In their quest for sound retail locations, many merchants are emphasizing geodemographics—the study of clustering the population according to ZIP codes.
- Area characteristic assessment is vital to the success of any potential retailing location.
- Shopping districts come in all sizes and shapes, with the downtown central district being the main one for city dwellers.
- Regional malls are found all across the country and feature a wealth of shopping opportunities as well as entertainment and dining facilities for their patrons.
- Mega-malls, such as the Mall of America, are huge retail environments that provide unique shopping and entertainment centers.
- Festival marketplaces, which feature fun shopping and dining, have opened in many formerly abandoned areas and facilities.

- In many cities' downtown shopping areas, vertical malls have risen to accommodate retailers who cannot find sufficient space in street-level locations.
- Freestanding stores are extremely popular for companies like Costco and Sam's Club, which have great customer appeal.
- Site selection is based upon the amount of pedestrian traffic that passes the location, neighboring stores that feature complementary goods, and the proximity of the site to public transportation.
- Retailers must carefully assess the advantages of leasing a store versus owning the property.

IMPORTANT RETAILING TERMS

anchor (278)
central shopping district (264)
community segmentation (262)
controlled shopping center (265)
demographic analysis (260)
fashion avenue (270)
festival marketplace (269)
freestanding store (276)
graduated lease (278)
mega-mall (265)
me-too store (262)
mixed-use center (267)
neighborhood cluster (275)
outlet center (265)
popular area destination (268)
power center (265)
rule of occupancy (279)
shopping mall (264)
strip center (275)
vertical mall (265)

FOR REVIEW

1. When retailers assess a general trading area, what is the first type of research that they should undertake?
2. Why is it necessary to determine the dominant ages of an area's population before any location decision is made?
3. Is it important to assess the stability of a trading area?
4. How does the geodemographics concept work?
5. What information can a retailer gain from ZIP code analysis?
6. How do area attractions benefit a retail operation?
7. What role does local legislation play in assessments of potential trading areas?
8. Why has the central shopping district remained as one of retailing's more important centers?
9. How have developers of downtown shopping districts solved the shortage of space there?
10. How can the Internet be used to learn the names and locations of outlet centers in the United States?
11. What is a mega-mall, and how does it differ from the traditional regional mall?
12. In what way does the festival marketplace differ from a traditional shopping center?
13. Why have airport terminals become important centers for shopping?
14. How does a neighborhood cluster differ from a strip center?
15. What type of retailer will probably have the most success as a freestanding store?
16. Are neighboring stores an important consideration when choosing a specific retail site?
17. How have many downtown vertical malls addressed the problem of parking facilities?
18. What is a graduated lease?

AN INTERNET ACTIVITY

One of the most important factors in the assessment of a trading area by brick-and-mortar operations is demographics. Before they can even consider a particular location for their stores, they must determine whether the people who inhabit the locale fit the customer profile necessary for success. The Internet can provide a wealth of information in this area and is regularly used in demographic research. Some of the information comes from governmental agencies, some from research firms such as Claritas (www.claritas.com), and some from industry periodicals such as *Stores* magazine, which may be viewed online at www.nrf.com.

Pretend that you are a small retailer who wishes to open another unit in an area that is different from the one in which your store is now located. Using any of the aforementioned Internet resources or any others that can be found on-line, prepare a report that outlines how you would go about researching the area under consideration. The paper should be typed and include a bibliography of your sources.

EXERCISES AND PROJECTS

1. By accessing Clarita's Web site (www.claritas.com) or by writing to the company, obtain information about consumers in the ZIP code in which you live. Once you have completed the information on a chart with headings as shown below, determine what type of retail operation would have a chance for success in that area and the reasons you believe it will be profitable.

| Clarita's "labels" | Households | Description | Interests |

2. From the following shopping districts, select four and prepare a chart that addresses distinguishing characterisics, primary tenants, location, and accessibility.
   - Downtown central district
   - Traditional mall
   - Outlet center
   - Mega-mall
   - Mixed-use center
   - Power center
   - Festival marketplace
   - Neighborhood cluster
   - Strip center
   - Vertical mall

After completing the chart, write a one-page paper about the district that you thought best served the needs of the shoppers and note the reasons for your selection.

THE CASE OF EXPANSION INTO A DIFFERENT SHOPPING ARENA

Tiny Elves, a fashion boutique for children, first opened its doors on one of Baltimore's main shopping streets. The location was typical of many such areas in that it featured a men's shop, women's clothing store, shoe store, bookstore, party favors shop, video rental outlet, stationery merchant, home furnishings center, gift shop, and two restaurants. Since none of the merchants competed with each other, they acted together to promote the area, and the shops became popular with customers.

With the immediate success of Tiny Elves in this location, owner Judy Franklin decided it was time to open another unit. She surveyed areas similar to the one in which the first store was located and decided that another main street 50 miles away would be perfect. After checking the shopper demographics she found that her instincts were right, and the second Tiny Elves store was opened. It was also a successful venture.

Based on the success of these two stores, she thought it might be time to expand once again. This time, one of the city's major malls was her goal. Given the popularity of these shopping centers and the throngs of people they attract daily, the location seemed to be a natural. With major department stores anchoring the mall, she believed she could spend less on advertising to generate interest in her store because the anchors' advertising expenditures brought a great deal of traffic to every merchant in the mall. The promotional dollars she saved could be used to pay the rental fee, which was somewhat higher than she was accustomed to paying.

A store that is similar in size to the company's other units has become available, and Judy is seriously considering leasing it.

Questions

1. Should Judy study the demographics of the areas from which the mall draws it customers or should she assume that they are the same as for her other stores?
2. What factors should she assess in terms of the specific site that is available to her?
3. What types of leasing possibilities for the new location might be different from the store's other two locations?

Mixing It Up
Sharon Edelson

June 28, 2007

Living above the store has always conjured up a variety of images, not all of them positive. Perhaps the most enduring is that of hard-working immigrants residing in tenements one story above their businesses. Mixed-use projects have changed that. Today, living above the store can mean owning a luxury condominium a few hundred yards away from Gucci or Burberry at Santana Row in San Jose, Calif., for example.

At the turn of the 20th century, the tenements of the Lower East Side of Manhattan housed waves of Eastern European Jews who sold linens and sewing notions from storefronts beneath flats they occupied. They have almost nothing in common with the residential properties of modern mixed-use developments, except that selling and living go on in the same complex.

For example, when residences in mixed-use properties are marketed and advertised, the word "luxury" often precedes the type of dwelling that is for sale, be it a condominium, town house or single-family home. There's usually a number of amenities such as restaurants, health clubs, swimming pools and spas.

Mixed-use design actually dates back further than the mid-to-late 1800s, pointed out Kenneth Himmel, president and chief executive officer of Related, which has developed mixed-use communities in Reston, Va., and West Palm Beach, Fla., and is working on projects in Phoenix and Los Angeles. For examples of mixed use, look no farther than Europe, "and that goes back thousands of years," he said. "In London, Paris and Rome, there are these extraordinary retail experiences where hotels are built over retail, or residences are built over retail, or office space is built over retail. It's a shame that so few of us practice the business with that European model. It's about combining extraordinary public spaces, art, landscaping and water features as the centerpiece for a retail street experience and restaurant street experience."

Himmel has tried to reinterpret that model with The Shops at Columbus Circle at Time Warner Center in Manhattan, where top restaurants such as Per Se, Masa and Café Gray share billing with Jazz at Lincoln Center and an Equinox health club. A fountain outside the Shops was designed by the same firm that choreographed the dancing fountains outside the Bellagio Hotel in Las Vegas.

It's easy to understand the appeal mixed-use projects holds for retailers. Stores in mixed-use settings have a captive audience of consumers who literally live over the store or within walking distance. Residents are mainly wealthy, a point underscored by the fact that developers said they charge a premium for condos and town homes in mixed-use communities, sometimes as high as 60 percent above market rates.

"Living over the store has become a wonderful asset," said Himmel. "There's the cachet of the names and brands. It's more interesting to live above Polo Ralph Lauren than above a drug store."

According to Himmel, Related targets home buyers in "the top 20 to 25 percent of the demographic. Our average household income in Phoenix's City North is $135,000 to $150,000 annually," he said. "That parallels the tenant mix and restaurants we go after, which is upper-bridge to luxury. These projects are expensive and more sophisticated. Anecdotally, when we sell condos in these projects they sell quickly and at premium prices."

Stores in mixed-use projects can be more productive than those in traditional shopping centers. General Growth Properties, which owns an interest in The Woodlands Mall, located at the 27,000-acre master-planned Woodlands community north of Houston, has said that sales increased by more than 403 percent between 1995 and 2006, in part because of the mixed-use nature of the project. The mall attracts more than one million people from within a 20-mile radius. According to an SEC filing last month, General Growth's total tenant sales in its portfolio have increased 7 percent in 2007, compared with a 4.1 percent increase last year. Sales per square foot as of March 31, 2007, were $458. The company attributed some of the gains to robust sales in shopping centers in mixed-use developments.

At The Shops at Columbus Circle at Time Warner Center, a vertical mixed-use development, retailers do sales of $1,500 per square foot on average, Himmel said. That's higher than traditional malls, where sales per square foot are in the $400 range, but lower than some jewelers and leather goods stores on Madison Avenue, where sales can reach more than $2,000 per square foot. With about 40 retailers at The Shops at Columbus Circle, a Whole Foods Market and eight upscale restaurants and bars, there's plenty for residents, tourists and office workers to do.

The development also includes a Mandarin Oriental Hotel, One Central Park luxury condominiums, 60 Columbus Circle offices and Time Warner world headquarters. Office workers visit the Shops an estimated six times a month, said Himmel, adding that residents go to the Shops an estimated four times a month. Eileen Fisher, Sephora and J. Crew consistently report that their Shops at Columbus Circle locations are among the top-ranking units in their portfolios.

"Any time you can incorporate mixed uses and enhance the consumer experience not only in terms of architecture and the environment, it's a good thing," said Mitchell Friedel, executive vice president of RKF Retail Property Advisors. "The more uses you can factor in, the better. Offices provide a lot of daytime traffic, residential is all day and night activity, and the hotel [means] tourists. There's no formula. [The elements] are specific to a certain market."

Friedel has been involved in the retail leasing at CityPlace in West Palm Beach, The Shops at Columbus Circle at Time Warner Center and SouthSide Works in Pittsburgh. He's also working on upcoming projects such as Bloomfield Park in Bloomfield Hills, Mich.; Mercato in Naples, Fla.; Westwood Station in Westwood, Mass.; New City in Chicago; Garden State Park in Cherry Hill, N.J., and an as-yet-unnamed venture in Miami.

Retailers including J. Crew, Gap, Banana Republic, Chico's, Ann Taylor, Talbots, Williams-Sonoma and Coldwater Creek are among those that have shown an interest in mixed use. "The tenants find them more intriguing and feel they can be more productive in them," Friedel said.

In some parts of the country, master-plan or mixed-use communities have stepped into the role of downtown. "Bloomfield Hills is a very affluent suburb of Detroit, which doesn't have a great downtown to speak of," Friedel said. "[Bloomfield Park] is almost serving as a downtown for Detroit. We have every tenant you can think of."

Demographers have estimated that about 20 million acres of development will be needed to provide housing for the 100 million additional people expected when the U.S. population reaches 400 million in 2045. (The population was 300 million in 2006.) At an International Council of Shopping Centers conference on mixed-use development, however, Ronald A. Ratner, president and chief executive of Forest City Residential Group, said that this approach would use just five million acres.

As the popularity of mixed use grows, though, projects have become more difficult to execute. High construction costs, increased competition, financial hurdles and the slumping condo market are among the obstacles.

"The one thing retailers get concerned about is making sure a mixed-use development is well thought out and staged appropriately," Friedel said. "'Do the developers have the wherewithal to pull this off?' It's the really experienced developers that the retailers rely upon."

• •

Luxe Goods on the Fly: Accessories Brands Tap Travel Retail for Growth
Katya Foreman

JULY 9, 2007

PARIS—Leather goods are set for takeoff in the travel retail sector, traditionally known for sales of perfume, liquor and tobacco.

Airport retailers and brand executives said that even though they are weighed down by luggage, travelers are still willing to splurge on that extra bag, regardless of the price tag.

And airport operators are zoning in.

For example, last November, British Airports Authority introduced its first concept area for fashion accessories, the World Duty Free Collection, in Gatwick North Airport in London.

The shop measures 900 square feet. "We decided that we needed an edgy concept that mixed the leather goods offer with jewelry and watches, but with tax-free prices," said Beta Palizban, a luxury buyer for the area.

The leather goods brands offered range from midlevel players such as Diesel and Tabitha to high-fashion labels including Chloé and Mulberry. "Roughly 80 percent of sales . . . comes from leather goods, but sunglasses also drive a lot of business," said Palizban.

"The leather goods category is thriving for a number of reasons: It offers a variety of price points, targets both men and women and generates good margins for retailers," commented travel retail specialist Martin Moodie, editor of The Moodie Report. "More retailers are giving both standalone and generic space to the category, a trend that is sure to accelerate in the future."

Moodie points to the "stunning" new Narita 5th Avenue shopping mall in Tokyo Narita Airport as an example. As host to 32 shops including Gucci and Burberry, its leather goods area, he said, has dwarfed space formerly used by liquor vendors, a longtime staple of Japanese duty free. "Everywhere in travel retail, the transition from traditional to more fashion-driven categories is an important dynamic—nowhere more so than Asia," said Moodie.

Though figures for 2006 have not yet been released, total sales for luxury goods in the travel retail sector in 2005 represented an estimated $9.8 billion, according to Generation Data Bank. Of this, $1.2 billion was generated from leather goods—a 40 percent increase from 2003. "I would expect an increase of around 50 percent for leather goods in the next three to four years," said Peter Williams, chief executive officer of Alpha Airports Group, a provider of catering and retailing services to airlines and airports in 17 countries. "Leather goods are definitely increasing at a faster rate than traditional travel retail."

With luxury brands wielding global identities, people expect access to them wherever they go—in a new city or an airport, he added. "Travelers now expect a shopping mall environment from airports."

With the ever-escalating number of travelers, notably from new markets such as Russia, India and China, Williams predicts the macro economy for growth is better for brands in airports than in city centers. "Travelers are often in a carefree mind-set where all of those rules about spending go out of the window," he said.

And brands are gearing up to cash in.

"Airports are the windows of the world. It's an extremely dynamic channel for maximizing revenue consolidation and creating brand awareness," commented Clemente Hernandez, commercial director for Spain's Loewe, which has 50 travel retail sales points, either as shops-in-shops or standalone boutiques. Seven more are planned for 2007.

Executives at French leather goods brand Longchamp, which has travel retail points in nearly all of the 80 cities where it is present, see the sector as strategic for lassoing new customers who would not necessarily go to its stores in the respective domestic markets.

"The [travel retail] sector fulfills two kinds of demand: a practical one for passengers who need a last-minute bag, as well as access for those who may have come into contact with campaigns on the domestic markets, but not necessarily the product," said Jean Cassegrain, general director of Longchamp, citing an ambitious plan to double the company's airport business over the next few years.

Mulberry is also stepping up its presence in the sector. The brand has even developed a mobile gadget designed to ease pre-flight purchases from the comfort of the airport lounge. A leather-clad computer screen on a stand will feature a touchscreen ordering system that's linked to the airport store via Intranet. "It will facilitate product to be delivered from the terminal store to the customer in the lounge or at the departure gate," said Lisa Montague, chief operating officer of the brand. Other options will include collection upon return flight or home delivery.

Mulberry is mulling international expansion into the busiest airport hubs via its own retail and franchise network, according to Montague. It is the first luxury brand to sign with BAA on a new site at Heathrow's Terminal 5 that will open in March, for example. Counting three airport stores to date in three of Heathrow's terminals, Mulberry also opened a store in Stansted Airport in June and is testing a boutique at the World Duty Free's new accessories area in Gatwick Airport.

Since airport retail is a volatile sector sensitive to economic and sociopolitical factors, flexibility is key, according to Montague, to accommodate shifting market trends.

"Mulberry's leather goods business [in travel retail] could climb from 7 to 15 percent of total sales, but that figure hinges on air-travel passenger numbers continuing to increase," she said.

Mirroring general buying trends, it is entry-level and luxury leather goods brands that do best in travel retail, retailers and brand executives concurred.

"The midprice ranges clearly lose out compared to very cheap and very exclusive products," said Ulrike Janett-Bachner, manager of corporate communications for the Nuance Group, the giant airport retailer. "There is an overwhelming demand for luxury goods in every area at this moment, be it leather goods, sunglasses or watches."

Small leather goods, she added, were particularly popular, given their lower price point compared with bags or luggage, making them affordable for a wide range of customers who are willing to spend on luxury. "At Zurich, one of our most important locations, small leather goods from the Bally, Burberry and Emporio Armani boutiques are particularly popular," she said. Emporio Armani recently opened its second airport shop in Zurich.

"Creating sophisticated retail experiences for traveling fashion consumers continues to be a top priority for the Armani Group," said John Hooks, group commercial director of Giorgio Armani. "We are very pleased with the positive performance and results of the Emporio Armani brand in the travel retail sector." Following openings in Buenos Aires' Ezeiza Airport in November, as well as at airports in Bangkok and Milan this year, its most recent addition was in Paris' Charles de Gaulle Airport in June.

Still, there are brands that are hesitant to enter the sector. Many attribute lofty rents and lack of sophisticated environments as factors behind the tardy arrival of certain high-profile luxury brands in airports, and many labels are sticking to stand-alone boutiques in strategic airports, namely in Asia.

Chanel, for example, operates only six boutiques in the travel retail space, primarily in Asia, that house ready-to-wear and leather goods. But the brand is looking to expand. "Travel retail gives us the opportunity to reach new customers, with people traveling more and more," said Bruno Pavlovsky, president of Chanel's fashion activities.

"Just as certain brands will choose to be situated on Bond Street or Rue Saint Honoré, say, they're very concerned about store environments and who they're going to be positioned next to," explained Williams, who has recruited design consultant HMKM to create a new 20,000-square-foot store in Manchester Airport in England. The firm has previously worked with high-profile fashion stores such as Harrods and Selfridges. "We're not yet actively targeting luxury brands, but we don't rule it out for the near future," said Williams.

Certain travel retailers are aggressively targeting leather goods brands, however, aiming to go head to head with department stores.

"Most luxury brands, with the exception of Louis Vuitton which does not distribute in any travel retail outlet, for now are distributing to at least one strategic airport across the world," commented Mathieu Daubert, manager of retail goods for Aéroports de Paris, which operates stores in both Charles de Gaulle and Orly airports.

Daubert was formerly a buyer of luxury goods for French department stores Le Bon Marche and Printemps. It's a retail phenomenon, he predicts, that is about to change.

"Our perfume sales outdo those of any [Parisian] department store and we believe we have the potential to achieve the same with leather goods," said Daubert.

Besides Hermès, its current main leather goods breadwinner, Ferragamo and Burberry are among the few luxury brands currently distributed by the firm. But there are plans to open two "major" accessories-only boutiques in both the Charles de Gaulle and Orly airports in 2008, and Daubert said he was angling to lure brands rarely seen in the travel context. "The stores will be multibrand but will stick to the corner logic," said Daubert. "With luxury brands having gone so far to establish an identity, we have a vocation to respect that."

Communication will focus on the sector's tax-free benefits. In terms of productivity, luxury, according to Daubert, will hold a slightly more important position. Targeting a limited offer of niche brands, such as Balenciaga, is also part of the strategy.

"It is important to cater to all types of customers, though I don't think it's the role of an airport to be a prescriber of trends," said Daubert, adding that he will nonetheless be seeking ways to stand out from competitors.

The firm also plans to have ultra-luxe goods at the ready.

"[Customer behavior] in other travel retail sectors has proved that there are no limits when it comes to spending in airports," said Maubert, citing a recent Chinese client who bought $30,000 worth of wine in one of the firm's boutiques.

"We are experiencing a rising number of travelers who have the means and the desire to splash out on exceptional goods."

CHAPTER 13
Designing the Facility

After you have completed this chapter, you should be able to discuss:

- The various elements that are part of a store's physical design
- The different types of window structures that retailers use in their brick-and-mortar operations
- Why open windows are used extensively by today's merchants
- The reasons why many retailers are using individualistic approaches to interior design rather than the traditional formats
- The basis for determining department locations
- The new fixturing concepts that are used in today's retail environment
- The various types of surfacing that merchants use in their stores
- Why nonselling departments play a secondary role in terms of location

Once a merchant has decided on a location for a new brick-and-mortar operation, he or she is ready to tackle the problems associated with facility design. With the enormity of the competition that retailers continue to face, it is imperative that a plan be in place to distinguish its concept and premises from the others. Relying upon old ideas and formats may not give the new retail entry a uniqueness or difference; using a me-too design no longer works.

First and foremost, merchants must differentiate themselves from their competitors by offering a merchandise plan that projects a specific image and has the potential to motivate customers to buy their goods. Once the plan is in place, attention must now focus on a store's design, where attractiveness and function interrelate. It is essential that the design and layout create a specific image that best shows the store's personality and reflects the potential productivity of the sales space.

As we travel from shopping center to shopping center, we are treated to a host of individual facility designs providing a combination of qualities that makes an impression on the shopper. It might be a **theme environment** like the Disney Stores use; a sophisticated, sleek look as seen in the Banana Republic stores; or a grand salon-like environment such as the American Girl Place in Chicago. Even supermarkets are transforming newer units into more visually appealing premises. Harris Teeter, the North Carolina–based food chain, has designed its newest markets to feature such elements as a circular island with meal solutions for the shopper who wants quick meals.

Looking back at the initial Banana Republic interior and exterior designs, consumers walked into safari-like environments, jeeps appeared as though they were coming through the display windows, and rattan and reed dominated the concept. This look served the organization until it decided upon a new merchandising format. That design was replaced with a sleek, contemporary look that would enhance the new product line. Management decided that designing a new facility was as important as the merchandise itself. The power of store design was deemed important to the success of the new road the company was to take. The total revamping of Banana Republic's stores was a great success in that it helped make the stores a destination that would motivate shoppers' to satisfy their clothing and accessories needs there. This is but one example of how store design plays a role in retailing. Sometimes a new focus must be initiated to underscore a change in company direction.

Throughout the United States, merchants of every size are making significant investments to provide their customers with new, exciting environments. Saks Fifth Avenue, for example, has invested millions of dollars in the refurbishment of its flagship in New York City and in many of its branches throughout the country. Belk continues to do the same so that its clientele will find shopping more pleasurable. Updating store designs is one way for retailers to bring excitement to their businesses in the twenty-first century.

It is important that retailers not only carefully design the new units in their organizations but also regularly evaluate the premises of existing outlets to determine if a facelift would prove beneficial to their images.

An examination of *Visual Merchandising and Store Design* (*VM+SD*) magazine and visits to trade expos such as **GlobalShop** prove that facilities design is reaching new heights. In each issue of the trade journal, everything from fixturing to lighting is presented, expressing the ways in which retailers can set off their brick-and-mortar units with unique designs that are both functional and eye-appealing.

EXTERIOR DESIGN CONCEPTS

The exterior design of a store is critical because it is this first impression that motivates a shopper to enter. Retailers who have taken this concept to an extreme include the Steuben Glass flagship on New York City's Madison Avenue, which has 25-foot-high windows that dramatically showcase the store's interior; Lord & Taylor on Fifth Avenue, which has display windows equipped with elevators to showcase a bi-level presentation in its animated Christmas displays; and the American Girl Place in Chicago, which has a museumlike façade. Each immediately conveys the message that there will be more dazzling treats to see inside the store.

Some of the major franchises have used their exteriors to attract consumers' attention. McDonald's golden arches is such an example. Drivers or pedestrians all over the world immediately recognize the sign and know exactly what to expect once inside.

Even movie theaters, considered by many to be a specialized segment of retailing, have added unique designs. They, like their merchandise-oriented counterparts, are faced with significant competition and need more than films to get their fair share of the market. One grand movie complex exterior is found at the Muvico Paradise 24 in Davie, Florida. At the grand entry, visitors see massive Egyptian columns and a pair of sphinxes. The fiber-reinforced, faux concrete calls to mind the ancient temple at Karnak, setting the complex apart from any other movie theater.

Of course, the impact made by these and other imaginative designs must deliver a sound merchandising concept once the consumer crosses the threshold. The interior should be an

TABLE 13.1
TOP 12 RETAIL DESIGN FIRMS

Company	Web Site	Major Clients
Callison Architecture Inc.	www.callison.com	Nordstrom, Saks Fifth Avenue, Seibu Department Stores (Japan)
Pavlik Design Team	www.pavlikdesign.com	Sears Grand, ShopKo
RPA	www.rpaworldwide.com	Adidas, Starbucks
Gensler	www.gensler.com	Aveda, Gucci
FRCH Design Worldwide	www.frch.com	Lazarus, Velvet Pixies, Discovery Channel
Carter & Burgess	www.c-b.com	AutoNation USA, Tower Square Food Court, Big Y World Class Markets
Little & Associates	www.littlearch.com	Harris Teeter Supermarkets, Fore The Links
Fitch	www.fitch.com	Timberland, Burger King
Entolo	www.entolo.com	Gateway, Duck Head
Design Forum	www.designforum.com	Lindt Chocolate, Gordman's 1/2 Stores, West Marine
MCG Architecture	www.mcgarchitecture.com	Sephora, Los Angeles Sporting Club
Walkergroup/CNI	www.wgcni.com	Iwataya Passage (Japan), Barnes & Noble, Neiman Marcus (Hawaii)

extension of what has been witnessed outside, making the whole environment a consistently pleasurable shopping experience. Numerous design firms throughout the United States are building new environments and are busily engaged in transforming established retail facilities into more exciting ones. The leaders in the retail design field are featured in Table 13.1.

STORE ENTRANCES

Before doing any actual shopping, a customer must pass through a store entrance. There are many types of entrances. Each is based on the shopping district it is in and the retail classification under which it falls.

Merchants whose operations face onto the street, as in downtown central districts, neighborhood clusters, power and strip centers, and many festival marketplaces, must feature doorways that open and close. Since the stores are confronted with different weather conditions throughout the year, these passageways are necessary. Stores that are sheltered from the street, as in enclosed malls, need not utilize traditional entrances and can simply provide open spaces that allow access to the selling floors.

Depending on the retailing concept, entrances are either functionally designed to enable store entry or are embellished with window structures that tell the shopper what he or she will find inside the store. Retailers such as Target, Kmart, Wal-Mart, and the warehouse clubs forgo display windows. Through extensive advertising, shoppers know exactly what to expect in these stores. On the other hand, department store flagships and other merchants of

The Lord & Taylor New York windows are home to extravagant displays.

The NBA storefront utilizes giant windows to give passersby an impression of the exciting merchandise inside.

fashion and seasonal merchandise make extensive use of their windows to attract shoppers. The exterior display stations are the **silent sellers** that help to presell the merchandise. They are designed in many different ways, with the final configurations based on space availability and the merchant's needs and creativity.

Window Structures

Each window structure serves a different purpose for the retailer. Some are constructed so that they serve as separations between the store's exterior and interior. Others are dividers that feature merchandise displays and also allow the shopper to look into the store.

Neiman Marcus has a host of parallel-to-sidewalk windows in its San Francisco location.

Parallel-to-Sidewalk Windows

Department store flagships are generally the primary users of **parallel-to-sidewalk windows**. These are the stages where such retailing giants put their best feet forward. The windows are usually 10 to 15 feet wide and up to 10 feet deep. They flank the store's main entrances. Flagships such as Lord & Taylor, Saks Fifth Avenue, and Macy's in New York as well as Neiman Marcus in San Francisco have several of these showcases built into their structures.

Open Windows

The antitheses of these display configurations are those typically found in the malls. With space at a premium in these locations, merchants generally resort to the use of glass walls that enable shoppers to see inside the store. The store itself is the display. In place of the formal visual presentations that are found in traditional display windows, merchants concentrate on making interiors as attractive as possible to call attention to the store's offerings. One retailer who embraced **open windows** was Brooks Brothers in its New York City Fifth Avenue flagship. Instead of the typical Brooks Brothers windows, this store's façade is a three-level sheet of glass. Its designer calls it "a vitrine for the architectural interior, enticing customers to come in and participate in a sophisticated, urban shopping environment." Its open, 35-foot atrium entrance glows with outside light that is filtered through a metal scrim lit from the outside.

Starbucks places its seasonal merchandise at the front of the store so that shoppers will see it immediately upon entering.

Another retailer that has taken to the glass wall concept is Levi's in its San Francisco flagship. Its expansive windows allow customers to see the entire store at a glance. At night, the huge upper glass panels are transformed into a 27-by-48-foot screen on which young, independent digital artists find an audience for their work. With the use of three projection screens, the stage is set to attract shoppers.

Also part of these structures is the use of open doorways that allow potential customers to enter without the need to open the door. This easy access often helps to generate customer traffic.

Miscellaneous Store Windows

Other type of windows include arcade fronts, angled windows, and corner windows. In the **arcade front** design, the store's entrance is set back about 10 or more feet from the building line so that two window showcases can be constructed to feature the merchandise. The **angled window** concept features glass panels that extend from the store's building line and end at the entrance way, which is set back about 5 feet. The **corner window** design benefits from traffic that converges from two streets and is also used for "islands" that are situated in a retailer's vestibule.

INTERIOR DESIGN AND LAYOUT

Today's seasoned merchants have taken design to a level that is more exciting than ever before. Relying on professional design teams has afforded retailers the opportunity to showcase their goods in environments that are both visually appealing and functional. Not only has the space been designed more creatively than in the past, it has also been developed to maximize customer comfort and shopping convenience. Whether it is the upscale fashion retailer, the value-oriented merchant, or some business in between, the aim is to offer appointments that will motivate shoppers to buy and to return again and again.

The creative forces must address aspects of design such as the location of the sales and sales-support areas, department layouts, and shopper traffic flow. Decisions must also be made as to the types of flooring, wall and ceiling materials, and lighting and fixtures that will be used.

By selecting a professional design team to create the environment, the retailer will more than likely meet the challenge to successfully compete in the marketplace. It is not always easy to select a design team because there are scores of creative possibilities. A good way to start the search is to contact the **Institute of Store Planners** by logging on to www.ispo.org.

Focus on . . .
Institute of Store Planners

THE INSTITUTE OF STORE PLANNERS WAS FOUNDED IN 1961 as a professional association for retail planning, design, and visual merchandising specialists. The organization includes more than 1,300 professional members and has 14 international chapters. Members include store planners, designers, visual merchandisers, associate planners, educators, industry contractors, product suppliers, and students preparing to enter the design field.

Retailers of all sizes and specialties utilize the Institute so that they can improve their status in the highly competitive global market. The design specialists in the group are not only creators of interiors; they also have a keen understanding of the retailers' merchandise needs and requirements. The design members understand what the merchants want their customers to experience and are able to advise retailers on how to save time, money, and effort in developing a new or remodeled store.

Carrying out the Institute's mission involves establishing and maintaining high standards and professional ethics, excellence in store planning and design, and the nurturing of the profession as a distinct discipline within the design community.

The Institute helps both design companies and retailers meet their goals. This is accomplished through a number of different means. First, its Web site features the latest news and developments pertaining to store planning. The site features an online version of the Directory of Store Planners and Consultants, which assists merchants in finding design firms in specific geographic areas with experience in particular types of projects.

Next, by holding monthly chapter meetings that include presentations by design professionals and contractors, members learn about design innovation and trends that can be passed on to their clients.

Other Institute programs include sponsoring competitions for store planners and employee referral services, which enable retailers to find competent store planners for their in-house teams.

Finally, through its cooperation with universities and technical colleges, the Institute provides lecturers, critics, and judges for the international student design competitions it sponsors.

Interior Design Concepts

Deciding upon a design that will make the store both functional and attractive is no easy matter. It is as difficult as the decisions the merchandising team must make in selecting the styles they will add to their product mix. Many merchants take the traditional path of store design and join the parade of me-too companies, repeating what has been constructed in the past. This is a safe approach to store design, but it doesn't offer the individuality that is key to success in today's competitive retailing environment. Others have chosen a new route, where a theme is the centerpiece of the design concept. This makes the store a more exciting place for customers to shop.

In the News . . .

"Aéropostale Updates Its Box," an article appearing on page 304 at the end of this chapter, should be read at this time.

The Traditional Approach

When shoppers enter many of today's retail operations, they are greeted with interiors that, while tried and true, are reproductions of many others in the field. Whether it is the department store with its traditional grid-like layout, or the supermarket where each product classification is found in an aisle that is identical to its competitors, standardization is the key. Of course, different materials subtly differentiate one from the other, but the sameness in each store is obvious.

Those who stay with the conventional approach generally do so because their selling arenas serve the purpose of satisfactorily housing all of the merchandise categories in the store.

During his address at Fairchild's 1999 CEO Summit in Carefree, Arizona, Ralph Lauren summed up the state of department store design best by accusing retailers of cheating shoppers of an exciting experience because they are afraid to take risks. "They're not in the business of passion," he charged. Instead, he said, they have become "boring and depressing."

Whether his comments initiated a change in department store design or whether the industry itself came to realize that change was needed in the new millennium is not certain. The same old homogenized stores are still there, but many are beginning to break the mold. The cookie-cutter approach is giving way to new ideas. One case in point is Saks Fifth Avenue's Boca Raton branch, which debuted as the new millennium was ushered in. Replete with the elegance of fixturing that rivals the finest in furniture and with grand lighting that not only effectively illuminates the store but also gives the impression that one is in a fine home, the new Saks store is indicative of what some department stores are doing to break the me-too mold.

Uniqueness of store design is especially important because there is an abundance of merchandising sameness in many of the stores. What might motivate the shopper to choose one store over another are the different environments in which they can shop.

The Individualistic Approach

It is in the specialty store arena that individuality is best being served. Merchants in large numbers are relinquishing the tired looks of their stores and are embracing new concepts in record numbers. Early purveyors of this approach include the first wave of Banana Republic stores and Ralph Lauren, who enhanced his signature styles with antique-laden selling floors.

Today, companies like Old Navy, Abercrombie & Fitch, OshKosh B'Gosh, and Sephora have redefined store design. Each has left the realm of sameness to provide its customers with new shopping arenas.

World of Disney uses a thematic approach in store design to enhance the company's distinctive image.

Individualism can sometimes be carried to the extreme, as in the case of REI's Denver flagship. The Seattle-based retailer, which appeals to sporting goods and outdoor enthusiasts, features an unusual and exciting environment for its operation. Using a brick power plant that previously housed the Denver Ramway Power Company, which provided electricity for the city's streetcar system during the first half of the 1900s, has made the company one that stands head and shoulders above the crowd. A local and state historic landmark—complete with pipes, ductwork, and brickwork that were part of the original building—was preserved and now serves as the setting for the nation's most exciting sporting goods concept. A mountain bike trail and a mammoth climbing pinnacle give customers the opportunity to test and compare products. It is this type of ingenuity that separates the stores of the future from the rest of the pack.

The uniqueness of the World of Disney store design took months of planning by people like the FRCH Design team.

Themes are also prominent in today's specialty retail operations. The NBA store on New York City's Fifth Avenue and the many Niketowns that are found across the country are examples of the thematic approach in retailing. Both of these organizations have designed their facilities to replicate the playing arenas in which their products are used. At the NBA store, for example, basketball hoops are available for use by would-be superstars before they buy a basketball. By providing these types of environments, the companies have taken their stores and the products they feature beyond the mainstream of retailing.

Upon entering the new OshKosh B'Gosh stores, shoppers find themselves inside a mini train station with boxcar fixtures, a ticket booth, and train-track graphics. These are all used to emphasize the company's origins as the makers of overalls for railroad workers. A caboose in which children may play while their parents shop is an exciting and functional addition to the design. The merchandise itself is featured on counters and racks that bear the same thematic design.

Retailers like these understand the need for individualization to make their stores unique within their product classifications.

Locating the Selling Departments

Every store has a limited amount of space in which to locate all of its departments. Most important to the success of the company is the amount of business it generates. Bearing this in mind, the most important areas are the selling floors. Aside from determining the amount of space that will be designated for selling, a plan must be established to place each department in an area that best serves its merchandise classification.

A series of meetings between management and the design team hired to execute the plan is essential in deciding where the particular selling departments should be located. Designers, although experts in their field, do not necessarily understand the specific needs of each retailer. In single-story operations, the placement is less complicated than for a multistory unit. Retail organizations that feature just one classification of merchandise (e.g., a shoe store) will not be as difficult to apportion as will department stores with their multitude of product lines.

> **In the News . . .**
>
> "Maximizing the Assets: Saks Flagship Charts Latest Set of Upgrades," an article reprinted on page 305 at the end of this chapter, should be read now.

Single-Story Operations

The amount of space found in these brick-and-mortar companies varies from relatively small spaces to cavernous ones. In the former category are the boutiques and specialty stores, where 4,000 square feet of space is commonplace. Somewhere in the middle are the units of such chains as Gap, Banana Republic, Casual Corner, Abercrombie & Fitch, Williams-Sonoma, and The Limited, where 6,000+ square feet is typical. At the other end of the spectrum are big box stores like Best Buy and Circuit City, category killers such as Toys "R" Us, and supermarkets and warehouse retailers such as Costco and Sam's Club. Each has its own needs in terms of where the placement of the different merchandise classifications will best serve the store's customers.

Gap, for example, generally uses the same department configuration in all its stores. The newest merchandise is arranged on islands close to the store's entranceway. After a few weeks in the store's spotlight, this merchandise is moved back to make room for newer arrivals. One side of the store features menswear; the other, ladies apparel.

Williams-Sonoma uses the front of the store as a place where its seasonal offerings are shown. As newer items come into the inventory, they take center stage.

Supermarkets, on the other hand, traditionally consist of a series of aisles, each featuring a specific product classification. The produce, meat and poultry, and deli departments are usually located at the store's perimeter. Harris Teeter, which specializes in freshly prepared dinner entrees, locates that department near the store entrance for the convenience of shoppers who have little time to spend in the store.

The key for any single-story retailer is to arrange its selling departments in a manner that addresses the most immediate needs first and then motivates shoppers to investigate the rest of the merchandise offerings.

Multistory Operations

The major full line and specialized department stores occupy at least two or three levels, with some using as many as eight floors for selling. The downtown flagships, where the companies feature their largest selections, are the ones with several levels; the branches are usually confined to two or three floors.

The locations of the selling departments are based upon the merchandise classifications that are featured. While there is no absolute standard arrangement, there are some considerations that must be addressed. In most

Counters of cosmetics usually dominate a department store's main floor.

multistory brick-and-mortar organizations, the main floor selling area is generally utilized for those departments that by their mere presence provide a motivational purchasing element. That is, when shoppers walk through the store, certain products are likely to be purchased on impulse. For example, the cosmetics department is generally located on the first floor and takes up the majority of the space that is closest to the entrance. Counter after counter of marquee fragrances and makeup attract the customer who has just entered the store. Many are drawn to these areas because of the appealing displays. If these departments were located elsewhere, the spontaneity of the purchasing might be lost. Of course, the placement of the cosmetics department is not engraved in stone.

Focus on...
Bergdorf Goodman

ALTHOUGH CONVENTIONAL WISDOM dictates that cosmetics counters be located adjacent to the store's main entrance, Bergdorf Goodman, one of New York City's premiere fashion emporiums, has taken a different approach. With insufficient space on the main level to properly merchandise its vast line of cosmetics and fragrances, management moved the department to the lower level. With a 15,000-square-foot space that is a 250 percent enlargement of the original space, the company opened its Level of Beauty.

The challenge of transforming a basement into a viable selling floor was a formidable one for the Toronto design team of Yabu Pushelberg. Creating a venue that gives the impression of being in the home of a person with refined tastes required the use of elegant appointments such as custom-finished cabinetry, a 21-foot chandelier, and unique terrazzo flooring. The team used a neutral palette that exuded an air of elegance while also helping to brighten the space, which was devoid of windows. Internally illuminated glass display cabinets also helped to create a sense of light and space.

The selling floor was divided into key zones in a U-shaped path. Once the shopper arrives by escalator, he or she is greeted by a flower show leading to the first cosmetic section, which features new lines, and then on to the more traditional brands in a second room, and finally into a third space featuring more avant-garde offerings. A fragrance room, complete with a nail spa and optical center, is another attraction.

At a cost of $10 million, Bergdorf Goodman is betting that this unconventional department location will not only pay off but also help to recapture some of the sales of its rival, Sephora.

• •

Also typically found on the main floor is the jewelry department. Other product groups that are located on the main floor and account for spontaneous buying include shoes and handbags. The menswear department is also located on the main floor. Although items in this merchandise classification are not usually bought on whim, the male shopper is one who often likes to reach his department as quickly as possible; hence, this department is traditionally located within easy access to the store's entrance. In some stores, where space isn't always available to house the entire menswear collection, a **split department** is used to solve this problem.

Bloomingdale's—in its Chevy Chase, Maryland, branch—has taken a new approach to its men's department location. After the success of placing the department on the top floor of its San Francisco unit, it is doing the same for the Maryland store. By offering superior customer service and a compelling design, it is betting that male shoppers will actually travel past the main floor to shop.

The location of the rest of the departments is generally based upon the company's beliefs about what will better serve the needs of the shoppers. Furniture, for example, is most often found on the highest floor. Since this is a classification that doesn't rely upon **impulse buying**, its shoppers will be more likely to seek it out no matter where it is located. Housewares is often found on either a high floor or on the store's basement level. Sometimes retailers will actually have two different selling venues for these items, separating them according to price points.

One plan that many department stores use in the location of their individual departments is to have those products with some degree of compatibility located adjacent to each other. The same customers, for example, often visit the ladies shoes and handbag departments during a trip to the store. If a pair of shoes were selected first, it would then be easy to find a matching handbag. This increases the probability of a larger sale for the store. Sometimes stores even set up satellite cosmetics departments adjacent to women's clothing so that the shopper who has just made an apparel purchase can buy the right makeup to enhance her new clothing.

Focus on . . .
American Girl Place

THE 35,000-SQUARE-FOOT, THREE-STORY BUILDING that is home to a wealth of dolls and related products is American Girl Place in Chicago, Illinois, the first of the full-scale retail operations of the American Girl company. Today, the company has two other stores in New York City and Los Angeles. They also feature smaller venues known as American Girl Boutiques and Bistros. Primarily a catalogue company that was founded in 1986, its brick-and-mortar operation is a blend of retailing and entertainment that capitalizes on the American Girl culture. The challenge to the firm Donovan and Green, which designed the first store, was formidable and required the construction of a special home to unite the company's products with real American girls and their families. The idea was to design a space that presented the products in a memorable way.

Unlike the typical retail emporiums that dot the country, these environments include a bookstore, café, 150-seat theater, and photo studio, each of which is used to augment the merchandise it offers for sale. Individualized spaces were created to showcase the company's distinct merchandise categories that include the dolls, their clothing and accessories, and books and crafts. Each is housed in a boutique setting and is connected to the entertainment areas. The layout resembles a museum. Unlike most toy stores, where it is difficult to find an empty patch of space, the American Girl Place is a quiet, peaceful environment in which shopping is meant to be a pleasurable experience.

Upon entering the store, young girls and their families are greeted by a concierge desk. Adjacent to this area is a display of the only complete collection of American Girl dolls in the United States. Preprinted tickets accompany each doll and, when the ticket is presented to the cashier, the customer is given the selected doll. To the rear of the store is a theater where live, hour-long musical productions based upon the American Girl dolls are presented. The next level houses the bookstore and photo studio. All of the items available for sale are attractively featured on this level.

On the top level is the café, a hundred-plus seat restaurant where girls and their families can dine. For a touch of fun, doll-sized high chairs are attached to the tables so that the dolls can dine with the family.

The long lines of patrons outside the store (which is now owned by Mattel) signal that this is not a typical toy store but rather one in which continuous pleasure is being realized by little girls.

Departmentalization

Once the retailer has determined where the different merchandise areas will be located, the next step is to decide how the product offerings will be grouped. This is known as **departmentalization**. Should the merchandise in a particular classification such as sportswear be grouped all together, or should it be segmented according to brand or designer name? In single-story premises with limited floor space, little can be done to provide an individualism to the collections. In the multitiered operations, however, a different approach is sometimes the answer.

Standard Departments

By and large, after choosing the general area for a merchandise classification, retailers use the **standard department** arrangement. Department stores will have areas that are called Juniors, for example. The department will be designed to feature all of the products in the classification as a mix. No particular space is allocated for each manufacturer or designer. The same is true for other merchandise classes, such as home furnishings and housewares.

This plan makes it easy for the retailer to stock the department no matter which vendor is in favor at a particular time.

Stores within the Store

A departure from the aforementioned traditional approach is the one in which small boutiques or specialty shops are found within the store. One of the early proponents of this arrangement was Ralph Lauren. Stores that carried his collection were required to set aside a separate portion of their selling floors to merchandise his offerings. Whether it was through the use of glass partitions or different types of fixturing, the Ralph Lauren collection became a distinct department in the store.

The concept of designer in-store shops is widely used by merchants.

Today, this concept is widely used by many retailers. In stores like Saks Fifth Avenue, Bloomingdale's, Macy's, and Neiman Marcus, designer boutiques are the order of the day. Each has its own small store in which the collections focus on individual designers. Separate shops that feature Christian LaCroix, Donna Karan, Ralph Lauren, Calvin Klein, Chanel, and the like give shoppers the feeling that they are inside couture settings and not in large retail environments.

Of course, to qualify for such status department settings, the merchandise collections must have significant sales potential or provide the store with an image that separates it from the competition.

Fixturing

Brick-and-mortar organizations—unlike their catalogue and e-tailing counterparts, whose customers never set foot on the store premises—must create fixture designs that are functional as well as visually appealing. The standard, traditional fixtures that once were central to most retailers' facilities have, for the most part, been replaced with newer ones that are not only functional but can also better visually merchandise the store's products.

A case in point is the premises of Sephora, the French cosmetics purveyor that has taken the United States by storm. Instead of relying upon the typical vendor-supplied fixtures that are used to form cosmetic islands, Sephora's approach is quite different. Sephora employs the **open-sell concept**, where shoppers are able to help themselves instead of having to wait for a salesperson to assist them. The walls are lined with **universal fixturing** in which all of the vendor's products are arranged alphabetically. Also present is a perfume organ that entices women

TABLE 13.2
TOP STORE FIXTURE MANUFACTURERS

Company	Web Site	Clients
Leggett & Platt	www.leggett.com	Wal-Mart, Kmart, Sears, Best Buy, T.J. Maxx, Barnes & Noble, Gap, Abercombie & Fitch, Limited, Target
Harbor Industries	www.harborind.com	Sears Brand Central, Wal-Mart
IdX Corp.	www.idxcorporation.com	Reebok, Tourneau, J.Crew, Nordstrom, Gucci, H&M, Polo
FFr (Fasteners for Retail)	www.ffr.com	Wal-Mart, CVS, Target
Madix Store Fixtures	www.madixinc.com	Toys "R" Us, Ace Hardware, Kmart, Staples, Walgreens, Safeway, Whole Foods
Ontario Store Fixtures	www.osfinc.com	Tommy Hilfiger, The Limited, Canadian Tire, Perry Ellis
Sparks Custom Retail	www.sparksretail.com	JC Penney, Jos. A. Bank, Verizon Wireless
Penloyd	www.penloyd.com	Dillard's, Bass Pro Shops
Unarco Material Handling Inc.	www.unarcorack.com	Home Depot, Lowe's, Nike, Kay Bee Toys, Asics, Target

to sample hundreds of scents. The success of this concept is evidenced by the rapid expansion of the company in America. It debuted in 1998 with one store yet now has more than 500 in the United States and 140 more worldwide. It should be noted that the brands are the same as those that have been featured by other retailers for years and years, except for the Sephora private brand. It is the design concept and fixtures that have given the cosmetics a boost. Fixtures are available from a wealth of different producers. Each focuses on different products and designs. Table 13.2 lists the top fixture manufacturers.

Some of the unique fixture choices of the new millennium include those that grace the Movado Rockefeller Center store in midtown Manhattan. A Bauhaus-inspired design was chosen to showcase Movado's watches, jewelry, and glass art accessories. Augmented by a palette of marble tile flooring with mother-of-pearl chips, taupe-stained bird's-eye maple paneling, and satin-finished nickel along with museum-style niches, the modern classic design of Rockefeller Center is carried throughout the store. Overall, the shopper is treated to the jewel-box look of a fashionable boutique.

At the other end of the design spectrum is MacySport, a high-tech, high-energy, state-of-the-art shopping environment that imparts an exciting dimension to shopping. Instead of the lackluster fixtures traditionally used in this type of premise, the creative design team used stainless steel tubing to display the hanging items—all of which are visually enhanced by high-tech video displays and lively graphics.

With minimal fixturing, DKNY opened a flagship store on New York City's Madison Avenue. Unlike the fixtures that grace its competitor's stores in this upscale fashion arena, the designers opted for simplicity enhanced with chartreuse beanbag chairs, lamps with orange nylon shades, and kitschy fixtures to hold the merchandise. Clothing is hung from tubular rods. The décor's shock value separates the store from its competitors in the area.

Finally, Nordstrom has undertaken a reinventing process through the use of fixtures. Rather than the typical walnut wood furniture and cases, metal fixtures with splashes of white and color merge with flea-market finds. Nordstrom's designers believe that a fun environment is just what is needed to reverse the store's previous, often stodgy image.

Although these fixturing approaches might not satisfy the needs of most retailers, unique design is one way for a merchant to distinguish itself from the rest of the field in today's marketplace.

Whatever approach is used, it is imperative that retailers follow certain guidelines to make sure that they are selecting the most effective store fixtures for their selling floors. In an interview conducted by *The Retail Challenge* publication with Madix Store Fixtures assistant marketing manager John Klotz, the following suggestions were offered for fixture selection:

Sephora has departed from the traditional vendor-supplied fixturing and instead uses the "open sell" concept, allowing customers to help themselves to the product. This design has contributed to Sephora's quick success in America.

- Identify what fixtures need to do.
- Review the space available for them.
- Select fixtures in styles and colors that will complement the merchandise and the store's décor.
- Keep sight lines in mind.
- Allow for good light penetration.
- Use fixtures that are interchangeable so that you can configure them in many ways.

These rules are particularly valuable for smaller merchants, who often make their own fixture selections.

Surfacing

The walls and floors of retail establishments can be dressed with traditional coverings as well as with a wide range of newer products. The purpose is to provide an aesthetic look to the premises along with a degree of functionality. Some of the materials, such as ceramic tiling, are more permanent in nature; others, such as paint, are more readily changed to fit the momentary needs of the environment. Designers painstakingly select the materials for both walls and floors that will help to further the concept that best highlights the retailer's image.

Floors

Walking through brick-and-mortar operations in the United States and abroad, one comes upon numerous types of floors that have been chosen by design teams. Each type provides some degree of attractiveness and comfort for shoppers and store employees. Carpet, rugs, wood, marble, and ceramic tile are popular materials.

There is nothing that treats the feet as nicely as carpet, which also conveys luxury. With an assortment of textures, grades, and colors available, it is generally the choice of interior design teams wishing to impart a feeling of warmth and comfort. Piles and flat weaves in various fibers and colors offer the merchant a diverse selection from which to choose. One benefit of using carpet is that it can easily cover floors that are not in the best condition. With a layer of heavy padding, blemishes are quickly concealed. Today's carpet is often color-sealed making it impervious to fading from sun and artificial light.

Although considerably more expensive to install than carpet, wood is a material that is now being used to a greater extent than ever before. Whether it is wooden planks that lie in a simple arrangement or intricate parquet design, the result not only assures a great degree of permanence but also provides aesthetic quality. Although wood does scratch easily, especially in high traffic areas, prefinished treatments of polyurethane make it virtually scratchproof. It is the artistry of the installers that can make the wooden floor a masterpiece in design.

Many types of rugs are being used on top of wooden flooring. Choosing from kilims, dhurries, Persians, and contemporary styles, designers are able to enhance any retail setting. Each type of rug has its own personality and imparts a flavor that can enhance the image of the environment. Rugs are practical in that they are easily cleaned and, when constructed of durable fibers, can withstand the abuse of constant abrasion.

Marble is certainly a product that has enormous resistance to any type of customer traffic. It is extremely impressive and tends to impart an air of elegance. It is, of course, one of the more costly floor coverings and so is used primarily in upscale fashion emporiums. It is hard on the feet and thus often augmented with area rugs.

Ceramic tile is another product that provides permanency for the selling floor. Traditional styles and designs are readily available, and a new breed of ceramics is being featured on many retail floors. The patterns are digitally imaged and can provide just about any feeling a designer wishes to impart. For example, the Frey Boy cigar store in New York City's Grand Central Terminal uses smoke tiles that were produced from stock photography of smoke and further enhanced to create the images for the 16-inch tiles. This floor creates the illusion that the customer is walking through a cloud of smoke.

Linoleum, brick, stone and poured terrazzo, and concrete are just some of the other materials that are being used on retail selling floors. They, along with the others that have been discussed, offer the interior designer a host of options to choose from in creating environmental schemes.

Walls

Typically, walls are covered with paint, wallpaper, fabric, wood, or mirrors. Each imparts a different feeling and must be selected with the overall design concept in mind.

Paint is the most widely used product because of its comparative low cost, ease in application, and ability to be quickly refreshed. A wealth of new formulas has given rise to paint that can take on many different textures and surfaces. Ralph Lauren, for example, has created a line of paint that can give the impression of denim, chambray, suede, linen, antiqued leather, or crackling.

Paint is extremely practical in stores that often change wall colors to complement the particular selling season. In a matter of hours, a department can be quickly transformed into one that signals something new is happening.

Wallpaper is another material that can almost immediately transform a mundane setting into one that provides interest. A large number of patterns, ranging from the traditional to the contemporary, are available.

Fabrics are used on walls to create a sensation of warmth that is usually unachievable via paint or wallpaper. They come in many different weaves, with each providing a particular look that will enhance the store's image. Jacquards, for example, might be used in areas to impart a feeling of luxury, while denim, with its rugged appearance, would best serve the surroundings of departments that feature outerwear.

A more permanent wall covering is wood. The natural beauty of the material immediately conveys richness. Whether it is the traditional paneling that can be quickly installed or narrow planks of actual wood, the effect is an everlasting one. New wood products are being developed so that difficult curved surfaces can be easily covered. Color Wall Prefinished Wall Covering, by Ventee of Chicago, is flexible wood sheeting that can be used on rounded walls. Its flexible fabric backing makes it easy to fit rounded contours, and it is held in place with special adhesives instead of nails.

Mirrors are also used in areas as a means of visually enlarging the space. Entire walls are covered with mirrors that range from the clear variety to the more elegant, antiqued types. These, too, are relatively permanent, maintenance-free materials that can add considerably to the ambiance of store interiors.

Lighting

Whether it is used for general illumination or to dramatically enhance the store's visual presentations, lighting is the one element that can immediately add excitement to the retail premises. The range of products available to today's designers is enormous. Every retail establishment has a wide variety of lighting fixtures and bulbs from which to choose. The requirements of each merchant necessitate different types of lighting installation. Some, such as the vast barnlike warehouse clubs and the big box merchants, are primarily concerned with cost-efficient products. At the other end of the spectrum are the upscale, fashion merchants whose requirements include a wide array of light fixturing, ranging from elegant crystal chandeliers to **halogen pin spots**.

Crystal chandeliers impart elegance in store lighting.

Lighting is important not only for purposes of general illumination but also to highlight visual presentations. Because of its significance in visual merchandising, a more detailed overview of its use is discussed in Chapter 18.

Locating the Nonselling Areas

To make certain that the store is perfectly merchandised and managed, certain areas that are out of the shopper's sight must be carefully planned. These **nonselling areas** include offices that house the management staff, receiving rooms, and storage facilities for merchandise that is waiting to be placed on the selling floor.

These spaces are found in a number of different places in the store. In the major department stores, for example, the buyers and merchandisers are more likely to occupy one or more separate stories in the flagships. Macy's flagship in New York City uses the first eight floors in the store for selling, with several above them used for various organizational managers and merchandisers. With retail space becoming extremely expensive to lease, some merchants have moved their management teams to other locations that are outside of the retailing forum. Belk, for example, maintains a separate facility for merchandisers, buyers, and advertising executives. This leaves in-store space primarily for selling and receiving. In cases where on-site availability is a must, as with store managers and the human resources team, a portion of an upper floor is set aside to house these people. Sometimes there are also very small offices adjacent to the selling floor in which staff members perform some of their daily tasks.

Receiving rooms are located adjacent to the store's loading docks. Depending upon the methodology used by the individual retailer in marking the goods and getting them onto the selling floors, the amount of space needed varies. Stores that use outside sources to mark their goods require less space, whereas those that perform all their own receiving tasks require more.

Merchandise warehousing is another element for which space must be reserved inside the store. The trend today is for merchants to minimize the amount of inventory that is kept in-house. This improves turnover rates (a concept that will be discussed in Chapter 16, The Concepts and Mathematics of Merchandise Pricing) and also frees up more space for the selling floors. In cases where some inventory is stored, it is usually found behind the respective merchandise department. The key is that primary focus be placed on the location and size of the sales areas, with less important spaces set aside for nonselling purposes.

Once the designers and retailers have finalized their plans, the stage has been set for the buyers and merchandisers to fill the premises with the product assortments that will transform shoppers into customers.

CHAPTER HIGHLIGHTS

- Given the competition that retailers face today and the similarity of merchandise assortments in the stores, one of the only ways that retailers can distinguish themselves is through individualistic premises design.
- Exterior designs are beginning to reflect the creativity of innovative teams that keep retailer brick-and-mortar operations from being mundane.
- More and more retailers are opting for the open store entrance, which enables shoppers to see the store's interior from the outside.
- With space limitations imposed on many merchants, there is a need to carefully assign selling departments to locations that will bring the most positive sales results.
- Some major department stores are making extensive use of separate small boutiques in their stores to give extra clout to marquee designers and provide customers with a more intimate shopping experience.
- The fixtures that a store uses must not only be functional but must also be attractive and carry out the desired image.
- Floor and wall surfacing, while traditionally made of standard materials, have more recently been made from a variety of new and innovative products.
- Nonselling departments, although necessary to the success of any retail operation, must not use the primary spaces reserved for the store's selling departments.

IMPORTANT RETAILING TERMS

angled window (291)
arcade front (291)
corner window (291)
departmentalization (297)
GlobalShop (288)
halogen pin spot (301)
impulse buying (296)
Institute of Store Planners (291)
nonselling area (301)
open window (290)
open-sell concept (297)
parallel-to-sidewalk window (290)
silent seller (290)
split department (295)
standard department (297)
theme environment (287)
universal fixturing (297)

FOR REVIEW

1. How does the "theme design" approach differ from the more traditional concepts used by most brick-and-mortar operations?
2. What was the first change that Banana Republic initiated to transform its image?
3. Why is the exterior design concept for a store so important?
4. How might a new retailer, or one that is considering a renovation, go about finding the companies that specialize in retail design?
5. Define the term *silent seller*.
6. Why are so many merchants opting to use open windows rather than the more traditional parallel-to-sidewalk variety?
7. What are the aims of the Institute of Store Planners?
8. Discuss the term *me-too designs*. Why do they poorly serve the purposes of the retailing industry?
9. Name some of the companies that have created interest through the use of individuality of store design.
10. Which departments in a store should take preference in regards to location?
11. Why is it more difficult to determine and design department location in multistory operations?
12. What innovative designs have some cosmetic merchants utilized?

13. Why do some retailers make use of split departments rather than placing all the merchandise for a particular classification in one area of the store?
14. How does the store-within-the-store concept differ from the traditional approach of departmentalization?
15. In addition to visual appeal, what must the retailer consider when selecting store fixtures?
16. Why do nonselling departments take a back seat to selling departments when it comes to department location?

AN INTERNET ACTIVITY

Pretend that you are about to open a new brick-and-mortar operation or redesign one already in existence. In order to make certain that you consider new design approaches, you wish to evaluate the various design team specialists in the field. With your attention focused on day-to-day management, your time is limited. To make a comparatively fast analysis of prospective retail design firms, you turn to the Internet.

Explore the Web sites of the retail design firms listed in Table 13.1. After logging on to each site, select the firm(s) that you believe should be considered for the job.

Write a brief paper on your findings. Be sure to include the following:

1. The type of store you are opening or refurbishing
2. The location of the store
3. The design company you have selected to create the facility
4. The different clients already served by the company
5. The reasons for your choice

EXERCISES AND PROJECTS

1. Visit any mall, downtown central shopping district, neighborhood cluster, or other retail venue to observe the storefronts and window configurations used by the retailers. Once you have observed a fair number of these brick-and-mortar establishments and studied their structures, select the five that you find most interesting. Take a photograph of each and mount your photos on a foam board. Note the store name, window configuration, and outstanding features of each and be prepared to give an oral presentation that compares the different structures.
2. Visit any shopping arena in the city where you live. The purpose of this trip is to observe the different types of flooring used in the stores. Carpet, wood, and tile are typical flooring materials, but you might find some newer types that are attractive as well as functional. Once you have selected five stores with different surfaces, complete a chart with the following headings:

Name of Store	Type of Flooring	Compatibility with Décor

Write a one- or two-page paper offering your analysis of each type of flooring and how it conveys the store's image.

THE CASE OF REDESIGNING A STORE'S INTERIOR

After being in business for more than 40 years, the Wagman Supermarkets notice that sales in most of their stores have decreased. After opening its first unit, the company was considered by industry professionals and consumers alike to be the most modern food chain in the areas it served. Its popularity helped it grow from a single-unit organization to one that now includes 40 stores.

Although the chain's interior design was traditional in nature, its fixturing, lighting, flooring, and other merchandising components were top of the line. Cash registers were placed at the front, with a variety of aisles used to feature different product classifications. Produce, meat and poultry, and dairy and deli sections were situated around the perimeter, making the stores very shopper-friendly.

Management's concern about poor sales figures was expressed at the company's annual meeting. After the operation's figures were shared with those attending the meeting, including store and department managers as well as buyers and merchandisers, a general discussion invited suggestions on how the problem could be corrected.

Some of the managers offered the following ideas:

- Current nonfood lines could be expanded to bring greater profitability to the company.
- Prepared food offerings could be increased to cater to those who have less time to make their own meals.
- A new design could be created, transforming the present environments into ones that provide better shopping surroundings.

After the daylong session, it was concluded that all three suggestions should be considered. The one that seemed to generate the most interest was the concept of a new store design. Everyone agreed that a more modern approach would transform the stodginess of the stores into more appealing environments.

Those in attendance offered the following suggestions:

- A few design teams should be contacted for ideas.
- A prototype should be constructed and tested before any large-scale renovations take place.
- More space should be given to new departments that feature pets and pet supplies, catering facilities, and gourmet products.

The company is still in the midst of considering these suggestions.

Questions

1. Do you think that any of the ideas offered by the management team warrant further consideration? If so, which ones?
2. How would you go about assessing some design firms before calling them in to make formal presentations?
3. How might the Wagman supermarket chain learn more about trends in interior design before they proceed with the impending project?

Aéropostale Updates Its Box
Jessica Pallay

April 9, 2007

WAYNE, N.J.—Aéropostale finally unveiled its new store format—the first of its kind in the New York City metropolitan area—to financial analysts last week at the Willowbrook Mall. The 4,200-square-foot store is one of 11 of the teen retailer's 736 doors to be converted to the new format.

Executives from New York City–based Aéropostale, including chief operating officer Tom Johnson, senior vice-president of marketing Scott Birnbaum and the newly appointed chief merchandising officer Mindy Meads, were on hand to show off the updated prototype.

"We love our old format," Johnson told the crowd, referencing a model the company has used since 1998. "But with the upgrade, it's more relevant to the shopper. There's a sense of discovery now. The store feels much warmer, and that makes kids want to hang out longer."

The conversion consists of obvious upgrades, such as decorating the formerly white walls with marketing graphics as well as creating a less-cluttered selling floor. But there are more subtle changes too, including lengthening wall cabinets to 6 feet from 4 feet to allow for enhanced merchandising opportunities, and adding more mannequins. "It communicates to the customer, particularly on the guys' side. If it's on a mannequin, they'll buy it," explained Johnson. The tactic seems to be working in the stores that have already been converted, he added. "Our men's productivity has been elevated in terms of its contribution to overall sales."

Other changes included moving the fitting rooms—complete with smoke-fogging "magic" doors—to the back of the store, concealed behind the cash wrap in an intimate lounge setting.

Overall, Johnson continued, the new store formats have either met or exceeded Aéropostale's past incarnation, which averaged $540 in sales per square foot.

The update has been in the works for nearly a year, with the first attempt launched last June in Aéropostale's store in the Woodfield Mall in Schaumburg, Ill. "We were careful not to roll out all of our new formats immediately," said Johnson, instead correcting mistakes such as an initial window-obscuring exterior screen. "The screens drove us crazy," he said, gesturing to a mannequin-clad window that now serves as an exterior instead.

Analysts in attendance seemed pleased with Aéropostale's result. "This store is much more sophisticated," said Jeff Klinefelter, senior research analyst at Piper Jaffray. "The consumer and the merchandise had already moved in a more sophisticated direction, and now the store format has caught up. In this environment I could see a consumer paying more for a product."

The store format is not the only venue where Aéropostale is evolving. The company recently hired Meads, a Limited Brands veteran, to head up its merchandising, and has experimented with a variety of promotional tie-ins under the marketing direction of Birnbaum, who joined last fall from Cole Haan. In February, Aéropostale collaborated with rock band Fall Out Boy to sell CDs at the store, and is now offering free Verizon LG Chocolate phones with a $50 purchase. Birnbaum explained, "We want to hook up with relevant partners that can connect with our audience."

Executives didn't address the lagging progress of Jimmy'Z, Aéropostale's celebrity-bent concept whose current 14 doors hardly seem on trend to reach the company's initial plan of 500 to 700 locations. But its flagship Aéropostale brand may have righted itself after what Johnson called its "hiccup in 2005." By the end of 2008, Aéropostale expects to have a Canadian presence, with at least 10 stores planned to open above the border in late summer and early fall. And despite Jimmy'Z's performance, the company's fiscal 2006 earnings, released on March 15, soared by 27 percent to $106.6 million, while sales jumped 17 percent to $1.41 billion.

Still, Eric Beder, Brean Murray, Carret & Co.'s teen and specialty retail analyst, cautions that Aéropostale's challenging comparisons in the second half of 2007 could lead to some difficulty for the retailer. "They're running out of store space for Aéropostale, and Jimmy'Z isn't the answer either," he said. "The company is bouncing back from tough times, but I'm not sure it's sustainable for the long term."

• •

> **Maximizing the Assets: Saks Flagship Charts Latest Set of Upgrades**
> **David Moin**

MARCH 28, 2007

It's not the grandiose master plan once envisioned, but the Saks Fifth Avenue flagship has a fresh round of renovations in store and a new manager to orchestrate the changes.

The strategy, while cautious and proceeding piecemeal, includes a doubling in size and relocation of the shoe department, a new bridal salon and the remodeling of the third level that houses the evening and fur salons and the Fifth Avenue Club for personal shopping and designer collections such as Akris, Chado Ralph Rucci, Dolce & Gabbana, Giorgio Armani, Gucci, Marc Jacobs and Oscar de la Renta.

Also on the drawing boards: rebuilding the behind-the-scenes infrastructure, developing closer connections to customers through technology and a remodeling of the restaurant on floor eight with a "state-of-the art" kitchen that also caters Saks parties.

"We want to make sure our flagship represents Saks and our designers in the best way possible and that we're doing that in the right time frame," said Suzanne Johnson, who became group senior vice president and general manager of the Fifth Avenue flagship last month. "It's probably not as fast as the original plan because of the sheer economics. It's an old building. Whatever we do is very expensive."

The 646,000-square-foot flagship, with roughly 340,000 square feet for selling, is Saks' biggest asset. It's critical for the chain's revival, accounting for about 20 to 25 percent of sales, or roughly $650 million to $700 million of the chain's total volume, which came to $2.94 billion last year. Between 12,000 and 15,000 people visit the store on a typical day, though the count can be as high as 20,000. Despite the wear and tear, it's said to be in better shape than most other old buildings. Opened in 1924, the store was expanded into the Swiss Tower on Madison Avenue in 1989. Some major renovations have already occurred in the last few years, including building a perimeter of designer accessory shops, a larger fine jewelry department on the main floor and an updating of designer sportswear on two, with the addition of new shops for Ralph Lauren Black Label, Piazza Sempione, Armani Collezioni, Dusan and Loro Piana.

The plans for the flagship come amid reports that private equity firms and some retailers have been kicking the tires at Saks, which has been showing improved results lately. Anyone considering buying the business would first focus on the flagship, which is owned by Saks and is estimated by real estate sources to be worth over $1 billion.

Considering it has landmark status, is opposite Rockefeller Center and across the street from St. Patrick's Cathedral, there's no opportunity to add higher floors, so it's a question of maximizing the existing space, which poses enormous logistical and service challenges.

In addition to the third floor and shoe renovations, Johnson outlined significant changes, including:

- A new bridal salon on five due in June.
- The installation of a Web-based clienteling system to increase communications with the public and generate increased transactions. The system just went live.
- Possibly rebuilding infrastructure for processing deliveries and getting goods on the floor faster and more efficiently.

According to Johnson, the new shoe floor will have an express elevator to eight, to where shoes will be relocated from their current space on the fifth floor. There will also be a shoe repair service and quicker access to storage and retrieving the shoes for the selling associates. "This is where the back of the house has to be perfect," Johnson said. "You have to be able to put the shoes back quickly. We've got to really be running that shoe inventory and there has to be lots of seating." The restaurant will remain on eight.

The third floor will see improved adjacencies and key vendors will be given more space, Johnson said. And commenting on the upgraded bridal salon, she said, "It will be comfortable enough to support the bride and her entourage."

The flagship's 1,500 selling associates have been trained on a Web-based clienteling system that connects to Federal Express so deliveries can be tracked and customers can know when to expect their purchases.

Meanwhile, there's an intensified calendar of designer personal appearances ahead. The Rachel Roy collection was introduced at Saks last week with a party for the designer; Donatella Versace and Alber Elbaz will appear for their fragrances next month, and Graeme Black for his collection also next month.

Aside from all the front and center partying, Johnson is making infrastructure a priority and has an anecdote to illustrate the point. "On my first day, I was here very early. I walked around the whole block at 6:45 a.m. I started my rounds in the basement and worked my way up and learned that the freight elevator was broken. It had been broken for 30 days. It was just old," Johnson said. "Night crews were loading and unloading trucks on the street," including merchandise destined for the Off 5th outlet division. "Merchants wanted to know where their merchandise was," and some of it was languishing on the 49th Street side of the store.

"One of the biggest challenges I have is to assess the whole support infrastructure for processing merchandise—the back of the house," Johnson said. "We don't have enough space to process the quantity of inventory that is coming into this building. There is not enough back space to process it efficiently."

Arriving merchandise must be unpacked, accounted for and hanged. "The whole reengineering of that is not the most glamorous thing, but it is most important if we want to bring the flagship to a new level," Johnson said. She added that the company is considering processing merchandise to get it floor-ready at a different location, possibly in the city, or in Aberdeen, Md., at the Saks distribution center.

Her last Saks job had its less glamorous side, too. Since 2002, she ran Off 5th, based on 31st Street and Ninth Avenue, a remote location compared with midtown Fifth Avenue. "When you boil it right down, I sold the markdowns. That was my job," Johnson said.

Discussing her promotion to the flagship, she gets animated. She's responsible for getting a strategy in place to grow the flagship business, executing the sales plans, and said she spends 80 percent of her time on the selling floor or in stock areas. When she's back at her office, Johnson is checking the hourly flash, and that often drives her back on the selling floor, particularly if the store is falling short of plan, to encourage managers to get the business in gear.

She's also sentimental about the flagship because her father, a former psychiatrist, bought his army uniform at Saks for World War II. Her mother was a jazz singer.

Johnson, 51, has been with Saks for a total of 21 years. She joined the company in 1983 as assistant general manager in Cincinnati, ran branch stores in different parts of the country and rose to a senior vice president and regional director of stores, at times in different regions. She's from Whitefish Bay, Wisc., and currently lives in Westport, Conn. She was director of stores for J. Crew from 1992 to 1996, before returning to Saks.

"I always wanted this job. It's a dream job. Steve knew I wanted to run this store," she said, referring to Steve Sadove, the chairman and chief executive of Saks Inc. Next to Sadove and Ron Frasch, president and chief merchant, Johnson as the flagship representative would be among the more visible executives at the company.

"I didn't push that hard, but I really wanted this job for 10 years," Johnson said. "It's the greatest store in the world."

PART FOUR

Buying and Merchandising

No matter what principles and philosophies are established by today's merchants in running their operations, none are quite as important as the merchandise that is on hand to motivate the shopper to become a customer. Without the appropriate merchandise mix, there will simply not be an audience to patronize the company.

The ever-important roles of buyers and merchandisers are carefully addressed throughout this section. In Chapter 14, Buying Domestically and Abroad, the duties and responsibilities of the buying team are examined to show the importance of these positions in retailing. We will show how carefully the buyers must involve themselves in forecasting and also how diligently they must prepare before any purchasing can be accomplished. Also significant, as will be seen in this chapter, is the wealth of merchandise that is globally available. Where buyers once only shopped domestic markets, the far reaches of the world are now their marketplaces.

Purchasing merchandise that is available from vendor resources is often the main purchasing activity, but another area requiring buyer attention is product development, which is explored in Chapter 15, Private Labeling and Product Development. Buyers are often responsible for helping in the creation of private label items. Although most are not professionally trained as designers, their buying trips familiarize them with everything that is out in the marketplace; by carefully observing these offerings, buyers may bring ideas back to their companies that can be considered for new products.

Finally, if merchandise is not carefully priced, it will not bring the expected profits to the company and the purchase will not be considered successful. Chapter 16, The Concepts and Mathematics of Merchandise Pricing, explores the various concepts of merchandise pricing as well as the mathematics required to make certain that the right prices are charged.

CHAPTER 14
Buying Domestically and Abroad

After you have completed this chapter, you should be able to discuss:

- The buyer's numerous tasks in acquiring the best merchandise assortment to satisfy the customer's needs
- Which internal resources the buyer addresses in planning purchases
- Why past sales play such an important role in future purchasing considerations
- The need for the retail buyer to use external assistance when undertaking future purchasing plans
- The way in which quantitative and qualitative elements are addressed in the planning of inventory acquisition
- How "open to buy" calculations are accomplished and why they are so important to inventory replenishment
- Market week visits and their importance to the buyer's assessment of industry offerings
- How buyers who are unable to make trips to the market for their purchases learn about new offerings
- The value of business-to-business Web sites in terms of product overview
- Use of chargebacks to vendors by professional buyers
- The manner in which purchases are negotiated with merchandise suppliers

The merchandise available to today's retailers is by far greater than in any other time in history. No matter what the product classification, merchants have a significant number of resources from which to choose. Wealth of individual items gives buyers vast selection opportunities, but it also tends to complicate the selection process. Choosing from all that is available requires a great deal of expertise to recognize which products have the potential for the greatest profits.

The global nature of the resources from which purchases may be made puts further strain on the buying process. In the recent past, retailers shopped wholesale markets that were close to their operations for the majority of their goods. Regional markets were in operation in many parts of the country, making regular buying trips routine. Just about anything was available in manufacturers' showrooms, wholesalers' sales offices, or trade expositions. When market trips were inconvenient for the buyers to make, "road" selling staffs visited the stores. Today, purchasing is anything but a routine task. With the intense competition in brick-and-mortar retailing, catalogue, and Web site operations, merchandise selection has become more challenging than ever before. In their quest for merchandise that is unique or profitable, buyers must embark upon trips to the far corners of the globe. It is not unusual for fashion buyers and merchandisers to head to Third World countries to locate items that will be exclusively theirs. Trips to the world's fashion capitals to purchase cutting-edge items are also commonplace.

Overseas merchandise sourcing is not limited to fashion apparel entrepreneurs but also involves buyers of gourmet food items, electronics, and home furnishings. A look at the labels on many of these items reveals that the countries of origin are not limited to our shores. In fact, for many product classifications, it is more likely that offshore suppliers outnumber domestic suppliers.

It is generally conceded by industry professionals that proper merchandising is the lifeblood of the retail business. Although such factors as location, staffing, promotion, and the like contribute considerably to the success of the retail operations, it is the merchandise that draws shoppers. Without the proper product assortment achieved by excellence in sourcing, neither brick-and-mortar operations, catalogues, nor Web sites would be able to satisfy their shoppers' needs.

In the News . . .

The article titled "Tackling the Sourcing Conundrum," on page 337 at the end of this chapter, should be read now.

BUYERS' DUTIES AND RESPONSIBILITIES

The task of bringing the best available merchandise to their companies is the job of the buyers and merchandisers. They are charged with difficult decision making and must be able to carry out their roles to ensure that shoppers will be satisfied with the products they find.

The depth and breadth of the various functions of a buyer depend upon a number of different factors. These factors include the size of the organization, the merchandise classification, the nature of the company, the manner in which business is transacted, the goals that have been established, the number of available staff assistants and associates, and the outside professional market specialists involved in product analysis.

Planning the purchases, making trips to the global marketplaces, vendor selection, communication with market specialists, price structuring, and interaction with in-house management teams are just some of the day-to-day responsibilities that buyers are called upon to perform. Each duty presents a different challenge and must be carefully addressed to guarantee that the end result will be the most profitable position for their company.

While most buyers are responsible for all of the aforementioned duties, it should be understood that buyers for brick-and-mortar retailers often are held accountable for tasks that their catalogue and Web site counterparts are not. Without selling floors, display windows, sales staffs, and "physical" departments to manage, the buyers employed off-site primarily concentrate on merchandise procurement. This is not to say that their roles are less challenging. On the contrary, the very nature of catalogues and Web sites makes the buyers' tasks formidable but different.

Keeping in mind the differences, the following overview offers a general account of the various roles played by professional buyers. Each of these areas is more fully examined in this and in other chapters.

Assortment Planning

A key duty of a store buyer is the planning of assortments prior to any purchases. The buyer must know exactly what the store's needs will be so that he or she can offer the "model stock" that will best serve customers and bring a profit to the company. The manner in which assortments are determined is discussed later in this chapter.

Purchasing

First and foremost for every buyer is the selection of merchandise that will ultimately be offered to the consumer. In order for the right items and assortments to be purchased, buying plans must be initiated. This involves careful scrutiny of the vendors in the field to make certain that the ones chosen provide the necessary cooperation to foster a good, professional relationship. It also involves careful selection of items in the suppliers' lines that will generate the greatest sales. The ability to negotiate the best prices and terms is also essential to successful purchasing.

The buyer is responsible for choosing the best merchandise available in the marketplace.

Merchandise Pricing

Because they operate in a competitive arena, buyers must be aware of their competitors' pricing on identical or similar merchandise. Although specific markups are necessary to bring a profit to the company, prices that are not in line with what other retailers are charging could be problematic. The expansion of the catalogue industry and the nature of online selling have helped to better educate the public on merchandise availability and prices. The ease with which consumers can compare prices by these two methods makes it even more important for brick-and-mortar buyers to price their offerings appropriately. Of course, such factors as image, product perishability, and buyer judgment each contribute to pricing.

Product Promotion

The use of advertising is important to the sale of much of a store's merchandise. It is the store buyers who are often responsible for the selection of the items to be advertised, promoted through special events, and visually merchandised. The buyer, by virtue of the fact that he or she is the product expert, is called upon to complete advertising request forms so that the right information will be presented to the public. Buyers are generally provided with 6-month advertising budgets that they must carefully manage in order for funds to be available to properly promote the goods in their departments.

In-House Department Management

Although fewer and fewer buyers are being held responsible for the management of store departments, some companies still make this a buyer responsibility. It is especially true in smaller stores where the buyers oversee the selling floor. When management centralization is part of the overall plan and buyers function from locations that are outside of the store, the in-store department responsibility is in the hands of department and assistant department managers. In the supermarket arena, buyers are never part of the store operations but instead utilize information from managers that is made available through faxes, e-mail, and other communication devices.

Interaction between the buyers and the in-store managers is regularly maintained so that purchasing can reflect the recommendations of those who interact with the customers.

Product Development

Major retailers of most merchandise classifications generally create private-label items as part of their overall product mixes. Whether it is apparel, wearable accessories, home fashions, or food, carrying one's own brands gives the retailer a degree of exclusivity. In many companies, the buyers are charged with the **product development** of items that are earmarked to become part of the overall inventory.

This concept has caught on with retailers across the country. The fundamentals of such programs, and the role that buyers play in their development, will be closely examined in Chapter 15.

PLANNING THE PURCHASE

Once a company has established its goals and parameters, those responsible for purchasing must follow them when buying decisions are made. Unless the company is a very small business—such as a boutique, where the buyer and proprietor are one and the same and purchasing decisions are made on the spot—there are guidelines that must be followed before any actual purchasing can be done.

Such preplanning includes the in-house tasks studying past sales records, forecasting sales, focusing on staff support interaction. It also involves outside assistance from industry professionals such as resident buyers, fashion forecasters, reporting service specialists, and the editorial staffs of retail trade and consumer periodicals.

Internal Planning Resources

Although the professional sources outside of the retail operation are important to most companies' functioning, none play a role as important as those available inside the business itself. Once these internal planning resources are addressed, the buyer generally focuses on the external group.

Past Sales Records

Nothing provides as much pertinent information in the area of buying as past sales records. The computer has made the study of past sales records much simpler than it was in the early days of retailing. Prior to the advent of computer-generated reports, retailers used a host of hand-recorded inventory methods to produce reports that would assist the buyer in gaining an insight into merchandise ordering and stock replenishment. With new technology providing detailed information based on past sales figures, buyers are better able to assess their merchandising needs for the future. At any time of the day, store purchasers can immediately access up-to-the-minute data that reflects sales experiences and trends.

With these reports in hand, information concerning vendor performance, price-point analysis, colors and sizes, and other pertinent areas serves as the basis of purchasing plans. Sales forecasts, either in whole or in part, are formed with the use of these reports.

Even though sophisticated reporting procedures have improved the usefulness of computerized reporting documents, buyers are prone to rely on other, more personalized sources of information during the planning stages.

Merchandise Management Input

Oftentimes, buyers call upon their supervisors to review their purchase plans. Since their superiors—namely the general and divisional merchandise managers—have come up from the buyer ranks, they are completely knowledgeable about the planning that their subordinates have undertaken. They can lend professional support with regard to adding new vendors, eliminating those suppliers who have served them in the past, analyzing future product trends, restructuring price points, and so forth. With their expertise, the buyer is more likely to proceed upon a buying path that will be beneficial to the company.

Staff Support

Many retail operations have management level personnel, in addition to senior merchandisers, who act as advisors to the buyers and merchandisers in the formulation of their purchasing plans. Fashion retailers, for example, often employ fashion directors whose responsibility it is to scout the market before the buyer enters it and to discover what trends will be at the forefront of the industry. Through visits to designers, vendor showrooms, textile mills, forecasting studios, and market specialists, helpful information can be obtained before any market visit is made.

Sometimes department managers serve as liaisons between buyers and customers. Through regular shopper contact, department managers and their sales teams are able to assess what's hot and what's not. Computer-generated reports are able to relate what has sold and in what quantities, but they cannot tell the buyer what items have been requested that weren't part of the inventory. The human factor plays an important part in preplanning and should be used to augment computer reports.

External Planning Assistance

Although the basis of planning is internally oriented, sources outside of the company also play a vital role in terms of future merchandise acquisition plans. There are many different types of market specialists who are under contract with retailers to keep them abreast of the industry climate and of any initiatives that will help them make better merchandising decisions. In addition, the editorial pages of consumer and trade publications, when examined thoroughly, also provide additional pertinent information.

Retail Consultants

In many retail classifications, especially those primarily engaged in fashion merchandise, there are numerous organizations that can supply a wealth of information to the retailer's buyers. Most notable are the **retail consultants**, formerly known as **resident buying offices**. Retail consultants collectively perform a host of activities that enable the retailer and its buying staff to make better decisions in the procurement of merchandise. Overall, the vast majority of these groups perform the following preplanning activities for their member merchants.

Retail consultants offer valuable advice to store buyers regarding the pulse of the market.

VENDOR ASSESSMENT

In retailing there are always new merchandise resources that come into the marketplace. Many just starting out are either too small to gain immediate recognition or are located in places where there is no convenient buyer access. The retail consultants, with their favorable locations inside the wholesale market, are able to scout these newcomers. After meeting with the vendors and examining their collections, they can report to their clients about the vendors' potential to become a merchandise resource. Because buyers are often preoccupied with what seems to be an endless array of chores, this service can help them study the new vendor without having to make time-consuming trips to its premises.

PRESCREENING LINES

Trips to the wholesale arena are challenging and time-consuming activities for most retail buyers. The time spent during the beginning of the purchasing period, known in many industries as **market week**, can be limited and insufficient for satisfactory visits to all the vendor showrooms trade expositions. In order to maximize the time spent in the market, the retail buyer often relies upon his or her **market consultant** or **resident buyer representative** to evaluate the lines and recommend those that seem worthy of adding to the merchant's product line. In this way, attention can be focused on the collections that seem to warrant the closest inspection.

EVALUATION OF MATERIALS' PRODUCTION

Each new season, especially in the soft goods arena, new materials are being readied for introduction to creative design teams and manufacturers. Although retailers have little to say in terms of which materials make their way into the actual products that will be designed, learning about them will help retailers better plan their merchandise assortments. Visits to mill and textile companies, leather processing plants, and other places of raw material conversion help consultants gain an overview of the next season's offerings. They can then alert the retail buyer to what's hot and what's not. In this way, the buyer will be ready to evaluate the manufacturer's and designer's lines in a more educated manner.

> **In the News . . .**
>
> "A Prominent Presence: Walking the Show Floor with Abby Doneger," an article that appears on page 338 at the end of this chapter, should be read now.

The Web site for Doneger, a major consulting firm, provides a description in Spanish of HDA, its international office.

INTERNATIONAL MARKET EVALUATION

With the ever expanding global merchandising opportunities available to today's merchants, no preplanning would be complete without a look at the vendors and merchandise being offered through international venues. Although buyers often visit overseas centers to make some of their purchases, often the preplanning phase doesn't include these on-site visits. The larger retail consultants maintain offices in many of the major international markets and call upon their representatives to provide market and merchandise overviews. With this information in hand, the brick-and-mortar, catalogue, and e-tailer buyers are able to determine whether visits to such purchasing arenas are necessary to their merchandise plans.

DEMOGRAPHIC ANALYSIS

Every merchant, particularly those that conduct their business exclusively via brick-and-mortar operations or who use other means to enhance these sales, are vitally interested in learning about any consumer changes that might affect their purchasing decisions. Such factors as population shifts, changes in the makeup of the potential consumer markets they serve, consumer spending patterns, and changes in lifestyles and tastes all contribute significantly to the buyer's ultimate purchasing decisions.

When such information provided by the retail consultants is carefully addressed, the buyer's merchandise plans will more likely bring favorable results to the company.

Focus on...
Barnard's Retail Consulting Group

KURT BARNARD, president of the consulting organization that bears his name, is an economist who for more than 40 years has specialized in the study of retailing and consumer behavior. He launched his firm in 1984 after serving as the founding CEO of the Federation of Apparel Manufacturers and CEO of the International Mass Retail Association.

Considered by many professionals to be one of the most important "voices" of retailing in America, his company is actively engaged in forecasting retail industry trends and consumer spending patterns, developing retail marketing strategies, and consulting with advertising agencies on retail industry issues and companies.

Buyers and merchandisers are made aware of the company's research by means of its Retail Trend Report. This publication is read by the management teams of more than 1,200 leading U.S. retailing chains, department stores, discount and specialty retailers, and shopping center developers. It is particularly valuable to retail buyers, who must be aware of trends in the field. Through its interpretation and analysis of these trends, merchandisers and buyers are able to steer clear of the hurdles that lie ahead.

The knowledge offered enables better focusing on ways to address the competitive nature of the industry. Buyers are equipped to understand the changes that are taking place in the economy and how they will affect future purchasing. With too many stores carrying too much of the same merchandise while battling for the customer's attention and share of the pocketbook, a thorough understanding of the problem enables better merchandise planning.

Specifically, the Barnard Consulting Group performs the following services for its client base:

- Economic analysis of consumer propensity to buy
- Development of marketing strategies
- Analysis and forecasts on consumer spending patterns
- Analysis and forecasts on changing consumer tastes and lifestyles
- Reports on what product lines will gain strength or weaken
- Competitive analysis of retail chains

The organization promises to answer the questions faced by management and merchandising teams in order to master the challenges in today's retail arena.

With its significant roster of clients, it is obvious that this is an invaluable resource for merchants to use in their problem solving.

Fashion Forecasters

Another important outside resource for fashion buyers are **fashion forecasters**. These groups, located in major fashion capitals all over the world, regularly scout the industry and bring back pertinent news to their clients. Buyers of fashion merchandise, especially those who

Fashion forecasters provide buyers with trend information based on industry research.

specialize in fashion-forward products, learn about trends as far as 18 months in advance of the selling season. By digesting this information, they are better able to assess which styles will be more than likely headed for customer acceptance, thus making their purchasing decisions more realistic.

Trade Publications

Numerous **trade publications** offer a wealth of information that helps to guide the buyer in his or her quest for up-to-the-minute news on products, vendors, and merchandise trends. They range from those that are published five days a week, such as *Women's Wear Daily*, to those that are published once a month, such as *Stores* magazine. These formats are the simplest and least expensive means of keeping pace with industry news. For the price of a subscription, buyers and merchandisers are able to get the latest scoop from editorial press coverage and the numerous vendor ads.

Consumer Newspapers and Magazines

These are also invaluable sources of information for the buyer. In their pages, writers often address such issues as the economy, new products on the horizon, merchandise recommendations, and the like, each of which can help the buyer better understand what consumers are likely to buy. The *New York Times* and other leading newspapers, as well as a host of magazines, are faithfully read by retailers so that they can learn what information is being fed to the consumer and how their purchases may be affected.

No source of information should be overlooked by the buyer. Each presents a different angle and slant and must be digested so that proper decision making will follow.

Trade publications such as *Women's Wear Daily* provide buyers with up-to-the-minute news about segments of the apparel industry.

Development of Assortments

Once the internal and external sources needed to formulate the buying plan have been reviewed, the buyer is ready to embark upon the task of developing the merchandise mix most likely to maximize the company's profits.

One of the initial undertakings is to produce an all-encompassing merchandise plan that will incorporate all the essential products to satisfy the customer's needs. The outline that is produced is known as the **model stock**. It includes the breadth and depth of the merchandise offerings for each of the product classifications for which the buyer is responsible. It is a complex blueprint that addresses the organization's goals and the merchandise needed to achieve them. The better the plan is formulated, the more likely it will lead to realizing projected sales.

In the model stock plan, the buyers must address elements that are both qualitative and quantitative in nature. That is, they must know *what to buy, how much to buy, from whom to buy*, and *when to buy*.

What to Buy

In companies that deal with **staple merchandise**—that is, products that are ordered over and over again without seasonal or fashion considerations—the decision is less problematic. Buyers of groceries such as canned goods, as well as those who purchase small appliances or some hosiery, are not terribly concerned with consumer buying patterns. On the other hand, buyers and merchandisers who are charged with the responsibility of purchasing for fashion or

Stores	GM%		Aug	Sep	Oct	Nov	Dec	Jan	Fall Total/Feb BOM	YTD Total/ act% to plan sis Fall
74	26.7	Actual Sales	1.6	1.2	1.3	2.8	3.8	1.3	12.0	12.0
		Planned Sales	2.7	2.1	1.8	2.3	5.0	1.1	15.0	80.1%
		BOM INV	6.2	4.6	16.8	19.1	18.9	12.4	16.4	
		Planned BOM INV	12.9	15.2	14.5	15.7	17.2	15.4	14.7	
141	19.7	Actual Sales	1.2	1.7	1.7	3.9	6.7	3.1	18.3	18.3
		Planned Sales	2.9	3.5	1.7	3.4	6.8	1.0	19.3	94.6%
		BOM INV	10.3	15.2	25.9	33.1	30.7	20.2	20.9	
		Planned BOM INV	17.5	18.4	16.2	18.9	22.0	14.5	11.8	
142	2.1	Actual Sales	1.5	1.3	0.8	1.9	2.5	1.5	9.6	9.6
		Planned Sales	2.7	2.1	1.8	2.3	5.0	1.1	15.0	63.8%
		BOM INV	12.3	10.7	16.8	19.6	18.7	14.3	17.8	
		Planned BOM INV	12.9	15.2	14.5	15.7	17.2	15.4	11.8	
202	14.7	Actual Sales	2.6	2.6	1.9	3.6	4.6	1.2	16.5	16.5
		Planned Sales	3.2	2.5	2.1	2.7	5.9	1.5	17.9	92.4%
		BOM INV	10.8	8.4	24.8	32.2	26.4	18.1	20.2	
		Planned BOM INV	12.9	14.7	13.6	14.5	15.6	12.9	11.8	
239	4.8	Actual Sales	0.9	1.0	0.6	1.5	3.2	1.3	8.5	8.5
		Planned Sales	2.7	2.1	1.8	2.3	5.0	1.1	15.0	56.7%
		BOM INV	10.0	9.0	15.2	18.0	17.4	12.2	13.7	
		Planned BOM INV	12.9	15.2	14.5	15.7	17.2	15.4	11.8	
534	29.1	Actual Sales	1.2	1.8	1.5	3.2	5.0	1.1	13.8	13.8
		Planned Sales	3.2	2.5	2.1	2.7	5.9	1.5	17.9	77.0%
		BOM INV	8.8	7.8	21.0	26.3	23.2	15.1	14.1	
		Planned BOM INV	12.9	14.7	13.6	14.5	15.6	12.9	16.0	
		Tot Actual Sales	9.0	9.7	7.9	16.9	25.8	9.5	78.7	78.7
		Tot Planned Sales	17.4	14.8	11.3	15.7	33.6	7.3	100.1	78.6%
	July	Tot BOM INV	58.4	55.7	120.4	148.3	135.2	92.3	103.1	0.0
	eom margin	Planned BOM INV	82.0	93.4	86.9	95.0	104.8	86.5	77.9	0.0
	17.3	Margin%	21.3%	21.8%	23.2%	17.0%	18.2%			

Reports of past sales help buyers plan future purchases.

seasonally oriented product classifications rely heavily on the information generated from past sales reports and other sources.

Printouts are routinely obtained by even the smallest entrepreneurs, who can study them before making future buying decisions. Brick-and-mortar operations, especially those that are of medium size or larger, are privy to information that is fed into the computer every time a purchase is made. Through the use of scanners or other technological means, data regarding prices, styles, and colors are immediately recorded and available in the numerous merchandise reports. Catalogue companies and e-tailers also utilize the latest in technology to record their sales and make the information available to the buying team that will make the new purchases.

In addition to giving the buyer information about specific products, automated systems also reveal such information as the time it took for a product to sell once it became part of the inventory, the percentage of the assortment that sold at full price, the amount of merchandise marked down for disposal, and a profile of each vendor in terms of its product's performance.

With all of this information in hand, the buyer can begin to lay out the plans for new purchases. This, of course, is insufficient for complete decision-making plans.

Many sources external to the company—some of which have already been mentioned—also provide additional pertinent information. The recommendations of market specialists and the editorial press, for example, provide economic forecasts, overviews of fashion forecaster predictions, and anything else that might help with the buyer's final decisions. Companies like the Doneger Group, for example, provide information to their clients concerning hot items and new resources. Available either through mailings or online, the information is up-to-date and can help the buyer quickly alter purchasing plans. *Chain Store Age, Stores, Women's Wear Daily*, regional publications such as the *California Apparel News*, and others all contribute their take on the state of the industry and how buyers might approach the next purchasing season.

Other external sources of information include governmental reports on the state of the nation—such as the census, which is taken every 10 years—and trade association findings that could affect the nature of future purchasing.

How Much to Buy

Once the data concerning qualitative considerations have been digested and a merchandise concept for the next purchasing period has been put in place, quantitative considerations are the next factors to consider in the planning phase.

Buyers are appropriated specific dollar amounts to spend on merchandise. The sum comes from the buyer's superior, the divisional merchandise manager if the company has an extensive merchandising division, from an owner if the business is a small venture, or from some other intermediary depending on how the operation is organized. In any of these cases, the amount earmarked for purchasing must be translated into different product classifications, with attention focused on ensuring that every product category is adequately covered to satisfy shopper needs. Retail sales forecasts, company plans for expansion or curtailment of the merchandise classifications in question, and economic indicators generally direct the amounts that will be given to the buyer to spend.

In times when unemployment is on the increase, there might be a tendency to spend less on career apparel. Similarly, if times are prosperous then more dollars might be expended for luxury items. There is no hard-and-fast rule in terms of what dollar amounts will be available to the buyer.

It should be understood that in every retail organization there is always merchandise available for sale. Companies do not completely sell off their entire inventory before they replenish the stock. Each and every day, companies sell goods to the consumer and replace them with newly arrived items. New merchandise is always being bought by the buying teams whether those purchases involve goods that warrant reordering or consist of entirely different products that will be added to the inventory.

Thus, buying is an ongoing process that requires constant attention by the retailer's purchasing staff. Although many retailing segments place the bulk of their orders during specific time periods, many days in the year will be used to add newer products. The most difficult problem for buying professionals is to maintain a merchandise level that doesn't cost more than the allocated funds. In order to best control their inventories, buyers utilize a concept known as **open to buy**.

Technically, open to buy is the difference between the merchandise needed for a particular selling period and the merchandise that is available. This concept considers not only the amount of **merchandise on hand** but also the **merchandise commitments** already made by the buyer. Thus, if a buyer is restricted to $100,000 for a particular time frame and has $60,000 on hand and $40,000 on order, there is no money left for that purchasing period. Keep in mind, however, that sales are made constantly in many large organizations, changing the dollar amounts in the inventory. Therefore, it is easy to see that the open-to-buy amount changes virtually every time a sale is made.

It should also be understood that, in most retail operations, the merchandise needed for a particular period changes. Holiday seasons warrant greater inventories whereas sale times require less. To achieve proper inventory levels, the buyer—in conjunction with his or her supervisor—must plan accordingly to have the proper merchandise levels needed to meet consumer demand.

Open to Buy

Month: May
Dept 370 Moderate Collections

							Plan Purchases							
						Net Receipts	27.8	30.2	15.2	24.9	6.9	8.2	13.3	12.0
Vendor	P.O. Number	Ship Date	Cancel Date	MU %	Total Units	Total $	Description	141	142	202	239	149	151	463	490
IZOD	320448805	4/25	5/25	64.3	2284	95.9	Microfiber Short	3.5	3.5	3.5	3.5	2.2	2.2	2.2	2.2
								84	84	84	84	52	52	52	52
IZOD	622710903	4/25	5/25	62.1	720	20.9	Swim	3.5	3.5	3.5	3.5	2.3			
cancelled 4/7 re-approved 4/27							120	120	120	120	80				
IZOD	420448803	4/25	5/25	62.5	3432	164.7	Golf	7.3	7.3	7.3	7.3	4.6	3.5	3.5	3.5
JULIAN	668245802	4/25	5/15	69.8	2238	85.8	Father's Day Promo	6.4	3.9	5.1	5.1	2.6		3.9	5.1
BUNGALOW	282827808	4/25	5/25	63.6	6300	216.1	May Fashion	7.4	7.4	7.4	7.4	6.0	4.4	7.4	6.0
								222	222	222	222	174	126	222	174
BUNGALOW	754091903	4/25	5/25	58.7	882	17.6	T-Shirt Reorders	0.7	0.7	0.7	0.7	0.6	0.4	0.7	0.6
								36	36	36	36	30	18	36	30
IZOD	811780907	4/25	5/25	64.3	1738	73.0	Merc. Knit	4.0	4.0	4.0	4.0	1.8	1.8	2.2	2.7
cancelled 4/7 re-approved 5/01							96	96	96	96	42	42	52	64	
BUNGALOW	936578800	4/25	5/25	58.3	822	39.5	Bedford Cord MF Pant	1.2	1.2	0.9	1.2	1.2	0.9	1.2	1.2
								24	24	18	24	24	18	24	24
Total								32.8	30.3	31.5	31.5	20.1	12.3	19.9	20.1
OTB								-5.0	-0.1	-16.3	-6.6	-13.2	-4.1	-6.6	-8.1

Computerized open-to-buy records give buyers current information about inventory and funds available for further purchases. Part of an open-to-buy report is shown here.

In each of these cases, planned inventories and sales figures are determined from which the buyer must calculate his or her open to buy. The following example illustrates this concept.

On February 1, the ladies shoe buyer for Bentley's Emporium wanted to determine how much money was available for additional purchases for the time period that would end on February 28. Her figures revealed the following:

Merchandise on hand	$216,000
Merchandise on order (commitments)	$ 54,000
Planned end of month inventory	$270,000
Planned sales	$108,000
Planned markdowns	$ 9,000

What was the shoe buyer's open to buy on February 1?

Merchandise needed for February
planned end-of-month inventory	$270,000
planned sales	$108,000
planned markdowns	$ 9,000
Total merchandise needed	$387,000

Merchandise available (June 1)
merchandise on hand	$216,000
merchandise on order (commitments)	$ 54,000
Merchandise available	$270,000

Merchandise needed − Merchandise available = Open to buy
$387,000 − $270,000 = $117,000 OTB

The open-to-buy calculation can be performed at any time, not only at the beginning of the month. It can also be quickly calculated by inputting the buyer's actual figures into a specialized computer program.

Buyers need to stay within their open-to-buy parameters for a number of reasons, including supervisory merchandisers' mandates and the need to avoid overbuying, which often leads to unplanned, high markdowns. Of course, even the best planning can not account for unforeseen conditions. When plans call for specific purchasing levels and then something unpredictable occurs that affects the planning—such as the terrorist attacks on the United States on September 11, 2001—significant markdowns might be warranted. The 2000 Christmas selling season was expected by most merchants to exceed the previous year's sales figures. Given an upbeat economy, buyers' purchasing plans called for larger inventories. However, with a sudden economic downturn and looming threats of a recession, higher sales never materialized for most retail companies. The vast majority of retailers had to take significant markdowns to move goods and make way for new products.

Major retail entities have their own in-house staffs to examine purchasing and sales information pertinent to determining open-to-buy levels, but their smaller counterparts generally do not have this level of resources. In such cases, outside companies are available to help. One such company is OTB Retail Systems, which offers an online system for retailers of all sizes. By logging on to their Web site, www.otb-retail.com, a potential user can get a firsthand look at the system they employ.

After learning about such benefits of open-to-buy calculations as proper inventory levels, higher returns, reduced markdowns, and increased cash flow, the user is taken through a number of different screens that will help to produce a better profit picture. The first screens deal with eliminating buying confusion, the prevention of overbuying, and reduction in markdowns—each of which can help improve the company's **bottom line**. Next, individual statements featuring a plan to set up departments, projected stock turn rates, ideal inventory levels, inventory comparisons between the actual and projected figures, and projected markdowns lead to the final open-to-buy calculation.

Programs like this enable less experienced retailers to grasp the importance of open to buy in their quest to maximize profits.

From Whom to Buy

With the **qualitative** and **quantitative decisions** now made, the buyer must perform yet another task on the road to developing a viable **buying plan**. There are numerous resources from whom to buy merchandise, including tried-and-true suppliers as well as newcomers to the playing field. Even those that have been mainstays of a buyer's vendor list do not always continue to be used as a supply source if their track records have been negative in the past selling period. To determine whether those presently being used should remain as suppliers, an evaluation of each one's recent record must be undertaken.

Vendors' lines must be assessed regularly to make certain their goods fit into the buyer's plans.

The research involved for the study of regularly used vendors is relatively simple. Sales records for each vendor are examined to see whether sales numbers were achieved and the maintained markups were as expected. Those that pass the test are likely to remain part of the resource roster, whereas those that haven't proved to be successful will likely be eliminated from further purchasing consideration.

Before a purchasing strategy can be finalized in terms of resource selection, it is necessary to review the different classifications of vendors from whom merchandise can be procured. Typically, product acquisition is made from one or more of many supplier groups. These include manufacturers, full-service and limited-function wholesalers, rack jobbers, retailer-owned production companies, market specialists, and private-label producers. The nature of the retail operation generally dictates from which of these classifications purchasing will be made. Appliance retailers most often buy from wholesalers, while fashion merchants generally use manufacturers for their merchandise. Retailers who sell greeting cards and stationery rely on rack jobbers. **Rack jobbers** are actually wholesalers that provide a number of services to retailers such as on-site inventory adjustments.

Table 14.1 lists **purchasing channels** and the merchandise that is typically obtained from these resources.

It should be understood that the merchants are not restricted to just one supply group. Different circumstances could contribute to their using some from which they wouldn't ordinarily purchase. For example, manufacturers generally require minimum orders for their merchandise. If a particular item is needed in a smaller quantity then the purchase would be made from a wholesaler, whose order requirements are less stringent.

Having decided which current vendors should be used and which should be eliminated, the buyer must always be ready to bring new ones on board. It might be a supplier whose products are unique or whose prices are better than the rest of the field. Before any new relationships are established, it is essential to assess the companies and their ability to make deliveries as promised. Retailers who subscribe to market specialist organizations, such as resident buying offices and reporting agencies, or are members of trade associations are in the best position to

TABLE 14.1
RETAILER SUPPLIERS AND PRODUCTS OFFERED

Suppliers	Products
Manufacturer	Apparel, wearable accessories, home fashions
Full-service wholesaler	Appliances, food products
Limited-function wholesaler	Major and small appliances
Rack jobber	Greeting cards, paperback books, stationery supplies
Retailer-owned production company	Private brand merchandise
Market specialist	Private label fashion items for clients affiliated with resident buying offices
Private label producer	Products made for the exclusive use of individual retailers

promptly evaluate new resources. These groups are always interacting with manufacturers and other suppliers and are therefore in a position to determine their potential as good vendors. Trade paper perusal is also a means of learning about new resources. Those that seem likely to succeed are often written up in these publications.

Geographic location is another consideration when selecting a resource. If the manufacturer is domestically based, faster receipt of goods is more likely than if the production is done overseas. Today, however, the bulk of merchandise such as clothing, accessories, furniture, and the like is outsourced offshore, giving the retailer little choice in terms of purchasing venues. When time is of the essence, as is the case with most fashion merchandise, prompt delivery is a factor to consider. Of course, placing orders earlier than required will generally alleviate delivery problems.

While off-shore suppliers sometimes offer merchandise that is unique and priced lower than what can be obtained in this country, it is important to consider that there will be a **landed cost**.

Unlike goods that are produced and bought in the United States and sold at specific wholesale prices, goods that are produced in overseas venues have a number of add-ons that actually increase their cost to a retailer. For example, many items are **dutiable**—that is, they have **tariffs** applied to the original price that can increase the cost by as much as 50 percent. Additional costs are added for commission fees, insurance, shipping, and so forth. Thus, an item that is initially priced at $50 can actually cost the retailer $100! Another factor that affects the wholesale price is the fluctuation of the dollar. Every day the value of the American dollar fluctuates against foreign currencies. During volatile periods there might be a great deal of change that can severely affect the price of goods. The dollar fluctuation coupled with the landed costs can place merchandise outside the range the retailer is able to charge to bring a profit to the company. This is not to say that global purchasing should be abandoned. It is just that extreme caution must be exercised whenever these purchases are made.

When to Buy

Timing the purchase is a critical part of the planning stage. If goods are purchased too soon and are placed on the selling floor before they are actually needed, their early arrival will affect the buyer's **stock turnover rate** (to be discussed later in the chapter). If the merchandise arrives later than needed, it will most likely result in lost sales. It is thus the buyer's responsibility to time purchases carefully so that they will be available exactly when their customers expect them.

Silver Edition Spring 20XX 6 Month Flow Plan							
ASST A	Feb	Mar	Apr	May	June	July	TTL
BOM	25.0	28.3	31.1	33.5	35.7	27.7	181.2
SALES	2.5	3.3	2.8	4.3	10.0	2.3	25.0
	10.0%	13.0%	11.0%	17.0%	40.0%	9.0%	100.0%
PURCHASES	6.8	7.3	6.3	8.1	6.0	7.0	41.5
	16.4%	17.6%	15.2%	19.5%	14.5%	16.9%	100.0%
MARKDOWNS	1.0	1.3	1.1	1.7	4.0	0.9	10.0
EOM	28.3	31.1	33.5	35.7	27.7	31.5	31.3

Average Invty 30.4
Turnover 1.22
Markdown % 40%
Stores: 74, 109, 141, 534

The 6-month flow plan provides information about the value of inventory at the beginning and end of each month.

The actual decisions for when purchases should be made are based on several factors such as the amount of production time needed, the time it takes to physically deliver the goods, when the goods are needed on the selling floor, and what (if any) discounts are awarded for early delivery.

In some retail segments, such as those that sell fashion merchandise, orders are placed as much as 6 months in advance of their need on the selling floor. For foreign-produced items, the lead time might be from 9 months to a year. The actual timing comes from the buyer's past experience and the standard industry practices. A **flow plan** helps the buyer keep track of these factors.

VISITING THE MARKET TO MAKE THE PURCHASE

Armed with all of the preplanned information, the buyer is ready to embark upon the actual purchasing of the merchandise. Many buyers choose to visit wholesale markets in their quest for the season's latest offerings, while others opt for alternative methods of merchandise procurement. In retail organizations like department stores and specialty chains, where fashion merchandise is their forte, trips to the marketplace are the order of the day, especially when a new season is dawning. In supermarkets and other operations where staple goods are the main products, ordering is usually done at the company's home offices through vendor visits. For other merchants, the goods may be bought in the store from **road sales staffs**. Still others may use online resources to fill their merchandise requirements.

A trip to the market often takes approximately one week and involves numerous meetings with market specialists and vendors. In order to accomplish the desired goal, the buyer must make an itinerary that details the arrangements before leaving his or her home base. The plans include arranging for travel, hotels, and appointment scheduling.

Market Week Visits

In many merchandise classifications, specific periods of time are set aside each year when new lines of merchandise are previewed for the retail buyers. In arenas all around the globe,

Itinerary for: Donna Lombardo													
Travel to: New York Holiday Market													
Sun	**04/09**	**Mon**	**04/10**	**Tues**	**04/11**	**Wed**	**04/12**	**Thurs**	**04/13**	**Fri**	**04/14**		
8:30		8:30		8:30		8:30		8:00		8:00			
								8:30	Greg Norman 609 5th Ave b/w 40th & 6th ave	8:30	Recap meeting		
9:00		9:00	IZOD 200 Madison Ave b/w 35th & 6th	9:00	Perry Ellis 1114 Ave of Amer b/w 5th & 6th	9:00	Claiborne 1441 Broadway 212-777-3456	9:00		9:00			
10:00		10:00	16th floor 212-777-3456	10:00	36th floor 212-777-3456	10:00		10:00		10:00			
11:00		11:00		11:00		11:00		11:00		11:00			
12:00		12:00	Alexander Julian 1350 6th Ave b/w 55th & 6th	12:00		12:00		12:00		12:00			
1:00		1:00	12th floor 212-777-3456	1:00		1:00		1:00	Cutter & Buck 80 w 40th Ave & 6th 212-777-3456	1:00			
2:00		2:00		2:00	Bungalow Brand 1071 Ave of Amer 11th floor 212-777-3456	2:00		2:00		2:00			
3:00		3:00 3:30	Ashworth Warwick Hotel 65 E. 54th Street 212-777-3456	3:00		3:00	Chaps 90 Park Ave b/w 39th & 40th 12th flr 212-777-3456	3:00		3:00			
4:00		4:00		4:00		4:00		4:00	J Khaki N44 140 57th Street b/w 6 & 7th 212-777-3456	4:00			
5:00		5:00		5:00		5:00		5:00		5:00			
		IZOD dinner		Perry dinner		Claiborne dinner		Cutter & Buck dinner					

Itineraries for market visits are preplanned to make sure the buyer will see all the important vendors and other resources.

vendors ready their lines and hold their collective breath awaiting the buyers' arrival. The pace during market week is hectic, with buyers converging from many parts of the world in the hope of finding just the right merchandise mixes to bring profits to their companies.

In order to maximize the effectiveness of these ventures, most buyers first arrange meetings with outside retail specialists who will help them address the merchandise selection problems that lie ahead. Most often, retailers of soft goods (and some who buy hard goods) enjoy affiliations with market consulting groups such as resident buying offices or with those in expanded roles from purchasing specialists to generalists advising on every aspect of retailing. The largest of these advisory groups that support retailers is the Doneger group.

Focus on...
The Doneger Group

FOUNDED IN 1946 BY HENRY DONEGER, this company has gone on to become the largest of its type in the world. It originally served as a resident buying office for women's specialty retailers in the United States. Today the company counts as its members department stores, family apparel stores, mass merchandisers, and discounters in America and in many overseas nations.

In 1980, the company was one of 50 buying offices that all offered similar types of service and information. Today, the Doneger Group is considered by most retailing professionals to be the most dynamic resident buying office and fashion consulting firm in the industry. The company advises hundreds of retailers on merchandising concepts and specific trends and offers sourcing capabilities and a breadth of other opportunities. With more than 7,000 retail locations served throughout the world, Doneger generates annual sales of more $25 billion.

Although the organization began as one oriented toward women's apparel and accessories, it now also specializes in men's and children's apparel, accessories for the family, and home furnishings. In meeting its obligation of providing the best information to their retail clients, the company provides a great deal of services to help clients make the right merchandising decisions and meet the ever changing challenges of the fashion and retail business. The ultimate Doneger goal is to help retailers generate greater sales, increase profits, and gain market share.

Located in the heart of the **garment center** in New York City, the company's ten divisions are supported by a staff of industry experts with years of experience in market research, merchandising, and trend forecasting.

When buyers come to Doneger headquarters in preparation for market visits, there are many individual conference and presentation rooms in which they can meet with company executives and preview the merchandise highlights for the season. Individual client work areas are also available when the need arises for a quiet space in which to rework plans. Augmented by an art department that prepares advertising layouts for in-staff and client use, a digital photography studio that can quickly record images of merchandise, and in-house print production rooms that can generate varied direct-mail pieces, the company is a comprehensive resource for retailers who must make merchandising decisions.

A relatively new addition to the services already offered by the company is the Doneger Web site. It was launched to provide clients with access to the company's market research and analysis efforts, product recommendations, and trend forecasting. In addition, the site offers manufacturers the opportunity to present products to retailers in a virtual showroom via the Internet. The Internet service also provides newsletters, merchandising concepts, market overviews, new resources, key item identification, reorder activity, and special offerings.

Buying Venues

Buyers have a number of different places in which to preview collections and make their buying decisions. These include permanent vendor showrooms, trade expositions, and temporary selling facilities.

Permanent Vendor Showrooms

Designers and manufacturers maintain selling environments in many parts of the globe. They are housed within buildings that are located in the wholesale markets or in special marts. The Chicago Apparel Mart is one such merchandising tower in which buyers from the Midwest may shop the lines. In New York City, the major wholesale market for fashion merchandise in the world, the garment center—often referred to as Seventh Avenue—stretches for many streets and houses the collections of a large number of producers. Each building is typically occupied by vendors offering similarly priced items within a given merchandise classification. This enables visiting buyers to more quickly cover the lines in which they are interested. Often these selling arenas are also home to the creative teams that design the lines.

Permanent vendor showrooms are found in all major markets and often occupy entire buildings.

Trade Expositions

Many product classifications are found in various **trade expositions**, or trade shows, around the world. In places like Las Vegas, home to one of the largest of these expositions, WWD MAGIC, buyers are able to screen the lines of vendors they are already using in their merchandise assortments and also evaluate new manufacturers' collections. This format enables the purchasing agents to cover an entire market without going from one building to another.

Other trade shows are regularly held all over the world and represent a wealth of different products. Some are based in one location, while others are presented in different locales to attract local buyers. More information about these shows can be obtained by accessing their Web sites. Tables 14.2 and 14.3 list a number of trade expositions that attract buyers from all over the world as well as some of the locations in which they may be seen.

Temporary Facilities

Some manufacturers operate relatively small businesses and cannot afford the costs of a permanent showroom. Instead, they opt to lease temporary spaces during peak selling periods. Some of the merchandise marts and commercial hotels in a city offer space to these companies on a limited basis. At other times such vendors try to sell their lines through resident buying offices and by calling on the retailers in their places of operation.

The buyer then visits the companies, screens the lines, and records all observations before any ordering is completed. This approach is necessary so that every line may be considered prior to any purchasing decision.

Trade expositions are held throughout the world. The show seen here took place in Spain.

TABLE 14.2
SELECTED DOMESTIC TRADE SHOWS

Exposition (Category)	City	Web Site
Georgia Bridal Show	Duluth	www.eliteevents.com
FFany Collections (shoes)	New York	www.ffany.org
WSA Show (shoes/accessories)	Las Vegas	www.wsashow.com
Designers & Agents	New York	www.wesignersandagents.com
Nouveau Collective (men's)	New York	www.noveaucollectivetradeshows.com
Moda Manhattan (apparel)	New York	www.modamanhattan.com
Lingerie Americas	New York	www.lingerie-americas.com
Intermezzo Collections	New York	www.enkshows.com
Printsource New York (fabric)	New York	www.printsourcenewyork.com
ECO Trade Show (apparel)	Las Vegas	www.globalecosghow.com
Kid Show (children's)	Las Vegas	www.spectrade.com
WWDMAGIC (women's)	Las Vegas	www.magiconline.com
Imprinted Sportswear Show	Atlanta	www.issshows.com
Shoe Market of the Americas	Miami Beach	www.smota.com
Sole Commerce (shoes)	New York	www.enkshows.com
Swimshow	Miami Beach	www.swimshow.com
Chicago Shoe Expo's Footwear and Accessories Show	Chicago	www.chicagoshoeexpo.com

TABLE 14.3
SELECTED INTERNATIONAL TRADE SHOWS

Exposition (Category)	City	Web Site
São Paulo Fashion Week (women's wear)	São Paulo	www.saopaulofashionweek.com.br
Pitti Immagine Uom (men's)	Florence	www.pittimmagine.com
Milan Fashion Week (men's)	Milan	www.cameramoda.it
Paris Fashion Week (men's)	Paris	www.modeparis.com
Tranoi Homme (men's)	Paris	www.tranoi.com
Munich Fashion Fair (men's)	Munich	www.munichfashionfair.de
Premium Berlin (women's)	Berlin	www.premiumexhibitions.com
SIMM (jeans/sportswear)	Madrid	www.semanamoda.ifema.es
ISPO RUSSIA (athletic wear)	Moscow	www.isporussia.com
ITKIB Turkish Fashion Fabric Exhibition	London	www.itkib.org.tr
Ready to Show (apparel)	Milan	www.readytoshow.it
Who's Next (men's/women's)	Paris	www.whosnext.com
Le Cuir a Paris (leather/fur)	Paris	www.lecuiraparis.com
CASABO HOMME (men's)	Paris	www.pretparis.Com
Hong Kong Fashion Week (apparel)	Hong Kong	www.hkfashionweekss.com

ALTERNATE METHODS OF MERCHANDISE PROCUREMENT

Although market visits are considered to be the best way to evaluate the state of the market and to screen available lines, the extent of buyer duties and responsibilities might prohibit such excursions except in the case of new season openings. The distance from these wholesale centers to the buyer's home bases also makes frequent visits difficult to work into the schedule.

In order to avail themselves of a continuous flow of new goods, retail buyers resort to on-premise meetings with road sales staffs as well as catalogues and business-to-business Internet Web sites.

In-House Buying

Most manufacturers and wholesalers maintain either their own road sales staff or contract with **manufacturer's representatives** to make regular visits to retail operations. The former group is a part of the producer's company while the latter is an independent seller who may represent several different manufacturers. In either case, the purpose is to get to those clients who have not visited the marketplace or to **cold canvass** for new accounts.

In addition to not having sufficient time for firsthand market coverage, some buyers prefer purchasing from these road sellers because the lines they represent have usually been pared down to leave only the best sellers in the collection. Those who travel from retailer to retailer usually do so after the new lines have been presented during the aforementioned market weeks. During these periods, the collections are first shown in their entirety, whereafter a gradual weeding out takes place. Only those items that have captured the attention of the buyers remain. Thus, when the sales reps hit the road, they take with them only those products that have the best chance for success with the consuming public. Therefore, buyers who opt for purchasing in-house are shown only the potential winners and need not make judgments on the entire line that was first presented.

Of course, waiting to buy after the initial market showings often leads to later deliveries. Since the earlier purchasers have the opportunity to receive their goods first, later purchasers must wait a little longer. When time is of the essence in terms of delivery, as is the case with many fashion-forward retailers, visits to the market at the very start of the selling season is the only way to guarantee timely delivery.

Catalogues

Many lines that are sold to retailers are done so through catalogues. Products for the home, for example, are often marketed in this manner. Manufacturers and wholesalers publish catalogues that accurately describe their offerings.

Many buyers prefer this manner of ordering because it allows them to do so during their own time frames. As previously discussed, market visits are time-consuming and visits by reps may come at inopportune times. Yet, catalogues may be examined at any time that suits the buyer.

The disadvantages of catalogue ordering include the potential for the actual product to differ somewhat from what was ordered and that buyers do not have the opportunity to have their questions answered. Of course, contact with the sales reps is always possible via telephone, fax, or e-mail.

One of the major clearinghouses, RetailExchange.com is a business-to-business Web site that helps buyers find off-price merchandise.

Business-to-Business Web Sites

Today's technology makes purchasing easier than ever before. Just as a wave of consumers is making use of the Internet for their personal needs, professional buyers are also using online purchasing at **business-to-business Web sites** for merchandise acquisition. Many manufacturers, wholesalers, retail consultants, and surplus sellers have Web sites that retailers may log on to and buy the merchandise being offered.

In the closeout arena, www.tradeout.com, the world's leading online business surplus marketplace, offers a wealth of products to merchants that include apparel, computer products, food and beverage items, health and beauty products, and housewares. Buyers simply log on to the Web site and access the product classification in which they are interested. A computer retailer might wish to view any one of a particular group of merchandise that TradeOut has available. After examining the availability list—which includes the seller name, the quantity remaining, the regular price, and the end date by which the merchandise must be sold—the potential buyer types in a bid and finds out if he or she has been sold the merchandise. The system is similar to that used by consumers on the eBay Web site, but this site is restricted to professional merchants who can buy in large quantities.

TradeOut offers its buyers a number of different advantages. These include service, side-by-side price comparisons, and an enormous product offering—all without additional cost to the buyer.

Another major **clearinghouse** is www.Retailexchange.com. Unlike the auction businesses, this company provides a managed negotiation format that lets the purchaser negotiate and control all of the terms of the deal. The Web site provides sales team assistants who take purchasers through every step of the buying process. It is the fastest way for clients to access the world's largest selection of off-price consumer goods in 16 categories from the world's most prominent vendors.

A visit to www.doneger.com reveals a number of unique buyer online services, the newest of which allows buyers to screen the lines of numerous resources. By clicking on the Marketplace Exhibition Center, retail buyers are able to view digital images of products through **virtual showrooms**. Users are able to select a particular manufacturer or product category to review for style, color, sizing, price, and delivery information. They can build and edit a line sheet as they shop the various manufacturers' collections, creating a merchandise assortment tailored to their specific company's needs.

Virtual showrooms act as extensions of the physical showrooms and are readily available for those who are too busy to make in-person trips to the market.

The doneger.com site is used by clients who pay a fee for all of the company's services. Retailers who are not Doneger members can visit the showrooms as guests of a manufacturer who is a member. Each user is assigned a log-in number as well as a password that enables them to access the site.

The Doneger online directory guides users to a variety of company services and allows buyers to view virtual images of products.

NEGOTIATING THE PURCHASE

Once the buyer has shopped the market and narrowed the offerings to fit allocated dollar amounts, it is time to consummate the deal. This is not simply a matter of selecting the items that seem to fit the buyer's needs; the process may also include price negotiation and a discussion of shipping terms, delivery dates, and chargebacks.

Price Negotiation

The price that is quoted by vendors is sometimes negotiable. But even when suppliers are willing to give clients special price considerations, they are generally prohibited from doing so by the **Robinson–Patman Act**. This federal legislation was enacted to limit price discrimination and to protect small businesses from the industrial giants who would otherwise be charged lower prices. Under the law, all buyers must pay the same price except when:

- The price reduction is made to meet competition.
- The price is reduced because savings result from sales to particular customers.
- The merchandise is damaged or is part of a **closeout**—an assortment of end-of-season merchandise that the vendor sells at reduced prices.

Working within this framework, the seasoned buyer may be able to agree on a better price for the merchandise by taking discounts for prompt payment, quantities, early acceptance of merchandise, advertising, and promotion.

Purchase Order Worksheet									
Vendor: Greg Norman		Dept#: 376		Start Ship: A/O		Terms: N30			
Vendor #: 3201501		PO #: TBD		Cancel: 01/25		OTB Month: Jan 5			
STYLE #	DESCRIPTION	TTL PER STYLE	COLOR	UNIT COST	UNIT RETAIL	MKUP%	ASST 1 UNITS	COST	ASST 1 RETAIL
GNS9J004	Microfiber Crew Neck Windshirt	170	401—Navy	$23.40	$78.00	70.0%	12	$281	$936
GNS9J004	Microfiber Crew Neck Windshirt	170	604—Red	$23.40	$78.00	70.0%	12	$281	$936
GNS0J010	Microfiber Full Zip (Reversible Jacket)	170	614—Black	$32.40	$110.00	70.5%	12	$389	$1,320
GNS0J011	Nylon Full Zip Jacket	142	328—Hunter	$22.20	$75.00	70.4%	10	$222	$750
GNS0J011	Nylon Full Zip Jacket	142	401—Navy	$22.20	$75.00	70.4%	10	$222	$750
GNS0J011	Nylon Full Zip Jacket	80	423—Royal	$22.20	$75.00	70.4%	10	$222	$750
GNH0J060	Windshirt "Windstopper" 1/2 Zip	40	001—Black	$26.40	$88.00	70.0%	8	$211	$704
		914					74	$1,828	$6,146
						Extension	370	$9,138	$30,730

The purchase order worksheet summarizes the details of the purchase. A portion of a worksheet is shown here.

Prompt Payment Discounts

In order to encourage buyers to pay their bills quickly, vendors generally offer different types of discounts. **Cash discounts** are provided for merchants who pay their bills by the end of a particular time frame. This is typically 30 days but may be longer. If the invoice is paid on or before that time, the buyer receives a discount that could run as high as 8 percent in some industries.

When suppliers are extremely anxious for payments they sometimes offer an extra discount known as **anticipation**. This discount might be an additional 1 or 2 percent. It helps manufacturers get their money quickly so they can use it to reduce operating costs, and it also enables the retailer to achieve a better profit margin.

Quantity Discounts

Many manufacturers and wholesalers offer pricing structures based upon quantities. As the size of the purchase increases for each item, the per-item cost to the buyer goes down. When goods are needed over a long period of time, the buyer can sometimes purchase them in the quantities needed for the entire period but only accept shipments as required, thereby enabling them to obtain the lower price.

Seasonal Discounts

When seasonal merchandise (like swimsuits) is purchased prior to the beginning of the retail selling season, vendors are likely to offer **seasonal discounts** for early delivery. There are several reasons why suppliers propose such discounts. Acceptance of early delivery allows the product to be tested prior to the main selling season, giving the retailer an opportunity to reorder the best sellers. It also enables the vendor to be paid sooner and helps alleviate problems associated with limited storage space.

Advertising and Promotional Allowances

One of the ways in which buyers can gain an important advantage is through the negotiation of dollars for advertising and promotion. Given in the form of **cooperative advertising**, the vendor usually pays for a percentage of an ad with the remaining expense coming from the buyer's budget. The percentage is determined as a result of buyer–vendor negotiation. With advertising costs continually spiraling upward, this is an important aspect of negotiation.

Slotting Allowances

One area of negotiation that has garnered a great deal of attention is **slotting allowances**. Buyers are paid by a vendor for featuring its merchandise in prime locations in stores or on Web sites. The practice occurs primarily in supermarkets and bookstores. In brick-and-mortar operations, items that are placed at the end of an aisle or featured in a prime display area generally sell better than if they were mixed in with other merchandise. Even on Web sites, vendors are often willing to pay extra sums to have their titles prominently displayed. Because the cost of slotting is often high, it is something that only major suppliers can afford.

Shipping Terms

Whenever an order is written, it is important for the buyer to specify the required method of shipping as well as who will pay for the shipping.

There are numerous shipping arrangements from which the buyer may choose. Some, while less expensive than others, may entail a longer time before the goods arrive. Conversely, the faster the delivery, the more costly it is. Not every shipment requires the same speed of delivery. Buyers must predetermine exactly how long they are willing to wait for delivery and how much they are willing to spend on this service.

Shipping charges are generally borne by the retailer. However, some negotiators are able to persuade the vendor to absorb the shipping costs in return for a larger merchandise commitment.

Specific terms such as **FOB shipping point** and **FOB destination** must be written on the order so that payment will be assigned to the proper party. Under the former designation, the buyer must pay all of the shipping costs from the place of origin. In the latter situation, all costs are the responsibility of the vendor.

Delivery Dates

When buyers finalize their purchasing plans, they earmark the delivery of merchandise for specific time periods. Merchandise that arrives after the required time creates problems. An advertising campaign might have been developed that requires the merchandise to be on hand for that time frame, or it might be a major selling season, such as Christmas, when the merchandise must be available to meet shoppers' needs.

If the merchandise is in stock, as is the case with many wholesale operations, delivery is not a serious problem. It is merely a matter of having the goods packed and shipped according to the buyer's instructions. On the other hand, if the goods are to be manufactured for the retailer then delivery terms must be carefully noted. Often there is a beginning and ending delivery period if the order involves a number of different items. If delivery isn't made by the promised date, then the buyer has the right of refusal. Of course, this results in a void in the inventory, with lost sales the most likely result.

Chargebacks

An area where the expert negotiator can gain an advantage on the vendor is the agreement about **chargebacks**. By convincing the supplier to offer allowances for merchandise that had to be marked down because of lackluster sales or shipping problems, the buyer is able to defray some of the merchandise's costs. The practice has become a standard occurrence in the fashion arena, with such retail giants as Lord & Taylor, Neiman Marcus, and Nordstrom always looking to improve their chargeback positions.

The seasoned buyer prenegotiates such amounts and is covered for any merchandising mishaps. The more detailed the purchase order, the better position the buyer is in to make certain that his or her purchasing plans will be realized.

It should be understood that many professional buyers do not finalize their purchases at the times the lines are being examined. They often just make notes about what they have seen, reserving final judgment until they have conferred with their divisional merchandise managers or supervisors, market representatives, or others who might provide assistance. **Note taking**, especially during market week, is a typical occurrence.

Once the orders have been reviewed, it is on to the vendor for processing.

EVALUATING THE BUYER'S PERFORMANCE

Buyers are evaluated in many ways, the most important of which is the actual markups they achieve and the stock turnover rate for their departments. The former will be addressed in Chapter 16 and the latter in this section.

The stock turnover rate is the number of times a store's average inventory is sold within a year. It is perhaps easiest to understand by examining two completely different product classifications. Bread that is baked every day is targeted to sell out completely every 24 hours. Thus, its turnover rate is 365. In contrast, precious jewelry, because of infrequent purchases, might sell out only once every 6 months, yielding a turnover rate of 2.

In the following example, the women's shoe buyer produced the following figures for last year.

Opening inventory (Jan. 1)...$ 660,000
Closing inventory (Dec. 1) ....$ 540,000
Sales for year...$2,400,000

The formula used to determine stock turnover is:

$$\frac{\text{net sales}}{\text{average inventory at retail}} = \text{stock turnover}$$

First the average inventory must be determined:

$$\frac{660,000 + 540,000}{2} = 600,000$$

Then:

$$\frac{2,400,000}{600,000} = 4$$

The turnover rate is 4 times every year.

In order to determine if this rate is appropriate, it would be compared with other departments in the store, previous years' rates, and the rates considered to be average for that merchandise classification in the industry. If the rate is above the standard that is expected, the buyer is doing an excellent job; if it is below, then investigation is in order to determine the problem.

Some of the contributing circumstances to poor turnover rates include:

- Retail prices that are too high
- Merchandise selections that aren't in line with customer preferences
- Poor-quality merchandise
- Inexperienced sales personnel
- Poor promotional techniques
- Lackluster visual merchandising
- Competition

An investigation should determine which of these potential causes is responsible for a poor turnover rate. Once the problems have been addressed and corrected, the turnover rate should improve.

A DAY IN THE LIFE OF A BUYER

The buyer studies past sales to predict future sales and gauge how much merchandise to reorder.

Reordering hot items ensures their availability to meet consumer demand.

A DAY IN THE LIFE OF A BUYER—(continued)

The buyer checks ads to make certain that they describe the merchandise accurately. Consumers expect to find the advertised items when they shop the store.

Regular communication with store personnel keeps the buyer abreast of merchandise needs.

Advance planning is the key to a successful market visit.

Store visits help the buyer determine whether displays are appropriate.

CHAPTER HIGHLIGHTS

- Purchasing by retailers, once a task that focused on domestic markets, now demands coverage of the vast global marketplace.
- The role of the buyer is considered by many industry professionals to be one of the most important in the retailing industry.
- Professional buyers perform a host of different activities, but the major one is purchasing merchandise.
- When purchase plans are formulated for the next buying period, major emphasis is placed on past sales records.
- Besides looking at internal sources of information when planning is undertaken, buyers seek assistance from numerous external sources.
- The most notable outside planning source for fashion merchandise is the resident buying offices, also known as retail consultants.
- Buyers develop model stocks that address both qualitative and quantitative needs.
- In order to ensure they remain within their allocated merchandise budgets, buyers regularly focus on the open-to-buy calculations.
- Retailers have a variety of suppliers from which to choose. They must evaluate each of them before any actual purchasing decisions are made.
- Stock turnover rates are important because they affect profitability.
- Most buyers place the bulk of the upcoming season's orders during a period called market week.

- Buying may take place at permanent vendor showrooms, trade expositions, temporary facilities, business-to-business Web sites, and the retailer's premises.
- Negotiating the purchase is the buyer's responsibility. If handled effectively, it can bring the retailer a better deal.

IMPORTANT RETAILING TERMS

anticipation (330)
bottom line (321)
business-to-business Web site (328)
buying plan (321)
cash discount (330)
chargeback (331)
clearinghouse (328)
closeout (329)
cold canvass (327)
cooperative advertising (330)
dutiable (322)
fashion forecaster (315)
flow plan (323)
FOB destination (331)
FOB shipping point (331)
garment center (325)
landed cost (322)
manufacturer's representative (327)
market consultant (314)
market week (314)
merchandise commitment (319)
merchandise on hand (319)
model stock (316)
note taking (332)
open to buy (319)
product development (312)
purchasing channel (321)
qualitative decision (321)
quantitative decision (321)
rack jobber (321)
resident buyer representative (314)
resident buying office (313)
retail consultant (313)
road sales staff (323)
Robinson–Patman Act (329)
seasonal discount (330)
slotting allowance (331)
staple merchandise (317)
stock turnover rate (322)
tariff (322)
trade exposition (326)
trade publication (316)
virtual showroom (329)

FOR REVIEW

1. Why is the time spent on purchasing in the marketplace more involved than in past years?
2. In addition to purchasing, what are some of the other duties and responsibilities performed by buyers?
3. Why are buyers often called upon to select the products that will be promoted?
4. What is the first source of information that the buyer utilizes in purchase planning?
5. To what extent are merchandise managers involved in the planning stages of purchasing?
6. Why do professional buyers use the services of external resources when planning their purchases?
7. What preplanning activities are provided by resident buying offices to their clients?
8. Why do some buyers use the services of fashion forecasters in their search for new merchandise?
9. What advantage does the reading of consumer periodicals afford the retail buyer?
10. What is a model stock?
11. List and briefly describe the four elements of buying.
12. Define the term *open to buy*.
13. How is open to buy calculated?
14. Should a buyer always use the same merchandise resources or should he or she continually look for new suppliers?
15. Which products are typically purchased by the retailer through rack jobbers?
16. Define the term *landed cost*.
17. How important is the stock turnover rate in evaluating a buyer's performance?
18. What is market week?
19. What advantage does a visit to a trade exposition provide the buyer that individual showroom visits do not?
20. If a buyer cannot get to the market to make purchases, what other means can he or she use?
21. How do the business-to-business Web sites differ from those used by consumers?
22. What is a chargeback?
23. How does the Robinson–Patman Act affect buyer–seller negotiation?
24. On what two criteria are buyers generally evaluated?

AN INTERNET ACTIVITY

The use of business-to-business Web sites by retail buyers is growing. Log on to any of those described in the chapter, such as www.tradeout.com, and prepare a summary of your findings as follows:

- List the name of the site and describe its function.
- Discuss how long it has been in business.
- Describe the types of merchandise it offers.
- Discuss the various types of businesses it attempts to sell to.
- Describe how you would become a member or user of the Web site.
- Discuss any fees or costs, other than those for merchandise, required of users.
- Describe the visuals used and how effective they are.
- Offer your comments about how effective a tool the site is.

EXERCISES AND PROJECTS

Visit or write to a retail buyer in your community to learn about how he or she plans purchases. If the retail operation is not headquartered in your city, find out from a local unit where its operation is located so that you may communicate with one of the buyers. It is not necessary to contact a major company; a small entrepreneurship would also be appropriate. The information that you obtain should be organized in a form similar to the one below.

```
Company Name _____
Buyer's Name _____
Merchandise Classification _____
Internal Planning Sources




External Planning Sources




Purchase Locations (showrooms, trade expos, on-premises, etc.)
```

THE CASE OF THE SEARCH FOR UNIQUE MERCHANDISE

With competition reaching an all-time high for Bancroft Department Stores, a fashion-oriented company, the merchandising team has decided it must venture in a new direction in terms of the lines featured in its stores. Ever since the store first opened in 1960, Bancroft's philosophy has been that the best approach to merchandising was to offer highly publicized national brands. Its stores are stocked with labels that include Liz Claiborne, Calvin Klein, Ralph Lauren, DKNY, Jones New York, and Ellen Tracy. Although each of these labels guarantees a high degree of consumer recognition and quality, the same products can be found at Bancroft's competitors. Other than its customer service, there really isn't any reason for shoppers to patronize Bancroft's over other stores.

To make matters worse, Bancroft's has witnessed an increase in its product lines being sold at the off-price stores in the same trading areas. Each of these labels is prominently displayed, and prices are considerably lower than what Bancroft charges. Although the merchandise arrives at these merchants much later in the season, the off-price merchants are still competitive in shoppers' eyes.

In order to distinguish themselves from other retailers who carry these lines, the company has decided to begin a program that features lesser-known names but to remain competitive in terms of fashion emphasis and quality. Because locating these lesser-known collections would be a major chore, the merchandising team is not certain of the best approach to take.

John Gallop, general merchandise manager, is an advocate of firsthand research to discover these new merchandise offerings and believes that visits to offshore venues would be the best place to start. He suggests that store buyers should travel to global centers such as Hong Kong, Korea, London, and Milan to see what's available that hasn't yet made an impact in American stores. Some of the buyers consider this to be a sound strategy. But top management, particularly CEO Marc Litt, believes the approach is too extravagant and costly to warrant consideration. He suggested that some other plan be adopted before foreign visits are made.

With the next season only 2 months away, a meeting was called by John Gallop. The meeting included his eight divisional merchandise managers and 80 buyers. Each person involved in the meeting was asked to prepare some notes about the direction the team should take in solving the merchandise acquisition dilemma. Specific remedies were expected from each of them at the planning session.

Questions

1. Pretend that you are one of the buyers asked to attend the meeting. What initial approach would you suggest be taken by the buyers and merchandisers before any offshore visits are made?
2. Do you believe that trips to foreign shores are necessary to locate new vendors that do not have marquee appeal?
3. What portion of the merchandise should be of the new variety, and why?

Tackling the Sourcing Conundrum
Evan Clark

April 9, 2007

MEMPHIS, Tenn—It might not be the sexiest side of the fashion business, but being able to get the right looks from the factories to the stores for the right price is every bit as important as beefy models and runways.

The vital backroom functions of sourcing, transportation and logistics were the focus of the American Apparel & Footwear Association's 2007 International Sourcing, Customs & Logistics Integration Conference in Memphis, Tenn.

Participants in the three-day conference, which was held at the Memphis Marriott Downtown late last month, emphasized the importance of some relatively straightforward ideas that can make all the difference when shipping goods around the globe.

Speakers said it was essential to be involved in the process each step along the way, to take quality assurance into account early, recognize that security and environmental concerns are now a part of life, and know that efficiency in the supply chain can trump the lowest price.

There are roughly 126 steps between when an idea springs into a designer's head to when the customer buys the product, said Rick Horwitch, vice-president of solutions and business development for consumer products at Bureau Veritas. However, audits for quality generally come around step 95 or 96, which is too late in the process.

"You need to address [quality assurance] and [quality control] issues upfront," he said, "Everybody says quality is important, yet quality is the last thing addressed."

Ensuring quality is not only important for maintaining brand image but also for avoiding retail chargebacks, which eat into the bottom line, he warned.

When it comes to sourcing, Horwitch said, the emphasis should be on efficiency, not just the lowest price.

"Everyday low cost to Wal-Mart does not mean give me the cheapest products," said Horwitch. "If Wal-Mart wanted to get it for free, trust me, there's some idiot out there who would give it to them."

Efficiency in apparel sourcing immediately conjures visions of China, which has charged onto the scene in a big way in recent years to capture more than one-third of the U.S. import market.

"It's not the least expensive [place to source], it's the most efficient," said Rick Helfenbein, president of Luen Thai USA, who also spoke at the conference. "You just need the right partner."

Helfenbein noted that China has good infrastructure, such as roads and ports, a skilled work force and plentiful raw materials. This has helped fuel a new kind of apparel manufacturing operation, "the supply chain city," of which Luen Thai is a pioneer.

"You can do everything in this one place," said Helfenbein, referring to Luen Thai's facility in Dongguan, which has all of the necessary components to make apparel, except fabric production. "Speed is the key ingredient," he said.

Relationship building and clear communication are also of paramount importance, said Jim Sciabarrasi, vice-president of sourcing, materials and logistics at New Balance.

Good partnerships can help get brands and their vendors together so that color, fit and other design issues can be worked out in advance and production can push forward without interruption, he said, stressing that the brand must lead the process.

Despite often vast cultural differences between the marketing and production departments within fashion companies, the two groups must decide who is in charge of the process so everybody can move forward with the same vision, he said.

"We don't share the same language, but we have to find a way to have the conversation," said Sciabarrasi.

When the business model does work and orders manage to get from the factory through the ports and customs and to the stores on time, production specialists need to take note, said Wendy Wieland Martin, vice-president of international trade services at Kellwood Co.

"Put a value on your wins," said Martin, who advocated very active management of the supply chain with very close record keeping. "We cannot look at the big picture if we're drowning in a sea of unfathomable paper," said Martin.

Once the goods hit American shores, fashion companies are then faced with a plethora of challenges moving them to the stores. With trade volumes increasing and finite port capacity on the West Coast, the transportation system, from ports and railways to roads, will continue to present big challenges that will require concerted and coordinated effort, said Robin Lanier, executive director of Waterfront Coalition. "We have no national freight policy," said Lanier. "This administration takes the view that transportation is not a federal policy. You can no longer ignore the transportation system in the United States."

Weighing in on trade policy for the duration of the Bush administration, Scott Quesenberry, special textile negotiator in the office of the U.S. Trade Representative, said a lot of energy would be spent on issues at the World Trade Organization, such as the Doha talks, which could reduce tariffs on industrial goods, like apparel, as well as agricultural products and services.

"We still have a lot of challenges as part of the Doha round," said Quesenberry.

Launched in the wake of the 9/11 terrorist attacks and intended to give a boost to developing countries, the talks have stalled numerous times as negotiators try to lessen the differences in their positions, particularly on agricultural issues.

"There is still a time frame out there where we can get this done within this administration," he said.

The Bush administration has negotiated and enacted a number of free-trade pacts, such as the Central American Free Trade Agreement, but working through the WTO, with 150 member nations, offers an opportunity to shape policy more broadly.

• •

A Prominent Presence: Walking the Show Floor with Abbey Doneger
Liza Casabona

APRIL 16, 2007

Walking through the aisles of the recent MAGIC trade shows with Abbey Doneger, president of the Doneger Group, is a bit like walking around a small town with its mayor.

Progress down the trade show aisles is slow as Doneger is stopped frequently by acquaintances, business colleagues and clients, or darts off to say a quick hello to someone he sees in the distance.

Rounding a corner into the Joseph Abboud booth, Doneger, distracted by another contact, drops behind. A public relations person says, "Marty's right here," and steps aside to reveal Marty Staff, Abboud's chief executive officer. He's wearing a yellow T-shirt that reads "Got Tequila" and a pair of cargo pants.

When Staff learns Doneger is not far behind, he becomes animated, and says, "Abbey Doneger is here! Where is he?" and bounds out of the booth to run and jump onto the dark-suited Doneger, squeezing him in a bear hug.

"We called each other this morning and coordinated our outfits," Doneger said, adding that he and Staff have known each other for many years. Their fathers were friends.

Staff's reaction, while more ebullient, is not dissimilar from the reactions of many in the apparel industry to the figure of Abbey Doneger in the aisles at MAGIC. Chief executives, chief operating officers, buyers and others all stop him to say hello.

The Doneger Group is a fashion merchandising, trend-forecasting and consulting company.

It provides business intelligence on global market trends and merchandising strategy to the retail and fashion industry. The company was founded as a buying group, but through acquisitions and expansions has grown to encompass trend forecasting, consulting on customized projects, trend and merchandising publications, a comprehensive Web site and complimentary trend services, advisory firms and publications such as Here and There, Carol Hoffman Associates and Tobe.

During the MAGIC show earlier this year, a major retailer flags Doneger down to compliment him on one of the firm's trend presentations earlier in the day. "Great presentation!" he says, pumping Doneger's hand.

In between company visits, Doneger strides quickly from booth to booth. He said his role at the show was largely to do just this, maintain his firm's broad relationships. He has a solid team of market analysts and trend forecasters who walk the floor without him whom he trusts to take care of day-to-day tasks that need to be accomplished at the shows.

"Our clients appreciate the big picture overviews," Doneger said. Both at the trade show and in the work the firm does year-round, staffers balance the big picture with the minute details of every category they are involved in. He encourages most of his clients to attend the show, he said, and it's an important trip for the Doneger Group, as well.

"If we weren't there, we would be missed. It's a very important part of what we do," he said. In particular, he said it had emerged as a very important event for men's and contemporary women's apparel.

Doneger's MAGIC work kicks off with the first of his firm's trend forecasts at 8 a.m. on opening day of the show. The trade show turns over a large meeting room to the Doneger Group to use for four of these seminar presentations over the course of the show, three trend forecasts and one report from the company's TOBE division.

The first one is standing room only as Doneger takes the podium to introduce his team of experts. During the presentation that follows most audience members appear to be taking assiduous notes. It's clear they are here to glean some insight.

Doneger hands the reins over to David Wolfe, the company's creative director, who details the directions for men's and women's apparel based on the shows for the year. Wolfe's presentation is followed by insight from the company's men's wear and West Coast teams, including Tim Bess and Janine Blain, who each present a snippet of the world they buy for and its trends.

As the presentation ends and the attendees move off to start walking the show floor, Abbey is surrounded by well-wishers and clients, many of whom he sees regularly in meetings in New York. He will also be present for the two remaining seminars the Doneger Creative team presents, one on women's wear and one on men's wear over the course of MAGIC.

Doneger said he sends roughly 20 people to MAGIC each season, and entrusts them with the nuts and bolts of working the show. There is so much going on, trusting his people to take care of the business that needs to be done allows Doneger the time and space to see the big picture. His focus at the show is to identify new trends, have time on the floor with clients and to work with them one-on-one. It's an important venue, he said, and remains a touch point even with clients who do the bulk of their business in New York or at other times.

Doneger's primary role at MAGIC is to walk the show floor, speak to everyone he can and get a better idea of the landscape of the industry, said Leslie Ghize, senior vice president. He leaves much of the day-to-day merchandise decisions to his team, he said, adding that he thinks in some cases they are better off without him.

Many of the Doneger Group's employees have been with the company for years. Doneger said he values "experience and youthful energy over just youth." And, indeed, even those employees who have been with him for only six or seven years have logged years or, in some cases, decades in the apparel industry. And the company starts early, recruiting interns and young employees from schools like the Fashion Institute of Technology.

Abbey's father, the late Henry Doneger, founded the Doneger Group in 1946 as a buying office primarily of women's wear. Over its 60-year-plus history, the company has moved into all the other apparel categories and has developed into a consulting firm that provides research and resources to the retail and fashion communities. Abbey joined the firm in 1973 and became president in 1980.

CHAPTER 15
Private Labeling and Product Development

After you have completed this chapter, you should be able to discuss:

- Some of the advantages of purchasing merchandise that bears a manufacturer's or designer's label or brand
- The beginnings of private branding and the concepts used by those retailers who first introduced them to their customers
- Why most retail organizations choose to use the proportional approach when stocking private brands and labels
- The store-is-the-brand concept and how it differs from the proportional approach used by most retailers
- The advantages for merchants who subscribe to some form of private branding and labeling
- How merchants avail themselves of privately branded and labeled merchandise
- The ways in which smaller retailers may participate in private labeling
- Several of the promotional techniques used by retailers to publicize their own brands and labels
- The importance of the name given to a company's private-label collection
- Why some merchants subscribe to licensed private branding

All over the United States, retailers are facing competitive challenges that have never before been witnessed in the industry. Not only are there large numbers of brick-and-mortar operations, there are also millions of catalogues being sent to consumers. To complicate matters, these two traditional forms of retailing face yet another competitive arena—retail Web sites.

In this age of multichannel retailing, when merchants are showcasing their offerings in their stores and catalogues and on their Web sites, the sameness of the merchandise that is available from a majority of retailers is troublesome. Shoppers—whether making visits to the stores, perusing the hundreds of catalogues that come into each home, or logging on to their favorite Web sites—find the same merchandise being offered over and over again. **Marquee labels** such as Liz Claiborne, Ralph Lauren, and Calvin Klein are in every major department store, making retail operations clones of each other. Although many shoppers prefer well-known labels to lesser-known brands, their presence often creates problems for retail outlets. Of paramount concern is the pricing factor. During slow selling periods, there is nothing to prevent a merchant from taking markdowns on these products. This, of course, may cause anguish for the retailer who isn't prepared to lower its price. Since shoppers often go from store to store to comparison shop, the store with the lowest prices wins. The end result is an inability to maintain the initial markup that is necessary to maximize profits. In a competitive society, it is imperative that different offerings be available to avoid the complications associated with identical product assortments.

In order to make operations more profitable, many retailers have taken the route of private labeling. Although most recognize the need to carry **signature brands**, many have opted for a portion of their inventories to be exclusively their own. For example, major companies like Macy's, Bloomingdale's, Belk, and Dillard's commingle nationally advertised brands along with their own products. Others, such as Gap, Banana Republic, Eddie Bauer, The Limited, and Abercrombie & Fitch have taken the private-label concept to its extreme and have become **store-is-the-brand operations**. That is, the entire merchandise assortment is exclusive to their respective companies.

Each of these retailers recognizes the need to distinguish itself from the others if it is to sustain a positive profit picture. Whether in brick-and-mortar operations, in catalogues, or on the Internet, product differentiation is necessary in order to maintain customer loyalty. Of course, other factors, such as service, play an important role in the success of any business, but it is the merchandise mix and its prices that help a consumer decide whether or not to patronize a retailer.

Private-label merchandising is significantly more difficult to manage than merchandising that focuses on national branding. The former requires a retailer to develop its product line or to have some outside resource provide the items. Buying merchandise from existing lines avoids the problems associated with product design and manufacturing.

In this chapter, attention will focus on the comparisons between manufacturer's and private brands, the trials and tribulations of private labeling, and the rigorous demands placed on those in the company who develop the products.

MANUFACTURERS' BRANDS AND LABELS

In most retail operations, be they brick-and-mortar, catalogues, or Web sites, the greatest proportion of the merchandise is produced by manufacturers. The products are not restricted to any one merchant, but sometimes their purchase comes with exclusivity terms for certain merchants. That is, the goods are restricted to specific retailers in a trading area.

Although the merchandising of these brands, many of which enjoy national and sometimes even global exposure, presents potential problems such as **price cutting**, their prominence makes them desirable. Some of the specific reasons why most retailers continue to use **manufacturers' brands** in significant amounts include the following:

Manufacturers' brands such as Dockers enjoy global exposure and improve retailers' profitability.

- *Exposure to the public.* Retailers who carry national brands benefit from the wealth of advertising and promotional endeavors undertaken by the manufacturers of these products.

Companies such as Calvin Klein have large budgets to help presell their products through advertising and promotion, motivating the consumer to purchase them. Retailers place these items on the selling floor, in their direct-mail pieces, or on their Web sites, and customers purchase them. This investment by the manufacturer helps retailers save their own advertising budgets to promote lesser-known brands or their own private labels.

Couture collections, such as Armani, appeal to shoppers who are motivated by prestige.

- *Reorder availability.* With the abundance of merchandise needed to satisfy the orders of merchants all over the country and sometimes those in foreign venues, many manufacturers keep an assortment of their best sellers on hand to quickly fill reorder requests. When time is of the essence—especially in the case of fashion items, whose shelf life is relatively brief—the prompt receipt of these goods will assure quick sales. In most retail organizations it is usually just a few items each season that capture the public's attention, and in-stock availability is crucial to satisfying customer needs. Without this immediate replenishment, sales could be lost and the company's bottom line could be adversely affected.
- *Quality assurance.* Manufacturers of branded merchandise are keenly aware that their products must be produced with the highest standards in order to protect their reputations and maintain interest in their offerings. Given this scrutiny, they can assure their clients that customers will receive goods that meet their needs. With adherence to quality control, the retailer will benefit by having fewer complaints about the merchandise and will thus be able to build regular patronage.
- *Consumer preference.* Through marketing research studies, retailers have been made aware that a significant percentage of consumers prefer national brands. Whether it is for food products, appliances, clothing, home furnishings, or other items, 45 percent of men and 35 percent of women prefer these products according to a study conducted by the National Advertising Bureau. Only when the retailers they patronize are looked upon as reliable do most customers begin to accept unbranded merchandise. Using questionnaires and focus groups, many retailers conduct similar studies of their own to determine manufacturer brand preference. The findings help merchants determine the ideal proportion of branded goods to the nonbranded variety.
- *Prestige.* Though value is in the forefront of the minds of many of today's consumers, and though more and more are looking to discounters and off-pricers to satisfy their needs, a large number of consumers are still motivated to buy certain marquee labels and brands. Price is not a factor with these consumers. They are motivated by the prestige and status of these products. A telling study concerning the purchase of prestigious automobiles revealed the extent to which some consumers would pay more for an identical product that bore a prestigious name than one that didn't. Study respondents were asked, "If you were able to purchase a Mercedes for 30 percent off the list price on the conditions that it wouldn't have the company logo or name on it and that the car would be taken away if you told anyone it was, in fact, a Mercedes, would you make the purchase?" The result was that 40 percent would rather pay the extra money to have the car emblazoned with its identifying trademarks. This is only one study, but it is safe to assume that prestige is an important factor in many purchases. Given this motivational aspect of buying, it is necessary for the retailer whose customer base is replete with prestige-motivated shoppers to merchandise such image products properly.

PRIVATE BRANDS AND LABELS

For many years, some retailers have opted to introduce **private brands and labels** into their merchandise mixes. The idea was to provide quality products, which were essentially the same as the nationally recognized ones, but at lower prices via the store's own brands. Proponents of this concept included A & P, the largest supermarket chain at the time, and Sears, America's leading catalog merchant. The former lined its shelves with a vast array of food items that bore its own name, and the latter merchandised hard goods such as appliances and tools under its own brands.

In both cases, the items that were marketed as private brands were almost identical to those that bore manufacturers' brands. These very same producers manufactured goods for Sears and A & P. The differences between these and brand-name products was in the packaging or in some minor feature. When using this type of merchandising, businesses weren't affected by price cutting or any of the other obstacles that came about through competition. After a great deal of promotional efforts brought favorable results, Sears made the Coldspot and Kenmore brands household names, and A & P did the same with its Ann Page labels.

Ironically, as the trend toward private branding and labeling caught fire in the 1970s, these two retail giants began to redirect their efforts toward regular brands. Sears, in particular, began to introduce nationally advertised manufacturers' products alongside its own brands primarily because its customers showed an interest in them. A & P began to lose its dominant position as a major supermarket chain and closed countless stores.

INC International Concepts is one of Macy's numerous private labels.

In any event, the wealth of private-label products that retailers began to feature in their assortments grew at significant rates. Macy's led the way with a large number of brands produced exclusively for its stores. Labels like Alfani and Charter Club coexisted with the likes of well-known brands and soon began to play a major merchandising role for the company. What many believe was crucial to their success was not only the quality and styling of the merchandise but also the choice of names coined to enhance each collection.

These names are not chosen by accident. A close inspection of the garments that were introduced with the Alfani signature revealed that the garments were actually produced in Korea. However, the Italian-sounding name gave them greater appeal. Rounding out the keen merchandising of the company was the introduction of the Charter Club label. The "clubby" sound of Ralph Lauren's collections had been bringing vast numbers of shoppers to the stores. Capitalizing on this merchandising phenomenon, Macy's developed its Charter Club label featuring styles that were quite similar to those of Ralph Lauren.

Private branding has become commonplace in most retailing classifications. In addition to department stores and apparel chains, other retailers such as discounters, off-pricers, and warehouse clubs have embraced the concept. Kmart has made headlines with its own Martha Stewart home furnishings lines; Costco has introduced its own brands, such as Kirkland; and so has Stein Mart.

It should be understood that the introduction of one's own brand or label requires a great deal of effort on the part of the retailer, beginning with the choice of a name that will motivate purchasing, a collection of products that can compete with the better-known manufacturers' offerings, and prices that are lower than those products that have already made their reputations.

The challenges of this type of merchandising are formidable and, in order to be successful, one must have the complete attention of the organization's staff. Aside from all that is required to make one's own private brand or label successful, there is also a need to determine to what extent these new offerings will be featured in the company's merchandise assortment.

In the News...

The article "Markets Say Proudly: It's Our Brand," reprinted on page 356 at the end of this chapter, should be read at this time.

The Proportional Concept

By and large, most retailers feature a merchandise mix that incorporates their own brands along with others that have either gained national prominence or are new manufacturers' designs with the potential for significant consumer acceptance.

Recognizing that a large percentage of their clientele seek manufacturer brands and labels, most retailers understand that the presence of these brands in their model stocks is a given. They set aside separate departments that bear these instantly recognizable names and locate them in spots that are easily accessed by customers. Liz Claiborne and Ralph Lauren, for example, have their merchandise featured in self-contained areas that resemble small shops and bear signage that announces their existence. With the sales volumes and ultimate profits achieved through the offering of such goods, their inclusion in the store's product mix is a must.

While these recognized merchandise collections are essential to the success of most companies, incorporating private brands and labels has also proven to be of paramount importance to retailers. The proportion of the overall inventory that should be devoted to these private brands is a matter of concern for retailers.

Most retailers gradually introduce their own labels into the mix, studying the results after each selling season. Stock of those that have achieved success is increased.

Table 15.1 lists some of the major retailers who subscribe to the **proportional inventory concept**.

Sometimes, as in the case of Macy's, the ratio of private brands to national entries is significant. Initially, the company began with a smattering of their own labels so that their impact could be tested. Each year the company seems to add more and more private labels, which now number more than 20. There is no real formula for what the proportions between private and manufacturer brands should be. It is up to management to determine what makes the most sense in terms of profitability.

Merchants generally must invest enormous promotional sums to publicize these brands so that customers will be motivated to buy. The national producers, on the other hand, promote manufacturers' brands and labels so that the public will be aware of them and seek out the retailers who sell them. Private-label offerings thus require extensive investments in terms of advertising, special events, and visual merchandising efforts because the products are sold only through the company's own outlets. It is essential to convince the public that these private offerings have the same or better quality than their national-brand counterparts.

The Store-Is-the-Brand Concept

All over the United States and sometimes in global venues, companies like Gap are reaping the benefits of total private-label merchandising. In these outlets, the need to determine proportionality between national brands and private labels is eliminated; the entire offering is the

TABLE 15.1
SELECTED RETAILERS WITH PROMINENT PRIVATE BRANDS

Company	Major Private Labels	Merchandise Classification
Sears	Kenmore, Coldspot, Craftsman	Tools, appliances
Kmart	Martha Stewart, Jaclyn Smith*	Housewares, linens
Costco	Kirkland	Food items
Macy's	Charter Club, Alfani, INC International Concepts	Apparel, bedding, jewelry
Dillard's	Preston & York, Daniel Creimeux	Apparel and accessories
Saks	St. John, SFA Folio	Apparel and accessories
Belk	J. Khaki	Apparel and accessories
Lord & Taylor	Kate Hill, Identity	Apparel and accessories
Bloomingdale's	Sutton, Aqua	Apparel and accessories
Nordstrom	Classiques Entier, BP, Caslon, Baby N, 81st and Park, Ewear	Handbags, apparel, shoes, juniors, men's clothing
Tiffany	Tiffany	Jewelry

*These private labels are part of licensing agreements. The names on the brands are well-known celebrities who, along with their designs, bring extra recognition to the products.

company's own. This concept is based on the philosophy that the organization's name and the brands that it features are one and the same. Once the brand name has been established, the public immediately comes to understand that only one brand is available.

The apparel and accessories segments of retailing dominate the store-is-the-brand concept. With companies such as The Gap Stores, Inc. (which features a host of private brands in different stores and catalogues under its umbrella), Eddie Bauer, Abercrombie & Fitch, American Eagle, and Nine West having a significant presence in the retail arena, it is certain that the consumer has confidence in this format.

Focus on..
Gap, Inc.

THE GAP WAS FOUNDED IN 1969 by Don and Doris Fisher with a handful of employees in a single store in San Francisco. Today, it is an international company with four distinct brands, Gap, Banana Republic, Piperlime, and Old Navy. Still headquartered in the San Francisco Bay Area, the Gap has product development offices in New York City and distribution operations and offices coordinating sourcing activities around the globe. It has become a household name for every member of the family. The Gap's cumulative revenues topped $15.9 billion in 2006.

By 1976, just eight years after Gap opened its first unit, the company went public with an offering of 1.2 million shares of stock. Little by little, additional labels were added to the Gap roster. First came GapKids in 1986, to be followed by babyGap in 1990. In 1983, Gap bought Banana Republic, a small retail operation that sold safari and travel clothing. It wasn't long before this retail entry was transformed into a more sophisticated concept that emphasized modern, versatile, and relevant apparel and accessories for style-conscious shoppers. In 1994, Old Navy was born with an emphasis placed on "fun, fashion, family, and value." Most recently, Gap has added Piperlime, an online shoe shop. In total, the company operates 7,100 stores.

One of the keys to the company's success is its ability to recognize the needs of the consumer and to offer products that fill those needs. Product development at the Gap begins with a cre-

Companies that apply the store-is-the-brand concept use only their own label on the merchandise they sell.

ative team of designers, product managers, and graphic artists who develop the look and feel of each season's merchandise. From color to concept, it all begins with inspiration. Whether it's people watching on the streets of Tokyo, a flash from a dream, or a visit to a local art gallery, the team translates the stimulus into salable designs.

Once the individual styles have been created, Gap provides them to third-party manufacturers for production. These producers are located in more than 50 countries around the globe, including the United States. Gap does not own any of these manufacturing facilities, but it has developed a Code of Vendor Conduct to ensure that the factories are not only capable of producing high-quality goods but also feature safe and humane working conditions. More than 80 company employees assure quality control and inspect the production facilities to make certain that they are in compliance with established policies.

In 2007 there were more than 3,100 Gap stores in the United States, the United Kingdom, Canada, France, Germany, and Japan.

The Private Label and Brand Advantage

Of course, exclusivity is the obvious reason why retailers subscribe to having their own brands and products available either as parts of their inventories or in the store-is-the-brand concept. Inherent in this exclusive approach to merchandising are specific advantages that make the approach profitable:

- There is no interference from vendors. Oftentimes, manufacturers with well-known brands require that a certain amount be spent on advertising or that the products be visually merchandised in a particular manner. Since the private-label retailer has the ultimate decision-making authority, there is no need to conform to anyone else's demands.
- Profitability is like to be higher because the costs of middlemen are avoided. By eliminating the vendor's markup on goods, the retailer can offer the consumer lower prices and also generate greater profits.
- Price cutting, which is often problematic for retailers, is avoided because the competition cannot obtain the same merchandise. In poor economic times or in situations where inventories might not move at the desired pace, competing merchants are sometimes prone to cut prices, and thus reduce the profits of traditional retailers.
- Suppliers cannot dictate the timing of markdowns or the setting of retail prices because only the retail operation can make those decisions.
- Purchasing requirements, as dictated by many vendors, are not present in privately branded merchandise. Some suppliers, especially those with marquee brands and labels, often require that purchases be made in predetermined assortments. For example, **prepacks** might be based on the manufacturer's concept of a particular size allocation to meet his or her own production requirements. Merchants, in accordance with their past sales records, might prefer a size breakdown that is weighted toward the large sizes while a vendor could demand the ordering of more smaller sizes. In such cases, the retailer is often left with unwanted sizes that ultimately turn up on the markdown racks, thus affecting profits.
- Customer **comparison shopping** is eliminated because the merchandise is of an exclusive nature. When national brands are inventoried, some consumers go from store to store in an effort to find the lowest price.
- Product specificity can be tailored to the company's individual needs. When buyers set out to purchase their inventories from independent suppliers, they are obliged to make selections that are earmarked for broader audiences. In the case of one's own brands, the exact product requirements will become part of the design.
- Customer loyalty can result from consumers being satisfied with a particular label or brand. If the item belongs to a nationally known manufacturer then the product may be purchased at many venues. In the case of retailer exclusivity through private branding, if the customer is satisfied then he or she is likely to patronize that store for those labels.

> **In the News . . .**
>
> The article entitled "The Power of the Private Label" appearing on page 358 at the end of this chapter should be read at this time.

LICENSED PRIVATE BRANDS

The typical type of private branding is the result of a retailer's initiative to produce or obtain products for its exclusive use. Retailers also use another approach: one that benefits from the names of well-known celebrities. Through **licensing agreements**, products are offered that

TABLE 15.2
SELECTED STORE-IS-THE-BRAND COMPANIES

Parent Company	Private Brand	Merchandise Classification
The Gap Stores, Inc.	Gap	Men's and women's casual apparel
	Banana Republic	Men's and women's fashion apparel
	Old Navy	Value apparel for the family
Limited Brands	Victoria's Secret	Intimate apparel
	Bath & Body Works	Body care products
The Spiegel Group	Eddie Bauer	Men's and women's apparel Home furnishings
Sears, Roebuck and Co.	Lands' End	Casual wear
Ann Taylor Stores Corp.	Ann Taylor	Women's apparel
Abercrombie & Fitch Co.	Abercrombie & Fitch	Men's and women's apparel
American Eagle Outfitters	American Eagle	Apparel
J.Crew Group	J.Crew	Men's and women's apparel
Jones Apparel Group, Inc.	Nine West	Shoes
Brooks Brothers	Brooks Brothers	Men's and women's apparel

feature famous people's names and are merchandised exclusively through one retailer's operation. The appeal of the personality's image often leads to significant successful sales of the products provided.

Several major retailers have successfully entered into these agreements, capturing the attention of their customers. One of the leaders in this approach is Kmart. Merchandise bearing the Martha Stewart label continues to dominate the bedding and linens departments of their stores. With her unofficial title as guru of good taste and the attention she receives from the media, her name has instant recognition with the public. Another licensed private label success story at Kmart is the Jaclyn Smith collection. As a former star of the television show *Charlie's Angels*, she continues to capture the attention of those who watched her fame rise. Her signature collection consists of fashion apparel. Those who admire her appearance and demeanor seem quick to embrace her line of merchandise.

Other licensed brands include labels by Madonna for H&M, Isaac Mizrahi for Target, Vera Wang for Kohls, and Todd Oldham for Gap.

The advantages of this type of private branding are numerous:

Isaac Mizrahi provides a line of clothes for Target.

- The merchandise does not require direct design or planning by the retailer as it does in traditional private branding and labeling.
- The advantage of name recognition immediately gives the retailer a selling edge.
- The quality of the merchandise is generally excellent because the celebrity whose name appears on the label doesn't want to ruin his or her reputation.
- A wealth of promotional **point-of-purchase** materials is generally available to use in windows and other visual presentations.
- Personal appearances by the celebrities, if part of the promotional package, guarantee crowds of potential customers.

The only requirement of such exclusivity involves a guarantee by the retailer to use a predetermined amount of goods for the year. Thus, it is the organization with a vast number of stores in the chain—and that uses other channels such as e-tailing to give broad exposure to the products—that typically benefits from this form of private branding. Companies like Kmart, Wal-Mart, Home Depot, Kohl's, and Target are all excellent candidates for such branding.

PRODUCT DEVELOPMENT

There are many different types of arrangements that retailers use in the acquisition of private labels and brands. In the vast majority of these endeavors, the retailer either produces the designs that ultimately are translated into products or works with outside resources in their creation. In certain situations, these exclusive merchandise assortments come from intermediary groups such as resident buying offices and retail consulting specialists. Whether it is through **company-owned production**, direct purchasing from national manufacturers who produce lines expressly for private-label merchants, or acquisition from **private-label developers**, the result is the same. That is, the retailer is afforded the exclusivity of private branding.

Company-Owned Production

The giants in the retail industry, especially those that subscribe to the store-is-the-brand philosophy, obtain their products from their own resources. Companies like The Limited that have many different divisions, requiring a continuous flow of their privately branded merchandise, typically own their own manufacturing facilities.

Focus on . . .
Mast Industries, Inc.

FOUNDED IN 1970 BY MARTIN AND DENA TRUST in their home in Canton, Massachusetts, Mast Industries has gone on to become one of the world's largest contract manufacturer's of men's, women's, and children's apparel. As of 2001, its revenues totalled approximately $1.3 billion at wholesale and $7.5 billion at retail.

In 1978, the company was acquired by Limited Brands and today produces the vast majority of the products featured in their retail outlets.

Unlike other contractors of the same nature, which are based in only a few countries, Mast Industries has offices in the United States, Hong Kong, Taiwan, Korea, Italy, Portugal, China, Indonesia, Sri Lanka, Egypt, Mauritius, Mexico, and the Philippines. All of the areas of the company, from design to manufacturing to distribution, are global. With this organizational structure, Limited is able to control all of the activities involved in the production of private-label goods and bring them to the consumer at the best possible prices. Through its ability to tap the resources of the numerous countries in which it is based, the company is able to satisfy the market demand for quality, quantity, and price.

With the extent of the globalization of Mast Industries, Limited is assured that on-time delivery will be exactly as needed regardless of unfavorable global events, unanticipated increases in product demand, or material shortages. The depth and breadth of their manufacturing facilities enables them to shift from one venue to another as the need arises.

In order to assure that it functions at the highest possible level, the company has developed many joint ventures and strategic partnerships. By doing so, Limited Brands is able to secure products that are manufactured in plants that have local involvement. This arrangement is considered by most industry professionals to be the soundest approach to overseas production.

Despite the seasonal demands of fashion merchandise and the intensely competitive nature of the retail community, Limited's outlets are able to meet the challenges of providing consumers with timely, high-quality products.

Purchasing from Private-Label Developers

Although in-house production affords the retailer many advantages, this route is not the one taken by most retailers. First and foremost in the decision not to proceed in this manner is the size of most retail operations, which are too small to warrant such privately held facilities. Moreover, the number of private brands or labels marketed by them is insufficient to maintain such facilities.

An alternative method to private brands and labels is to purchase from vendors who are strictly in the business of producing goods to the retailer's own specifications. Throughout the United States and many countries abroad, a significant number of manufacturers are set up to satisfy the specific needs of retail clients. With input from stores, catalogue companies, e-tailers, and the cable TV home-shopping channels, these suppliers produce exactly what is required.

One such fashion merchandise company, based in New York City, is Lizden Industries, Inc. With the help of well-known designers, Lizden is able to meet the challenges of

Independent design companies create products for exclusive use by many clients.

most retail organizations. They have access to the world's leading textile mills and production plants and are able to produce goods that are priced appropriately for their clients. One of their major customers is QVC, for whom they design a variety of products.

Purchasing from National Manufacturers

Throughout the world are numerous manufacturers in a variety of merchandise classifications that primarily produce goods under their own labels. Their principal focus is promoting their own brands and making them household names. However, some manufacturers also choose to accommodate clients by producing products that do not bear the manufacturer's label.

Supermarkets were among the first retail outlets to utilize the services of manufacturers of nationally branded products for their own private brands. They began by purchasing the **overruns** of well-known products and affixing their own labels to give the appearance that they were produced by the retailer itself. Today, many of a supermarket's private brands come not only from these overruns but also via contractual arrangements made with these producers.

More and more retailers of every merchandising classification are opting for well-known manufacturers to produce their goods. Some buy a proportion of their products under the marquee labels with the remainder produced by these very same companies—except that these items bear the retailer's own label.

Alternative Private-Label and Brand Acquisition

When none of the aforementioned practices are appropriate for the retailer, there are some other approaches that might be taken to acquiring private-label merchandise. Specifically, these are through the services of market consulting firms or by way of group purchasing.

Market Consulting Firms

The largest of these firms, the Doneger Group, advises clients on manufacturer sourcing and other pertinent information that assists their companies with the right decision making. It also produces collections for clients.

Through their own product developers, the Doneger Group creates styles and silhouettes, complete with the latest in fabrication and color, and contracts with manufacturers to produce them. Using a variety of its own labels—such as Lauren Matthews, Complements, and Greg Adams—the company presents lines to clients via in-house presentations, brochures, individual meetings, and the Internet. The purchase of these products assures exclusivity within a specific geographic area. That is, each retailer is guaranteed that the line will be his or hers alone without the fear of any competition.

It should be understood that this acquisition practice doesn't afford the retailer absolute private-label merchandise, as is the case when merchants develop their own lines. Instead, it might be considered a semiprivate label, since distribution is limited to only those who maintain noncompeting outlets.

Many manufacturers produce private brands, such as these sports logo products, along with their own lines.

Smaller retailers who are unable to tailor their own private-label collections, either because of their limited financial resources or their inability to market large quantities, often find this alternative plan satisfactory to their needs.

Group Purchasing

In many retail classifications, independent merchants join in **group purchasing** to gain the advantages enjoyed by their larger retail counterparts. That is, they pool their orders so that they can gain price advantages as well as other purchasing benefits. An additional practice that some of these buying groups have become involved with is in the private-label arena.

With the expenses of developing their own collections shared, smaller retailers are able to get into the business of private-label merchandise. They initially meet to discuss the nature of the merchandise that should be produced exclusively for their use and then, with this information in hand, employ the services of a designer or product developer to create the products. When the individual items have been evaluated, the line is then reduced to include only those that have appeal to the group. The identifying private label is chosen that best reflects the companies that have joined forces in the group venture.

The final step is selecting contractors who will carry out the production stage. It might be a local manufacturer or one that is based off-shore. As in the case of private-label acquisition from market consulting firms, this arrangement assures the participants a degree of exclusivity in their own trading areas.

PROMOTION OF PRIVATE BRANDS AND LABELS

In order to ensure that the consumer is aware of their latest merchandise collections, designers and manufacturers take it upon themselves to make the necessary promotional commitments. Major companies often have their own in-house publicity divisions to undertake these chores, while others opt for the use of public relations firms to do the job. Whatever the situation, the end result—if the campaign is professionally carried out—will be that the public is well aware of the product's existence. Labels and brands like Liz Claiborne, Nike, Ralph Lauren, Zenith, Del Monte, and Levi Straus have become household names and so require little promotion from retailers to make them known to their customers.

On the other hand, although the advent of private branding and labeling has given the retailer specific merchandising advantages, it doesn't guarantee that the line will achieve consumer recognition. Retailers must be willing to spend significant sums to promote their private labels and brands so that sufficient exposure will be achieved. They use a variety of techniques to publicize their own privately produced merchandise, beginning with its initial introduction and continuing with the building of public awareness. Some of these endeavors include the following:

Nike has opened giant retail facilities called Niketown to promote its own lines.

- *Advertising campaigns.* There is virtually no better way for retailers to inform their regular customers and potential purchasers about a private-label line of merchandise than through advertising. Generally, a multimedia campaign is developed that encompasses the use of both print and broadcast media. Through newspapers, magazines, television, and radio, a general audience is likely to be reached. For more focused campaigns, direct marketing is often the answer. With their own mailing lists of charge customers and other lists purchased from marketing research firms, the retailer is able to get its message across to a specific audience. The key to the effectiveness of these promotional endeavors is continuity. By regular blitzes, a percentage of those exposed to the different media approaches will ultimately be curious enough to find out more about the product line. Potential customers might do this through direct store visits or, perhaps, by checking out the company's Web site.
- *Stores within the store.* A retailer that wants to maximize exposure to its private collections sometimes creates an area called a **store within the store** that seems to be separate from the other departments. These self-contained selling areas are much like those that merchants set aside for their couture collections. Not only do these areas showcase the private brand, they also give greater importance to the line by moving it from the mainstream of typical merchandise offerings. Macy's, for example, generated a great deal of interest in one of its private labels, Charter Club, by giving it the appearance of a specialty store within the store.
- *Promotional tools.* The ingenuity of the retailer's in-house staff and that of outside sources can generate a variety of giveaways that often leave an indelible impression in the consumer's mind. One such promotional tool is a shopping bag emblazoned with the name of the new private label. If the bag is especially attractive and sufficiently sturdy for future use, many shoppers are apt to keep it for long periods of time. Each time they use it they are actually publicizing the company's name. Other promotional items that continue to serve as reminders to the users are small items such as pens. Every time the writing implement is taken in hand, it serves as a reminder of the new private label.

- *Special events.* A host of different activities, or **special events**, are usually mounted to serve as part of the new label's introduction process. The presentation of a fashion show featuring the new collection may present a vivid impression of the line. It might be a runway show that will introduce the collection with significant fanfare, or informal modeling for a specific number of days that serves to introduce the products throughout the store. The use of celebrities during the introduction phase could help generate considerable in-store traffic and motivate purchasing. One way that shopping channels have created consumer interest is by utilizing the services of a personality to motivate buying. QVC and the others have used this promotional tool with great success. The vast majority of the products introduced via this format are new to the public and are actually the end result of the work of designers who create them especially for these programs. They are, in fact, private labels that are not found in any other venues. With a large segment of the population captivated by celebrities, their use could prove invaluable in promoting the new private label.
- *Staff training.* While it is desirable to have those responsible for selling the merchandise completely knowledgeable about all of the company's merchandise offerings, it is especially important to make certain that they know how to discuss the merits of a new private label. Customers often have questions about new products, and only if they are satisfied with the answers will they opt to try them. The consumer is fully aware of the benefits of nationally advertised brands but must be convinced that the company's own brand will satisfy his or her needs.
- *Visual merchandising.* One of the ways that brick-and-mortar retailers catch the shopper's attention is through the use of window and interior displays. If carefully conceived, there is no better way to silently sell the new in-house brand. Professional visual installations are the motivating tools that can stop passersby and perhaps stimulate them enough to enter the store for a closer look at the goods. If the department's visual presentation is also carefully developed, it will bring the shopper one step closer to making the purchase.

The promotion of a new private collection is almost as important as the specific products themselves. It is the only way for retailers to bring these offerings to the attention of their clientele. The merchandiser must be able to peak consumer interest and stimulate customers to take a chance on the new items.

CHAPTER HIGHLIGHTS

- Competition among retailers has caused more and more of them to enter the arena of private brands and labels, thus providing them with more distinctive merchandise.
- Most retailers, especially department stores, have approached private labeling by using these brands as a proportion of their overall inventories.
- Merchandising private-label goods is more difficult than merchandising nationally branded goods because the former requires a great deal of development.
- Manufacturers' brands afford the retailer immediate exposure to the public, reorder availability, quality assurance, and in some cases prestige.
- Sears, although one of the earliest entries in private branding, has gone against the tide and now touts manufacturers' brands along with their own store brands.
- The store-is-the-brand concept is used by merchants who exclusively sell their own brands and label them with the company's name. Leaders in this area include Gap, Inc. and Limited Brands.
- The private brand and label approach promotes greater profitability for the retailer, avoids unfair price competition, eliminates the purchasing requirements typical of manufacturers' brands, reduces customer comparison shopping, and ensures product specificity.
- The giants in the private-brand arena maintain their own production facilities so that they can control every aspect of the operation and avoid middleman markups.

- Private-label goods, when not produced at the company's own plants, come from national manufacturers that also produce goods to order under the retailer's own labels. Goods also come from producers who are solely in the business of making products for private-label clients.
- One way in which smaller retailers may avail themselves of private brands is by purchasing the lines of market consulting firms. These lines are produced expressly for their customers.
- In order to make customers aware of private labels and brands, retailers undertake advertising campaigns, create separate shops within their stores, use a variety of promotional tools, plan special events to draw shoppers, and train their sales associates on the benefits of such products.
- One of the biggest factors in the success of a private label is the name that is given to it. More and more of those who are involved in the concept use names that sound like designers or celebrities as their signatures.
- Some retailers who have the potential to sell enormous quantities of merchandise, such as major value chains, enter into exclusive licensing agreements with celebrities who have merchandise collections bearing their names.

IMPORTANT RETAILING TERMS

company-owned production (350)
comparison shopping (348)
group purchasing (352)
licensing agreement (348)
manufacturers' brand (342)
marquee label (341)
overrun (351)
point-of-purchase (349)
prepack (348)
price cutting (342)
private brands and labels (344)
private-label developer (350)
proportional inventory
    concept (345)
signature brand (342)
special event (354)
store within the store (353)
store-is-the-brand operation (342)

FOR REVIEW

1. Why do most retailers primarily stock their inventories with manufacturers' brands?
2. Why can retailers be certain that manufacturers' brands will have the quality assurance expected by consumers?
3. Why is prestige an important motivational factor for some consumer purchases?
4. Which was the first major retailer to use private-brand merchandising for appliances?
5. What is meant by proportional use of private labels?
6. How does the store-is-the-brand concept differ from the proportional use of private branding?
7. Who are some of the most famous proponents of store-is-the-brand merchandising?
8. Is profitability generally higher or lower for private brands than for manufacturers' national brands?
9. Why do merchants who use their own brands avoid price cutting?
10. What is meant by the term *prepack assortments*?
11. Is customer loyalty more likely to come from private or manufacturers' brands?
12. How do licensed private brands differ from those typical of traditional private branding?
13. Which methodology of private brand and label development is the most difficult for the retailer to undertake?
14. What role does a market consulting firm play in private labeling and branding?
15. How might group purchasing help small retailers avail themselves of private-label goods?
16. Why do some merchants utilize stores within the store for private-label offerings?
17. What are some of the typical promotions that retailers use to publicize their own labels?
18. Why is it necessary to train the sales staff in terms of private-label benefits?
19. How important is the name that is given to a private-label collection?
20. What approach have some major retailers used to give their private brands a designer impression?

AN INTERNET ACTIVITY

Log onto the Web sites of 10 major U.S. department stores. Using your favorite search engine, do a search on department stores to locate these Web addresses.

Once you have logged on to these sites, research each one to learn whether it identifies merchandise that is its own brand.

Prepare a table to summarize the information you collect. Use the following column heads:

Retailer name	Are private brands identified?	Private brand name

EXERCISES AND PROJECTS

1. Visit five discount or value-oriented retailers in your city for the purpose of determining whether they have collections that bear the signatures of celebrities. If you are uncertain about a particular line, ask to speak to a manger to learn if the collection is exclusive to the company. Stores like Wal-Mart, Target,

Kmart, Home Depot, and Sears are typically participants in these licensing agreements. Complete a chart with the following headings, using the information you have gathered.

| Retailer | Signature private label(s) | Merchandise type |

2. Contact a major store-is-the-brand retailer for the purpose of determining how they come by their products. (Table 15.2 may be used as a guide for finding the one you would like to research.) You may obtain product information either by writing to the corporate headquarters or by logging on to its Web site. A two-page, typed, double-spaced report should be written containing the information you have gathered.

THE CASE OF DETERMINING THE APPROPRIATENESS OF PRIVATE LABELS

Caldwell and Fine is a specialized department store in the Northeast that has been in business since 1968. It operates a flagship store and 12 branch stores, all of which are located within a 500-mile radius of each other. Its forte is high-fashion designer apparel for women and men, with a merchandise assortment that includes couture, designer, and bridge collections. Featured among the numerous lines that it carries are such internationally known labels as Armani, La Croix, Lauren, DKNY, Versace, and others. Its reputation is flawless, and the store enjoys the continued loyalty of its customers.

With the opening of a few off-price merchants near some of its units and with Internet Web sites that feature some of its lines at discounted prices, Caldwell and Fine has begun to hear some complaints from its regular customers in the past 2 years. In addition, some of the lines it features—the bridge collections, in particular—were becoming more visible at many of its competitors. The increased visibility of these lines makes them less desirable for Caldwell and Fine customers, who prefer a greater level of exclusivity.

At Caldwell and Fine's last general merchandising meeting, the question of including private labels in its assortments came under discussion. With the problems surfacing about the proliferation of well-known brands in its trading areas, Janet Rogers—the divisional merchandise manager for women's bridge apparel—suggested that the time was ripe to develop some of its own collections. Philip Rivers, a buyer in that division, stressed that the store's reputation was built on fashion labels offering prestige to its customers and that perhaps the unbranded offerings would be inappropriate for the company.

After a great deal of discussion, the members of the merchandising team were asked to present their opinions on the possible inclusion of private labels and on how they believed their inclusion would affect overall sales.

Questions

1. If you were a member of the team, would you be in favor of private labels for the store? Defend your answer with sound reasoning.
2. If the decision is made to include private labels, what proportion of the inventory would you suggest be devoted to this exclusive merchandise? Why?
3. What methodology would you use in the development and acquisition of the private brand?

Markets Say Proudly: It's Our Brand
Jon Ortiz

NOVEMBER 11, 2007

One of the most profound yet subtle shifts in America's grocery industry starts in a nondescript beige stucco warehouse on Auburn's northern edge.

Inside, 17 workers for Mad Will's Food Co. concoct, bottle, box and ship nearly 100 so-called private label gourmet barbecue sauces, salad dressings and salsas that end up in grocery aisles around the country.

The company, based in San Francisco, represents a tiny sliver of a growing but intentionally obscure $45.5 billion industry that manufactures goods for supermarkets with tailor-made labels featuring each store's brand.

Mad Will's business is up, fueled by traditional grocers who are turning to private labels, once considered the lowest rung of retail, as a new weapon in the fight for consumer loyalty.

"Things are booming for us," said Tim Sullivan, Mad Will's products director. "And we think it's only going to get better."

Private labels and their humble generic brand cousins have historically screamed "Cheap!" with plain packaging, low prices and an also-ran quality that didn't measure up with shoppers like 59-year-old Elk Grove resident Georgia Rand.

"I always thought of them like I think of knock-off perfume," Rand said during a recent shopping trip at the Raley's on Elk Grove Boulevard. "Close, but not quite."

Experts say that marketing, not price or profit, has driven retailers to put more thought into private brands. Every bottle, every box, every bag carrying the store's brand is a direct message that implies shoppers have something that can't be purchased across the street. That builds loyalty.

So stores are demanding products with higher-quality ingredients and stylish packaging. They're also rolling out trendier fare such as organic food and serving up multitiered portfolios that hit low, middle and upper-end categories while still holding the line on prices when compared with nationally recognized brands.

Those efforts have boosted business for companies like Mad Will's as consumers switch from national to store brands. Nearly half of the 1,000 shoppers surveyed by the Nielsen Co. earlier this year said one of every four grocery items that they buy is a store brand. Some 41 percent of consumers said they were "frequent" private label buyers, up from 36 percent five years ago.

Rand's shopping cart tells the same story. Of the 19 items she purchased, the bread, bacon, mustard, bottled water, canned corn and grape jelly carried Raley's store labels.

"I used to shy away from (private labels)," she said. The reason for her conversion? "Simple. Costs less and tastes the same or better than the stuff I used to buy."

Consumers' change of heart has played out across the country. Supermarket store brand sales grew at a 5.3 percent clip last year, according to Nielsen figures, while overall sales grew just 4.6 percent.

"It only stands to reason that retailers who invest in their own store brands ... expect to maximize the advantage," said Dane Twining, spokesman for the Private Label Manufacturers Association, a New York City-based trade group.

In a bid to do just that, Pleasanton-based Safeway Inc. this year reorganized more than 70 different store brands into 10 "power" brands with updated packaging, including its O Organics, Safeway Select and Basic Red lines.

"The growth has been tremendous," said Safeway spokeswoman Teena Massingill. "We started O Organics last year with 150 items. It's now up to 200."

Save Mart Supermarkets, which carries more than 2,000 private label items, is rolling out a redesigned look for the Sunnyside Farms and Sunny Select brands that it shares with Raley's.

"The existing brand was old and tired and held minimal value," said Alicia Rockwell, spokeswoman for the Modesto-based chain.

Raley's, for its part, is trimming its Sunnyside Farms and Sunny Select lines in favor of its low-priced Everyday, midrange Raley's and higher-end Nob Hill Trading Co. brands.

"We've gone from virtually no (Raley's branded) private label items two years ago to about 2,000 today," said spokeswoman Amy Johnston.

The privately held company declined to provide specifics about its store brand development program, but Johnston said, "We're always looking for new products to add."

Private label products get to a store's shelves from various sources. Some national companies use their excess plant capacity to supply store brands. Some wholesalers and large retailers, like Safeway, own manufacturing plants and make their own goods.

Then there are the small, nimble companies like 18-year-old Mad Will's that make specialty product lines. A national manufacturer can take a year or more to bring a new sauce to market. Mad Will's can do it in seven weeks.

"We watch for emerging trends," Sullivan said. "We also talk to people who have their own recipes. When we see something with promise, we jump on it."

Mad Will's path to the grocery aisle takes two routes. Sometimes the company pitches a sauce to corporate decision-makers at food shows and industry conventions. Often it submits samples at the invitation of retailers looking for a specific kind of product.

New ideas go to the company's development staff. In a small back room lined with shelves stuffed with jars of spices and oils, they whip up test batches, stirring, tasting and critiquing.

Flavor is just part of the equation. The sauces have to be the right consistency, or the company's 150-gallon commercial mixers and bottling equipment will bog down. The recipe has to be cost-effective to mass produce. And the developers have to consider the finished product's shelf life.

What's on the bottle is almost as important as what's inside it, so Sullivan wrestles with what to name each concoction. He usually relies on a formula.

"Two words that give you the ingredients, two words that tell you what to do with the product," he said during a recent tour of the 16,000-square-foot Auburn plant and warehouse.

With this approach, Mad Will's sells "Honey Jalapeño Grilling Glaze," "Bourbon Peppercorn Steak Slather" and "Raspberry Mustard Pretzel Dipper," to name a few.

"This is all about marketing," Sullivan said with a chuckle. "We used to sell plain old Chinese Chicken Salad Dressing. Then we changed the name to 'Sesame Soy Ginger Vinaigrette.' Sales shot up 50 percent."

Indeed, the biggest expense to introducing a new product for companies like Mad Will's is marketing, said consultant Mark Lilien of Retail Technology Group in Stamford, Conn. "They already have the ingredients. They already have the bottles," Lilien said. "The real problem is virtually anyone can make barbecue sauce and salad dressing. So they have to do the missionary work of marketing it."

As a final check, Mad Will's often ships a sample case to a 10-member "tasting panel" for a final round of criticism.

"Retail executives, customers, a food broker, marketing people from the East Coast to the West Coast," Sullivan said. "One guy is a Swiss chef. He's made some terrific suggestions. What a palate."

Grocers invite private label manufacturers to submit specific samples for a "cutting," a contest that pits up to a dozen similar products against each other in areas that include flavor, appearance and price.

"Sometimes it's a bid process," Sullivan said. "A retailer may want something equivalent to an $8.99 Williams-Sonoma item to sell for $3.99 at the supermarket."

The intense competition between manufacturers is one reason store brands remain 10 percent to 15 percent cheaper than national brands, say experts. Another reason: Private labels don't carry their rival brands' heavy national marketing costs.

U.S. grocery store shoppers last year saved an estimated $15.8 billion by purchasing private label groceries, according to industry sales data.

Officials with the privately held Mad Will's wouldn't divulge the company's finances, but Sullivan noted that it sells "in every state except Hawaii, from mom-and-pop stores to some of the country's biggest chains."

As proof, he pointed to 20 thick rolls of customized bottle labels on a table in a staging area. Various grocery store brands, some in California, topped each label. But Sullivan decline to release the names.

"Wouldn't be good for business to let that out," he said.

The Power of the Private Label
William George Shuster

March 1, 2007

"Our store brand is our face in the market, the one we want people to know. So we try to do as much as we can to support it with our private labels, blending them with the store's strategic interests and advertising."

So says Virginia Beach, Va., jeweler David Nygaard. Like many jewelers, he uses private-label products—made by or for the jeweler and bearing the store name or trademark—to successfully imprint his store brand in consumers' minds. As he told the Virginia-Pilot in July 2006, "A jeweler needs a strong identity to separate [himself] from the pack." Nygaard tells JCK that he believes in supporting that identity by "our own brand's qualitative distinctions, rather than being value driven, like chains and mass merchandisers."

His strategy has been successful enough that, over the last two years, Nygaard expanded from one store to six.

St. Louis jeweler Michael George has sold his own branded products since the late 1980s. "Private-label is significant, because we're putting our name on something, setting us apart from other vendors," he says. "It enables consumers to look at us with a different eye, to see we don't have what everyone else has. There's prestige and advantage in having your own named line instead of someone else's branded product, whose pricing you can't control, making you less competitive."

"When one shops in a mall, it seems every store comes from the same cookie cutter, with variants of the same merchandise," notes Alan Grunwald, president of Belair Time, a leading manufacturer of private-label timepieces. "But independent jewelers are different. They offer unique products and personalized service. They need to tell that story, and private branding is the avenue to do so."

Self-branding is something major retailers have done for generations. What are "Cartier" and "Tiffany," after all, but private-label brands of jewelry stores successfully impressed on the public consciousness through their products and marketing. More recently, regional jewelry chains have set themselves apart with proprietary lines, diamond cuts, and products. More independents also see the value—and profit—in that. A 2004 JCK national survey of hundreds of jewelers found that two out of five had private-label products, and three out of five expected their sales to keep growing through this decade.

Private-label merchandise supports a store brand with exclusivity, prestige, and quality control, say jewelers.

Exclusivity is a significant competitive advantage. As jeweler Sandi Dahlquist, Poulsbo, Wash., notes, "Other stores don't have it, and it can't be price shopped." That brings in customers, both regular and new. Says Elizabeth Parker, of Curt Parker Jewelers in St. Louis, "Our CAPI jewelry is signature pieces you can only get at our store. People who see it on friends and want it must come here for it."

Consumers want items that are different, not generic, says Oklahoma City jeweler Arthur Gordon, who makes his own award-winning trademarked jewelry. "They see the same things everywhere, because more jewelry manufacturers sell the same designs under different names to guild stores, major chains, and mass marketers. We prefer to have things unique to us, that associate us in customers' minds with beautiful designs they can't get elsewhere."

Private-label exclusivity also helps watch retailing. Grunwald says private-label watches fit neatly into store branding. "With the right high-quality watch, a private brand can protect a jeweler's profits while enhancing the store image," he says. "Nothing is more embarrassing for a jeweler than to sell a brand-name watch to a customer who later sees it for less elsewhere. Such customers can be lost forever if they think the jeweler isn't competitive, and they may think twice when it's time to purchase a special diamond or expensive bracelet."

Grunwald says the Internet is devastating to jewelers selling brand-name watches because it makes it easy for consumers to price shop. "Private-label watches, though, can't be price shopped, which protects the jeweler's margin," he notes.

He also believes private-label watches are subliminal marketing tools. "How many times a day does someone look at his watch? If your store name is on it, how often does the wearer see it? When it's time to buy jewelry, who will that person think of?"

Private-label merchandise also helps jewelers address quality issues. "Many people are looking for quality in jewelry and not finding it, because many jewelry manufacturers use mass-production methods or have items made overseas, and the quality control isn't there," says Arthur Gordon. But, with private-label wares, notes David Nygaard, jewelers have "more control, from quality to the ability to better service what they sell."

Many jewelers say the attention they give to products with their own label ensures that customers get more for their money. "We don't use cheap materials in our jewelry," says Elisabeth Parker. She also notes that eliminating intermediaries keeps costs down. "When someone spends $1,000 on our CAPI jewelry, they get a better value." The CAPI label has several thousand original designs.

For such reasons, many jewelers are doing less with commercially branded jewelry and watches and more with self-labeled products.

San Antonio jeweler Ted Resnick, of Reznikov Jewelers, has manufactured jewelry of his own design stamped with his RFJ logo for 17 years. "We prefer to promote our own brand," he says. "In a town with 300 jewelers, it helps set us apart. We're noted for using the highest-quality gemstones and materials, which also sets us apart."

Nygaard's private-label Passion Fire pieces are designed in-house and manufactured outside. Passion Fire, which grew out of his Hearts Amore and Ageless Fire Ideal-cut diamonds, is "designed to be fast-selling, with triple markup, and three to four turns, leveraged with marketing and advertising," he says.

MSG Jewelers in St. Louis recently added a private-label line of 18k white gold and diamond rings, manufactured for it and hallmarked with its name and logo in the ring shanks. "More jewelry manufacturers are offering jewelers private-label jewelry," notes owner Michael George.

The store has also sold for 17 years MSG Originals, one-of-a-kind designs it guarantees won't be duplicated. They include ready-for-sale items and designs awaiting a buyer. They're marketed through in-store displays and promotions and occasional ads.

CHAPTER 16
The Concepts and Mathematics of Merchandise Pricing

After you have completed this chapter, you should be able to discuss:

- The way each merchant selects the pricing policy that best addresses his or her business
- How retailers calculate their markups
- The numerous factors that affect a retailer's pricing structure, with special emphasis on competition in the marketplace
- How competition can be eliminated through the use of private-label brands and exclusivity arrangements with vendors
- The importance of a retailer's image to pricing decisions
- How pricing strategies run the gamut from keystone pricing to the concept that allows for judgment on every item before it heads to the selling arena
- How merchants select price points or price ranges for their companies so that they can better serve the needs of a narrower market segment
- The relationship between markdowns and the original selling price, and why markdowns must be taken to dispose of less desirable merchandise

After the buyers and merchandisers have completed their purchases and decided upon the percentage, if any, of private label products, they must properly price the goods to maximize profit. The pricing philosophy is established by the company's management team, and is adhered to by the buyers and merchandisers, who must stay within mandated guidelines.

Retail operations utilize pricing procedures that best serve their company's format. For example, the traditional merchant that uses brick-and-mortar outlets for the vast majority of its business generally subscribes to larger markups than its discount or off-price counterpart. No matter what pricing structure is used, it must remain constant so that the consuming public will be able to determine if it is in line with its expectations. Those individuals who frequent the value shopping arenas, for example, want to be assured that the prices charged are rock-bottom. Those who patronize the more traditional venues or luxury stores will be less inclined to care about price but will more than likely expect services to be offered along with the merchandise.

In addition to the overall pricing concept of a company, there are numerous factors that eventually help management determine the actual prices that it will charge their customers. These factors include competition in the retailer's trading area, exclusivity of the merchandise, how quickly the merchandise sells (its turnover rate), specific characteristics of the merchandise, promotional endeavors of the organization, its image, the services that are rendered to the clientele, and **inventory shrinkage** due to internal theft and shoplifting.

Once these factors are analyzed, the organization is ready to decide upon the **markup** that will be needed to bring the company the profit it expects to achieve. Of course, as we will learn later in the chapter, not every item that is marked to retail for a particular price actually sells at that price. Often, **markdowns** are needed to dispose of some items because they can't attract customer attention. When these reductions are taken, the retailer is not able to achieve the initial markup that was applied to these goods but is actually left with a **maintained markup**—the actual markup that has been achieved based upon retail selling prices that were adjusted because of markdowns.

Markup and markdown mathematical computations are easily achieved through the use of computer programs. However, in order to give the reader a better understanding of the concepts, mathematical illustrations are presented here.

MARKUP

Once the merchandise has been purchased, it is necessary for each item to be priced at an amount that will hopefully bring a profit to the company. It begins with the concept of markup, which is the difference between the amount that is paid for the goods by the merchant and the price for which they will be sold to the consumer. It is essential that all of the company's expenses be carefully considered so that the markup will be sufficient to render a profit.

The following illustrates the mathematics of markup:

$$\text{Retail (selling price)} - \text{Cost} = \text{Markup}$$

For example, a dress that is purchased by the buyer for $100 and retails for $200 would have a markup of $100.

$$\$200 \text{ (retail)} - \$100 \text{ (cost)} = \$100 \text{ markup.}$$

This illustration addresses the **dollar markup**. In practice, retailers utilize a system that focuses on **markup percents** rather than dollar markups. These markup percents may be expressed as a function of either retail or cost.

Markup Percent on Retail

By far, the most widely used markup percent computations are based on retail. Through the efforts of the National Retail Federation (NRF) and numerous research organizations and universities, the markup percent on retail approach has become commonplace.

Markup percent on retail affords these advantages to the retailing community:

- Because sales information is much more easily determined than cost, a markup based on retail greatly facilitates the calculation of the estimated profits.

- Inventory taking requires calculation of the cost of merchandise on hand. The **retail method of inventory** used by most merchants is based on markup at retail and provides a shortcut for determining inventory at cost.
- Sales associates' commissions are based on retail, as are management's bonuses and other operating data. It is therefore practical to base markup on retail as well.
- When consumers speak of markup, the smaller the markup percent they believe they are paying the better. In pure mathematics, the percent rendered by the retail approach is significantly lower than if it were based on cost. Although this is a psychological matter, it suggests that the company is working on a lower markup.

To find the markup percent based on retail, the dollar markup, as we saw in the previous illustration, is divided by the retail price. For example, a pair of athletic shoes costs the retailer $50 and is marked to retail for $100. What is the markup percent based on retail?

For the solution, the dollar markup must first be determined:

$$\text{Markup} = \text{Retail} - \text{Cost}$$
$$\text{Markup} = \$100 - \$50$$
$$\text{Markup} = \$50$$

To find the markup percent based on retail:

$$\frac{\text{Markup}}{\text{Retail}} = \text{Markup \% based on retail}$$

Substituting the numbers:

$$\frac{\$50}{\$100} = 50\% \text{ based on retail}$$

By using the same dollar markup in the preceding example and the following one, we will be better able to understand the necessity of using the percent method and showing how identical dollar markups bring different returns to the retailer.

In the following illustration, a merchant purchases a set of luggage for $150 and sells it for $200. What is the dollar markup and markup percent based on retail?

To find the dollar markup:

$$\text{Markup} = \text{Retail} - \text{Cost}$$
$$\text{Markup} = \$200 - \$150$$
$$\text{Markup} = \$50$$

To find the markup percent on retail:

$$\frac{\text{Markup}}{\text{Retail}} = \text{Markup \% based on retail}$$

$$\frac{\$50}{\$200} = 25\% \text{ based on retail}$$

When we compare the two examples, we note that both reward the retailer with $50 markups. However, in the first example, the merchant had to invest only $50 to get the $50 markup, while in the latter, it had to invest $150 for the same dollar return. In the former it achieved a markup of 50 percent on retail; in the latter, this figure was only 25 percent. It is simple to see that the first method is far better than the second, further explaining the need to calculate markup percents rather than dollar markups.

Markup Percent on Cost

Although retailers most often use markup on retail, some in the industry rely upon the markup percent on cost computation. Typical of those who use this concept are the purveyors of produce, where fruit and vegetable prices vary from day to day according to the supply and demand of the wholesale market. Under such conditions, where the cost of inventories is relatively unimportant—because they sell out every few days and the profit and loss figures can be easily determined—the use of markup on cost is preferable. Others use the system simply because they have done so for many years and find change difficult to address.

For instance, a camera cost the retailer $66 and retails for $88. What is the markup percent based on cost?

To find the solution, first determine the dollar markup.

$$\text{Markup} = \text{Retail} - \text{Cost}$$
$$\text{Markup} = \$88 - \$66$$
$$\text{Markup} = \$22$$

To find the markup based on cost:

$$\frac{\text{Markup}}{\text{Cost}} = \text{Markup \% based on cost}$$

$$\frac{\$22}{\$66} = 33\text{-}1/3\% \text{ based on cost}$$

FACTORS THAT AFFECT PRICING

As we have just learned, the retail price of an item is based upon its actual cost from the vendor plus a sufficient markup that will yield a profit after covering the operating expenses of the business. Since management's prime responsibility is to maximize profits for the company (or for its principals or shareholders if it is a corporation), appropriate pricing is essential. Care must be exercised by those who have been given the responsibility to run the company in choosing the right pricing policy to assure the highest profit margins. This does not by any means warrant unusually high prices, since competition is always a key factor to any retailer's operation. If the prices are too high, consumers will certainly look elsewhere to have their needs satisfied. Understanding this, retailers must choose from a variety of pricing plans that will maximize profits. These plans range from the traditional retailers' approach, where relatively high markups are the order of the day because a host of clientele services are offered, to the value merchants' approach, where lower markups prevail in the hope that larger sales volumes will make up for the lower prices. Of course, there are other alternatives: those used by prestige retailers, where prices are high because their customers are willing to pay for the image that company offers and merchants who operate the **wholesale clubs**, charging less because they obtain a great deal of income from their membership fees.

Supreme Court Pricing Decision

In 2007, the Supreme Court of the United States handed down a decision that will probably have significant implications for the retailing industry. In a 5–4 ruling, the Court ended a 96-year-old ban on minimum pricing agreements, allowing brands to enforce the lowest price at which their products could be sold.

As a result, merchants such as discounters and off-pricers may no longer be able to market their merchandise at prices that they consider appropriate to their philosophies and merchandising concepts. Under this agreement, manufacturers would have the right to pull their brands from those stores that deviate from the prices established by the vendors. Small retailers, who often mark down items early in the season to move inventories, could also be affected.

Internet Web sites that use price as a major factor in their marketing plans would have to abide by the established prices, thus changing the nature of the way they do business. Many have established themselves on the concept of selling for less.

Consumer groups have declared that the decision will adversely affect shoppers, forcing them to spend an additional $750 to $1,000 annually for their purchases.

The Buyer's Judgment of the Merchandise's Appeal

If you have ever entered a brick-and-mortar operation, shopped the pages of a catalogue, or surfed the Web to make a purchase, occasionally a specific item may seem to be worth more than its retail price. This is not a typical occurrence, but it does happen. Although the buyer who was given the responsibility to price the goods stayed within the company's overall pricing strategy, he or she missed an opportunity to charge more for the particular item. By having a feel for creative pricing, the buyer might be able to add a few more dollars to the price, giving it the potential for greater profitability. Of course, pricing every piece of merchandise with added markup is not wise because goods don't always warrant extra dollars.

The buyer's ability to judge each item's appeal can result in higher markups—and increased profitability—for some items.

Prices are often set within specific minimums and maximums. These are in place to help the buyer use his or her own judgment. Being able to charge more for one item leaves room for the buyer to charge less for others that might be used for promotional purposes. It is really a juggling act and not one that is based upon automatic markups. It should be understood that a buyer is generally given an **average markup** to achieve. That average markup is based upon the entire inventory instead of just one item. If automation were used to price merchandise, then it wouldn't be necessary for retailers to employ individuals who have the instincts necessary to maximize profits. The buyer who has the skills to evaluate each piece of merchandise affords the merchant its greatest potential for profit. It must be remembered that every product that sells for a little more than the traditional markup helps to increase the company's maintained markup.

Competition

Having established that merchandise judgment is a factor to consider each time a product is being priced, it is also essential to understand that competition in one form or another can always take business away from the merchant. As we are discovering in the new millennium, competition is at an all-time high. Many brick-and-mortar operations within a given classification, such as the department stores, are often clones of each other. A walk through any of the major department stores quickly reveals Liz Claiborne, Ralph Lauren, and DKNY departments. The offerings are so familiar to the shoppers that they not only come to expect certain styles from them but are also aware of the exact prices to expect. Thus, the merchant who is foolish enough to price these collections at higher than traditional markups will certainly be met with customer resistance. A departure from the pricing norm for lines that are available almost everywhere would spell failure.

In order to make certain that the prices being charged for these widely distributed collections are in line with those being charged elsewhere requires a careful watch on the competition. It might come by way of a formalized approach that utilizes **comparison shoppers** who go from store to store to check out the competition or examines the catalogues and Web sites featuring the same goods. These shoppers make notes on the competitor's prices and bring them back to the buyers for further scrutiny.

Allowing their customers to discover identical merchandise at lower price points can cause irreparable harm to the merchant. Many retailers advertise that they will meet or beat competitors' prices, and this practice might encourage customers to shop around. Such retailers might have to reduce the price of some items in order to make good on their promise.

In an attempt to minimize the effects of widespread competition, more and more retailers are developing their own private brands and labels. With the **exclusivity** factor now a part of the overall merchandising scheme, the merchant can make up for the lower markups typical of nationally prominent brands. Private-label goods are not found anywhere but in the merchant's own premises, catalogues, and Web sites. Companies such as Macy's, Bloomingdale's, Marshall Field's, Dillard's, Belk, and Lord & Taylor continue to increase the proportion of their own brands in the overall merchandise mix. By doing so, they need not fear competitor price cutting.

Exclusivity

One way to achieve exclusivity is by private-label collections. This, however, is not the only means of stocking an assortment that is solely for a particular company. Oftentimes, relatively unknown manufacturers with limited production capability are eager to sign exclusive agreements for specific geographic trading areas. In this way, the vendor gains the advantage of having its product lines on the selling floor in quantities and assortments that are generally greater than if the lines were widely distributed. Retailers are often more inclined to expend significant promotional dollars on collections that are theirs alone. Bloomingdale's and other major department store organizations are always waiting to discover new designers whose collections can be exclusively theirs.

While it is possible for these lesser-known entities to offer exclusivity, this is not the case for marquee labels. Companies such as Ralph Lauren and Liz Claiborne, for example, will rarely ever grant the rights to a single merchant to solely represent their companies in a particular trading area. One notable exception is Tommy Hilfiger's deal with Macy's to limit this brand to that company only. However, a company might accommodate some of its better accounts by confining specific groupings within the collections to them. Thus, although the Lauren or Claiborne label is seen in every fashion-oriented department store, certain groups may be seen in just one area. This gives the vendor's most important clients the privilege of a certain degree of exclusivity.

With the knowledge that no other competing merchant may take advantage of competitive pricing, sole rights to particular products sometimes enable the beneficiaries to achieve better markups.

Membership Clubs

A growing value-oriented retail operation is the one that requires membership before any consumer purchasing may take place. Companies such as Sam's Club, Costco, and BJ's are examples of **membership clubs**; prices at these retailers are affected by the extent of their membership.

Focus on...
Costco

SINCE IT FIRST OPENED IN 1976—in a converted airplane hangar in San Diego—under the Price Club name, Costco has gone on to become the premier wholesale club in many parts of the globe. Its concept is to bring members the lowest possible prices on quality, brand-name products. It provides a wealth of different types of merchandise that includes but is not restricted to packaged and fresh foods, electronics, giftware, jewelry, accessories, automotive supplies, and wines.

It began as a company that served only small businesses but soon recognized that it could achieve significantly better buying clout by expanding its customer base to nonbusiness members. In 1993, Price Club and Costco merged and generated $16 billion in annual sales. Costco operates more than 500 warehouses around the world and today has sales of more than $59 billion.

It is interesting to note that the prices charged at Costco are considerably less for identical merchandise found in other operations. While the enormous volume it enjoys certainly contributes to its ability to sell for less, that is not the only key to its pricing strategy. The cost of each membership, $45 annually at the time of this writing, allows Costco to minimally mark up the goods offered for sale. Even if no profits are reaped from the sale of these items, the membership dollars alone would bring in sufficient revenue to turn a handsome profit for the company. By simply multiplying the $45 by the many millions of members it serves around the world, one can easily understand the nature of Costco's pricing structure. The single most important factor that affects its pricing is the membership fee.

Of course, the retail price charged for each item is above Costco's wholesale cost. The fee simply allows for a lower markup, making the company highly competitive with other merchants.

While price is certainly the single most important factor to the success of the company, Costco also provides other services to maintain a satisfactory relationship with its customers. The company provides real estate services, mortgage services, long-distance phone programs, check printing, auto sales, travel arrangements for all members, and special services to its executive members, including 2 percent savings on most purchases, business payroll processing, business equipment leasing, small business loans, business credit card processing, and health care programs.

But above all, it is the pricing of its offerings that brings the consuming public and business enterprises to Costco.

The Nature of the Goods

Different types of merchandise require different pricing considerations based on their characteristics. For example, some items plague the retailer with a certain degree of perishability, as is the case of fashion merchandise, while others require a great deal of security to safeguard them from shoplifters, as is the case with precious jewelry. Because of the nature of these classes of goods, they typically require higher markups.

Fashion Merchandise

The typical culprit in this product classification is women's apparel and accessories. Rarely does a specific item successfully transcend the seasons. While some styles gain immediate success and account for significant sales, others are not as readily accepted by the consumer. Even when early acceptance has taken place, there always seems to be end-of-season leftovers that need to be marked down to make way for the newer fashions.

In order to make certain that these short-lived styles help the retailer to maximize profits, it is essential that the initial retail price be sufficiently marked up. That is, a larger amount must be added to the wholesale price to make sure that, when the markdowns are taken at season's end, a certain degree of profitability will be maintained.

When merchandise of this nature is contrasted with the staples that many retailers stock in their inventories, it is apparent that the latter classifications are more likely to bring steady sales at the initially marked prices.

The business of fashion merchandise is a risky one. Retailers must always be prepared for the possibility that the choices their buyers have made will fail to attract customers. It might be the right silhouette but the wrong color or the right color but the wrong fabric. In terms of pricing, these fashion-oriented goods must be marked up as high as the competition will allow. When the figures are in, the winner's revenues should make up for the purchasing errors.

Markups on short-lived fashion products are normally high to compensate for end-of-season markdowns.

Seasonal Merchandise

Products that last for only a short selling period owing to their seasonal nature must, as in the case of fashion items, be sufficiently priced to make up for the inevitable markdowns at the end of the selling season. It might be swimsuits, raincoats, snow boots, or any other items that fall into the short-lived category. Like their fashion product counterparts, they must be disposed of at season's end to make room for the newly expected merchandise. One might assume that the unsold seasonal or fashion items could be stored and carried over to the next year, but the numerous design changes that regularly take place make this a risky business. Also negating the carry-over concept is the cost of warehousing. Retailers do not have the storage space necessary to stock merchandise for long periods of time.

The raincoat buyer may be plagued with a limited amount of rainfall in the spring, a time when rainwear sales generally peak; the swimwear buyer may be confronted with cool and rainy summer months; and skiwear merchants may be stuck with large inventories due to lower than expected precipitation. It is only then when higher markups can be appreciated. Adding additional dollars to the initial selling price allows for markdowns that will, it is hoped, move the slow sellers and still bring something of a profit to the company. If lower retail prices were initially affixed to these items, the end results would be disastrous.

Perishable Merchandise

The aforementioned seasonal products do bear a type of perishability, but others pose even greater risks to the merchants who sell them. A prime example of **perishable merchandise** is fresh-cut flowers. Florists must deal with time frames as brief as a few days in their retailing. Once the rose has faded, it is no longer salable. Thus, products of this nature must be priced to take into consideration that not everything will sell. A high markup will offset the losses.

Whether it is farm produce or fresh-baked breads and pastries, the appeal of truly perishable items is extremely short lived. Unlike leftover fashions, which may be marked down to encourage purchasing, these goods are often tossed into refuse containers. Their sellers must make certain that the items are sufficiently priced to offset the inevitable discards.

Bulky Merchandise

Of particular importance in this category is furniture, carpeting, and rugs. Because of their size and the space they require either in warehouses or on the selling floor—their merchandising necessitates higher markups. They must be priced so that this additional expense can be offset by higher markups.

Precious Jewelry

One of the cost factors that must be considered in the pricing of gemstones and precious metals is security. Because these items must be carefully secured and safeguarded from would-be shoplifters, state-of-the-art alarm systems are put in place. Not only is this a necessity as understood by the retailer, it is also a condition of most companies that insure such precious merchandise.

In addition to security systems that protect the showcases in which these items are displayed, large tamperproof vaults are maintained for storage at the end of the selling day. Merchants regularly remove their goods from the selling floor and place them in these vaults for safekeeping.

These protection costs are significant and must be considered when the merchandise is being priced. Hence, precious jewelry requires markups that are higher than most other goods.

Stock Turnover

As we learned in Chapter 14, the number of times an inventory totally sells out during the year is a major factor for the retailer. The standard rule that is addressed by the buyers who determine retail prices is as follows:

The higher the turnover rate, the lower the markup; the lower the turnover rate, the higher the markup.

Thus, prepared salads such as tuna fish sold in supermarkets, which generally sell out every day, require a low markup to be considered profitable. On the other hand, diamonds, because of their high prices, turn over at a low rate, requiring a larger markup.

Retailer Promotional Endeavors

Today's competitive environment necessitates a considerable amount of promotion whether it is at the brick-and-mortar operations, in catalogues, or on the Internet. Merchants must set aside large sums for advertising campaigns and for special events that bring attention to their businesses. Whether it is the use of the print or broadcast media or the development of special promotions such as fashion shows, the costs of such involvement are spiraling upward. These expenses must be taken into account by the retailer when selling prices are being established, but it should be understood that successful promotion also helps to generate more business, often enabling the retailer to be more profitable.

In any case, promotional budgets must be carefully considered when merchandise is being priced. The cost of the advertising and special events must be included when determining what prices must be charged in order to maximize profits.

Designer shops like Louis Vuitton mark up their merchandise at higher percentages than do value retailers because they know their customers are willing to pay high prices for prestige items.

Company Image

Although value shopping is a major trend for the new millennium, not every segment of the population patronizes a merchant because of the lowest selling price. In fact, there is also a trend in which more and more **prestige retailers** are cropping up throughout the country.

Looking at Fifth Avenue in New York City and Worth Avenue in Palm Beach, Florida, we observe many new retailers whose business centers on high-profile merchandise. Designer shops, along with companies like Nordstrom and Neiman Marcus, are undergoing extensive expansions to capture the market motivated by labels that bring image to the forefront. This does not mean that these retailers do not bring quality along with their prestigious labels. They do, indeed, but at the same time they add yet another dimension that stimulates purchasing.

The extra services offered to customers in stores like this fashionable Hong Kong shop often necessitate higher markups.

Just as designer logos became commonplace on the outside of apparel and accessories in the 1970s and 1980s, so have the image-building retailers. This phenomenon has enabled many merchants to use higher markups for their products. A few extra dollars might not bring the shopper a different item from what is available elsewhere for less, but it affords them the opportunity to bring prestige to their attire.

The retailer must establish this prestige image early on if it is to successfully merchandise its inventory with higher markups, just as its value-oriented counterparts must promote their discount and off-price images from the outset.

Services

The more services afforded the consumer, the more likely these will be reflected in the price of merchandise. As we note by shopping in stores, through catalogues, or online, multichannel retailers offer about the same services in each of their selling formats. For example, brick-and-mortar operations might offer free alterations, and companies such as Levi's feature "made to measure" jeans for their customers.

Whether it is alterations, concierge services, personal shoppers' gift registries, or any other service, all come at additional expense to the merchant. Such services do attract customers, but the expenses attributed to these offerings must be considered when selling prices are established. Customers who frequent the service-oriented merchants are often willing to pay the little extra that is being charged to make their shopping experience more pleasurable.

Pilferage

Shoplifting and internal theft, also known as **pilferage**, are among the most troubling factors to plague retailers. Naturally, brick-and-mortar merchants bear the brunt of the problem since they are the only retailers with on-premises customers. This is not to say that catalogue and e-tail divisions do not have problems with internal theft or losses due to unscrupulous online purchasers. In any case, the pilferage figures continue to climb. As we learned in Chapter 10, more and more state-of-the-art systems are being installed to help reduce the problem. Nonetheless, the losses must be offset in some way. Toward this end, merchants find that they must consider pilferage rates in their markups and ultimately in the prices they charge. The result is that honest consumers pay more in order to make up for these losses.

PRICING STRATEGIES

Before any retail operation gets off the ground, attention must be focused on the company's pricing strategy. Each merchant must consider all of the available approaches and decide upon the best one to satisfy the company's needs. Some of the strategies include keystone pricing, keystone plus pricing, overall uniform pricing, department pricing, individual merchandise pricing, negotiable pricing, and average pricing. Each can stand on its own merits and can be utilized to maximize the company's profits.

Keystone Pricing

Perhaps the simplest method for determining the selling price is through the use of **keystone pricing**. Retailers who subscribe to this strategy merely double the wholesale cost to determine the retail. Thus, if a product costs $25 it will be automatically marked $50. In many retail operations this approach covers the organization's expenses and brings the expected profit.

Keystone Plus Pricing

Similar to keystone pricing, **keystone plus pricing** takes the concept one step further. In cases where doubling the cost doesn't provide for sufficient expense coverage and shortfalls in profit, an additional amount is added to arrive at the selling price. For example, a merchant might double the cost and add an additional 10 percent. In this situation, a product that costs $25 would carry a retail price of $55. First, the cost ($25) is doubled ($50). Then an additional 10 percent ($50 × .10 × $5) is added for a selling price of $55.

Overall Uniform Pricing

Overall uniform pricing is the strategy used most often by off-price retailers. They do not necessarily look at specific merchandise classifications to make their pricing decisions but instead treat all items the same. Thus, if it is determined that a 48 percent markup will bring the

This worksheet shows that different styles command different markups.

best results to the company, every individual item is marked up exactly that amount. This is a simple, straightforward method that doesn't require any decision making.

Department Pricing

In most retail organizations, merchandise assortments are segmented according to the departments in which they will be displayed and sold. Full-line department stores, for example, feature a wealth of hard goods and soft goods, with each department called upon to utilize a specific markup formula. The reason why **department pricing** is prevalent in this type of retailing is that some departments, because of competition from the **big box operations**, must price their products competitively. In the selling of appliances, department stores, for example, must be able to compete with the prices being charged by the likes of Best Buy. Other departments within the same organization need not worry about this value pricing and are able to achieve higher markups on their items. Thus, when departments have their own pricing goals, they are able to bring the highest possible profit to their company.

Individual Merchandise Pricing

The ingenuity of pricing is often left to the discretion of the buyer. This is known as **individual merchandise pricing**. He or she is given a markup goal to maintain but is left to decide which merchandise should be marked up lower than usual, which should take advantage of higher markups, and which should be priced according to traditional practices.

Bearing in mind the optimal markup, with creative pricing the buyer considers such factors as the appearance of the goods, the competition for such products, and the exclusivity factor. When merchandise comes to the selling floor premarked by the vendor, few adjustments can be made. Hence, with lower than the typical prices the buyer might increase sales volume on other items, higher markups can be applied to offset subsequent markdowns. It should be remembered that individual pricing is only successful if the buyer has a complete understanding of the marketplace and the competition.

Negotiable Pricing

Negotiable pricing, the practice of the consumer being able to negotiate a price that is different from the asking price, is not commonplace in the United States except at automobile dealerships and jewelry stores. Haggling over prices is expected in many countries throughout the world, such as China and Mexico, but Americans have come to understand that the price on an item is the price that must be paid.

Average Pricing

It is the goal of the retailer to make certain that an optimum markup is achieved when the entire inventory is considered. No one system is always better than any other. It is imperative, however, that the **average pricing** goal be met. By averaging all of the markups that have been applied, the result must be one that produces the greatest revenue for the company. It takes careful planning, teamwork, and experience to achieve this pricing goal.

> **In the News . . .**
>
> "Retail Pricing Strategies," an article that appears on page 381 at the end of this chapter, should be read now.

PRICE POINTS

Just about every retail organization restricts its offerings to specific **price points** or **price lines**. That is, the range of prices charged by a company cannot be at just any level but must rather be at some established level that has been determined by management. Few brick-and-mortar operations—or, for that matter, catalogues and Web sites—attempt to make their merchandising appeal at every price point.

The reasons for these pricing restrictions are many and include the following:

- The size of the store generally limits the depth and breadth of price points within its merchandise classification.
- Goods in the same overall classification that are at opposite ends of the pricing spectrum generally require different visual merchandising approaches.
- Upper and lower price points require different types of merchandising strategies.
- When a company remains within a particular price range, customers are more likely to know what the company is offering before they enter the store, examine its catalogues, or log on to its Web site. In the brick-and-mortar operations, in particular, the overcrowding of a selling floor with shoppers who—because of the prices—will not buy makes the environment one that is less desirable for those who are apt to be purchasers.
- Price points facilitate purchase planning for the buyer. Since wholesale markets and merchandise collections are segmented according to price points, the necessity of covering many markets becomes time consuming and might warrant additional buyers for each range. Thus, the company's expenses will increase.

Bearing all of this in mind, it is necessary to carefully determine the outside merchandise parameters in terms of pricing. This is not to say that a single price is the only one to consider; instead, a range that addresses the needs of the company should be favored. In cases where the same merchandise classification has a wide span, the company must separate the goods according to prices. In women's apparel, for example, a major department store might feature separate departments with each concentrating on its own price points. Typically, the costliest items would be in the couture area. The designer department would follow, with bridge merchandise next according to price: "better" as the designation for moderately priced goods and "budget" for the lowest price points.

In this way, customers are made aware that a wealth of different price points are available under one roof and that each will offer the necessary assortment to satisfy their needs.

In more specialized companies there is usually only a single price point that is merchandised. Anyone entering the doors of The Limited or Banana Republic knows exactly what the price ranges will be. The popularity of the specialty chain underscores the practicality of limited price points and its inherent success in putting its products into the hands of the consumer.

MARKDOWNS

No matter how carefully buyers and merchandisers plan their purchases, there are always some items that do not sell as well as had been expected. Whatever the reasons for their inability to attract customer attention, they must be disposed of in order to make room for new products. Markdowns, or reductions in the selling price, are how these items are sold.

> **In the News . . .**
>
> "The Markdown Blues, Revisited," an article that appears on page 382 at the end of this chapter, should be read now.

Markdown Causes

The reasons why some items fail to bring the expected sales results are many. They include buying errors, poor selling techniques, inadequate visual presentation, insufficient promotional endeavors, inappropriate initial prices, adverse weather conditions, and poor fit with the overall merchandise assortment.

Buying Errors

It is the professional buyers and merchandisers who are charged with the responsibility of stocking their inventories with the best merchandise available in the marketplace. These seasoned professionals utilize a number of internal and external sources of information before they make buying decisions. Yet even with these preplanning procedures, errors are still made. It is safe to say that no amount of forecasting will guarantee success.

One of the errors that is often attributed to these professional purchasers includes **overbuying**. At the beginning of the season, especially for fashion merchandise, there is often an indication of a particular style or color that is expected to result in significant sales. In an industry where reorders of **hot items** are often slow in coming, buyers may try to anticipate the customers' reactions to such products and sometimes purchase more than they normally would so that their inventories will be adequately stocked to meet the anticipated demand. If the sales are significant, the buyer is a hero. However, if sales do not materialize as planned, then the markdown route is inevitable.

Where the merchandise is not fashion-oriented or seasonal, there is little need to dispose of it very quickly. **Staples**, or items that are purchased by consumers throughout the year, will eventually sell, making it unnecessary to take markdowns. Once the inventory of these slow sellers dissipates, they may be replaced with other items.

Another approach that could be troublesome—and lead to price reductions—is reordering too late in the selling season. When the success of a particular style makes it a **runner**, there is temptation to continue it in the merchandise assortment as long as possible. Because it is difficult to predict when customer interest will wane, the last shipments sometimes arrive too late and must be disposed of via the markdown route.

Poor Selling Techniques

One of the problems that continue to plague retailers is poor selling. Many retailers do not adequately prepare their sales associates to handle the questions posed by would-be purchasers or neglect to teach them the fundamentals of successful selling. The shoppers who walk through the sales floors of many of America's leading retailers are often ignored by sales associates. The mere presence of someone in the store is generally an indication that he or she is in the market to make a purchase. Even when there is a sales associate present, poor training may prevent him or her from bringing a sale to fruition. There might be an "I don't care" attitude or one that is too overbearing. While these are two extremes, the result is often the same—the shopper leaves the store without making a purchase.

Selling is required not only at brick-and-mortar operations; catalogue customers and e-tail shoppers sometimes also need to be sold a product. When a catalogue order is being placed, oftentimes there are questions that need answering before the transaction is completed. Without answers, the sale could be lost. Similarly, shopping on a Web site is not always automatic. Browsers may need to have certain concerns addressed before they are willing to make the purchase. Many Web sites have interactive capabilities so that such problems can be handled and sales will be made.

Inadequate Visual Presentation

Even the best merchandise requires high-level visual presentation if the company is to maximize its sales potential. Companies like Crate & Barrel, Pottery Barn, and Williams-Sonoma continue to grow not only because of the products they feature but also because of the manner in which they are visually merchandised. The merchant who fails to feature items in their best settings runs the risk of shoppers passing them by.

Visual presentations must appear in outside show windows and in interior areas in a manner that motivates passersby to make closer inspections. It is these silent sellers that often make or break the sale. In Chapter 18, attention will focus on how retailers use these display techniques to their best advantage.

Insufficient Promotional Endeavors

Whether it is the use of advertising or a special event, sufficient dollars must be budgeted so that maximum exposure to the product will be the result. Today, with operational expenses at an all-time high, many merchants try to curtail costs by reducing expenses associated with their products. This is a shortsighted approach in retailing. At a time when competition is extremely fierce, promotional endeavors are what brings the merchant's products to the customer's attention.

Inappropriate Initial Prices

When an overzealous buyer tries to capture early sales, he or she is sometimes likely to apply an extra markup. The thought is that, early in the season, shoppers are more willing to spend a little extra to get the latest merchandise. Of course, if the competition's prices for the identical merchandise are lower, the results could be disastrous. Customers may become wary of the store's higher prices, and the store could lose its patrons altogether.

The result is often to take markdowns, making the products less profitable. High initial prices should be avoided unless the merchandise is private label or part of an exclusivity plan that the buyer has arranged with the vendor. In any case, it is risky business.

Adverse Weather Conditions

When the merchandise is of a seasonal nature and its sale is dependent upon certain weather characteristics, any deviation from the norm can play havoc on the retailer. In the case of swimsuits, for example, a rainy summer could spell disaster. Similarly, a mild winter could reduce the demand for outerwear.

These conditions are no fault of the buyer. He or she must take the risks involved with such merchandise purchases or be caught short if the season's weather is typical. When the weather doesn't cooperate, the markdown route is inevitable.

Inappropriate Placement in the Assortment

As we learned in Chapter 14, the buyer carefully plans the model stock to make certain that it contains the elements to make the selling season a successful one. The products that have been assembled should bear some cohesiveness, whether as regards style, price point, color, or size. Sometimes, a buyer will stray from this preplanned assortment and be tempted to bring in a few items that do not necessarily fit with the remainder of the inventory. It is these items that are often rejected by the customers. Unless there is some evidence that such items will tempt shoppers to buy, including them in the merchandise mix should be avoided. It might be a price point that is atypical of the other goods, a color that doesn't work with the rest of the palette, or a style that doesn't fit with the others.

Timing Markdowns

No matter what the cause of the markdown, it is necessary to determine when it is appropriate to take the reduction. As we learned earlier, it is generally unwise to carry the unsold goods to the next season, thus making the markdown the only viable means of their disposal.

When to take the actual markdown is a matter of concern for all retailers. Traditionally, markdown periods have been around the Fourth of July and after Christmas. Although most stores no longer use this time frame as a hard-and-fast rule, some do. For example, Nordstrom—especially in its men's department—takes the semiannual approach. Other retailers, including department stores and specialty chains, have resorted more and more to reducing the prices of slow sellers as soon as they fail to bring positive results. It might be just a matter of a month or so that will warrant the markdown.

Early markdowns are favored by some because:

- The selling season may still be at its peak, providing the retailer with a multitude of shoppers.
- The revenues obtained from these sales can be used to purchase other goods that might be better received by the consumer.
- The selling floor is thereby emptied of slow movers, making room for new items.

Filene's Basement of Boston is famous for its automatic markdown system.

Later markdowns also have their proponents, for the following reasons:

- It sometimes takes longer than expected for merchandise to catch on with consumers. If this is the case, the early markdown will hamper profits.
- Some merchants—especially those, like Nordstrom, with a prestigious image—feel that the presence of markdown racks transforms their stores into places where value seekers make the shopping experience for their regular customers less appealing.

Automatic Markdowns

Although the concept of **automatic markdowns** is not widespread, it does have a place in retailing. Most notably, Filene's Basement, which initiated the concept, and Syms, which has used it in its women's department, have made it work successfully.

The idea is to dispose of the merchandise as quickly as possible and without further input from pricing decision makers.

Focus on . . .
Filene's Basement

THE CONCEPT OF AUTOMATIC MARKDOWNS began in the basement of Filene's department store in Boston, Massachusetts, in 1908. The idea was Edward A. Filene's way to rid the company of excess merchandise in the department store. Using the basement as his arena for these slow sellers and after-season leftovers, he priced everything to sell quickly—in fact, in a matter of 30 days.

Goods that came to the basement were attractively priced for this quick disposal. After a couple of weeks, if goods still remained then their price was automatically reduced another 25 percent. The price was systematically lowered each week until the product was sold. In the event that there were no takers at the end of 30 days, leftover merchandise was donated to charity. With the success of quick disposal of this merchandise from the upstairs store, other retailers and manufacturers soon joined the bandwagon and started bringing their unsold goods to Filene's. It is not unusual to see end-of-season inventories from prestigious retailers such as Neiman Marcus gracing the Basement's selling floor. Many consider this to be the birth of off-price retailing. Although it took 10 years for the Basement to operate in the black, it eventually went on to be one of the more profitable operations in retail history.

The popularity of the Boston operation can best be appreciated by the fact that it is considered to be the city's second most popular attraction. It is shopped by some 15,000 to 20,000 people a day. Its colorful history has made shopping there part art form and part sporting event. Shoppers line up before dawn for special sales, engage in tug-of-war contests over merchandise, and even try clothes on in the aisles. Celebrities often visit the store when they are in Boston.

Today Filene's Basement stores carry on the tradition in other cities. These stores operate under different management from the original Filene's Basement. Still, the lower level at the Boston store generates excitement for its faithful followers.

Determining the Markdown

The specific reductions taken by retailers to rid themselves of unwanted goods are by no means uniform in the industry. Some believe in the concept of starting with a small markdown, such as 20 percent, and then waiting until sales falter to proceed with additional markdowns, continuing in this manner until the inventory is disposed of. Others are of the mind that it is better to drastically slash prices—say, by 40 percent—so that quicker disposal of goods is accomplished.

It should be understood that minimal reductions in the selling price, such as 10 percent, rarely motivate shoppers to buy merchandise that otherwise wouldn't interest them.

Whichever approach is taken, it is a general rule that not every item in the inventory is marked down but only those in need of a little extra enticement. Some companies that wait for season's end to announce their clearances reduce their entire inventory in one fell swoop. The key to the success of any of these plans is understanding the needs of the retailer's clientele.

Markdown Recap Moderate/Better Collections

Month: Feb-2002

Dept.	Plan	First	Second	Third	POS	MUC	MKU/MKDR	Total
370	47.5	0.0	41.8	0.1	5.0	0.0	-1.6	45.3
373	115.5	77.2	26.9	1.3	0.0	0.0	-1.5	103.9
374	48.7	10.7	15.2	0.0	0.0	0.0	0.0	25.9
376	19.9	40.7	0.0	1.4	1.0	0.1	-1.3	41.8
Total	231.6	128.6	83.9	2.8	6.0	0.1	-4.4	216.9

This markdown recap form reviews markdowns by department.

The price-change printout shows the impact of markdowns on selected items.

Markdown Percent Calculations

Today's computer programs enable retailers to reprice merchandise very quickly. With the simple entry of the appropriate numbers, the results are easily calculated. It is necessary not only to compute the actual reduction but to also figure the markdown percent based upon sales.

The following example is given to simplify the computational aspect of markdowns and to show exactly how it works.

A merchant determines that, with sales far behind projections for the shoe department, it makes sense to mark down the entire footwear inventory by 30 percent. What is the markdown percent based on sales, assuming that all of the $100,000 inventory sells?

1. The dollar markdown must be determined.

$$\text{original retail} \times \text{reduction percent} = \text{markdown}$$
$$\$100{,}000 \times .30 = \$30{,}000$$

2. Next, the actual sales are determined.

$$\text{original retail} - \text{reduction} = \text{new retail}$$
$$\$100{,}000 - \$30{,}000 = \$70{,}000$$

3. The markdown percent on sales is then determined.

$$\text{Markdown \%} = \frac{\text{Markdown}}{\text{Sales}}$$

$$\text{Markdown \%} = \frac{\$30,000}{\$70,000}$$

$$\text{Markdown \%} = 42.86\%$$

It should be understood that this is an extremely simplified illustration. It is virtually impossible for a retailer to sell its entire inventory and be left with nothing, no matter how drastic the markdown.

More involved calculations address what proportion of the inventory sells and at what percents.

CHAPTER HIGHLIGHTS

- Markup is the difference between the retailer's cost and selling price; it may be figured as either a percent of retail or of cost.
- The factors that affect retail prices are numerous and include the buyer's judgment of the item's appeal, competition, the degree of exclusivity of the merchandise assortment, the nature of the goods, and the potential stock turnover rate.
- With the use of private brands and labels, retailers can pay less attention to competition than with products that are widely distributed.
- A company's image can contribute to the eventual prices it charges. Prestigious companies, for example, may take advantage of their name to charge higher prices; value merchants such as discounters and off-pricers will charge lower prices.
- As operating costs continue to escalate, many merchants are using larger markups than ever before to cover these expenses.
- Price points or ranges are essential in retailing so that the merchant can concentrate on a narrower wholesale market and tailor its operation to address this restricted price point.
- Markdowns are essential to moving slow sellers out of the inventory. By doing so, retailers are able to use the monies to buy new merchandise and to make room for incoming purchases.
- It is generally considered poor business practice to carry merchandise over to the next year, since customers' needs usually change.

IMPORTANT RETAILING TERMS

automatic markdown (377)
average markup (365)
average pricing (373)
big box operations (372)
comparison shopper (366)
department pricing (372)
dollar markup (362)
exclusivity (366)
hot item (374)
individual merchandise pricing (372)
inventory shrinkage (362)
keystone plus pricing (371)
keystone pricing (371)
maintained markup (362)
markdown (362)
markup percent (362)
markup (362)
membership club (367)
negotiable pricing (372)
overall uniform pricing (371)
overbuying (374)
perishable merchandise (368)
pilferage (371)
prestige retailer (370)

price line (373)
price point (373)
retail method of inventory (363)
runner (374)
staple (374)
wholesale club (365)

FOR REVIEW

1. What do consumers who patronize the more traditional types of retailers, and often pay full price for their goods, expect from the merchant in return for these higher prices?
2. What is the formula for dollar markup, and what does each of the three components of the calculation stand for?
3. Why do the vast majority of today's merchants use the markup percent based on retail?
4. How can the buyer's ability to judge the merchandise he or she has purchased affect the price the consumer will be charged?
5. Why does competition play such an important role in merchandise pricing?
6. In what way can a retailer avoid the pitfalls of competitive pricing?
7. What does the term *exclusivity* mean in retail merchandising, and how can it help the buyer achieve a higher than typical markup?
8. Which product classifications cause the retailer the most difficulty when it comes to pricing?
9. Can adverse weather conditions hamper the sale of merchandise? Give several examples.
10. Why does precious jewelry often warrant unusually high markups?
11. Does the retailer's image ever contribute to its pricing policy?
12. How does internal and external theft contribute to a company's pricing policy?
13. What is meant by keystone pricing? How does it differ from keystone plus pricing?
14. How does average pricing differ from overall uniform pricing?
15. What is meant by the term *price points*?
16. Why is it necessary for retailers to maintain price points?
17. Can markdowns be avoided in dealing with fashion merchandise? Why?
18. What are some of the causes of markdowns?
19. When is the best time for retailers to mark down their less desirable goods?
20. Under what circumstances is it appropriate to carry fashion merchandise from one season to the next?

AN INTERNET ACTIVITY

Using your favorite search engine, log on to a number of retail Web sites and determine whether or not they promote price in their online presentations. You should select three department stores such as Belk or Macy's, three off-pricers such as Burlington Coat Factory or Stein Mart, and three specialty stores such as Gap or Banana Republic. Prepare your report in chart form with the following headings:

Company Name	Web Site	Retail Classification	Emphasis on Price

EXERCISES AND PROJECTS

1. Plan a visit to three fashion-oriented brick-and-mortar operations for the purpose of determining whether they charge the manufacturer's list price. Well-known vendors such as Perry Ellis, Liz Claiborne, Ralph Lauren, Jones New York, and others include their own price tags on the merchandise. Some retailers observe this price while others feature prices that are lower. Complete a chart with headings as shown below for the three stores you have selected. List at least five vendor names that have preticketed their merchandise with their own tags.

Name of Store	Labels with Vendor-Designated Prices	Actual Retail Prices

2. Plan a visit to a supermarket and to a wholesale club in your area and see whether prices for the same products differ. Select ten products that are considered to be staple items, such as brand-name cereals, bottled water, soda, frozen items such as pizza, and so on. Make certain that the items you have chosen are of the same package size and weight so that you can compare prices fairly. Prepare a chart listing the products and their supermarket and wholesale club prices.

   Using the information you have gathered, write a summary indicating the price differences that you have found. Be sure to indicate the names of the stores you visited.

THE CASE OF THE MARKDOWN DILEMMA

One of the more successful department store operations in the Midwest is Finders and Wells, which has been in business since 1925. It has been well known throughout the region ever since it opened its first store, which is still its flagship operation. The recognition and loyal following it has always enjoyed are due to its wonderful merchandise assortment and the services it offers to its clientele.

As the company entered the new millennium, it had grown to 23 units, all of which are located within several of the Midwestern states. Its profit picture has been relatively steady, with economic downturns somewhat affecting the company as they do retailers across the country. Among the many pricing strategies that the company uses is the one that addresses markdowns. Its approach has been the traditional one in which retailers take markdowns twice a year, once after the Fourth of July and the other after New Year's Day. Its belief is that the use of markdowns for slow sellers at any other time of the year would hamper sales. While the less desirable merchandise might sell more quickly, customers might wait to see if the other merchandise would also be marked down before the end of the traditional selling period.

Mr. Robert Hampton, senior vice president for merchandising (a position he has held for the past 15 years), believes that the status quo has served the company well and doesn't want to fool with success.

Ms. Janet Woods—divisional merchandise manager for the retailer's most important classification, women's apparel, and a member of the management team for the past 2 years—firmly believes that the use of more frequent markdowns would better serve the needs of the company. She feels that merchandise that doesn't sell in a predetermined time period should be reduced so that it might be disposed of more quickly, making room for newer products.

For the past 6 months, the topic has been discussed at the regular merchandising and management meetings. Each of the two managers has followers on the management team, with the split approximately 50–50.

A decision must be made soon regarding the type of markdown philosophy the company should take.

Questions

1. What are the advantages of each of the plans?
2. Which executive's approach do you believe should be taken? Why?

Retail Pricing Strategies
Shari Waters

NOVEMBER 9, 2007

SET THE RIGHT PRICE

There are many outside influences that affect profitability and a retailer's bottom line. Setting the right price is a crucial step toward achieving that profit. Retailers are in business to make a profit, but figuring out what and how to price products may not come easily.

Before we can determine which retail pricing strategy to use in setting the right price, we must know the costs associated with the products. Two key elements in factoring product cost is the cost of goods and the amount of operating expense.

The cost of goods includes the amount paid for the product, plus any shipping or handling expenses. The cost of operating the business, or operating expense, includes overhead, payroll, marketing and office supplies.

Regardless of the pricing strategy used, the retail price of the products should more than cover the cost of obtaining the goods plus the expenses related to operating the business. A retailer simply cannot succeed in business if they continue to sell their products below cost.

Retail Pricing Strategies

Now that we understand what our products actually cost, we should look at how our competition is pricing their products. Retailers will also need to examine their channels of distribution and research what the market is willing to pay.

Many pricing strategies exist and each is used based on a particular set of circumstances. Here are a few of the more popular pricing strategies to consider:

Markup Pricing

Markup on cost can be calculated by adding a pre-set (often industry standard) profit margin, or percentage, to the cost of the merchandise.

Markup on retail is determined by dividing the dollar markup by retail.

Be sure to keep the initial mark-up high enough to cover price reductions, discounts, shrinkage and other anticipated expenses, and still achieve a satisfactory profit. Retailers with a varied product selection can use different mark-ups on each product line.

Vendor Pricing

Manufacturer suggested retail price (MSRP) is a common strategy used by the smaller retail shops to avoid price wars and still maintain a decent profit. Some suppliers have minimum advertised prices but also suggest the retail pricing. By pricing products with the suggested retail prices supplied by the vendor, the retailer is out of the decision-making process. Another issue with using pre-set prices is that it doesn't allow a retailer to have an advantage over the competition.

Competitive Pricing

Consumers have many choices and are generally willing to shop around to receive the best price. Retailers considering a competitive pricing strategy will need to provide outstanding customer service to stand above the competition.

Pricing below competition simply means pricing products lower than the competitor's price. This strategy works well if the retailer negotiates the best prices, reduces costs and develops a marketing strategy to focus on price specials.

Prestige pricing, or pricing above competition, may be considered when location, exclusivity or unique customer service can justify higher prices. Retailers that stock high-quality merchandise that isn't available at any other location may be quite successful in pricing their products above competitors.

Psychological Pricing

Psychological pricing is used when prices are set to a certain level where the consumer perceives the price to be fair. The most common method is odd-pricing using figures that end in 5, 7 or 9. It is believed that consumers tend to round down a price of $9.95 to $9, rather than $10.

Other Pricing Strategies

Keystone pricing is not used as often as it once was. Doubling the cost paid for merchandise was once the rule of pricing products, but very few products these days allow a retailer to keystone the product price.

Multiple pricing is a method which involves selling more than one product for one price, such as three items for $1.00. Not only is this strategy great for markdowns or sales events, but retailers have noticed consumers tend to purchase in larger amounts where the multiple pricing strategy is used.

Discount pricing and price reductions are a natural part of retailing. Discounting can include coupons, rebates, seasonal prices and other promotional markdowns.

Merchandise priced below cost is referred to as loss leaders. Although retailers make no profit on these discounted items, the hope is consumers will purchase other products at higher margins during their visit to the store.

As you develop the best pricing model for your retail business, understand the ideal pricing strategy will depend on more than costs. It is difficult to say which component of pricing is more important than another. Just keep in mind, the right product price is the price the consumer is willing to pay, while providing a profit to the retailer.

The Markdown Blues, Revisited
Ted Hurlbut

It's been a while since I've read anything quite like this. Part food fight, part mud wrestling, part theatre of the absurd.

A recent *New York Times* article ("First the Markdown, Then the Showdown" by Tracie Rozhon, February 25, 2005) recounted the tong war currently taking place between the major department store chains and their vendors. It seems they're fighting over markdowns.

"For holiday shoppers, there were bargains galore. By Thanksgiving weekend, Saks Fifth Avenue was offering 40 percent off; Macy's was selling furs for "40 and 50 percent off—plus an extra 15 percent." Now the stores and the clothing makers are arguing about who is going to pay for the profits lost because of all those markdowns."

"Merchants say they have no choice but to mark merchandise down because of the weak demand. Suppliers say the stores panicked, marking down items too soon. They claim the merchants should have stuck to the sales plan, which was hammered out between the merchants and suppliers before the stores even saw the designs."

For years, markdown money has been a part of the relationship between large retailers and their vendors. As originally conceived, markdown money compensated retailers when a specific style or grouping from a vendor turned out to be an unexpectedly weak seller. The retailer and the vendor shared the expense of liquidating the inventory.

But as time has gone along, things have changed. Retailers aren't just asking for markdown help on troubled merchandise now; they're asking for markdown help on everything. Markdown money has now become a revenue stream.

"Now, the merchants are demanding the difference between what they thought they would make as profit on clothes and what they received in the end, according to financial officers at several companies."

"In the annual ritual of price-slashing, analysts, bankers and clothing manufacturers agree: the fighting is a lot more intense this year."

In the retail trade, it's called "partnering with your vendors." The vendors might instead call it a good old-fashioned shakedown. Whatever you call it, however, there are some important things that smaller retailers can learn from all this pushing and shoving:

Vendor Management, Risk and Leverage

In any supply chain, in the short term, inventory risk will pool with the weakest link in the chain. In this instance, the weaker link is the vendors, as large retailers have gone through one round of merger and consolidation after another over the last decade and a half. Large retailers have the market leverage to force the financial risk of carrying inventory onto their vendors. Once they reached Thanksgiving in this case, the retailers had no in-

centive to hold the line on markdowns because they knew they could force their vendors to pick up the tab.

Conversely, 20 years ago when the retail industry was far more fragmented, vendors had the leverage to insist that retailers assume the financial risk of their purchases. If a retailer bought it, and it didn't sell, the retailer took the markdown hit.

Many smaller retailers may feel like the large retailers did back then. They feel like they need their vendors more than their vendors need them. But most smaller retailers have more leverage than they might think, if they manage their vendor base skillfully.

You can only be important to so many vendors, and you must be important to the vendors that you do choose to do business with. The volume you do with your vendors is almost surely more important to them than you think it is. Where else could they go to replace your business? Who else will represent their full line, and test all their new items? Who else do they have an open, honest and forthcoming relationship with like you? Who else do they have the confidence will be around for the long term because you've your i's dotted and t's crossed?

Understanding leverage in your vendor relationships is not so much about taking advantage as much as it's about building solid business relationships to work together to serve the customers' needs. And while in the short term risk will pool with the weakest link, in the long term it is not in any vendor's interest to put their customer's sales and margins under stress.

Merchandise Management, Buried Costs and the Customer

Underlying this battle over markdown money is one inescapable conclusion: When Thanksgiving rolled around, the retailers had too much merchandise. Without any markdown risk of their own, the retailers had no reason to prudently manage their inventory. Buy a big number, sell what you can before Thanksgiving at your planned margins, and after Thanksgiving slash away as deeply as you need to sell it all through.

Their vendors went along, as they always do, because of the size of the purchase orders. For a long time, the vendors understood how to play this game; they simply built the markdown money into their prices upfront, wink-wink, and everybody was happy. Except the retailers treat markdown money just like revenue; they expect to run increases every year.

Contrast this to a recent quote from a Wal-Mart spokesman. "We expect our suppliers to drive the costs out of the supply chain. It's good for us and good for them." (*New York Times*, "Don't Blame Wal-Mart" by Robert Reich, February 28, 2005)

Excess inventory is excess inventory. It doesn't matter whether the cost of marking it down later has been buried in the purchase price. All that does is inflate the retail price, shrink the gross margin, or both. And the carrying cost of retail inventory, which includes costs of storage, financing, insurance, handling, shrink, damage and obsolescence, is typically 2 percent to 2 and a half percent a month.

To be truly successful, smaller retailers must carefully plan their sales and inventories, communicate those plans to their vendors, not over-commit to too much inventory at any one time, and constantly update their plans as business develops. Like Wal-Mart, they must continually challenge their merchandise management practices to eliminate unnecessary costs and protect margins.

After reading Ms. Rozhon's article, it's no wonder that so many large retailers have struggled for so long. There doesn't seem to be a whole lot of focus on the customer.

"Experts say calculations over markdown money are one reason customers are complaining that all the clothes in department stores look alike—both manufacturers and retailers are increasingly playing it safe, avoiding "way out" fashion and chance-taking."

Smaller retailers can learn from this, just as they can learn from the successes of companies like Wal-Mart, and so many others: You must offer your customers quality products, compelling value and outstanding customer service each and every day, no matter what your niche. And if you do, you can thrive against any competition.

PART FIVE

Promotion and Customer Service

Having taken care of all of the decision making in terms of management, facilities design, and purchasing, it is imperative that the retailer's potential market be made aware of the company's existence.

Most professional merchants recognize that, without the appropriate promotional endeavors, their companies will not attract the masses needed to make them successful. To that end, considerable sums for advertising are set aside by many retailers as well as for special promotional events that will, it is hoped, motivate customers to venture into the stores. Equally important is properly servicing those who are interested in patronizing the retailer.

In Chapter 17, Advertising and Promotion, the different types of advertising and special events projects that retailers use are discussed. From those that cost very little money to those that are extravagant in nature, this chapter shows how retailers of every size may subscribe to some form of advertising and promotion.

Taking an item and presenting it in the best possible light is the job of visual merchandisers. Their ability to transform the mundane into something exciting in a visual setting makes their role in retailing invaluable. In Chapter 18, Visual Merchandising, all principles and elements are carefully addressed so that even the novice can try his or her hand at it.

Today's merchant is totally aware of the competitive nature of the game of retailing. With many inventories similar from one company to the next, it is service that can separate one from the other. By carefully providing personal selling that instills confidence in the customer and by offering a host of traditional and customized services that make the shopping experience pleasurable, a retailer is likely to engender customer loyalty. In Chapter 19, Customer Service, the numerous services that are afforded by retailers are discussed along with why they help to bring customers back again and again.

CHAPTER 17
Advertising and Promotion

After you have completed this chapter, you should be able to discuss:

- The various components that make up a retailer's sales promotion division
- Advertising and how it differs from selling, visual merchandising, and publicity
- How the major retailers organize their advertising departments and the functions of these departments
- The different elements of an advertisement
- The effectiveness of single ads and ad campaigns in terms of the sales they generate
- The role of the advertising agency
- Media choices for retailers and the different benefits derived from each
- Special events and how retailers use them to promote their products and images
- How publicity helps promote a retailer's image without the costs of advertising

Consumers from every walk of life are in need of products that run the gamut from basic necessities to those that make living more pleasurable. Whether it is the food that sustains them or the luxuries that only some can afford, there is a multitude of retail establishments ready to offer this merchandise. Brick-and-mortar operations, catalogues, Web sites, and cable TV shopping channels all vie for the consumer's attention in hopes of turning a profit for their companies.

The merchants who make up these various retail outlets are many. In fact, there has never been a retailing climate in which so many have competed for the consumer's dollars. It might be one's favorite department store, a traditional specialty organization, a value operation such as a discounter or off-pricer, a wholesale club, a store-is-the-brand merchant, a franchise operation, an Internet Web site, a catalogue, or still other outlets to whom the public turns for their purchases. With all of these retailers competing for the sale, it is safe to say that choosing one is not generally an automatic response for the consumer. Of course, a percentage of the population regularly patronizes a particular supermarket for grocery needs, or a department store for apparel. By and large, however, much of the retail dollar is up for grabs.

Through direct and continuous efforts to make the public aware of their operations, retailers can be more assured that they will have a chance to capture a segment of the market to whom their products are targeted. These endeavors are primarily through **advertising** and promotion. Without regular notification to the public of their existence, few retailers would be able to maintain favorable sales volumes. It might seem that retailers, such as supermarkets, that supply the basics should not need to expend large advertising budgets to call attention to themselves. However, by the number of print and broadcast advertisements these outlets place every week it is obvious that these ads are necessary to guarantee that shoppers fill their stores.

Merchants spend untold hours making certain that they have focused their operations on sound retailing principles and that their decisions are worthy of the clienteles to whom they are appealing. They establish strategies that help to achieve their goals, buy the merchandise that is appropriate for their regular and potential customers, and offer services that will bring the shoppers back again and again. All this planning is obviously necessary to develop a sound business, but it is also imperative that merchants create advertisements and promotional tools that will encourage the consumer to choose their stores instead of the competition.

The matter of advertising and promotion is not a simple one. It requires experts to develop approaches that not only gain the attention of the consumer markets but also convince them that a particular retailer will satisfy their needs better than other retailers.

It should be understood that these advertising and promotional endeavors are not restricted to the country's major retailers; they are also utilized by those small entrepreneurs who compete for the consumer's dollars. The depth and breadth of these undertakings are of course different for each of these players. Each must find the way that publicizes its existence with the dollars that have been set aside for this purpose. Whereas the major retailer will have its own sales promotion division to oversee the **publicity** aspect, the small, independent merchant will either handle its own promotional endeavors or call upon an outside specialist such as an **advertising agency** for guidance.

THE SALES PROMOTION DIVISION

Given that a company is a major one in retailing, it is the rule that a separate division be established to oversee everything that is of a promotional nature. This includes the development of advertising approaches that are of a distinctive nature, campaigns that cover all media, special events that will create interest for customers, visual presentations that are attention getters, and publicity that will present the retailer's name in the marketplace.

A typical organization chart for the sales promotion division of a department store.

To successfully carry out all these endeavors, a company must first establish its goals and organize its division so that the plans will be faithfully executed. In the largest retail organizations, the sales promotion division is a major function of the organizational structure. Its tasks are generally divided among four major departments with each headed by a manager, as seen in the chart on page 388.

The overall operation is managed by a divisional leader who interacts with the other divisional leaders in the organization to make certain that the promotional plans best present the company's merchandise. Thus, the sales promotion division head regularly meets with the general merchandise manager whose responsibility is to supply the company with the most suitable products. With these two divisional leaders in sync, sales goals are more likely to be achieved.

In this chapter, attention will focus on the advertising, special events, and publicity departments. Visual merchandising, since it has become such an important force in the brick-and-mortar operations, will be discussed separately in the next chapter. Of course, the coordination of all of these efforts is essential so that the greatest sales potential will be realized.

ADVERTISING

Many industry professionals are in agreement that, aside from the merchandise itself, advertising is the lifeblood of retailing. As defined by the American Marketing Association, advertising is "any paid for form of nonpersonal presentation of the facts about goods, services, or ideas to a group." Unlike selling, which requires interaction between two people, or visual merchandising, which requires the display of actual merchandise, advertising merely requires the use of artwork and **copy** to get its message across. Also, unlike publicity (which is free), advertising is paid for.

The main duty of a copywriter is to provide the written portion of the ad.

In-House Advertising Departments

The size of a company's **in-house advertising department** depends on the amount of advertising it undertakes and the types upon which it focuses.

Retailers who are more restricted in their advertising needs are likely to have a department that is organized along the lines of the one featured in the chart on page 388. Whether for print or broadcast advertising, the advertising manager has complete control and oversees each aspect of the program.

In the giants of the retail trade, a more segmented approach is utilized. With their involvement in every aspect of advertising, individual departments handle periodical, direct, broadcast, and sign (or mass) advertising. Each department has its own manager who is responsible only for his or her own particular media outlet, as depicted in the chart on page 391. The actual copy and artwork needed by each of the departments, as well as the production

The copy and art experts develop the layout of the ad to make it visually appealing.

The advertising manager checks the copy for accuracy and appropriateness.

requirements such as proofreading, are found in a common area that services all media departments.

This is by no means the only format that retail giants use. In actual practice, each utilizes a plan that best serves the company.

Whatever the organizational arrangement, the preparation of the advertisement requires several components. These include, but are not limited to, the following:

- *Writing copy.* Written advertising copy may be used by itself in an ad or to augment any artwork.
- *Preparing artwork.* The illustrations that appear in most ads are either photographs of the actual merchandise or drawings that have been created by artists.
- *Developing the layout.* The art and copy that have been created are physically arranged in a layout that has significant eye appeal.

Not too many years ago, the vast majority of the work needed to create advertisements was hand-rendered. That is, layouts were a matter of creating pasteups, which required a great deal of time and effort. Today, the traditional light boxes and other tools have become a thing of the past, replaced by computers that can more quickly and efficiently create effective advertising designs.

External Sources of Advertising Assistance

In smaller retail operations, the luxury of an in-house advertising department is not an option. With the limited amount of dollars available for such promotional endeavors, the costs

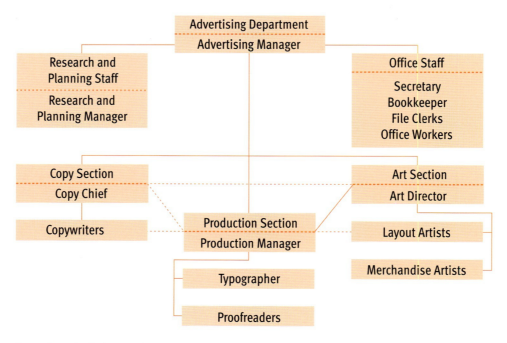

Areas of a typical in-house advertising department.

Advertising and Promotion | CHAPTER 17   391

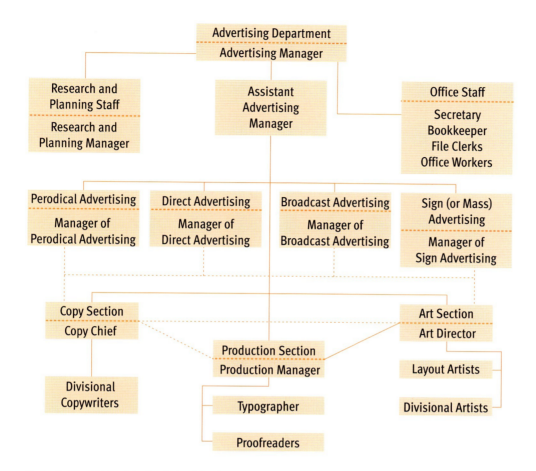

Many retailing giants organize their advertising department following this structure.

Buyers provide the product information that is the basis for advertising copy and artwork. In large firms like Belk, this information is generally recorded on a requisition form.

The retailer's advertising commitment form, like this one from Belk, spells out the cost of the ad along with other important details of the sale.

outweigh the need. This, however doesn't take the minor players out of the game. They turn to outside specialists to assist with their advertising needs. The following are just some of the routes taken by these merchants to help with their advertising requirements.

Advertising Agencies

These companies are the specialists in the field. They are in business to assist clients with a wide variety of services needed to make their companies and products better known to the public. They create single print or broadcast ads, complete campaigns, or anything else of a promotional nature. The remuneration they receive is often based upon a percentage of the cost of the ad's placement. That is, the media, rather than the retailer, pays them based on the space they purchase in a newspaper or magazine or on the time purchased for an ad that airs on television or radio. Sometimes, as in the case of creating a direct-mail piece, there might be a flat fee. It should be understood that advertising agencies service not only smaller merchants but also major retailers that have their own in-house staffs.

Vendors

Recognizing that retailer success is required if product manufacturers are to sell their merchandise, vendors are often willing to provide sample advertisements for their accounts to use. These computer-generated ads are complete in terms of illustrations and copy. The only elements omitted are the retailer's name and the retail prices. The user of these ads is at liberty to insert its own name or logo in the space provided and the retail price that it will charge.

This is a simple and cost-free approach to advertising, but it does run the risk of having others use the identical ad in the same print publication. That would take away from the exclusive nature of the advertisement, rendering it a me-too promotion.

Freelancers

In every aspect of advertising there are individuals who, for a set fee, will create an ad that is appropriate for the retailer. He or she might be a generalist who can develop every aspect of the ad or a specialist who can create the layout and employ others to prepare the artwork and copy. Some **freelancers** specialize in one medium, such as direct mail, while others may plan each of the media. Using this approach to advertising assures the retailer that the ad will be developed exclusively for its business, without worrying about others using it for their own promotions.

Media Services

Most of the print and broadcast media maintain departments that offer **media services**, including planning and actual development. These services are generally free, with the revenue coming from the actual ad placement.

The smaller, local, independent newspapers or shopping publications—which are predominantly used by small retailers—are heavily involved in these services. They recognize that such entrepreneurs can afford neither their own advertising experts nor the services of freelancers.

Advertising Classifications

Retailers have choices in terms of what approach they would like to emphasize in their advertisements. The approach might center on specific merchandise or, to

One typical promotional advertisement is the clearance sale ad.

perhaps a lesser extent, the company's image. The former is known as **promotional advertising** and the latter as **institutional advertising**.

Promotional Advertising

Most retailers want to get an immediate response to the ads or commercials they place in the print or broadcast media. To accomplish this goal they rely upon the promotion of specific products featured in their inventories. The promotion might be an ad that highlights an item from a particular designer collection, a sale that announces significant price reductions, or, in the case of supermarkets, a flyer that lists the specials for the week.

The intention is to tempt the shopper to visit the store and buy the advertised goods or to order them from a catalogue or Web site.

Institutional Advertising

At the other end of the spectrum is advertising that is intended to promote the retailer's image. It might be to emphasize the services the merchant offers that make the shopping experience a pleasurable one, to show its commitment to American-made products, or to salute a particular event or charity. Such advertising depicts the retail operation as a humanitarian organization and not one that is solely interested in profits.

Typically, institutional advertising is used more sparingly than is promotional advertising. The return on this type of advertising investment is difficult to measure, so it is only used as an adjunct to the other.

Combination Advertising

Sometimes, the retailer utilizes a format that combines both promotional and institutional advertising. By using **combination advertising** the company can implant an idea that is institutional in nature but at the same time helps to sell a product. Fashion merchants often use a message that brings attention to the fact that the store is dedicated to fashion merchandise (the institutional portion) while featuring a particular style (the promotional portion) that it wishes to sell.

Events like Macy's annual flower show attract shoppers to the store. Yet because they contribute only indirectly to the bottom line, the proportion of the advertising budget allocated to institutional advertising is relatively small.

Advertising Campaigns

The occasional use of an ad is not likely to bring the results that the retailer is seeking. If advertising is sparingly or irregularly used, it will not have much impact on the consumer. As we examine the wealth of print publications and broadcast media, we see that retailers advertise again and again to attract attention. A one-time ad might be missed by a large number of readers or viewers at a particular day or time, wasting the dollars that have been expended for it.

By blitzing the media with a central theme or merchandising concept, the company's name, product lines, and image will soon be indelibly etched in the minds of the consumer. In this way, whenever shopping needs must be fulfilled, the customer might recall the retailer's name and head for that particular brick-and-mortar operation, catalogue, or Web site to make a purchase.

The best **advertising campaigns**, if budgets allow, are the ones in which all of the media are used. This is especially true if the retailer is introducing a new line, announcing a major sales event, or refocusing its image. By using newspapers, magazines, direct-mail pieces, television, radio, or any of the local communication outlets, the company is certain to gain the exposure needed to make the event a successful one.

Cooperative Advertising

One of the concerns of many of those responsible for retail advertising is cost escalation. Buyers of print space and airtime are finding that their dollars no longer go as far as they once did. Always looking for industry support to promote their companies and the products they sell, buyers and merchandisers are generally involved in a concept known as **cooperative advertising**. In this arrangement, the vendor and the retailer share the expense of advertising. The way it works is that a formula is developed that provides promotional funds to be used for advertising purposes. Generally, the amount is based on the dollars that the retailer spends with the vendor. A portion of that amount, say 10 percent, will translate into promotional dollars. Once the actual amount has been determined, it is applied toward the cost of an ad—with each party paying for half of the ad's cost, up to the predetermined amount.

The following example is typical of a cooperative advertising arrangement. The buyer of menswear for Stewart's Department Store has purchased $100,000 worth of goods from Arlington Industries. Both parties have agreed to a cooperative advertising arrangement of 5 percent on purchases. The allowance would be as follows:

$$\$100,000 \times .05 = \$5,000$$

Stewart's would then be able to apply the $5,000 to an advertisement. Thus, if an ad costs $10,000, each party would be responsible for one half. It should be noted that if the ad were to cost more than $10,000, Arlington's responsibility would remain at $5,000, the percent based upon the purchase. If the ad cost $3,000, the vendor's portion would only be for $1,500, the one half originally agreed to. The remaining "unused" amount of $3,500 would be carried over for use in another advertisement.

The advantage of this type of arrangement is that it benefits both the vendor and the retailer. The vendor gets the brand name out to the public, and the retailer is able to promote his or her store along with the featured merchandise.

Seasoned buyers and merchandisers are always in the market for these promotional dollars because they can thereby effectively double the amount of money that has been allocated to them by management. One cautionary remark that merits attention is that purchases should never be made simply because of the advertising allowances that are offered. Only after it has been determined that the goods are suitable for the buyer's model stock should a cooperative advertising arrangement be negotiated.

Crossover Advertising

The vast majority of the major brick-and-mortar retailers in the United States spend a great deal on advertising in the hope that it will encourage potential customers to come to their outlets. Today, however, in-store shopping is not the only game in town. More and more of these high-profile merchants are depending upon their Web sites to bring additional sales to the company.

In an effort to beef up these off-site sales, merchants are using their print and broadcast ads to remind shoppers who are unable to make store visits that there is a Web site for their purchasing pleasure. This is known as **crossover advertising**. Somewhere in these advertisements the company's Web site is prominently featured. It is the merchant's way of reminding the shopper that a Web site does exist for their use. The hope is that those who log on will eventually find their way into the stores, where the selections are generally broader.

Advertising Media

Many different communication outlets are available for the promotion of a company and the merchandise it sells. The nature of the retailing operation dictates which medium is best suited for putting the company's name and merchandise before the consumer. Although one medium might be better suited than another to a specific retail classification, this is not to say that each merchant should follow suit when choosing where to expend its promotional dollars. Some make use of all media, while others might restrict their advertising to just one. Department stores, for example, generally utilize a mix of newspaper, magazine, direct-mail, television, radio, and Internet advertising to reach their targeted audiences, whereas the small retailer may only subscribe to the direct-mail route.

By examining each of the media in terms of its advantages and disadvantages, the retailer is able to choose one that is best suited to the store's needs.

Newspapers

Although the use of television and direct mail by retailers has increased in recent years, the newspaper remains the leading medium used by the vast majority of the industry. Whether it is print ads in the country's biggest newspapers, such as *The New York Times* or the *Los Angeles Times*, or in the small local publications that serve communities nationwide, this format usually brings the best sales results.

The advantages of print ads may be summarized as follows:

This ad for a small, single-unit retailer appeared in a community newspaper, whose advertising department prepared it for the advertiser. Using this medium enabled the retailer to reach its target market at a low cost per potential customer.

1. The diversified offerings provide interest for every family member. Whether it is the sports enthusiast, the teenager who often faithfully reads the advice columns, the would-be gourmet cook who seeks out new recipes, or the investor who religiously checks his or her stocks, there is potential for each of them to see the advertising.
2. When costs along with the actual number of prospective customers that can be reached are considered, the cost per consumer is lower than other media.
3. The life of the newspaper is relatively long. For the dailies it is 24 hours until the next edition is published; for the Sunday edition, which features the greatest amount of advertising, the life is often until the next weekend edition is produced. Compared to radio and television, where messages are but fleeting moments, the newspaper has longevity.
4. Acquiring a newspaper is often automatic. Through a vast number of subscriptions, there is a guarantee that it will regularly be delivered to the household or office without the need to find a place from which to purchase it.

5. A newspaper can be read at any time—while commuting, during a break, or at the end of the day.

There are also some disadvantages to the newspaper.

1. The amount of time that is spent reading the newspaper has decreased in many families. Women, for example, are working outside of the home in greater numbers than ever before, which means there may be limited time to enjoy the newspaper. Teenage readership has also declined, with more and more getting their news via radio or the Internet.
2. A great deal of attention has been focused on the Internet, where increasing numbers of families are logging on to buy merchandise, follow their investments, chat with others, and so forth. All of this replaces the time that was once spent reading the newspaper.
3. The limitations of newsprint stock makes for poor reproduction quality.

> **In the News . . .**
>
> "The Newspaper Cemetery" article, on page 408 at the end of this chapter, should be read at this time.

Magazines

Primarily used by manufacturers of products that have significant market appeal, magazines are not the choice of many retail operations. Since the costs are relatively high and since the trading areas covered by most retailers are generally smaller than the reach of the magazine's circulation, it is not usually a place where merchants expend their promotional dollars. There are, however, exceptions to the rule, with some of the giants in the industry utilizing the magazine to get their messages across. Companies like Sears and JCPenney, with outlets all across the nation, reach markets via magazine advertising. Fashion retailers, too, such as Saks Fifth Avenue, sometimes enter the magazine arena even though their trading areas do not often cover the print publication's consumer market. These retailers use this format as a means of presenting their fashion image to travelers who come to such places as New York City and Chicago, where the companies have flagships. By doing so, they are preselling these travelers on the idea of making in-store visits when they come to these cities.

In order to concentrate on narrower marketplaces, those retailers whose companies are in smaller geographic areas and wish to advertise in magazines often opt for **regional editions** of the publications. For example, a home furnishings retailer that is based in the South—and wishes to reach a market in that portion of the country—might choose a regional edition of *House & Garden* to do so.

The long-lasting nature of magazines is without rival. With the newspaper lasting but a day before it becomes obsolete, and the message on radio or television quickly vanishing, the magazine affords the advertiser continuous inspection that might last a few months. Further value is placed on this periodical because it is often passed from one family to another, accounting for a readership that is greater than the official circulation figures in magazines.

Because of the long life it offers to the advertiser, the ads featured in magazines are typically institutional rather than promotional. Readers' attention is sought over a long time period. In newspaper advertising, the opposite is true. Consumers are expected to immediately react to a featured product and come to the store to make the purchase while the supply lasts.

Unlike their print counterpart, newspaper, magazines require a great deal of **lead time** for the publication of an ad. Whereas the lead time for the placement of a newspaper advertisement is often 48 hours prior to publication, the same for a magazine can be a few months. Thus, when timely ads are the desire of the retailer, the magazine is not selected.

Television

Nothing else quite compares to the combination of sight and sound that is television. It brings realistic as well as stylized commercials into households all across the nation in a manner that no other medium can accomplish. Of course, its considerable expense limits usage to just a few of the major players in the field, with the lion's share of the advertising going to producers of consumer products.

The cost, however, is considerably reduced when the retailer can limit its commercials to a narrow marketplace. This is possible because of the pauses that programs utilize during their shows to sell the sponsor's merchandise. The use of one sponsor for an entire program has faded in the industry, so more and more advertisers are resorting to **spots**. Many local advertisers are taking this a step further by contracting for only that part of the television audience that is within their trading area to see the commercial. The way it works is that, during the time periods when the networks revert back to their local affiliates, a multitude of different commercials are aired. In this way, a midwestern chain might buy this local time to reach its audience, while a southern merchant might use the same time to make its appeal to potential shoppers. Winn Dixie and Publix, supermarket chains whose stores are located in the South, will opt to show their commercials to those southern viewers.

Even with the regional option that reduces the cost and with the incomparable messages it imparts to viewers, television is used sparingly as a medium for retail advertising.

Radio

When the Sony Walkman first came onto the scene, it opened an avenue for retailers to recapture the radio listening audience, which was then in somewhat of a decline. The new device enabled joggers, walkers, exercise enthusiasts, and those who lounged at the beaches and poolside to keep abreast of the day's happenings. Added to this was the ever increasing growth of automobile travel, which holds motorists captive in their cars during gridlock periods and the regular driving times required by their daily commutes. Of course, a segment of the population still listens to the radio at home or in the workplace.

With all of these occurrences favorably affecting radio usage, its relevance to retail advertisers began to spiral upward. Consumers of all ages commit some of their time to tuning in to their favorite stations and programs. In particular, teenagers and young adults became less and less enthralled with the newspaper, became important listeners, and so became eventual purchasers of products that were advertised on the wave-lengths.

With costs relatively modest, particularly when compared to television and the print media, the radio became a viable means to reach targeted markets even for small retailers with limited budgets. Utilizing the regional approach, restaurants, department and specialty stores, entertainment centers, and others found this advertising niche a winner for their needs. Stations that featured rock and rap zeroed in on the younger market, while more serious listeners regularly began to tune in to the talk shows.

Radio is now considered by many merchants a perfect communication outlet for their needs, at costs that are affordable and with little lead time necessary to place most advertisements.

Direct Mail

One needs only to check the mailbox each day to find that he or she is being inundated with an abundance of material from retailers. Coming in such forms as catalogues, brochures,

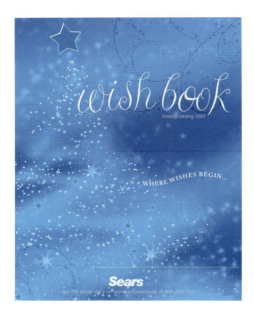

Direct mail catalogues are fast becoming a major advertising medium for multichannel retailers as well as direct marketers.

broadsides, pamphlets, and many other types, direct mail is considered to be one of the more important media outlets.

With expenses that range from low-cost one-page flyers to the more costly, ambitious catalogues that run over 100 pages, direct mail has become an extremely important income-producing outlet for merchants involved in multichannel retailing as well as for those that confine their sales to direct marketing.

Department stores use this form of advertising extensively when they send customers their end-of-month billing statements. By enclosing a motivational piece along with the bill, they are able to appeal to a clientele that has been satisfied in the past. This captive audience often uses the enclosed order forms to make additional purchases.

Catalogues have become a vital outlet for retailers of every size. Hundreds upon hundreds of these sales booklets find their way into homes throughout the year. The competition in catalogue retailing has become so keen that it rivals the experience of merchants in their brick-and-mortar environments.

Through the use of store mailing lists or those that have been purchased from marketing research companies, the retailer is able to zero in on a targeted market that can be customized for the store's own needs. Of course, the lists that are maintained by the retailer's own company include the names and addresses—and now telephone and fax numbers, as well as e-mail addresses—of the store's own customers. Those purchased from list houses may also be tailored to the retailer's needs. Such characteristics as family income, type of employment, level of education, size of the family, and other demographic and psychographic classifications are researched to deliver a list that will include those individuals who could become customers.

Finally, direct mail affords the retailer the opportunity to place the advertisement directly in the consumer's hands to be read at his or her leisure.

Production of direct mail requires careful attention to the quality of the printing because customers rely on the printed image for their impression of the appearance of the advertised products.

Text Messaging

More and more retailers are "instant messaging" their customers to alert them about new offerings, special sales, promotions, and so forth. With cell phones being used by almost everyone in the country, this is yet another way to reach customers. The messages can't be the usual run-of-the mill advertisements; they must alert shoppers to something unique. For example, a message that offers discount coupons for a limited time could bring immediate customer response. As discussed in Chapter 1, Moosejaw—a company that sells outdoor gear and whose customers are tech-savvy—uses instant messaging to communicate with them.

Web Sites

While still in its infancy in terms of the sales its produces for the retail industry, the Internet has become a medium that offers many advantages to merchants. With tens of thousands of retail Web sites, consumers can log on to find exactly what they need without leaving the comfort of their homes.

Whether that of a Web-only merchant, such as Amazon.com, which sells only via this medium, or that of a merchant who toils in the multichannel game, the Web sites are often more diverse than the brick-and-mortar operations we have become used to patronizing.

Surfing the Web reveals a variety of formats that retailers have chosen to use. Some merely advertise a brick-and-mortar or catalogue operation and direct the motivated surfers to visit the store or obtain a catalogue to make purchases. At the other end of the spectrum are those that maintain page after page featuring a host of products that can be instantly ordered. Some are even interactive Web sites in which there is communication between the retailer's representative and the consumer.

As is the case with any form of advertising, Web site quality varies considerably. With more and more specialists using this medium to challenge their design abilities, the level of creativity is continuously improving.

These days, retailing industry professionals consider this form of advertising a necessary addition to the more traditional approaches to advertising.

Outdoor Advertisements

These types of ads include billboards, posters on public transportation vehicles, and backlit transparencies. Such **outdoor advertisements** are gaining popularity with retailers all over the nation.

Outdoor advertisements on backlit transparencies and signs on buildings, as well as transit ads on buses and at bus stops, are popular with retailers.

Billboards along interstates or major thoroughfares often bring drivers and passengers information about companies that will soon be in the vicinity. While this is by no means a major form of advertising, it does serve the purposes of some businesses. Restaurants, in particular, make their presence known to hungry motorists by this means. Other retailers, such as automobile dealers and shopping center groups, are beginning to make more use of the billboard. Posters, which are smaller versions of the typical billboards, are regularly found on the sides and backs of buses, alerting pedestrians and those waiting to board these vehicles of retailers in the area.

Backlit transparencies are excellent attention getters. They are illuminated from within and are highly visible at all times.

Outdoor advertising is relatively inexpensive, and offers the retailer the ability to capture the consumer's attention 24 hours a day.

Advertising Cost Analysis

At the top of the list in terms of expense is television advertising, followed by magazines, newspapers, the Internet, radio, direct mail, and the outdoor entries. The retailer must consider the expenses involved and the return on investment that such advertising could bring.

After studying the advantages and disadvantages of each and deciding which would bring the most positive results, the merchant must choose from everything that is available in each classification that would best serve the company's needs. The consumer magazine category, for example, features more than 3,000 entries from which to choose. Each provides a different cost and readership profile that must be analyzed by the retailer to make certain that the best one is selected. The same factors apply to newspapers and to any broadcast medium that is chosen.

One of the easiest ways to make comparisons among all of the potential communication outlets is through the use of the **Standard Rate & Data Service (SRDS)**.

Focus on . . .
SRDS

SINCE 1920, the Standard Rate & Data Service has provided media rates and data to the advertising industry. The company offers comprehensive coverage on the traditional media such as magazines, newspapers, television, and radio as well as today's alternative marketing opportunities such as online, out-of-home, and direct marketing. SRDS is a steady source of information for every segment of the business world, and it helps individual clients grow by providing high-quality data and advanced functionality.

SRDS is the leading information provider in the high-powered advertising industry. It is a member of the VNU family, a $3 billion international company with over 9,000 employees in the United States and 20,000 worldwide. Making SRDS even more valuable to the potential advertiser is that it is part of the ACNielsen company.

When merchants are researching potential outlets for advertisements, SRDS affords them the largest and most comprehensive database of media rates and data available in the world. The company catalogues more than 80,000 media properties and 30,000 direct marketing lists in all. To keep information current, SRDS verifies each listing 20 times a year and issues more than 25,000 listing updates every month. These updates keep subscribers current with changes in advertising rates, circulation information, and personal contacts. It also provides information on new advertising opportunities including magazine launches and alternative media options such as Web sites.

The importance of SRDS to the advertiser may be best realized by the fact that 95 percent of all advertising agencies—including Ogilvy & Mather, J. Walter Thompson, and McCann Erickson—rely on SRDS products.

Some of the benefits of SRDS to retailers are:

- More than 3,200 detailed listings for newspaper dailies and specialized papers
- More than 3,400 magazine listings that cover 85 subclassifications

- More than 30,000 direct-mail listings organized into 223 market classifications
- More than 4,000 TV and cable listings
- More than 10,000 AM/FM station listings
- More than 2,200 marketing vehicles for Spanish-speaking audiences in the Hispanic market listings
- Thousands of online advertising possibilities in SRDS's sources

By consulting SRDS's print publications or its Web site, a merchant can quickly compare its advertising opportunities and the cost of each.

Evaluation of Advertising

Having carefully considered the alternative advertising techniques and having made the decision to follow a particular route, the retailer must make certain that the expended dollars have been wisely spent. In order to decide whether or not a particular ad or campaign improved sales, an evaluation is in order.

For the smaller merchant with perhaps a one-unit operation, the task is relatively simple. Because of the personal contacts with their clienteles, these merchants are able to get verbal acknowledgments of the ads when consumers patronize the store. While this is by no means a scientific approach, it does quickly let the entrepreneur know if it is the ad that has brought the customer into the store.

In larger companies, the evaluation process is approached more technically. Many have in-house research departments that can set up the evaluative procedures. One method that is extensively used is to compare the sale of the advertised products before and after the ad runs. If sales increase after the ad's publication, then it is assumed that the ad was the reason for the additional sales. Additional research might also focus on the amount of the increase and whether or not the sales revenues offset the cost of the advertisement.

Another evaluative measure that is used focuses on store traffic for advertising placed by a brick-and-mortar operation. In some campaigns, the theme of the ad is not for specific merchandise but rather to call attention to the store itself or to a particular department within the store. If this is the case, the research department could use an observation tool that measures customer traffic before and after publication of the ad.

Advertising is a costly expense to the retail industry. It must continually be evaluated to determine if the company's expenditures are appropriate in terms of the profits they generate or if changes must be made to maximize the profit potential.

PROMOTION

In addition to advertising as a means of motivating shoppers to become customers, most retailers utilize a variety of promotional endeavors to augment the ads and bring greater attention to the company and the merchandise it offers for sale. A blending of different promotional tools helps the retailer achieve the sales levels necessary to bring a profit to the company. In addition to visual merchandising, an extremely viable promotional tool that will be explored in the next chapter, the vast majority of these endeavors involve special events.

Special Events

As the name implies, these promotional features are not routinely offered by the retailer but are presented as limited occurrences that are both special and often unique. Their creation and

Special events are one way to get attention, and a major cost of a special event is advertising it.

development generally lie with an in-house staff if the company is a large one or an outside agency if it is a smaller one. In either circumstance, experts are called upon to lend their talents to the creation of events that will draw attention to the retailer's operation. The expenses involved in such promotional endeavors range from modest sums to extravagant amounts. Macy's, one of the world's major users of promotion, budgets huge sums for its special events programs. With such annual presentations as its Thanksgiving Day Parade, the fireworks display on Independence Day, and its springtime flower show, the monetary outlay runs into the millions. For the flower show alone, more than a million dollars are spent to transform the store into a botanical garden. With the in-store traffic that is generated by these events and the sales that follow, it is safe to assume that the ends justify the means.

Typically, retailers use a variety of formats for their special events programs. Included are fashion shows, celebrity appearances, trunk shows, demonstrations, sampling, charitable functions, holiday parades, community programs, and others such as special sales.

Fashion Shows

For the fashion retailer there are few other special events that bring out the shoppers like fashion shows. Running the gamut from runway presentations to informal modeling, the sales results are usually worth the cost and effort of the production. Most typical are the runway shows that take place somewhere in the store. It might be within the department of the featured merchandise so that, when the production ends, attendees can closely examine the goods and purchase them if they like. Some merchants have special events centers in which the show takes place. These usually provide more room for customers and thus can bring greater sales. Another runway option is in the store's restaurant. While customers are enjoying their meals, the models are displaying the merchandise.

The runway production costs vary from presentation to presentation. If professional models are used, the costs could escalate. Some retailers make use of in-house employees, thereby reducing the modeling expense. Other than building the runway and providing music in the form of live entertainment or tapes, there is little extra expense.

Retailers are inclined to use formal productions when they are part of fund-raising events. With the commitment to charities providing excellent public relations, this is a sound investment. Oftentimes outside auditoriums or ballrooms are used to feature these events. There might be a large stage erected to show the models in their attire, along with a runway. These are generally the most elaborate shows presented by retailers. With professional models, music, commentary, and the like, these shows often cost several thousand dollars.

A fashion show at the store's mall entrance invites customers to try on the items being modeled.

Informal modeling is not typically considered a fashion show but rather a way in which apparel is modeled throughout the store. Live "mannequins" stroll throughout the store carrying signs and telling onlookers where the merchandise may be found.

Companies like Nordstrom, Macy's, Bergdorf Goodman, and other fashion image retailers make use of all of these fashion show formats.

Celebrity Appearances

A great number of consumers react positively when the announcement is made that one of their admired celebrities will make an in-store appearance. The bigger the name, the bigger the crowd that assembles. It might be a particular designer, an entertainment personality, a sports figure, or anyone else with the potential to attract attention.

Belk Department Stores reaped the rewards of having Tommy Hilfiger appear in one of its locations when he was launching his new fragrance. Not only did the company enjoy record crowds, but fragrance sales skyrocketed.

Trunk Shows

One of the fastest growing special events is the **trunk show**. Designers or their representatives visit the stores and bring with them their latest collections. Customers are notified by mail or by some media form such as the newspaper that the event will take place.

The concept requires the merchant to set aside space in the store where the trunks filled with merchandise will be featured. Some might be modeled and others simply shown and described by the company representative. Customers are sometimes invited to have merchandise adjusted to their personal preferences and thus customized. Other merchandise is there to be ordered, as shown, for

Trunk shows bring the manufacturer's latest collection to the store, often generating orders even before the store stocks the new merchandise.

future delivery. These events usually take place at the season's opening so that the customers will be the first to enjoy them.

Most retailers who participate in these events report that they generally result in significant sales.

A recent variation on the in-person trunk show is the use of a virtual rendition. Since it is generally impossible for designers to visit all of the retail shops in which they would like to promote their collections, some use virtual trunk shows. Net-a-porter, a promotional organization, has been one of the leaders in virtual trunk show production. One of their major efforts was to feature the collection designer Roland Mouret. A video team recorded the live version of a fashion show in Paris, complete with commentaries and interviews, to produce a virtual trunk show version. In 4 days, customers from 22 countries placed preorders of $500,000.

High-fashion retailers such as Bergdorf Goodman, Neiman Marcus, and Saks Fifth Avenue have similarly created online trunk shows that allow customers to preorder from a designer's collection.

Demonstrations

One way that the cosmetics industry, in particular, helps to generate business is through the use of makeup application. Leading manufacturers send cosmeticians to the major retailers who spend their time demonstrating the use of their latest products. Individuals are invited to act as models and learn all about the company's offerings as the makeup is being applied. Sales come not only from the participants but also from the onlookers. When the names of the marquee brands are advertised in the newspapers, many potential customers are likely to make their way to the store.

Other demonstrations that manufacturers offer to retail clients run the gamut from the use of vacuum cleaners to the latest entries in computers.

"How to" Clinics

One effective promotional endeavor that brings immediate sales to retailers is a clinic that teaches consumers how to solve their problems. Home Depot offers a number of different clinics of this nature ranging from how to install ceramic tile to maintaining a garden. Scores of different "how to" clinics are listed in the stores on a bulletin board that gives the dates and times of each event. The end result of these programs is the purchase of the necessary tools and supplies to complete each project.

Sampling

When consumers walk through the aisles of many grocery stores or warehouse operations like Costco or Sam's Club, they are likely to be treated to a variety of different food products for sale. Stations that feature skillets or microwave ovens and cooks who prepare the foods are constantly serving samples for passersby to taste. The intent is to motivate shoppers to purchase the products they have just sampled.

Other sampling techniques involve the aforementioned cosmetics industry. Vendors supply the retailers with attractive items that are either given away free with any purchase or are made available at a nominal cost. In this way the vendor can introduce the new product lines and help the retailer introduce them to its clientele.

Charitable Functions

Major retailers regularly use charitable functions as part of their promotional programs. These vehicles serve two purposes: first, they help to build the retailer's image as a leader who is interested in serving the needs of the community; and second, they provide a wealth of potential customers who frequent these events.

Retailers such as Bloomingdale's, Macy's, Nordstrom, Dillard's, and the like feature charitable functions that include fashion shows, dinners, dances, celebrity appearances, and other events.

Some typical charitable functions that have gained widespread attention are:

Charity events are widely sponsored by retailers; they allow a retailer to improve its image while achieving greater sales.

- Bloomingdale's benefit for colon cancer research that featured the *Today* show's Katie Couric, whose husband died of the disease
- JCPenney's promotion to benefit the Susan G. Komen Breast Cancer Foundation
- Nordstrom's various events on women's health issues
- Neiman Marcus's in-house events that raise money for cancer research

Holiday Parades

The most prominent of these parades are featured on Thanksgiving Day. Although the Macy's extravaganza is the best-known, others are presented by major retailers throughout the United States. These events are used to signal the beginning of the Christmas selling season.

The Macy's entry, produced in conjunction with NBC, is a multimillion-dollar event that features stars of stage, screen, television, and the sports world. Entranced by the now-famous balloon characters that tower above and by bands from every part of the country that have competed for the right to participate, the crowds that assemble number several hundred thousand. With television coverage, the happening also announces to the viewing audience that the time has come to begin holiday shopping.

Macy's Thanksgiving Day parade brings throngs of shoppers to the flagship store; broadcasting on national television provides institutional publicity far beyond the flagship's trading area.

So enormous is the commitment to these parades, and so successful are they in terms of promoting their stores, that the retail participants begin planning the next year's event immediately after the current one has been presented.

Community Programs

Many merchants recognize the need to either sponsor community events or participate in their presentation to the public in their retail environments. Educational institutions, for example, are often invited to promote their programs through these endeavors. One event that is typical of these community presentations is the fashion show. Either in a selling department that has been cleared to make room for the show or in areas that are adjacent to the store, high school and college students participate in modeling the store's latest apparel collections. Not only does this bring good will to the company, it can also introduce the store to new customers.

"Promoting" the Promotion

The creation and presentation of special events generally requires a large commitment of time and money. Their occurrence, however, does not guarantee that audiences will be there to appreciate them.

In order to assure that these happenings will be well attended, it is necessary to publicize them through newspaper ads, spot announcements on radio and television, and direct-mail pieces. The ads might offer additional motivation to attend by describing prizes that will be offered or any other incentives that will bring in the crowds.

Promotion is one way for retailers to distinguish themselves from their competition. Although merchandise offerings in many of the competing operations are identical, the special events provide the impetus to gain in-store visits. With the proper "promotion" of the promotions, it is likely that store traffic will increase, giving the merchant the opportunity to distinguish its operation from the others.

PUBLICITY

Every major player in the retailing industry has in-house publicists whose jobs it is to present the company in the best light and to attract shoppers. The people involved are public relations experts who know how to achieve these goals.

Unlike advertising, special events, and visual presentations, which all come about as a result of spending budgeted dollar amounts, publicity is a means of spreading awareness to the consumer without any direct cost.

By contacting the editorial press, public relations experts are able to get their messages to would-be customers. Some of the vehicles they use are press releases and press kits. Where these had typically been sent via the traditional mailing route, today's publicity professionals use e-mail to instantly get their ideas across to those who might spread the word. Of course, whichever technique is used, the intention is to sufficiently motivate these "communicators" to relay the messages to their readerships and listeners.

In the News . . .

"Gale Group: Blurring the Lines," an article on page 410 at the end of this chapter, should be read at this time.

MULTIMEDIA CAMPAIGNS

Although individual advertising and promotional endeavors still have a place in retailing, more and more merchants are utilizing multimedia campaigns that incorporate a variety of these tools to promote their businesses and merchandise offerings. This integrated approach can have a major impact on consumer markets and generally results in increased on-site and off-site sales.

One of the proponents of this approach is Sears. As the end of 2007 neared, the company entered into a major multimedia campaign to create a positive shopping atmosphere for the holiday shopping period. Not only did it dovetail national TV, radio spots, magazine inserts, its Web site, direct mail, circulars, and catalogues, Sears also collaborated with Yahoo! using a holiday-themed social networking site as well as "widgets" and text messaging to alert customers to its special promotions and added services for the holiday shopping season.

CHAPTER HIGHLIGHTS

- Through direct and continuous promotional efforts by retailers, the public will be aware of their operations and their merchandise. This assures retailers that they will have a chance of capturing the market segment they are targeting.
- The sales promotion division of a major retailer is generally divided into separate departments that are responsible for advertising, special events, visual merchandising, and publicity.
- Major retailers have in-house advertising departments, while their small store counterparts use outside sources for their advertising needs.
- External advertising assistance comes from vendors, the media, ad agencies, and freelancers.
- Advertising takes two forms: promotional and institutional.
- Cooperative advertising is a joint venture between merchandise suppliers and retailers.
- Although some of the other media have gained in importance in retailing, newspapers remain the most important communications outlet.
- The radio has become an increasingly important advertising medium.
- Special events are activities such as fund-raisers, holiday parades, and celebrity appearances that retailers use to promote merchandise and improve their images.
- Publicity comes as a result of something that a retailer does that is newsworthy. It catches the attention of the editorial press which, in turn, passes the news on to its readers and viewers.

IMPORTANT RETAILING TERMS

advertising (388)
advertising agency (388)
advertising campaign (393)
combination advertising (393)
cooperative advertising (394)
copy (389)
crossover advertising (395)
freelancer (392)
in-house advertising department (389)
institutional advertising (393)
lead time (396)
media services (392)
outdoor advertisement (399)
promotional advertising (393)
publicity (388)
regional edition (396)
spots (397)
Standard Rate & Data Service (SRDS) (400)
trunk show (403)

FOR REVIEW

1. Name the departments that usually comprise a sales promotion division of a retail operation.
2. How does advertising differ from publicity?
3. Generally, what four components make up the preparation of an advertisement?
4. From whom does an advertising agency receive its remuneration?
5. In what way does a vendor assist the retailer with its advertising endeavors?
6. What is the difference between promotional and institutional advertising?
7. Does the retailer ever combine promotional and institutional advertising in an ad? If so, what is it called?
8. Why is it often necessary for the retailer to use an ad campaign rather than a single advertisement?
9. How does cooperative advertising work?
10. Define the term *crossover advertising* as it is used in this chapter.
11. Which of the media generally commands the lion's share of the retail advertising budget?
12. Which types of retailers are more likely to make use of magazine advertising?
13. Why is radio important to the retailer?
14. How can a direct-mail advertiser assemble a mailing list if it hasn't maintained its own?
15. How does a retailer determine the success of a single ad or an advertising campaign?
16. What is meant by the term *special event*?
17. Why do merchants use charitable functions as part of their promotional endeavors?
18. Which segment of the fashion industry uses the demonstration technique to attract a passerby's attention?
19. Give an example of a community program that a retailer might use as part of its special events agenda.
20. What is meant by the term *publicity*?

AN INTERNET ACTIVITY

Many of the search engines that we use on the Internet are involved in promoting retail Web sites and help direct the consumer to them. Log onto five of them, and prepare a chart with the following heads to indicate the names of the merchants to whom the surfer is directed.

Search Engine	Retailers Cited

EXERCISES AND PROJECTS

1. Using one of the major newspapers that serve your community, select three advertisements: a promotional ad, an institutional ad, and a combination ad. Each advertisement should be mounted on foam board and be accompanied by your comments indicating why it falls into a particular category.

2. Contact a major department store or chain organization near your residence to learn about their calendar of special events for the next month. From the list, choose an event to attend for the purpose of evaluating its effectiveness. A report should then be prepared that includes the following:
   - Advertisements that preceded the event
   - Type of event
   - Breadth and depth of the presentation
   - Size of the attending audience
   - Your evaluation of its effectiveness

THE CASE OF THE FASHION ENTREPRENEUR WITH LIMITED PROMOTIONAL FUNDS

Surrounded by fashion-oriented retailers who seem to spend untold sums on special events that promote their merchandise, the owner of Amanda's Boutique is at a loss as to how her store can promote itself without spending large sums of money.

The merchant does a minimum amount of advertising in local publications as well as through some direct mailings that are sent to the customers who have frequented the store. Although this approach has been satisfactory in terms of the dollars expended, it has not brought new customers to the store.

One of the promotional endeavors that owner Amanda Gallop is considering is the use of a fashion show aimed at women in the community. After running this initiative by some of her key employees, Amanda decided to plan a budget that would bring positive sales results to her boutique. When all of the costs were figured—including the expense of hiring professional models, using a trio to provide the musical accompaniment, program development, and the like—the costs were far greater than she could afford. She was now faced with the likelihood of canceling her fashion show plans and trying another means of promotion to better serve her business interests.

Questions

1. Should Amanda forgo her fashion show plans? Why or why not?
2. Would another special event be more cost-effective?
3. If a fashion show is the tool that will best serve her interests, how might Amanda go about producing such a show with minimal expense?

The Newspaper Cemetery
Naseem Javed

MAY 23, 2007

Despite all denials, newspapers all over the world are simply dying. The gravity of the problem is not that the competing media like TV or Internet are at play it's rather that the public all over the world prefers moving pictures in the palms of their hands over deciphering or reading between the lines of nicely arranged words spread out on a paper blanket.

THE CHILDREN OF THE MILLENNIUM

Historians will regard our current centuries as volatile, innovative and dynamic, yet the Paleontologist would agree that during the last millennium, we have hardly evolved at all. There go all the IQ tests. As a result, we are still the same homo-sapiens, although erectus but still scared of the dark, carrying the same chains of emotions and fears, like babes in the woods, very cautiously we tread on this little planet. As children of this new millennium we now have new toys to play with, and some new buttons to push, while minds stay trapped in ancient behavior, responding to external stimuli with great caution.

The human mind naturally gravitates towards the easy flow of colorful moving pictures, where it likes to become a receptacle, while reading words forces the cerebrum to create imaginary moving pictures with its own logic, and exercise its own craft. But with regular watching, a kind of mental numbness takes over and the mind tries to go to sleep. Like watching very late night TV and getting out of body experiences.

PRINT-SOCIETY TO CYBER-SOCIETY

If you are reading the newspaper today, then it is obviously yesterday's news. The cumbersome process of cutting forests down all the way to print and distribute takes some many thousands of critical steps and this system perfected over a century is still too slow to feed the voracious appetite of the info-hungry creatures that walk the planet now. The sudden explosion of technology in the last few seconds on the clock of human evolution may appear to make us look suave over what we looked like a few minutes ago, but we are certainly trapped where we were hours ago. Where are you Darwin when we need you?

SOUND BITE CULTURE

The short and crisp doses of sound bites have made us, around the world, a very well-informed and highly educated population, in sound-bites only. That's it. The abbreviated versions of very complex issues demanding deeper and richer understandings are eliminated by short headlines, nicely arranged to fit cute small screens, as words are further corrupted and abbreviated to comply with this new lingo. Today the universe of text messaging is where the once-powerful print society of the last century was. Everything and all things are compressed into sound bites. The diversity and variety of trivial issues has taken over discussion and any chance for in-depth analysis.

Today's youth is fully conversant about some 100 issues, as long as no detailed explanations are required. This cursory knowledge incubates further fears and lack of confidence and also makes us gullible to any heavy bombardment of any strong and highly-repetitive message. The Orwellian model is passé, it's more like the DigiSapians en masse preparing for our brains to shrink to the size of our fancy PDA's. Miniaturization anyone?

THE SURGERY TABLE

Denials about the print medium will not cure the main problem. Like the much earlier resistance by the media barons for having absolutely nothing to do with websites to display their newspaper contents has already proven very wrong. Here are three surgical procedures. Oxygen please.

CYBER-BRAND FOR CYBER-SOCIETY

Most newspaper corporations are convinced that by simply having a website with complicated layouts and complex graphics, they are deeply immersed into e-commerce, and some flashy, jumpy website with a weird looking format and foot long silly twisted URL is a hip cyber-branding strategy in action. It's really time to go back to school. The books that teach about cyber-branding are not published yet. An in-depth discovery of the real cyber-branding and the complex cyber-society is a prerequisite.

RE-POSITION FOR RE-POSITIONED MIND SHARE

Most formats are just copies of each other; the same news, and same formats are only repeated to death until the minds shut off. Reformat the contents and build a brand based on today's realities and the pioneering old print society thinking. Re-train the organization to a mega cultural change. Mass merchandising concepts are fading to One-to-one, making advertising a very selective targeting process.

RE-CLAIMATION OF THE TRUTH

Most newspapers have desperately tried to copy or simulate the other mediums and have failed big time. The fake sensationalization of breaking news or twisting truth in an attempt to get some attention, or acting hip and childish to attract the youth must be replaced by a solid, confident approach. The news is not a movie, and a movie is not the news. Chasing and accurately delivering the truth would be a good start.

100% GLOBAL OWNERSHIP

Most newspapers named after towns or generic names like The Ledger, Tribune, Journal, or Dailies are now lost in the web-jungle of thousands of similar names all over the world. Less than 1% of newsprint names are unique or worthy for global branding, while the rest are expensive luggage and going nowhere. Discover the Five Star Standard of Global name identities and also what makes an absolute 100% ownership of a brand to provide an umbrella and to park your future underneath.

THE WINNERS & LOSERS

There are some very fine survivors of this fierce transition, the biggest pain came from the print media's lingering in a state of denial. Now that the cat is out of the bag and the demise of print is an open subject the winners are the surgeon at the marketing strategy and editorial teams that are embracing the revolution as an opportunity and completely re-inventing themselves. The losers are the public, as they have replaced the communication of articulated printed words and elaborate concepts to flashy, but watered-down, moving pictures. The emerging and far away lands are still very dependent on newspapers but the explosion of mobile technologies spread faster than the sluggish delivery of newspapers.

SUMMARY

Though in reality, newspapers will always stay some part of our lives, but will certainly not be the drivers of our morning agenda, and more likely become a weekly or monthly recap of in-depth analysis of serious matters, limited to the highlights of the day in soundbite format. There are new frontiers and new challenges to be embraced by new players. Let's read more about them in the papers. But first the Breaking News on TV: The Democrat's poodle bites the Republican's hound, so the both owners jump in and bite each other . . . let's watch the live footage and join the panel discussion.

• •

Gale Group: Blurring the Lines
Rachel Strugatz

JULY 2, 2007

Holding up the new graphically driven brochure and sample of Styli-Style's latest beauty innovation and triple threat—an eye shadow and eyeliner that is waterproof, smudge-proof and activity-proof—Mindy Gale, founder of the advertising and public relations hybrid Gale Group, stresses the importance of creative mailing to her staff.

"We never send a dry product or press release to an editor," said Gale, a Philadelphia native, during a recent production meeting. "We always send a press release, product and graphic all together to catch the eye."

While Styli-Style's Shadow 24 promises to withstand any challenges encountered in a woman's day, Gale says it's her job to make sure Gale Group provides this information to editors across the country.

Gale has come a long way from her Hofstra University coed days with a major in medical illustration. With a main office in New York and a satellite office in Los Angeles, Gale Group has grown into an agency that infuses the "perfect proportions" of advertising and P.R. with the aim of giving clients little reason to go elsewhere.

"When we first started this concept, we did have resistance, because clients would think, 'How could you be great in P.R. and how could you still be great in advertising services?' But the two really go hand in hand, and today more than ever the line blurs," Gale explained.

Gale said potential clients could have been hesitant because disciplines and staffing for advertising and P.R. vastly differ. "People that tend to be in publicity are different than creative and production people," Gale said. "And I guess in retrospect the biggest challenge was in figuring out how to harness all this talent."

Gale admits there was a learning curve, and said her current staff of 22 is almost evenly split between the two fields. "We do have different teams of people and they do work together," said Gale, a brunette with striking green eyes and the mother of seven-year-old twins. "We'll sit around at a staff meeting and the people in P.R. that are talking to magazines every day might share trends in graphics or color stories while the advertising department says, 'Hmm, that's interesting,' or vice versa."

Gale said her business has to "evolve and change, and move with your clients' needs and what's happening in the industry. Business always changes so you can't get stuck in your way of doing things. You need to be ahead of the game."

Gale's business evolved from an early eighties "magalogue" she created in order to weld together interests in publishing and fashion. She created a cohesive publication aptly titled "Fashion Avenue" that was full of editorial content. As self-proclaimed editor in chief, Gale pioneered blurring the lines between advertisements and editorial nearly two decades ago. Peak circulation hovered around 300,000.

For Gale, an average day consists of a combination of production, creative and P.R. meetings, new business directional meetings (to secure new clients) and additional meetings with staff and clients (both established and potential), as well as media lunches. A large portion of her time is spent directly in the creative element, whether it be art directing, overseeing casting or attending photo shoots. In the few free moments she has, Gale tries to return the seemingly never-ending e-mails and phone calls she is inundated with on a daily basis.

In addition to her daily workload, Gale also leads seminars and participates in panels relating to brand cohesion, usually coinciding with a major trade show. "My seminars are directed toward brand owners, retailers and/or manufacturers that want to understand how to get their message out," said Gale. "We talk about how to layer P.R. and creative visuals, point of purchase, showroom environment, sales people and how everything can and should have the same message throughout."

At a recent staff meeting, K-Swiss was next on the agenda. The classic footwear brand, responsible for the first leather tennis shoe, is in the midst of encapsulating a new marketing decision, said Gale. K-Swiss, once associated with a certain age demographic, is now being branded as a "premium sport" brand, conjuring up images of classic California, and a younger, hipper customer of both genders. So far, Gale Group has produced two TV commercials (the first running now and the next later in July), as well as outdoor media light boxes and print ads featuring the new K-Swiss products.

Next up for Gale is a new business directional meeting with Liz Cohen, who works on business development at Gale Group, and Maria Ashe, the president of BeautyADDICTS, a new line of makeup whose mission is to create "beauty made simple." The purpose of the meeting was to "get the ball running and tighten up direction" on what Gale Group aims to achieve in terms of advertising and P.R. promotions for the new brand. Ashe, a self-proclaimed beauty junkie who studied theatrical makeup in college, explained that the objective of BeautyADDICTS is to base all makeup on attitudes and moods, rather than seasons.

Later that day, Gale makes a quick change to a black-and-white ensemble consisting of a chic black wrap blouse that ties around the waist with fitted white jeans for a K-Swiss event. The new showroom, boasting a roof deck overlooking the city and state-of-the-art design, was filled with K-Swiss' spring 2008 line of clothing and colorful sneakers. There were models walking around sporting leggings, tanks and zip-ups from the updated line, as well as Champagne, wine and hors d'oeuvres.

"The opening of the showroom is part of the culmination of a project we have been working on for a long time with the Gale Group, which is really about the global positioning of our brand," said K-Swiss executive vice president David Nichols at the launch party. "We have had growth in Europe, Asia and the United States over the last several years, and now we're at a point where we have momentum in each market, so the important thing is to make it one global brand."

After numerous phone calls, e-mails and meetings, as well as the party, Gale calls it a day. Balancing career and family while tackling future strategies for her company, it's clear Gale is ambitious and was career-driven from a young age.

"Honestly, I was always the kid in high school with a portfolio in one hand, a guitar in the other hand and a button to vote for me for class president on my chest," she said. "I was always in the creative and communication areas, so it's kind of natural that I ended up in advertising and P.R."

CHAPTER 18
Visual Merchandising

After you have completed this chapter, you should be able to discuss:

- The different approaches retailers take to assure themselves of the most beneficial visual presentations
- Why, in major retail brick-and-mortar operations, the visual merchandising chores are left to in-house staffs
- Why most large chain organizations utilize the concept of centralized visual merchandising
- Why the focal point in any merchandise installation is the merchandise and not the display props
- How components such as lighting, signage, graphics, mannequins, props, and color are used to augment displays
- The five design principles utilized by visual merchandisers: balance, emphasis, proportion, rhythm, and harmony
- Why visual merchandisers must check on interior installations daily

Capturing the attention of passersby or the numerous browsers who constitute the traffic inside a retail operation is a formidable task but, if done properly, these lookers are transformed into customers. The merchandise on the selling floors reflects the buyer's many hours of planning, but its visual presentation often leaves much to be desired. Lackluster displays sometimes present a product in a manner that will not attract the attention of would-be customers. Of course, this is not true of every retail establishment. Some, by virtue of their visual merchandising teams and their dedication to eye-catching presentations, are able to take what would otherwise be mundane offerings and enhance their presence with traffic-stopping results.

Although the department store has been the greatest proponent of visual merchandising—as can be seen in the sometimes extravagant downtown flagship stores—other retailers have joined them, creating interiors where magic is often performed to lend excitement to the merchandise. A walk through stores like Crate & Barrel and Pottery Barn immediately reveals that everyday dinnerware, glassware, and household accessories take on a new and exciting look that is bound to attract attention. Close inspection of many of the featured items shows that these are just practical items that have taken on a special pizzazz because of the manner in which they are shown. In the gourmet retail cooking arena, another sense of excitement is generated by

Lord & Taylor uses lavish Christmas displays to attract large crowds.

the in-store displays of Williams-Sonoma. Taking a variety of cooking utensils, dining elements, table accessories, and other items for the home and then featuring them in eye-catching table and countertop settings makes shoppers stop in their tracks and significantly motivates them to make a purchase.

With the enormous amount of competition in retailing today, the need for individual approaches is great, and none can better serve the merchant than imaginative visual merchandising. That is not to say that large budgets are the only route to successful product presentation. On the contrary, some of the better visual efforts come at relatively low cost. At Pottery Barn, for example, the use of a particular color scheme that transcends many of the offerings does not rely on a monetary investment. Instead, the approach focuses on showing items in abundance, giving them greater eye appeal. Whether it's the cobalt blue theme that regularly abounds in its glassware department or the emerald green that is often featured, the visual impact is striking. It doesn't cost a penny more to use color as a central theme; it only requires the attention of a professional to underscore its value as a visual merchandising tool.

Even supermarkets, at one time the least likely to engage in visual merchandising to promote goods, are now taking extra steps to improve their visual presentations. Chains like Harriss Teeter have made their premises more appealing with special displays that feature pre-cooked meals and departments that present the products in visually enhanced settings. Hence customers are drawn to these areas and are motivated to buy what they see displayed.

Where budgets have been reduced in many of retailing's brick-and-mortar operations, the end result is often unimaginative, lackluster visual presentations. It is the creativity of seasoned professionals that can overcome this insufficient funding and deliver dazzling themes.

Vitrines are used on selling floors to allow viewing from many angles.

DEVELOPMENT OF THE VISUAL CONCEPT

In order to differentiate one's premises from others in the retail industry, merchants must carefully develop a concept that is unique to their operations. In the larger companies the task is left to the **in-house display staff**. The staff is supervised by a visual merchandising director, who at many retail operations enjoys the title of vice president and acts at the same level as merchandise and store operation executives.

The visual merchandising director—along with a team of display installers, signage experts, carpenters, and others—is responsible for both exterior and interior visual merchandising. Whether it is the exterior windows that need spectacular installations or a department that requires product arrangements that will gain shopper attention, the tasks are carried out each and every day of the year.

In smaller retail organizations, these tasks are usually carried out by the owner or given to a freelancer, whose primary function is to create window displays that will entice pedestrians to come into the store. By and large, it is these itinerant professional visual merchandisers who plan and execute the display windows. In some cases they are also called upon to spruce up the interiors to make them more appealing to the clientele.

Whether it is the in-house team or the professional freelancer, the overall goal is the same: to make the environment one that generates business.

The Department Store Approach

Compared to other retail classifications, the department store has the largest visual merchandising budget. Department stores regularly change their display windows, especially in the downtown flagships, where sizes and configurations are unrivaled. In addition, the staff is responsible for every visual presentation ranging from **vitrine** to countertop displays. Daily **walkthroughs** are also part of the routine to make certain that the selling floor is refurbished each day and to make any necessary adjustments to displays that might have been damaged by overzealous shoppers.

This task is not only for the flagship but also for each of the branches in the organization. Their presentations must echo those of the main store and be carefully executed.

The size of the visual team varies from company to company. The major players, especially those that are convinced that visual merchandising is truly the silent seller that many retail professionals believe it is, often have staffs that number more than 50 people, with specialists performing in every aspect of the department's endeavors. Companies like Lord & Taylor and Neiman Marcus, for example, are typical of the larger departments. Others, without the same commitment to visual merchandising, have in-house staffs that employ fewer people who each perform several functions. Some department store visual teams have separate staffs for their flagships and branches. The former houses the director and those that create the actual props to be used in the installations, as well as display people who trim the windows. The latter generally has just a few installers who follow the directions that come from the company's main store.

In some department stores, in-house artists create unique display props.

Centralized Visual Merchandising

In the case of chain operations, there is generally a different approach to the visual merchandising procedure. Just as the buying, merchandising, and management functions are centralized, so is the one that deals with visual presentations.

Typically, the concept is developed by a team that is housed in the company's corporate headquarters. Headed by a director who creates the concepts and is assisted by a few individuals, the team develops sample display presentations. It might be a window display, countertop presentations, props, specific signage, or any element that will be needed by all of the units in the chain. Once installed, the sample displays are photographed and, along with directions for installation, are forwarded to either regional visual teams or directly to the stores, where they are reproduced by managers, who faithfully follow the plans that

Williams-Sonoma centralizes the management of its visual merchandise; presentations are designed at company headquarters and are duplicated in each store.

have been sent to them. The key to this visual approach is uniformity. Each store in the chain must have the same appearance in order to give it a universal image. By assigning the creative responsibilities to the team at central headquarters, the company is assured of having competent professionals carry out the developmental stage, and others, at the store level, who follow their instructions.

Companies like Gap, Pottery Barn, and Williams-Sonoma utilize the centralized approach to visual merchandising.

Small Store Visual Arrangements

Just as small retailers cannot afford the expense of in-house specialists to perform their buying, merchandising, and promotional activities, neither can they undertake the cost associated with in-house staffing to carry out their visual presentations. Instead, they use freelancers to make their installations or use simple approaches that they themselves can install. Sometimes a freelancer is used at the beginning of each season to create a design that can be adapted periodically by the entrepreneur. For example, it might be a spring or autumn theme that will remain until the following season. Only the merchandise is changed, not the background props. In this way a professional touch is given to the display area.

Freelancers

As already mentioned, the freelancer is a professional whose business specializes in developing visual presentations for retailers. This visual professional does everything from the development of the creative concept to the installation of the displays. A freelancer might work on a one-time basis for his or her clients or on contracts that cover a full year's efforts. The better known of these individuals generally require a contract for their services.

COMPONENTS OF VISUAL PRESENTATIONS

Every seasoned merchant recognizes that there must be a balance between the products offered in their model stocks and the backgrounds and props that are used to highlight them. First and

Attention-getting props in Christmas displays draw the shopper's eyes to the featured merchandise.

foremost, the merchandise must be the primary focus of a visual presentation and never be upstaged by any of its elements. Display props should be used only to enhance the merchandise.

Once the merchandise has been selected (except in the case of institutional presentations that center on image-building ideas or community dedication and are generally void of merchandise), the other components must be selected to complete the display. Elements such as props, mannequins, lighting, color, signage, and graphics are employed as the enhancements.

Table 18.1 features selected suppliers of elements that are used in visual merchandising. Those unable to visit the showrooms may get a taste of the offerings though visits to the companies' Web sites.

Props

Ranging from the elegant, professionally crafted entries to more simply developed items, a wealth of props are available to transform empty window shells and counter surfaces into environments that stop traffic.

The vast majority of the country's visual merchandisers visit trade shows each year that give them ideas for new themes and also introduce them to the abundance of new props and materials available for use. NADI, a major visual merchandising trade show held twice a year in New York City, attracts vendors from all over the world exhibiting scores of display props that range from simple to ornate. Many props are also tailored specifically by these resources for individual retailers. NADI is the subject of the following *Focus*.

TABLE 18.1
SELECTED VENDORS OF VISUAL MERCHANDISING PRODUCTS

Vendor	Specialization	Web Site
The Eagle Line	Banners, flags, and pennants	www.eagleregalia.com
AdMart Custom Signage	Signs and graphics	www.admart.com
Bernstein Display	Display props	www.bernsteindisplay.com
Carol Barnhart	Display forms, mannequins	www.carolbarnhart.com
Clearr Corporation	Illuminated signage	www.clearrcorp.com
Display Boys	Custom displays	www.displayboys.com
Ferrari Color	Large format graphics	www.ferraricolor.com
Flynn Signs & Graphics, Inc.	Sign systems	www.flynnsigns.com
Greneker	Mannequins and forms	www.greneker.com
JustPedestals, Inc.	Display pedestals	www.justpedestals.com
LightBoxCity.com	Light boxes	www.lightboxcity.com
Meisel Visual Imaging	Graphic specialists	www.meisel.com
Opto International, Inc.	Display systems	www.optosystem.com
Patina-V	Mannequins	www.patinav.com
Rootstein	Mannequins	www.rootstein.com
Sachs Lawlor	Sign manufacturing	www.sachs-lawlor.com
Scenery West	Themed environments	www.scenerywest.com
Spaeth Design Inc.	Animated presentations	www.spaethdesign.com
Swirling Silks, Inc.	Custom soft signage	www.swirlingsilks.com
Visual Fabrics Inc.	Display fabrics	www.visualfabrics.com

Source: *VM + SD*, January 2002. Courtesy of VM+SD Magazine/ST Media Group International, Cincinnati, OH.

> ### Focus on...
> ### NADI

THE NATIONAL ASSOCIATION OF DISPLAY INTERIORS (NADI) is one of the largest visual merchandising trade shows in the world. Retailers of all sizes visit the show to learn about the latest in the industry's offerings and translate them into ideas for their own visual presentations. Companies that provide mannequins, display props, lighting, store fixtures, materials, and other products that make up interior and window presentations interact with visual merchandisers, store planners, display installers, and lighting professionals at NADI's premises.

Unlike many trade shows, this one includes many major New York showrooms. Both domestic and global brands are featured in individual settings, where display professionals come to see the latest offerings. Major companies such as Adel Rootstein Mannequins, Bernstein Display, DK Display, Goldsmith, Lifestyle, Patina-V, and Visual Merchandising International are some of the regular participants.

In addition to the "stock" offerings of these companies, each offers tailor-made products ranging from individual props to complete presentations. A visual merchandiser may learn about trends in the industry and thus become better prepared for the best possible display ideas season after season.

• •

The more creative of the visual merchandisers use their artistic talents to either create props themselves, refresh shopworn pieces that were initially used for other purposes, or use everyday items. In the shopworn category, old picture frames, chairs, rusted watering cans, and the like—when enhanced with a fresh coat of paint—make excellent props with which merchandise can be presented. Everyday items such as ladders, flowerpots, musical instruments, and others make excellent choices when used in windows and interior displays. When any of these items are used in abundance, the impact they make is particularly appealing.

> ### In the News...

"Integrating Art into the Storefront," an article reprinted on page 432 at the end of this chapter, should be read at this time.

• •

> ### Focus on...
> ### Spaeth Design

WHENEVER A MAJOR DEPARTMENT STORE OR REGIONAL MALL wishes to create dramatic excitement that utilizes an animated theme, it more than likely heads for the studios of Spaeth Design. In business since the 1940s, the company continues to captivate the public with its extravagant, artistic **animated installations** that are seen in many parts of the world. The company brings the ideas and dreams of visual merchandisers to life with these dramatic installations. A staff of creative and innovative designers, sculptors, model makers, welders, and craftspeople executes projects of any proportions.

Spaeth's client list includes overseas companies such as HarborCircus Mall in Kobe, Japan; Maykal Instaat Ve Ticaret A.S. in Istanbul, Turkey; Selfridges & Co in London, England; and Engelhorn & Sturm in Manheim, Germany. Domestically, it is best known for the magnificent windows during the Christmas season at Lord & Taylor, Saks Fifth Avenue, Marshall Field's, Macy's, and Nordstrom.

The designs the company has created have gained awards for many of its clients, including *The Nutcracker* windows at Saks Fifth Avenue and *A Christmas Carol* at Lord & Taylor.

So involved are the development of the Christmas productions that the actual design and execution begin in July so that the installations can take place immediately after Thanksgiving. This early start means that each retailer will be assured of an individual design.

The success of these animated productions can best be appreciated by the attention they receive from the public. During the Christmas season, 90 percent of the company's designs are featured. The retailers install ropes to control the enormous crowds that wish to see them. Oftentimes, the crowds wait more than half an hour to view the displays.

After they've seen the displays, a majority of the onlookers head for the store's entrances, making the expense of the display worthwhile for the retailer.

Mannequins

In the fashion arena, nothing presents a complete ensemble as dramatically and realistically as a mannequin. The mannequin choices are numerous and range from those that faithfully represent the human form to more **stylistic mannequins** that embody the latest in artistic expression. The price of mannequins ranges from a few hundred dollars to more than a thousand dollars for state-of-the-art offerings.

Dramatic mannequins show how apparel looks on the human form.

In choosing mannequins that are appropriate for their stores, the visual team must first determine if the budget mandates standard mannequins that fit every display situation or if it allows for a variety of different types. The major mannequin companies such as Roostein, Patina-V, Silvestri, and Greneker have showrooms in many countries.

In situations where budgets are limited and little is available for mannequin replenishment, alternative solutions may be needed to solve the problem. One approach is to create one's own mannequins. With the use of a few basic elements such as a coat hanger, wire, and some pieces of lumber, even a novice can produce a form that will satisfy a display's needs.

In the News . . .

The article "Redesigning Mannequins for an Upscale Image" appears on page 433 at the end of this chapter and should be read now.

Signage and Graphics

A look into most brick-and-mortar windows or a walk through most of their premises immediately reveals a host of different signs and photographic enlargements that are quite striking.

Signs are used for a number of reasons that include the identification of the particular departments in the stores and announcements of special events. They are featured in many different formats including poster boards, banners, backlit transparencies, and pennants. They are either temporary, to be used for short time periods in display windows or for special events, or permanent, used for last-

A combination of graphics and signage attracts attention and provides product information.

Backlit transparencies are being used in malls to present timely, informative messages.

ing identification purposes in departments. The major retailers generally have in-house staffs that produce the signage. Others rely upon external companies that produce everything from simple paper products to the more extravagant types.

One of the mainstays of many retail operations is **hanging and framing systems**. These are installations that enable the merchant to quickly and easily make changes that will benefit his or her operation. They are particularly useful to retailers whose customers have a minimal amount of time to spend in their stores. Since the average customer spends only 9 minutes in a store, it is essential that he or she know exactly where to go to make the purchase. Another fact that underscores the need for directional signage is that 80 percent of the shoppers entering a store know exactly what they would like to buy but only 50 percent know where to find it. The hanging and framing systems are perfect to use for getting the customer to the point of purchase quickly.

Uptons, a Georgia-based retailer, installed such a system and found that it not only brought positive results to the company but also reduced signage costs.

Today, more and more retailers are using photography as a means to dramatize their display windows and interiors. Retailers like Abercrombie & Fitch and Gap regularly use these graphics in both their windows and internal environments. They are modest in cost, can be quickly and inexpensively installed, and may be changed with little effort. Often they are made available by the vendors without cost to the retailer.

The most recent innovation in this aspect of visual merchandising is digital graphics, which can be tailored to fit the budgets of both large and small retailers. On the grander scale are the graphics used in the Polo Sport flagship on Madison Avenue in New York City. The project was co-produced by Polo Sport Services and Duggal Color Projects. They teamed up to design and fabricate eight high-resolution photographic prints that went on to stop pedestrians in their tracks. The images were output using Cymbolic Sciences' Lightjet printer, which produced prints that were actually sharper than traditional photography.

For companies that are smaller, less expensive approaches can prove equally effective. Chiasso, a small regional giftware chain in Chicago, used a Mother's Day promotion that involved 20 fabric banners, each measuring about 30 by 60 inches, that were produced using Adobe Illustrator and the Raster Graphics 5442 electrostatic printer. The end result was a show-stopping display that cost relatively little.

Of course, stock photos provide images that may be quickly obtained at modest prices. Retailers like Gap and Eddie Bauer, for example, use them in many of their visual presentations. Among the more widely used resources are Adstock Photos, The Image Bank, and FPG International. Samples are available through catalogues, by logging on to Web sites, or from CDs that many of the companies provide.

Focus on . . .
Clearr Corporation

ONE OF THE MORE EXCITING CONCEPTS in signage involves images that are illuminated in some manner. Ever since Clearr Corporation entered the signage business in 1959, its products have captured the attention of a variety of retailers as well as the consuming public. Today, the company is the leading manufacturer of backlit and edgelit graphics.

Featured in department stores, specialty chains, shopping malls, outdoor environments, restaurants, banks, and other retail forums, their quality is unparalleled. Central to its production is the backlit format. With the aid of a lightbox, photographic transparencies immediately come to life. The vibrancy that is achieved through this medium has not been duplicated by any other form of signage. What makes this type of presentation even more exciting to the retailers is the cost factor and simplicity of production. Any slide, transparency, or color negative can be converted to a large transparency that fits the requirements of the lightbox. The film is placed in a fixture that houses fluorescent bulbs to uniformly light the image from behind.

Drawing on the success of the stationary fixture, Clearr Corporation has taken the process one step further with motion capability. Macy's, in the children's department of its New York City flagship at Herald Square, uses Clearr's three-message scrolling backlit displays, MOVING PIX, as a focal point. With vibrant backlighting and mesmerizing motion, they continue to captivate the viewer's attention. Through specially designed computer controls, all of the images change in unison.

Aside from the backlit entries that gained the company prominence in the signage industry, it also produces simulated neon signs, edgelit displays, and outdoor illuminated signs.

Since many of its users report sales increases of 20 percent or more, it is obvious that an investment in their products would be well founded.

• •

Lighting

As discussed in Chapter 13 lighting is an essential part of facilities design as well as visual presentations. The dramatic effects that lighting offers quickly transform an otherwise routine visual presentation into one that is enhanced.

One trend in display lighting is hiding the fixtures that house the bulbs. Fixtures were formerly almost always exposed to the viewer, as in the case of **fluorescent fixtures**, **track lighting** systems, and **spotlight cans**. The fixtures themselves were considered to be important design elements as well as sources of necessary light for the displays.

Track lighting can be easily directed to highlight merchandise.

TABLE 18.2
LIGHT SOURCES

Classification	Uses	Advantages
Fluorescent	General overall lighting, wall washing, display illumination	Low cost; long lamp life
Incandescent	Spotlighting, overall illumination (floodlighting)	Enhances true color and textures; reduces heat (low volt variety)
High-Intensity Discharge (HIDs)	Unusual lighting	Small in size but produces more light per watt than either fluorescents or incandescents
Neon	Outdoor signage, indoor sculptured effects	Relatively maintenance-free; vivid colors easily sculpted into shapes
Halogen	Extremely bright illumination	One-fourth the size of an incandescent, ideal for enhancing merchandise

The hidden light sources offer a blend of ambient and accent lighting, both of which are essential to perfectly light any display area and the merchandise within it. Generally, visual merchandisers use strong focal lighting on the products they wish to sell. Also, a little ambient light is used on the walls so that the goods will be separated from the backgrounds. One formula involves using halogen lights to provide the dramatic intensity needed to enhance the merchandise together with hidden fluorescent reflectors to wash the walls. In any situation, experts are essential to make certain that the right lighting choices have been made to maximize the display's effectiveness.

The antithesis of the hidden light concept is the use of customized light fixtures that identify a retailer's image. Such retailers as Old Navy effectively use such fixtures in both their exterior and interior environments. With the Old Navy tagline, "Old Navy Covers the World," the creator of the light fixtures designed globe wall sconces of stainless steel with laser-cut continents and glowing white acrylic oceans. This unique fixturing not only gave the store its own image but dramatically illuminated the selling areas as well.

Light Sources

No matter which approach to lighting is used, it is essential that the appropriate light sources be selected. There are several to choose from including fluorescents, **incandescents, high-intensity discharge lamps** (HIDs), **halogen**, and **neon**. Each has its own specific advantages that must be considered by lighting specialists and visual merchandisers before they can be used.

Fixtures and Systems

There are numerous fixtures and systems from which to choose. Typically used are recessed systems, in which containers that hold either fluorescents or incandescents are set into the ceiling track lighting, a system that allows for the adjustment of lighting fixtures to the exact position needed for proper illumination; and decorative lighting, such as chandeliers, used to add a visual impact to the overall store design. The use of more than one of these types of fixtures and systems provides an aesthetic as well as a practical means of lighting.

It is the type of retail operation that dictates which lighting is best for illumination purposes. Recessed fluorescent fixtures, for example, are extensively used in supermarkets where overall lighting is essential. At the other extreme is the upscale fashion emporium, where chandeliers are often used not only to provide sufficient, dramatic lighting but also to enhance the store's elegant environment.

In the broad spectrum of retail operations, track installations are mainstays. Their adjustable nature serves the retailer's various needs, and the multitude of available types makes them easy to blend with the style chosen by interior designers in the company's fixturing.

Color

Without incurring any extra expense, color is the one element that can dramatically affect a visual presentation. Visual merchandisers are keenly aware of the excitement that color can generate and how it can transform an otherwise routine merchandise display.

Color has a great effect on our emotions. This makes the skillful use of it a plus in any visual display. It not only generates interest but may also motivate us to buy. Different colors can create different moods, thus stimulating certain responses. For example, blue—the favorite color of most people—suggests coolness and serenity whereas red often generates excitement. Although color selection is not an exact science, the professional visual merchandiser generally knows which ones will provide that extra incentive to stimulate a positive reaction from the observer.

Used in its purest form, color may not always provide the exact tone necessary to maximize display effectiveness. Different **values** (the lightness or darkness of the color) and **intensities** (the brightness or dullness of the color) must be determined when creating the exact tones to enhance the merchandise that is paramount to the success of a display.

One way for a novice to select the best color combinations or harmonies for a visual presentation is by understanding the **color wheel**. This device helps us understand the relationships of colors so they can be applied in the most effective manner. Using the wheel, color schemes or harmonies can be quickly selected with less chance of error. For example, arrangements that are monochromatic, analogous, or complementary can be determined and applied appropriately to whatever merchandise is being displayed.

The color wheel has six main **hues** from which the visual merchandiser may choose for arrangements: the **primary colors** (red, yellow, and blue), and the **secondary colors** (orange, violet, and green). Mixing two adjacent primaries results in the secondaries, while mixing a primary and secondary results in a tertiary color. By also adding neutrals to the scheme, still other effects can be achieved.

The six major arrangements are as follows:

Monochromatic Color Scheme. The use of only one hue in the scheme.
Analogous Colors. Colors that are adjacent to each other on the wheel.
Complementary Colors. Two colors that are opposite each other on the wheel.
Split Complementary Color Scheme. One color and the two colors that are on either side of its complement.
Double Complementary Color Scheme. Two sets of colors that are opposites on the wheel.
Triadic Color Scheme. Arrangement of three colors that are equidistant from each other on the wheel. (The primary colors form a triad, as do the secondary and tertiary colors.)

Table 18.3 gives some examples of these harmonies and their effects.

Of course, the use of color has no limitations. Professionals often come up with harmonies and schemes that defy the color wheel's scientific approach but nonetheless result in dramatic,

TABLE 18.3
COMMON COLOR ARRANGEMENTS

Color Harmonies	Examples	Effects
Monochromatic	All one color, such as red	Visual elegance
Analogous	Red, red-orange, and orange	Visual excitement
Complementary	Yellow and violet	Color intensity is heightened
Split complementary	Yellow, blue-violet, and red-violet	Creative visual impact
Double complementary	Yellow-orange, yellow-green, red-violet, and blue-violet	Magnetic effects
Triad	Yellow, red, and blue	Intensive color effects

eye-catching arrangements. They may be taken from fabrics of which the merchandise is made, wallpapers that are used as backgrounds, or display fixtures. By concentrating on these colors, the display will achieve a harmony between the background and the featured merchandise.

Additional interest may be achieved through color by using tints or shades of the hues, different intensities, and the "neutrals" such as black, white, gray, or tan.

DESIGN PRINCIPLES

In order for a visual presentation to achieve the results that it wishes to convey to the consumer, it must be developed with the many design principles that constitute a good display firmly in mind. Balance, emphasis, proportion, rhythm, and harmony are the design principles that must be followed by visual installers to ensure the best results.

Balance

The assignment of exact weights on two sides is not exactly what visual merchandisers are trying to achieve in their presentations. Their goal is rather to give the illusion of equal distribution.

To achieve this balance, an imaginary line is drawn down the center of the area that is about to be visually presented. It might be an exterior store window, a shadow box, a vitrine, an interior platform, or any other setting that holds a display. If satisfactorily accomplished, the merchandise and/or props on one side of the imaginary line should equal those on the other side. This illusion or visual effect may be achieved in one of two manners: the balance may be either symmetrical or asymmetrical.

Symmetrical Balance

Also known as formal balance, **symmetrical balance** is the easier of the two to accomplish. It involves the placement of identical items on either side of the imaginary line that has been envisioned. If a mannequin is used on one side, then another is used to balance it on the other. While this is relatively simple to achieve, it sometimes leads to unimaginative presentations. Except for novices who are uncertain in terms of more creative installations, this type of balance is not typically used in store displays.

Asymmetrical balance

Although the equal distribution factor is also essential to **asymmetrical balance**, the proper use of this type of balance leads to more creative and exciting environments. Often referred to as informal balance, it allows the professional to produce less structured display arrangements. While still requiring an equality of merchandise or prop distribution, the pieces need not be placed in a mirror-like setting. The sum of the different elements on one side of the imaginary line must equal the sum of those on the other. If a mannequin is used on one side, for example, it might be balanced by a prop such as an artificial tree on the other. The ingenuity of the installer is most evident in asymmetrically balanced displays.

Emphasis

When we approach a store window or an interior display of merchandise, the viewer's eye should be immediately drawn to a particular item: the one that is supposed to be dominant. The emphasis or focal point should be on the merchandise and not on the backgrounds against which it is being presented. If the props are what capture the shopper's attention and his or her eyes remain focused there, then the display is considered to be a failure. The purpose of any visual presentation is to sell the merchandise, not the materials that are used as enhancements!

Asymmetrical balance, as seen here, allows for creativity and informality while maintaining the stability of the presentation.

In order to create design emphasis, a number of approaches are used. One might be to accent or highlight the item that is central to the theme with the use of a halogen spotlight that separates the targeted item from the rest. Another would be to place emphasis on a piece of merchandise by selecting it in a color that differs from everything else in the display. If a red sweater, for example, is surrounded by white merchandise, the red item will become the focal point.

Stores like Pottery Barn use color as their means of creating emphasis. An abundance of one color is often used to attract attention.

Proportion

It is essential that the size of the objects featured in a display be in **proportion** to the size of the venue in which it they are being featured. A case in point is mannequins that are too tall for small showcase windows. They immediately give the viewer the impression that the installation was not carefully planned. Similarly, very small items should never be placed by themselves in large showcase windows; their presence is quickly lost in such settings.

Rhythm

When all of the elements of the display help to move the eye smoothly from one to the other, **rhythm** has been achieved. It is up to the installer of the presentation to make certain that this visual movement will result. There are several methods by which rhythm can be achieved, including repetition, continuous line, progression, radiation and alternation.

Repetition. This is achieved through the use of multiples of the same shape.

Rhythm may be achieved by using multiples of the same item.

The arrangement of ties on the round table forms a rhythmic radial design.

Continuous line. Linear devices such as a garden hose coiled through the merchandise provide a continuous line that moves the eye from one element to another.

Progression. When there is a gradation of shape, size, or color, progression is being utilized. For example, when one color such as red is featured in tints such as pink that gradually progresses to deeper tones, the eye automatically moves from one to the other.

Radiation. Round props, which are often used to display small items, encourage the observer's eye to move outward from the central point of the installation.

Alternation. When shapes or colors are used alternately, rhythm can be achieved. By using a background of black and white, for example, a design rhythm is the result.

Harmony

When the visual merchandiser has successfully incorporated all of the display elements to form a cohesive picture, the principle of harmony has been accomplished. It generally requires the use of a central color scheme, props that enhance the merchandise, lighting that attractively and dramatically illuminates the presentation, signage that provides additional information, and anything else that yields an effect that is eye-catching.

THEMES

Most department stores rely on changing themes like Valentine's Day in their visual programs.

Today's retailers subscribe to three approaches to setting a picture for the merchandise they offer. The traditional, standard approach involves changing themes to depict different seasons, holidays or special events. Typically, department stores rely upon this concept to make the transition from one period of time to the next. This revitalizes a store and signals the shopper that the next season's merchandise has arrived.

Many merchants refrain from this ever changing visual concept and opt for one that identifies the store with a single theme throughout the year. This is known as the thematic approach. In such endeavors, retailers must make certain that the concept is a lasting one because it will be the centerpiece of their operations for a long time. The initiator of this idea was Banana Republic. When they began their business, the founders' merchandising approach centered around safari-type clothing with khakis as the main emphasis and a permanent set of props and fixtures that would enhance these products.

Finally, there is a trend for many merchants to forgo most visual merchandising and design interiors tied to their product assortments. Even the use of temporary props has been abandoned, with the merchandise itself the only means of attracting attention. This approach is hardly a visual merchandiser's dream, but it does work for stores like the aforementioned Banana Republic, whose premises are minimally designed and perfectly suited for the sophisticated merchandise it offers.

TABLE 18.4
VISUAL MERCHANDISING APPROACHES FOR SELECTED STORES

Company	Approach	Example
Macy's (New York City flagship)	Traditional	Transformation of main floor with $1,000,000 in flowers to introduce spring
Disney Stores	Thematic	Entire store embellished with Disney characters and props
Banana Republic	Minimalist	No obvious display props, lighting is major visual enhancement
OshKosh B'Gosh	Thematic	Railroad depot utilizes a wealth of props to echo the product line
Ralph Lauren (Madison Avenue flagship)	Thematic	Mansion setting with a multitude of antiques to enhance merchandise
Ann Taylor	Minimalist	Basic fixturing without help from seasonal props

Table 18.4 describes selected retailers and the visual merchandising approaches they have chosen for their stores.

STEPS TO ASSURE VISUAL MERCHANDISING SUCCESS

The dollar investment in visual merchandising is often enormous in some retail organizations. If we examine the efforts of some of the country's major department stores, we realize that such expenses run in the millions. Of course, the costs are well worth the expenditure if the expected results are achieved. In order to maximize the effectiveness of window displays and interior installations, a procedure must first be established and then strictly adhered to by the staff.

Areas of concern that must be continuously addressed include refurbishment of the components that are imperative to sound visual merchandising, removal of displays that have outlived their timeliness, cleanliness of the environment in which a new installation is ready to be presented, daily refreshing of in-store displays, attention to merchandise offerings that are on self-serve counters, and the regular moving of merchandise to other areas in the department so that each product may be sufficiently exposed to the shoppers who are merely passing by.

Component Refurbishment

Consider the carefully executed window display that fails to impress those who pass by because the spotlights used to accent the merchandise have burned out, or the poorly coifed mannequin's wig that detracts from the clothing intended for display. These are but a few of the distractions that can make an otherwise effective display one that is below par. If it is an exterior window or a vitrine within the store, it is essential that the glass be perfectly clean. Light bulbs must be new enough to assure that they will last the time allotted for the installation, and mannequins must be free of chips or scratches so as not to present a shabby image. Every component should be carefully scrutinized before it is used.

Timeliness of the Display

When Christmas has passed or Valentine's Day has seen its final hours, the corresponding seasonal displays must immediately be withdrawn from their venues. Not only is the use of such space wasteful, it prevents showing merchandise that is timelier to the company's merchandising efforts. Immediately after Mother's Day, for example, the summer season is in full swing and swimwear might be the product that should take center stage. Since there is no longer any interest in Mother's Day items, no further sales will result from such visual merchandising.

Cleanliness of the Environment

If you have ever looked into a store window you might have noticed some pins or price tags strewn on the floor. Carpet floor might hold loose threads, and wooden floors might be scratched. These might be considered minor details, but they do detract from the overall presentation. Such simple problems are easy to correct and should be every time an installation is mounted. Image is a factor that is critical to the success of any retailer. Any disregard of cleanliness will give the impression of slipshod retailing.

Displays, particularly in high-traffic areas such as store entrances, should be regularly checked for tampering.

Refreshing the In-Store Displays

With customers regularly pacing through the store, there is a tendency for many to tamper with the merchandise that has been carefully placed in a visual presentation. If a mannequin is used on the selling floor, oftentimes the passerby feels the fabric or closely inspects the different apparel pieces in the display. At the end of the day, the installation is no longer as fresh as it was at the start, and it becomes less attractive as the days pass. To make certain that a fresh quality is still part of the presentation, daily walkthroughs should be taken by a member of the visual merchandising team to make the necessary adjustments.

Care must also be exercised in supermarkets, where self-service displays need continuous merchandise replenishment. The purchasing and handling of products like produce must regularly be cared for so that the displays are always fresh. In this way, the shopper will be treated to a feast for the eyes and might be motivated to buy something that wasn't initially planned for. If this is not a routine practice, the end result will be lower sales and the impression of a poorly managed retail operation.

Continuous Maintenance of Self-Service Fixtures

Many brick-and-mortar operations have severely reduced the size of their sales staffs. Instead, they are turning to open counters from which the consumers may make their selections. While this does help control expenses, the end result is often a counter that is left in total disarray.

Two stores that utilize the self-selection concept are Gap and Banana Republic. Each uses a visual merchandising approach that revolves around islands where merchandise is abundantly displayed according to color. The items are carefully folded to add greater appeal and motivate shoppers to examine them. Of course, with this understood touch-me concept, the merchandise often ends up as a jumbled mess, with items no longer in their assigned places.

To ensure that this unappealing situation is quickly corrected, it is essential that folders always be on the selling floor. It is really a simple matter to solve the problem. All it takes is a determination by management to address the issue and instill in those on the selling floor the need for a perfect look.

Merchandise Rearrangement

Every department in a store has prime selling locations as well as locations with less visibility. Merchandise that is featured in prime locations often catches the attention of those who are passing through on their way to another area. In this case, unexpected sales are often produced. In order to assure that each inventory item receives the benefit of a prime selling location, it is essential that the different products be rotated. Of course, if one style is a hot number then it should hold center stage until its salability wanes. Once this occurs, the item should be quickly replaced by others with greater sales potential.

Gap is a firm subscriber to this philosophy, placing the newest items at the front of the store. They are replaced when that inventory is about to sell out, moving these items farther back on the selling floor to make room for the new arrivals. This rotation always gives the shopper something new to look at and purchase.

VISUAL MERCHANDISING: THE LINK TO ADVERTISING

As those in retailing know, advertising is supposed to alert consumers to a retailer's merchandise offerings. When the various media are used to advertise products, sales should come to the brick-and-mortar operation either by mail and telephone orders or from in-store visits. For the most part, merchants with stores would rather motivate the shopper to make personal visits because such sales are often greater than those that result from off-site outlets. With assortments usually wider than any catalogue or Web site can offer, the chances for bigger sales are greater.

Thus, advertising is designed to motivate the consumer to come to the store and satisfy his or her shopping needs. Once this trip is made, it is up to the visual merchandising team to continue the effort.

Major department stores, which are the traditional proponents of advertising, use large parallel-to-sidewalk windows—especially in their flagships. These are the showcases that house the merchant's most important attractions. Oftentimes the visual merchandisers take their cues from the buyers who have expended advertising dollars in the promotion of specific merchandise or special events. Buyers might want to promote the introduction of a new designer, the heralding of the new back-to-school collections, or the welcoming of spring. Once the ads have run, they are often tied into these show windows. The ads announce the event, and the display presents the merchandise to the consumer who has been motivated to come to the store to see the advertised merchandise. Coupling the ad and the visual presentation gives the promotion the much needed one–two punch. The visual effort doesn't stop when the shopper enters the store. Once in the department that sells the items, creative interior displays further entice the customer. If all goes as expected, the team effort results in a purchase and a satisfied customer.

Thus, promotional dollars are best spent when the various components of the retailer's promotion division act in unison. Many companies produce calendars that list the various events the store is developing, the different media and visual components that will be used, and the dates of the presentations. In this way, the visual team has sufficient time to design installations that will not only make for eye-catching displays but will also enhance the concepts laid out in the ads.

If the buyers have carefully chosen the merchandise, then these collaborative efforts will maximize sales.

CHAPTER HIGHLIGHTS

- In large retail organizations, the visual concept is developed and carried out by a team of in-house visual merchandisers.
- Many chain organizations subscribe to the concept of centralized visual merchandising. Displays are developed and photographed at the home office and then sent to individual units for the installations to be carried out by the store's manager.
- Small retailers who are unable to employ their own visual merchandisers either use freelancers to carry out the display installations or develop their own plans.
- The most important component of any visual presentation is the merchandise. All the other elements used are enhancements.
- Lighting is crucial for any visual display. It highlights the merchandise by setting the appropriate mood for the viewers.
- Graphics are becoming more and more important to today's visual environment. One of the leading types is called the backlit transparency, which is illuminated from within to provide an exciting image.
- Color is one element that is free to the user. If properly utilized it can create eye-catching displays that motivate purchasing.
- There are several design principles used by visual merchandisers. When all of them are correctly applied, the end result will be a display that is totally harmonious.
- If a display is to achieve its maximum potential, it must be carefully scrutinized to make certain that it is free of imperfections.

IMPORTANT RETAILING TERMS

analogous colors (423)
animated installation (418)
asymmetrical balance (424)
color wheel (423)
complementary colors (423)
double complementary color scheme (423)
fluorescent fixture (421)
halogen (422)
hanging and framing system (420)
high-intensity discharge lamp (HID) (422)
hue (423)
incandescent (422)
in-house display staff (414)
intensity (423)
monochromatic color scheme (423)
neon (422)
primary color (423)
proportion (425)
rhythm (425)
secondary color (423)
split complementary color scheme (423)
spotlight can (421)
stylistic mannequin (419)
symmetrical balance (424)
track lighting (421)
triadic color scheme (423)
value (423)
vitrine (415)
walkthrough (415)

FOR REVIEW

1. Who is generally responsible for the visual merchandising concept in a department store?
2. How does the centralized visual merchandising concept work?
3. Since most small retailers cannot afford their own in-house visual design staff, how do they utilize the services of display professionals?
4. Which component of a display is the most important and why?
5. In addition to store-bought props, what others can a visual merchandiser use to create effective presentations?
6. How do stylistic mannequins differ from the traditional types?
7. What is a backlit transparency, and how does it differ from the traditional signage found in retail operations?
8. What are hanging and framing systems?
9. Define the term *hidden light sources*.
10. In what way do fluorescents and incandescents differ?
11. Why do most visual merchandisers turn to halogen lighting for their installations?
12. What purpose does the color wheel serve in visual presentations?
13. How do monochromatic and analogous color schemes differ?
14. How can a monochromatic color scheme be expanded to make window and interior displays more interesting?
15. What is the difference between symmetrical and asymmetrical balance?
16. Distinguish between continuous line rhythm and rhythmic radiation.
17. What is meant by a thematic approach in visual merchandising?
18. Why must display components be continually refurbished?
19. What is visual merchandising's link to advertising?

AN INTERNET ACTIVITY

One of the challenges of visual merchandising is to select the appropriate components to enhance the merchandise being featured. With so many sources available, it is often difficult and time-consuming to select the best vendors to satisfy a retailer's display needs.

The advent of the Internet has made this task an easier one. Retailers need not make multiple vendor visits to find products for their display installations.

Using the Web sites listed in Table 18.1, choose one display component (such as lighting or mannequins) and ascertain the extent of vendors' assortments. Prepare a chart with the following heads, using the information you have obtained on the Internet. If you find any other Web sites, they may be used in place of the ones listed in Table 18.1.

Vendor	Web Site	Product Line

EXERCISES AND PROJECTS

1. The most important silent seller that a retailer uses to entice consumers to enter its premises is the exterior display window. Ranging from large parallel-to-sidewalk types to those that are more like shadow boxes, the merchant can put his or her best foot forward. Plan to visit three of the most important brick-and-mortar operations in your area to evaluate the effectiveness of their exterior window displays. The following should be used in a report that will be delivered orally to the class:
   - Photographs of the displays
   - Concept used to attract attention
   - Types of signage and graphics, if any, that were used
   - Effectiveness of the lighting
   - Attention paid to the various design elements
   - Cleanliness of the venue in which the display was featured

   Upon completing each visit and addressing each of these points, mount the photos on three individual foam-boards. In addition, your evaluation of each of the displays should be presented.

2. Today's supermarkets are using a good deal of visual merchandising to present their products. In fact, many are using new fixturing, lighting, and other enhancements to better display their goods. Visit three supermarkets to determine the level of visual merchandising being used in the stores. List your findings on a chart with the following heads:

Company Name	Fixturing	Lighting	Unique Display Features

Compare all three stores to determine which one is best suited to attract customers and sell more merchandise. Be sure to list the reasons for your selection.

THE CASE OF CREATING A VISUAL ENVIRONMENT TO REFLECT A NEW COMPANY DIRECTION

When Home Décor opened its first store, it decided that the best approach in terms of visual merchandising would be to build a facility that was strikingly simple. Not knowing exactly what would dictate its future merchandising needs, store management believed the minimalist approach would be best.

The stocking of basic accessories for the home—such as traditional glassware, dinnerware, tableware, and the like—seemed to perfectly fit into this type of environment. As time passed, the company began to open other units and today has a total of 28 stores in the chain. Remaining faithful to its original merchandising philosophy, the company continues to carry a wide assortment of sterling silver and silver-plated tableware, crystal glassware, and china.

During the past few years, the buyers and merchandisers began to see that fashion had come to home furnishings. The same designers who created apparel were now crossing over into this aspect of retailing. The product mixes invariably took on a fashion-forward look, with a great deal of the items having a contemporary feel. Instead of the basic neutral colors that were the mainstays of the home products' industry, new collections were replete with bold colors and imaginative designs. In addition to management's awareness of this new trend, customers also became more cognizant of it and began asking for such items. Little by little, the new items were added and eventually filled more space than the traditional wares.

One of the glaring deficiencies at Home Décor concerned its visual presentations, which were lackluster and no longer appropriate for this new look. The problem confronting the company was how to transform the present store appearance into one that visually enhanced the new merchandising direction without incurring considerable expense.

Questions

1. Which physical components might be used to transform the premises of the stores and give them a more contemporary flair?
2. Without spending much and while retaining the same fixtures, how can the overall look of the store be updated to create more visual excitement?

Integrating Art into the Storefront
David Moin

June 26, 2007

NEW YORK—Bloomingdale's and Macy's are chasing contemporary art almost as vigorously as fashion exclusives.

The art is for windows and catalogues as a backdrop for merchandise, and to dress up store interiors.

"We are not looking to become a gallery," said Jack Hruska, executive vice president of creative services for Bloomingdale's. "We're looking to recognize art and artists as important contributions to the lives of our customers."

"It's about the fusion of art and fashion," said Nicole Fischelis, vice president and fashion director, Macy's East.

At Bloomingdale's 59th Street flagship, there is a different kind of glamour and sensuality in the windows—erotic photographs of model Margarita Svegzdaite, sprayed in gold paint, dripping gold beads of perspiration, posed naked or in a metallic bikini, or wrapped in solid gold vines. The photos are juxtaposed with designer gowns that seem restrained in comparison.

The exhibit, more bacchanalian than Ian Fleming, is called "Liquid Gold" and is the work of photographer Bettina Rheims of Paris. It's a prelude to a Bloomingdale's strategy that takes off this fall to promote artists, particularly emerging ones, and incorporate art into marketing. A September catalogue called "Artrageous" will spotlight trends of the season and will be followed by "Art Seen" catalogues for ready-to-wear, large sizes, New View bridge looks, men's wear and beauty. The flagship's windows will exhibit artists from Aug. 27 until the start of the holiday season, when the windows will switch to displaying large reproductions of children's art from The Children's Museum of Manhattan and The Children's Museum of Art.

Bloomingdale's will also support the New Museum of Contemporary Art, opening in November, with pop-up stores inside the 59th Street and SoHo units selling gift-oriented items from the museum shop.

To decorate Bloomingdale's stores around the country, photographers have long been hired to capture the communities. "We still do that, but we have also started to make large-scale purchases of art, which began with the opening of our San Francisco store last fall," Hruska said. "Now that our store design is more modern, there's a greater opportunity to apply art. Our stores have more amenities, open spaces to relax, lounges and seating areas where a beautiful piece of art enhances the space."

Macy's is advancing its "Art Under Glass" concept, where the Herald Square flagship's windows become a sidewalk gallery for contemporary and cutting-edge artists. "The point is you don't have to go to a museum or a gallery to experience art," said a Macy's spokeswoman.

The program, which started last fall, has its second installment July 9 through 25 and continues this fall. It's curated by Gabrielle Bryers, an art dealer, and conceptualized with Paul Olszewski, director of windows for Macy's Herald Square, and Fischelis. The July windows will showcase 11 contemporary and cutting-edge artists, including Federico Uribe's flock of outsized mosquitoes and a 20-minute video called "Paper Dolls" by Shannon Plumb, who portrays herself as model, photographer, magazine editor and fashionista, and stages a runway show with paper fashions.

Other artists are Nicholas Howey, Misaki Kawai, Cassandra Lozano, Taylor McKimens, Alex Nahon, Devin Powers, Lucas Reiner, Silas Shabelewska and Russell Young. "It's a very comprehensive collection in a variety of media, from paintings to paper sculpture to glass spheres and Super 8 loops," Kazan said.

On July 10, Macy's will hold a private cocktail reception for the artists as well as Anna Sui, who will preview several art-inspired looks from her retrospective exhibit coming to Macy's in the fall. Sui's designs—along with other better, bridge and contemporary designers and brands, such as O Oscar, Tahari, INC, Calvin Klein, Michael by Michael Kors, and DKNY—sold at Macy's are showcased with the artwork in the windows.

"Macy's has a long history of integrating fashion with art," Macy's East chairman and chief executive officer Ron Klein said in a statement. "One of our first forays into showcasing contemporary art came in 1942 when Latvian-born American painter and printmaker Mark Rothko unveiled his latest paintings at Macy's Herald Square. With the summer 2007 'Art Under Glass' exhibition, we have now come full circle, as one of the featured artists has looked to Rothko's work as an inspiration, affirming the timeless impact of art."

"Liquid Gold," a traveling exhibition sponsored by Chablis, stays at Bloomingdale's until Monday, moves to the New York Palace Hotel for the rest of July, and winds up in Grand Central Terminal, at the Metrazur restaurant, from Sept. 18 to Oct 15. Rheims is known for her powerful and controversial images capturing intimate moments of famous women. "This is something I love to do: taking photos of naked women," Rheims said. "Working on the body has always been part of my work."

Redesigning Mannequins for an Upscale Image
David Moin

MARCH 7, 2007

NEW YORK—So what if they don't speak or move? Mannequins must have a point of view.

That's become the mantra at Lifestyle, a manufacturer of mannequins as well as forms, decoratives, visual accessories and specialty fixturing, which is reinventing its product line and moving the image upscale.

"We're taking Lifestyle to a new level," said Salvatore Lenzo, creative director and vice president of sales and marketing, during an interview at the firm's 3,500-square-foot showroom at 151 West 25th Street here.

Since September, Lenzo has been reinventing Lifestyle, a small, privately held business that's been around for some 40 years, but began to lose its edge. He's renovated the showroom, designed new products, culled a lot of the old, designed a booth for the GlobalShop visual trade show this week in Las Vegas, upgraded the collateral materials and has been revamping the Web site.

"Before I got here, there was no point of view," Lenzo said. "There wasn't a creative person here to really focus the business. Now we're taking what I did in fashion and retailing and applying it to Lifestyle. It's becoming more design-driven," so the product reflects what retail customers seek and what the trends dictate.

"Retailers are using a lot more mannequins. They're trying to differentiate," Lenzo said, particularly those retailers with limited expansion opportunities or those undergoing consolidations or mergers, and attempting to generate greater sales and traffic from existing locations, he added.

At GlobalShop, Lifestyle is concentrating on its mannequins and previewing two new collections: Chelsea, which includes women's and men's styles, and the Deco collection, for women's, which will include men's, tweens' and children's in the fall. Both mannequin collections are in black lacquer. Chelsea is realistic and sculptured, while Deco is abstract.

Currently, accessories are big at retail, Lenzo noted, so at GlobalShop, Lifestyle also is displaying accessory forms as well as decorative porcelain-finished urns that are as tall as 70 inches.

The company also manufactures handbag risers, belt bolsters and hat heads. Among Lifestyle's biggest clients currently are Macy's private label program, Ann Taylor, Mimi Maternity and Lucy's.

When Lenzo joined Lifestyle last fall, "our first challenge was to renovate the showroom and pull together a December show, which we successfully did. I wanted to show something different, [something] other than headless white mannequins, being that we are in an accessory moment at retail. I thought, Why not show beautiful forms along with decoratives? I wanted people to walk in and really see a change, but I also wanted to spark ideas. Creative people always need to be stimulated. The idea was to start a conversation, but not necessarily buy what was being shown."

There's a new tag line, "The Shape We're In," which is visible in the showroom and on marketing materials. It's a play on words referring to the company's transformation. Chuck Rosenthal is president and majority owner of Lifestyle, which is projecting $18 million to $20 million in sales this year.

Prior to joining Lifestyle, Lenzo was vice president of visual merchandising at Burberry, and before that, at Saks Fifth Avenue for eight years in a similar capacity. Earlier in his career, he worked at Lord & Taylor.

"All I've ever done is visual merchandising and store design. That was my entire career," he said.

When the opportunity arose to join Lifestyle and take a career turn, Lenzo pounced. "Reinventing a company sounded like a very exciting thing for me to do. The owners have really, really given me carte blanche."

CHAPTER 19
Customer Service

After you have completed this chapter, you should be able to discuss:

- ▶ Why personal selling is imperative in a wide variety of retailing establishments
- ▶ The reasons why many stores that once subscribed to the self-selection concept are recognizing the importance of the sales associate and are now expanding their sales forces
- ▶ The rules of the selling game, which include a positive appearance, motivational skills, enthusiasm, knowledge of the product and the company, communication skills, and tactfulness
- ▶ How retailers are training their sales staffs to better serve customers
- ▶ The importance of selling in the various off-site retailing ventures, which are now more important than ever
- ▶ The different types of charge accounts and credit card services that are provided to consumers
- ▶ How retailers serve customers by way of traditional as well as customized services
- ▶ Why call centers play an important role in retailing

As we closely examine the retail playing field, we recognize the vast number of different operations that are vying for a share of the consumer's dollar. Whether it is the brick-and-mortar companies, catalogues, Internet Web sites, or cable television shopping networks, there are many opportunities for the shopper to have his or her needs quickly satisfied. How a consumer decides which of these merchants to patronize is, of course, based upon merchandise assortments, pricing, ease of making the purchase, and, in the case of brick-and-mortar operations, their design and physical layout.

Given the intense competition, another factor that often plays a significant role in motivating the customer to select one merchant over another is service. All too often, retailers have neglected to satisfactorily address the needs of the customer. They spend considerable sums maintaining management teams that direct business operations and train them to meet the challenges of producing sufficient revenues. However, those who interact daily with the company's clientele are not as carefully trained. When one enters a store, it is often difficult to find a sales associate, and when one does appear, he or she is sometimes ill prepared to answer the simplest questions. The problem of properly serving the customer is not limited to brick-and-mortar operations alone but applies to off-site retailers as well. It is hard to understand why merchants spend so much on advertising and other promotional endeavors to attract shoppers to the store only to let them get away without making a purchase.

It is a relatively simple matter to correct. Through proper orientation of new employees, meaningful training, and competitive remuneration to attract above-average personnel, the problem can be quickly resolved.

An inattentive salesperson can lose a sale even though shoppers seem interested in the products.

The other way that merchants can distinguish themselves is by providing services that go beyond the attention offered by sales associates. There is a wide disparity among retailers in terms of the services they offer to shoppers. Of course, the extent of these services will vary according to the different retailer classifications. The traditional department store, for example, is more likely to offer services that the discounter cannot. The former, with the benefit of larger markups, will have the funds necessary to make the shopping experience more pleasurable than in an off-price store, where customers are more interested in bargains than extras.

Each retailer, in order to remain competitive in its classification, must examine the plusses and minuses associated with providing services to customers and then use those services to distinguish itself from the others in its class.

The material presented in this chapter focuses not only on selling but also on the broad spectrum of services offered by retail operations.

PERSONAL SELLING

In the not-too-distant past, a customer who entered a store was routinely greeted by a sales associate who was ready and able to guide the shopper to the right merchandise, assist with the purchasing decision, and transform the shopper into a satisfied customer. It was not unusual to find a large percentage of consumers who could be considered loyal customers. In the 1970s and 1980s, the era of this type of personalized service began to give way to the concept of self-selection. Retailers began to alter their environments by installing open counters from which shoppers could help themselves. In many retail operations, gone were the traditional counters that necessitated sales assistance. This concept enabled retailers to reduce the size of their sales staff and, in turn, the expenses associated with **personal selling**.

While the cost of doing business was reduced, the relationships between customer and sales associate waned. Many customers preferred this type of shopping, but others felt they weren't properly attended to—especially if questions needed to be answered.

Now the personal selling approach is resurfacing. Merchants are finding that sales associates not only help make the sales but often are also responsible for bigger sales because of their ability to suggest additional merchandise to shoppers who seek their assistance. Even those who opted for the self-service route are turning to personal selling so that they can successfully compete in today's overcrowded marketplace. Even stores that pride themselves as off-pricers, selling the best for less, are hiring sales associates to interact with the shoppers. One such retailer is Stein Mart. While many of Stein Mart departments have a **skeleton sales crew** on hand to assist shoppers, its boutique department offers personalized service to any one who wants it.

Many chain operations, such as Ann Taylor and Banana Republic, approach selling in a less formalized manner. Shoppers are greeted as they enter the store and are asked if they need assistance. The level of the seller–buyer relationship is determined by the customer. If close attention is wanted, full assistance is available.

Focus on . . .
Nordstrom

STARTING ON THE SITE OF AN OLD SHOE REPAIR SHOP, John Nordstrom invested $5,000 to establish a shoe store in Seattle, Washington, in 1901. With $1,500 to fix up the store and $3,500 for inventory, he was on his way to introducing American consumers to one of the most prestigious retail ventures in retailing history. From his very first day in business, when he had to take a pair of shoes from the window to sell to a customer, he hit upon the principle of doing whatever it takes to take care of the customer. It is this principle by which Nordstrom still runs today. In the 1960s the company, now with other units, expanded into apparel.

The centerpiece of the operation is service, with personal selling in particular at the forefront. Its attention to customer needs remains unparalleled in retailing. While others continue to capitalize on the Nordstrom approach, few if any have reached the heights of personal selling as has Nordstrom.

Unique to the company is the concept that sales associates may sell merchandise to their customers from any department in the store. That is, they take care of the customer from start to finish. If, for example, a shopper has purchased a dress and is also in the market for a pair of shoes, a handbag, or hosiery, the dress salesperson will take her from department to department helping with the other selections. Nordstrom believes that once a sales associate has established a rapport with the customer, that associate should be able to help with all of the customer's wardrobe needs.

The company is one of the few in the United States to pay its sales employees on commission. In this way, those who are self-starters and sufficiently motivated are paid according to their ability. Commission sales, along with bonuses, enable the sales staff to work harder and establish their own customer followings. Those who meet or surpass pre-established sales volume goals achieve the status of Pacesetter. Target figures are adjusted annually, with about 8 to 12 percent of the people in each division reaching Pacesetter goals. Those who achieve this level are recognized with a special certificate, an event or outing in their honor, business cards designating their Pacesetter status, and an increased employee discount for a full year.

Those who are at the top of the selling game at Nordstrom do not wait for customers to come to the store. Most Pacesetters use the telephone to keep in touch with the clientele they have established. Asking for permission to call the clients makes their relationship even stronger. It might be to chat about some new item that seems perfect for the customer or perhaps about a special sales event. The concept works well in that customers come to rely on these calls to keep them abreast of what's happening at Nordstrom.

Once these relationships have been established, future sales come as a result of a number of different circumstances. It might be a call from someone's private plane or from an overseas venue requesting a suit that will be needed in a couple of hours. Knowing the client's measurements and tastes from previous meetings, the order can be quickly filled.

Recognizing that personal attention is the key to success for both the merchant and the sales associate, Nordstrom goes the extra mile in making the sales staff feel special. It supplies them with thank-you notes that may be sent after a sale has been completed, postcards, personalized letterheads, and address lists to help them follow up with customers.

In an industry that is often characterized by low salaries, Nordstrom is the exception. That sales associates' salaries often reach $100,000 or more indicates that special attention to serving the customer can bring monetary rewards usually reserved for management personnel.

The Rules of the Game

A salesperson who greets a shopper must first carefully prepare for the meeting. First and foremost, it must be understood that the sales associate represents the company. The initial dialogue is extremely important. If successfully mastered, it can mean the difference between a sale and a walkout. Of paramount importance for the sales associate are appearance, enthusiasm, communication skills, product knowledge, company knowledge, tactfulness, and self-control. All these attributes (except appearance) are as important to off-site venues as they are to brick-and-mortar operations.

Appropriate dress is an essential part of working on the selling floor.

Appearance

A sales associate's appearance is very important. Many retailers, in orientation sessions for new employees, stress appropriate dress and grooming for salespeople. Some retailers don't address this issue and take the risk of having someone on the selling floor who doesn't foster a proper image for the company. What is appropriate dress? Each of us has his or her own standards that may or may not fit with the image that the merchant is trying to impart to the customer.

Today, retailers require far less structured attire than they did years ago. In the past, pants for women were taboo and bright colors were frowned upon. A more cloned look was the order of the day. Nowadays, many merchants subscribe to a more relaxed manner of dress much the same as various business environments, such as investment banking and law. In fact, more and more retailers are encouraging their staffs to wear the merchandise that is featured in the store. Often a shopper will admire a salesperson's attire, and this helps make a sale. In the Ralph Lauren flagship in New York City, sales associates are given monthly dollar allowances to purchase the store's merchandise and wear it on the selling floor. The sophisticated dress of the Lauren sales associates often inspires shoppers to buy the same items. At chains like Gap and Banana Republic, the sales staff is also encouraged to wear their company's offerings. While those at Gap are casually dressed in attire appropriate for that store, in other retail venues this mode of dress might not be considered appropriate.

It should be noted, however, that Bloomingdale's maintains a strict dress code that requires people on the selling floor to wear black. The company feels that any other color is a distraction.

The rules of dress must be spelled out at the time of employment. Once they have been clearly established and understood by new employees, a positive appearance will likely follow.

Enthusiasm

Having an enthusiastic attitude should not be confused with the hard-sell approach. Shoppers should not be overwhelmed, as in the case of the stereotypical used car salesperson, but should feel that the seller has a real feeling for the merchandise. A lethargic approach will often dampen the spirit of the shopper and discourage purchasing. A warm, friendly smile along with a bright, cheerful greeting will sometimes transform a looker into an interested customer.

By considering two different reactions to the same film, we can better understand the value of enthusiasm. When two friends are asked about the same movie, each might have a different way of displaying their approval. One might say it was really good. The other might describe it as a must-see film with fabulous acting and great scenery. Of course, the latter description will more likely motivate the individual who asked the question to buy a ticket.

Enthusiasm seems to transfer from one individual to another. If properly used on the selling floor, the sales associate has a better chance to make the sale.

Communication Skills

Using the right language and proper diction are extremely important when first greeting the shopper and while trying to make the sale. This doesn't mean that the language used should be extraordinary—just sufficiently simple and clear that a seller–shopper dialogue results.

The use of slang should be avoided. Although slang may be appropriate in private conversation, there is no place for it in the business world. Learning to speak correctly is a matter of study. Through courses, videos, audiotapes, and CDs, those interested in mastering the language will be able to do so and become better salespeople.

Product Knowledge

Over the course of any selling day, some shoppers are likely to inquire about the specifics of a product. This is especially true for companies that sell electronics. Living in a technological society requires the sales associate to know all the nuances of the latest technology. Whether selling a computer, television, VCR, camcorder, DVD player, Palm Pilot, or any other device, the details of the product should be known.

Product information is necessary not only in the realm of electronics. It is also essential to know about fabrics, styles, silhouettes, and color harmonies in the world of fashion. A shopper might want to know if the item being considered for an overseas trip will require ironing or if a particular garment's shape will remain in style for more than one season.

Product information is available to the salesperson from a variety of sources. Colleges and universities offer specialized courses that concentrate on a host of products. Videos are also a popular way to learn about products. Videos are often available from vendors that wish to make the retailer's employees better informed. Information on specific merchandise classifications is available through trade associations and business groups. Those interested in learning more about gems, for example, can obtain a booklet produced by the Gemological Society. Online resources can also be used to obtain information.

When the sales associate is adequately prepared to answer any merchandise questions, a sale is more likely to be achieved.

Company Knowledge

One should never have to call upon a manager to answer questions concerning company policies. A salesperson should be well informed about return policies, credit availability, alterations, special order merchandise, and the like. Not only will this inform the shopper about the company's policies and philosophies, it will also help establish confidence in the store and its sales staff.

This information is generally available in new employee orientation sessions as well as through ongoing discussions with the management team.

Tactfulness

With knowledge of psychology, the seller is more likely to approach sensitive problems more easily. If an overweight shopper, for example, is deciding between two outfits, the salesperson should "sell" the shopper on the more flattering one. Only if there is persistence by the shopper for the wrong item should the seller acquiesce. Allowing the "wrong" purchase means the sold merchandise will likely be returned. Not only will the sale be voided, but the end result could be a dissatisfied customer.

Leading the customer in the right direction—without implying that he or she is making the wrong decision—requires tact. If carefully approached and if the right words are used, the customer will purchase appropriate merchandise and the chances of that individual becoming a regular patron are increased.

Tact is second nature to some people, but others need continual training to get it right, as discussed in the next section.

Self-Control

Even the most mild-mannered salesperson has come across a situation in which he or she is ready to verbally or even physically react to a customer's demands. Bearing in mind the **customer-is-always-right concept**, this reaction must be avoided at all costs. Losing one's temper will not only result in the loss of the sale at hand, it might affect future business for the company as well.

Those with short fuses shouldn't consider a career in sales; they will be wasting their time. Such individuals will not be up to the challenge and may quickly find themselves unemployed.

Perfecting the Persona

The proper sales training is critical. All too often, sales training is either accomplished during a brief time frame or not at all. Arguments for not giving adequate training include the cost, the probability of rapid employee turnover, and the lack of trainers to accomplish the task. Of course, ill-prepared sales associates will lose many sales and may even discourage shoppers from returning to the store.

Merchants who properly train their sales staff can accomplish the task several ways, which include role-playing, videocassettes, on-the-job training, vestibule training, and online training.

Role-Playing

No sales training technique other than **role-playing** parallels an actual sale. It is a methodology that involves two individuals: one poses as the buyer and the other as the shopper. The scenario may be played on the retailer's premises or at an off-site professional training venue. Whichever location is used, it is essential that a trained evaluator oversee the performance. At the end of the presentation, the evaluator rates the level of selling in terms of the customer approach, communication skills, and the ability to handle the customer's objections. Recording the session makes an indelible impression on the trainee. By playing the video back, the trainer and trainee are better able to discuss each aspect of the presentation and amend those that need improvement. Reviewing the video will enable the newly hired sales associate to hone his or her selling skills.

To make the session even more meaningful, the evaluator should design a form that addresses each of the essential elements of a professional sale and provide the trainee with a copy of it. This will serve as a future reference point that, like the video, may be referred to many times. In addition to the written evaluation, a careful verbal assessment should be delivered to the new seller. In this way, any constructive criticism can also be incorporated into real selling situations.

Professional Videocassettes

Today, more than ever before, a wealth of professionally prepared materials are available to retailers for use in training their sales associates. High on the list are videocassettes that instruct viewers on everything from preparing to sell to the actual stages of a sales demonstration. The advantages of these tools include low cost, the ability to use the tapes repeatedly and off-premises, and limiting the time necessary for in-person training.

On-the-Job Training

While pretraining is generally an essential aspect of sales personnel readiness, it alone doesn't always place the trainee in a real-life situation. Oftentimes, human resources managers use one of the pretraining techniques in conjunction with **on-the-job training**.

The best of these arrangements involves a mentoring system in which a retailer's seasoned sales associate closely watches the new employee make his or her way through an actual selling situation. The mentor is given the responsibility of evaluating the sales attempt, making suggestions for improvement, and providing the little extras that would improve the performance.

If this approach is used, it is imperative that the mentor not be involved in the actual sales situation but be close by to assess the performance. Interference during the sales attempt might give the shopper the impression that the salesperson was ill-prepared and also could cause a drop in the employee's morale.

Vestibule Training

It should be understood that selling is not merely a conversation between the seller and the potential customer. It generally involves a host of other responsibilities. Learning to use the company's systems, especially the computerized sales terminal, is essential to the organization's inventory and sales recording controls. If not properly handled, the problems that arise could hamper proper recording of the sale, giving either the customer or employee an unwarranted disadvantage.

The vast majority of today's retailers find that credit card purchases significantly outdistance cash sales. Even supermarkets, the last of the cash-and-carry merchants, are finding that many of their customers are opting for credit or debit card transactions. Proper training in the use of "plastic" assures that only those customers who have been approved will receive the merchandise.

Even the task of proper packing should be carefully taught. This will ensure the safe arrival of breakables and the arrival of soft goods as perfectly as when they were purchased. This procedure can be quickly and easily accomplished and need not take endless hours to perfect.

The use of any number of forms can be easily taught in this **vestibule training** venue. Today's merchants are busy satisfying the customer's needs by making available special order goods, arranging for alterations, having goods delivered to the home, or trying to locate merchandise from another store. It becomes a problem on the selling floor if a sales associate is ill-prepared to handle these tasks. An otherwise simple task can take unnecessary time and result in cancellation of the purchase.

Online Training

One of the newest sales training methods is **online training**. Many companies that recognize both the need for such training and the retailer's inability to provide it have made a variety of training approaches available. In addition to specific course packages that are available in an Internet format, some training groups also provide CD-ROMs if that is a company's preference.

One vendor in this field is MOHR Learning, a division of Provant, America's leading performance solutions company. One of its more popular products is Quick-Start, a tool that is available either as an Internet course or a CD-ROM. It involves a sports-themed selling game that challenges the user in the art of selling. It concentrates on four key areas: greeting the shopper, product knowledge and selling benefits, handling objections, and closing the sale. One of the program's advantages is that it can be tailored to other merchandise classifications such as clothing, electronics, and housewares. The programs can also be personalized for each retailer by providing MOHR with the merchant's specific policies and responsibilities. Retailers can access its Web site at www.mohrlearning.com.

The Selling Experience

Although some people have a natural instinct for selling, there are no sales shortcuts. Of course, if a shopper enters the store, selects his or own products, and brings them to the sales associate to finalize the sale, this is a simple sale to complete. On the other hand, when a shopper is moving through a department without giving an indication whether he or she is really there to buy, it is the seller's challenge to transform the shopper into a customer. By arming oneself with the proper approaches, needs assessment, and product information, a sale is more likely to result.

Basically, the selling experience involves a number of different stages. These include greeting the customer, determining what his or her needs are, presenting the merchandise that will satisfy those needs, handling any objections that might prevent the sale from being realized, and closing the sale.

A pleasant greeting can set the stage for a successful sales presentation.

Greeting the Customer

Unskilled sales people often use the approach that begins with "May I help you?" The danger of this approach is that the response might be "No." If the shopper replies negatively to the sales associate, there is nowhere else to go. Questions that might yield negative responses should be avoided at all costs.

The correct approach might begin with just a smile. This could be followed with, "Good morning. If there's anything I can help you with, please let me know. If you need any sizes, I'll be more than happy to help you with that. If we don't have the size or style you want, please let me know and I'll do my best to accommodate you." This type of greeting is basically the treatment that sales associates themselves would like to receive when they shop.

Service-oriented retailers like Nordstrom teach this type of approach during training sessions and have learned that it works best when trying to begin a sales presentation. It helps put the shopper at ease and takes the hard-sell, overbearing attitude out of the selling mix. The dialogue needs to begin on a positive note and to carry through until the sale has been consummated.

Needs Assessment

When a salesperson has been successful in approaching the customer, a specific item may be requested. In these cases, it is pointless to try to determine the customer's needs. Often, however, the shopper is not so forward; in this case, an associate needs to question the customer to determine what he or she is looking for. In the case of the individual who has accepted the seller's offer to help with the purchase of a computer, the first question might be "Is the computer for your home or office?" Once this has been established, it might be followed with "What types of tasks are you expecting to perform on the computer?"

In a fashion operation, where the customer is looking for a dress, the first question should be, "Is there any special occasion that you need the dress for?" If the response is for a party, it could be followed by "Is it a formal affair or one that is semiformal?" The next question might be, "Do you have any color preference, or would you like me to show you the popular colors for this season?" Once the customer's needs have been established, the time is ripe to present the appropriate merchandise.

Merchandise Presentation

Merely showing an item or two doesn't often motivate the customer to make a purchase. This art of the sales presentation might warrant a demonstration or at least a discussion concerning why particular items have been chosen to bring to the customer's attention.

In the case of electronics, a demonstration is generally in order. If the purchase in question is a television, a comparison of two different models would be in order. Then the prospective purchaser can assess visual clarity, sound, and other features such as picture in picture. Offered two choices, the customer is able to make a comparison that could lead to a sale.

If a customer is interested in a particular line of cosmetics, then an application could immediately reveal which products were better suited to the individual. It might be a matter of color choice or ease of use. For fragrances, applying a few different products could provide the customer with choices.

Some products, such as apparel and footwear, need to be tried on. In these situations, the sales associate should lead the customer to the fitting room and inquire whether or not assistance is necessary.

In every case, a continuing dialogue should occur. This will help the seller assess the customer's acceptance of the items and determine which of them have a chance to be purchased. Sometimes it is a matter of reinforcing the customer's own decisions or suggesting an alternative that is likely to better serve the individual's needs.

It is most important that a positive attitude be maintained at all times by the seller. Not every shopper is a pleasure to serve, and some might need more attention than others. Oftentimes, objections pertaining to the merchandise must be professionally handled to close the sale.

Handling Objections

When a customer is not ready to commit to a purchase, it is often necessary to find out the reasons why. He or she may be interested and simply need more time to decide. Whatever the circumstances, a sales associate must be able to handle the objections and try to turn them into selling points.

There are several techniques that are standard for overcoming objections in retail. One is the **agree and counterattack method**, whereby the seller agrees with the objection but then uses some selling points that refute it. This is sometimes called the **"yes, but" technique**. In a selling situation that involves the purchase of an automobile, the customer might object to the leather seats, stating that they are too cold in the winter. A seller using this technique would agree only to respond with "Heated seats are standard on this model and will provide excellent comfort during the cold months."

When a shopper professes that the price of the dress is higher than expected, the seller's response might be "Yes, it is a little more expensive, but it is so basic that it could be worn for many occasions."

Another approach to customer objections involves asking questions. This must be carefully done so as not to put the individual on the defensive. If, for example, a customer is not in agreement with the type of sofa that have been suggested, the sales associate might ask, "What period of furniture would your prefer?"

Unless you are absolutely certain that the customer's objections are ill-founded, you should not disagree. If you are positive that the objection is incorrect, then denying it is permissible. Of course, care must be exercised when using this methodology. In the case of price, for example, if the customer states that your competitor sells the identical item for less and you are certain that this is not true, the objection might handled with, "No, I believe that our prices are the same, but I am willing to check to make certain."

It should be noted that not every sale can come to a satisfactory conclusion—even if all objections are carefully handled. Not everyone can be sold, but keeping the discussion on a positive level may encourage the customer to come back another time.

Closing the Sale

When the seller believes that he or she has satisfied all of the preceding stages of the presentation, the time could be ripe to attempt concluding the sale. Of course, this does not always bring the sale to a favorable end. Choosing the right time is often a matter of trial and error. The first attempt, if unsuccessful, is considered to be a trial close. That is, others should be tried until every approach has been exhausted.

Sometimes the customer gives a clue that signals a willingness to buy. It might be, in the case of a furniture purchase, "Will I be able to buy the set on credit?" For a dress, the clincher could be, "How quickly can I have it altered?" Another clue might be "I'm looking for a wedding gift. How long would the couple have to make another selection?"

When all closing attempts have not resulted in the culmination of a sale, the seller either stops trying or, in certain cases, suggests that a manager take over. With automobile sales, it is common practice that, when the salesperson hasn't been able to close the deal, the manager is brought in. He or she might be able to offer a better price or otherwise satisfy the customer's demands.

Whatever the end result, courtesy is imperative so that future business might be forthcoming.

The Follow-Up

In many retail operations, especially those that are prestige or service oriented, it is common practice for the sales associate to write to customers thanking them for their business. Companies like Nordstrom and Neiman Marcus, for example, provide their associates with notepaper so that they can communicate with satisfied customers. It is a gesture that takes a little bit of time, but the payoff could be significant. People in the retail sales arena often build up clienteles that ask for assistance each time they enter the store. In many cases, a rapport might be established that brings future business in ways other than in-store appearances.

At Nordstrom, for example, one Pacesetter revealed that a regular customer rushed to catch a flight to Washington, D.C., for a wedding only to discover that he had packed the pants from one suit and the jacket from another. Knowing the customer's measurements and style preferences, the sales associate had a new suit, which was perfectly altered, waiting when the customer's car arrived. It is this type of seller–customer relationship that brings further sales to the retailer.

Handling Returns

Just as it is necessary to treat the customer in a positive manner when making a sale, it is equally important to properly handle merchandise returns. If the customer is treated fairly and in a pleasant manner, the chances are that he or she will return again to shop. Too often, employees are shortsighted regarding the importance of pleasantries when handling returns and thus discourage the shopper from becoming a repeat customer.

When returns are being made by mail, it is best for the store to offer **return labels** that simplify the procedure. Exchange postage should be free, with a prepaid label provided for merchandise that was ordered by phone or from the store's catalogue or Web site. At Nordstrom, for example, the return policy is very simple. Log on to www.Nordstrom.com, where the details are carefully spelled out.

OFF-SITE SELLING

Selling to the consumer via means other than in brick-and-mortar stores is nothing new to retailing. Companies like Sears established themselves as catalogue merchants, serving the needs of those who were unable to visit its stores. As the population continued to grow—and people not only lived too far from the stores but were also too busy at work to make such time-consuming trips—more and more merchants offered catalogues to their customers. Numerous catalogue-only retailers joined the fray. With the availability of catalogs at an all-time high, it has become a successful way for consumers to satisfy their needs.

At this point in time, the Internet continues to increase in importance as a means of selling. Merchants with store operations and catalogue divisions are opening Web sites in record numbers to sell to a wide consumer market. Known as multichannel retailers, their task is to sell by any means possible.

Finally, a great number of merchants have developed programs for cable television that regularly attract huge numbers of viewers who buy their products.

In each of these formats, there is a need to sell to the consumer. Much as in the case of traditional in-store retailing, questions must often be answered before any sale will be consummated. Of course, much of the business is transacted anonymously and without the need for personal interaction. In cases where direct communication is needed, it should be handled in a professional manner.

Catalogue Selling

When a potential customer wishes to place an order by telephone, oftentimes the decision to buy is not a straightforward one. Just as in the case of the in-store shopper, questions about the merchandise may need to be answered. Those who handle these orders have an advantage over their brick-and-mortar counterparts: because it is the catalogue purchaser who initiates the sale, the personal approach that characterizes face-to-face contact is unnecessary. However, the catalogue representative must be able to answer any questions that the customer might have. Since these sales reps do not generally have the merchandise on hand to discuss their benefits, they must carefully study the catalogues, the company's philosophies in terms of pricing, and any rules and regulations regarding such aspects as returns.

Like those who work in the store, these people are not merely order takers but company representatives who are often called upon to answer questions and satisfy the customer's needs. If this role is performed satisfactorily, the shopper may well patronize the retailer again and again.

Internet Selling

While much of the ordering is handled automatically on the Internet, some purchases require interaction between the customer and the company representative. Any number of questions may be on the shopper's mind before making a final decision. Many companies address this possibility by establishing an interactive mode where the buyer and the seller can communicate. One user of this concept is Lands' End. In addition to having a carefully organized Web site that addresses a host of potential inquiries, they also feature a service called "Lands' End Live." By accessing this feature, customers are able to communicate with company representatives either by telephone or through an online chat. It is at this point that the seller must be able to answer any questions that might be posed and then try to bring the sale to a successful conclusion.

As in the case of in-store and catalogue selling, the more professionalism that is utilized the more likely that repeat business will follow.

Home-Shopping Selling

Whether it is QVC, HSN, or any of the other cable networks that sell merchandise, there is a great deal of interaction between the show's personalities and those who wish to purchase. In this case, unlike the catalogue and Internet venues, the sellers are seen by the viewers. Thus, appearance is an essential factor along with the ability to answer the caller's questions. Oftentimes these chats are lengthy and require the same selling process used in the stores. This is not only a one-on-one presentation but might also involve thousands of silent viewers. The vast majority of those who shop via these home-shopping networks call in their orders without any direct communication. They are, however, often listening to the interaction between those who actually do make calls and the show's representatives who offer the answers. A motivating response to one caller might close not only that sale but numerous others as well.

Whether it is an in-store presentation or one that is made through an off-site venue, it is imperative that the company rep be knowledgeable, courteous, forthcoming, and enthusiastic.

CUSTOMER SERVICES

When a customer enters a brick-and-mortar operation, logs onto a Web site, telephones a catalogue company, or interacts with one of the many home-shopping cable channels, there is an expectation that these companies will provide services to make the shopping experience a pleasurable one.

Easy-to-locate customer service areas make shopping more convenient, thereby encouraging customer loyalty.

As we have underscored throughout the text, the new millennium challenges every merchant to do his or her best to gain a share of the consumer's disposable income. Merchandise assortments are key to the success of every retailer, but with identical or similar merchandise available in many places, it is the "extras" that motivate an individual to buy from one merchant rather than another. Thus, the key to a retailer's success is often the services provided to its customers.

Many retailers have emerged as service leaders and have reaped the rewards from this image. Nordstrom, the ultimate service provider, has set the standard in the field of upscale fashion emporiums and has made enormous numbers of people regulars because of that service. Many other merchants—even off-pricers and discounters—benefit from attending to customer service. Each company makes a determination of how best to serve their customer base and so bring them back on a regular basis.

The services offered in the retail arena are numerous. Many are free, while others carry a charge. Some of them are typically found in most retail operations, whereas others are less frequently employed.

In the News . . .

"Dynamic Web Content: Giving Customers What They Want" is an article appearing on page 455 at the end of this chapter that should be read now.

This child cart pick-up and return is a service to shoppers who are accompanied by children.

Maximizing Shopper Satisfaction

Establishing meaningful customer services is a necessity for retailers that wish to maximize profitability. It is also important to evaluate the shopper's experience both in the store and online, acting as soon as possible after the shopper's visit. By doing so, management can move in a timely manner to correct any problems and make the adjustments necessary to ensure that future visits are more satisfying.

Retailers may use their own in-house staffs to handle these matters, or they may employ the services of an outside agency. One such company is Mindshare Technologies of Salt Lake City. They report that, although some customer responses are positive, most are on the negative side and should be dealt with immediately.

Customer feedback is a must. The A & P supermarket chain makes customer response cards available in all stores; the filled-out cards are examined immediately by the managers. The company also encourages shoppers to mail the cards back to corporate headquarters.

Another method used by many retailers is the mystery shopper. These are individuals who pose as customers and use checklists of questions during their store visits.

Whatever the method, the need for evaluation is imperative for the continued success of any retail operation.

Traditional Customer Services

There are numerous services that are offered both by brick-and-mortar operations and off-site retailers. These services are made available to customers in order to make their shopping experience a well-rounded one.

Gift Registries

Stores of almost every type offer **gift registries** for couples who are about to be married or are expecting a child. The individuals either come to the store to examine the offerings or make their selections online. They complete a wish list and then wait for their friends and relatives to purchase from it. The purchasing may take place in the store or through the retailer's Web site. The benefit to the celebrant is that no unwanted gifts will have to be returned. For the purchaser, it is a quick and easy way to provide recipients with gifts of their own choosing. This service is especially valuable for those who do not reside in the same city as those who are celebrating the upcoming event. Through the use of the retailer's Web site or by way of telephone or fax, the purchase can be simply accomplished.

The merchants themselves are less troubled with gift returns because the choices have been preselected. Another benefit is that potential new customers are introduced to the company.

Merchandise Alterations

Most full-line and specialized department stores offer merchandise alterations to their customers. Sometimes the service is free and sometimes it carries a nominal cost. In either case it relieves the customer's need to find a professional tailor to perform the alterations.

More and more smaller retailers are offering this service as a means of competing with larger stores. The availability of a professional tailor is often the difference between making a sale and losing it. Uncertain shoppers sometimes need the assurance that the garment can be perfectly tailored to fit their figures before they decide to buy.

Personal Shopping

Most major department stores as well as upscale specialty organizations that have a significant fashion orientation provide a service known as **personal shopping**. It is especially suited to the needs of those who have little time to shop or for those who need special assurance that the purchases they are about to make are appropriate.

With most companies that offer this service, it merely takes a phone call to obtain assistance. For example, a shopper who needs a suit for an important business meeting might not have the time to go through everything available in the store. By phoning ahead, the customer gives the store's shopping specialist her preferences in terms of color, price, and style and indicates at what time she can come to the store. Upon arrival, she is met by the consultant in a special place where the merchandise has already been assembled for her to look at and try on. Bergdorf Goodman, one of New York City's high-fashion emporiums, has numerous private rooms in which the customers are shown preselected merchandise. Food and beverages are also made available in these private surroundings so that those with time limitations can make the most of their shopping experience.

Customers tend to spend more when purchasing with credit cards.

Sometimes personal shopping is used not for a complete ensemble but solely for a particular item that will enhance an outfit the customer already owns. Macy's encourages such clients to call in their requests; when he or she arrives, a selection of the appropriate items will be on hand.

At Nordstrom, the personal shopping role is the practice of every sales associate. Each is ready to take a customer through the store and suggest merchandise or to provide this service via the telephone. It is not unusual for a Nordstrom employee to receive an emergency call that warrants delivery of merchandise directly to the customer's place of business, home, or hotel. It is because of these accommodations that Nordstrom has thrived.

Credit Accounts

Although these programs, for the most part, bring additional revenues to the company, they are nonetheless considered to be services for the customer. Most large retail operations offer a variety of plans ranging from those that are interest free for customers who pay their bills within 30 days to those that require interest and are payable over a period of time.

Bloomingdale's offers a proprietary card.

The purpose is not only to provide shoppers with extended times in which to pay their bills but also to increase the size of the purchase. When compared to cash purchases, credit card transactions are generally larger.

Living in a world of plastic makes the offering of charge plans a must for most retailers. Without them it is likely that the vast majority would not be able to remain in business.

The types of retail credit that are offered are the **proprietary credit card** and **third-party card**. Tables 19.1 and 19.2 describe each classification and their features.

Dining Facilities

Many large retailers offer dining services to their customers. These include upscale types as well as self-service ventures. Most department stores feature one or more of these eating

TABLE 19.1
PROPRIETARY CREDIT CARDS

TYPES	EXAMPLES	FEATURES
Charge accounts	Most department stores	Customers are given lines of credit and must pay their bills within 30 days.
Revolving credit accounts	Most department stores and chain organizations	Lines of credit are established; customers make monthly payments and can make additional purchases as long as the total doesn't exceed the established line of credit.
Installment credit	Most major department stores, electronics, and furniture chains	For major purchases, the store sets up a monthly payment plan that must be paid in full at the end of the prescribed period.

TABLE 19.2
THIRD-PARTY CREDIT CARDS

TYPES	EXAMPLES	FEATURES
Travel and entertainment	American Express, Diners Club	Unlimited credit, but user must pay off entire bill at the end of the billing period.
Bank cards	MasterCard, VISA	Cards are issued by banks and are usable at most retail operations. Credit limit is established for each account. Minimum payment is due every month until balance is paid. Users can buy and pay as long as they remain within their credit limit.
Cash reward cards	Discover Card	Similar to bank cards, except that the user receives a rebate at the end of the year based upon his or her spending.

venues. Even companies like Sam's Club have food counters at which patrons may purchase food and beverages.

The concept provides the retailer with a profit and also encourages the shopper to stay in the store for a longer period of time. If the store doesn't feature dining facilities, when hunger strikes the shopper will more than likely leave the store and not return for additional shopping.

Bloomingdale's opened an upscale restaurant in its South Coast Plaza store in Costa Mesa, California, in 2007. Following in the footsteps of its successful flagship dining spot in New York City, which features the culinary delights of star chef David Burke in a venue called Burke Bar Café, the company has partnered with chef extraordinaire Charlie Palmer of Aureole fame. The company's belief is that in-store dining should not merely be a quick fix but one that centers on luxury dining, as in upscale stores such as Selfridges or Harrods in London and Bon Marché in Paris. It is hoped that this will help to keep customers in the store much longer and will also put them in a better shopping frame of mind.

Leased Departments

Many major retailers have **leased departments** in which they rent a portion of their premises to outside companies who specialize in services that are not typical of the store's offerings. These include travel services and beauty salons.

These departments often carry the names of established companies and sometimes motivate the consumer to come to the store to avail themselves of their services. World-famous hair stylist Frederick Fakai, for example, operates a leased department in Bergdorf Goodman. It is the retailer's plan that, once inside the store for these services, the shoppers will also purchase the company's own goods.

Customized Services

While many retailer services are typically found in the large companies and serve an important need for their clienteles, others are unique to individual companies. The intention is to distinguish one store from another and hope that these special services will sufficiently entice shoppers to patronize the stores that offer them.

Special Shopping Times

Some merchants periodically set aside specific hours to cater to a particular segment of their market. It might be a few hours before the normal shopping day for handicapped shoppers to come to the store to purchase or a special time when only men can enter the store to make holiday purchases.

Special shopping night themes help attract a desired audience.

Henri Bendel, the upscale fashion emporium in New York City, has a Girls' Nites program that features exclusive workshops on beauty, weddings, and other fashionable subjects. Recognized authorities such as national makeup artist Eric Jimenez, designer Diane Von Furstenberg, and *New York Magazine* editor in chief Caroline Miller are just a few of the invited guests who have made the Girls' Nites special.

Interpreter Programs

The continued influx of visitors from all over the globe has created a demand for people who are able to communicate in foreign languages. These shoppers often spend considerable sums in the stores on themselves and on gifts that they will bring back home. Harrods, perhaps the world's most famous fashion retailer, provides interpreters for just this purpose. Just about any foreign visitor can be assigned an individual who is perfectly able to communicate in the necessary language. Macy's, in its New York City flagship, also provides language experts who can communicate in most any language. Without any charge to the customer, the interpreter will not only assist with purchases but also arrange for immediate alterations, help with currency exchanges, and provide anything else that will make the visitor's shopping experience more pleasant.

Corporate Gift Service

Many retailers, particularly those that are located in the major commercial cities, provide special services to accommodate businesses that regularly need gifts for their employees and clients. At Christmas, in particular, some companies spend enormous sums on gifts to thank their customers for past patronage. Macy's provides a **corporate gift service** in which expert consultants help in the selection of client gifts, incentive offerings, and retirement awards. Through the use of a special Macy's corporate account, the user is entitled to volume purchase incentives and other service amenities.

Choosing One's Own Sale Day

In order to reward customers for their patronage, Bloomingdale's has developed a program that focuses on the faithful. Shoppers receive notification through the mail of special days that have been set aside for them to receive a 15 percent discount on everything that is purchased for one day. The particular day is left to the consumer since the company is aware that not everyone may be available at the same time to take advantage of the offer. After entering the store, the customer takes the shopping pass to any Bloomingdale's sales associate who will then activate it. All day long the discount can be taken on merchandise.

Child Care Facilities

Shopping is necessity for consumers, but many face the problem of finding free time to accomplish this task without interruption from others. In particular, children often prevent parents from spending the time needed to make their selections. Retailers recognize that, the more time available for uninterrupted shopping, the more likely the sale will be greater. To accommodate shoppers, IKEA—the furniture and housewares chain with branches throughout the United States—has solved the problem by offering a fully protected fun environment where parents may leave their children while shopping. This specially designed area is managed by trained people who have complete responsibility for the children left in their charge. Each child is marked with a special tag for identification and is released to the parent only when matching identification is shown.

Each retailer must assess its own clientele's needs and develop those service programs that bring greater sales to the company.

The 10 Commandments of Customer Service

Put Your Customers First
Retail stores cannot exist without customers . . . so welcome them and make them feel valued.

Make It Easy ...
for shoppers to get into and out of your store, to find a sales associate, to gather merchandise and to locate fitting rooms, restrooms, and the return desk.

Know Your Customers
Embrace every opportunity to notice them, listen to them, and remember them.

Keep It Simple
Discount store shoppers don't expect piano music, and commissioned sales help won't fly in a warehouse club, but a friendly smile, a bit of empathy, and a willingness to help work in every environment.

Cultivate a Service Culture
Passion for customer service must be part of the culture, not just part of the mission statement.

Be Consistent
Multichannel is industry jargon. Customers expect customer service, prices, and return policies to be consistent regardless of whether they shop your store, catalogue, or Web site.

Play Fair
Do what you say you'll do, when you say you'll do it, at the price you promised.
If you advertise something, have it in stock. If it's out of stock, provide comparable alternatives.

Empower the Front Line ...
to make decisions and deliver results, and counsel them when mistakes arise.
Take care of the people who are charged with taking care of your customers and they will take care of your business.

Use Technology ...
to aid and abet customer service, not to replace it.

Recover Quickly
Mistakes will happen. The true measure of good customer service is how quickly you can turn a negative into a positive.

The 10 commandments of customer service.

Call Centers

Recognizing the need for customer service is obvious by the number of different types retailers offer. Addressing customer problems is a necessity, but the expense involved in handling these concerns continues to escalate. Many merchants have also discovered that finding the right people to perform this service is becoming more and more difficult.

The answer for many retailers has been the use of call centers, centralized facilities that are operated by external companies. One of the global leaders in corporate networking solutions and services is Avaya, Inc. Among the many retailers it services, in terms of interacting with consumers and handling problems, is Home Depot. Through Web chat, e-mail, and telephone—all of which originate from a call center managed by Avaya—Home Depot is able to relieve their in-store personnel from handling problems, freeing them to pay more attention to making sales. Home Depot provides information about all its products to Avaya, which in turn uses it to satisfy customer inquiries and complaints. In addition to the problem-solving nature of these and other call centers, the information that is gathered from the consumer may be used to better understand buying patterns and preferences. In this way, Home Depot and other retailers can tailor their operations to satisfy customer needs.

Guidelines for Better Service

Establishing **service guidelines** and making certain that employees are familiar with them makes the shopping experience more pleasant for the shopper and more profitable for the retailer. Some areas of service and how they should be implemented include the following:

- Serving the customer is a given, but it requires a sufficient number of associates to be on the selling floor to make the shopping experience quick and meaningful. In a time when many shoppers do not have the luxury of spending endless hours shopping, the retailer must make certain there is enough staff available to efficiently handle customer inquiries. When customers wait too long, often they lose their desire to shop.
- Training is essential in order to make certain the store's "rules" are followed. This is especially important when part-time employees are on the selling floor. They should receive a pamphlet outlining the principles of good service, an instructional DVD that they can view over and over again, and/or in-store training by service managers.
- An enthusiastic approach, as discussed earlier in the chapter, is essential for motivating the shopper to listen and ultimately make the purchase. Make certain that shoppers are made to feel at home.
- The old cliché of "Do unto others . . ." goes a long way in serving the customer. Employees should picture themselves when shopping and then transfer that insight to the customer's perspective.

In the News . . .

The article "Merchants Struggle to Define Customer Satisfaction," on page 457 at the end of this chapter, should be read now.

CHAPTER HIGHLIGHTS

- Customer service is not only important in brick-and-mortar operations, but in the off-site organizations as well.
- When some merchants changed their selling formats from service to self-selection, sales began to decline.
- Nordstrom has set the standard for excellence in retail selling as well as in customer service.
- The rules of the selling game include proper appearance, communications skills, tactfulness, motivational expertise, and enthusiasm.
- Product knowledge can be acquired by taking courses and through technology.
- Sales training may be achieved through role-playing, professional videocassettes, on-the-job training, vestibule training, and online training.
- Proper selling involves appropriate customer greetings, needs assessment, merchandise presentation, handling objections, and attempts at closing the sale.
- Some Web sites are providing online help so that a customer's questions can be answered directly.
- Retailers provide a wealth of traditional services to make shopping more pleasurable.
- Customized services are provided by retailers who wish to go the extra mile to make their customers feel special.
- Retail credit is provided either by the merchants themselves or through third-party creditors.

IMPORTANT RETAILING TERMS

agree and counterattack method (443)

corporate gift service (451)

customer-is-always-right concept (440)
gift registry (447)
leased department (450)
online training (441)
on-the-job training (441)
personal selling (436)
personal shopping (448)
proprietary credit card (449)
return label (445)
role-playing (440)
service guidelines (453)
skeleton sales crew (436)
third-party card (449)
vestibule training (441)
"yes, but" technique (443)

FOR REVIEW

1. Why are many retailers improving their customer services?
2. In the 1970s and 1980s, what changes took place in terms of service on the selling floor?
3. Which retailer is said to epitomize personal selling and customer service?
4. Why is appropriate appearance such an important part of the salesperson's preparation?
5. How can a sales associate learn proper communication skills if in-house training is unavailable?
6. What are the areas of company knowledge that a sales associate should be familiar with in order to make a better sales presentation?
7. Describe how tactfulness helps generate future business.
8. Why is role-playing considered by many to be the best way to learn selling techniques?
9. What is meant by the term *vestibule training*, and what purpose does it serve?
10. Upon greeting a customer, what is important to remember?
11. Discuss two techniques that are typically used to overcome customer objections.
12. Is it always possible to close every retail sale? Why or why not?
13. Why do some upscale retailers use follow-up techniques for customers who have just made purchases?
14. Does any actual selling take place in the off-site retail environments? Explain.
15. What are some of the traditional services offered by the major retailers in the United States?
16. What is the difference between typical department store charge accounts and revolving credit accounts?
17. Distinguish between bankcards and cash reward cards.
18. Why do some retailers offer interpreter services to their shoppers?
19. How does the corporate gift service differ from typical gift registries?
20. Why do some merchants set aside space for child care facilities in their stores?
21. In what way do call centers improve upon in-house customer servicing?

AN INTERNET ACTIVITY

Along with brick-and-mortar enterprises and catalogue companies, retailers with Web sites are now offering a variety of services to their users. Once a venue where automatic purchasing was the primary focus, many Web sites now offer different services to augment purchasing. These companies may be divisions of multichannel retailers or merchants that use the Internet as their sole means of selling.

In this assignment, you should access a number of different retailers who sell merchandise on their Web sites. Companies that operate both brick-and-mortar operations and Web sites should be explored as well as companies that are solely Internet based.

Select one multichannel and one e-tail merchant to compare the services they offer online. Prepare a report using a form with the following heads to list each of the traditional and customized services offered on the Web. Summarize your conclusions about why one retail source is better than the other in terms of customer service.

Retailer	Traditional Services	Customized Services

EXERCISES AND PROJECTS

1. Visit two stores that are in the same retail classification (e.g., department stores, chain organizations, or supermarkets). Each of the chosen companies should then be assessed in terms of the services provided to their customers. Once you have recorded your findings, prepare a comparative analysis that describes these services along with your conclusion as to which company is more customer-oriented and why.
2. Pretend that you are in the market for a consumer product that requires some personal selling. It might be a computer, a television, a camera, or any other high-ticket item. Visit two stores and assess the selling assistance that was provided. When finished, write a one-page paper describing the approaches used in each of the selling presentations; select the one that you think was handled best and give the reasons for your choice.

THE CASE OF DEVELOPING A CUSTOMER SERVICE PROGRAM THAT BEST SERVES CONSUMERS

Ever since the rush of off-price merchants entering the retail arena, consumers have more and more places in which to find bargain merchandise. Joining the fray in 1980 was Paramount Specialty Shops, which marketed fashion-oriented items that paralleled the inventories of the most sophisticated, traditional fashion emporiums. Collections that included names like Ralph Lauren, Anne Klein, Perry Ellis, and other marquee labels were commonplace at Paramount. The success of the operation can best be measured by the number of new units it continued to open. There are now 125 units.

Taking its cue from the early entries into this value-shopping format, the company built its facilities as bare-bone environments devoid of any services other than the acceptance of third-party credit cards. With its success continuously spiraling upward, the company envisioned a chain that would ultimately double its present numbers. During the past 2 years, however, other companies that catered to value shoppers began to open, competing with many of Paramount's units. Not only did these competitors offer the same type of merchandise mix at bargain prices, but some designed facilities that were more consumer-friendly and offered a host of services.

Although business in most of the Paramount stores continued to be successful, management was worried that the new competition might result in the loss of some of its regular patrons. Through informal research Paramount learned that, while customers were most interested in price, more and more expected some level of customer service.

David Michaels, the company's CEO, was not in favor of introducing any services because he believed it would adversely affect the bottom line. Price, he stated, was the only real reason for the clientele to patronize its stores. Amy Alexander, the company COO, was in total disagreement. While conceding that price was most important to shoppers, she argued that the need for some customer services was imperative because of the new competition in this arena. Amy believes that, even though the cost of these services would hamper the store's profits at present sales levels, the new approach would attract more customers and increase sales, allowing the same (or a better) profit picture to prevail.

Questions

1. With whom do you agree? Defend your position with sound reasoning.
2. If some services are offered, what method would you use to introduce them to the company?
3. Which services might be both appropriate and cost-effective for Paramount to offer?

Dynamic Web Content: Giving Customers What They Want
John Lovett

JULY 2, 2007

Effective Web content provides targeted messaging to attract customers onto a Web site followed by consistent, timely and relevant information to guide them through the online experience. The goal of these actions is to culminate in a desired result such as a sale, qualified lead or submitted application.

Findings from a recent Aberdeen Group benchmark report, Online Content Speaks Volumes, show that the firms enjoying Best-in-Class prominence are going beyond static Web content—where information and images rarely change—to continuous updates and dynamic content delivery. Seventy-four percent of Best-in-Class companies currently deliver non-static Web pages through combinations of the following: updating online content continuously, refreshing content on each visit, altering content based on referral site or navigational path and varying content in real time based on user behavior.

MARKETING TAKES THE REINS

The delivery of dynamic content reflects advances in technology as well as a shift in corporate culture, where Web content management E-Mail Marketing Software-Free Trial. Click Here. Latest News about content management is predominately a function of the marketing group, rather than an IT discipline. In fact, marketing owns Web content management for 76 percent of Best-in-Class companies. Many of today's content management solutions share a common feature: easy-to-use interfaces that place content management and creation in the hands of the marketing department. This provides better control for targeted messaging and frees up resource constraints from IT or other operational departments.

To improve Web content management effectiveness, companies are deepening their understanding of customers and their behavior to provide targeted messaging for specific customer segments. Companies that demonstrate maturity with online content transform the presentation of static content to a dynamic delivery model, where content changes based on user interests, actions, behavior and history.

This delivery model is possible, in part, through segmentation, used by 64 percent of Best-in-Class. Using segmentation, different individuals visiting a site will receive alternative content based on factors such as: where they were referred from, if they are a new or returning visitor, or what pages they've visited previously.

NO PIECE OF CAKE

Delivering dynamic content in a relevant and timely manner is a difficult task. Even Best-in-Class companies struggle with common problems associated with content management and delivery issues. The dominant frustration for 68 percent of all companies, including 72 percent of Best-in-Class, is that they do not possess enough resources to manage Web content. Other frustrations include the ability to segment relevant content for specific market segments effectively, which is a struggle for 51 percent of Best-in-Class.

Finally, 36 percent of all companies are challenged by the fact that their Web content strategy is not defined and understood throughout their organizations. This problem is most prevalent among Average and Laggard companies, who have not succeeded in building a unified corporate strategy or aligning common goals for Web content management. Companies that begin with those building blocks for delivering content across one site, multiple sites, or a network of partners, will have greater success because of working towards a defined and measurable goal.

BEHAVIORAL TARGETING AND CONTEXTUAL CONTENT

Online retailers are uniquely suited to delivering dynamic Web content due to the deep relationships they have with their customers. Survey results show that behavior-driven content delivered in a real-time manner is in the nascent stages of adoption, as only 20 percent of Best-in-Class currently use this capability. However, this number will rise to 40 percent within the next 12 months and to 100 percent adoption for Best-in-Class within the next 24 months. It's important to note that there are different methods for delivering relevant content to users based on what is known about their habits and behaviors:

- Unique User Profiles. Unique user profiles are currently used by 60 percent of Best-in-Class retailers, allow Web sites to track individual customers through a cookie, which stores all of their user information such as purchase history, contact information, browsing behavior, promotions received and click through rates. Unique user profiles provide a wealth of information to deliver relevant cross-sell/up-sell merchandise dynamically and personalize the online experience for each customer based on their preferences and behavior.
- Contextual Content. Contextual content is delivered differently than pages generated from a unique user profile. Contextual content can be delivered to customers as soon as their first Web site visit by interpreting their behavior and serving relevant blocks of content. For example, a Web site visitor who navigates to a page selling widgets is automatically offered products that other site visitors who landed on that page purchased previously. A key advantage to this approach is that no prior history is required to provide content recommendations, yet it works for both new and returning visitors. Further, there is no need for marketers to review reports to decide what's effective. Instead many contex-

tually driven content systems are delivered in an automated fashion.
- As described above, many companies are leveraging the marketing power of collective wisdom and unique user profiles, made possible through Web analytics, to perform complex tasks such as affinity based recommendations, behavior driven content, contextual presentation of content for new visitors and multivariate testing. Although adoption of these tools may be lagging today, deployment of Web content tools will experience growth of 55 to 300 percent within the next 12 to 24 months.

RECOMMENDED ACTIONS

- Develop a strategy for online content management and delivery and ensure that all parties invested throughout your organization understand and are committed to the program. This holds true regardless of whether you have an in-house developed content management system, or work with a vendor partner. Currently, only 43 percent of Laggards have a defined process in place for Web content management and many are struggling as a result.
- Use segmentation to instill a process of dynamic content delivery vs. static content presentation. The strategy of altering content delivery to different market segments is the second most prevalent strategic action for both Average and Best-in-Class companies. Segmentation provides companies the ability to target the needs and wants of different users, to improve the efficiency of the online experience, to aid in product or information discovery and to enhance the overall experience.
- Go beyond dynamic content presentation to personalized delivery. Sixty percent of retailers are building and maintaining profiles for unique users to provide a better online experience. Adoption of unique user profiles will grow to 100 percent within the next two years, showing that understanding customers on an individual level is important to all online retailers. User profiles are built on past purchases, online and offline experiences and preferences. They can be used to target content and information by offering relevant messaging to users both in the form of dynamic content and outbound email campaigns.

• •

Merchants Struggle to Define Customer Satisfaction
Maria Halkias
Amy Conn-Gutierrez

Customer service isn't what it used to be.

That's a lament expressed by many consumers, convinced that a golden age when the customer was always right is long past.

But that statement is also a fact of life for businesses—and retailers in particular: Customer service doesn't mean what it used to mean.

After a decade of overwhelming change for retailers—online shopping, globalization, the Wal-Mart effect, self-service checkout aisles—companies are recalibrating their customer service while trying to define it.

The good news: There's a growing realization that improving customer service is the best way companies can distinguish themselves in a crowded, competitive, built-out marketplace.

Today, improvements and declines in customer satisfaction can show up faster than ever on a company's bottom line and, yes, in its stock price.

An article in the *Journal of Marketing* last year showed that companies with high customer satisfaction ratings in the University of Michigan's American Customer Satisfaction Index beat the stock market as a whole.

In an era of globalization and the low-price revolution, customer service is one of the few levers companies have left to raise prices, said Claes Fornell, director of the university's National Quality Research Center.

"Companies don't have much pricing power unless there is shrinking supply or higher customer satisfaction," Dr. Fornell said. "Companies may begin to see narrowing profit margins unless there is further improvement in customer satisfaction."

The National Retail Federation, the industry's largest trade group, recognizes this. Last month, it released a set of customer service competency standards to be used in training centers, schools and colleges. It offers a professional certification in customer service at its new NRF University Web site and has opened retail skills training centers in a few states.

"This industry traditionally churned our employees. Now we're trying to make them aware that it's not just an industry you pass through," said Kathy Mannes, managing director of workforce development at NRF. "We haven't been thinking enough about the skills needed for retail, and that's obvious when customers walk out the door."

BY DEFINITION

So what is good customer service these days?

Does it mean getting a customer out the door fast? Or having a sales assistant help find the right item, size and color? Or keeping costs as low as possible?

Is it about minding expiration dates so consumers don't have to? Keeping the restrooms clean? Self-checkout? No self-checkout?

Is it having the latest stuff shoppers don't even know they want until they see it? Making a delivery on time? Fixing errors and having a reasonable return policy? Having a live person answering the phone?

"The phrase means everything, and it means nothing," said Pamela N. Danziger, an authority on consumer insights and author of several books on the shopping experience. "It's whatever is important to the consumer."

There's no one formula that works for everyone. Customer service is one thing if you're in a Neiman Marcus and something else inside a Dollar General.

"Everybody knows it when it's not happening. It's like what the court says about pornography. It knows it when it sees it," said Phil Rist, vice president at BIGresearch, a firm that surveys more than 7,000 shoppers a month for the largest retail trade organization.

"It's all about expectations," J.C. Penney chairman and chief executive Mike Ullman said. "Southwest Airlines has never been considered a full-service airline, but it has a high delivery on its promise. It has high customer satisfaction because it fulfills its promise."

Penney is working hard to improve its customer satisfaction scores by retaining good employees and teaching them to make shoppers feel welcome. Its marketing message, "Every Day Matters," shouts that it wants to supply the daily needs of life.

At the same time, Penney is one of the industry's biggest users of technology designed to have the right product available at the right price. Its cash registers are wired to the Internet, so if housewares doesn't have the color you want, the sales assistant can order it right there for delivery to your door.

Customer service "is easier said than done, and it's a lot of different pieces," Mr. Ullman said. "If the register doesn't work, it doesn't matter how friendly the person is. If the price isn't right, the restroom isn't clean and the dressing room isn't tidy, those are all disqualifiers."

Jorge Leis, a retail expert and partner in the Dallas office of Bain & Co., said the retailer's perspective is that service is just one element of a total customer experience that a retailer develops over time. That would include a culture that takes care of the customer.

"The customer isn't this monolithic thing. Customers differ. Stores differ, and it varies even inside the same box," Mr. Leis said. "Some departments need better-trained employees than others.

So the expectations are even different inside the same store."

"ALWAYS SMART"

Although some companies still practice "the customer is always right," a more relevant approach today is "the customer is always smart."

Technology is empowering shoppers, making them more knowledgeable, demanding and resourceful.

As a 40-year-old college graduate and mother living in a Dallas suburb, Victoria Rice of Allen is a highly sought-after retail demographic. She does a lot of shopping.

But she says she hasn't had many negative retail experiences.

Why? She picks her merchants carefully and knows what to expect from them. If she's buying a camera, she not only researches the cameras, she finds out the store's return policy ahead of time.

Customer service "is such an integral part of a company's business plan, and it's fascinating to me that there are so many patterns a store can follow. There are only so many companies I'll do business with, especially online," Ms. Rice said.

Making a customer mad enough to promise never to return isn't just a loss of one. Today, it means thousands may read their experience online.

Social networking sites such as MySpace, YouTube, Amazon.com, Yelp.com and Angieslist.com mean that consumers can spread the compliments and complaints fast. Such sites are visited at least once a month by about 25 percent of the U.S. online population, according to a study by market research firms iProspect and Jupiter-Research.

Highly coveted moms in high-spending years are busy, technologically connected and more savvy about marketing messages. As a result, they depend more and more on fellow customers' recommendations.

"It's not just a couple ladies talking across the back fence anymore," BIGResearch's Mr. Rist said.

DELL'S STORY

Computer maker Dell Inc.'s recent history shows the importance of customer service.

For years, fast-growing Dell could do no wrong on Wall Street—until reports of declining customer satisfaction started showing up in 2004 surveys after call hold times lengthened and tech support moved outside the U.S.

"These things have long tails, and it takes time to build and to dissipate," said John Spooner, an analyst with Technology Business Research Inc. "In the last year or so, they've worked to reverse the trend by beefing up the tech support and shortening times that people are on the phone by letting staffers go off-script with more knowledgeable customers."

FLEXIBILITY IS A BIG KEY

Ms. Danziger, who last year wrote *Shopping: Why We Love It and How Retailers Can Create the Ultimate Customer Experience*, recently went to a major home-goods retailer for a shower gift.

She decided to buy the couple something that wasn't on their list.

"They wouldn't gift-wrap it because it wasn't from the registry," she said. "That policy is insane. They don't deserve my business.

"That doesn't fly in today's world," she said. "Some companies have draconian policies. They need to give people that they hire the power to say yes to the customer. The luxury hotel industry is a model retailers should study."

Understanding the audience is also important.

Andrew Ethridge has worked in retail for several years, mostly in clothing stores. But when he went to work in Best Buy's computer department almost two years ago, he quickly realized that he would have to help shoppers who knew more than he did and those who knew very little.

"You have some people who come in with pages of paper and challenge your knowledge level, and then you have others who barely know what a computer is," Mr. Ethridge said.

Helping the two customer extremes, and those with proficiencies in between, means sales assistants really have to know their stuff and communicate at the right level, he said.

The ability to chat in real time with knowledgeable staffers is boosting customer satisfaction scores for online retailers.

Dallas-based CompUSA said that after initiating a chat, 60 percent of customers added an item to their cart from the section they viewed before the chat. As part of their training, CompUSA's online chat agents work in a store for three weeks, taking customer questions face-to-face before they go online.

PREPARING FOR 2015

Differing levels of technological proficiency among consumers complicate the customer service equation.

For those who can handle it—both among consumers and companies—technology is going to keep making the whole proposition better, said Al Meyers, senior vice president at TNS Retail Forward Inc., a retail research firm that's studying what the industry will look like in 2015.

"It has to, because the industry can't find enough people, train enough people and the customer isn't willing to pay for better service when a competitor has it for a lower price," he said.

"We're not saying that the trusted salesperson will be replaced at a Saks, Neiman's or a Nordstrom, but in most of retail, providing service with people is going to make it harder for them to compete.

"It won't be long before we are scanning entire grocery carts and paying for its contents with a thumbprint," he said. "Mirrors will send images to friends from dressing rooms to replace that salesperson with a vested interest in telling you it looks good."

People are already doing that with cellphone cameras, he said.

But change can be frustrating.

Over the last decade, technology has increased customers' access to information and helped drive down prices. The Internet has enabled people to buy virtually anything they want and have it delivered to their homes overnight. (It gets better: Amazon is testing same-day delivery in some cities for orders placed before 11 a.m.)

Conflicts between technology's benefits and frustrations will continue to be customer service issues.

"To many, technology is the nasty, endless, black hole loops of telephone inquiries that never result in connecting with a human being or being in a store with a broken kiosk . . . or pushing a help button and having no one respond," Mr. Meyers said.

"The same companies that provide bad customer service will provide bad technology and vice versa."

APPENDIX
Careers in Retailing and Related Fields

After reading this book, it should be obvious that many different types of roles must be played in order to manage any retail operation. Those who are motivated to enter the field, and some of those that are directly related to it, will have the opportunity to involve themselves in the areas that seem most appropriate for their skills and motivations.

Whether it is a small or large brick-and-mortar operation or one of the off-site ventures that are significantly affecting the industry, there is a wealth of opportunity ahead. With its promise for greater globalization, retailing is one of the few careers that does not restrict its participants to a rather limited geographic region. Small towns, big cities, and domestic and foreign venues all provide ample opportunity to make a significant contribution to the field.

Working as a team member in retail operations of any size has its own rewards, as does starting one's own business. Each offers a degree of excitement and monetary remuneration that is based upon individual ability, knowledge, and the determination to achieve success. It is a career that doesn't require the ultimate educational achievements demanded by other professions—just a certain level of competency and individual motivation. Those who enter this arena with a willingness to work diligently and play by the rules of the game will undoubtedly have the opportunity to reach the top.

Before entering the field it is imperative that an exploration be undertaken so that one's abilities and desires can be best matched to the specific positions within the field.

JOB CLASSIFICATIONS

One need not look further than the pages in this text to become familiar with the wealth of jobs that are performed in retailing. Each brick-and-mortar operation, catalogue, Web site, and home-shopping service is home to every level of management, merchandising, and product development. Even those off-site ventures that seem to focus on self-selection often require a certain degree of personal selling. Of course, it is the stores that require the greatest degree of professional salesmanship.

Bearing in mind that retail careers cross over into these different arenas, the reader should carefully examine each career classification and pursue the specific venue that appears to bring the greatest excitement and potential for success. Thus, whether it is a department store, specialty chain, supermarket, franchise, discount operation, off-price venture, catalogue, Web site, or home-shopping service, the jobs offered by the organization are more or less the same.

It should also be noted that many of today's merchants participate in multichannel retailing, where different divisions vie for the consumer's dollar. By seeking employment in this type of company, there is even greater potential for the individual to explore the various types of opportunity without having to move from one company to another.

Typically, careers in retailing are centered on the areas of *merchandising, management, operations, promotion,* or *finance.* Parallel careers—such as those available in market consulting firms, marketing specialist groups, and fashion forecasting services—feature a host of opportunities, many of which are similar to those found in retail operations and others that are exclusive to their particular types of businesses.

The following discussion will focus on the management and mid-management levels of employment that are open to those who have satisfactorily fulfilled the obligation of entry-level positions.

Brick-and-Mortar and Off-Site Job Opportunities

Each of these venues offers a potential for advancement and salaries that is commensurate with educational background, experience, and a willingness to perform at the highest possible level.

Merchandising

If the excitement of purchasing merchandise that appeals to the consumer and brings a profit to the company is the goal, then merchandising is the most appropriate career to pur-

TABLE A.1
MERCHANDISING CAREERS

POSITION	DESCRIPTION
General Merchandise Manager	Heads the merchandising division; oversees the company's entire merchandising budget; leads management team in determining company product mix, pricing strategies, and merchandising philosophy.
Divisional Merchandise Manager	Heads several related divisions in the company, oversees buyers, allocates budgeted dollars to individual buyers, sets tone for division's merchandise assortment, and assists buyers in the division with major purchasing decisions.
Buyer	Develops model stock, visits wholesale markets, buys merchandise, and is often involved in product development of private-label merchandise.
Assistant Buyer	Often purchases staple goods, reorders merchandise, places special orders, and assists the buyer with purchasing decisions at home and in the wholesale market.
Fashion Director	In companies with fashion orientations this is most often a staff position in which specialists advise the merchandising team on the present status of new collections and trends in the market.
Comparison Shopper	Another staff position, the role is to compare prices of merchandise at competing companies.

TABLE A.2
MANAGEMENT CAREERS

Position	Description
Store Manager	Overall management functions, which include services and management team selection; also responsible for carrying out company policy.
Department Manager	Responsible for individual departments and their personnel, scheduling, and employee evaluation.
Assistant Department Manager	Aids department manager in running department, sells, handles complaints, and is responsible for end-of-day receipt tallying.
Human Resources Manager	Provides company with competent employees and oversees all aspects of human resources management.

TABLE A.3
OPERATIONS CAREERS

Position	Description
Operations Manager	Responsible for areas such as security, plant maintenance, traffic, receiving, supplies purchasing, and workrooms.
Security Chief	Develops loss prevention systems and manages the security team.
Maintenance Manager	Responsible for housekeeping, construction and facilities alteration, ventilation, and maintenance of mechanical equipment.
Receiving Manager	Oversees incoming merchandise, checking and marking, and invoicing.
Purchasing Manager	Buys equipment and supplies for the company's operation.
Workroom Manager	Responsible for clothing alterations, merchandise repairs, and restaurants.

sue. In major retail organizations, this division consists of line and staff positions. In smaller companies, the limited amount of business dictates fewer positions and the absence of staff or advisory people. Table A.1 is based on the needs of the major retailers in the industry.

Management

Those who manage the retail operations are in areas that cut across the entire organization. Some of these positions are listed in Table A.2.

Operations

This division generally maintains the physical plant and the management of its employees. Table A.3 lists several careers in operations.

Promotion

The company's promotional and publicity endeavors are imperative to informing the consumers and press about their latest innovations. Managers who fulfill these responsibilities head a number of different areas of expertise, some of which are included in Table A.4.

TABLE A.4
PROMOTIONAL CAREERS

Position	Description
Director of Promotion	Oversees and coordinates all promotional efforts of the company and the managers of each promotional department.
Advertising Manager	Responsible for all media planning, development of campaigns, and management of personnel in division.
Visual Merchandising Manager	Develops window and interior visual concepts, oversees installations, hires artists and trimmers, and coordinates efforts with other promotional managers.
Special Events Manager	Creates concepts for company's special events, including fashion shows and in-store celebrity appearances.
Publicity Manager	Prepares press releases and interacts with the press.

Finance

The success of any retail operation in terms of profit comes from close control of its financial expenditures and the manner in which it offers credit to its customer base. Those who manage these endeavors are described in Table A.5.

Careers That Parallel Retailing

Aside from those who work directly in any retail organization are those who have careers in external companies. Whether the company is comparatively small or a giant in the field, outside resources are often necessary to get an impartial handle on what is taking place in the industry. In the fashion arena, for example, marketing specialists, the largest of which are the market consulting firms, continually feel the pulse of the wholesale industry through research and make their findings known to their clients. In this way, merchants are able to better understand what is ahead of them in terms of merchandise availability, trends, and the like. Reporting services also serve the retailer's needs by apprising them of the competition's merchandising focus and the general state of the marketplace. Others such as fashion forecasters assist the retailer's buying and merchandising team by predicting which styles will be coming to the forefront so that the proper purchasing plans can be developed.

Each of these parallel industries features careers that may attract those who are enamored with retailing but would like to pursue a challenge that is not directly focused on consumer interaction. Some of the careers in this category are listed in Table A.6.

TABLE A.5
FINANCE CAREERS

Position	Description
Accounting Manager	Responsible for formulating accounting procedures and practices and for hiring subordinates.
Payroll Administrator	Develops and coordinates payroll procedures and practices.
Credit Manager	Manages every aspect of credit; oversees credit policies and credit authorization.
Inventory Controller	Develops methods for inventory taking and management of the procedures.

TABLE A.6
MARKET SPECIALIST CAREERS

Position	Description
Market Consulting Firm Merchandise Manager	Oversees a wide product classification, prepares programs for market weeks, and manages buyers in division.
Market Consultant	Assesses wholesale market, advises retail buyers on merchandise availability, prepares buyers for market trips, and prescreens merchandise collections.
Assistant Market Consultant	Follows up retail orders, handles retailer adjustments and complaints, prescreens lines, and accompanies buyer to marketplace.
Product Developer	Develops private-label items.
Fashion Forecaster	Predicts the direction up to 18 months before the season so that buyers may plan their needs well in advance of the market weeks.
Reporting Service Manager	Studies the sales of current merchandise and reports the hot items to clients for possible inclusion in their inventories.

PLANNING FOR THE CAREER

Anyone who wishes to pursue a career in a retail operation or in one that parallels the industry must be fully prepared. This preparation involves a number of areas, including educational background, learning about the company, developing materials such as résumés that will help to gain an interview, and refining the qualities needed for the interview. A significant preplanning effort will bring the best results.

Educational Background

The better educated one is for any career, the more likely he or she will excel. Some industries, such as law and medicine, require substantial formal education before entry is permitted. Retailing, on the other hand, is considerably less stringent in its educational requirements. Nonetheless, those who are better educated will more than likely be the candidates of choice.

For entry-level positions such as sales, most merchants do not look for special diplomas or degrees but rather for a desire by the individual to meet the challenges of face-to-face interaction with the consumer. For those who perform diligently at this lower-level position, promotions to more responsible positions are likely. Many a department manager has risen to that level by showing the dedication necessary to meet the company's standards.

Those who wish to enter at a more professional level will need to have completed a particular course of study that culminates with a degree. Some companies require associate degrees whereas others require baccalaureates as a minimum. Some seeking managerial candidates who will eventually run their company may require a master's degree. In most retail operations with mandatory educational requirements, retailers typically enable employees to work and attend college at the same time so that they can complete the necessary degree. Many will pay for some of the tuition, making schooling less burdensome on the employee.

Introduction to the Company

In order to learn about educational expectations and other company information, those seeking positions should make a thorough investigation to learn if the company is appropriate for their consideration and also to fortify themselves with the necessary knowledge for the interview.

Such information may be obtained by writing to the company or, in today's world of advanced technology, through the Internet. By and large, most retail organizations have sections on their Web sites that invite potential employees to learn about employment opportunities. By logging on to them, one can quickly find an employment application that can be transmitted to the company and evaluated. In Chapter 9, an overview of such employment information is offered.

If the company that is being considered for employment is within close proximity to the interested party, then an in-person visit is in order. In particular, brick-and-mortar operations may be entered with complete anonymity. The visit allows the candidate to assess the work environment and the types of employees that are already in place as well as their mode of dress. This can be a simple yet invaluable source of information that helps determine whether or not the company should be pursued. If the indicators seem appropriate to the job seeker's needs, then a trip to the employment office is in order to learn more about the company. This might also be a good time to set up an interview appointment.

Gaining an Interview

Being granted an interview depends on supply and demand. As we entered the new millennium, there were considerably more jobs that needed filling then the number of applicants seeking them. Of course, this is not always the case. In times of a recession or during downturns in the economy, the reverse is true: more people are seeking positions than are available. Conditions can change at any time, so there must be a plan to secure the interview that best meets the goals of the individual seeking to initially enter the field.

Different approaches are used to break into a new company. These include examining the classified ads in the newspapers, visiting employment agencies that specialize in retailing, and networking. Networking involves calling on friends or relatives to discover which ones have access or connections to the retail organizations. Doors often open to those who come with recommendations.

No matter which route one takes to gain an interview, significant planning must be undertaken to make certain that the candidate is well prepared for the meeting. Part of this preparation involves writing a résumé and a cover letter to accompany it.

Résumés

A résumé gives the individual responsible for hiring a general picture of the candidate. It is this document that either gives the go ahead for an interview or the reason to deny the candidate the opportunity. Thus, developing a "perfect" résumé is essential to a candidate's potential employment with the company.

Résumé writing requires total competence. It may be accomplished by the individual if he or she has the writing skills necessary to succinctly present the appropriate information. Oftentimes it is best to employ the services of a professional who has mastered résumé writing and is able to present the individual's characteristics in the perfect format.

There are numerous resources from which to obtain information about résumé writing on the Internet. Free assistance is available quickly and easily by logging onto www.askjeeves.com and then clicking on The Resume Dolphin. To search for a professional résumé writer, go to www.jobsearchpro.com. At www.resumeservice.net, the user can view a step-by-step procedure that will help one write his or her own résumé. On the same Web site help is also available for a fee. One can also e-mail a résumé preparation company, such as info@resumedotcom.com, to get advice or a complete résumé for a nominal fee. These are but a few of the hundreds of professional services available to job applicants; it is then simply a matter of examining many of them and deciding which one provides the service for a cost that is appropriate.

Additionally, numerous books on résumé writing are available at libraries and bookstores. These written materials provide a wealth of forms that can be used to tailor a résumé to one's own needs.

Cover Letters

Accompanying each résumé should be a cover letter that states *why* the potential candidate is submitting a résumé to the company. The letter might include information on your desire to work for that particular company or the name of someone familiar who has recommended you as a potential employee. It is unnecessary to include any of the information that is already part of your résumé. This would only be redundant and time-consuming for the company representative to read.

The Interview Follow-Up

Once the interview has been completed, it is always appropriate to thank the interviewer for his or her time. Not only is this a courtesy, it also shows a candidate's level of interest in the position.

This thank-you should be in the form of a letter that is as painstakingly prepared as the résumé. The resources used to prepare the résumé are also available to provide the necessary formats for professional follow-up letters.

The proper use of these documents will help make the impression necessary to gain the interview and then, perhaps, employment with the company.

Figure Credits

Chapter 1
- p. 5 — Tim Boyle/Getty Images; James Leynse/CORBIS
- p. 8 — AP Photo/Sears Roebuck and Co.; AP Photo/Elise Amendola, File
- p. 9 — AP Photo/Paul Sakuma; Tim Boyle/Getty Images
- p. 10 — Oleg Nikishin/Getty Images
- p. 11 — Courtesy of The Kittery Outlets
- p. 12 — AP Photo/Donna McWilliam
- p. 13 — © Erin Fitzsimmons
- p. 17 — Rebecca Sapp/Getty Images
- p. 18 — Courtesy of Fairchild Publications, Inc.
- p. 19 — LAURENT FIEVET/Getty Images
- p. 20 — John Sciulli/Getty Images
- p. 21 — Courtesy of Fairchild Publications, Inc.
- p. 24 — Getty Images
- p. 25 — Visit Jacksonville
- p. 27 — © Clover/SuperStock

Chapter 2
- p. 37 — Peter Kramer/Getty Images
- p. 39 — AP Photo/Stacie Freudenberg
- p. 40 — Lightworks Media/Alamy
- p. 42 — Courtesy of Harris Teeter; Tim Boyle/Getty Images
- p. 43 — James Leynse/CORBIS
- p. 44 — AP Photo/Paul Sakuma
- p. 46 — Ellen Isaacs/Alamy
- p. 48 — Stein Mart
- p. 49 — Tanger Outlets Rehoboth Beach, DE
- p. 50 — Dimas Ardian/Getty Images

Chapter 3
- p. 57 — 2008 Zappos.com, Inc.
- p. 59 — Courtesy of Steve Madden.com
- p. 60 — Courtesy of Eddie Bauer
- p. 62 — © 2008 EBAY INC. ALL RIGHTS RESERVED; Spiegel Brands, Inc.
- p. 63 — AP Photo/Joel Page
- p. 64 — AP Photo/Shiho Fukada; Courtesy of Fairchild Publications, Inc.
- p. 65 — AP Photo/Jennifer Szymaszek, File
- p. 67 — Courtesy of Lands' End
- p. 68 — Courtesy of Red Envelope
- p. 69 — Courtesy of Lillian Vernon
- p. 71 — Courtesy of Victoria's Secret
- p. 72 — Courtesy of HSN

Chapter 4
- p. 80 — Travelpix Ltd/Getty Images; Erik Freeland/CORBIS
- p. 81 — Jon Arnold Images Ltd/Alamy
- p. 82 — STEPHEN HIRD/CORBIS
- p. 83 — Travel Ink/Alamy
- p. 84 — TWPhoto/CORBIS; Courtesy of Fairchild Publications, Inc.
- p. 85 — George Pimentel/Getty Images
- p. 86 — snappdragon/Alamy
- p. 90 — Alessandro Garofalo/CORBIS
- p. 91 — AP Photo/Marty Lederhander
- p. 92 — China Photos/Getty Images
- p. 93 — Joe Raedle/Getty Images
- p. 94 — Kevin Foy/Alamy

Chapter 5
- p. 110 — Kay Nietfeld/CORBIS
- p. 111 — AP Photo/Marcio Jose Sanchez
- p. 112 — Courtesy of Fairchild Publications, Inc.; Pascal Le Segretain/Getty Images
- p. 113 — Larry Williams/CORBIS
- p. 114 — © VALS
- p. 116 — Courtesy of Fairchild Publications, Inc.; Ralf-Finn Hestoft/CORBIS
- p. 123 — Courtesy of National Retail Federation
- p. 125 — Stuart O'Sullivan/Getty Images

Chapter 6
- p. 132 — David P. Hall/CORBIS
- p. 134 — Ted Soqui/CORBIS; Justin Sullivan/Getty Images
- p. 135 — Courtesy of Fairchild Publications, Inc.; Steve Azzara/CORBIS
- p. 136 — Courtesy of Flori Roberts
- p. 139 — Jeremy Horner/CORBIS
- p. 140 — Courtesy of *Amsterdam News*; AP Photo/JET Magazine

Chapter 7
- p. 157 — Belk, Inc.
- p. 159 — Council of Better Business Bureaus
- p. 160 — TONY GENTILE/CORBIS
- p. 161 — Courtesy of Fairchild Publications, Inc.
- p. 162 — TEH ENG KOON/Getty Images; AP Photo/Damian Dovarganes
- p. 163 — Michael Prince/CORBIS
- p. 164 — Barry Austin Photography/Getty Images

Chapter 8
- p. 174 — Home Depot
- p. 175 — Sustainable Cotton Project/Academy of Art University, San Francisco; Courtesy of Fairchild Publications, Inc.

470 Figure Credits

p. 176	Daniel Berehulak/Getty Images; Giant Eagle
p. 178	JEFF HAYNES/Getty Images; Courtesy of Barneys New York; Patagonia
p. 180	Pete Springer; Brad Barket/Getty Images
p. 181	Nike; Vittorio Zunino Celotto/Getty Images
p. 182	Courtesy of The Collective

Chapter 9

p. 197	Courtesy of Fairchild Publications, Inc.; Courtesy Monster.com
p. 199	AP Photo/David Zalubowski
p. 200	Tim Boyle/Getty Images
p. 205	ChinaFotoPress/Getty Images
p. 206	Van Maur
p. 207	Mark Peterson/CORBIS
p. 209	AP Photo/Elaine Thompson

Chapter 10

p. 223	Sensormatic
p. 225	Sensormatic; Scott Olson/Getty Images
p. 226	Sensormatic; © Image Source/SuperStock
p. 228	USSearch.com, Inc.
p. 229	Tim Boyle/Getty Images
p. 232	Peter Essick/CORBIS
p. 233	Walter Hodges/CORBIS; Sean Justice/Getty Images

Chapter 11

p. 240	Helen King/CORBIS
p. 242	© UpperCut Images/SuperStock
p. 244	Justin Sullivan/Getty Images
p. 249	VEER

Chapter 12

p. 261	Courtesy of Fairchild Publications, Inc.
p. 262	VISUM Foto GmbH/Alamy
p. 263	Kevin Foy/Alamy
p. 264	Courtesy of Fairchild Publications, Inc.
p. 265	Alan Schein Photography/CORBIS
p. 266	Tim Boyle/Getty Images
p. 267	Danita Delimont/Alamy
p. 268	wim wiskerke/Alamy; AP Photo/John Russell
p. 269	Richard Cummins/CORBIS
p. 271	JHP Signs/Alamy
p. 275	AP Photo/Tracy Hollis
p. 276	Andria Patino/CORBIS

Chapter 13

p. 289	AP Photo/Mark Lennihan; Ambient Images Inc./Alamy
p. 290	Justin Sullivan/Getty Images; AP Photo/Jennifer Graylock
p. 293	Courtesy of Lee McKee, Le Grand Photography; Courtesy of FRC Design Worldwide
p. 294	YOSHIKAZU TSUNO/Getty Images
p. 297	Alex Segre/Alamy
p. 299	Jeff Greenberg/Alamy
p. 301	Juice Images Limited/Alamy

Chapter 14

p. 311	Radius Images/Alamy
p. 313	Blend Images Photography/VEER
p. 314	Courtesy of Fairchild Publications, Inc.
p. 316	Digital Vision Photography/VEER; Courtesy of Fairchild Publications, Inc.
p. 321	Blend Images Photography/VEER
p. 325	Getty Images
p. 326	Courtesy of Fairchild Publications, Inc.
p. 328	RetailExchange
p. 329	The Doneger Group
p. 333	Dennis Cooper/CORBIS; Tim McGuire/CORBIS
p. 334	Zefa Photography/VEER; Tim McGuire/CORBIS; Alloy Photography/VEER; AP Photo/Zack Seckler

Chapter 15

p. 342	Steve Jennings/Getty Images
p. 343	Courtesy of Fairchild Publications, Inc.
p. 344	Marvi Lacar/Getty Images
p. 347	AP Photo/Terry Gilliam; AP Photo/Paul Sakuma; AP Photo/Paul Sakuma
p. 349	Courtesy of Fairchild Publications, Inc.
p. 351	David P. Hall/CORBIS
p. 352	AP Photo/Keith Srakocic
p. 353	AP Photo/Ben Margot

Chapter 16

p. 365	Flirt Photography/VEER
p. 368	Getty Images
p. 370	JEAN-PIERRE MULLER/Getty Images; AP Photo/John Stanmeyer/VII
p. 376	AP Photo

Chapter 17

p. 389	Directphoto.org/Alamy; RubberBall/Alamy; UpperCut Images Photography/VEER
p. 390	VEER
p. 392	Courtesy of Fairchild Publications, Inc.
p. 393	AP Photo/Jennifer Graylock
p. 395	Courtesy of Fairchild Publications, Inc.
p. 398	Digital Vision Photography/VEER; fStop Photography/VEER
p. 399	TOBY MELVILLE/CORBIS; Frank Schwere/Getty Images; Evan Agostini/Getty Images
p. 403	AP Photo/Chris Pizzello; Steve Eichner/CORBIS
p. 405	Kevin Winter/Getty Images; Keith Bedford/CORBIS

Chapter 18

p. 414	Brad Barket/Getty Images; © Photononstop/SuperStock
p. 415	AP Photo/Charles Rex Arbogast; AP Photo/Chitose Suzuki
p. 416	MIKE CLARKE/Getty Images
p. 419	James Leynse/CORBIS; AP Photo/Paul Sakuma
p. 420	Philippe Hays/Alamy
p. 421	HECTOR MATA/Getty Images
p. 425	JEAN-PIERRE MULLER/Getty Images; Marvi Lacar/Getty Images
p. 426	Julio Lopez Saguar/Getty Images; AP Photo/Jennifer Graylock
p. 428	Shannon Stapleton/CORBIS

Chapter 19

p. 436	Stewart Cohen/Getty Images
p. 438	© Clover/SuperStock
p. 442	Colorblind/Getty Images
p. 446	AP Photo/Damian Dovarganes
p. 447	Michael Reynolds/CORBIS
p. 448	Marcus Mok/Getty Images; AP Photo
p. 450	Jamie McCarthy/Getty Images; Jemal Countess/Getty Images

Index

Page numbers in italics refer to figures or tables.

A

A & P, 8
Abboud, Joseph (designer): "focus on," 19
Abercrombie & Fitch: as chain organization, 6; "focus on," 82–83; and global market demand, 104; as a limited-line store, *5*; and reevaluation of tech choices, 30
ACNielsen, 133, 142; "focus on," 124
ACORN® (A Classification of Residential Neighborhoods), *261*, 262
acousto-magnetic (AM) systems, 224
acquisitions: as method for expansion, 21
advertising, 389–401: agencies, 392; assistance for smaller retailers, 390, 392; campaigns, 393–94; combination, 393; cooperative, 331–32, 394; cost analysis of, 400; crossover, 394–95; direct mail, 397–98; ethics in, 160; evaluation of, 401; freelancers, 392; green retailing practices, 180–81; and Hispanic market, 147–54; infomercials, 56; institutional, 393; in-store, 128–30; magazine, 396–97; misleading price claims in, 160–61; in multicultural markets, 140–41; newspaper, 25, 140, 395–96; 408–10; outdoor, 399–400; promotional, 393; radio, 141–42, 397; for recruitment purposes, 196–97; and strategic planning, 15; television, 141, 397; and text messaging, 25–26, 399; and visual merchandising, 429; and Web sites, 399
advertising departments, 389; media services, 392; structures of, *390–91*
Aéropostale: and interior store design, 304–5
African Americans (as a consumer group), 132; and direct marketing, 142–43; and magazines, 140–41; and newspapers, 140; and radio, 141–42; and television, 141
age classifications: as a factor in consumer group assessment, 109
agent order takers, 81
airport terminals: as retailing locations, 271, 275, 283–86
Allied Media Corp.: "focus on," 132–33
alligators. *See* hard tags
alterations, 448
American Eagle Outfitters, *21*; and teenager demographic, 110; and utilizing new technology, 29–30
American Girl: "focus on," 70–71; as a multichannel retailer, *65*
American Girl Place: and exterior design, 288; "focus on," 296. *See also* American Girl
America Online: and virtual catalogues, 66
Amsterdam News (newspaper), *140*
anchor stores, 39–40
angled windows, 291
animated installations, 418
Ann Taylor: and PETA, 167; and young adult demographic, 111
anticipation, 330
apparel retailers: online popularity of, 75–78; targeting ethnic minorities, 135
apparel shops: as chain organizations, 43–44
applicant screening, 228
Arbitron, Inc.: "focus on," 142
arcade front, 291
Armani. *See* Giorgio Armani (company)
Armani Exchange, *92*. *See also* Giorgio Armani (company)
Asian Americans (as a consumer group), 132; and direct marketing, 142–43; and magazines, 141; and newspapers, 140; and radio, 141–42; and television, 141
assortment: development, 316; planning, 311
automatic markdowns, 377
Avaya, Inc.: and call centers, 452–53
average pricing, 373

B

baby boomers, 109
bait-and-switch, 160
balance (in visual presentation): asymmetrical, 424, *425*; symmetrical, 424
Banana Republic, 45, 89; and manufacturer-owned outlets, 11; and merchandise mix, 24; and visual merchandising approach, *427*; and young adult demographic, 111
bar codes, 225
Barnard's Retail Consulting Group: "focus on," 315
Barnes & Noble, 45
Barneys: and green retailing practices, 186
Bath & Body Works: as a chain organization, 6; and Web site redesign, 60
Belk Inc.: and codes of ethics, *157*; "focus on," 7; and private labeling, 342
benefits (for employees), 211
Benetton: and franchising, 10
Bergdorf Goodman: "focus on," 295; and lower-upper class demographic, 116
Best Buy: Canadian presence, 85; as category killer, 13; as discount store operation, *9*; and Hispanic market, *137*; and rational buying motives, 121; and recruitment, 199, *200*; and teenager demographic, 110; and young adult demographic, 112
Better Business Bureau (BBB), 158; "focus on," 159
big books, 8; in U.K. market, 81

big box operations, 372. *See also* category killers; warehouse clubs
billboards. *See* outdoor advertisements
Blockbuster: success in U.K. market, 82
Bloomingdale's, 37, 38, 89; and catalogue selling, *71*; and charitable events, 405; and private labeling, 18; and upper-middle class demographic, 116–17; and visual merchandising strategies, 432–33; and young middle-aged demographic, 112
bodegas, 139
Body Shop: success in U.S. market, 81
bookstores: as chain organizations, 45–46
Borders, 45; and teenager demographic, 110
boutiques, 12
branch stores, 7, 39–40
branding: exclusive, 73; private, 17–18. *See also* private labeling
brick-and-mortar retailing, 35–50; catalogue divisions of, 71; and location analysis, 259–79
bricks and clicks, 64
Brooks Brothers: and global market demand, 103, 105–6; and marking systems, 250; and Thom Brown, 18
Brookstone: and 3D online consumer sales presentations, 26
Brown, Thom (designer), 18
Bulgaria: as emerging retail market, 88
bulky merchandise, 369
Burlington Coat Factory: as off-price retailer, 9
business-to-business Web sites, 328
buyers: analyzing what and how much to buy, 317–21; analyzing when to buy, 322–23; "day in the life of," *333–34*; duties and responsibilities, 310–12; and internal planning resources, 312; judgment of merchandise appeal, 365; and market evaluation, 314–15; and open to buy concept, 319–20; performance evaluations of, 332–33; and prescreening lines, 314; and price negotiation, 329–32; and resident buying offices, 313; and retail consultants, 313; and vendor selection, 321–22; and visits to vendors, 323
buying (by retailers), 309–32; alternative methods, 327–29; venues, 325–26. *See also* price negotiation
buying motivations: consumer, 120–22
buying plans, 321
buying power: as factor in consumer assessment, 133

C

call centers, 452–53
Calvin Klein (company), 44: and designer flagships, 13; and off-price stores, 9; and outlet malls, 49; and PETA, 167; and spin-offs, 21; and upper-middle class demographic, 116
carbon footprint, 174
carbon neutral, 175

careers (in retailing and related fields), 461–67; finance, *464*; and the interview process, 466–67; job classifications, 461–62; management, *463*; market specialist, *465*; merchandising, *462, 463*; operations, 463; opportunities, 27; planning for, 465–66; promotional, *464*
Carrefour, *94, 95*; 102; and green retailing practices, 188
cart abandonment: in online retailing, 60
casual Fridays, 113
category killers, 13, 47, 294. *See also* power centers
cataloguers, 68–71: with brick-and-mortar outlets, 70; and e-tailing, 63; popularity of, 68–69; unique offerings of, *69*. *See also* Fingerhut; Lands' End; L.L.Bean; Spiegel
catalogue selling, 8, *398*, 445; virtual, 66
celebrities: and exclusive retail collections, 19; and home-shopping channels, 72; and sales promotions, 403
centralized operations, 14
centralized receiving, 245
chain organizations, 40–41; history of, 5–6; and international expansion, 41; list of top 10 U.S., *41*; and tables of organization, 15; traditional, 41–46
chain store organizations. *See* chain organizations
chargebacks, 331–32
check fraud, 230. *See also* TeleCheck
children: as a consumer group classification, 110
Chile: as emerging retail market, 87
China: as emerging retail market, 87; low-cost sourcing concerns, 169–72
Christmas displays, *414, 416*
Claiborne, Liz, 20. *See also* Liz Claiborne (company)
classified ads, 196, *197*
clearinghouses, *328*, 328–29
Clearr Corporations: and signage, 420–21
closed-circuit television (CCTV), 222–23, 228
closeouts, 49, 329
Coach: and manufacturer-owned outlets, 11
coded signals, 226
codes of ethics, 155; development of, 156; trade association, 158. *See also* ethics
cold canvassing, 327
Collaborative Planning, Forecasting, and Replenishment Committee (CPFR), 241–42
The Collective, 182
collective bargaining, 212
color: common color arrangements, *424*; in visual merchandising, 423–24
Combs, Sean "Diddy," *135*
commissions, 209
community segmentation, 262. *See also* multicultural market segments

company-owned production (of private labels), 350
comparative price, 160
comparison shopping, 366: and e-tailing, 57; and private label operations, 348
compensation (of employees), 208–11; list of various plans, *210*; profit sharing, 210; salary plus bonuses, 210; straight commission, 209; straight salary, 209; wage plus commission, 209–10
competition: and global retail expansion, 89; local, 91; and site selection, 277; and visual merchandising, 414
conflicts of interest, 156; in product procurement, 161–62. *See also* ethics
conspicuous spenders, 116
consumer behavior, 120–25; buying motives, 120–22;
consumer groups: and age classifications, 109; assessment of, 108–20; children, 110; dual-earner couples, 119; and education, 115; empty nesters, 120; elderly, 113; identification, analysis, and research, 107–25; and income, 115; and geographic location and climate, 109; lower class, 117; lower-lower class, 117; lower-middle class, 117; lower-upper class, 116; middle class, 116–17; older middle-aged, 112; and population concentration, 109; single earner couples, 119; single parents, 118; and social class, 115; teenagers, 110; upper class, 115–16; upper-lower class, 117; upper-middle, 116–17; upper-upper class, 116; young adults, 111; young middle-aged, 112. *See also* demographics; lifestyle profiles; psychographics
consumer research, 123–25; and focus groups, 125; governmental resources, 123; informal, 144; in-house, 124, 133; observation-based, 125; questionnaires, 124–25; samples, 125; trade organizations, 123. *See also* ACNielsen; Arbitron, Inc.; market research groups
consumers: behavior of, 120–25; buying motives, 120–22; country-by-country differences, 91; and researching purchases online, 57–58; variety of purchasing outlets, 1. *See also* consumer behavior; consumer research
control access, 225–26
controlled shopping center, 265
conveyor systems, 247–48
copywriter, *389*
corner windows, 291
corporate gift service, 451
cooperative advertising, 331–32, 394
Costco, 10, *96*; Canadian presence, 85; "focus on," 367; as freestanding stores, 276; and upper-lower class demographic, 117

counterfeiting, 162
cover letters, 467
Crate & Barrel: as chain organization, *5, 6*; and young adult demographic, 111
credit cards, 448: ethics involved in, 161; proprietary versus third-party, *448*
crossover advertising, 394–95
customer-is-always-right concept, 440
customer service, 435–53; guidelines, 453; in online environment, 455–57; personal selling, 436–38; and selling experience for customer, 442–45; and shopper satisfaction, 447, 457–60; and services provided to customers, 446–52, 10 commandments of, *452*. *See also* sales associates
customized shopping services, 450–51
CVS, *42, 99*; as chain organization, 6; and elderly demographic, 113

D
delivery dates, 331
demographics, 108, 132–34, 398; distinction from psychographics, 129; and location analysis, 260–62. *See also* psychographics
departmentalization, 297
department pricing, 372
department stores, 6–7, 36; full-line, 37; list of top 10 U.S., *37*; and one-stop shopping, 7; specialized, 38; and visual merchandising, 415, *426*
design (of retail facilities). *See* facility design
designer flagships, 13
Designeroutlet.com, 62
design principles, 424–26: balance, 424; emphasis, 425; harmony, 426; proportion, 425; rhythm, 425–26
destination area shopping, 268
detacher, 223
Dillard's: and private labeling, 18
direct mail advertising, 397–98
direct marketing: to multicultural markets, 142–43
direct selling, 35. *See also* direct-to-consumer sales
direct-to-consumer sales, 32
discounters, 48; and older middle-aged demographic, 113. *See also* Kmart; Target; Wal-Mart
discount operations. *See* discounters; discount stores
discounts: and anticipation, 330; cash, 330; quantity, 330; seasonal, 330
discount stores, 9. *See also* discounters; Target; Wal-Mart
distribution (of merchandise). *See* merchandise distribution
diverse marketplace, 132
Dolce & Gabbana: and Designeroutlet.com, 62
Doneger, Abbey, 338–40
Doneger Group, *314, 329,* 338–40; "focus on," 324–25
DKNY: and fixturing, 298; and off-price stores, 9; and outlet malls, 49; and upper-middle class demographic, 116

drugstores, 42–43
drug-testing, 229
dual-earner couples: as consumer group, 119

E
eBay, *62*
Ebony (magazine), 140
eco-conscious production, 175
eco-friendly, 174
eco-friendly suppliers, 181
e-commerce businesses. *See* Web site–only retailers
economic downturns: and global retail expansion, 91
eco-only merchandising, 179–80
Eddie Bauer: and innovative Web site, *60*
education: and consumer group assessment, 115
elderly: as consumer group classification, 113
electronic article surveillance (EAS), 223; components of, 225
electronic asset protection (EAP), 224
electronic data interchange (EDI), 240, 245
electronic magnetic (EM) systems, 224
electronic retailing. *See* e-tailing
emotional motives: and buying, 121
emerging markets, 85–88
employee pool, 193
employment agencies, 198–99
empty nesters: as a consumer group, 120
energy efficiency, 176–77
environmental activism, 175
environmentally friendly, 173
environmentally responsible practices. *See* green retailing
equal opportunity employment, 194–95
esteem needs: in Maslow's Hierarchy of Needs, 123
e-tailing, 55–68; and catalogers, 63; interactive, 66; online, 57–58, 74–75; as a percentage of overall sales, 35; reasons for popularity, 57; and Web sites, 59–60
ethics: in advertising, 160; conflicts of interest, 156; and credit, 161; and hiring practices, 162; misleading price claims, 160–61; questionable products, 163, 167–69; in retailing, 155–65. *See also* bait-and-switch; codes of ethics; conflicts of interest; low-cost sourcing; price fixing; price gouging; puffery; short shipments
ethnic diversity, 131
ethnic minorities: as consumer groups, 131–32. *See also* multicultural market segments
evaluation (of employees), 207–8
exclusivity, 366
executive search firms. *See* headhunters
executive trainees, 205
expansion: arrangements in foreign markets, 92–94; attractive emerging markets for, 85, 87–88; through acquisition, 21; multichannel retail,

23; offshore, 17, 88–90; and strategic planning, 15
exterior retailer design, 288–91; store entrances, 289; window structures, 290–91

F
facility design, 287–301; exterior, 288–91; interior, 291–302; store entrances, 289–90; window structures, 290. *See also* exterior retailer design; Institute of Store Planners; interior retailer design
factory outlets. *See* manufacturer-owned outlets
family life cycle, 117
fashion avenues, 270–71; table listing, *272–74*
fashion forecasters, 315–16
fashion merchandise, 368
fashion shows, 402–3
fast-food industry: and franchising, 10
Federal Express (FedEx), *244*
Federal Trade Commission (FTC), 42
festival marketplaces, 269
Filene's Basement: and automatic markdown system, *376*; "focus on," 377
Fingerhut, 68
fixturing, 297–99; manufacturers of, *298*; universal 297–98
flagship stores, 7; designer, 13
flea markets, 11–12, 271
Flori Roberts (company), *138*
flow plans, 323
FOB shipping destination, 331
FOB shipping point, 331
focus groups, 125
food products: and multicultural markets, 139
franchising, 10, 93
fraud: internet, 67–68
freelancers: advertising, 392; visual merchandising, 416
freestanding stores, 276
French retailers, 83. *See also* Carrefour; Printemps
friendship stores, 87. *See also* China
Fuentes, Daisy: and Kohl's, 19, *135,* 143
full-line department stores, 37

G
Gale Group, 410–12
Galeries Lafayette, 101: in Dubai, 92; New York City branch, 90, *91*
Gap (company): as a chain organization, 6; and control access, 226; and exclusive contracts with upscale designers, 18–19; "focus on," 44, 346–47; and global expansion, 89; and global market demand, 104; and low-cost sourcing, 169–72; and manufacturer-owned outlets, 11; and marking systems, 250; and merchandise mix tailored to location and climate, 109; and product development, 346–47; and online presence, 77; and refocusing

organizational structures, 24; and retail clearance centers, 50; and store-is-the-brand operations, 342; and teenager demographic, 110; and Todd Oldham, 349; and wholly owned subsidiaries, 93; and young adult demographic, 111
GapKids, 110
general stores, 4–5; distinction between department stores and, 6
generation X, 109
generation Y, 109
geographic location and climate: as a factor in consumer group assessment, 109
Giant Eagle: "focus on," 177; and green retailing practices, 176, 177
gift registries, 447
Giorgio Armani (company), 84: and designer flagships, 13; Russian presence, 86. See also Armani Exchange
glass ceiling, 194
globalization: pitfalls for retailers, 90–91; and retailing, 79–94; and strategic planning, 15
global retailers: importance of international travel to, 89; keys to future success, 101–3; prominent, 80–85, 94; top 20, 95–99
GlobalShop, 288
global sourcing, 23
going green, 23, 173–84; definition of, 174; pros and cons, 183. See also green retailing
graduated leasing, 278–79
graphical merchandising: in online environment, 60
Granoff, Jill, 31–32. See also Liz Claiborne (company)
"gray heads." See elderly
Great Atlantic & Pacific Tea Co., 8; as first U.S. chain organization, 5. See also A & P
Greenloop, 180
green retailing, 173–84, 186–87; advantages and disadvantages, 183; consumer awareness of, 180–81; and eco-friendly products, 177–78; energy efficiency, 176–77; European leaders in, 188–90; and plastic bag usage, 175–76; recycling, 180; researching sources, 183–84; terms associated with, 174–75
group purchasing, 352
Gucci: in airport terminals, 284; and manufacturer-owned outlets, 11; in Las Vegas, 267
Guess: and off-price stores, 9
Gymboree: and merchandise distribution, 243

H

H&M: and eco-friendly products, 178, 186; and exclusive contracts with upscale designers, 18–19; and low-cost sourcing, 169–72; and Madonna, 19; success in U.S. market, 80
hanging and framing systems, 420
hard tags, 223, 225
Harry Winston (company): and lower-upper class demographic, 116
headhunters, 198–99
Hermès, 112; at airport terminals, 285
Hindmarch, Anya (designer): and white canvas tote design, 175, 176
hiring practices, 162; interviewing, 202–3; reference checking, 202; selection process, 201. See also recruitment (of employees)
Hispanic advertising agencies, 147–54
Hispanic magazines: list of top 10, 141
historical overview of retailing in the United States, 4–13
Holt Renfrew, 85, 218
home centers, 43
Home Depot, 43, 95; Canadian presence, 85; and drug-testing, 229; and green retailing, 174; and spin-offs, 22
home furnishings: and young adult demographic, 111
home-shopping channels, 71–72
hot items, 374
household mean income: as factor in consumer assessment, 133
HSN, the television shopping network, 71–72, 446; "focus on," 72–73
human resources departments, 195–97; and hiring, 201-3; and maintaining satisfactory working conditions, 211; and recruitment, 195–97; software used in, 212, 218; and training, 203–4
human resources management, 193–212; and equal opportunity employment, 194–95
hypermarkets, 13; popularity in France, 83

I

IKEA: and green retailing practices, 176, 180; success in U.K. market, 82; and young adult demographic, 111
impulse buying, 42, 296
incentive award programs: in theft prevention, 226–27
income: and consumer group assessment, 115
India: as an emerging retail market, 85
individual merchandise pricing, 372
infomercials, 56
informal research, 144
in-house distribution, 245–46; and centralized receiving, 245; and regional receiving, 245
Institute of Store Planners: "focus on," 291–92
intellectual property, 157
interactive e-tailing, 66
interenterprise collaboration, 240–41
interior retailer design, 291–302; concepts, 292–93; departmentalization, 297; fixturing, 297–98; lighting, 301–2; surfacing, 299–301
intermodal transportation, 244
internal sourcing (for recruitment purposes), 196
internal theft, 162–63, 227–231
International Council of Shopping Centers: "focus on," 270
international travel: and global retail expansion, 89; and older middle-aged demographic, 112
internet fraud, 67–68, 231–32. See also PayNet Secure
internet selling, 445–46
internships, 199
interviews: final, 203; preliminary, 202; rail, 202
inventory: planning, 240; retail method of, 363; shrinkage, 362
invoice checking: and vendor theft prevention, 233
Italian retailers, 84–85. See also Giorgio Armani (company)

J

Japanese retailers, 83–84. See also kimono stores; Takashimaya; terminal stores
JCPenney: and charitable events, 405; and Hispanic market, 60, 136; and multicultural markets, 135; and online presence, 76–77; and recruitment, 199; and repositioning, 24; and shoplifting, 236
J.Crew: as cataloguer with retail outlets, 71; and young adult demographic, 111
JET (magazine), 140
job analysis: in recruiting and hiring, 195
job applications, 201
job descriptions: in recruiting and hiring, 195, 196
job satisfaction, 211, 215
job sharing, 211
job specifications: in recruiting and hiring, 195
joint ventures, 92
Jos. A. Bank: "focus on," 6

K

Kellwood (company): and Phat Fashions, 32–33
Kids "R" Us, 110
Kimono stores, 84
kiosks, 12
kleptomania, 222
Kmart: and Hispanic market, 136; and older middle-aged demographic, 113; and lower-middle class demographic, 117; and marking systems, 250; and recruitment, 199; and upper-lower class demographic, 117
Kohl's: and Daisy Fuentes, 19, 135, 143; and Hispanic market, 136; and multicultural markets, 20, 135; and Vera Wang, 18, 349

L

Lands' End, 60; e-tailing operations, 63; and shopping consultants, 66; and virtual try-on service, *67*
Latinos (as a consumer group), 60, 132; and direct marketing, 142–43; major metropolitan markets, 134; and magazines, 141; and newspapers, 140; and radio, 141–42; targeting strategies to reach, *136–37*; and television, 141
Latvia: as an emerging retail market, 87
Law Enforcement Retail Partnership Network, 236
lead time, 396–97
leased departments, 450
leasing, 278–79
Levi Strauss (company), 44
licensing, 93–94; and private labels, 348–50
Lids (company): and start as a kiosk, 12
lifestyle centers: and Jos. A. Bank, 6
lifestyle profiles, 114; and trading area selection, 261. *See also* ACORN
lighting, 301–2, 421–23; fixtures and systems, 422–23; and nonselling areas, 301; types of, *422*
Lillian Vernon (company), *69*
The Limited: as a chain organization, 6; and store-is-the-brand operations, 342; and young adult demographic, 111. *See also* Limited Brands
Limited Brands, 6; and organizational structures, 24; and PETA, 167. *See also* Bath & Body Works; The Limited; Limited Too; Victoria's Secret
limited-line stores, 5
Limited Too, 110
line and staff positions, 14
list price, 160
Liz Claiborne (company), 31–34: and empty nester demographic, 120; "focus on," 20; and green retailing practices, 181; job satisfaction at, 216–17; and joint ventures, 92; and manufacturer-owned outlets, 11, 49; and off-price stores, 9; and refocusing organizational structures, 24
L.L.Bean, 60, *63*
location analysis, 259–79; community segmentation, 262; demographic, 260–62; occupancy considerations, 278–79; shopping districts, 263–64; shopping malls, 264–65; and site selection, 276–78; trading area, 260–63
"location, location, location," 259
Loehmann, Frieda, 9. *See also* Loehmann's
Loehmann's, 9; and utilizing latest technology, 16
logos: and counterfeiting, 162
Lord & Taylor: and Joseph Abboud, 19; and retail clearance centers, 50; and technology, 16; and window design, *289, 414*

Los Angeles: as a major Hispanic market, *134*
loss prevention, 221–34. *See also* acousto-magnetic (AM) systems; detacher; drug-testing; electronic article surveillance (EAS); electronic asset protection (EAP); electronic magnetic (EM) systems; hard tags; internal theft; radio frequency (RF) systems; ticket switching; two-way mirrors; vendor theft; warning signs
Louis Vuitton (company): and counterfeiting, *162*; and designer flagships, 13; and emotional buying motives, 121. *See also* LVMH
low-cost sourcing: and China, 169; ethics of, 161
lower class: as a consumer group, 117
lower-middle class: as consumer group, 117
lower-upper class: as consumer group, 116
Lowe's, *97*; Canadian presence, 85
LVMH (Moët Hennessey Louis Vuitton): and Sephora, 64; and succeeding in global markets, 102

M

Macy's, 37, 80; and codes of conduct, 157–58; and expansion, 7; "focus on," 38, 157–58, 241; and holiday parades, *405*; and Hispanic market, *137*; logistics and operations, 241; and online presence, 76–77; and partnering, 22; and PETA, 169; and private labeling, 18, 342, *344*; and utilizing latest technology, 16; and Tommy Hilfiger, 19; and visual merchandising approach, *427*, *432–33*
Madonna, *19*, 349
magazine advertising, 396–97
magnifying mirrors, 225
mail-order retailers, 7–8
mail-order selling, 7–8
Malaysia: as emerging retail market, 87
Mall of America, 269
Mall of Georgia, 266, 269
malls. *See* shopping malls
mannequins, 419: ethnic, *142*, 143; innovative design of, 433–34
manufacturer closeout stores, 49–50
manufacturer-owned outlets, 11
manufacturers: as retailers, 20. *See also* private labeling
manufacturer's brands: reasons for continued use, 342–43
manufacturer's representatives, 327
manufacturer suggested retail price (MSRP), 382
markdowns, 362, 374–79, 382–84; and assortment problems, 376; automatic, 377; calculating, 377–79; maintained, 362; and ineffective promotion, 375; and ineffective selling, 375; and initial prices, 375; timing, 376; and

visual presentation failures, 375; and weather conditions, 375–76
market consultants, 314
marketing: site-to-store, 25
market research groups, 124. *See also* ACNielsen; Arbitron, Inc.
markets: global, 101–3; emerging, 85–88
market segmentation: multicultural, 20. *See also* multicultural market segments
market week, 314; buyer visits during, 323–24
marking (of merchandise), *249*; re-marking, 250. *See also* Monarch Marking Systems
Marks & Spencer, 82; green retailing practices, 188–90; in India, 85
markups, 362–64; average, 365; calculating, 363; on short-lived products, *368*
marquee labels, 44, 341
Marshalls: as off-price retailer, 9; and off-site training, 204; and older middle-aged demographic, 113
Mary-Kate and Ashley collection, 19
Maslow, Abraham. *See* Maslow's Hierarchy of Needs
Maslow's Hierarchy of Needs, 122–23
Mast Industries, Inc.: "focus on," 350–51
McComb, William L., 31, 33. *See also* Liz Claiborne (company)
McDonald's, 10, *93*; "focus on," 207
mega-malls, 265, 269
membership clubs, 367. *See also* Costco; Sam's Club; warehouse clubs
Men's Wearhouse: as an off-price retailer, 9; and training, 219–20
merchandise: bulky, 369; fashion, 368; perishable, 368–69; precious jewelry, 369; seasonal, 368
merchandise commitments, 319
merchandise distribution, 239–50; and high-tech innovation, 240; in-house, 245–46; and interenterprise collaboration, 240–41; quality checking, 248–49; receiving and marking operations, 246–50; and transportation methods, *244*; vendor–retailer, 243–45. *See also* Collaborative Planning, Forecasting, and Replenishment Committee (CPFR); Voluntary Interindustry Commerce Standard Association (VCIS)
merchandise diversification: in strategic planning, 15–16
merchandise exclusivity: and multicultural markets, 135
merchandise mix: broadening, 24; and eco-friendly product additions, 177–78; and proportional inventory concept, 345
merchandise on hand, 319
merchandise pricing. *See* pricing

merchandise supply chain, 241–42: performance, 245. *See also* merchandise distribution
merchandising: eco-only, 179–80; and multicultural markets, 134–35
mergers and acquisitions: in strategic planning, 16
me-too stores, 262
Mexico: as an emerging retail market, 87
Mexx stores, 92
Microsoft, 16
middle class: as consumer group classification, 116–17
mid-sized organizations, 14
Mikasa: and manufacturer-owned outlets, 11
minimum wage, 209
minorities. *See* ethnic minorities
mirrors: in theft prevention, 225
mixed-use centers, 267, 281–83
Mizrahi, Isaac: and Target, *349*
mobile fashion sales, 26
model stock, 316
Monarch Marking Systems: "focus on," 249–50
monster.com, *197*
Montgomery Ward & Co.: as an early mail-order retailer, 7
morale (of employees): in the retail industry, 215–17
multichannel retailing, 65–66; and technology integration, 66
multiculturalism: in retailing, 131–44
multicultural market segments, 20, 134; and advertising, 140–41; and cosmetics and fragrance companies, 138; and direct marketing, 142–43; and food products, 139; and merchandising, 134–35; targeting strategies, 134–44; and visual merchandising, 142–43
multimedia campaigns, 406
multiple-member/shared households, 118
multistory operations, 294–95
mystery shoppers, 228

N

National Association of Display Interiors (NADI): "focus on," 418
National Association of Ethical and Responsible Independent Retailers (NAERIS), 158
National Retail Federation, 108, 110, *123*, 362
negotiation pricing, 164
neighborhood clusters, 275
Neiman Marcus: and online presence, 76; and retail clearance centers, 50; and upper-middle class demographic, 117; and window design, *290*; and young middle-aged demographic, 112
newspaper advertising, 25, 140, 395–96, 408–10
Nicole Miller (company): and Designeroutlet.com, 62

Nike: and eco-friendly products, *181*; and promotional activities, *353*
Nine West: and manufacturer-owned outlets, 11, 49
nonselling areas, 301
Nordstrom: and charitable events, 405; and commissions, *209*; "focus on," 39, 437–38; and green retailing practices, 187; and marking systems, 250; and personal selling, 437–38; and retail clearance centers, 50; and utilizing new technology, 29–30
Nordstrom, John W., 39
North Face: and direct-to-consumer sales, 32; and green retailing practices, *181*
noveau riche. *See* lower-upper class

O

observation research, 125
occupations: and consumer group assessment, 113–14
Office Depot: and rational buying motives, 121; and young adult market, 112
off-price retailers, 48–49; and lower-middle class demographic, 117
off-price stores, 9
offshore expansion, 17; list of retailers with significant, *18*
offshore retail operations: analysis of, 88–90
off-site purchasing, 55
off-site retailing, 17, 55–78
off-site selling, 445–46
off-site training, 204
older middle-aged: as consumer group classification, 112
Oldham, Todd (designer), 18, 349
Old Navy, *44*, 45, *347*; and control access, 226; and lighting, 422; and rational buying motives, 121; and teenager demographic, 110
"one size fits all" philosophy, 131
one-stop shopping, 7
online consumer sales presentations, 26
online retailers: list of successful, *61*
online retailing, 57–58; advantages for consumers, 74–75; big eight internet outlets, *58*; escalation of, 23; popularity of apparel in, 75–78
open-sell concept, 297
open to buy (buying concept), 319
open windows, 290
opportunistic buying: as practiced by off-price retailers, 48
organic cotton, 174, *175*
organic labeling, 174
organizational charts, 14
organizational formats: large-sized, 14; mid-sized, 14; small-store, 14
organizational structures, 14; of branch stores, 40; refocusing, 24
OshKosh B'Gosh, 246, 293
outdoor advertisements, 399–400
outlet centers, 48, 49, 265, 268; developers of, 52–54

outlet malls. *See* outlet centers
outside marking (of merchandise), 243
outside sourcing (for recruitment purposes), 196
outsourcing: of private label operations, 23; in strategic planning, 15–16
overbuying, 374
overruns: and private label operations, 351

P

parallel-to-sidewalk windows, 290
parking facilities: and site selection, 277–78
partnering, 22
Patagonia (company): "focus on," 178; and green retailing, *178*
patronage motives, 122
PayNet Secure, 231–32
peddlers: as an example of early retailers, 4
pedestrian traffic: and site selection, 276
perishable merchandise, 368–69
Perry Ellis (company): and manufacturer-owned outlets, 11
personal selling, 436–38, 448
PETA (People for the Ethical Treatment of Animals), 167–69
Phat Fashions, 32–33, 135
physiological needs: in Maslow's Hierarchy of Needs, 122
pilferage, 371
planning: inventory, 240
plastic bags: and green retailing, 175–76
point-of-purchase: and private label operations, 349
political risk: and global retail expansion, 91
Polo Ralph Lauren. *See* Ralph Lauren (company)
population concentration: as a factor in consumer group assessment, 109
Pottery Barn: as chain organization, 6; "focus on," 111–12; and young adult demographic, 111; and visual merchandising, 375, 414
power centers, 265, 270, *271*. *See also* outlet centers
Prada: and Designeroutlet.com, 62; Russian presence, 86
precious jewelry: as a merchandise category, 369
prestige retailers, 370
prêt-à-porter, 83
price cutting, 342
price fixing, 163
price gouging, 163
price negotiation, 329–33; chargebacks, 331–32; delivery dates, 331; discounts, 330; shipping terms, 331
price points, 373–74
pricing, 361–78; average, 373; as buyer duty, 311; and company image, 370; department, 372; factors affecting, 364–66; individual merchandise, 372; misleading, 160–61; negotiable, 372; and retailer services, 370–71;

and stock turnover, 369; strategies, 371–73, 381–82; and Supreme Court decision, 365; and working-class discrimination, 164–65; zone, 165. *See also* markdowns; markups; price points; pricing strategies
pricing strategies, 381–82; discount, 382; keystone, 371, 382; keystone plus, 371; overall uniform, 371–72; psychological, 382
Printemps, *83*
private brands. *See* private labeling
private labeling, 17–18, 358–60; advantages of, 348; developers, 351; outsourcing of, 23; and product development, 341–60; and promotional activities, 352–54
prize money (PM), 210
product development: as buyer duty, 312; and private label operations, 350–52
product mix: at supermarkets, 42
profitability: and global retail expansion, 90
profit sharing, 210
promotion from within, 196
promotion (of products): as buyer duty, 311; of private labels, 352–54. *See also* sales promotions
proportional inventory concept, 345
psychographics, 128–30, 398. *See also* demographics
psychological testing (of employees), 229
publicista, 148
publicity, 406
public transportation: and site selection, 277
puffery, 160, 161
purchasing: buyer duty, 311; channels, 321; planning, 312–13; and private label operations, 351–52. *See also* buyers; buying (of merchandise)

Q

quality checking, 248–49
questionnaires: and consumer research, 124–25
Quick Response (QR) inventory planning, 240
QVC, 71, *351*, 446

R

rack jobbers, 321
radio advertising, 141–42, 397
radio frequency (RF) systems, 224
radio frequency identification device (RFID), 224, *225*
Ralph Lauren (company), 44; and emotional buying motives, 121; and Designeroutlet.com, 62; "focus on," 86; and off-price stores, 9; and outlet malls, 49; and PETA, 167; Russian presence, 86; and upper-middle class demographic, 116; and visual merchandising approach, *427*; and young middle-aged demographic, *112*
rational motives: and buying, 121

receiving docks, 247
receiving (of merchandise), 245–48
receiving records, 247
receiving rooms: ethical practices in, 163–64
recruitment (of employees), 195–97; employment agencies, 198–99; external sources, 196–97; internal sources, 196
recycling, 180
Red Envelope, *68*
reference checking, 202, 228
regional receiving, 245–46
Regulation Z, 161
repositioning, 24–25
research: consumer, 123–25; consumers using, 57; green retailing, 183–84; and lifestyle profiles, 114; samples, 125; top 10 Web sites used by consumers for, *58*. *See also* consumer research
resident buying offices, 313
résumés, 466–67
retail clearance center, 50
retail consultants, *313*
retail design firms: top 12, *289*
retailers: and buying, 309–32; catalogue, 68–71; and celebrities, 19; challenges for, 3; and consumer demand, 107–8; and consumer research data, 108; and facility design, 287–301; freestanding, 276; French, 83; global, 80–85, 94; and going green, 23, 173–84; Italian, 84–85; Japanese, 83–84; and location analysis, 259–79; and loss prevention, 221–34; mail-order, 7–8; and morale issues, 215–17; and merchandise distribution, 239–50; and multicultural market segments, 146–47; and new concepts, 21, *22*; off-price, 48–49; with overseas presence, *18*; and ownership, 279; prestige, 370; with private brands, *346*; and site selection, 276–78; small-scale, 46–47; structure complexity, 14; and 3D online consumer sales presentations, 26; top 10 U.S., *13*; top 20 global, *95–99*; traditional, 36–47; U.K.-based, 81–82; utilizing new technology, 26, 29–30; value-oriented, 47; and visual merchandising, 413–29; Web site–only, 56, 62
RetailExchange.com, *328*
retail exclusivity, 18–19
retailing: American domination of, 13; brick-and-mortar, 35; careers in, 27, 461–67; codes of ethics, 156; current trends in, 17–25; and customer service, 435–53; "doors," 79; ethics in, 155–65; and exclusive contracts with upscale designers, 18–19; future trends, 25; and globalization, 79–94; and global market demand, 103–5; history of, 3–34; multichannel, 65–66; multiculturalism in, 131–44; off-site, 55–78; online, 23; store-is-the-brand, 44
retail method of inventory, 363

Retail Technology Group, 16
reusable supplies, 175
rhythm (in visual presentation), *425*, 426
road sales staffs, 323
Robinson–Patman Act: in price negotiations, 330
role-playing, 205, 440
rule of occupancy, 279
runners, 374
rural communities: and general stores, 5; and peddlers, 4
Russia: as emerging retail market, 86

S

safety needs: Maslow's Hierarchy of Needs, 122
Saks Fifth Avenue: "focus on," 203–4; and global markets, 101, 103; and lower-upper class demographic, 116; and marking systems, 250; and merchandise distribution, 253–56; and private labeling, 18; redesigning interior space, 305–6; and retail clearance centers, 50; and technology, 16; and training practices, 203–4; and upper-middle class demographic, 117; and young middle-aged demographic, 112
sales associates: appearance, 438; communication skills, 439; company knowledge, 439; enthusiasm, 438–39; new, 204–5; product knowledge, 439; self-control, 440; tactfulness, 440, training, 440–42. *See also* customer service; selling techniques; training
sales channels: in strategic planning, 15–16
sales promotions, 401–6; charitable events, 404–5; celebrity appearances, 403; community programs, 405; demonstrations, 404; division structure overview, 388–89; fashion shows, 402–3; holiday parades, 405; how-to clinics, 404; sampling, 404; special events, 401–2; trunk shows, *403*, 404
Sam's Club, 10; Canadian presence, 85; as freestanding stores, 276; and Hispanic market, *137*; and upper-lower class demographic, 117
Saudi Arabia: as an emerging retail market, 87–88
Sean John (brand), 135
Sears, *96*: Canadian presence, 85; as a mail-order retailer, 7, 8; and marking systems, 250; and multicultural market segments, 20, *134*; and recruitment, 199; success in U.K. market, 82
seasonal merchandise, 368
selection process, 201
self-actualization needs: in Maslow's Hierarchy of Needs, 123
Selfridges, *81*
self-service displays, 428
selling: catalogue, 8, *398*, 445; home-shopping, 446; off-site, 17

selling techniques: agree and counterattack, 443; "yes, but," 443
Sensormatic Electronics Corp.: "focus on," 224
Sephora: and fixturing, 297–98, *299*; "focus on," 64–65. *See also* LVMH
shipping terms, 331
shoplifting, 221–22; deterrents, 222–27; gangs, 236–37
shopping consultants: in e-tailing, 66–67
shopping districts, 263–64; central, 264; destination, 268
shopping malls, 264–65; developers of, 52–54, 265–66; in casinos, 267; traditional, 266–67. *See also* International Council of Shopping Centers; vertical malls
shopping services (for customers), 447–51
shopping tours, 26
short shipments, 163. *See also* receiving rooms
signage and graphics, 419–20
signature brands, 342
signing bonuses, 199
Simon Property Group: "focus on," 265–66
single-earner couples: as a consumer group, 119
single parents: as a consumer group, 118
single-store receiving, 246
single-story operations, 294
site-to-store marketing, 25
skeleton sales crew, 436
slotting allowances, 331
small store organizations, 14, 46–47
social classes: and consumer group assessment, 115
social needs: in Maslow's Hierarchy of Needs, 122
souks, 88
sourcing: global, 23; low-cost, 161; and quality assurance, 337–38
Spaeth Design: and animated installations, 418–19
special events, 401–2
specialization: of merchandise, 15–16
specialized department stores, 38
specialty stores. *See* limited-line stores
Spiegel, *62*, 68; catalogue, 8; e-tailing operations, 63; and retail clearance centers, 50
spin-offs, 21: in strategic planning, 16
spots: in television advertising, 397
split department, 295
staffing, 193–94: multicultural, 143
standard departments, 297
Standard Rate & Data Service (SRDS): and advertising cost analysis, 400–401
staple merchandise, 317
staples: as a merchandise category, 374
Staples (company): and recycling, 180; and rational buying motives, 121; and young adult market, 112
Stein Mart, 48; and corporate ethics, 156–57; and personal selling, 436
Steve Madden (company): and innovative Web site, *59*

stock options, 211
stock turnover, 322, 369
store-is-the-brand retailing, 44, 342, 345–46, *347*; companies using, *349*
store within a store: and use by department stores, 36; designing, 297; and private labeling operations, 353
strategic planning, 15
strip centers, 275
subclassification, 44
supermarkets, 8, 41–42; and e-tailing, 64; and green retailing practices, 177; list of top 5 U.S., *43*; and multicultural markets, 139; and plastic bag usage, 176; and private labeling operations, 356–58
surfacing, 299–301; floors, 299–300; walls, 300–301
sustainability, 175
swapmeets. *See* flea markets
Syms: as an off-price retailer, 9; and older middle-aged demographic, 113

T

tables of organization. *See* organizational charts
Takashimaya, *84*
Target, 9, 48, *96*; "focus on," 198; and global market demand, 105; and Hispanic market, *136*; and Isaac Mizrahi, *349*; and low-cost sourcing, 169–72; and lower-middle class demographic, 117; and multicultural markets, 20, 135; and older middle-aged demographic, 113; and recruitment, 198; and upper-lower class demographic, 117
tariffs, 322
technology: multichannel integration, 66; use of, 16, 26
teenagers: as a consumer group, 110; spending habits of 127–28
Telecheck, 231, 232
television advertising, 141, 397
terminal stores: in Japan, 84
Tesco, 82, *96*; and green retailing practices, 189
Texaco: hiring and promotion practices, *162*
text messaging, 25–26, 399
theft prevention. *See* loss prevention
theme environment, 287
third-party certification, 175
through-the-wall security systems, 230
ticket switching, 226
Tiffany & Co.: success in Japanese market, 84
Timberland: and becoming carbon-neutral, 181
T.J. Maxx, 47: as an off-price retailer, 9; and older middle-aged demographic, 113
TJX (company), 48, 49. *See also* T.J. Maxx
Tommy Hilfiger (company): and exclusive contract with Macy's, 19; in India, 85
town centers, 25, *265*

Toys "R" Us, *110*; as a category killer, 13, 47; as a chain organization, 6; and recruitment, 199; success in U.K. market, 82
Trade Association Codes (of ethics), 158
trade expositions, *326*; selected domestic, *326*; selected international, *327*
trade publications: and buyers, 316; want ads, 197
trade shows. *See* trade expositions
trading area analysis and selection, 260–63
trading posts, 4
traditional chains, 41–46
traditional retailers, 36–47
training (of employees), 219–20; in-house, 203–4; off-site, 204; online, 441–42; on-the-job, 441; retraining, 206–7; vestibule, 441
transportation (of merchandise): intermodal, 244; modes, *244*
trolley conveyors, 248
trunk shows, 403
Truth in Lending Act, 161
Tunisia: as an emerging retail market, 88
turnover rate, 196, 218
two-way mirrors, 225

U

U.K.-based retailers, 81–82. *See also* Body Shop; Marks & Spencer; Tesco
Ukraine: as emerging retail market, 87
unique products: in the fashion industry, 90
upper class: as a consumer group classification, 115–16
upper-lower class: as a consumer group, 117
upper-middle class: as a consumer group, 116–17
upper-upper class: as a consumer group, 116
Urban Outfitters: and estimating global market demand, 105
U.S. Census Bureau, 123, 133
U.S. Department of Commerce, 109–10

V

VALS™ system, 114
value-oriented retailers, 47; international success of, 48; list of top 20 U.S., *47*
value shopping, 20, 23; and older middle-aged demographic, 113
vendor-managed inventory (VMI), 241, 245
vendor–retailer physical distribution, 243–45
vendor showrooms, *325*
vendor theft, 232–34
vertical malls, 265, 267
VF Corp.: and direct to consumer sales, 32
Victoria's Secret, 21, 24, *71*, 89; as a chain organization, 6
video surveillance systems, 222–23

Vietnam: as an emerging retail market, 87
virtual catalogues, 66
virtual showrooms, 329
virtual try-ons, 67
visioning workshops: in strategic planning, 15
visual merchandising, 413–29; and advertising, 429; centralized, 415–16; department store approach, 415; development of, 414–16; and facility design, 288; and freelancers, 416; in-house display staff, 414; and multicultural markets, 142–43; and private labeling operations, 354; success in, 427–29; and themes, 426–27; vendors of products for, *417*. *See also* design principles; visual presentation
visual presentation: and color, 423–24; components of, 416–24; and hanging and framing systems, 420; and lighting, 421–23; and mannequins, 419; and props, 417; and signage and graphics, 419–20. *See also* design principles
vitrines, *414*, 415
Voluntary Interindustry Commerce Standard Association (VCIS), 241

Von Maur: "focus on," 206; and executive training, 206

W

Walgreens, *40*, 42, *98*; and elderly demographic, 113
walk-ins (by job seekers), 199
Wal-Mart, 9, 47, 48, 80, *95*; "focus on," 143, 182; and global expansion, 89; and global market demand, 103; and green retailing practices, 182, 187; and Hispanic market, 60, *136*, 148; and low-cost sourcing, 169–72; and lower-middle class demographic, 117; and marking systems, 250; and Mary-Kate and Ashley collection, 19; and multicultural markets, 20, 135; and older middle-aged demographic, 113; and shoplifting, 236; and staffing, 143; and upper-lower class demographic, 117
Wang, Vera (designer), 135: and contract with Kohl's, *18*, 349
warehouse clubs, 10; and pricing, 365
warning signs: in theft prevention, 226
watchdog agencies, 158
Web site–only retailers, 56, 62
Web sites: as advertising medium, 399; business-to-business, 328; and customer satisfaction, 455–57; innovative directions for, 59–60; navigation, 67; for recruitment purposes, 197
Whole Foods, *8*; and eco-friendly products, *178*, 187
wholesale: and blurring of line with retail, 20, 31–34
wholesale clubs. *See* warehouse clubs
wholly owned subsidiaries, 93
Williams-Sonoma: as a single-story operation, 294; and visual merchandising, 375, 414, *415*
window design, 290–91
World of Disney, *293*

Y

young adults: as a consumer group, 111
young middle-aged: as a consumer group, 112
yuppies: and rational buying motives, 121

Z

Zalia: "focus on," 138–39
Zappos.com, *57*; "focus on," 62–63
zone pricing, 165